Introducing Linguistics

Everything we do involves language. Assuming no prior knowledge, this book offers students a contemporary introduction to the study of language. Each thought-provoking chapter is accessible to readers from a variety of fields, and is helpfully organized across six parts: sound; structure and meaning; language typologies and change; language and social aspects; language acquisition; and language, cognition, and the brain. The book's companion website also offers three brief chapters on language and computers; animal communication; and dialectal varieties of English outside of North America.

The chapters feature illustrative tables, figures, and maps, along with three types of pedagogical boxes (Linguistic Tidbits; Pause and Reflect; and Eyes on World Languages) that break up the text, contextualize information, and provide colorful accents that give real data from languages across the globe. Key words are bolded and defined in a glossary at the end of the book, while end-of-chapter summaries and practice exercises reinforce the key points discussed.

Joyce Bruhn de Garavito is a Professor Emeritus of Hispanic Studies and Linguistics at the University of Western Ontario and an Adjunct Professor at the University of Ottawa. She is the recipient of the Western University Pleva award for excellence in teaching and the Graham and Gail Wright Distinguished Scholar award. Her research interests include theoretical linguistics (syntax, language acquisition, Romance languages); languages in contact (language change, bilingualism, Amerindian languages); and applied linguistics (language teaching, methodology).

John W. Schwieter is a Professor of Spanish and Linguistics and Faculty of Arts Teaching Scholar at Wilfrid Laurier University where he directs the Language Acquisition, Multilingualism, and Cognition Laboratory and Bilingualism Matters at Laurier. His research interests include: psycholinguistic and neurolinguistic approaches to multilingualism and language acquisition; second language teaching and learning; translation and cognition; and language, culture, and society. He is the Executive Editor of the book series *Bilingual Processing and Acquisition* (Benjamins) and Co-Editor of *Cambridge Elements in Second Language Acquisition*.

Introducing Linguistics

Theoretical and Applied Approaches

Edited by

JOYCE BRUHN DE GARAVITO
University of Western Ontario

JOHN W. SCHWIETER
Wilfrid Laurier University, Ontario

CAMBRIDGE
UNIVERSITY PRESS

CAMBRIDGE
UNIVERSITY PRESS

University Printing House, Cambridge CB2 8BS, United Kingdom

One Liberty Plaza, 20th Floor, New York, NY 10006, USA

477 Williamstown Road, Port Melbourne, VIC 3207, Australia

314–321, 3rd Floor, Plot 3, Splendor Forum, Jasola District Centre, New Delhi – 110025, India

79 Anson Road, #06–04/06, Singapore 079906

Cambridge University Press is part of the University of Cambridge.

It furthers the University's mission by disseminating knowledge in the pursuit of education, learning, and research at the highest international levels of excellence.

www.cambridge.org
Information on this title: www.cambridge.org/9781108482554
DOI: 10.1017/9781108696784

© Cambridge University Press 2021

First published 2021

Printed in the United Kingdom by TJ Books Limited, Padstow Cornwall

A catalogue record for this publication is available from the British Library.

Library of Congress Cataloging-in-Publication Data
Names: Garavito, Joyce Bruhn de, editor | Schwieter, John W., 1979- editor.
Title: Introducing linguistics : theoretical and applied approaches /
edited by Joyce Bruhn de Garavito, John W. Schwieter.
Description: Cambridge, UK ; New York : Cambridge University Press, 2020. |
Includes bibliographical references and index.
Identifiers: LCCN 2020019010 (print) | LCCN 2020019011 (ebook) | ISBN
9781108482554 (hardback) | ISBN 9781108696784 (ebook)
Subjects: LCSH: Linguistics. | Applied linguistics.
Classification: LCC P121 .I57 2020 (print) | LCC P121 (ebook) | DDC
410–dc23
LC record available at https://lccn.loc.gov/2020019010
LC ebook record available at https://lccn.loc.gov/2020019011

ISBN 978-1-108-48255-4 Hardback
ISBN 978-1-108-71065-7 Paperback

Additional resources for this publication at www.cambridge.org/introducing-linguistics.

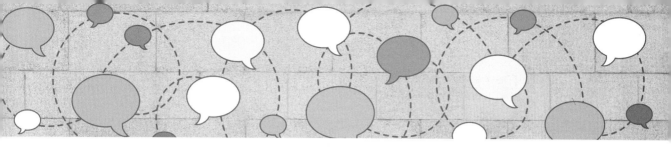

CONTENTS

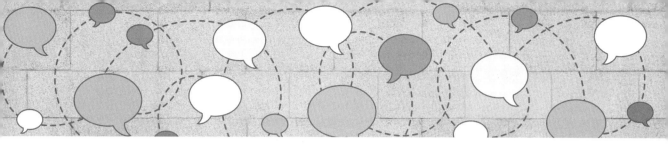

PREFACE

Have you ever wondered how you learned your language as a baby? Perhaps a better question is whether you remember doing so at all. How is it possible – and more difficult – to learn another language later in life (and why is this second language often less 'native-like' than the mother tongue)? How do we use language creatively to negotiate meanings in different stages of our life? You may not realize it, but language is involved in almost everything we do. It truly is what separates us from other animals that have far less sophisticated ways of communicating compared to humans. *Linguistics* – the study of language – is interested in these and many other related questions.

Imagine that you are in a crowded metro in a country where you do not speak the local language. There are many people around you speaking their language and since you don't understand it, for the most part, you tune it out. After all, why would you try to listen in on people's conversations if you understand nothing? But imagine that all of a sudden someone far away, but still within hearing distance, says "You're kidding!" in a language that you speak. Chances are, you will immediately turn your attention towards this individual. Why is this? Is it because you hear strings of sounds that you recognize? Maybe. Is it because you hear something different from everything else being spoken? Maybe but probably not, or everyone else would also turn their attention. Is it because "You're kidding" may trigger an emotional or heated response that could provide some entertainment that is worth eavesdropping on? Again, maybe. Is it because language is part of who you are and as a human, you are naturally drawn to those who share the same language? Linguists, in addition to numerous other issues, are interested in situations such as this in order to better understand humans and language.

Target Audience

This book is not only intended for individuals studying linguistics, perhaps as a major program or elective in their university, but it is also geared towards those who are interested in language and communication in general. In other words, the book assumes no prior knowledge of linguistics. To this end, we have built a comprehensive introductory textbook on linguistics that we hope will appeal to the widest audience possible.

Structure and Contents

The book contains 15 in-print chapters and three brief chapters that are available on the book's companion website. **Part 1: Introduction** includes *Chapter 1: Introducing Linguistics*, which contextualizes important foundations of modern linguistics. It presents the development of the field and offers insight on the importance of studying linguistics. You will also read about some common misconceptions about linguistics and linguists.

In **Part 2: Sound**, *Chapter 2: Phonetics* studies how sounds are articulated using our speech-producing system (i.e., the vocal cords, tongue, lips, etc.). You will learn about the International Phonetic Alphabet (IPA), a universal way of transcribing all human speech sounds. The chapter also introduces you to the acoustic properties of sounds, for example, the difference between vowels and consonants and some of the processes we use to make speaking easier. In *Chapter 3: Phonology*, you will learn about sound patterns and contrasts in specific languages. The chapter begins by defining a phoneme, or individual sound. You will then read about more detailed properties of sounds, both at the individual sound level and within syllables. You will see that analyzing larger units such as syllables and words is also part of what phonology studies. In fact, many rules governing phonetic change rely on syllables and elements such as stress for their application.

The first chapter in **Part 3: Structure and Meaning** is *Chapter 4: Morphology*, which familiarizes you with the study of word structure. You will read about the differences between simple and complex words in addition to how words are formed through different types of word formation processes. You will also learn about compound words and other ways of constructing words. *Chapter 5: Syntax* introduces you to phrase and sentence structure. You will first study the classification of words (e.g., noun, verb, adjective, etc.) and how certain classes of words can naturally form what are known as *constituents*. The chapter then shows you how constituents are merged together to form phrases and sentences. You will also learn about how constituents may undergo movement in order to do or mean something different (e.g., *Bert does speak German* vs. *Does Bert speak German?*). Finally, *Chapter 6: Semantics* acquaints you with the study of meaning. The chapter begins by comparing and contrasting different types of meaning in language. You will read about how meaning is captured in words and how they are related to each other based on meaning. The chapter also describes how we put together word meanings to come up with phrase meaning and how syntax is used to create meaning. Finally, you will learn about some current theories on how meaning is accomplished in language.

Part 4: Language Typologies and Change begins with *Chapter 7: The Classification of Languages*, in which you will come to an understanding of the historical relationships among languages and linguistic typologies. The overarching question of the chapter is how languages can be classified. To answer this question, you will read about the genetic and typological classifications of languages. You will also learn about linguistic typology and change along with some typological similarities that apply to all world languages. Following this, *Chapter 8: Historical Linguistics*, will introduce you to how languages develop and change over time. In doing so, you will review types of language changes with respect to sound, structure, and meaning. You will have the opportunity to compare current language forms with past forms by applying methods such as comparative reconstruction. The chapter also talks about the reasons for language change and how we can gain knowledge of unattested languages.

Opening **Part 5: Language and Social Aspects** is *Chapter 9: Sociolinguistics*, in which you will read about how language functions in society. The chapter begins by defining important concepts that are used in studying language variation. You will discover factors that influence how distinct groups of people speak and the different ways they change their manner of speaking according to social needs. You will also learn about language variation in bilingual societies. In *Chapter 10: Pragmatics and Discourse Analysis*, you will become acquainted with language, meaning, and society, along with the different genres and styles of discourse. You will also learn about how and why spoken and written language are coherent. Finally, in *Chapter 11: Writing Systems*, you will read about the emergence of writing in human languages, how it is used, and how it has changed since its origins.

Part 6: Language Acquisition begins with *Chapter 12: First Language Acquisition*. In this chapter you will read about issues such as how phonology, vocabulary, morphology, syntax, and communicative development occur in a first language (L1). You will also read about what can affect L1 acquisition such as a critical period for language acquisition, innate knowledge, and general cognition. The chapter concludes with a discussion on atypical language development, bilingual L1 acquisition, and some of the methods used to study language in infants and children. In *Chapter 13: Second Language Acquisition*, you will compare and contrast L1 and second language (L2) acquisition, read about how sounds, words, and structure develop in an L2, and learn about teaching pedagogies that are used in L2 learning. You will see that learning an L2 is affected by many internal and external factors (e.g., age, gender, motivation, etc.). The chapter ends by describing some of the frameworks and methods that are used in L2 research.

In **Part 7: Language, Cognition, and the Brain**, *Chapter 14: Psycholinguistics* introduces you to how language is processed and represented in the mind. You will also read about how sounds, words, and sentences are processed and you will consider innovative methods used in psycholinguistic research. The chapter ends by presenting how the bilingual mind processes more than one language. *Chapter 15: Neurolinguistics* explores language and the brain. The chapter begins with a look at the anatomy of the human brain. You will then read about the brain areas that are most involved in language. The chapter also reviews the methods and technologies used to study the brain, including lesion studies and autopsies, hemispheric connections, neuroimaging techniques, and measures of electric and magnetic fields. You will also read about language impairment from neurological trauma such as non-fluent and fluent aphasias, acquired dyslexia, and acquired dysgraphia, along with some of the techniques used in the rehabilitation of language(s) in impaired individuals.

Finally, **Part 8: Brief Chapters** is available on the book's accompanying website. *Chapter 16: Animal Communication and Language*, begins with a discussion on the difference between language and communication. In doing so, you will see that the information conveyed in animal communication is different, yet similar in many ways, to that of humans. You will also read about how we can decode animal signals and how research is conducted on animal communication using prairie dogs and honeybees as examples. *Chapter 17: Computational Linguistics*, will offer you insight on how humans and computers interact through language. The chapter begins by defining natural (i.e., human) languages and languages of computers. You will read about the effects of language ambiguity on computation, how computation is done, and which aspects of human languages are of most interest to computational linguists. *Chapter 18: English Varieties Outside of North America*, will broaden your perspective of how English came to be a world language historically. You will learn about the types of English that are spoken outside of North America and understand how Englishes are differentiated from native-, second-, to foreign-language varieties.

The book's accompanying website also includes additional information to enrich the material found in the main chapters for those of you who wish to satisfy your curiosity about language a bit more. For example, in relation to *Chapter 1: Introducing Linguistics*, on this site you will find a short section on different approaches to how language evolved. In the online materials for *Chapter 10: Pragmatics and Discourse Analysis*, you can read about how language helps us distinguish between old and new information. Complementary materials for *Chapter 12: First Language Acquisition*, include different methodologies for studying how children acquire pragmatics. And so on.

Linguistics Intersects with Many Other Disciplines

As you will see, linguistics is pertinent and complimentary to many (if not all) fields of study. Here are just a few examples – in no particular order – of how other fields and professionals can learn from linguistics:

- Speech and language pathologists, along with professionals working with individuals with speech impairments, can learn a great deal from phonetics (Chapter 2), phonology (Chapter 3), psycholinguistics (Chapter 14), and neurolinguistics (Chapter 15), to inform and improve assessment and treatment for their patients.
- Sociologists, anthropologists, community service personnel, and non-profit organizations can benefit from learning about how language works in society, how it functions and varies across cultures, how it shapes who we are as individuals

(Chapter 9: Sociolinguistics), and in the case of English, how it varies in other places (Chapter 18: English Varieties Outside of North America).

- Business professionals and individuals working in communication studies and global relations may learn important things about human interaction such as appropriateness, politeness, and discourse patterns (Chapter 10: Pragmatics and Discourse Analysis) and meaning in general (Chapter 6: Semantics). These individuals will learn that these issues do not always transfer across other languages and cultures.
- Historians, geographers, and archeologists, among others, can gain a deeper understanding of the historical context of language, including language evolution (Chapter 8: Historical Linguistics), the emergence of writing in human languages (Chapter 11: Writing Systems), and the historical relationships among languages (Chapter 7: The Classification of Languages).
- Biologists, zoologists, and those working in the natural sciences can gain a deeper understanding of the complexities of human language and communication by comparing how this works among other animal species (Chapter 16: Animal Communication and Language).
- Cognitive psychologists, medical professionals, and health care providers can inform their practices by learning about how the mind processes languages (Chapter 14: Psycholinguistics) and how the brain stores languages – which can be greatly affected if trauma occurs to certain brain areas (Chapter 15: Neurolinguistics).
- Developmental psychologists, teachers, educational administrators, and language policy makers can sharpen their understanding of how infants and children (Chapter 12: First Language Acquisition) and adults (Chapter 13: Second Language Acquisition) develop language. In turn, this can inform theories of human development across the lifespan, teaching practices, and important policies on language.
- Individuals working in math or computer science will appreciate the computational nature of language. If these individuals work on tasks such as equation building and computer programming or modeling, they will enjoy learning about how words are built (Chapter 4: Morphology), how sentences are structured (Chapter 5: Syntax), and how computers and humans communicate with one another (Chapter 17: Computational Linguistics).
- And much more!

Pedagogies and Special Features

There are several features that make this book the ideal tool to introduce you to the field of linguistics. Here are just a few of these that you will have at your fingertips:

- Every so often, you will come to a *Pause and Reflect* box which asks that you briefly stop for a moment to contemplate what you have just learned. These boxes often ask you a question based on your personal experience.

- *Eyes on World Languages* boxes introduce you to how languages (other than English) work across the globe. These boxes, which are related to the text around them, encourage you to think about how different or similar languages function compared to the one(s) you speak.
- *Exercises* at the end of the chapter provide a series of problems designed to help you understand and apply the core concepts.
- To pique your interest about linguistics, *Linguistics Tidbits* boxes offer you situations reminiscent of the question "Did you know that … ?".
- The book includes a complete *Glossary* of the main terms used in the text. These terms are bolded throughout the text to make you aware of their importance.
- *Answers* to *Pause and Reflect* boxes are found at the end of each chapter.
- *Answers* to *Exercises* are available with instructor access on the book's accompanying website.

PART 1

INTRODUCTION

1 Introducing Linguistics

Joyce Bruhn de Garavito and John W. Schwieter

OVERVIEW

In this chapter, you will develop a better understanding of the field of linguistics. Our objectives are to:

- **examine how to approach linguistics as a scientific process of inquiry;**
- **contrast language and other forms of communication;**
- **compare the notion of *prescriptive grammar* to *descriptive grammar*;**
- **develop a general idea of the roots of modern linguistics; and**
- **explore some of the different approaches to the science of linguistics.**

1.1 What Is Linguistics?

Linguistics is the scientific study of language. Although linguists agree on this definition, not all of them agree on what the objectives of linguistics should be.

1.1.1 Linguistics and Science

What do we mean when we say linguistics is *the scientific study of language*? Let us first examine the definition for **science** found in the Oxford English Dictionary Online:

> The intellectual and practical activity encompassing the systematic study of the structure and behaviour of the physical and natural world through observation and experiment. (https://en.oxforddictionaries.com/definition/science).

From this definition, we can extract the following points that are relevant to the science of linguistics:

- Science is an activity. As with all other sciences, linguistics is something we do, it is a process of inquiry. It is the pursuit of knowledge, not a body of truths that must be accepted. The aim of linguistics is not only to describe language, but also to explain why it is as it is.

- Science uses a systematic approach to each field (the study of language, in our case). Linguistics is systematic in the types of methodology it uses, examining data, examining the existing body of knowledge, forming hypotheses (conjectures about possible answers, proposed explanations), testing the hypotheses (evaluating the evidence), constructing theories, and making predictions.
- Science may involve the study of structure and behavior. You will read about both of these aspects of linguistics in this textbook. On the one hand, we discuss the structure and meaning of sounds, words, and sentences in language, and on the other hand, we look at how language is used to communicate and how it is processed. The aim is to explain structure and behavior through general principles.
- Science focuses on the physical and natural world. In our case, language is a physical activity that involves actions by several parts of the body, depending on the type of linguistic expression. For example, sign language (see 1.1.9 below) relies heavily on movement of the hands and arms in relation to the body and on movement of face muscles. Oral communication involves the breathing apparatus, the larynx, the mouth, etc. Writing involves the hands, fingers, and arms. In all cases, the activity of the body is generated and controlled by the brain. Language is essentially a form of knowledge in the mind/brain which constitutes part of the natural world and that is used for social purposes.
- Science uses experimentation and observation. This is an important point because in order to understand how language works, we must rely on data. Data may often be imperfect, so we must construct experiments that are appropriate for explaining the data. Although this is quite easy to discern in the case of language acquisition studies or psycholinguistics, experimentation is also common in areas such as syntax, in which we construct both acceptable and unacceptable sentences with the objective of understanding the underlying principles.

PAUSE AND REFLECT 1.1

Consider the following two linguistic hypotheses and the evidence provided for each. Focusing on what you have learned about linguistics as a science, is the evidence in each case sufficient to support the hypotheses? Why or why not?

i. Hypothesis: Ancient Nahuatl (Aztec, a language spoken in Mexico) and Ancient Greek are related languages.

Evidence: In both Nahuatl and Ancient Greek, the word for god is quite similar: *teo* in Nahuatl (as in the ancient city of Teotihuacan near Mexico City) and *theos* in Greek.

ii. Hypothesis: All of the following languages are related: the Germanic languages (English, German, Danish, Dutch, etc.), Latin and languages derived from it (Spanish, French, Portuguese, etc.), Greek, Persian, and Sanskrit (see Chapter 7 The Classification of Languages and Chapter 8 Historical Linguistics).

Evidence: for hundreds of words, and with no exceptions, there are correlations between how words are pronounced in one set of languages and how they are pronounced in another set. For example, the sound /p/ is systematically pronounced as /f/ in the corresponding words of Germanic origin, as shown in the following examples, which all mean *foot*:

PAUSE AND REFLECT 1.1 (*cont.*)

English: *foot*	Latin: *pes*
Dutch: *voet* (pronounced foet)	Spanish: *pie*
German: *Fuss*	French: *pied*
Danish: *fod*	Greek: πουσ (pronounced pus)
Norwegian: *fot*	Sanskrit: *pada*

1.1.2 Linguistics and Language

Although we have explained what we mean by *a scientific study,* we have not explained what **language** is. When asked, most of us would define language as the form of **communication** used by humans. We define communication as the transfer of information from a sender to a receiver.

Strangely enough, linguists do not agree that language and communication are at all equivalent. This is because we now understand that there is a system of knowledge underlying our use of language. Although how we use language to communicate is of the utmost importance, we must also consider the knowledge that allows us to do so. Many of the chapters in this book aim at describing the fundamental linguistic knowledge that we need in order to communicate. We will have more to say about this knowledge below.

However, no linguist would argue that communication is not crucial to the study of language. How we interact with others, how language is used in social groups and communities, how it allows us to express our innermost feelings and ideas, are fundamental areas of study in linguistics (see Chapter 9 Sociolinguistics).

We must also distinguish between *language* and *a language*. English is a language, as are Portuguese, Mohawk, Navajo, Cree, and sign language. Languages vary from each other in their structure and how they are used. However, many linguists go beyond the study of individual languages to examine how language works in the mind and what properties can be considered universal. For example, in all languages, meaning depends on how words are organized in sentences. All languages also include some form of negation and ways of indicating that an utterance is a question, among other properties. If you are interested in the evolution of language, read 'Delving Deeper' in Chapter 1's resources on the website to accompany this book at www.cambridge.org/introducing-linguistics.

In short, for many linguists, though certainly not all, an important objective in linguistics is to understand knowledge of language, although very often the only way to do so is to examine how a particular language is used. Linguistics makes a distinction between **competence** and **performance**. Competence refers to our unconscious

LINGUISTICS TIDBITS: WHAT IS A LANGUAGE?
Most of us agree that English is a language. However, as you will read in Chapter 9 Sociolinguistics and Chapter 18 English varieties outside of North America, the dialect or variety of English that you speak is different from the ones that others speak, although none is superior. In some languages, varieties may be so different that communication becomes difficult, as in Mandarin and Cantonese. In other cases, people that consider they speak different languages can communicate quite easily, as is the case with Galician (spoken in Northwest Spain) and Portuguese, or Norwegian and Swedish. In other words, the definition of *a language* is often a question of politics and power more than a linguistic question. For this reason, it is often said that *a language is a dialect with an army and a navy.*

knowledge of language and performance describes how we use language. For example, imagine that someone loses the ability to produce sounds. We would not say the person's knowledge of language had been affected, their competence would remain intact. However, their performance in speech production would be greatly affected.

1.1.3 Language: A Grammar and a Lexicon

We have said that the linguistic knowledge that constitutes competence is unconscious. By this we mean that we can't necessarily explain how we build sentences, we just know how to do it, because the rules to do so are in an inaccessible part of our minds (Jackendoff, 2002; Paradis, 2009; Ullman, 2001). In its simplest form, language knowledge consists of the mental representation of a grammar and a lexicon, or our mental dictionary. We will explain these terms below, noting that each of them has a somewhat different definition in linguistics than in our everyday usage.

1.1.4 Prescriptive Grammar

In everyday usage, the term *grammar* refers to what we learned early on in school. You may also think of grammar as something that refers to the rules of how we should speak and write. In many cases this advice is useful, for example in a job interview or when writing an essay. However, we often break many of these supposed grammar rules because they rely on someone's opinion about how we ought to speak, rather than on how language really works. Because these rules are often arbitrary, they may lead to confusion.

We use the term prescriptive grammar to refer to the set of rules that tells us how we ought to speak.[1] The term prescriptive grammar is often contrasted to **descriptive grammar** which describes how we actually use language. Linguists will never tell you how you should speak, in the same way as a biologist will not tell a plant how to grow. They will, however, examine how you speak, and how your speech may differ from the speech of other people.

---

[1] See https://www.theguardian.com/books/2014/aug/15/steven-pinker-10-grammar-rules-break for an amusing look at some prescriptive rules by Steven Pinker.

EYES ON WORLD LANGUAGES: PRESCRIPTIVE GRAMMARS IN DIFFERENT CULTURES

Cultures have distinct views on the need for prescriptive grammars. In some countries, we find academies charged with maintaining a certain standard and often defending the purity of a language. For example, the *Accademia della Crusca* 'Academy of the Bran' that regulates the use of Italian was founded in Florence in 1583; *L'Académie Française* 'The French Academy' was established in 1635 in Paris; *La Real Academia de la Lengua* 'The Royal Academy of the Language' was founded in 1713 in Madrid; and *L'Office Québécois de la Langue Française* 'The Québec Office of the French Language' was founded in 1961 in Québec. Today, these institutions are all going strong, producing dictionaries and grammars that continue to be useful to specialists and the general public alike.

There is no equivalent of these academies for English. In fact, the first attempts at standardizing English spelling only took place in the mid-eighteenth century. English has always accepted foreign words without problem, although in the twentieth century, it has begun to be more of an exporter of words rather than an importer.

However, whether there are official entities in charge of language or not, most people have very strong feelings about the 'correct' way of using a language. People often criticize the speech of others living a few kilometers away. Let's face it, most of us are language snobs.

1.1.5 The Term *Grammar* as Used by Linguists

Language can be analyzed at various levels. For example, the sound system constitutes one level and the way sentences are built constitutes another. Linguists use the term **grammar** to refer to our unconscious mental representation of language at all levels, including sounds (see Chapter 2 Phonetics, which looks at how linguistic sounds are produced and heard, and Chapter 3 Phonology, which looks at how languages organize the basic units of sound); words (see Chapter 4 Morphology, which looks at how words are formed); phrases and sentences (see Chapter 5 Syntax, which looks at organizing words into larger units); and meaning (see Chapter 6 Semantics, which studies the meaning of what we hear or produce).

PAUSE AND REFLECT 1.2

Determine if the following statements are examples of prescriptive grammar or whether they belong in a linguistics book.

i.   The verb *will* should be used with second and third persons only (*you will, he will*). With first person the correct form is *shall* (I shall).
ii. In many dialects of the British Isles, the sound /h/ is not pronounced at the beginning of words.
iii. Second language learners of English often leave off the /s/ of third person verbs: *he say; she come.*
iv. In some regions of Canada, French speakers refer to a truck as *le truck* instead of the correct form, *le camion*. In France, speakers may use the term *weekend* instead of the correct form, *fin de semaine*.
v.   In many dialects of English the negation of the verb *to be* in the present is produced as *ain't*.

1.1.6   The Lexicon

The **lexicon** includes all words that make up our vocabulary. However, besides what we all consider to be vocabulary items, the lexicon also includes grammatical information about words. For example, the lexicon includes information about the meaning of a word like *make* (that it can mean 'to assemble or construct') and information about the type of sentence the word may appear in (i.e., the sentence must include information about who is doing the making and what is being made). In other words, the lexicon tells us what type of verb *make* is. An example of the use of the word *make* is seen in (1).

(1)   a. Jorge made a pie.
     b. *Jorge made.
     c. *Made a pie.
     d. *Made.

You will notice that examples (1b), (1c), and (1d) are preceded by an asterisk *. You may have already seen or used the * in this way when texting a friend. The * indicates that these sentences are somehow wrong in English. (1b) sounds incomplete because it does not indicate what is made, (1c) sounds incomplete because it does not indicate who does the making, and (1d) sounds wrong because it does not include either. The information in the lexicon is what allows us to make these judgements.

Besides knowledge of a grammar and a lexicon, other types of information are also necessary to use language, including social factors (see Chapter 9 Sociolinguistics) and pragmatic factors (see Chapter 10 Pragmatics and Discourse Analysis). These additional elements also constitute knowledge of language, and in many cases, although not all, they fall beneath the level of consciousness too.

1.1.7   Language and Communication

If the foundation of language is a form of knowledge, where does that leave **communication**?

Nobody denies that we use language to communicate. The problem is that we can have communication without having knowledge of a grammar. Imagine you are driving along the highway and you see a sign like the one in Figure 1.1.

Figure 1.1 Moose road sign

Think about the information that Figure 1.1 conveys to drivers. It tells drivers that they are going through an area where moose are likely to cross. As a consequence, drivers know they should slow down and be very attentive. However, there is no grammar involved. We usually pass driving tests to prove that we can interpret signs like this. Therefore, the knowledge involved is conscious and learned.

PAUSE AND REFLECT 1.3

They say a picture is worth a thousand words. Do you think this is accurate? Try to illustrate the following sentences through a drawing (it does not have to be artistic). Do you think the drawing is a true representation of the sentence? Do you think everyone would understand it in the same way? Why or why not?

i. There isn't a small hippopotamus in the classroom.
ii. I believe it may rain.
iii. Look out the window on your left.

1.1.8 Animals and Communication

Another problem with the use of the word *communication* to define language is that we now know that, in the natural world, communication between animals is common (see Chapter 16 Animal Communication and Language). In other words, animals transfer information to each other. To do so, they develop signals that can be interpreted by other animals. These signals can be of several types: visual (e.g., the use of color to repel or attract; showing teeth to ward off other animals); smell (e.g., to attract mates or repel danger); sound (e.g., singing to attract a mate or growling to repel an enemy); tactile (e.g., touching to bond); movement (e.g., gesturing and posing to indicate dominance or submission); etc. Needless to say, none of these forms include a complex grammar, although, as you will read in Chapter 16 Animal Communication and Language, a careful analysis of the communication system of some animals, such as prairie dogs, lessens some of the differences between animal and human communication. Below you will find a few examples of animal communication:

- Ants lay down pheromones (chemical signals) to tell other ants where they may find food;
- Vervet monkeys have different calls to warn other monkeys about the presence of different types of predators;
- Chimpanzees signal the presence of a threat by raising their arms or slapping the ground;
- The color of some frogs (also some insects and snakes) is a warning to other species that the animal is poisonous and should be avoided;
- Many primates groom one another very frequently, forming social bonds among group members;
- Fireflies glow to attract mates;

- Cobras inflate their hoods (like cats arch their backs) to appear bigger and/or intimidate;
- Birds have complex songs that may differ from region to region. Birdsong may be used to attract mates, to warn off other males, or to call to the fledglings;
- You will find many examples of whale song on YouTube and there is currently a great deal of interest in this topic. Whales are able to communicate over great distances. As with birds, they may be attracting mates or warning other whales.

PAUSE AND REFLECT 1.4

Give three examples of non-linguistic communication among humans. In other words, come up with examples where no words or grammar are involved.

Animal Communication vs. Human Language

You probably do not need to be further convinced that animal communication is not necessarily like human language. However, besides the presence or absence of a grammar, there are noteworthy differences between animal communication and human language. In Chapter 16 Animal Communication and Language, you will find that some of these differences do not always apply.

- As you will see throughout the textbook, language is characterized by having at least two main levels. The first consists of a sound system (or a sign system in sign languages) made up of units that do not have any intrinsic meaning. For example, the sound /l/ has no meaning on its own. The second level happens when sounds are combined into words and phrases that do have meaning.
- Animal communication is about the here and now. A monkey uttering a cry to warn other monkeys is doing so because right now there is a snake coming through the grass, not because he is retelling a story from last week. Human language escapes the present context. We can talk about past and future, what could happen, what may happen, what we wish would happen, etc.
- Animal communication is not generally linked to mental concepts. That is, the monkey sees a specific snake and detects present danger. He does not generalize the concept of *snake* or, in fact, the concept of *danger*. Humans, on the other hand, have a very rich system of concepts. Just think about the difference between the *birds* ostrich and canary.
- Human language allows for creativity. A grammar constituted by a limited set of principles or rules, combined with an unlimited number of words, allows us to express ideas, thoughts, feelings, etc., that have never been expressed before. That is, we don't just repeat things. Animals are much more restricted in this sense, not only because of the limited number of signs, but also because they do not permit new combinations.

- Animal communication is ideal for the context in which animals live. It is made, so to speak, for the niche in nature that they occupy. They do not need a more sophisticated form of communication. For millions of years, their communication has contributed to their survival. Humans, in contrast, have traveled the world and have learned to adapt to different environments. As profoundly social animals, humans need language. And as profoundly curious animals, humans need to understand what the gift of language consists of.

1.1.9 Sign Language

As with oral languages, **sign languages** include a grammar and a lexicon, and they serve the same communicative purposes. Look at the following list showing that sign language, just like oral languages, is also considered *a language* as we have defined it:

- Sign languages have a system of basic signs that, although they do not have meaning of their own, when put together form meaningful utterances. These signs are equivalent to the sounds in oral language and often obey similar rules.
- There are fully developed and quite complex systems of grammar in sign languages.
- Sign languages include a sophisticated lexicon.
- There are no limits to what you can express with sign languages.
- Sign languages are different from each other, in the same way English is different from German.
- Sign languages are not based on spoken languages.

1.2 Development of Modern Linguistics

It is important for any scientific field to understand its roots. As you will see below, the roots of linguistics go far back in time, although many of the scholars involved would not have called themselves linguists.

1.2.1 Brief Overview of the History of Linguistics

People often have very specific ideas as to what language is, how it is learned, and what it says about humans. If we look at records of the past, we will see that this has always been the case. Among other things, in order to develop writing, people had to understand how

LINGUISTICS TIDBITS: GEORGE BERNARD SHAW AND HENRY SWEET

In 1913, the play *Pygmalion*, by the British playwright George Bernard Shaw, was first presented in London. It was later made into a musical and a movie under the title *My Fair Lady* (1964). The play tells the story of Eliza Doolittle, a woman who sells flowers in the market and wants to learn 'proper English' so that she can work in a shop. She goes to a linguist, Professor Henry Higgins, to ask for his help. The character of Henry Higgins is based on a real linguist, Henry Sweet, who is famous as one of the developers of the notion of a phoneme, a unit of linguistic sound, as you will read in Chapter 3 Phonology.

Other movies that include linguists are *Still Alice* (2014), about a linguist who is diagnosed with Alzheimers, and *Arrival* (2016), about a linguist who must help interpret an alien language. There are also linguists featured in several *Star Trek* episodes and movies.

the sound system and words (or parts of words) of a language interacted. Writing was developed independently at least four times (Babylonia, ancient Egypt, China, and Mesoamerica) (see Chapter 11 Writing Systems). Four thousand years ago, what was perhaps the first dictionary was developed in Sumeria (Babylonia).

Other cultures have also left information about their understanding of language. In the Hindu tradition, Pāṇini, who lived around 500 BCE, gave us rules for the formation and pronunciation of words in Sanskrit that are still valuable today. Many of our ideas about how language is structured are derived from Greek and Latin linguistics. Arabic grammarians focused on the formation of words and sound systems and greatly influenced European thinkers in the Middle Ages and Renaissance. In the late seventeenth and early eighteenth centuries, we saw the birth of systematic approaches to the history of languages and how they relate to each other (see Chapter 8 Historical Linguistics).

Modern linguistics, as understood in this textbook, started to take shape at the end of the nineteenth and early twentieth centuries. At this time, linguists shifted their focus from how languages evolve over time to considering them as autonomous systems which should be studied individually. In part, this was a consequence of the realization that the indigenous languages of the Americas exhibited systematic differences from widely studied languages spoken in Europe and elsewhere.

Scholars who laid the groundwork for modern linguistics include Franz Boaz (1858–1942), Edward Sapir (1884–1939), and Leonard Bloomfield (1887–1949). One of the most influential linguists of this time was Ferdinand de Saussure (1857–1913), a Swiss linguist who argued that language is a system of arbitrary signs. His work has been very influential on European thinkers outside of linguistics.

1.2.2 Modern Linguistics: Main Questions

Each subfield of linguistics has a set of main questions. However, there are some that are fundamental to the field. These basic questions are the following:[2]

(1) What is language?
(2) How is language acquired?
(3) How is language used?
(4) How is language represented in the brain?

[2] Recently a fifth question has received a lot of attention: How did language evolve?

You will not be surprised to know that linguists may differ in important ways in their approaches to these questions. Furthermore, as you will see during your journey learning about linguistics, these questions are tightly linked to each other. In other words, the answer to one question may lead to a particular answer for the others, as we will see below.

1.2.3   The Questions of Linguistics: Theories

There are several theories about language, and these theories have bearing not only on the answers that are given but also on how the issues are framed. However, disagreements in science are not a sign of a weakness. They represent strength in any field of study.

Why do these theories matter? Imagine that you have misplaced a book. If you have absolutely no idea where it is, you could imagine it is at school, in Singapore or Argentina, or that a little green linguist goblin stole it. In other words, there is no limit to the hypotheses you formulate. On the other hand, you may have some idea: you did not leave the house yesterday and you remember reading at home, so the book must be somewhere in the house. This theory reduces considerably the search space for you, making it more precise. You may now develop hypotheses about where the book is. Perhaps you put it under your pillow before going to sleep last night, or perhaps your roommate moved it when cleaning. These hypotheses allow you to constrain your search even more. Hypothesizing and narrowing possibilities applies in all sciences. We need to develop theories about our subject to narrow our search space and make our questions manageably testable. Simplifying somewhat, we can divide the different approaches to the study of language into two main branches: functional accounts and generative accounts.

1.2.4   Functional Accounts of Language

Generally, **functional theories of grammar** refer to a variety of approaches that argue that the main function of language is to communicate. Therefore, the main objective of linguistic analysis is to determine how language works during interactions between people. Functionalists look at how language helps us accomplish our goals in society.

Behaviorism

In the middle of the twentieth century, **behaviorism**, a psychological theory of learning, was very influential in North America. In 1957, one of the main proponents of behaviorism, the psychologist B. F. Skinner, published a book on language and language learning titled *Verbal Behavior*. According to Skinner and his followers, language is no different from any other form of human activity, from learning to ride a bike to learning physics. Like other organisms, humans learn by responding to stimuli. If the response to the stimulus is positively reinforced, it is learned. If the reinforcement is unpleasant, the situation will be avoided.

As you can imagine, for behaviorists, the input and environment are critical in establishing the set of habits which, according to this view, make up language, because it is only by frequent reinforcement that language can become habitual. Reinforcement can take many forms, from receiving nourishment to simply being understood. Imitation is fundamental to this approach as you will read in Chapter 12 First Language Acquisition and Chapter 13 Second Language Acquisition.

As an example, imagine that a child is hungry. Hunger represents the stimulus. If the child's response is the word *milk*, he/she may be fed and will therefore associate the reward with the word uttered. If, however, the child responds with a word that sounds like *ball*, s/he will not be rewarded, so the association will not be made.

PAUSE AND REFLECT 1.5

Try to apply behaviorism to one of your activities (a sport, reading, playing video games). What is the stimulus for this activity? How do you respond to the stimulus? What reinforcement do you receive? Is the reinforcement enough to make you want to continue the activity, even when it is difficult?

The evidence for the Stimulus, Response, Reinforcement view of language learning fails to adequately explain language acquisition and/or use. As you will learn in Chapter 12 First Language Acquisition, it is not that children do not imitate what they hear, some imitate quite a lot. However, child grammars develop over time and imitation seems constrained by the stage the child is in at a particular point in time. A child at the two-word stage will imitate *I will throw the ball* as *Throw ball*.

To summarize, for behaviorist approaches, language is viewed as a set of habits that are acquired through the reinforcement of certain responses to stimuli.

Usage-based Models of Language

In the twenty-first century, the most important model of language based on language use in social interactions is by Michael Tomasello (2003). This approach focuses on specific events in which communication takes place. According to Tomasello, it is during these interactions that language is learned and used. The linguistic skills that people may have are the result of all the interactions that they have been involved in throughout their life. The linguistic units that people use are identified by watching what people actually say. These units may consist of anything from whole constructions that are acquired as chunks (e.g., *How's it going? What's up?*) to highly complex structures (e.g., *I forgot to send Mary the gift*). Unlike most behaviorists and emergentists, as you will read below, Tomasello argues that language use leads to the development of linguistic rules in a speaker's mind.

To summarize, usage-based approaches consider language a complex phenomenon that includes a grammar but also whole units that may be analyzed into parts or not. Language is acquired mainly through repeated use.

Emergentism

Emergentism has been used as a source of explanation in many fields, including biology, evolution, economics, cognition, literature and art, and linguistics. Based on complex mathematical descriptions, emergentists argue that certain systems, including language, emerge naturally from multiple factors that interact at several levels. However, what emerges at any given level is not completely understandable in terms of the previous level(s). For example, in biology, although at one level bodies are made up of atoms, bodies cannot be completely explained by their atomic constitution.

Emergentism makes widespread use of online simulations to model its descriptions. The linguistic application of this theory assumes that knowledge of language constitutes an emergent property that is arrived at mainly through analogy and association. We make use of analogy when we realize that a phrase such as *the blue car* is similar to the phrase *a yellow submarine*. We use association when we say that the phrase *a yellow submarine* is associated, for example, with a particular meaning.

Language learning is best represented by **connectionist models**. For connectionists, diverse sociolinguistic, communicative, cognitive, and psychological factors, among others, interact with the structures of the brain (see Chapter 15 Neurolinguistics). Mediated by a learning mechanism based on neural connections, these structures produce the apparent regularities of language. Connectionist models are derived from computer simulations of the brain that are used to test language learning modules.

To summarize, similar to other functional theories, connectionist models are based on the notion that all linguistic units are acquired through language use. In these usage-based perspectives, the acquisition of language is the piecemeal learning of many thousands of constructions. Unlike most usage-based approaches, however, connectionism assumes that there is no real underlying grammar.

PAUSE AND REFLECT 1.6

Artists have often created whole universes and occasionally languages to go with them. Examples are Elvish, created by the author of *Lord of the Rings*, J. R. R Tolkien; Klingon developed for *Star Trek* by linguist Mark Okrand; and Dothraki and Valyrian, developed for *Game of Thrones* by another linguist, David Peterson. In many cases people have learned these as foreign languages.

Although these languages were first created on paper, fans often hold meetings in which they practice communication.

Consider usage-based theories of language. Would learning these languages be any different from learning other human languages? Will they become more "natural" with time? Would the language change the more it is used?

1.2.5 Generative Approaches

The view that language is a form of knowledge is embedded in **generative approaches**. These approaches are referred to as generative because they explain how humans can *generate* an infinite number of sentences of a language. Noam Chomsky (1928–), one of the most cited scholars in modern times, is the founder of this school of thought, although some of his ideas can be traced far back in the history of language studies.

There are three main components of the generative approach that explain our knowledge of language: an innate (genetic) component; experience with the language; and general principles, including principles of learning and processing (Chomsky, 2005).

1. **Innate (genetic) component**. Language acquisition by children is constrained by an innate set of principles that is commonly referred to as **Universal Grammar (UG)**. We say it is universal in the sense that it does not vary across languages or different times (Mendívil-Giró, 2018). UG is part of our endowment as humans, in the same way as we are endowed, in the majority of cases, with the ability to see. In fact, Chomsky often speaks about the distinctly human language faculty. The language faculty grows in a similar fashion to other faculties. UG serves to constrain the search space for the child that is learning a language. No human language has been found to violate UG.

2. **Experience**. We must be exposed to language in order to acquire it. In this respect, functionalist and generativist approaches agree.

3. **General principles**. Besides the linguistic principles that make up UG, we also need learning principles, which may be encoded in the structure of our minds/brains (see Chapter 15 Neurolinguistics), and a way to process the information from the linguistic representations (see Chapter 14 Psycholinguistics).

As Chomsky (2005) points out, this is not different from the growth of any of the organs of the body. In order for your arms to grow, you need the genetic code, you need the environment (eating, for example, is crucial), and you need principles of growth that are general to the world of organisms.

What evidence do we find for the presence of an innate linguistic component for humans? The main argument comes from what is generally referred to as ***the logical problem of language acquisition***. Basically, the logical problem says that children acquire knowledge that goes beyond what can be inferred from the input. Input includes not only the language the children hear but also the context in which it is produced. The main issue is whether children can only acquire what they have heard in a specific context, or whether they develop a more complex grammar. In particular, whether children develop knowledge of what is possible and not possible in their language. If they are able to learn more than is clear from the input, we may assume the input is not sufficient and we must hypothesize that there is another source for the knowledge of speakers, UG. This insufficient input is often referred to as the **poverty of the stimulus**.

Linguists are rigorous in determining what constitutes evidence for UG. They try to design questions that show that the input cannot be the source of knowledge. As an example, consider the sentences in (2).

(2) a. I believe that Ernest stole the money.
     b. I believe the claim that Ernest stole the money.
     c. What do you believe that Ernest stole?
     d. *What do you believe the claim that Ernest stole?

Your intuitions probably tell you that (2a), (2b), and (2c) are acceptable sentences in English, but that (2d) sounds wrong. Why do we have this intuition? We can understand (2d) so it is not the meaning that is problematic. Furthermore, we have probably never been told that sentences such as (2d) are impossible. Therefore, the origin of knowledge about these sentences must be addressed.

PAUSE AND REFLECT 1.7

The sentences in (2) are examples of a violation of grammar that can nevertheless be interpreted. However, it is possible to produce sentences that have excellent grammar but no interpretation. One of the most famous sentences of this type was created by Chomsky: *Colourless green ideas sleep furiously.*

Another famous instance is a poem from *Alice in Wonderland*, written by Lewis Carroll: Jaberwocky. Although the words do not make sense, the grammar allows us to interpret far more than expected.

Here are the first two verses of the poem. Except for names, replace all the nonsense words with real words.

Then, compare yours to a classmate's to see if you replaced them with the same type of word.

> 'Twas brillig, and the slithy toves
>   Did gyre and gimble in the wabe:
> All mimsy were the borogoves,
>   And the mome raths outgrabe.

> "Beware the Jabberwock, my son!
>   The jaws that bite, the claws that catch!
> Beware the Jubjub bird, and shun
>   The frumious Bandersnatch!"

Now consider the following: little children often overgeneralize irregular verbs. They say things like *goed* and *breaked* instead of *went* and *broke*. This is not evidence for UG. Although generally these forms are not part of the input, you do not need to appeal to UG to explain this fact; human brains are very well suited to find patterns and to generalize in all domains.

To end, we must acknowledge that both functionalist and generativist approaches to language have been fruitful, advancing our understanding of the issues in far reaching ways. Although we have presented both approaches as opposed to each other, the reality is that linguists are found along several places in a continuum, according to how much importance they assign to input and/or to innate abilities.

EYES ON WORLD LANGUAGES: BIRTH OF A NEW LANGUAGE

Before the late 1970s, deaf people in Nicaragua were mainly isolated. This situation was remedied when, between 1977 and 1980, two schools for the deaf were opened in Managua, the capital. Some of the deaf children who attended the school used some type of home signs to communicate, but the teachers were instructed to focus on teaching Spanish, using lip reading and fingerspelling. They were not successful. However, outside the classroom, the children developed a system of signs to communicate. As the American linguist Judy Kegl found, the younger children who entered the school quickly made the basic sign system used by the older children into a full-fledged language. In this way, Nicaraguan Sign Language was born. It has been argued that children applied UG principles to develop the grammar of this new language.

1.3 Why Study Linguistics?

As you may have gathered from this chapter, linguistics contributes to our understanding of how the human mind/brain works and how humans communicate. Curiosity about language is what fascinates many linguists. However, there are also practical applications that may be appealing. Here is a brief list of the opportunities that linguistics may open for you. For a more comprehensive list visit the page of the Linguistic Society of America https://www.linguisticsociety.org.

- Linguistics has many applications in the area of digital technologies including speech recognition, artificial intelligence, digital communications, etc.
- Many NGOs use linguists for field work or interpretation. For example, those fighting for the preservation of endangered languages often employ linguists for advice.
- Linguists are often employed to help in translation, although current technologies often rely on non-linguistic approaches.
- Linguists may be employed by government agencies. For example, the FBI and the CIA or their counterparts in other countries often advertise for speakers of other languages with an understanding of linguistics.
- In applied practice, linguists can specialize in fields such as language pathology, forensic linguistics, or consultantships for medicine or law.
- University students majoring in areas such as anthropology, archeology, (international) business, communication studies, education, global studies, literature, neuroscience, philosophy, psychology, sociology, and more, can complement their studies by linking these fields to linguistics.

1.4 Some Myths about Linguistics and Linguists

After reading this chapter, we hope that you know that the following impressions about linguistics are false:

- Myth 1: *Linguists speak many languages.* It is often said that the most common question linguists get asked is: how many languages do you speak? As a beginning linguist, you understand that the aim of linguistics is to understand how language works, not to learn as many languages as possible.
- Myth 2: *Linguists are experts at telling you how to speak and how to improve your writing.* Linguists do not criticize how people use language; they describe and explain what we know as speakers and how we use what we know.
- Myth 3: *Rules of grammar have to be taught in order to be used correctly.* This is false because we know that children learn language without explicitly being taught, and in fact second language learners can also do this. Most of us do not consciously know the rules of our mother tongue.

1.5 A Roadmap to *Introducing Linguistics*

Throughout this chapter we have mentioned many branches of linguistics that will be discussed in this textbook. To summarize these again, the list below briefly defines these branches in the order in which we will explore them:

- Phonetics studies acoustic and articulatory properties of sounds.
- Phonology examines sound patterns and contrasts.
- Morphology looks at word structure.
- Syntax explores phrase and sentence structure.
- Semantics studies meaning.
- The classification of languages is interested in understanding the historical relationships among languages and linguistic typologies.
- Historical linguistics looks at the development and change of language over time.
- Sociolinguistics examines language in society.
- Pragmatics explores meaning and social appropriateness in context. Discourse analysis is concerned with how language users produce and understand coherent discourse. These ranches are often studied together.
- Writing systems define how script is used to communicate and how it has changed since the time of hieroglyphics.
- First language acquisition studies the development of a mother tongue.
- Second language acquisition examines the development of a non-mother tongue.
- Psycholinguistics studies language processing and cognition.
- Neurolinguistics explores language and the brain.
- Animal communication studies the ways in which non-humans communicate.
- Computational linguistics is interested in how natural language can be processed using computer algorithms.
- English varieties outside of North America will introduce you to the dialectal variations found in English.

SUMMARY

We began the chapter by defining linguistics as a science. As is typical in other sciences, in linguistics, we ask questions about an object in the natural world (in our case, language). Linguists also follow a precise method of inquiry that includes the following: constructing theories and proposing hypotheses; examining previous research; looking for evidence to refute or support hypotheses; and suggesting explanations for findings. In short, linguistics investigates and seeks to explain the nature of various aspects of language.

We also explained that defining the concept of language is not as straightforward as it seems. Although *language* is used for communication, it cannot be reduced to *communication* if by communication we mean the exchange of information. As we saw, most living organisms communicate in one way or another, but only humans have a highly sophisticated language.

The chapter also covered several important terms such as:

- *Competence and performance.* Competence refers to the unconscious knowledge of language; performance is the use of language in many types of contexts.
- *Prescriptive and descriptive grammar.* Descriptive grammar is what linguists generally do. That is, linguists try to understand how language works and how it is used; prescriptive grammars are grammars that try to impose a certain usage on others.
- *Grammar and lexicon.* As linguists understand them, grammar consists of the unconscious knowledge speakers have of the principles or rules that govern language; the lexicon consists not only of the lists of words in a language, but also the grammatical properties that are often attached to those words.
- *Language vs. a language.* Language is generally equated with the faculty of language; a language is a particular language with its own grammar and lexicon.
- *Functional and generative approaches to language and language acquisition.* Functional approaches argue that the basis of language is to be found in the way we use language to interact with other people; generative approaches believe that, although interactions may be necessary to acquire language, another ingredient must be present: knowledge of an innate set of linguistic principles, UG. Although these two positions are generally presented as opposed to each other, for many linguists, it is simply a question of whether the main focus is on input or on knowledge.

In the rest of this textbook, you will deepen your understanding of this exciting field, and hopefully your curiosity will be aroused.

EXERCISES

1.1 A policeman is called to the home of someone who was killed. He thinks the criminal is probably a robber who was caught by the owner of the house because there have been a series of robberies in the neighbourhood. The policeman takes photographs of the victim and the surroundings, questions the family, and looks for fingerprints. The family tells him several valuable items are missing. He finds fingerprints of a well-known thief who is later arrested.

    i.   What is the policeman's hypothesis in relation to the crime?
    ii.   What is the basis for the hypothesis?
    iii. What methodology did he use to solve the crime?
    iv. What evidence did he find?
    v.   Did the evidence support his hypothesis?

1.2 In Italian, unlike in English, it is not necessary to always express the subject of a sentence (the person who does the action). A researcher wants to know how often two-year-old children acquiring Italian in normal circumstances omit subjects. Other linguists have found that English children omit subjects about 30 percent of the time. The researcher therefore predicts that Italian children will also omit subjects this often. She records several two-year-old Italian children speaking to their caretakers. She finds that the children omit subjects 90 percent of the time. She concludes that this is due to the underlying grammar of Italian, which allows speakers to drop the subject.

    i.   What is the researcher's hypothesis?
    ii.   What is the basis for this hypothesis?
    iii. What methodology did the researcher use?
    iv. Did the evidence support her hypothesis?
    v.   What was her explanation for the results?

1.3   Imagine you are a linguist conducting a study of Inuktitut, a language spoken by the Inuit in the Canadian north. You want to know if Inuktitut, as it is spoken today, is like Italian, a language in which you can omit subjects, or like English, in which you can't. Inuktitut is in intense contact with English. Research has shown that contact with another language may lead to grammatical changes.

    i.   What do you think your hypothesis should be? Why?
    ii.   What methodology could you use to test your hypothesis?

1.4   Consider the lyrics to *Another Brick in the Wall*, a well-known song by Pink Floyd:

We don't need no education
We don't need no thought control
No dark sarcasm in the classroom
Teachers leave them kids alone
Hey! Teachers! Leave them kids alone
All in all it's just another brick in the wall
All in all you're just another brick in the wall.

    i.   If you are producing a prescriptive grammar, what could you say about these lyrics?
    ii.   If you are a linguist, how would your attitude change regarding these same lyrics?

1.5   Based on what you have learned in this chapter, determine whether the following statements are true or false. For those that are false, give a correct statement.

    i.   A descriptive grammar will have a rule that says: *You should never …*
    ii.   Science consists of a set of proofs that you cannot argue with.
    iii. Linguistics is not a science because language is not part of the natural world.
    iv. The following is an example of faulty performance: After drinking several beers someone says *Losht my keysh* 'I lost my keys'.
    v.   The following shows that knowledge of language is often unconscious: I know that the following sentence is not possible in English, but I don't know why it is not possible: *When you can help me?*
    vi. The plural marker /s/ (*shoes*) is part of an English speaker's lexicon.
    vii. Bees use very sophisticated dances to communicate the location of a source of food. In other words, they use language.
    viii. Generative approaches to language assume that input is not important.
    ix. Children learn mainly through imitation.
    x.   Sign languages are not real languages.

REFERENCES

Chomsky, N. (1959). Review of "Verbal Behavior" by B. F. Skinner. *Language, 35*(1), 26–58.
Chomsky, N. (2005). Three factors in language design. *Linguistic Inquiry, 36*(1), 1–22.
Gardner, R., & Gardner, B. (1969). Teaching sign language to a chimpanzee. *Science, 165*, 664–672.

Jackendoff, R. (2002). *Foundations of language: Brain, meaning, grammar, evolution*. Oxford: Oxford University Press.

Mendívil-Giró, J.-L. (2018). Is Universal Grammar ready for retirement? A short review of a longstanding misinterpretation. *Journal of Linguistics, 54*, 859–888.

Paradis, M. (2009). *Declarative and procedural determinants of second languages*. Amsterdam/Philadelphia, PA: Benjamins.

Premack, A., & Premack, D. (1972). Teaching language to an ape. *Scientific American, 227*(4), 92–99.

Savage-Rumbaugh, S. (1991). Language learning in the bonobo: How and why they learn. In N. Krasnegor, D. Rumbaugh, R. Schiefelbusch, & M. Studdert-Kennedy (Eds.), *Biological and behavioral determinants of language development* (pp. 209–234). Hillsdale, NJ: Erlbaum.

Skinner, B. (1957). *Verbal behavior*. New York, NY: Appleton-Century-Crofts.

Terrace, H. (1979). *Nim*. New York, NY: Knopf.

Tomasello, M. (2003). *Constructing a language: A usage-based theory of language acquisition*. Cambridge, MA: Harvard University Press.

Ullman, M. (2001). The neural basis of lexicon and grammar in first and second language: the declarative/procedural model. *Bilingualism: Language and Cognition, 4*(1), 105–122.

PART 2

SOUND

2 Phonetics

Christine Shea and Sarah Ollivia O'Neill

OVERVIEW

In this chapter, you will develop an understanding of the linguistic field of phonetics and will:

- explore how sounds are produced;
- learn how to describe and transcribe the sounds of the world's languages using the International Phonetic Alphabet;
- examine how sounds change when they are part of flowing speech;
- understand the physical properties of speech; and
- learn to interpret spectrograms.

2.1 What is Phonetics?

Phonetics is the study of human speech sounds. Phonetics also forms the basis for the field of phonology, the topic of the next chapter.

This chapter begins with a discussion of how sounds are produced, key to understanding how to describe and transcribe linguistic sounds. As you read, make sure to produce aloud all sounds and words. Phonetics is one of the more 'hands-on' fields of linguistics and you can actually feel and see phonetics in action when you say and hear sounds and words. For example, say the word *cat* out loud. Pay attention to the first sound. Can you feel how the middle of your tongue rises up to touch your soft palate? That is how you articulate the first sound in the word *cat*.

2.2 Speech Production

Speaking is something most of us do all day without giving it much thought. In fact, producing speech involves careful coordination of a highly sophisticated system for producing speech sounds. In Figure 2.1 below, you can see a diagram of this speech production system. Speech sounds are generated when air is pushed through the **vocal tract**. The vocal tract is the area from the nose and the nasal cavity down to the vocal

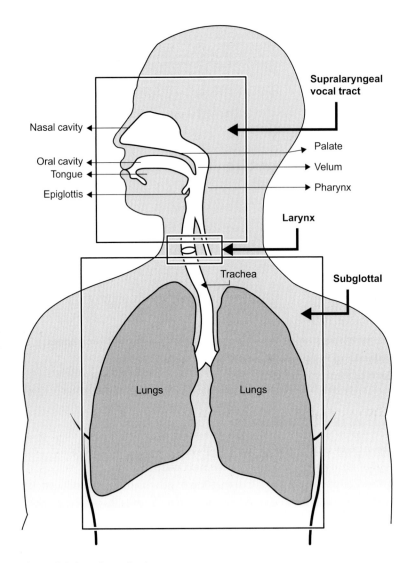

Nasal cavity

Oral cavity
Tongue
Epiglottis

Supralaryngeal vocal tract

Palate
Velum
Pharynx

Larynx

Trachea

Subglottal

Lungs   Lungs

Figure 2.1 Speech production system

cords deep in the throat. As the air passes through the vocal tract, it moves through the larynx, the pharynx, the oral cavity, and the nasal cavity.

2.2.1 Articulators

In spite of the diverse number of sounds that exist in the world's languages, humans use a small set of **articulators**, or speech organs (e.g., jaw, tongue, teeth, lips, hard palate) to produce all human speech sounds. The articulators are all located in the upper portion of the speech production system, above the larynx. Figure 2.1 shows the parts of the speech production system.

There are two types of articulators:

- **Active articulators**: move during the production of a speech sound to form a closure of some type in the vocal tract. For example, when we articulate the first sound in the word *tea*, our tongue moves to the roof of our mouth, just behind our teeth. The tongue, in this case, is the active articulator because it moves towards the roof of our mouth, which does not move and is the passive articulator.
- **Passive articulators**: do not (typically) move and are often the point of contact for an active articulator. For example, when English speakers produce the sound 'g', the back of the tongue is the active articulator and the velum (see Figure 2.1) is the passive articulator. When we name sounds, we typically refer to the passive articulator.

In Table 2.1 you can see some examples of speech sounds produced by different combinations of passive and active articulators.

PAUSE AND REFLECT 2.1

Though the vocal tract is responsible for all *speech sounds*, it is not responsible for all *language production*. What other forms of language production do you think exist that do not rely on the vocal tract? Do these forms of language production also rely on a small set of "articulators"?

2.2.2 The Lungs and Airstream

The vast majority of speech sounds are produced by air flowing from the lungs up through the vocal tract, or an **egressive pulmonic airstream**. Egressive refers to the action of pushing air out and pulmonic refers to the use of the lungs. A certain level of

TABLE 2.1 Passive and Active Articulators

Active Articulator	Passive Articulator	Speech Sounds
lower lip	upper lip upper teeth	**b**an, **p**an **f**ine, **v**ine
tongue tip/tongue blade	alveolar ridge alveolar ridge/hard palate	**t**ie, **S**ue, **n**ight **r**ing, a**rr**ow
front of the tongue	alveolar ridge+hard palate hard palate	**sh**eet, mea**s**ure, ju**dge** **y**ou, **y**ellow
back of the tongue	soft palate	**c**at, **g**o, ri**ng**
root of the tongue	uvula	no corresponding word in English Arabic word for 'story' **q**isa
vocal folds	glottis	**h**en, **h**at

air pressure is needed to keep the air flowing. The pressure is maintained by the action of muscles in the abdomen, known as **intercostals** (the muscles between the ribs) and the **diaphragm** (the large sheet of muscle separating the chest cavity from the abdomen). The intercostals raise the ribcage to allow air to flow into the lungs during inhalation, while the diaphragm helps to control the release of air so that we can speak for a reasonable period of time between breaths.

The next section of the speech production system begins above the larynx (see Figure 2.2) and is where most of the individual sounds of language are formed. This section is called the supralaryngeal, or **supraglottal** (i.e., above the glottis) articulatory system. This diagram is commonly called a **midsagittal diagram**. It is called as such because it represents a cross-sectional view of the vocal tract, divided from the tip of the nose to the back of the head.

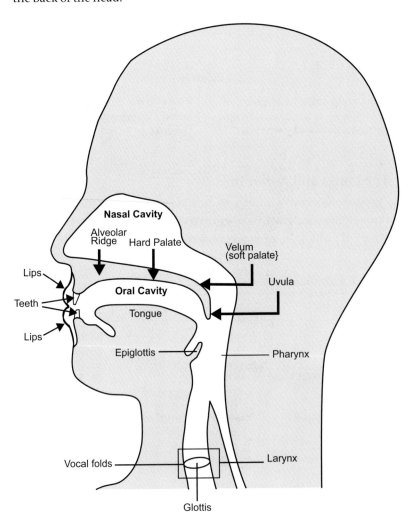

Figure 2.2 Midsagittal diagram of the supraglottal articulatory system

2.2.3 The Larynx

When air is expelled from the lungs, it passes through the **trachea (windpipe)** and then through the **larynx**. The larynx is a box-like structure made of cartilage and muscle, commonly known as the voicebox or Adam's apple. The larynx consists of the thyroid cartilage, which sits on the ring-shaped cricoid cartilage. The vocal folds (or cords) are along the side of the thyroid cartilage and are opened or closed by the muscles attached to the arytenoid cartilages. Figure 2.3 shows the larynx from the front.

As air is pushed through the space between the vocal folds, or the glottis, different types of voicing occur, depending upon the position of the vocal folds. When the vocal folds are held tightly together, they vibrate very rapidly when air passes between them as seen in Figure 2.4(a). This produces **voiced** sounds. Voicing is a low buzzing or vibrating sound that accompanies vowels and some consonants. These include [z], [g], [v], and many others.

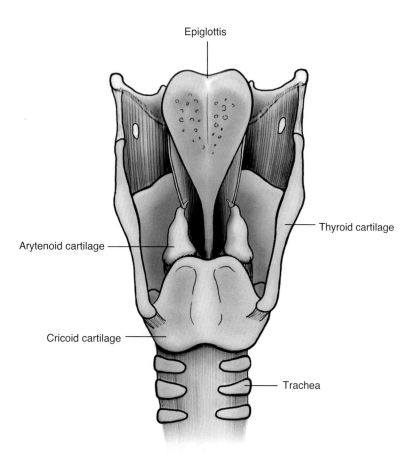

Epiglottis

Thyroid cartilage

Arytenoid cartilage

Cricoid cartilage

Trachea

Figure 2.3 The larynx from the back

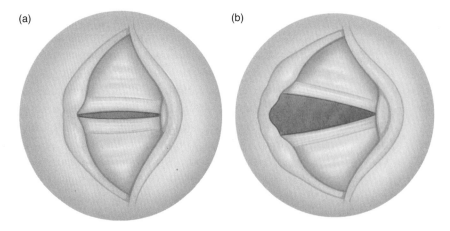

Figure 2.4 The larynx as seen from the top when producing (a) voiced (b) voiceless sounds.

If the vocal folds are pulled apart, air passes through them easily as shown in Figure 2.4(b). The vocal folds do not vibrate, the airstream is relatively unaffected and the sounds that result are **voiceless sounds**. Voiceless consonants in English include [s], [k], and [f].

PAUSE AND REFLECT 2.2

i. To determine whether a sound is voiced or voiceless, place your fingers on your neck, near your vocal cords, and feel for vibration as you speak. Do not whisper. Pay attention to the vibration of your vocal folds while you say the beginning and end of the word *shush* or the last part of the word *whisk*. You should not feel any vibration. Now try the words *zig zag* and *vigor*. You should be able to feel that your vocal folds vibrate for the duration of the word. Now compare the words *bag* and *tag*. What do you notice about the first sounds of those words? Which one is voiced and which one is voiceless? Do the same for the pair *fan* and *van*.

ii. In English, 's' and 'z' distinguish between words (e.g., *Sue* and *zoo*, *sap* and *zap*). This is not the case in all languages, however. In Latin American Spanish, for example, 'z' and 's' are both pronounced as 's'. What do you think this might mean for Spanish speakers learning English?

We can produce many different kinds of voicing (e.g., singing, shouting, changing our voice to imitate a small child or to imitate an evil villain). These voicing options, also known as **phonation**, can be realized in different ways across languages. English sounds are produced using **modal voicing**, characterized by moderate airflow from the lungs and vibration along all or most of the vocal folds.

Breathy voice is another type of phonation used in the world's languages. For breathy voice, there is strong airflow from the lungs and the vocal folds are not fully pulled together. In English, breathy voice is often used when the speaker wishes to sound romantic or seductive (see Linguistics Tidbits 'The Breathy Bombshell'). Example

(1) provides samples of breathy vowels from the Mexican indigenous language Jalapa Mazateco (Otomanguean, spoken in Jalapa de Díaz, Oaxaca). Example (2) is from Hindi (India, 370 million speakers) and has a breathy consonant at the beginning of the word.

(1)   Jalapa Mazateco   *horse*   http://www.phonetics.ucla.edu/vowels/chapter12/ mazatec.html

(2)   Hindi   *confusion*   http://www.phonetics.ucla.edu/vowels/chapter12/ hindi.html

LINGUISTICS TIDBITS: VOCAL FRY

Vocal fry, or creaky voice, was originally associated with voice pathology (people who had disordered speech) but it has recently become common in the speech of young women in Canada and the United States. It is common in the speech of young females and males and has received a great deal of attention in the popular and academic press ("Vocal fry may undermine the success of young women in the labor market", Anderson, Klofstad, Mayhew, & Venkatachalam, (2014), and "Rise of the 'vocal fry': Young women are changing how low they talk to sound more like Kim Kardashian and Katy Perry", see http://www .dailymail.co.uk/sciencetech/article-3559946/Rise-vocal-fry-Young-women-changing-low-talk-sound-like-Kim-Kardashian-Katy-Perry.html#ixzz4GwQJLSs5). As can be seen by the article and the video, the use of creaky voice by young females is often assigned certain social values by others. Creaky voice in itself does not carry any social value. As discussed above, there are languages that use creaky voice as part of their sound system, in which no social value is attached to it at all. The use of creaky voice by young females on the other hand, can carry negative social associations, suggesting that it is not valued when used by women. Vocal fry is but one example of how society assigns social values to the way individuals or groups of individuals speak. Can you think of any other examples? Does anyone you know use vocal fry? Do any male speakers that you know use it in their speech?

Another type of phonation is **creaky voice** (also known as vocal or glottal fry), characterized by irregular vibration of the vocal folds that sound as if they are popping open and closed. While English does not use breathy or creaky voice as part of its phonetic inventory of sounds, English speakers do use creaky voice at times as a social marker, as discussed in the Linguistics Tidbits Box on vocal fry.

Numerous indigenous languages spoken in North America use creaky voice as part of their phonetic inventory. Some examples are languages from British Columbia, Canada, such as Nuxalk (Salishan family, also known as Bella Coola) and Nuu-chah-nulth (Wakashan family, formerly known as Nootka), among others. Jalapa Mazateco uses both creaky and breathy voice to distinguish different sounds.

After passing through the larynx, air moves through the **pharynx**, located in the upper section of the throat. The pharynx may be constricted, resulting in **pharyngeal** sounds. These sounds are rare in English, existing only in a few dialects, but are common in Semitic languages such as Arabic and Hebrew.

2.2.4 The Nasal Cavity and the Oral Cavity

Above the pharynx is the **velum,** which lies between the entrances to the **nasal cavity** and the **oral cavity** (refer back to Figure 2.2). When the velum rises, it blocks the nasal cavity and air passes only though the mouth. This produces **oral** speech sounds. If the velum is not raised, air flows through the **nasal cavity**. Say the English nasal sound [m] and pay close attention to your mouth and nose. You should notice that your

LINGUISTICS TIDBITS: THE BREATHY BOMBSHELL

To imagine breathy voice, simply imitate the voice of Marilyn Monroe. Breathy voice is the result of bringing the vocal cords together, but relaxing them enough so that some air can escape. In many languages (see Examples (1) and (2)), this constitutes a third voicing option for consonants. In English, however, breathy voice is employed for socio-phonetic reasons. It makes the speech sound as though it comes from younger, thinner vocal cords.

mouth is closed and that air passes only through your nasal cavity. On the other hand, it is possible to hold your nose shut and successfully produce words that contain only oral sounds, such as *capital* and *brush*, even though they sound odd.

Your answers to questions in Pause and Reflect 2.3 show that in English, one sound can correspond to different letters and different letters can match a single sound. How do phoneticians deal with this inconsistency? The answer to this question is in the next section.

PAUSE AND REFLECT 2.3

i. Without looking at Table 2.1 above, think of a word that starts with a sound that corresponds to all the passive articulators. Do the same for the active articulators. For example:

    Active articulator: tongue tip   word: day

    Passive articulator: soft palate   word: singer

ii. How many individual sounds and individual letters are there in the following words?

    (a) next   (b) change   (c) these   (d) enough   (e) saw   (f) ache

iii. What is the relationship between spelling and sounds in English?

iv. Think of different ways of pronouncing the sounds that correspond to the letter 'c' (hint: there are at least four, five if you count silent 'c'). Think of all the different spellings for the sound [s].

2.3 The International Phonetic Alphabet: Transcribing the World's Languages

Phoneticians study how the sounds of human language are produced and how to characterize them. Importantly, the field of phonetics studies **all** human languages. That means that finding a way to transcribe these sounds that is independent of one particular writing system or linguistic sound system is necessary.

In 1887, a group of phoneticians who were members of the International Phonetic Association decided to create the International Phonetic Alphabet (IPA). The IPA is based on a set of principles, two important ones being:

- *The alphabet would be unambiguous.* Each sound would correspond to only one symbol and each symbol would correspond to only one sound.
- *The alphabet would be universal.* There would be a symbol to represent every sound in every human language.

2.3.1 Unambiguous: Letters and Sounds Don't Always Match

As we saw above, in English the same letter or combination of letters can often correspond to very different sounds. For example, the letter 'i' can correspond to a number of different sounds, as in the following set of words: *fit, ride, piece*. We also have the opposite situation, where one sound can correspond to many different letters and combinations of letters. For example, the vowel sound in the word *feet* can also be written with *ie* and *ea*, as in *receipt* and *eat* or as *y*, as in *pretty*. Indeed, if you are a native speaker of English, you may have had the experience of not knowing how to pronounce a word until you have heard it spoken by someone else. This is because English has an **opaque orthographic system**. English has very irregular sound-spelling correspondence. The IPA allows phoneticians to transcribe the vowel in *feet, receipt*, and *eat* using the same symbol, [i].

Related to this are dialectal differences. Within the same language speakers may read the same word but pronounce it very differently. If you travel from Sydney to Dallas to Toronto, you will hear a variety of different pronunciations of the same word. Phoneticians must be able to capture this variability in sounds across dialects of the same language and also across individuals who speak the same dialect.

PAUSE AND REFLECT 2.4

The English playwright George Bernard Shaw used the following anecdote to characterize the problem with English spelling-to-pronunciation correspondence. Imagine a new word comes into the English language that is spelled *ghoti*. How should English-speakers pronounce it? Shaw argued that the word could be pronounced as *fish*. Using the pronunciations in the words *enough, women*, and *nation*, explain how Shaw could claim that *ghoti* could be pronounced as *fish*.

Needless to say, Shaw was an active proponent of spelling reform.

2.3.2 Universal (a): Not All Languages Use Letters

Not every language has a writing system that uses letters. While English uses a fixed set of letters to write words, there are other languages, such as Mandarin, in which letters are not used at all. Instead, Mandarin uses logograms, which represent word meanings rather than pronunciations. Japanese and Korean use symbols that correspond to syllables rather than individual sounds.

2.3.3 Universal (b): Different Sounds in Different Languages

And finally, there are many more languages other than English that phoneticians and linguists must be able to transcribe, many of which have sounds that do not correspond to any English letter at all. In the Mohawk language (Iroquoian, spoken in Ontario, Quebec, and northern New York, with 3,500 native speakers) vowels can be long and short. This is similar to the difference between the vowels in the English words *b**a**t* and *b**a**d*. In *bat*, the vowel is shorter than in *bad*. In Mohawk, long vowels are also associated with changes in tone, whereby the voice rises or falls when the vowel is pronounced. For example, the word *kaná:ta* "town", which has a long '*a*' sound as well as a higher tone, or a rise in pitch. In written Mohawk, the symbol for this is '*á:*' English has no sound similar to this, nor, obviously, do we have a written symbol that could capture it. You can hear a recording of this word and others at the following website: https://www.firstvoices.com/explore/FV/sections/Data/Kanehsat%C3%A0:ke/Mohawk/Kanien'k%C3%A9ha%20(Mohawk)%20[Eng]/learn/words/10/1.

2.3.4   The IPA in Action

Phoneticians refer to the sounds of speech (i.e., what reaches the listener's ear) as **phones** (from Greek *phone* 'sound, voice') or **speech sounds**. When we are transcribing speech, we need a way to distinguish the IPA symbols from regular letters or writing. To do this, the IPA symbols are placed within square brackets [ ]. For example, the word 'soon' is transcribed using three phonetic symbols: [sun].

From this point on in the chapter we will be transcribing phones and therefore we will use the square brackets consistently. Remember, *all phonetic transcriptions must be between square brackets*. Otherwise, they are a series of letters or symbols, but not transcriptions of speech.

The most recent version of the IPA can be found on the website for the International Phonetic Association. Since many of the symbols used by the IPA are not part of the Roman *alphabet*, phoneticians use a special font for transcriptions. It can be downloaded from the IPA website and can be found in Chapter 2's resources on the website to accompany this book at www.cambridge.org/introducing-linguistics. As you work through this section, consult the webpage http://web.uvic.ca/ling/resources/ipa/charts/IPAlab/IPAlab from the Linguistics Department at the University of Victoria for audio samples for most of the IPA sounds and explanations of various symbols and other additional marks that provide more detail. These marks are called **diacritics**.

2.3.5   Transcribing the World's Languages

When phoneticians transcribe the sounds of a language, they do so using either **broad** or **narrow transcription**, depending upon the level of detail they seek. Broad transcription uses the basic symbols that appear in the main section of the IPA table (see Table 2.2) while narrow transcription adds diacritics to provide more detail. When you are transcribing words that you hear, you must know whether you need to transcribe using broad or narrow transcription.

PAUSE AND REFLECT 2.5

Pronounce the following words, paying close attention to the first sound. What does the first sound of each group of words have in common? Think about *where in your mouth* the sound is produced. Are you using the back of your mouth or the front? Think also about *how you are producing the sound*. Is it a continuous sound? Or is it a short burst?

i)   pay, may, bay
ii)   die, sigh, tie
iii)   sign, fine, shine
iv)   buy, day, girl

So far, you have learned why we need the IPA and have also started to think about how individual sounds are produced and how to describe them (Pause and Reflect 2.5). In the next section, you will learn how to transcribe **consonants** and **vowels**, the basic categories of sound for human speech.

2.4 Transcribing Consonants and Vowels

Sounds can be divided into consonants and vowels:

- Consonants have some type of constriction when they are articulated. For example, [b] has a constriction at the lips and [s] has constriction at the alveolar ridge (the ridge you feel just behind your teeth).
- Vowels are produced with no constriction. To produce [o], your tongue is in the middle of your mouth and there is no blocking of the air flow at all.

In Figure 2.5, you can see that the largest section of the IPA includes **pulmonic consonants**, produced with air pressure from the lungs. In the first row, across the top, are columns that refer to the **place of articulation** of sounds (e.g., [f] is produced using your upper teeth and lower lip, which is why it is a labiodental sound). The first column on the left refers to how sounds are produced, or the **manner of articulation**. For example, nasal sounds are produced by forcing the air out through the nasal cavity, hence the name. In cells where there are two symbols (e.g., [t] and [d]), the one on the left is voiceless and the other is voiced.

In Figure 2.5, there are certain cells that are empty and others that are colored grey. The empty cells represent sounds that could exist in human language but do not. Grey cells are sounds that are humanly impossible to articulate.

CONSONANTS (PULMONIC)

	Bilabial	Labiodental	Dental	Alveolar	Postalveolar	Retroflex	Palatal	Velar	Uvular	Pharyngeal	Glottal
Plosive	p b			t d		ʈ ɖ	c ɟ	k g	q ɢ		ʔ
Nasal	m	ɱ		n		ɳ	ɲ	ŋ	N		
Trill	ʙ			r					ʀ		
Tap or Flap		ⱱ		ɾ		ɽ					
Fricative	ɸ β	f v	θ ð	s z	ʃ ʒ	ʂ ʐ	ç ʝ	x ɣ	χ ʁ	ħ ʕ	h ɦ
Lateral fricative				ɬ ɮ							
Approximant		ʋ		ɹ		ɻ	j	ɰ			
Lateral approximant				l		ɭ	ʎ	L			

Symbols to the right in a cell are voiced, to the left are voiceless. Shaded areas denote articulations judged impossible.

Figure 2.5 IPA pulmonic consonants. From: http://www.internationalphoneticassociation.org/content/ipa-chart, available under a Creative Commons Attribution-Share Alike 3.0. Unported License. Copyright © 2018 International Phonetic Association

2.4.1 How to Transcribe Linguistic Sounds

Transcription is an important skill that you need to study phonetics and also phonology. An added bonus is that once you begin to hear different sounds and are able to identify them, you will start to notice dialect differences in a whole new way. We promise that you will never hear someone speak in quite the same way again. Below we focus mainly on the sounds of English because we assume that all readers of this text are at least familiar with English, not because it is easier than any other language.

How to transcribe words from English:

- Be familiar with the sounds English uses. Just because you speak English does not mean you are consciously aware of its sounds. North American English consonants are listed in Table 2.2. Go through the table and pronounce each word, carefully noting the different pronunciations of the sounds.
- Pay special attention to sounds that are written with two letters. For example, *sh* corresponds to one symbol, [ʃ], the same for *th*, which can be voiced (***th**ose* [ð]) or voiceless (*wi**th*** [θ]).
- Remember that the same vowel sound (and therefore IPA symbol) has several spelling equivalents. For example, the words *piece* and *feat* have the same vowel [i]. Take care to transcribe sounds, not letters.
- Related to this, *sounds are not letters*. You must start to hear sounds through the IPA.
- When you are given a word to transcribe, slowly pronounce it. Ask yourself what sounds you hear. Try to write the word out using IPA notation, without referring to your IPA chart. Make sure to use square brackets [ ] around your transcription.
- Go back to the chart to check what you have transcribed. How close were you? Which sounds caused you problems?

PAUSE AND REFLECT 2.6

i. Using the consonant symbols in Table 2.2, provide the transcription for the following underlined letters. For example: r<u>i</u><u>ch</u> [ɹ] [t͡ʃ]

a) be<u>d</u>	g) pa<u>c</u>e
b) wi<u>sh</u>	h) enou<u>gh</u>
c) <u>s</u>cript	i) na<u>ti</u>on
d) gara<u>g</u>e	j) ba<u>ck</u>
e) <u>J</u>une	k) ma<u>ss</u>ive
f) <u>y</u>awn	l) fu<u>nn</u>y

ii. Find two words for each of the following consonant sounds:

a) [ʃ]   b) [ʒ]   c) [θ]   d) [t͡ʃ]   e) [k]
f) [ŋ]   g) [ɹ]

iii. Write the IPA consonant symbol that corresponds to the following descriptions:

a) voiced palatal stop
b) voiced bilabial nasal
c) voiceless postalveolar fricative
d) voiced labiodental fricative
e) voiceless velar stop
f) voiced uvular fricative

TABLE 2.2 English Consonants

	Word-initial position	Word-medial position	Word-final position
Stops (plosives)			
[b]	bay	fabulous	tab
[d]	day	hidden	mad
[g]	gay	tiger	fig
[t]	tail	attach	heat
[k]	kale	maker	tack
Fricatives			
[f]	foe	muffin	tough
[θ]	thought	ether	with
[s]	sow	dresser	piece
[ʃ]	show	washer	wish
[h]	hoe	ahead	—
[v]	vote	ever	give
[ð]	though	father	bathe
[z]	zoo	razor	phase
[ʒ]	—	Asian	beige
Approximants (glides and liquids)			
[w]	whale	awake	—
[j]	you	higher	—
[l]	lay	miller	fill
[ɹ]	ray	terror	for
Nasals			
[m]	may	summer	sum
[n]	neigh	winner	win
[ŋ]	—	singer	thing
Affricates			
[t͡ʃ]	cheer	macho	witch
[d͡ʒ]	jeer	wager	edge

2.4.2 Pulmonic Consonants: Place and Manner of Articulation

In this section, you will learn how to describe and transcribe the **consonants** of English and some consonants from other languages. In the upcoming tables, the consonants used in English are marked in bold. Examples are provided for all the English consonants and for some of the consonants not used in English.

Stops (Also Called Plosives)

Stops, also called *plosives* are produced with a full constriction in the vocal tract, followed by a brief burst when they are released into the vowel. Bilabial stops are produced with constriction at the lips, hence the name "bilabial". English has two bilabial stops [p] and [b]. The English stops [t] and [d] are produced by contact between the alveolar ridge and the tip of the tongue. English velar stops [k] and [g] are produced when the back of the tongue touches the velum. We also have the glottal stop [ʔ] that occurs at the beginning of each syllable in the expression *Uh oh!*. Uvular stops are common in other languages, such as Tlingit (Na-Dené, British Columbia, and Alaska, 500 speakers) as in [qákʷ] *screech owl* (Maddieson et al., 2001). You can see the plosive consonants in Table 2.3. Remember, we have put the ones used in English in bold.

TABLE 2.3 Stops (Plosive Consonants)

Bilabial	Labiodental	Dental	Alveolar	Post-alveolar	Retroflex	Palatal	Velar	Uvular	Pharyngeal	Glottal
p b			**t d**		ʈ ɖ	c	**k g**	q ɢ		ʔ

How Is [t] Different from [d]?

Across different languages, stops at the same place of articulation are often represented by the same symbols in broad transcription. However, when narrow transcription is used, differences across languages emerge, often related to the **phonetic context** of the sound. The phonetic context refers to the sounds that are around the target phone, the phone's position in the word (at the beginning of the word, between vowels, or at the end), and also whether it occurs in a stressed or unstressed syllable.

In English, phonetic context affects the production of bilabial, alveolar, and velar stops in a particularly important way. The difference between voiced and voiceless stops is related to **Voice Onset Time**, or **VOT**. VOT refers to the length of time that passes between the release of a stop and the onset of voicing for the following sound.

English voiceless stops at the beginning of a word have long VOTs. This is called aspiration. Aspiration is a small puff of air that is exhaled when producing these sounds. Aspiration is represented with an [ʰ] diacritic just after the stop symbol, as in [pʰɑt] *pot*. Compare this to the [b] at the start of the word [bɑt] *bought*, which does not have aspiration. When [p t k] occur as the second member of a consonant cluster, as in the word *school* [skul], they are not fully aspirated and are produced with a short VOT. And when they occur at the end of a word, voiceless stops are often unreleased, indicated with the diacritic [˺], as shown below in (3). Pronounce the following words and note the differences across each phonetic context.

(3) IPA   Word   Phonetic context
     a. [bæt̚]   bat   end of the word; unreleased
     b. [pʰæd]   pad   start of the word; aspirated
     c. [skul]   school   second member in consonant cluster; short-lag VOT

LINGUISTICS TIDBITS: UVULARS IN KLINGON
Uvulars have a distinctive sound that sticks out strongly to English speakers, often perceived as harsh or angry. This is most likely the reason why uvulars are common sounds in Klingon, the fictional language from the *Star Trek* franchise. In the series, the language is spoken by a war-loving alien race.

For more practice and in-depth information on aspiration and VOT, consult the folder "Speech Analysis using PRAAT" in Chapter 2's resources on the website to accompany this book at www.cambridge.org/introducing-linguistics.

Nasals

Nasals are different from other consonants because the airflow comes out of the nasal cavity rather than the oral cavity. Nasals are stops, however, since there is full obstruction at a certain point in the vocal tract, even if the air is expelled through the nasal cavity.

English has three nasal phones at bilabial, alveolar, and velar places of articulation (see Table 2.4). The bilabial and alveolar nasals can occur at the beginning, in the middle, and also at the end of words in English. The velar nasal [ŋ] appears at the end of words or syllables as the symbol for the final sound in the word *singing* or *sing*. There are no words or syllables that begin with [ŋ] in English. The palatal nasal occurs in Spanish words such as *año* [aɲo] "year" and French words such as *agneau* [aɲo] "lamb".

Trills and Taps/Flaps

Trills are made by holding the active articulator tense (whether the lips, or tongue tip, or uvula) and then exhaling strongly to make the active articulator and the passive

TABLE 2.4 Nasal Consonants

Bilabial	Labiodental	Dental	Alveolar	Post-alveolar	Retroflex	Palatal	Velar	Uvular	Pharyngeal	Glottal
m	ɱ		**n**		ɳ	ɲ	ŋ	N		

articulator vibrate. The bilabial trill [ʙ] is similar to what we associate with the "rasp-berry" sound and is very rare as a linguistic sound across the world's languages (see Table 2.5). The language Medumba (Niger-Congo, Cameroon, 210,000 speakers) has a bilabial trill in the word for *dog*. The labiodental flap [ⱱ] is found in languages of Central Africa and it is one of the newest symbols to be added to the IPA, in 2005 (Zsiga, 2012).

The alveolar trill [r] is a very distinctive sound in Spanish, as in the words *arriba* [ariβa] "up" and *perro* [pero] "dog". The alveolar trill can also be found in the speech of Scottish English speakers, particularly noticeable in words such as *girl* and *farm*. However, younger generations of Scottish English speakers are weakening their [r] and producing it closer to the retroflex sound found in other English dialects (see https://www.bbc.com/news/uk-scotland-33585096 for discussion of this sound change in process). The uvular trill [ʀ] is used in Québecois French and European French in words such as *rue* [ʀy] "road". Remember that the North American English sound that corresponds to the sound in the word *room* is the retroflex consonant [ɹ].

North American English speakers most often use the alveolar **tap** [ɾ] instead of [t] and [d] in words such as *pretty* [pɹɪɾi], *automatic* [ɑɾomæɾɪk], and *ladder* [læɾəɹ] (see Table 2.6). The alveolar tap is produced by tapping the tip of the tongue quickly against the alveolar ridge with no pressure build-up at all. The terms "tap" and "flap" are often used interchangeably.

TABLE 2.5 Trills

Bilabial	Labiodental	Dental	Alveolar	Post-alveolar	Retroflex	Palatal	Velar	Uvular	Pharyngeal	Glottal
ʙ			r					R		

TABLE 2.6 Taps (Flaps)

Bilabial	Labiodental	Dental	Alveolar	Post-alveolar	Retroflex	Palatal	Velar	Uvular	Pharyngeal	Glottal
	v		ɾ		ɽ					

PAUSE AND REFLECT 2.7

i) What is the phonetic context for the alveolar tap [ɾ] in North American English (neighboring sounds, relationship to stress)?

ii) Listen to a news broadcast from England and note the pronunciation of the phones [t] and [d] in the words where Canadians and Americans produce the flap [ɾ]. What do you notice?

iii) Listen to a news broadcast from Australia and New Zealand. What version of [t] and [d] do these speakers produce?

Fricatives

Fricatives (see Tables 2.7 and 2.8) are produced with a continuous airflow through the mouth. Compare the pronunciation of [tʰ] in *tip* to the [s] in *sit*. The stop [tʰ] is articulated with a fast release while the fricative [s] is long, continuous, and is produced by pushing air through a narrow opening at some point in the vocal tract.

The dental, alveolar, and alveopalatal fricatives are all **coronal** sounds. Coronal sounds are articulated with the tip of the tongue. For the dental fricatives [θ ð], the tongue tip is flat and pressed against the teeth, as in the words *thin* [θɪn] and *then* [ðɛn]. For [s z ʃ ʒ], as in *Sue* [su], *zoo* [zu], *shoe* [ʃu], and *beige* [beʒ], there is a small groove in the tongue that creates friction when these sounds are produced. This extra friction is why [s z ʃ ʒ] are termed **sibilants**.

The palatal fricatives [ç j] are produced with the body of the tongue against the hard palate. These sounds do not occur in North American English but the voiceless palatal fricative [ç] does occur in the German word *ich* [iç] "I" (1p.sing.). Scottish Gaelic (Celtic, spoken in Scotland, about 57,000 native speakers) uses the voiced palatal fricative [j] at the beginning of certain words. In (4) and (5) you can hear examples:

(4) a dhìth   [əˈjiː]   lacking, needed

(5) ò dhìol!   [oˈjiːəl]   o God!

Source: http://learngaelic.net/dictionary/index.jsp

The uvular fricatives do not occur in North American English but [χ ʁ] do occur as variants of the uvular trill in French. Words such as *rouge* [ʁuʒ] "red" can be produced with either the uvular trill or the uvular fricative, depending upon the speaker. Many languages also have fricatives that are produced even further back in the mouth, at the pharyngeal place of articulation. Voiced and voiceless pharyngeal fricatives [ħ ʕ] occur in many Semitic languages, such as Arabic and Hebrew. The Arabic words [ħuruwb] "wars" and [saʕala] "coughed" have these sounds in word-initial and word-medial position, respectively. Finally, the voiceless glottal fricative [h] is found in many English words, such as *hot* and *hotel*.

TABLE 2.7 Fricatives

Bilabial	Labiodental	Dental	Alveolar	Post-alveolar	Retroflex	Palatal	Velar	Uvular	Pharyngeal	Glottal
ɸ β	f v	θ ð	s z	ʃ ʒ	ʂ ʐ	ç j	x ɣ	χ ʁ	ħ ʕ	h ɦ

TABLE 2.8 Lateral Fricatives

Bilabial	Labiodental	Dental	Alveolar	Post-alveolar	Retroflex	Palatal	Velar	Uvular	Pharyngeal	Glottal
			ɬ ɮ							

Lateral fricatives occur in many indigenous languages of the Pacific Northwest (northwestern United States and Canada). Lateral fricatives are produced as an [l] sound but with additional friction that makes them into fricative [ɬ]. In (6) you can hear some samples of the Dene language, spoken by the Dene Sų́łiné people who live in northern Manitoba, Saskatchewan, and Alberta, Canada (Na-Dené, about 12,000 speakers), that has lateral fricatives as part of its inventory.

(6)   a. lateral fricative in onset position   [ɬ]ur   *scab*
       b. lateral fricative in word final position   bį̃[ɬ]   *snare*

Source: http://www.firstvoices.com/en/Dene

Approximants

Approximants are sounds that involve a constriction in the vocal tract but do not have complete closure or any frication. In English, approximants can be divided into laterals and rhotics. **Laterals** are sounds related to [l]. If you pronounce the first sound in the word *late*, you will notice that there is a constriction at the alveolar ridge, but at the same time, there is also airflow around the edge of your tongue. That is why the sounds are called "laterals" (see Table 2.9).

In English, there are two lateral phones, a "light" lateral sound that occurs at the beginning of words, such as *loose* [lus] and a "dark" lateral [ɫ] that only appears at the end of syllables and before other consonants, as in the words *milk* [mɪɫk] and *fill* [fɪɫ]. The "dark" [ɫ] is produced with the back of the tongue touching the velum. Try producing the words *call* and *gall* with the tip of your tongue and then again with the back of your tongue touching the velum. Practice some more with the words *level*, *lentil*, and *lilt*, which have both light [l] and dark [ɫ].

The second category of approximants in English includes sounds related to [ɹ], or **rhotic sounds** (see Table 2.10). For example, the sound at the beginning of the English word *red* [ɹɛd] is an alveolar rhotic. Some English speakers produce this sound by bunching up the back of their tongue instead of making contact with the alveolar ridge. Pronounce the words *red* and *right* and think about which way you produce the rhotic sound at the beginning of these words.

TABLE 2.9 Lateral Approximants

Bilabial	Labiodental	Dental	Alveolar	Post-alveolar	Retroflex	Palatal	Velar	Uvular	Pharyngeal	Glottal
			l		ɭ	ʎ	ʟ			

TABLE 2.10 Rhotic Approximants

Bilabial	Labiodental	Dental	Alveolar	Post-alveolar	Retroflex	Palatal	Velar	Uvular	Pharyngeal	Glottal
	ʋ		ɹ		ɻ	j	ɰ			

Glides

A type of sound that shows properties of both consonants and vowels is called a **glide** (see Table 2.11). Glides may be thought of as rapidly articulated vowels that move quickly into another sound, as in the words *you* [ju] or *wet* [wɛt]. The [j] is a palatal glide and is articulated in a similar fashion to the vowel [i]. The glide [w] is made with the tongue raised and pulled back near the velum and with the lips protruding, or **rounded**. For this reason, it is sometimes called a **labiovelar**.

Because glides are very close in articulation to vowels, they are sometimes called semi-vowels or semi-consonants. As a group of sounds, linguists are not always in agreement regarding how to transcribe glides or how best to describe them.

> **LINGUISTICS TIDBITS: WHICH WITCH WEARS WHITE?**
> Some speakers of English also have a voiceless (labio)velar glide, transcribed [ʍ], in the words *when*, *where*, and *which* (but not in *witch*). For speakers who do this, the [w] glide is aspirated slightly, as if they were saying 'whooo'. The [ʍ] pronunciation is common in Scotland and North America, but is rare elsewhere.

Affricates

There is another category of sounds that the IPA represents as a combination of two symbols. These sounds are called **affricates** and they occur in English words such as *chose* [t͡ʃuz] and *June* [d͡ʒun]. As you can see in Table 2.12, the symbols that are used to represent affricates are essentially a stop + fricative, with a tie bar above them, showing that affricates are a combination of the two sounds. Affricates in English can be voiced and voiceless and are articulated at the postalveolar place of articulation (matching the fricative portion of the affricate).

Affricates occur across many different places of articulation and in both voiced and voiceless forms. The indigenous language Haida (**language isolate**, British Columbia, 20 native speakers) has a wide variety of affricates, both pulmonic and non-pulmonic (ejectives, see below). Example (7a) is a voiceless alveolar lateral affricate, (7b) is a voiced alveolar lateral affricate, and (7c) is a voiceless alveolar affricate.

(7) a. [t͡ɬ]   **tl**áal   husband
    b. [d͡ɮ]   **dl**áamaal   licorice fern
    c. [t͡s]   ka**ts**   hair

TABLE 2.11 Glides

Labial	palatal
w	**j**

TABLE 2.12 Affricates

Postalveolar
t͡ʃ d͡ʒ

Let's try practicing some of these consonant place and manner contrasts discussed in the preceding section. The answers can be found in the footnote.[1]

a) For each of the following sets of IPA symbols, identify the place of articulation that they share:

i) [p b m]   ii) [ʃ ʒ]   iii) [g ŋ]

b) For each set of words, identify the underlined sounds that share a place of articulation.

i) ar<u>ch</u>aic <u>q</u>uestion <u>th</u>ink   ii) <u>s</u>ue <u>d</u>o <u>t</u>wo

c) Write two words that contain a sound at the following places of articulation:

i) postalveolar   ii) labiodental   iii) glottal

d) For each of the following sets of IPA symbols, identify the manner of articulation that they share.

i) [ʃ ð z ʂ]   ii) [ŋ ɳ m]   iii) [ɹ w j l]

e) For each set of words, identify the underlined that sounds share a manner of articulation.

i) <u>c</u>ake <u>Ch</u>ristmas <u>k</u>ite   ii) <u>j</u>ury <u>ch</u>air   iii) na<u>ti</u>on enou<u>gh</u> philoso<u>ph</u>y

f) List all the English sounds that correspond to the following manners of articulation:

i) glides   ii) laterals   iii) stops

EYES ON WORLD LANGUAGES: SOUNDS IN NAHUATL

Nahuatl (Uto-Aztecan, 1.5 million speakers of various dialects in Mexico, Central America, and Mexican communities in the United States) is a Native American language spoken mainly in Mexico and many of its dialects retain the voiceless lateral affricate [tɬ]. Numerous Nahuatl words have been borrowed into the Spanish spoken in Mexico. Some Nahuatl words have also been borrowed into English, many of which originally had the [tɬ] sound in them: *coyote* (from Nahautl *coyotl*), *avocado* (from Nahuatl *ahuacatl*), and *tomato* (from Nahuatl *tomatl*).

2.4.3 Non-Pulmonic Consonants

While languages such as English only use the lungs as a source of air for producing speech, other languages use non-pulmonic sources. There are three types of non-pulmonic consonants: ejectives, implosives, and clicks.

---

[1] a) i) bilabial; ii) postalveolar; iii) velar. b) i) velar; ii) alveolar. c) answers will vary. d) i) fricative; ii) nasal; iii) approximant. e) i) stops/plosives; ii) affricates; iii) fricatives. f) i) [j w]; ii) [l]; iii) [p b t d k g ʔ]

Ejectives

Ejective sounds are represented by adding the apostrophe symbol ' directly after another phonetic symbol. For example, [p'] is the symbol for the bilabial ejective. Ejectives occur in about 20 percent of the world's languages (Ladefoged, 2005) and are common in Northwest North American indigenous languages as well as in East and Southern Africa. To articulate an ejective sound, speakers make two closures, one at the larynx and one at the particular place of articulation. The double closure creates a pocket of air. The speaker then raises the larynx and releases the oral closure. The added air pressure created by raising your larynx creates a pop sound when the oral closure is released. For this reason, ejectives are voiceless and are either stops or fricatives.

In the sound files for this chapter (8a–b), you can hear examples of implosives and their ejective counterparts from Haida.

(8)   a.   alveolar   [t]áw   grease
      b.   alveolar ejective [t']ál   yellow seaweed

In the chapter soundfiles (9a–b), you can hear examples of an alveopalatal fricative ejective and an alveolar lateral fricative ejective, both from the Athabaskan language Gwich'in (spoken in Alaska and Yukon Territory, 300 native speakers).

(9)   a.   [tʃ'] aachi   two-year-old beaver
      b.   [tɬ']èethoh   skirt

Implosives

Implosives are similar to the sound we make when we are surprised and pull air in. They can be thought of as the opposite of ejectives. To produce an implosive sound, you make the constriction and then pull your larynx down, which creates an expansion in the oral cavity and lowers the pressure in your mouth. When the oral closure is released, air rushes in, sort of like the *huh* sound we make when surprised. Implosives occur in about 13 percent of the world's languages and are represented in the IPA with a small hook on the upper part of the symbol: [ɗ]. Implosives are found in West African languages such as Fula (Niger-Congo, spoken in Senegal, Mali, Niger, among other countries, 24 million speakers) and Hausa (Afro-Asiatic, spoken in Nigeria, 44 million native speakers).

Clicks

Clicks are produced with a closure of the tongue body against the velum or uvula and a second closure at another point in the oral cavity. Clicks occur in only about 1.8 percent of world languages. They are produced by pushing the back of your tongue against the soft palate and then making another closure further forward in the oral cavity. The center part of the tongue is then lowered, enlarging the air space and creating a partial vacuum between the two closures. The closure at the front of the mouth is then released and because the pressure of the air inside the mouth is lower than the pressure outside, the air abruptly rushes into the mouth, creating the click noise.

The bilabial click [ʘ] is familiar to non-click language speakers because it is very similar to the kissing sound we often make, but without the lip-rounding. The dental click [ǀ] is similar to the sound made when you are sucking on the back of your teeth to express frustration or anger. The language !Xóõ (Tuu, Namibia, and Botswana, 2,600 native speakers) has 83 varieties of clicks, across different places of articulation and combinations with other sounds.

For a video on the phonetics of non-pulmonic consonants, consult the 'Ling Space' series on YouTube at https://www.youtube.com/watch?v=JKP10ARLnzM .

2.4.4　Vowels

Vowels are different from consonants first and foremost because there is no obstruction of air when they are produced. Since there is no closure, place of articulation is not useful and almost all languages use voiced vowels, which also makes the voice/voiceless distinction less important. More on voiceless vowels can be found in 'Delving Deeper' in Chapter 2's resources on the website to accompany this book at www.cambridge.org/introducing-linguistics. So how do we describe vowels, then? Phoneticians describe vowels in terms that roughly align with the position of the tongue in the mouth, along two dimensions:

- height (high, mid, low)
- degree of backness (front, center, back)

Keep in mind that there may be some variability in terms of exactly what you say (or hear in your region) – perhaps more distinctions or fewer. As well, remember that the same vowel sound should be represented by the same symbol, independent of the way a word is spelled. This means that if two words are spelled differently but sound the same, they should have exactly the same phonetic transcription. Visit the webpage http://web.uvic.ca/ling/resources/ipa/charts/IPAlab/IPAlab from the University of Victoria Department of Linguistics to see the IPA symbols used to transcribe the vowels of the world's languages.

Figure 2.6 presents a chart for the vowels found in most English dialects spoken in North America. The vowel chart reflects the shape of the mouth facing towards the left and shows where each vowel is produced. Across the top, you can see the backness descriptors, which refer to the position of the tongue relative to the horizontal dimension in the oral cavity (the lips are at the front). On the left side are the dimensions that refer to tongue height, or the vertical dimension of the oral cavity.

- The high vowels [i] *teeth* and [u] as in *tooth* are produced with the tongue high, almost touching the roof of the oral cavity (but not touching – it is a vowel!). [i] is front and [u] is back. The vowel [ɪ] occurs in words such as *fit* and *bit* while [ʊ] occurs in words such as *foot* and *book*.
- The mid-vowels are produced with the tongue slightly lower in the mouth. The mid-high vowels [e], as in *paid* and [o], as in *hope*, are produced with the tongue in the

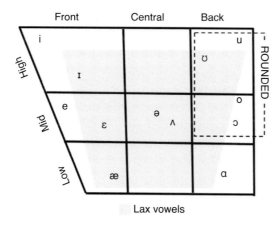

Figure 2.6 Vowels of North American English

middle of the mouth, either towards the front (for [e]) or the back (for [o]). The mid vowel [ɛ], as in *pet* is produced at the front of the mouth, with the tongue in mid-position. English has a number of different mid-vowels and they are discussed in more detail later on in this section.

- The low vowels [æ] *bat* and [ɑ] *bought* are produced with the tongue low in the mouth.

Table 2.13 shows some examples of words that include the vowel sounds found in North American English.

TABLE 2.13 North American English Vowels

Vowel	Examples
[i]	heat, beet, piece, lenient
[ɪ]	hit, bit, pit, trick
[e]	wait, made, maid, daily
[ɛ]	head, bet, red, set
[æ]	hat, man, pad, ram
[ɑ]	father, bother, cod
[ʌ]	but, mud, suck, tongue
[o]	toad, lode, home, tone
[ɔ][1]	coffee, law, caught
[ʊ]	book, look, could, foot
[u]	food, tooth, moon, rude

[1] this vowel is only found in some dialects of North American English, particularly in the North Eastern United States, in cities such as New York and Boston.

If you look at the IPA vowel chart at http://web.uvic.ca/ling/resources/ipa/charts/IPAlab/IPAlab, you will notice that the IPA prefers the terms "close" and "open" for vowels. However, today the majority of linguists prefer the terms "high" and "low".

When linguists describe vowels, they talk about **vowel quality**, or what distinguishes one vowel from another (along one or more dimensions). For example, the vowels [i] and [u] differ across the dimension of backness and therefore have different vowel qualities. Vowel quality is just another way of talking about differences among vowels. Across the world's languages, vowel systems with five different qualities are the most common and are found in languages such as Egyptian Arabic (Modern Standard Arabic), Semitic (Egypt, 55 million speakers) and Spanish (Romance, Spain, Latin America, United States; approximately 350 million speakers). The Spanish vowel system, for example, has [i], [e], [a], [o], and [u] for a total of five different qualities.

EYES ON WORLD LANGUAGES: VOWELS AROUND THE WORLD

The World Atlas of Language Structures (WALS) online (Dryer, & Haspelmath, 2013, available at http://wals.info) is a large database that includes descriptions of languages gathered from different sources by a team of 55 linguists. According to WALS, the average number of vowels in languages included in the database was just below six. Yimas (Lower Sepik-Ramu, Papua New Guinea, 300 native speakers) has the smallest vowel quality inventory with only two. British English has 13 and North American English varieties typically have between 11–13, depending upon the dialect.

Tense and Lax Vowels

In English and many other languages, vowels can be further distinguished by being **tense** or **lax**. Compare the words *feet* [fit] and *fit* [fɪt]. The vowel [i] is tense while the vowel [ɪ] is lax. Tense vowels tend to be slightly longer and higher than their lax counterparts. In most varieties of English, there are at least three pairs of tense-lax vowels. They are presented in Table 2.14.

In English, there is a simple test that helps determine whether vowels are tense or lax. Words with one syllable cannot end in lax vowels. To test this, take a look at what

TABLE 2.14 Tense and Lax Vowels in English

	Front		Back	
	tense	*lax*	*tense*	*lax*
High	[bit] beat	[bɪt] bit	[but] boot	[bʊk] book
Mid	[bet] bait	[bɛt] bet		

happens when we add different vowels to the sound [s]. When we add tense vowels, the result is a real word: *see* [si], *Sue* [su], *so* [so], and *saw* [sɑ]. When we add lax vowels, we come up with ungrammatical words: *[sɪ], *[sɛ], *[sʌ], *[sʊ] or *[sə]. So if you are not sure if a vowel is tense or lax, put [s] in front of it to see if it is a real word or not.

Rounded Vowels

If you say the words *hoo* and *hee*, you will notice that both vowels are high but [u] is back while [i] is front. Another key difference between these two vowels is what happens with your lips: [u] is rounded but for [i], your lips are exended out to the side.

North American English has three **rounded** vowels: [u], [o], and [ʊ]. In some varieties, the vowel [ɔ], a low-mid rounded vowel, also exists, in words such as *saw* [sɔ] and *bought* [bɔt] (see "Low Vowel Merger").

French, distinct from English, has rounded and unrounded front vowels that contrast words as shown in (10).

(10) a.   [li]   lit   bed
       b.   [ly]   lu   read (past participle)
       c.   [lu]   loup   wolf

Source: http://www.vowelsandconsonants3e.com/chapter_15.html

Mid-Vowels, Stress, and "Schwa": The Most Relaxed Vowel of All

The production of a mid-central or mid-back vowel in English depends upon whether it occurs in a stressed syllable and whether it is followed by a rhotic sound as in the words *girl* and *fur*. For stressed syllables, English speakers use the *wedge vowel*, or [ʌ], as in the word *b**u**t* [bʌt]. The **schwa**, or the upside down *e* symbol [ə], is used for unstressed syllables, such as in the words *a**bout* or *s**u**pply*. Schwa is the neutral vowel in English and is the sound that speakers produce when the tongue is in the center of the mouth, neither high nor low, neither back nor front. If you relax your mouth, put your articulators in a neutral position and make a vowel sound, you are producing a schwa. The schwa is very characteristic of English and plays an important role in contrasting stressed and unstressed syllables. For example, if you produce the word *about* without pronouncing a schwa, it sounds like you are talking about *a bout*, i.e., an actual bout, or a short period of intense activity!

Mid-Vowels and r-Coloring

Another notable difference in the production of mid-vowels is related to dialect. English dialects differ as to whether speakers produce full "r" sounds at the end of syllables. Those dialects that produce full "r"s are called **r-full dialects**. These are by far the most common in the English spoken in Canada and the United States. Speakers of r-full dialects produce words such as *car* [kɑɹ], *here* [hiɹ], and *beer* [biɹ] with the full alveolar approximant sound at the end. For the schwa [ə] and mid-back [ʌ] vowels, the [ɹ] has an

TABLE 2.15 Examples from r-less and r-full Varieties

Symbol	Example	Spelling	Context
[ʌ]	[mʌd]	mud	Stressed syllable
[ə]	[bəliv] [əbaʊt]	believe, about	Unstressed syllable
[ɜ]	[fɜ] [hɜdə]	fur, herder	In r-less dialects including Boston and BBC English
[ɝ]	[fɝ] [hɜˑdɚ]	fur, herder	In r-full dialects, such as General North American English; stressed syllables
[ɚ]	[ˈfɑðɚ] [ˈtitʃɚ]	father, teacher	In r-full dialects, such as General North American English; unstressed syllables

effect that is called r-coloring. The r-colored schwa [ɚ] and r-colored central vowel [ɝ] occur in words such as *dinner* [dɪnɚ] and *her* [hɝ].

There are other dialects of United States English (e.g., some parts of the Southeast, Boston, and New York – listen to how Robert DeNiro speaks for an example of New York r-dropping), Australia, New Zealand, and the United Kingdom whose speakers do not produce [ɹ] in syllable- and word-final position. For speakers of these r-less dialects, the word *beer* would be pronounced closer to [biə]. Table 2.15 shows you examples of r-colored vowels of General North American English and r-less varieties (Zsiga, 2012, p. 63).

Low Vowel Merger

The low vowels found in Standard North American English are [æ] *pat* and [ɑ] as in *body*. The low vowel [ɑ] also participates in what linguists call the low-back merger. This refers to a collapse of the distinction between the back vowels [ɔ], as in *caught*, *paw*, and *thought* with the vowel [ɑ] in words like *lot*, *cot*, and *Tom*. In certain British dialects and most northeastern United States dialects, these two phones maintain a distinction. In other US English dialects and all Canadian English varieties, this distinction has merged and the vowel [ɑ] is used exclusively. For example, *lot* and *thought* rhyme, while *cot* and *caught*, *stock* and *stalk*, and *don* and *dawn* sound alike but are spelled differently.

Nasal Vowels

As with nasal consonants, nasal vowels are articulated with air flowing out of the nose and mouth. In some languages, such as French and Portuguese, nasalization of vowels can change the meaning of a word. Languages such as English and Spanish have nasal vowels as the result of the influence of neighboring sounds.

In standard French and Québecois (spoken in the province of Quebec, Canada) French, oral vowels alternate with nasal vowels in contrastive fashion. In examples (11)–(14) you can hear sets of contrasting words:

(11) a. [lɛ]   laid   ugly
 b. [lɛ̃]   lin   flax

(12) a. [lœʀ]   leur   their
 b. [lœ̃di]   lundi   Monday

(13) a. [la]   las   tired
 b. [lã]   lent   slow

(14) a. [lo]   lot   prize
 b. [lõ]   long   long

Source: http://www.phonetics.ucla.edu/vowels/contents.html

Vowel Length

In many languages, a vowel that is held for a longer time alternates with a shorter version of the same vowel (or one similar enough to be considered basically equivalent) and can change the meaning of the word. Inuktitut (Inuit, Eskimo-Aleut, spoken in Canada in Nunavut, Northwest Territories, Quebec, Newfoundland, and Labrador, approximately 34,000 native speakers) is one of the four official languages of the Canadian territory of Nunavut. Inuktitut has three vowels that differ based on length. Long vowels are written with double letters to distinguish them from their short counterparts. In examples (15)–(17) you can hear samples of words in the Inuinnaqtun dialect, using different vowel lengths. For ease of exposition, these are presented in the Roman alphabet.

(15) a. [a]ttak   aunt (father's sister)
 b. [a:]ppaka   father

(16) a. [i]glu   house
 b. [i:]nmuktuq   8 o'clock

(17) a. gyuk   bearded seal
 b. [u:]gaq   cod

Source: http://www.tusaalanga.ca/glossary/inuktitut

Diphthongs

Languages can also combine two vowel sounds into one syllable, to form a **diphthong**. For example, the word *buy* only has one syllable but the vowel portion of *buy* actually has two parts. Try pronouncing the word *buy* very slowly: buuuuuuyyy. You hear that the main vowel sound is [a] but at the end of the vowel, you probably notice that it transitions into and ends with a high vowel [i]. Notice as well how your tongue moves from the bottom of your mouth to the front. English has three diphthongs:[2] [aj] as in *buy*, [aw] as in *now*, and [ɔj] as in *toy*. Other languages have different combinations of vowels that form diphthongs, and even triphthongs, which are combinations of three vowels.

In various languages, including English, we distinguish between true diphthongs and vowels that have been diphthongized. The words *may* [mej] and *you* [juw] have [j] and [w] following the [ɔj] main vowel. These sounds are offglides and are very common in English but they do not serve to contrast words and therefore are not considered diphthongs of English (Zsiga, 2012).

At this point, you should be able to identify and describe the sequence of speech sounds that make up a word or utterance and to use a universal set of symbols (the IPA) to transcribe them. In the next section, we move beyond the phonetics of individual sounds to a more detailed examination of how sounds change when they occur in particular phonetic contexts.

2.5 Speech Processes

When we produce a word, each sound in the word affects the production of its neighboring phones. We rarely (if ever) produce a phone that is completely unaffected by its phonetic context.

There are several ways that phonetic context can influence the production of a sound. These are known as **speech processes**. Some speech processes make articulation easier by altering individual sounds so that it requires less effort for the mouth to produce the sequence. Other speech processes make perception easier by altering individual sounds so that it is easier for the listener to understand what is being said.

Several different factors can affect how much sounds change, such as how quickly the individual is speaking, how carefully they are speaking, how formal the situation is, or what the sounds are that come before and after the phone itself.

2.5.1 Coarticulation

Remember that the vocal tract includes various articulators, such as the vocal cords, lips, tongue, etc., that are involved in the articulation of specific sounds. However, real speech is not quite this neat and tidy. If speakers simply waited until the previous sound was released before they began to move into position, speech would be choppy and slow. To make the transitions between sounds smoother, articulators sometimes move *in anticipation* of an upcoming sound. For example, when we say the word *flower* [flawɚ], we do not pronounce [f] [l] [aw] [ə] [ɹ] as separate segments. The place of articulation of [f] overlaps with that of [l] and the [ə] in turn is influenced by the [ɹ] that follows. These overlapping gestures are what we call **coarticulation**. Coarticulation is a common process and speakers are largely unaware of the fact that they are doing it.

---

[2] There is some variability in terms of how diphthongs are transcribed.

PAUSE AND REFLECT 2.8

Pronounce the [kl] portion of the word *clear*. What exactly is happening when you produce these sounds at the beginning of the word?

2.5.2 Assimilation

In **assimilation**, one sound becomes more similar to a nearby sound. The result is easier articulation because it requires less effort to transition from one phone to the next if they are similar. Assimilation can affect the voicing, manner, or place of articulation of a sound, or a combination of the three. It can often be difficult to draw a clear line between coarticulation and assimilation.

In English, for example, a nasal stop has the same place of articulation of the consonant that comes after it. When a nasal comes before a bilabial consonant, such as [p], it is produced as a bilabial nasal, [m], as in *camp* [kæmp]. On the other hand, nasal stops before alveolar consonants, such as [d], are alveolar, [n], as in *candy* [kændi]. This process is known as **nasal assimilation**. Nasal assimilation is so regular that it is reflected in the spelling of many words in English. You can also hear nasal assimilation when the word *in* is followed by a consonant in fast speech, for example in the phrase *in peace* [ĩmpis].

Our examples of *candy* and *in peace* show **regressive assimilation**, because the influence of one sound is spread *backward*. The speaker is anticipating the upcoming sound and adjusts her pronunciation to reflect it. If the voicing, manner, or place of a sound spreads to the next sound (i.e., it is spread forward), it is an example of **progressive assimilation**. In (18) There are more examples of regressive assimilation (18a) and progressive assimilation (18b).

(18) a. bilabial: impatient   in Portugal   [mp]
         alveolar: indirect   in debt   [nd]
         velar: incorrect   in cages   [ŋk]
     b. voiced stop + [s]   kids   legs   [dz]/[gz]
         voiceless stop + [s] kits   licks   [ts]/[ks]

PAUSE AND REFLECT 2.9

During fast speech, English speakers often produce the voiced interdental fricative [ð] as a voiced alveolar fricative [z] when it follows [s]:

How would you describe this assimilation process? Is it progressive or regressive? Does it show voicing, manner, or place assimilation or some combination of the three?

- What's the special today?   [sz]
- Why is that sign crooked?   [z]

Palatalization is another frequent form of regressive assimilation and it also involves the assimilation of place of articulation. Palatalization occurs when a palatal glide [j] follows another consonant and regressively assimilates its place of articulation. For example, when [d] and [j] are together in the speech stream, speakers often produce the affricate [d͡ʒ], which is produced further back in the mouth than [d], a result of the palatal [j] that follows. Practice pronouncing the sentences in (19).

(19) Which one di<u>d y</u>ou pick?   [d͡ʒ]
Couldn'<u>t y</u>ou do something?   [t͡ʃ]

Nasalization is also the result of regressive assimilation. Nasalization occurs when a nasal consonant comes after a vowel in the same syllable. The nasalization spreads backward from the consonant to the vowel, which becomes a nasal vowel. A nasal vowel is produced with the velum lowered, so air moves through both the nasal cavity and the mouth. If you say the words *dim* and *dip* very slowly, you should be able to feel air flow through your nasal cavity for *dim*, but not for *dip*. The same thing occurs for *can* and *cat*.

2.5.3 Dissimilation

Until this point, we have talked about speech processes that facilitate articulation by making speech sounds more similar to the sounds around them. However, speakers may also make a sound *less similar* to a nearby sound, a process known as **dissimilation**. One example of dissimilation in English can be found in the word '*ae<u>sth</u>etic*'. In this word, the voiceless alveolar fricative [s] comes before the voiceless interdental fricative [θ]. However, the sequence [sθ] is difficult both to produce and to perceive. For many speakers, the second fricative [θ] undergoes dissimilation and becomes a voiceless stop, [t]. Dissimilation helps the listener clearly recognize the difference between two sounds.

2.5.4 Epenthesis

Speakers can also make the transitions between speech sounds easier by adding an additional sound between them, a process called **epenthesis**. The inserted, or epenthesized sound can be a vowel, [ə] in the word *athlete*, which can be pronounced as *a-the-lete* ([æθəlit]) to ease the difficult transition of [θ] to [l]. The added sound may also be a consonant, as in *something* and *hamster*. In fast or casual speech, a [p] is produced between these two sounds; the words are produced as [sʌmpθɪŋ] and [hæmpstɚ]. This production of *hamster* is so common that many English speakers accidentally spell the word as **hampster*.

2.5.5 Deletion

In fast or casual speech, speakers may also remove a sound completely, a process known as **deletion** (also called **elision**). Deletion is likely to occur in frequent words or phrases and can result in utterances that are much shorter and include fewer segments than speakers or listeners realize. In (20), you can see some examples of deletion:

(20)	*gimme*	*give me*	deleted: [v]
	I dunno	*I don't know*	deleted: [t]
	I see 'em	*I see them*	deleted: [ð]

PAUSE AND REFLECT 2.10

Processes of deletion get rid of sounds altogether. Why do you think these processes are more common in frequent words or phrases than in less-frequent words or phrases? That is, why do we often delete the [v] in *give me* to produce *gimme* but do not typically delete the [v] in *cave mammals* to produce phrases like *camammals*?

2.5.6 Metathesis

Metathesis is another phonetic process that occurs in many languages and involves the reversal of the order of sounds in a word. Methathesis can often result from the regularization of mispronunciations that become part of the language's regular system. For example, it is common in English to hear the word *iron* [aɪɹən] pronounced as [aɪəɹn].

Another example occurs in the English word *ask*, which is often pronounced as [æks]. Up to now you have learned about the different sounds of language, including how to describe them and how they change when they are combined together into words and sentences. In the next section, you will learn how the speech system shapes the air that is produced from our lungs into meaningful sounds.

2.6 **Source Filter Theory**

When we produce language, we do not just open our mouth and breathe out. Producing language involves a complex process of breathing and movement of the glottis and articulators. Air moves from the lungs through the trachea to the larynx, where it may or may not cause the vocal folds to vibrate. When vocal folds do vibrate, they produce sound. If you think of your vocal tract as a tube, the shorter the tube (i.e., as for a child or a woman), the faster the tube will vibrate. For longer tubes (i.e., for a man), the vibration will be slower. The basic vibration of the vocal folds comes from the glottis, and is perceived as vocal **pitch**, a sound property similar to musical notes that ranges from low to high.

Our vocal folds vibrate the same way for all voiced sounds. Therefore, we need a way to modify these vibrations, or resonances, in order to produce the different sounds of human languages. The vocal tract above the larynx does this by acting as a filter that shapes the way sound is emitted. The vocal tract amplifies certain parts of the source and diminishes other parts. For example, to produce [i], we raise and push our tongue forward. To produce [u], however, we raise our tongue, pull it back, and round our lips. Different configurations of the vocal tract allow us to produce the distinct sounds of speech. You can think of speech as the result of both a source (lungs and larynx) and a filter (vocal tract) that shapes the sound.

To help you understand this, think of our vocal tract as a hallway. When people (air molecules) start to move through the hallway, it is possible to funnel them to one side or the other by putting barriers to channel people along the hallway. In our vocal tract, the articulators act like the channels, by funneling air molecules instead of people, according to the articulation involved. When air molecules are forced together on their way out of the vocal tract, bands of energy, or **formants**, result. Formants are narrow concentrations of energy that happen at different **frequencies**. Frequency refers to how rapidly the sound wave moves through the air and is measured in Hertz (Hz). Higher formants will have higher frequencies (see the left side of the spectrogram in Figure 2.7). Vowels (and some consonants) have distinct formant structures, reflecting the particular shape of the vocal tract when they are articulated. For vowels, phoneticians typically analyze the first three formants, F1, F2, and F3, numbering from the lowest to the highest.

Just as it is possible to manipulate the filter characteristics, we can also modify the source characteristics. Remember the source is the energy produced at the larynx and it is called pitch. By manipulating the source, we have the same vowel produced at low pitch and again at higher pitch. An example of this would be a man producing the word *heat*, followed by a child producing the same word. The relationship between the formants remains the same; otherwise we would not perceive the two versions as the same word. Read 'Delving Deeper' in Chapter 2's resources to learn more about how humans hear sound on the website to accompany this book at www.cambridge.org/introducing-linguistics.

2.6.1 Spectrograms

In Figure 2.7, you can see a representation of vowel formants using a **spectrogram**. Spectrograms represent the frequency of a speech signal (y-axis) over time

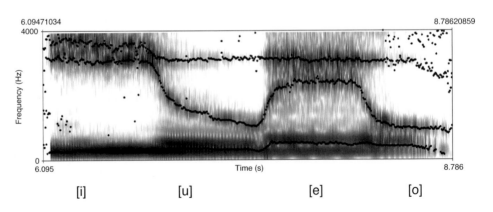

Figure 2.7 Spectrogram and formants for vowels [i]-[u]-[e]-[o] (female voice)

(x-axis). Figure 2.7 shows how manipulating the filter affects the formant structure of the resulting vowels. The vowels represented in this spectrogram are [i]-[u]-[e]-[o]. The solid black lines indicate the bands that correspond to the first, second, and third formants.

The spectrogram in Figure 2.7 shows the changes in formant structure between the high front vowel [i], as in *feet*, the low vowel [ɑ], as in *father*, the mid-high vowel [e] as in *wait* and the back mid-rounded vowel [o], as in *hope*.

Look closely at the shifts in formants, which are always numbered from the bottom up. Notice that for the vowel [i], F1, the first formant, is at the same height as for [u]. For the mid-vowels [e] and [o], however, F1 rises slightly. The first formant correlates to vowel height: higher vowels have lower F1. The second formant, or F2, correlates to backness: front vowels have higher F2 than back vowels. Rounding also lowers formants overall.

On a spectrogram, voicing is represented by vertical lines. Each line represents a single glottal pulse, or a single puff of air moving through the glottis. It is sometimes possible to see a "voicing bar" in the very low frequencies. Voiceless sounds do not (typically) have any striations, or voicing bar.

Formant Transitions

As stated above, speech is not a series of isolated sounds. Sounds flow together, overlap, and influence each other in articulatory and acoustic terms. The intermediate stage between a consonant and a following vowel is called the **transition**. These transitions change as the vocal tract reshapes to produce new sounds. This is an important part of the speech signal and listeners use it to identify sounds.

In Figure 2.8 you can see spectrograms for the words *bab*, *dad*, and *gag*. For each word, the same low front vowel [æ] occurs in different consonant contexts. Look closely at the formant transitions into the vowel (i.e., from the consonant to the vowel) and out of the vowel (i.e., from the vowel to the consonant) for each word, and across each place of articulation.

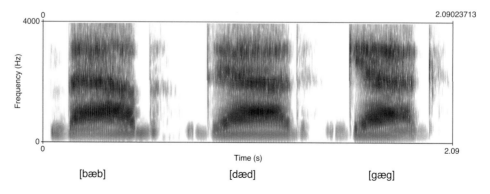

Figure 2.8 Spectrogram of stop formant transitions

In Figure 2.8, notice how the F2 transitions from the initial [b] and into the final [b] in *bab* both point down. In *dad*, F3 points up at the transition out of and into [d]. For *gag*, however, the F2 and F3 initially start out together and then F2 falls into the final [g]. This initial F2 and F3 position is called **velar pinch**. In general, labials have downward pointing transitions (usually all visible formants, but especially F2 and F3), velars tend to have F2 and F3 transitions that pinch together (hence velar pinch), and the F3 of coronals tends to point upward. This will also depend on the vowel that follows, along with variation among individuals.

Fricatives are relatively easy to identify on spectrograms, given their high frequency random noise. The high frequency noise is most present in the sibilant fricatives. Typically, [s] has a concentration of energy at the top of the spectrogram while [ʃ] has most of its energy concentrated at slightly lower ranges. The voiced fricatives [z] and [ʒ] have a voicing bar across the bottom and slightly less amplitude of frication. Figure 2.9 shows the wave and spectrograms for the words [su zu ʃu ʒu], respectively, the four sibilant fricatives in English.

Approximants are the sounds that are closest to vowels and they share many characteristics of vowels including formant patterns. In English, the approximant sounds are [l ɹ w, j]. In Figure 2.10 you can see approximants [w j] and in Figure 2.11 you can see the approximants [l ɹ].

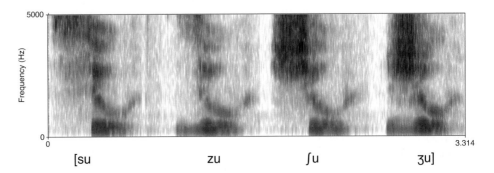

Figure 2.9 Spectrogram of English sibilant fricatives

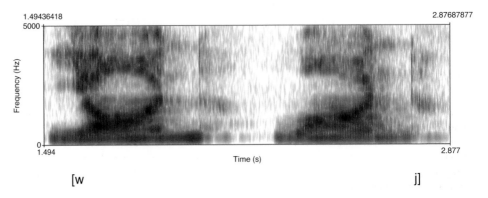

Figure 2.10 Spectrogram of approximants [w j]

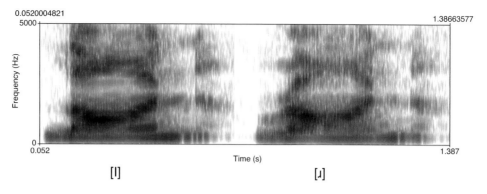

Figure 2.11 Spectrogram of approximants [l ɹ]

Notice how the formant transitions move into and out of each approximant and how the presence of formant structure in the approximant itself distinguishes them from stops and fricatives above.

How to recognize some sounds on a spectrogram:

- Vowels usually have very clearly defined formant bars. F1 corresponds to vowel height. F2 corresponds to vowel backness. For example, the vowel [i] has a high F1 formant and a low F2 formant.

- Non word-initial stop consonants will have a blank period on the spectrogram that corresponds to the closure phase of articulation. Voiced stops will (possibly) have a voicing bar. Voiceless stops will not.
- Nasals and [l] will look like faint vowels.
- Fricatives will have high frequency energy. Voiced fricatives will have a voicing bar. Voiceless fricatives will not.

> **LINGUISTICS TIDBITS: THE MCGURK EFFECT**
>
> Read Chapter 2's 'Delving Deeper' on the website to accompany this book at www.cambridge.org/introducing-linguistics to learn more about the close relationship between what we see and what we think we hear and what happens when these two do not match (www.cambridge.org/introducing-linguistics).

In this section, you learned about how the production of speech can be interpreted as a source (the larynx and lungs) and a filter (the vocal tract). You also read about how the resulting sounds are shaped by their context and formant structure. In the next section, you will learn about the suprasegmental features of speech that are above the level of individual sounds.

> **PAUSE AND REFLECT 2.11**
>
> Speech perception involves comparing words and sounds we hear to words and sounds we have heard previously. What happens when we learn a new language? We need to establish new sound categories, different from the sounds in our native language. Yet, not all new sounds are created equal.
>
> When you think about learning to perceive the sounds of another language, which sounds are most difficult? Totally new sounds or sounds that are close to sounds in the first language? Think about the rounded front and back vowels in French that you heard in examples (11–14).

2.7 Suprasegmentals

Suprasegmentals are not connected to specific sounds, which is why they are called supra (i.e., "above") segmentals. For example, we can say *John studies linguistics* as a regular statement, for example as an answer to the question *What does John study?*. We can also use the same words to ask the question *John studies linguistics?*, if we are surprised to hear that news (perhaps he had been studying engineering and switched to linguistics). The difference between these two utterances is the **intonation** pattern. One is related to a statement (your voice goes down at the end) and the other is expressing surprise (your voice rises at the end).

Another example can be found with the two questions *Do you love linguistics?* and *Do you know the IPA?*, for which you use the same intonation pattern – rising voice at the end to indicate a yes-no question. This tells us that intonational patterns are not linked to specific words or segments but rather sit above them. The same happens with stress. For example, we can stress the first syllable in the word *record* or the second, depending upon whether it is a noun or a verb. Visit http://web.uvic.ca/ling/resources/ipa/charts/IPAlab/IPAlab to see the IPA symbols used to transcribe suprasegmental features of world languages.

2.7.1 Stress

For spoken language, **stress** refers to how prominent syllables are within a word. In English, stress can be used to contrast words, as in ***re**cord* vs. *re**cord*** and ***con**vert* vs. *con**vert***. Linguistic stress is relative. For example, the word *linguistics* has three syllables. Say it out loud and ask yourself which syllable has the main, or primary stress? You probably heard that the second syllable has primary stress. However, the only way to perceive the second syllable as receiving primary stress is by hearing it relative to the other two syllables. Remember that vowels in reduced, or unstressed syllables are represented by the schwa [ə].

PAUSE AND REFLECT 2.12

Compound words are two words combined to make one (see Chapter 4 Morphology). For example, *greenhouse* and *hotdog* are compound words. These types of compounds are stressed on the left-most syllable. There are other types of compounds as well, that occur as phrases: race car driver, river boat captain, ice skating rink. Can you think of other examples like these? Where does stress fall on these types of compounds?

Phonetically, stress is considered *abstract* because there is not one invariant phonetic correlate to stressed syllables across the world's languages or even within the same language. Native English speakers tend to use the following acoustic cues to differentiate between stressed and unstressed syllables:

- Syllables with primary stress tend to be longer, louder, and have higher pitch than the other syllables in a word.

- Another key acoustic cue to stressed syllables is the quality of the vowel. The schwa [ə] only occurs in unstressed syllables. In other words, primary and secondary stressed syllables never have schwa. Thus, for native English speakers, vowel quality is an important acoustic cue to stress.

Most languages use stress, and linguistic stress patterns can be classified as lexical, paradigmatic, or positional. Lexical stress is mostly unpredictable and speakers of these languages (and second language learners) must learn where to place the correct stress for each word. Russian is often claimed to be a lexically-stressed language. Other languages, such as English, have a more predictable stress system that is heavily influenced by word form and class. That is why they are called paradigmatic stress systems. Finally, there are languages like Hungarian that always stress the first syllable of the word while languages like Polish stress the second to last. These languages have what is called a positional stress system, where stress is consistently predictable and does not move. Much of the theory related to stress assignment is part of phonology (see Chapter 3 Phonology).

PAUSE AND REFLECT 2.13

Where would you place the primary, or main stress in the following made-up words?

How did you decide where to place the stress? Can you think of real words that follow these same patterns?

trotment	trotmental
nonimpt	nonimption
stoil	stoiler

Sentence/Prosodic Stress

Up to this point we have discussed stress at the word, or lexical level. Stress also plays a role at the sentence level, however, and this is called sentence, or **prosodic stress**. At the sentence level, stress can be used to contrast or emphasize words. If speakers want to mark a contrast with something that was previously said, they will use contrastive sentence stress to do so.

Examples (21) and (22) show phrasal and contrastive stress:

(21) Phrasal stress
   a. The house on the **cor**ner
   b. The corner **house**

(22) Contrastive stress
   a. **Mi**chael went shopping. (not Susie)
   b. Michael went **sho**pping. (not to the movies)

2.7.2 Tone

Tone is the use of pitch as a way to distinguish between words. Tone is different from intonation because intonation is not used to contrast words. Tonal languages are found all around the world and are particularly common in Africa, East Asia, and Central American/North American indigenous languages. In tonal languages, each syllable has a pitch or pitch contour connected with it. The IPA represents tones using different diacritics to indicate the range from extra high to extra low. Visit http://web.uvic.ca/ling/resources/ipa/charts/IPAlab/IPAlab to see the IPA symbols used to transcribe tone. In Navajo (Na-Dene, spoken in Arizona and New Mexico, approximately 170,000 native speakers), syllables are produced with high and falling tones. Yoruba (Niger-Congo, spoken in Nigeria and Benin, 28 million speakers) has a system of three level tones (high, low, and mid). The high tone is represented with the accent marker *á* while the low tone is marked by the accent marker *à*. In the examples found in (23) you can hear samples of some tone combinations in two-syllable Yoruba words:

(23) a. àgbá   wheels
     b. àgba   elders
     c. àgbà   high

Mandarin Chinese is the tonal language with the greatest number of speakers (Sinitic, spoken in most of China, approximately 960 million native speakers). There are many different dialects of Mandarin Chinese and no two dialects share exactly the same set of tones. Nonetheless, it is possible to identify a minimal tone set in Mandarin as consisting of five tones: a high level tone, a mid-to-high tone, a low tone that falls and then rises, a falling tone, and a neutral tone. In this language, these tones can be used to contrast words, as the examples in (24) show:

(24) a. mā   mom/mum   high level tone
     b. má   hemp   mid-to-high tone
     c. mǎ   horse   fall-rise tone
     d. mà   scold   falling tone
     e. ma   (an interrogative particle) neutral tone

The website https://en.wikipedia.org/wiki/Tone_(linguistics) provides examples of the tones in Mandarin.

2.7.3 Intonation

Languages such as English make various uses of **pitch** to communicate information about how we feel and what type of function our speech has. For example, questions seem to raise and declarations (statements) seem to fall. Pitch is perceived functionally as **intonation**. By changing intonation across words and phrases, we can change their function (e.g., from a statement to a question) and their emotive content (e.g., angry vs.

excited). In written language, punctuation fulfills many of the functions that intonation does in spoken language. Try saying the sentences in (25) on the left with the appropriate intonation to elicit the responses on the right.

(25) a.   You are American?   (yes, I am)
b.   YOU are American.   (yes, HE is British)
c.   You are AmERican!   (yes, did you hear me talking about the US?)
d.   You are American.   (neutral)

PAUSE AND REFLECT 2.14

Upspeak, or the use of high-rising intonation where a declarative sentence would normally end in falling intonation, is a feature of some varieties of English. Popular media has reported that speakers who use upspeak are exhibiting insecurity and this can undermine their communication style. This is similar to what we mentioned regarding vocal fry and really begs the question of why female-identified speech patterns are automatically identified as lacking seriousness or professionalism. See the comment by Mark Liberman (Linguistics Professor at the University of Pennsylvania) regarding upspeak. http://languagelog .ldc.upenn.edu/nll/?p=568

Do you know of any other intonation patterns that are highly gendered? What is your impression of speakers who use upspeak or vocal fry?

EYES ON WORLD LANGUAGES: PITCH ACCENT IN JAPANESE

Japanese uses pitch accent to distinguish between words. For example, *sake*, "fermented rice alcohol" and *sake*, "salmon" are distinguished only by their pitch accent. Interestingly, the Anglicized name for the alcohol, sake, sounds more like the Japanese word for "salmon". Visit https://www .youtube.com/JapaneseEng101 to hear the pronunciation of *sake* and other Japanese terms.

SUMMARY

Phonetics is the field of linguistics that studies how sounds are produced and perceived. Phoneticians characterize the sounds that make up world languages. To do this, phoneticians use the IPA to transcribe words. The IPA is a system of symbols that represent the sounds of all spoken languages, in order to transcribe words. The IPA allows linguists to overcome sound-spelling inconsistencies that are common to the writing systems of most languages. Language is not a series of isolated sounds, however. All sounds occur in particular phonetic contexts and these contexts can change the way sounds are pronounced through processes such as coarticulation and assimilation. Sounds are produced when speakers raise their diaphragm and push air out of the lungs (the source). The air passes through the larynx (where the vocal cords are found) to the supralaryngeal articulatory system, which acts as a filter for creating the distinct sounds that make up world languages. As the active articulators move, different sounds are produced. Languages also have phonetic features that occur above the segment, called suprasegmentals, that include word and phrasal stress and intonation.

EXERCISES

2.1 Each of these transcribed items corresponds to at least one spelled word in English. Say each item aloud and spell out all words to which it corresponds.

   a. [feɹ]
   b. [bor]
   c. [si]
   d. [ajl]
   e. [əˈlawd]
   f. [sɛnt]
   g. [t͡ʃuz]
   h. [t͡ʃɪli]
   i. [ɹajt]
   j. [klɑz]
   k. [bit͡ʃu]
   l. [nu]
   m. [tʰul]
   n. [ðeɹ]

2.2 Each of the following spelled items corresponds to two words with different pronunciations. Using the IPA, transcribe the two possible pronunciations of each word.

   a. close
   b. read
   c. wound
   d. live
   e. minute
   f. moped
   g. tear
   h. wind

2.3 Read aloud each of the words transcribed in IPA. For each item, write the English word to which the transcription corresponds.

   a. [əˈlɛkʃən]
   b. [ˈwʌndɚ]
   c. [ˈnɑləd͡ʒ]
   d. [kəˈmoʃən]
   e. [ˈɹajrɚ]
   f. [juθ]
   g. [ˈbluri]
   h. [klɑk]
   i. [ɹɑŋ]
   j. [bi]

2.4 Read aloud each of the following sentences transcribed in IPA. For each item, write the English sentence to which the transcription corresponds.

   a. [ʃilɪvzɪnfloɹɪrə]
   b. [wibarənuhaws]
   c. [kʌmtuðəmuvizwɪθmi]
   d. [ajkæntəfoɹdəvekeʃən]
   e. [hudujuθinkjuɑɹ]

2.5   Provide the IPA transcription for each of the following words in English.

    a.   shoulder
    b.   happiness
    c.   measure
    d.   favorite
    e.   theorize
    f.   gated
    g.   packing
    h.   mission
    i.   quickly
    j.   there
    k.   college

2.6   In each of the following words, determine whether the vowel is a monophthong or a diphthong. The recording is 2.6. Recordings are provided on the website if you would like to listen to the items.

    a.   boot
    b.   beet
    c.   buy
    d.   bout
    e.   boy
    f.   bat
    g.   bet

Are any of these items diphthongs in one English dialect but monophthongs in another?

2.7   For each of the following words, provide IPA transcriptions and mark the primary stress and secondary stress (if applicable).

    a.   examination
    b.   artificial
    c.   commitment
    d.   responsibility
    e.   conclude

2.8   Each of the following items has two possible pronunciations, depending on the placement of stress.

    i.   Provide two transcriptions for each item, marking the stressed syllable.
    ii.   Briefly explain the difference in meaning between the two items. Do you notice any pattern in the relationships between the words?
       a.   refuse
       b.   project
       c.   insult
       d.   convict
    iii.   Think of five more word pairs which differ only in stress placement. Do they follow the pattern you identified in part A?

2.9   Read each of the transcribed sentences and identify the segments that have been elided, epenthesized, or altered due to articulatory processes.

    a.   I already did all my homework [ajɑɹɛdidɪdɑlmɑhomwɚk]
    b.   Can her hamster do any tricks? [kʰænɚæmpstɚduənitrɪks]
    c.   I'm stayin' in bed today. [ajməsteɪmbɛdtəde]

2.10 Use your knowledge of vowel formants to match each spectrogram to the appropriate word.

    a.   reed
    b.   rude
    c.   rad
    d.   red
    e.   rod
    The spectrogram images are in the folder "Files for Chapter Exercises" in the online sound files folder. Image files: Spectogram 10.1–10.5.

2.11 Examine the five following spectrograms and determine which word each spectrogram represents. Think about the differences between stops and fricatives as well as the differences between voiced and voiceless consonants. Listen to the files on the site to find out if you were correct.

    a.   teal
    b.   deal
    c.   feel
    d.   veal
    e.   reel

    The spectrogram images are in the folder "Files for Chapter Exercises" in the online sound files folder. Spectrogram 11.1–11.5. The original sound file is also provided.

2.12 In Chapter 2's resources on the website to accompany this book (www.cambridge.org/introducing-linguistics), you will find a folder called "Speech analysis using PRAAT.". Complete the exercises in this folder to gain practice using Praat, an open-access program for carrying out acoustic analyses.

REFERENCES

Burnham, D., & Dodd, B. (2004). Auditory–visual speech integration by prelinguistic infants: Perception of an emergent consonant in the McGurk effect. *Developmental Psychobiology*, *45*(4), 204–220.

Dryer, M., & Haspelmath, M. (Eds.) (2013). *The world atlas of language structures online*. Leipzig: Max Planck Institute for Evolutionary Anthropology. Available online at: http://wals.info.

Flege, J. (1999). Age of learning and second language speech. In D. Birdsong (Ed.), *Second language acquisition research: Second language acquisition and the Critical Period Hypothesis* (pp. 101–131). Mahwah, NJ: Erlbaum.

Ladefoged, P. (2005). *A course in phonetics* (5th Edition). New York, NY: Thomson Wadsworth.

Maddieson, I. (2001). Phonetic fieldwork. In P. Newman & M. Ratliff (Eds.), *Linguistic fieldwork* (pp. 211–229). Cambridge: Cambridge University Press.

Medina, J. (2008, March 6). *McGurk Effect (with explanation)* [Video file]. Retrieved from: https://www.youtube.com/watch?v=jtsfidRq2tw .

Zsiga, E. (2012). *The sounds of language: An introduction to phonetics and phonology*. West Sussex, UK: Wiley.

3 Phonology

Sound Patterns and Contrasts

Joyce Bruhn de Garavito

OVERVIEW

In this chapter, you will develop an understanding of how sounds are organized in different languages. Our objectives are to:

- understand the concept of a *phoneme*, that is, a distinctive sound segment in a specific language;
- understand how the phonemes of a language are organized in systematic ways;
- identify the phonemes of a language by using contrasts in meaning;
- recognize the differences in distribution of phonemes across languages;
- distinguish between phonemes and *allophones*, that is, the different forms phonemes take as the result of sound changing processes;
- recognize the distinctive features of phonemes and how these allow us to organize sounds into natural classes;
- examine and represent the structure of syllables; and
- practice representing phonological rules.

3.1 What Is Phonology?

Both phonetics (Chapter 2) and phonology (this chapter), deal with the sounds of language. However, these two branches of linguistics focus on different aspects. Phonetics, as we have seen, looks at the physiological and acoustic properties of sounds in the languages of the world; specifically, how sounds are produced and perceived. The unit of interest in phonetics is the phone or sound segment, which is generally represented in square brackets. **Phonology** focuses on the patterns of sounds in a particular language or dialect. Phonology looks at how a specific language selects segments and organizes the sound system. The unit of interest here is the phoneme (see below), which is represented between slashes, for example /k/.

TABLE 3.1 Phonetics and Phonology

Phonetics	Phonology
Unit is the [phone].	Unit is the /phoneme/.
Describes the articulatory and acoustic properties of the sounds used in the languages of the world.	Examines which sounds form part of the inventory of a particular language.
Classifies the different sounds according to their articulatory and acoustic properties.	Determines what the distinctive units (phonemes) of a particular language are.
Is concerned with the physical properties of sounds.	Is concerned with the way sounds are represented in the mind.
	Determines which sounds can go together in a particular language.
	Establishes how sounds change in different phonetic environments in a particular language.

Table 3.1 summarizes the differences between phonology and phonetics. As you can see, phonology studies the ways in which phones form systems and patterns in particular languages, and determines the rules that govern their interactions.

To better understand these differences, consider the sounds [p] and [pʰ]. Phonetics tells us that both of these sounds are: bilabial, pronounced by bringing together the lips; voiceless, that is, produced without vibration of the vocal chords; stops, that is, produced by bringing the lips together and building up pressure that is then released. The two segments differ in that the second, [pʰ], is also aspirated, that is, it is accompanied by a small puff of air. Phonology then uses this information to examine these sounds in specific languages such as English, French, and Punjabi. The phonologist will find that both sounds are found in English, that is, they are part of the **inventory** or complete set of sounds that we use to produce English. However, most people are not aware that the use of [p] or [pʰ] depends on the sounds around them. At the beginning of a word speakers will produce [pʰ], but after [s] they will produce [p].

In French we only find [p]. The segment [pʰ] is not part of the inventory of sounds of this language. In Punjabi, we find both sounds, but unlike English, the distinction leads to different words with different meanings. In other words, in Punjabi, [p] and [pʰ] are not only part of the inventory, they are distinctive units. In Persian, all voiceless stops are aspirated. As you can see, the status of these two sounds varies among languages.

3.2 The Phoneme

Consider the following words:

(1) a.   /kæn/   can
    b.   /tæn/   tan
    c.   /pæn/   pan
    d.   /mæn/   man

The words in (1) differ from each other in the first consonant. The meaning of the word changes as the consonant changes. The sounds /p t k m/ serve to distinguish between words in English.

The words in (2) also differ by one sound, in this case the vowel. Again, the meaning is different in each case. The vowels /æ i ɪ ɛ/ also help to contrast between words in English.

(2) a.   /tæn/   tan
    b.   /tin/   teen
    c.   /tɪn/   tin
    d.   /tɛn/   ten

Finally, the change of meaning of the words in (3) depends on the last consonant, so we can add [ŋ] and [n] to our list of contrastive units.

(3) a.   /sɪn/   sin
    b.   /sɪŋ/   sing

LINGUISTICS TIDBITS: PHONETIC AND PHONOLOGICAL TRANSCRIPTION

Phonology builds on phonetics (Chapter 2). Naturally, both use the International Phonetic Alphabet (IPA) that you learned in phonetics. In many cases, the phonetic and phonological (phonemic) transcriptions of a word will be the same, as the following examples show:

i.   [skul] = /skul/   school
ii.   [ful] = /ful/   fool
iii. [bif] = / bif/   beef

However, in many cases the phonetic and phonological representations will be different, as seen below.

iv.   [pʰæt] ≠ /pæt/

Phonemes are the contrastive sound segments of a language. *Contrastive* means that phonemes can distinguish between words that have different meanings. We write the phonemes of a language between slashes: /p/, /t/, /k/, /m/, / ŋ/, /n/ for some English consonant phonemes; /æ/, /i/, /ɪ/, /ɛ/ for vowels.

Compare these changes in sound and meaning with the following (the diacritic over the vowel represents nasality):

(4) a.   [kʰæn]   [kʰæ̃n]   can
    b.   [mæn]   [mæ̃n]   man

The word *can* in (4) may be pronounced with more or less nasality on the vowel. This is also the case for *man*. However, changing the nasality does not change the meaning of the word. Nasality on the vowel does not contribute to changes in meaning in English, so vowel nasality is not **phonemic** (related to phonemes) in English.

PAUSE AND REFLECT 3.1

On the basis of the following list of words, find new phonemes in English that you may add to the partial inventory we have so far. How are the phonemes written using IPA?

i.	fan
ii.	Dan
iii.	ban
iv.	van
v.	ran
vi.	thin
vii.	gin
viii.	chin

As we saw, phonemes can only be identified in relation to a specific language. Phonemes are part of what a speaker of a language knows. We showed above that vowel nasality does not lead to contrasts in meaning, that is, it is not phonemic in English. Compare this with vowel nasality in French.

(5) a.   /gʁɑ̃/   *grand*   big
     b.   /gʁɑ/   *gras*   fat
     c.   /bo/   *beau*   beautiful
     d.   /bõ/(or /bɔ̃/)   *bon*   good

The examples in (5) show that vowel nasality does help us distinguish between words in French. Unlike in English, /ɑ̃/ and /ɑ/, /õ/ and /o/ are phonemes in French.

3.2.1 Identifying Phonemes through Minimal Pairs

In order to determine whether a segment is a phoneme we look for **minimal pairs**. A minimal pair consists of a pair of words in a particular language that differ by only one sound segment in the same position. The difference in the sound segment leads to a difference in meaning. Looking back at the English examples in (1), (2), and (3), all constitute minimal pairs. Some contrasts based on minimal pairs in English can be seen for consonants in Table 3.2 and for vowels in Table 3.3.

Note that vowels that may be described phonetically as diphthongs, [ej] and [ow], are here transcribed as /e/ and /o/. In English, these vowels are diphthongized but we will continue to transcribe them as monophthongs to facilitate comparison with other languages and to avoid including features that are predictable.

The major diphthongs in English (see Chapter 2 Phonetics) are /ɔj/ as in /tɔj/ *toy*; /aw/ as in /maws/ *mouse*; and /aj/ as in /fajn/ *fine*. These are not predictable.

TABLE 3.2 Some Examples of Minimal Pairs for English Consonants

/p/	/pɪn/ pin	/ɹajp/ ripe	/pæt/ pat	/pɪt/ pit	
/b/	/bɪn/ bin		/bæt/ bat	/bɪt/ bit	
/t/	/tɪn/ tin	/ɹajt/ right		/tɪt/ tit	
/d/	/dɪn/ din	/ɹajd/ ride			
/k/	/kɪn/ kin		/kæt/ cat	/kɪt/ kit	
/g/			/gæt/ gat (a type of gun)	/gɪt/ git	
/f/	/fɪn/ fin	/ɹajf/ rife	/fæt/ fat	/fɪt/ fit	
/v/			/væt/ vat		
/s/	/sɪn/ sin	/ɹajs/ rice	/sæt/ sat	/sɪt/ sit	
/z/		/ɹajz/ rise		/zɪt/ zit	
/θ/	/θɪn/ thin				/iθəɹ/ ether
/ð/		/ɹajð/ writhe	/ðæt/ *that*		/iðəɹ/ either
/ʃ/	/ʃɪn/ shin				/fɪʃən/ fission
/ʒ/					/vɪʒən/ vision
/t͡ʃ/	/t͡ʃɪn/ chin		/t͡ʃæt/ chat	/t͡ʃɪt/ chit	
/d͡ʒ/	/d͡ʒɪn/ gin				
/m/	/mɪn/ Min	/ɹajm/ rhyme	/mæt/ mat	/mɪt/ mitt	
/n/		/ɹajn/ Rhyne	/næt/ Nat	/nɪt/ knit	/sɪn/ sin
/ŋ/					/sɪŋ/ sing
/l/	/lɪn/ Lyn	/ɹajl/ rile		/lɪt/ lit	
/ɹ/			/ɹæt/ rat	/ɹɪt/ writ	
/j/					/haj/ high
/w/	/wɪn/ win			/wɪt/ wit	/haw/ how
/h/			/hæt/ hat	/hɪt/ hit	

TABLE 3.3 Some Examples of Minimal Pairs for English Vowels

/i/	/bit/ beat	/lik/ leek	/ɹid/ read
/ɪ/	/bɪt/ bit	/lɪk/ lick	/ɹɪd/ rid
/e/	/bet/ bait	/lek/ lake	/ɹed/ raid
/ɛ/	/bɛt/ bet		/ɹɛd/ red
/æ/	/bæt/ bat	/læk/ lack	/ɹæd/ rad
/u/	/but/ boot	/luk/ Luke	/rud/ rude
/ʊ/		/lʊk/ look	
/o/	/bot/ boat		/rod/ road
/ɑ/	/bɑt/ *bought*	/lɑk/ lock	/rɑd/ rod
/ʌ/	/bʌt/ *but*	/lʌk/ luck	

There are several things to note about Tables 3.2 and 3.3.

- There are gaps in the tables. Some of these are accidental. There is no reason, for example, why words such as /nɪn/ and /ɹʌd/ should not exist in English.
- Gaps may be due to the rarity of some phonemes. There are few words that make the contrast between /θ/ and /ð/. However, the contrast is not impossible to find: /θaj/ *thigh* and /ðaj/ *thy*. In the same way, it is difficult to find contrasts that include the phoneme /ʒ/. In cases where it is impossible to find minimal pairs, we often make do with near-minimal pairs, that is, pairs that may differ by two phonemes. The contrast between /vɪʒən/ *vision* and /fɪʃən/ *fission*, in the last column of Table 3.2, is a near-minimal pair.
- In some cases it may be impossible to find a minimal pair because the relevant context is never found. For example, in English, the phoneme /h/ is only found before vowels in the same unit, and /ŋ/ is only found after vowels. You will never find a word in English that begins with /ŋ/ or one that ends in /h/. We categorize these segments as phonemes of English because we do find contrast with other sounds.
- The vowel sound /ə/ has not been included in Table 3.3 because it occurs in non-stressed positions. It is therefore difficult to find minimal pairs with other vowels.

LINGUISTICS TIDBITS: PHONEMES AND LANGUAGE VARIETIES

Dialects or varietes may vary in their inventory of phonemes. A well-known case is the difference between European and Latin American Spanish. Latin American dialects do not include the phoneme /θ/, while European Spanish makes a contrast between /θ/ and /s/ in minimal pairs such as /abraθar/ "to hug", and /abrasar/ "to burn". These two words sound the same in Latin America (they are homophonous): /abrasar/.

Similarly, for many speakers around the world, *cot* and *caught* are pronounced in the same way. In other dialects these words contrast the vowels /ɑ/ and /ɔ/ (see Chapter 2 Phonetics).

- Remember not to confuse letters with sounds. As Tables 3.2 and 3.3 show, one phoneme, transcribed by using one symbol, may be spelled with different combinations of letters (Chapter 2 Phonetics).

In Table 3.4 we show the English phonemic consonants, and in Table 3.5 the English phonemic vowels.

TABLE 3.4 English Phonemic Consonants

Manner	Voicing	Labial	Labiodental	Interdental	Alveolar	Post-alveolar	Velar	Glottal
		Place of articulation						
Stop	voiced	/b/			/d/		/g/	
	voiceless	/p/			/t/		/k/	
Fricative	voiced		/v/	/ð/	/z/	/ʒ/		
	voiceless		/f/	/θ/	/s/	/ʃ/		/h/
Affricate	voiced					/d͡ʒ/		
	voiceless					/t͡ʃ/		
Nasal	voiced	/m/			/n/		/ŋ/	
Approximant	voiced lateral				/l/			
Approximant	voiced rhotic				/ɹ/			
Glide	voiced					/j/ (palatal)	/w/	

TABLE 3.5 English Phonemic Vowels

	Front	Central	Back
High	/i/ /bit/ *beat* /ɪ/ /bɪt/ bit		/u/ /but/ boot /ʊ/ /bʊk/ *book*
Mid	/e/ /bet/ bait /ɛ/ /bɛt/ bet	/ə/ hʌntəd/ hunted /ʌ/ /hʌntəd/ hunted	/o/ /bot/ boat /ɔ/* /kɔt/ caught
Low	/æ/ /bæt/ bat		/ɑ/ /kɑt/ cot

*This sound is not in all dialects.

PAUSE AND REFLECT 3.2

Using the IPA, make a phonemic transcription of the following words. Then find two minimal pairs for the initial consonant of each word. Do the same for the vowel.

i.	hat
ii.	gun
iii.	zip
iv.	seat
v.	desk
vi.	very
vii.	she
viii.	vine

3.2.2 Allophones

Tables 3.4 and 3.5 above show the phonemes to be found in most dialects of English. We know from Chapter 2 Phonetics that there are many other segments that we use, such as [pʰ], which is the sound at the start of the words *pot* and *pit*. However, this sound following /s/, as in the word *spin*, no longer has the same puff of air. All native speakers of English will produce that puff of air when /p/ occurs at the beginning of a word or stressed syllable. It is completely regular and fully predictable. Sounds that change their pronunciation based upon a predictable context are **allophones**. However, these sounds do not lead to a contrast in word meanings. They are often the result of articulatory processes, that is, how a segment may change due to the environment in which it appears. Consider the words in (6).

(6) a.   /kæt/   [kʰæt]   cat
     b.   /skæt/   [skæt]   scat
     c.   /pɪt/   [pʰɪt]   pit
     d.   /spɪt/   [spɪt]   spit
     e.   /tʌn/   [tʰʌn]   tonne
     f.   /stʌn/   [stʌn]   stun

In (6), the first column shows the phonemic transcription of the words, the second the phonetic transcription. A comparison shows that, in English, the voiceless stops /p t k/ are realized in two ways: as an aspirated stop at the beginning of a word or a stressed syllable and as a non-aspirated stop after /s/. In other words, the voiceless stops in English have at least two allophones. There are no minimal pairs that contrast in meaning due to the presence of [p] and [pʰ]. We represent the relationship between the phoneme and the two allophones in (7). The environment that conditions the realization of each allophone is included below it.

(7)   Aspirated stops and their allophones.

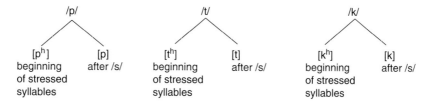

[pʰ]   [p]
beginning   after /s/
of stressed
syllables

[tʰ]   [t]
beginning   after /s/
of stressed
syllables

[kʰ]   [k]
beginning   after /s/
of stressed
syllables

EYES ON WORLD LANGUAGES: ASPIRATION IN HINDI

Consider the following examples in Hindi. Does the aspiration of stops represent allophonic variation or are aspirated and non-aspirated stops different phonemes? What is the evidence?

i.	[bal]	hair	[bʰal]	forehead
ii.	[pal]	care for	[pʰal]	knife blade
iii.	[pəl]	fruit	[pʰəl]	moment
iv.	[kapi]	copy	kʰapi]	meaningful

The presence of these minimal pairs in Hindi is strong evidence that aspirated and non-aspirated stops are phonemes in this language. For a speaker of Hindi /b/ and /bʰ/, /p/ and /pʰ/, and /k/ and /kʰ/ sound quite distinct. Not so for an English speaker, for whom the contrast is allophonic and thus would not result in two differing words.

3.2.3 Complementary Distribution

Allophones do not contrast with each other, they appear in contexts that do not overlap. In other words, a phoneme will be realized by a particular allophone in one context and another allophone in another context. When this happens we say that they are in **complementary distribution**. Two sounds are in complementary distribution if they cannot occur in the same phonetic environment. You can think of this like Spiderman and Peter Parker: where one is, the other cannot be at the same time.

As an example, let us return to the aspirated stops in English. In (8) we find a summary of their distribution.

(8)   a. Voiceless stops are aspirated at the beginning of (stressed) syllables.
       b. Voiceless stops are not aspirated after another consonant, typically /s/.

Although an English speaker is not conscious of the two allophones, we can predict which allophone will be produced in each environment: an aspirated voiceless stop will never be realized after /s/ but it will always be realized at the beginning of a (stressed) syllable. This is what is meant by complementary distribution.

PAUSE AND REFLECT 3.3

In Language X the segments [p] and [b] are allophones of a single phoneme. Which of the following may be true? Explain your answer.

i. The words [puman] and [buman] both exist in language X with different meanings.
ii. The /p/ in the word /puman/ is produced as [b], [buman], before a vowel.

Allophones of the same phoneme generally share most of their phonetic properties. For example, we should not assume that the glottal fricative /h/ and the velar nasal /ŋ/ are allophones of a shared phoneme simply because /h/ is generally found at the beginning of a syllable while /ŋ/ only appears at the end. Nevertheless, care must be taken to rely on objective criteria for determining whether two sounds are allophones of the same phoneme or of separate phonemes. Sounds that seem to be different in one language may not be perceived as such by a speaker of another language.

LINGUISTICS TIDBITS: /d/ AND /ð/ IN QUÉBEC ENGLISH

Many English-French bilinguals and some monolingual English speakers in Québec alternate between pronouncing /d/ and /ð/ in the same words, as illustrated in the following examples:

i.	the	[də]	[ðə]
ii.	this	[dɪs]	[ðɪs]
iii.	then	[dɛn]	[ðɛn]

For these speakers, /d/ and /ð/ are in free variation. There are factors external to the grammar that determine the choice of one pronunciation over the other, such as level of formality, level of proficiency, identity, etc.

3.2.4 Free Variation

Free variation occurs when a phone is pronounced in different ways but the phonetic context does not change. Consider the following data. Note that there is variation in the way the /p/ phoneme is pronounced: In the first example, the final voiceless stop /p/ is unreleased; in the second it is released; and in the third it is aspirated. The realization of these allophones is not phonetically conditioned, rather it is an example of free variation.

(9)   a.   [stap̚]   "Always stop there"
        b.   [stap]   "Stop, please"
        c.   [stapʰ]   "Stop!"

You may read more about free variation in 'Delving Deeper' in Chapter 3's resources on the website to accompany this book at www.cambridge.org/introducing-linguistics.

PAUSE AND REFLECT 3.4

Consider the following data. The phoneme /ɹ/ is devoiced in certain consonant clusters. Are the two allophones of /ɹ/, [ɹ] (voiced) and [ɹ̥] (voiceless), in free variation or are they in complementary distribution? If they are in complementary distribution, what is the phonetic context in which each is found?

The best way to proceed is to determine the phonetic contexts for each of the sounds. In all the words listed, the sound following /ɹ/ is a vowel, therefore we will concentrate on the preceding segments. As a guide, we have included a table you can fill in with a list of the preceding consonants.

i.	[kɹæk]	crack	ii.	[pɹæm]	pram
iii.	[tɹæm]	tram	iv.	[kɹim]	cream
v.	[tɹʌk]	truck	vi.	[pɹuv]	prove
vii.	[fɹʌm]	from	viii.	[gɹæm]	gram
ix.	[bɹæn]	bran	x.	[dɹim]	dream
xi.	[dɹon]	drone	xii.	[gɹɪn]	grin
xiii.	[bɹejv]	brave	xiv.	[əpɹuv]	approve
xv.	[əfɹejd]	afraid	xvi.	[ajskɹim]	ice cream
xvii.	[ɛntɹəns]	entrance	xviii.	[ɪngɹejt]	ingrate
ixx.	[ɨmbɹejs]	embrace	xx.	[əndɹɛs]	undress

We find [ɹ̥] after the following consonants:	We find [ɹ] after the following consonants:

What do the consonants in the first column have in common? How do they differ from those in the second column? Now complete the following representation of the phoneme /ɹ/ in consonant clusters:

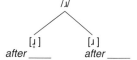

/ɹ/

[ɹ̥]   [ɹ]
after _____   after _____

3.2.5 Points to Remember

As we conclude this section, it may be helpful to summarize a few key points.

- Phonemes are contrastive units of a specific language.
- Allophones are the different realizations of phonemes.
- Allophones are conditioned by the environment in which they appear, unless they are in free variation.
- Allophones share most of their phonetic traits.
- Allophones that are conditioned by the phonetic environment are typically in complementary distribution.
- What constitutes a phoneme in one language may be an allophone in another, and may not exist in a third: /pʰ/ is a phoneme in Punjabi; [pʰ] is an allophone in English, and [pʰ] does not exist in French.
- The environment that conditions the realization of particular allophones may also vary from language to language. In English, nasal vowels are produced by regressive assimilation (see Chapter 2 Phonetics), that is, they become nasalized when followed by a nasal consonant in the same syllable. In Warao (Venezuela), nasalization of vowels and consonants is progressive, that is, the presence of a nasal consonant triggers nasalization in the following segments.

Please consult the appendix at the end of this chapter for a tutorial on how to explore a sound system of a language you do not know.

3.3 Features

The set of data found in (10) reflect what is generally referred to as **Canadian Raising**, although it is also present in other dialects. In the United States it is often heard in New England, New York, Pennsylvania, Maryland, and Delaware. Canadian Raising consists of the production of the diphthongs /aj/ and /aw/ as [ʌj] and [ʌw].

(10) Raised diphthongs [ʌj] and [ʌw]   Non-raised diphthongs /aj/ and /aw/

[pɹʌjs]	/pɹajs/	price	[pɹajz]	/pɹajz/	prize
[hʌjp]	/hajp/	hype	[hajv]	/hajv/	hive
[lʌjf]	/lajf/	life	[lajv]	/lajv/	live
[hʌjt]	/hajt/	height	[hajd]	/hajd/	hide
[hʌws]	/haws/	(the) house (N)	[hawz]	/hawz/	(to) house (V)
[lʌwt]	/lawt/	lout	[lawd]	/lawd/	loud
[kl̩ʌwt]	/klawt/	clout	[klawd]	/klawd/	cloud
[mʌwθ]	/mawθ/	(the) mouth (N)	[mawð]	/mawð/	(to) mouth (V)
			[flaj]	/flaj/	fly
			[baj]	/baj/	buy

In (10) you saw the phonetic representation of words produced with both raised and non-raised diphthongs. In other words, in varieties of English that include Canadian Raising the diphthongs /aj/ and /aw/ have two allophones (11):

(11) Canadian Raising

How do we express the conditioning environment? We could simply list the phonemes where the rule applies, something along the lines of "Canadian raising applies to the diphthongs /aj/ and /aw/ before /p t k f θ s/. No raising takes place when these diphthongs precede the segments /b d g v ð z/." However, this is not very enlightening because a list does not provide an explanation. So what do these phonemes, /p t k f θ s/, have in common? And how do they differ from /b d g v ð z/? You will have realized at once that the first list consists of phonemes that are voiceless, while the second are voiced. So what matters here is not the particular phonemes, it is not /p/ or /t/ that triggers Canadian Raising but rather the fact that these sounds are voiceless.

   In phonology, the term **feature** refers to a phonetic property of a phoneme. Features are binary, that is, they are either present in a phoneme or set of phonemes, or absent. We represent the presence of a feature with a plus sign, the absence with a minus sign. The phoneme /b/ is [+voice], which means it is voiced; /p/ is [–voice], which means it is voiceless. By focusing on one of the features in a group of sounds, we have arrived at a generalization that not only simplifies our description but also allows us to be more precise. Features such as [+/–voice] play a very important role in phonology. They constitute the building blocks of the sound systems of language. We have abstracted away from individual phonemes, which we can now view as bundles of features, in the same way as living entities are made up of bundles of cells.

Returning to our description of Canadian Raising, we may say that it is triggered by the feature [–voice]. We can now write a simple rule (12):

(12) Descriptive rule for Canadian Raising:

- /aj/ and /aw/ are realized as the allophones [ʌj] and [ʌw] before [–voice] consonants.
- /aj/ and /aw/ are realized as the allophones [aj] and [aw] elsewhere.

As another example of an important feature in English, consider the phonemes /m, n, ŋ/ on the one hand, and /b, d, g/ on the other. These phonemes are all voiced, but the first set is comprised of nasal consonants, while the second is made up of oral consonants. We refer to the feature that /m, n, ŋ/ share as [+nasal]. Nasality in consonants is also an important distinctive feature of English. A **distinctive feature** is a feature that serves to distinguish between two phonemes or groups of phonemes in a language. The feature [+/–voice] differentiates between /b/ and /p/, the feature [+/–nasal] differentiates between /b/ and /m/.

To summarize, features such as [+/–voice] and [+/–nasal] allow us to generalize across categories of sounds, to group phonemes into classes, and to explain phonological processes with greater precision. Features are the most basic characteristics of the sound units of languages and they are fundamental to our understanding of the rules that govern these systems.

PAUSE AND REFLECT 3.5

Consider the two following sets of phonemes. What major property do you think distinguishes the two sets?

  i.   /p t k b d g m n ŋ v f s z .../
  ii. /i ɪ e ɛ æ ʌ ə u ʊ .../

In Pause and Reflect 3.5, the first set of sounds is made up of consonants. All the sounds in this set have the feature [+**consonantal**]. In contrast, the sounds in the second set are all vowels. We say vowels are [+**syllabic**], because, as we shall see, vowels typically constitute the core of the syllable. Vowels are [–consonantal] [+syllabic], most consonants are [+consonantal] [–syllabic].

3.3.1 Natural Classes

Features allow us to classify sounds into natural classes. **Natural classes** are sets of phonemes that share a number of features and participate in certain regular processes of the phonological system of a language. For example, in English the phonemes belonging to the natural class made up of [+consonantal, –syllabic, –voice, –nasal] stops (/p t k/) are aspirated at the beginning of a syllable when immediately followed by a stressed vowel; [+nasal] consonants tend to assimilate to a following consonant under certain conditions; elements that are [+syllabic] (vowels) may nasalize when they precede a nasal consonant, etc.

3.3.2 Major Features

The features [+/–consonantal] and [+/–syllabic] are very important because the natural classes they define are general and universal. Another major feature is [+/–sonorant]. **Sonority** is a way of classifying sounds depending on how open or closed the vocal tract is. Sounds that are [+sonorant] are produced with very little constriction so that the flow of air is not interrupted or made turbulent. The English phonemes that belong to this class are the vowels, nasals, and approximants (/l ɹ w j/). Sounds that are [+sonorant] are often contrasted with obstruents, sounds that are produced either with a complete obstruction of the vocal tract (stops), a narrowing that leads to turbulence (fricatives), or a combination of both (affricates). Sonorants are typically voiced.

PAUSE AND REFLECT 3.6

Try to sing the phonemes /m/ and /t/. Which of the two is sonorant?

In Table 3.6 we illustrate the classification of some of the phonemes of English using the important features we have seen so far.

TABLE 3.6 Example of Features as Applied to Some of the Consonants

	[+/–consonantal]	[+/–syllabic]	[+/–sonorant]	[+/–voice]
/p/	+	–	–	–
/t/	+	–	–	–
/k/	+	–	–	–
/b/	+	–	–	+
/d/	+	–	–	+
/g/	+	–	–	+

TABLE 3.6 (cont.)

	[+/–consonantal]	[+/–syllabic]	[+/–sonorant]	[+/–voice]
/v/	+	–	–	+
/m/	+	–	+	+
/n/	+	–	+	+
/ŋ/	+	–	+	+
/l/	+	–	+	+
/i/	–	+	+	+
/ɛ/	–	+	+	+
/u/	–	+	+	+

PAUSE AND REFLECT 3.7

As we did in Table 3.6, complete the following table showing, for each phoneme, the value that applies for each of the major features.

	[+/–consonantal]	[+/–syllabic]	[+/–sonorant]	[+/–voice]
/f/				
/θ/				
/ð/				
/ɹ/				
/s/				
/z/				
/ʃ/				
/ʒ/				
d͡ʒ				
/t͡ʃ/				

We have stated that the approximants, /j, w/, are sonorants. At the same time, they are [–syllabic] because they cannot constitute on their own the nucleus of a syllable. That is, you can find short words such as *tap* /tæp/ in which [æ] is the nucleus, but you will never find a word such as /tjp/ or /twp/. These phonemes are also [–consonantal] because they can form part of a diphthong that will make up the nucleus in words such as *type* /tajp/, in which the nucleus is /aj/ (see Chapter 2 Phonetics).

The phoneme /h/ is a unique form unlike the phonemes we have seen so far in that it is [–syllabic], [–consonantal], and [–sonorant]. So is the glottal stop /ʔ/, if this is a phoneme in your language or dialect.

PAUSE AND REFLECT 3.8

Consider the following phonemes of English. Do you think they form a natural class? Why or why not?

i.	/b p ŋ/
ii.	/m s d͡ʒ/
iii.	/d͡ʒ t͡ʃ/
iv.	/i ɪ u ʊ/

3.3.3 Distinctive Features in English Consonants

In this section we will examine all the features that serve to describe the English consonantal system. A summary of these features is found in the Feature Matrix of English consonants, Table 3.8. A **feature matrix** is a table that shows, for each feature, the value, either [+] or [–], assigned to each phoneme. You will find it is a useful resource.

We have already seen the major features, [+/–consonantal], [+/–syllabic], and [+/–sonorant]. Recall that articulatory phonetics classifies segments according to manner of articulation, voice, and place of articulation. We will classify the features in the same way.

Manner of Articulation Features

- [+*continuant*] sounds are produced without a complete blockage of airflow in the vocal tract. The [+**continuant**] phonemes include the vowels, glides, approximants, and fricatives. All other segments are [–continuant].
- [+*nasal*] sounds are produced by lowering the velum, allowing air to escape through the nose. Included are the nasal consonants (/m n ŋ/). In some languages nasality is also a distinctive feature in vowels. In English nasality in vowels is allophonic. All other segments are [–nasal].
- [+*lateral*] are sounds formed by the tongue tip touching the roof of the mouth, with air escaping from one or both sides of the tongue. /l/ and its allophones are [+lateral]. All other segments in English are [–lateral].
- [+*delayed release*] (DR) is a feature used to distinguish the affricates (/d͡ʒ t͡ʃ/) from other obstruents, which are [–DR]. Recall that affricates are [+**DR**] formed by a complete constriction followed by a fricative-like release of air.

Table 3.7 summarizes the manner of articulation features as they apply to English natural classes. All vowels are [+continuant].

TABLE 3.7 Manner of Articulation Features of Some English Consonants

Members of class	[+/−continuant]	[+/−nasal]	[+/−lateral]	[+/−DR]
/f/, /v/, /θ/, /ð/, /ʃ/, /ʒ/	+	−	−	−
/dʒ/, /tʃ/	−	−	−	+
/m/, /n/, /ŋ/	−	+	−	−
/l/	+	−	+	−
/ɹ/	+	−	−	−

EYES ON WORLD LANGUAGES: PROGRESSIVE ASSIMILATION OF THE FEATURE [+NASAL]

The feature [+nasal] is quite unique in some of the world's languages. In some languages a nasal consonant spreads to all the following segments, making them nasal. This process is often halted by an obstruent. Below you can see this property of nasality in Warao, a language spoken in parts of Venezuela, Guyana, and Suriname (data from Piggott 1992).

i.	inãw̃ãh̃ã	summer
ii.	mõỹõ	cormorant
iii.	mõãũ	give it to him
iv.	mẽh̃õkohi	shadow
v.	mõãũpu	give them to him

As you can see, after the [+nasal] consonants (/m/ or /n/) everything takes on the feature of nasality. However, as the examples in (iv) and (v) show, this copying of nasality is stopped when it reaches /k/ or /p/, both obstruents. This copying or spreading could not be explained if we did not consider nasality as a separate feature.

Laryngeal Features

Laryngeal features are those that relate to the activity of the larynx, in particular the vocal folds.

- [+/−*voice*]. You are already familiar with this feature. Recall that in the production of [+voice] segments the vocal folds are pulled together and the air passing through causes vibration. Vowels are typically [+voice]. All the voiceless segments are characterized by the feature [−voice].
- [*Spread glottis*] (SG). The vocal folds are spread far apart in [**+SG**]. The phoneme /h/ is [+SG], as are the aspirated consonants [pʰ tʰ kʰ]. These last are considered [+SG] because the vocal folds remain open after the closure in the vocal tract is released. For example, when producing [pʰ], the vocal folds are still open after the lips have separated, which

accounts for the little puff of air we find with aspirated consonants (see Chapter 2 Phonetics). All other sounds besides the aspirated consonants and /h/ are [–SG].

- [*Constricted glottis*] (CG). The vocal folds are tightly constricted. The only segment in English that is [+**CG**] is the glottal stop, /ʔ/. All other segments are [–CG].

PAUSE AND REFLECT 3.9

Complete the following table with the English consonants according to whether they are [–voice] or [+voice].

	English consonants
[–voice]	
[+voice]	

Place of Articulation Features: Consonants

We will examine the place features of consonants separately from those that distinguish vowels although some place features are shared by both classes.

Consonant place features. The main place features for consonants are [+/–anterior], [+/–coronal], [+/–high], [+/–back], [+/–round]. We include a fifth feature here, [+/–strident], although it does not technically belong among place features.

- [+/–*anterior*]. This feature distinguishes between segments according to where the primary constriction of the airflow in the vocal cavity is found. Phonemes that are [+anterior] are articulated with the primary constriction at the alveolar ridge or in front of it, in other words, all alveolars, interdentals, labiodentals, and labials are [+anterior]. All other segments are [–anterior].
- [+/–*coronal*]. This feature distinguishes between segments according to whether the articulation involves the tip or blade of the tongue. Interdentals, alveolars, and post-alveolars are [+coronal], all other segments, including the palatal /j/, are [–coronal].

LINGUISTICS TIDBITS: THE GLOTTAL STOP

Recall from Chapter 2 Phonetics that the glottal stop is the sound we produce when saying *uh-oh*. In North American English, the glottal stop is used as an allophone of /t/ when pronouncing certain words such as *button* [bʌʔn̩] (the [n̩] is syllabic in this context). Pronouncing the /t/ as a glottal stop is common in most urban varieties of Britain. However, the glottal stop is a phoneme in languages such as Arabic.

PAUSE AND REFLECT 3.10

i. In the following list, indicate which segments are [+anterior].
/p b t d k g f v s z θ ð ʃ ʒ t͡ʃ d͡ʒ m n ŋ l ɹ/

ii. Now indicate which segments are [–coronal] /p b t d k g f v s z θ ð ʃ ʒ t͡ʃ d͡ʒ m n ŋ l ɹ j w h/

- [+*high*] segments are those that are produced with the body of the tongue raised above the resting position. Besides the [+high] vowels that we focus on in 3.3.4, the [+high] consonants include /k g kʰ/ and the glides. All other consonants are [–high].
- [+*back*] segments are produced with the tongue retracted to the back of the mouth. In English the consonants /k kʰ ŋ w/ are [+back]. All other consonants are [–back].
- [+*round*] segments are produced with the lips tightly rounded. Besides the back vowels, there is only one segment to which this applies, the glide /w/, which is also [+back]. All other consonants are [–round].
- [+*strident*]: Unlike most of the features we have seen, stridency does not refer to the articulation of segments but rather to their acoustic properties. Phonemes that are [+strident] are produced with high turbulence in the air flow. This feature is easiest to understand with the segment /s/, which produces something similar to the white noise made by sizzling oil in a frying pan. In fact, both /s/ and the sound of oil in a pan will block out almost all other sounds. As you may guess, the segments /s z ʃ ʒ t͡ʃ d͡ʒ/ are [+strident], all other consonants are [–strident].

PAUSE AND REFLECT 3.11

Complete the following statements.

i.   The consonants /   / and /   / are [+anterior], [+coronal], [+strident].
ii. The consonants /   / and /   / are [+voice], [–anterior], [+coronal], [+strident].
iii. The consonant /   / is [+nasal], [+back].

Table 3.8 shows the feature matrix for English consonants.

3.3.4 Distinctive Features in English Vowels

All vowels are characterized by the major class features [–consonantal], [+sonorant], and [+syllabic]. They are also [+voice] and [+continuant]. They are distinguished by the following place features:

- [+/–*high*]: In the articulation of [+high] segments the body of the tongue is raised above its normal position. The vowels /i ɪ u ʊ/ are [+high], all other vowels are [–high].
- [+/–*low*]: In the articulation of [+low] segments the body of the tongue is lowered below its normal position. The vowels /æ ɑ ɔ/ are [+low], all other vowels are [–low].
- [+/–*back*]: The body of the tongue is retracted to the back of the oral cavity in the articulation of [+back] segments. The set of [+back] vowels includes both the central and back vowels /ə u ʊ o ʌ ɔ ɑ/. All other vowels are [–back].
- [+/–*round*]: The lips are protruded when producing [+round] segments. Included in the set of [+round] vowels are /u ʊ o ɔ/. All other vowels are [–round].

TABLE 3.8 Feature Matrix for Consonants in English (Phonemes and Some Allophones)

		p	pʰ	b	t	tʰ	d	k	kʰ	g	f	v	s	z	θ	ð	ʃ	ʒ	t͡ʃ	d͡ʒ	m	n	ŋ	l	ɹ	j	w	h	ʔ
Major class	[consonantal]	+	+	+	+	+	+	+	+	+	+	+	+	+	+	+	+	+	+	+	+	+	+	+	+	+	−	−	−
	[sonorant]	−	−	−	−	−	−	−	−	−	−	−	−	−	−	−	−	−	−	−	+	+	+	+	+	+	+	−	−
	[syllabic]	−	−	−	−	−	−	−	−	−	−	−	−	−	−	−	−	−	−	−	−	−	−	−	−	−	−	−	−
Manner	[nasal]	−	−	−	−	−	−	−	−	−	−	−	−	−	−	−	−	−	−	−	+	+	+	−	−	−	−	−	−
	[continuant]	−	−	−	−	−	−	−	−	−	+	+	+	+	+	+	+	+	−	−	−	−	−	−	+	+	+	+	−
	[lateral]	−	−	−	−	−	−	−	−	−	−	−	−	−	−	−	−	−	−	−	−	−	−	+	−	−	−	−	−
	[DR]	−	−	−	−	−	−	−	−	−	−	−	−	−	−	−	−	−	+	+	−	−	−	−	−	−	−	−	−
Laryngeal	[voice]	−	−	+	−	−	+	−	−	+	−	+	−	+	−	+	−	+	−	+	+	+	+	+	+	+	+	−	−
	[SG]	−	+	−	−	+	−	−	+	−	−	−	−	−	−	−	−	−	−	−	−	−	−	−	−	−	−	+	−
	[CG]	−	−	−	−	−	−	−	−	−	−	−	−	−	−	−	−	−	−	−	−	−	−	−	−	−	−	−	+
Place	[anterior]	+	+	+	+	+	+	−	−	−	+	+	+	+	+	+	−	−	−	−	+	+	−	+	−	−	−	−	−
	[coronal]	−	−	−	+	+	+	−	−	−	−	−	+	+	+	+	+	+	+	+	−	+	−	+	+	+	−	−	−
	[high]	−	−	−	−	−	−	+	+	+	−	−	−	−	−	−	+	+	+	+	−	−	+	−	−	+	+	−	−
	[back]	−	−	−	−	−	−	+	+	+	−	−	−	−	−	−	−	−	−	−	−	−	+	−	−	−	+	−	−
	[round]	−	−	−	−	−	−	−	−	−	−	−	−	−	−	−	−	−	−	−	−	−	−	−	−	−	+	−	−
	[strident]	−	−	−	−	−	−	−	−	−	+	+	+	+	−	−	+	+	+	+	−	−	−	−	−	−	−	−	−

Note: /pʰ/, /tʰ/, and /kʰ/ are not phonemes in English, they are allophones. They have been included in the table to illustrate the feature [SG]. In the same way [ʔ] represents the feature [CG].

- [+/–*tense*]: More muscular effort is required to produce [+tense] segments. Included in this set are /i e u o ɑ/. All other vowels in English are [–tense].
- [+*reduced*]: The only [+reduced] vowel in English is [ə].

Remember that features are binary, they are either [+high] or [–high]; [+low] or [–low]; etc. This allows us to characterize mid-vowels as [–high], [–low]. Binary features allow us to make better generalizations.

PAUSE AND REFLECT 3.12

Complete the following statements.

i.	The vowels /	/ and /	/ are [+back], [+high].
ii.	The vowels /	/ and /	/ are [–high], [–low], [–back].
iii.	The vowel /		/ is [–back], [+low].
iv.	The vowel /		/ is [+reduced].

In Table 3.9, we show the feature matrix of all English vowels. Recall that /ɔ/ is not used in all dialects.

TABLE 3.9 Feature Matrix for English Vowels

		i	ɪ	e	ɛ	æ	ʌ	ə	u	ʊ	o	ɑ	ɔ
Major class	[consonantal]	–	–	–	–	–	–	–	–	–	–	–	–
	[sonorant]	+	+	+	+	+	+	+	+	+	+	+	+
	[syllabic]	+	+	+	+	+	+	+	+	+	+	+	+
Manner	[continuant]	+	+	+	+	+	+	+	+	+	+	+	+
Laryngeal	[voice]	+	+	+	+	+	+	+	+	+	+	+	+
Place	[high]	+	+	–	–	–	–	–	+	+	–	–	–
	[low]	–	–	–	–	+	–	–	–	–	–	+	–
	[back]	–	–	–	–	–	+	+	+	+	+	+	+
	[round]	–	–	–	–	–	–	–	+	+	+	–	+
	[tense]	+	–	+	–	–	–	–	+	–	+	+	–
	[reduced]	–	–	–	–	–	–	+	–	–	–	–	–

EYES ON WORLD LANGUAGES: ROUND AND BACK VOWELS

In English all [+round] vowels are also [+back] (but not vice versa). However, in French and other languages (e.g., German) there are also vowels that are [−back] and [+round]. Furthermore, as we saw, French also has [+nasal] vowels. In order to complete a feature matrix for French (and other languages) we have to make certain changes and additions, as you may see by comparing the feature matrix table of French in Table 3.10.

TABLE 3.10 Feature Matrix for French Phonemic Vowels

		i	y	e	œ	œ̃	a	ã	u	o	õ
Major class	[consonantal]	−	−	−	−	−	−	−	−	−	−
	[sonorant]	+	+	+	+	+	+	+	+	+	+
	[syllabic]	+	+	+	+	+	+	+	+	+	+
Manner	[continuant]	+	+	+	+	+	+	+	+	+	+
	[nasal]	−	−	−	−	+	−	+	−	−	+
Laryngeal	[voice]	+	+	+	+	+	+	+	+	+	+
Place	[high]	+	+	−	−	−	−	−	+	−	−
	[low]	−	−	−	−	−	+	+	−	−	−
	[back]	−	−	−	−	−	−	−	+	+	+
	[round]	−	+	−	+	+	−	−	+	+	+
	[tense]	+	−	+	+	+	−	−	+	+	+

3.3.5 Economy and Features

Avoiding redundancy, which we call **economy** in linguistics, is very important for stating linguistic rules and describing sounds. As in other sciences, simple is better.

In the present case, we see the importance of avoiding redundancy in two ways: (a), we use only the number of features that is absolutely necessary to describe a segment; and (b), we use rules to express phonetic processes that are predictable. We will examine each of these in turn.

Number of Features

When we describe phonemes or phonetic processes we do not use all the features from the feature matrices given above. On the contrary, we use as few features as possible.

Natural classes can generally be described with few features. The larger the number of members in a class, the fewer the number of features. Individual phonemes need a larger number of features to define them.

Imagine that you are playing the game *20 questions*. If you guess the answer in fewer than 20 questions you win. We will try to guess the phoneme /k/ from all the phonemes of English:

/p, b, t, d, k, g, f, v, s, z, θ, ð, ʃ, ʒ, t͡ʃ, d͡ʒ, m, n, ŋ, l, ɹ, j, w, h, i, ɪ, e, ɛ, æ, ʌ, ə, u, ʊ, o, ɑ/

You will first ask about the major class features.

1. Is the phoneme I am looking for [+consonantal]? The answer is yes. Your search area has now been reduced: all the vowels, the glides, and /h/ have been excluded.

   /p, b, t, d, k, g, f, v, s, z, θ, ð, ʃ, ʒ, t͡ʃ, d͡ʒ, m, n, ŋ, l, ɹ, j̶, w̶, h̶, i̶, ɪ̶, e̶, ɛ̶, æ̶, ʌ̶, ə̶, u̶, ʊ̶, o̶, ɑ̶/

2. Is the phoneme [+voice]? The answer is no. Now you have eliminated several other segments:

   /p, b̶, t, d̶, k, g̶, f, v̶, s, z̶, θ, ð̶, ʃ, ʒ̶, t͡ʃ, d͡ʒ̶, m̶, n̶, ŋ̶, l̶, ɹ̶, j̶, w̶, h̶, i̶, ɪ̶, e̶, ɛ̶, æ̶, ʌ̶, ə̶, u̶, ʊ̶, o̶, ɑ̶/

   You will not ask whether the phoneme you are trying to guess is [+sonorant], [+syllabic], [+nasal], or [+lateral] because all the segments with these features have already been eliminated by the feature [voice]. Now you turn to the manner features.

3. Is the phoneme [+ continuant]? The answer is no. Your search space is now reduced even more:

   /p, b̶, t, d̶, k, g̶, f̶, v̶, s̶, z̶, θ̶, ð̶, ʃ̶, ʒ̶, t͡ʃ, d͡ʒ̶, m̶, n̶, ŋ̶, l̶, ɹ̶, j̶, w̶, h̶, i̶, ɪ̶, e̶, ɛ̶, æ̶, ʌ̶, ə̶, u̶, ʊ̶, o̶, ɑ̶/

   You now have to choose between /p, t, k, t͡ʃ/. The place features allow you to narrow the search space considerably.

4. Is the phoneme [+anterior]? The answer is no.

   /p̶, b̶, t̶, d̶, k, g̶, f̶, v̶, s̶, z̶, θ̶, ð̶, ʃ̶, ʒ̶, t͡ʃ̶, d͡ʒ̶, m̶, n̶, ŋ̶, l̶, ɹ, j, w, h, i, ɪ, e, ɛ, æ, ʌ, ə, u, ʊ, o, ɑ/

   With only four questions, you have guessed that the phoneme you were looking at is /k/. In other words, /k/ is characterized by the features [+consonantal], [–voice], [–continuant], and [–anterior].

   You will need even fewer features to define natural classes as shown in some examples found below:

- the natural class made up of /m, n, ŋ/ needs only one feature to define it: [+nasal] (in French it would need more);
- the natural class of approximants, /l, ɹ/, is defined as [+consonantal], [+sonorant], and [–nasal];
- the glides, /j, w/, are defined as [–consonantal], [+sonorant], [–syllabic];
- the natural class consisting of /p, b, t, d, k, g/ is defined as [+consonantal], [–sonorant], [–continuant], [–DR];

- the natural class consisting of /p, t, k/ is defined as [+consonantal], [–voice], [–continuant], [–DR];
- the two affricates in English may be defined simply as [+DR];
- the natural class consisting of the vowels /i, ɪ, u, ʊ/ is defined as [+syllabic], [+high].

PAUSE AND REFLECT 3.13

Define the following natural classes with a minimum number of features:

i.   /f v s z θ ð ʃ ʒ/
ii.   /e ɛ ʌ ə o/
iii. /θ ð/
iv.   /u ʊ/

Predictability of Rules

We have mentioned that, in English, at the beginning of a syllable immediately followed by a stressed vowel, the phonemes /p t k/ are produced with a puff of air, that is, they are aspirated. This happens automatically when we speak. Aspiration is entirely predictable from the phonetic context. In fact, speakers are not conscious of the fact that the syllable initial phonemes in words such as /kæt/ *cat*, /pæt/ *pat*, and /tæt/ *tat* are realized as [kʰæt[, [pʰæt], and [tʰæt]. /kæt/, /pæt/, and /tæt/ are the phonemic or underlying representations, what we know about the pronunciation of these words.

The phonetic realization, what we actually pronounce, is [kʰæt[, [pʰæt], and [tʰæt]. The phonemic representations are part of our linguistic competence (see Chapter 1 Introducing Linguistics). The phonetic form, the way the vocal tract produces the sound, is generally predictable. Features are very helpful in describing the rules that account for the difference between what we have in our minds, the phonemes, and what we actually produce, the phones.

In order to describe this type of predictable rule we must focus on three things:

1. the input to the rule, that is, the features of the phonemic or underlying representation;
2. the output of the rule, that is, the features that change;
3. the phonetic environment that conditions the change.

We summarize this information with the following template for rules (13): "A" represents the input, that is, the phonemic representation; "B" represents the output, the features that have changed; and after the slash you find the phonetic context that conditions the change. The arrow means something like *becomes*. In short, we are saying that A becomes B when it is between Y and Z. Some examples can be seen in (14)–(17).

(13)   A → B/Y _____ Z

Let us apply this template to changes we are already familiar with (σ is the symbol for syllable).

- **Aspiration.** The voiceless stops /p t k/ (input to the rule) become (→) aspirated (change) at the beginning of a syllable (see the section on syllables below) when immediately followed by a stressed vowel.

(14) Rule for aspiration of consonants in English.

$$\begin{bmatrix} +\text{consonantal} \\ -\text{voice} \\ -\text{continuant} \\ -\text{DR} \end{bmatrix} \rightarrow [+\text{SG}] \ /\sigma \underline{\hspace{1cm}} \begin{matrix} V \\ [\text{stressed}] \end{matrix}$$

- **Vowel nasalization.** Vowels (input to the rule) become [+nasal] (output), when followed by a nasal consonant in the same syllable. This change is seen in examples such as *sing* /sɪŋ/ which, in some dialects, is realized as [sĩŋ]; *ran* /ɹæn/ → [ɹæ̃n]; *Rome* / ɹom/ → [ɹõwm]. Recall that [+/−nasal] is not a distinctive feature for vowels in English.

(15) Rule for vowel nasalization in English

[+syllabic] → [+nasal] / _____ [+nasal] σ

- **Vowel lengthening.** Vowels in English (input to the rule) are produced with greater length (change) when followed by a voiced consonant in the same syllable (conditioning environment), as seen in the examples below (the diacritic ":" indicates lengthening).

[bæt]	bat	[bæːd]	bad
[flis]	fleece	[fliːz]	fleas
[lif]	leaf	[liːv]	leave
[bet]	bait	[beːð]	bathe

The rule is shown in (16).

(16) Rule for vowel lengthening.

$$[+\text{syllabic}] \rightarrow [+\text{long}] \ / \underline{\hspace{0.5cm}} \begin{bmatrix} +\text{voice} \\ +\text{consonantal} \\ -\text{sonorant} \end{bmatrix}^{\sigma}$$

- **Devoicing of approximants.** The approximants /l, ɹ/ (input to the rule) become voiceless (change) following a voiceless stop (conditioning environment).

(17) Rule for devoicing of approximants in English.

$$\begin{bmatrix} +\text{consonantal} \\ +\text{sonorant} \\ -\text{nasal} \end{bmatrix} \rightarrow [-\text{voice}] \ /\sigma \begin{bmatrix} -\text{voice} \\ +\text{consonantal} \\ -\text{continuant} \\ -\text{DR} \end{bmatrix} \underline{\hspace{0.5cm}}$$

PAUSE AND REFLECT 3.14

Consider the following data from Spanish. In this language [z] and [s] are in complementary distribution.

(i) Phonemic representation of /s/ in Spanish.

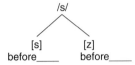

/s/

[s]   [z]
before____   before____

Now look at the data in (ii) (we have omitted some irrelevant allophonic changes). Determine the conditioning environment for the occurrence of [s] vs. [z]. First, write the conditioning environment under the branches in (i) representing the phoneme /s/. Using the rule notation form we have learned, indicate the rule that governs the change from /s/ to [z] in the table below. As usual, you should start by making a list of the conditioning environments. You will see in these data, /s/ is always preceded by a vowel and followed by a consonant, you should concentrate on the consonants.

(ii)   [estudiar]   to study
       [kosto]   cost
       [mizmo]   same
       [peska]   fishing
       [azbesto]   asbestos
       [tiznar]   to blacken
       [izla]   island
       [dezde]   since
       [restar]   to subtract
       [esfumar]   to disappear in smoke
       [esperar]   to wait
       [peskisa]   inquiry
       [razgar]   to tear

3.4 The Syllable

A **syllable** is a unit of phonological structure that consists of a vowel that may be preceded and/or followed by one or more consonants. A word may be made up of one or more syllables. Examples of words broken down into syllables are found in (18). Note that the boundary between syllables is marked with a dot.

(18) a.   tendency   /tɛn.dən.si/
     b.   window   /wɪn.do/
     c.   stops   /stɑps/
     d.   contract   /kɑn.tɹækt
     e.   landing   /læn.dɪŋ/

Native speakers of a particular language find it relatively easy to identify the syllables that make up the words of that language. They are very accessible to the conscious mind. In fact, it has been found that illiterate speakers of a language find it very difficult to manipulate phonemes but have no trouble with syllables. Syllable structure is important because many phonological rules operate at the level of the syllable, as we have seen, including rules related to the placement of stress or relative emphasis of one syllable in comparison to others.

PAUSE AND REFLECT 3.15

Use your intuition to divide the following English words into syllables.

i.	strange	/stɹend͡ʒ/
ii.	examination	/eksæmɪneʃən/
iii.	impressive	/ɪmpɹɛsɪv/
iv.	gymnastics	/d͡ʒɪmnæstɪks/
v.	truthfulness	/tɹuθfəlnɛs/

3.4.1   The Parts of a Syllable

The peak or **nucleus** of the syllable is a [+syllabic] segment. Recall that [+syllabic] phonemes are usually vowels. The nucleus represents the peak of sonority in a syllable. Recall that sonority is related to amplitude or loudness (Chapter 2 Phonetics). The nucleus is the one part of the syllable that is universally obligatory.

The nucleus may be made up of a single vowel or a diphthong, which is usually constituted of a vowel followed by a glide (/j/ or /w/). In (19) we show the nuclei of syllables in bold.

(19)	about	/ə.b**aw**t/
	tendency	/tɛn.dən.s**i**/
	am	/**æ**m/
	pat	/p**æ**t/
	moth	/m**ɑ**θ/
	rose	/ɹ**o**z/
	two	/t**u**/

The consonants that follow the nucleus of the syllable are referred to as the **coda**. The coda is optional. In (20) we show in bold the codas of syllables for the same words we saw above.

Notice that the first syllable in *about* has no coda, nor does the last syllable in *tendency* or the one-syllable word *two*.

(20)	about	/ə.baw**t**/
	tendency	/tɛ**n**.dɛ**n**.si/
	am	/æ**m**/
	pat	/pæ**t**/
	moth	/mɑ**θ**/
	rose	/ɹo**z**/
	two	/tu/

The consonants that precede the nucleus are referred to as the **onset**. Like codas, onsets are optional in English. Notice the lack of onset in the first syllable of the words *about* and *am*.

(21) about   /ə.**b**awt/
     tendency   /**t**ɛn.**d**ən.**s**i/
     am   /æm/
     pat   /**p**æt/
     moth   /**m**ɑθ/
     rose   /**ɹ**oz/
     two   /**t**u/

3.4.2 The Structure of Syllables

As is generally the case in language, the structure of syllables is not flat. Rather, the different parts are organized in a hierarchy. The nucleus (N) and the coda (C) constitute the **rhyme** (R). The nucleus and the coda are closely linked, and together they contribute to important properties such as stress. The onset (O) does not make this contribution.

The rhyme and the onset together make up the syllable. Remember that the syllable is represented with the symbol σ. The template for the structure we have described is found in (22).

(22) The structure of syllables.

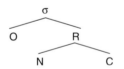

The structure of syllables is binary, that is, each node (O, R, C) can only have a maximum of two branches. Languages, however, impose constraints on which parts of the syllable can branch, as we will see.

3.4.3 Representing the Structure of Syllables

There are three main steps in drawing the representation of syllable structure. First we determine what the nucleus is. Recall that the nucleus is constituted by a [+syllabic] element, typically a vowel. You link this element to N(ucleus), and then to R(hyme). Finally, you extend the link to σ. An example with the word *train* is in (23).

(23) a. The nucleus: /tɹen/ *train*

Next, we can determine the onset. In this example we find a branching onset made up of the consonants /t/ and /r/. The onset is linked directly to the syllable σ.

b. The onset: /tɹen/ *train*

The last step is to identify the coda, which will consist of any consonant to the right of the nucleus that is in the same syllable as the nucleus. The coda constitutes the second branch of the rhyme.

c. The coda: /tɹen/ *train*

Recall that the elements of a syllable can only be binary branching. If, instead of the word *train* we tried to represent the word *strain* there would be a problem because there are three sounds in the onset. We confront a similar problem with codas that include three or more segments, as in *bumps* /bʌmps/ or *limped* /lɪmpt/. However, the shape of these extended onsets and codas is quite restricted. The only element that can appear in the onset before two consonants is /s/. Although less restricted, not everything can appear at the right edge of a coda with three or more segments. These facts have led linguists to suggest that these elements are part of the syllable but not part of the onset or coda, as shown in the representation of *strained* below. The initial /s/ is extrasyllabic and is appended to the syllable level as in (24).

(24) /stɹend/ *strained*

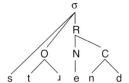

PAUSE AND REFLECT 3.16

First show the phonemic representation of the following words using IPA. Divide each word into syllables. Then, draw the syllabic representation of *plant*.

   i.   plant
   ii.   contract
   iii.   inclusion
   iv.   incredible

3.4.4   General Rules for the Structure of Syllables

We have already seen that the structure of syllables is constrained to two branching nodes. Besides this requirement, there are two more rules that apply to the world languages: the Sonority Scale and the Maximum Onset Rule.

Sonority Scale

Segments within a syllable are typically organized around a sonority scale. The **sonority scale** is a requirement that, when there are complex onsets or codas, the segments with the highest degree of sonority (amplitude or loudness) should be closest to the nucleus. The sonority hierarchy is shown in (25). The number of asterisks above the segment class indicates the degree of sonority: the more asterisks, the more sonorous the sounds. Vowels are represented by four asterisks because they constitute the peak of sonority: they are the least constricted sounds, and they resonate a lot more loudly. Obstruents (oral stops, fricatives, affricates) have no sonority.

(25)   Sonority hierarchy

				*
			*	*
		*	*	*
	*	*	*	*
obstruents	nasals	approximants	glides	vowels

The sonority hierarchy predicts that sonority will rise in the onset, as you approach the nucleus, and decline in the coda, as you move away from the nucleus. English allows /s/ before the onset and some [–voice] obstruents at the end of the coda, leaving these segments somewhat outside the sonority scale, as expected if they are extrasyllabic. In (26) you will find some examples.

(26) a.   tramps

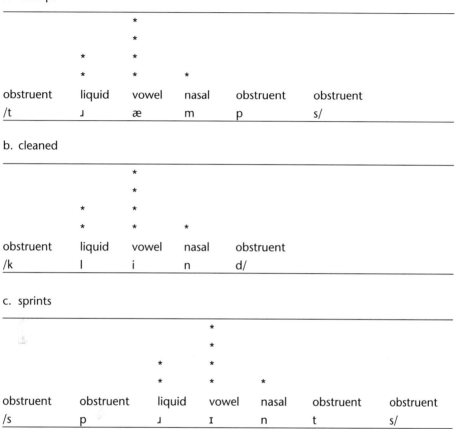

		★			
		★			
	★	★			
	★	★	★		
obstruent	liquid	vowel	nasal	obstruent	obstruent
/t	ɹ	æ	m	p	s/

b. cleaned

		★		
		★		
	★	★		
	★	★	★	
obstruent	liquid	vowel	nasal	obstruent
/k	l	i	n	d/

c. sprints

			★			
			★			
		★	★			
		★	★	★		
obstruent	obstruent	liquid	vowel	nasal	obstruent	obstruent
/s	p	ɹ	ɪ	n	t	s/

PAUSE AND REFLECT 3.17

Using IPA, show the phonemic representation of the following words, then indicate the sonority scale for the whole word.

i.	prize
ii.	school
iii.	blame
iv.	when

Maximum Onset Rule

According to the **Maximum Onset Rule**, as many consonants as possible should be syllabified in the onset, as long as the resulting sequence is allowed in the language.

Consider the word *constrain*. We know that there are two syllables because there are two nuclei: /ə/ is the nucleus of the first syllable and /e/ is the nucleus of the second. We also know that /k/ constitutes the onset of the first syllable. However, we have to determine what the onset of the second syllable is among four consonants: /nstɹ/. Do they all form the onset of the second syllable? The Maximum Onset Rule tells us to fit as many phonemes as possible into the onset of the second syllable while maintaining the syllable structure allowed by English. Does English allow these four consonants in the onset?

In order to determine which consonants form part of the second syllable we can ask whether there are any words in English that begin with /nstɹ/. The answer is no, which is evidence that /nstɹ/ cannot be the onset. We then ask whether any words begin with /stɹ/. The answer is yes, for example in the word *straight*. Therefore we conclude that /stɹ/ is the onset. The remaining nasal /n/ constitutes the coda of the preceding syllable. The syllabification of *constrain* is therefore: /kən.stren/. Native and very proficient speakers of English will have intuitions about this, but others may have more difficulty.

EYES ON WORLD LANGUAGES: EXAMPLES OF SOME CONSTRAINTS ON SYLLABLE STRUCTURE

- Italian: allows single codas that consist of approximants or nasals, and only when the nucleus is not a diphthong. Examples: /par.te/ "part"; /al.to/ "high"; /kon.to/ "count". Italian onsets are less restricted, allowing up to three elements. Examples: /spre. d͡ʒa.re/ "to despise"; /zblok.ka.to/ "unblocked".
- Spanish: generally allows single codas, typically approximants or nasals. Examples: /lar.go/ "long"; /al.to/ "high"; /ba.lon/ "ball". Spanish also allows only two phonemes in the onset. Examples: [blaŋ.ko] "white"; [prisa] "hurry".
- Japanese: strongly favors a CV syllable. It allows single codas made up of nasals. Examples: /pan/ "bread"; /hon.too/ "truth". It also allows single consonants in the onset. This is most visible in the case of borrowings from other languages, in which typically, vowels are inserted to break up clusters of two or more consonants. Example: /in.to.ro.da.ku.sjon/ "introduction" (recall that /j/ is [–consonantal] and therefore /jo/ is a diphthong, part of the nucleus).

Syllabification in Other Languages

In order to syllabify words in other languages you must know both the universal rules and the language specific rules. Let us look in detail at language specific rules that differ from English rules: the rules of Spanish.

In English, the word *instructor* is divided into syllables as followings: /ɪn.stɹʌk.tɚ/. The Maximum Onset Rule demands we assign to the onset as many consonants as possible, and English specific rules allow us to include /stɹ/ but not /nstɹ/ in the onset. However, examine the following data from Spanish.

(27)

English		Spanish	
/skul/	school	/eskwela/	*/skwela /
/splɛndɪd/	splendid	/esplendido/	*/splendido/
/stɹɪkt/	strict	/estrikto/	*/strikto/
/sofə/	sofa	/sofa/	
/sɛns/	sense	/sentido/	

In (27), notice that in Spanish, though words may begin with /s/ followed by a vowel, they may not begin with /s/ followed by a consonant. This is evidence that /s/ + consonant is not allowed as part of the onset of a syllable in Spanish. The only option to syllabify *instructor* in this language is /ins.truk.tor/.

EYES ON WORLD LANGUAGES: EFFECTS OF FIRST LANGUAGE SYLLABLE STRUCTURE ON SECOND LANGUAGE USE

You may have noticed that Italian speakers of English often add a schwa to the end of words that end in a consonant, for example pronouncing *club* as /klʌbə/. In the same way, Spanish speakers add /e/ at the beginning of words. For example, they may say /estʌdɪ/ for *study* and /eskul/ for *school*. These pronunciations are the result of transferring, usually unconsciously, the first language syllable structure to the second.

Maximum Onset Rule in Phrases and Sentences

So far we have focused on the syllable structure of words. However, in many languages, there is a second pass at syllabication when we string words together. For example, consider the following combination of words: *an apple*. In isolation, each word is broken into syllables as shown in (28). In this example [l̩] fills the role of nucleus.

(28) an apple

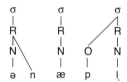

When we produce the words *an apple* together, the coda of the word /ən/ becomes the onset of /æpl/, thus satisfying the Maximum Onset Rule. We say /ə.næ.pl̩/. The new structure is seen below in (29).

(29) an apple

3.5 Above the Syllable: Stress

The syllable is not the only unit above the segment that phonology analyzes. As you saw in Chapter 2 Phonetics, we are also interested in the phonetic and phonological structure of words, phrases, and sentences. We refer to these as **suprasegmentals**. We will focus on word stress in this section.

In many languages, including English, one syllable is perceived as prominent in words such as nouns, verbs, adjectives, or adverbs. By this, we mean that the most prominent syllable is pronounced with greater length, volume, or higher pitch than the other syllables. We say that this syllable carries **stress**. We mark the stressed syllables with a superscript vertical line placed directly before the syllable that bears the stress, as you may have seen in some dictionaries:

(30) Examples of stress placement in English

/ˈte.bl̩/	table
/ˈstu.dənt/	student
/ˈwɪn.do/	window
/ˈtɹæ.vəl/	travel
/kən.ˈsʌlt/	consult
/dɪs.ˈtɹɔj/	destroy

As we will see in Chapter 4 Morphology, English sometimes uses the placement of stress to distinguish between verbs and nouns, as shown in (31).

(31)

/kən. ˈvɛɹt/	(to) convert, verb
/ˈkɑn.vɛɹt/	(a) convert, noun
/səb.ˈd͡ʒɛkt/	(to) subject, verb
/ˈsʌb.d͡ʒɛkt/	(a) subject, noun

In English, in words with three or more syllables, stress is often assigned to more than one syllable. However, one of the syllables will always be the most prominent, receiving primary stress, while the other stressed syllable receives secondary stress. We indicate secondary stress with a subscript vertical line directly before the syllable, as shown in (32).

(32)

/ˈsɛ.kən.ˌdɛ. ɹɪ/	secondary
/ˌlɪŋ.ˈgwɪs.tɪks/	linguistics
/ˌtɹʌ.ˈdɪ.ʃə.nəl/	traditional
/ˌfʌn.də.ˈmɛn.təl/	fundamental
/ˌdɪs.ˈtɹæk.tɪŋ/	distracting

You may notice that the vowel in the syllable that is not stressed may change, often to the reduced vowel /ə/. Note, for example, the vowel changes in (33):

LINGUISTICS TIDBITS: STRESS AND VARIATION

Note that it is sometimes possible to recognize the first language of a second language speaker of English because of stress placement. For example, a native English speaker refers to the capital of Canada as 'O.tta.wa, a French speaker will often say O.tta.'wa, and a Spanish speaker may say O.'tta.wa.

(33) /ˈfo.to/   photo
      /ˈfo.tə.ˌgɹæf/   photograph
      /ˈfə.ˈtɑ.gɹə.fi/   photography
      /ˈfo.tə.ˈgɹæ.fɪk/   photographic

In fact, sometimes the unstressed vowel may be dropped completely, as in the British English frequent pronunciation of *secretary*: [ˈsɛ.kɹə.tɹɪ]. Compare this to North American English, in which there is secondary stress on the third syllable: /ˈsɛ.kɹə.ˌtɛ.ɹi/.

SUMMARY

In Chapter 2 Phonetics, we learned about the articulatory and acoustic properties of human languages. In Phonology, we have seen that individual languages or language varieties may use only some of the possible sounds and organize them in different ways. A sound inventory of a language will include sounds that are used to contrast words with different meanings. We call these sounds phonemes, and we recognize them because we can use them to form minimal pairs. Minimal pairs are words that differ in one segment only but have different meanings. For example, the words *pat* and *bat* constitute a minimal pair. Minimal pairs such as this one allow us to determine that /p/ and /b/ are phonemes in English.

However, phonemes are not always realized in an identical way in the string of speech because the phonetic environment in which they are found may condition certain changes. We refer to the different forms that a phoneme may adopt in different phonetic contexts as allophones. For example, the /p/ in *pat* is produced as an aspirated [pʰ]. In most cases, the type of allophone that is produced is predictable and rule-governed. However, it is important to note that what may be an allophone in one language (for example, nasal vowels in English), may be phonemes in another (nasal vowels in French). Furthermore, the conditioning environments may be different across languages.

Although the phoneme is an important unit in a language, it is possible to deepen our understanding of phonological processes if we recognize that different phonemes share particular features. Considering features allows us to group sets of phonemes into natural classes that participate in general phonological processes. For this reason we refer to these features as the building blocks of the phonological system of a language.

Phonology also examines the constitution of larger units such as syllables and words. In fact, many of the rules governing phonetic change rely on syllables and suprasegmental elements such as stress for their application. In Chapter 4 Morphology, we will see that the phonology of a language may interact with morphology (how words are put together).

Appendix

How to Discover the Sound System of a Language

Imagine that you have been asked to analyze the phonology of a language, in this case Brazilian Portuguese (BP). The first thing you must do is to determine the phonemes. Recall that to do this you must look for minimal pairs, which are evidence that the two sounds in question are contrastive.

Below is a list of words in BP, including their phonetic transcription, their spelling in BP, and the English translation.

1. The first question you are asked to consider is whether the distinction between nasal and oral vowels is contrastive, that is, whether both nasal vowels and oral vowels are distinct phonemes, or whether, as in English, they are allophones of the same underlying phoneme. In order to determine this you should:

(a) List the vowels you find.
(b) Look for minimal pairs. Do you find minimal pairs for all vowel contrasts?
(c) List the vowels that you found in minimal pairs. These will be the vowel phonemes.

Transcription	Spelling	Translation
[sĩ]	sin	yes
[sẽ]	sem	without
[sãtʊ]	santo	saint
[vidə]	vida	life
[fa]	fa	fa (musical note)
[ẽ]	em	in
[bõbə]	bomba	pump
[vĩdə]	vinda	arrival
[bõ]	bom	good
[fã]	fã	fan

Transcription	Spelling	Translation
[mudʊ]	mudo	mute
[tetə]	teta	teat
[tẽtə]	tenta	tries
[mũdʊ]	mundo	world
[boba]	boba	silly
[verdad͡ʒi]	verdade	truth
[t͡ʃivi]	tivi	I had

Your list of vowels will include the following oral vowels: [a e i o u ʊ ə] and the following nasal vowels: [ã ẽ ĩ õ ũ]. You will also have found the following minimal pairs:

[vidə]	life	[vĩdə]	arrival
[fa]	fa (musical note)	[fã]	fan
[bobə]	silly	[bõbə]	bomb
[mudʊ]	mute	[mũdʊ]	world
[tetə]	teat	[tẽtə]	tries

You may conclude that both the oral and the nasal vowels are phonemes in Brazilian Portuguese: /a e i o u ã ẽ ĩ õ ũ/. However, you may have noticed that there were no nasal counterparts for the vowels [ʊ ə].

2. Returning to the list of words given above, focus on the two vowels that did not have nasal counterparts: [ʊ ə]. You will notice that there are no minimal pairs that rely on these two vowels for contrast, not even near-minimal pairs. Your working hypothesis is that these are allophones. You are asked to decide whether these two vowels are in complementary distribution. In order to determine if this is the case you should list the words where you find these vowels. In this example, the conclusion is fairly obvious: the phones [ʊ, ə] are found only at the end of words that have more than one syllable. Because you should take phonetic similarity into consideration, you conclude the two vowels [ʊ, ə] can be considered allophones of /o/ and /a/ respectively.

3. To continue, consider the consonants in the following list of words from BP.

a. Determine whether /t/ and /d/ are phonemes or allophones. Show your evidence.

[nadʊ]	nado	swim
[od͡ʒiʊ]	odio	hate
[pat͡ʃinar]	patinar	skate
[fatʊ]	fato	fact
[dadə]	dada	due
[tez]	tez	complexion
[dez]	dez	ten
[d͡ʒigʊ]	digo	I say
[teɲʊ]	tenho	I have

[natʊ]	nato	born
[datə]	data	date
[kwatrʊ]	quatro	four
[foxt͡ʃi]	forte	strong
[unidʊ]	unido	united
[t͡ʃivi]	tivi	I had
[fadʊ]	fado	fate
[d͡ʒiŋejrʊ]	dinheiro	money
[t͡ʃiʊ]	tio	uncle
[verdad͡ʒi]	verdade	truth

You will find several minimal pairs distinguished by only the two sounds in question. This is evidence that /t/ and /d/ are phonemes in BP.

[natʊ]	born	[nadʊ]	swim
[fatʊ]	fact	[fadʊ]	fate
[tez]	complexion	[dez]	ten
[datə]	date	[dadə]	due

b. Using the same list of words, determine whether /t͡ʃ/ and /d͡ʒ/ are phonemes or alophones. Again, you will search for minimal pairs. There are none, so your hypothesis is that these are not phonemes. You must determine what the conditioning environment may be and whether they are in complementary distribution with the phonemes /t/ and /d/. Make a list of words that include [t͡ʃ], [d͡ʒ] and a list of those with /t/ or /d/.

Words including [t͡ʃ] and [d͡ʒ]	Words including [t] and [d]	[nadʊ]	swim
		[fatʊ]	fact
		[fadʊ]	fate
[od͡ʒiʊ]	hate	[teɲʊ]	I have
[pat͡ʃinar]	skate	[natʊ]	born
[t͡ʃivi]	I had	[datə]	date
[verdad͡ʒi]	truth	[kwatrʊ]	four
[t͡ʃiʊ]	uncle	[tez]	complexion
[d͡ʒigʊ]	I say	[dez]	ten
[foxt͡ʃi]	strong		

You will notice in the first column that [t͡ʃ d͡ʒ] always appear before /i/. In the second column, [t d] never appear in this context. In other words, the contexts do not overlap, meaning that [t͡ʃ d͡ʒ] are in complementary distribution with [t d].

Recall that a condition of allophony is that there are articulatory or acoustic similarities between a phoneme and its allophones. Note that [t͡ʃ] and [t] are both [–voice], while [d͡ʒ] and [d] are both [+voice]. You therefore conclude that, in BP, the phoneme /t/ has two allophones: it may be realized as [t] or as [t͡ʃ]. In a similar fashion, the phoneme /d/ may be realized as [d͡ʒ] or [d].

We can show the visual representation of allophones of /t/ and /d/ as such:

	/t/			/d/	
[t͡ʃ]		[t]	[d͡ʒ]		[d]
before [i]		elsewhere	before [i]		elsewhere

The contrast between the pronunciation of [t͡ʃ] and [t] on the one hand, and [d͡ʒ] and [d] on the other is illustrated here:

a.	/patinar/	[pat͡ʃinar]	skate	
b.	/data/	[datə]	date	
a.	/odio/	[od͡ʒiʊ]	hate	
b.	/dez/	[dez]	ten	

We may account for these facts with a more general rule using features. In the rule given below, in (iii) [+/– voice] means that the output will match the input in voicing. If the input (the phonemic representation) is [–voice], that is, /t/, the output (the phonetic realization) will also be [–voice], that is, [t͡ʃ]; if the input is [+voice], that is /d/, the output will also be [+voice], that is [d͡ʒ].

The phonological rule that explains the allophonic variation of /t/ and /d/ in BP is:

$$
\begin{bmatrix} \text{+ consonantal} \\ \text{–sonorant} \\ \text{–continuant} \\ \text{+coronal} \\ \text{+/– voice} \end{bmatrix} \rightarrow \begin{bmatrix} \text{+DR} \\ \text{+/–voice} \end{bmatrix} / \underline{\hspace{1cm}} \begin{bmatrix} \text{+syllabic} \\ \text{+high} \\ \text{–back} \end{bmatrix}
$$

Summarizing, to analyze a language's sound system, you should carry out the following steps:

1. Determine whether the segments in question are phonemes by checking for minimal pairs.
2. If they are not phonemes and if they are phonetically similar, you must determine whether they are allophones. To do this, check whether they are in complementary distribution.
3. If they are in complementary distribution, describe the environment that conditions the realization of each of the allophones.
4. Write a rule that is as general as possible.

EXERCISES

3.1   Consider the groups of English phonemes below. In each case you should:

    a.   Indicate the phoneme that does not belong in the natural class.

    b.   Using the fewest number of features, describe the natural class.

    i.   /p ŋ b m/

    ii.   /f v s z ð θ ʒ ʃ w/

    iii.   /l h ɹ/

    iv.   /b p l d t g k/

    v.   /i ɪ e ɛ ʌ/

    vi.   /u ʊ o i ɔ/

3.2   Consider the following data from Japanese. (/ɯ/ represents a high, back, unrounded vowel)

    i.   Determine whether the segments [t t͡ʃ t͡s] are phonemes.

    ii.   If they are not, determine whether they are in complementary distribution.

    iii.   State the environment in which each is realized.

    iv.   Choose the segment used in the greatest number of contexts to represent the phoneme. How would you represent the relation between [t t͡ʃ t͡s] in a branching diagram?

[hatake]	dry field
[takay]	high
[soʃite]	and then
[t͡sɯki]	moon
[t͡ʃitori]	one person
[t͡ʃikara]	strength
[kɯt͡sɯʃita]	socks
[nekɯtay]	necktie
[kut͡su]	shoe
[it͡ʃi]	one
[tambo]	paddy
[hat͡ʃi]	bee
[t͡suri]	fishing
[itoko]	cousin
[te]	hand

3.3   The following data are from Spanish. The segments [i] and [ɪ] are allophones of an underlying phoneme /i/. What conditions the realization of one or other allophone?

[lindo]	pretty
[lɪtro]	liter
[fin]	end
[vɪno]	wine
[imposɪble]	impossible
[pɪsar]	step on
[pintura]	painting
[siŋko]	five
[refɪnar]	refine
[anfɪtrjon]	host
[fɪnal]	ending
[timbrar]	ring
[iŋkoŋgrwente]	incongruent

i.   List the environments for [i] and [ɪ]. Are the two segments in complementary distribution?
ii. Diagram the relation between the two allomorphs. Do not forget to indicate the conditioning context.

3.4 There are some dialects of English in which /ɹ/ is dropped or very reduced in certain contexts. Determine under which conditions the /ɹ/ is dropped. (Recall that ":" indicates vowel lengthening, which occasionally happens when /ɹ/ is dropped.)

ron	[ɹɑn]
hurry	[hʌɹɪ]
clearing	[kl̩ɹɪŋ]
parrot	[pʰærət]
star	[stɑ:]
harder	[hɑ:rə]
clear	[kɪ°]
striker	[strajkə]
rear	[ɹi:]
park	[pʰɑ:k]

i.   List the environments under which the /ɹ/ is pronounced or dropped.
ii.   Using your knowledge of syllable structure, explain in words the conditions that trigger ɹ-drop.
iii. Write a rule that summarizes the data.
iv.   Write the phonemic representation of the word *rear*.

3.5 The following data are from Quechua, a language spoken in Peru and Ecuador. [q] stands for a voiceless uvular stop and [χ] for a voiceless uvular fricative.

Part A

First try to determine the status of the sounds [i] and [e] by answering the questions below.

[qateχ]	descendant
[suti]	name
[teχwaj]	pluck
[api]	take
[t͡ʃilwi]	chick
[χwirti]	strong
[fit͡ʃa]	date
[wasi]	house
[t͡ʃaki]	foot
[qent͡ʃa]	enclosure for sheep
[t͡ʃit͡ʃi]	herb
[rinrint͡ʃeχ]	our ear
[waleχ]	poor
[qet͡ʃun]	he argues
[wawqe]	brother (of a man)

i.   List any minimal pairs found. Based on your answer decide whether [i] and [e] are phonemes or allophones.
ii.   List the phonetic environments in which [i] and [e] are found.
iii. Which segment, [i] or [e], is the least restricted (appears in more contexts)? The segment you choose will represent the phoneme.
iv.   What is the conditioning environment for the allophones?
v.   What is the phonemic transcription of the word [qet͡ʃwa]?

Part B

In a similar fashion, examine the vowels [o] and [u] in the following data from Quechua.

[wajʎoq]	lover
[t͡ʃoχlu]	corn cob
[moqo]	runt
[pʰulu]	blanket
[alqoχ]	dog
[plaku]	thin
[runku]	round
[wiqru]	crooked
[ukut͡ʃa]	mouse
[tuktu]	flower
[surqoj]	extract

i.   List any minimal pairs found.
ii. List the phonetic environments in which [o] and [u] are found.
iii. Which segment, [o] or [u], is the least restricted (appears in more contexts)? The segment you choose will represent the phoneme.
iv. Can you generalize your description to include the four vowels [i e o u]?
v.   We know that /a/ is a phoneme in Quechua. Which are the phonemic vowels in this language?

3.6 The following data (simplified) are from Korean (thanks to Dr. Young-He Kim for help with the data). Focus on [l] and [r] which are allophones of the same phoneme in Korean. Then answer the questions. (Nominative means it is the form that appears in subject position.)

[nal]	day
[nari]	day (nominative)
[seul]	Seoul
[ilgop]	seven
[rubi]	ruby
[saram]	person
[pʰal]	arm
[seolda]	to cut
[sal]	rice
[sari]	rice (nominative)
[salgama]	bag of rice
[param]	wind
[ratjo]	radio

i.   Consider the syllables in which each allophone, [l] and [r], are found. Are they in the onset or the coda?
ii. Write a formal rule assuming /l/ is the phoneme.

3.7 The following data are from Italian (thanks to Dr. Maria Laura Mosco for her help with the data). Like English, Italian allows branching onsets that obey the sonority scale, plus a left edge addition (i.e., appendix) of a sibilant that attaches directly to the syllable.

Part A

Focus on the alternation between [s] and [z] in this left edge extrasyllabic position.

[spakko]	I split
[strano]	strange
[zgretolare]	to crumble

[skrepolato]	cracked
[zdrajato]	laid back
[spredʒare]	to despise
[zblokkato]	unblocked

i.   List the environments in which [z] and [s] occur as a left edge extrasyllabic position.
ii. In words, describe the environments that condition each of the allophones.
iii. Write a formal rule assuming /s/ is the phoneme.
iv. Draw the syllable structure for the second syllable of the word [aspro] *bitter*. Be sure to remember the Maximum Onset Rule.

Part B

When [z] and [s] occur as the regular part of syllables the situation is a bit different. Consider the following additional data from Italian.

[fuzo]	melted
[fuso]	spindle
[kjeze]	churches
[kjese]	s/he asked
[frantʃeze]	French
[inglese]	English
[sano]	healthy
[filozofo]	philosopher

i.   What is the status of [s] and [z] as part of the inner structure of the syllable? What is your evidence?
ii. Give the phonetic transcription of /diskretsjone/ *discretion* and /disbrigare/ *to dispatch*.

3.8 As you saw in Chapter 2 Phonetics, North American speakers often use the alveolar tap [ɾ] in certain cases. In the following English data, focus on the alternation of [t], [d], and [ɾ].

[ˈstændɪŋ]	standing
[ˈstʌɾi]	study
[pʰɹiˈstin]	pristine
[ˈhiɾɪŋ]	heating
[ˈpʰɹɪɾi]	pretty
[ˈhɪstəɹi]	history
[əˈdɪʃən]	addition
[ˈsɪɾəɹ]	sitter
[dɪˈtʰʌmɪn]	determine
[ˈpʰestɪŋ]	pasting
[ˈæɾəm]	atom
[ˈkʰæptɪn]	captain

i.   List the environments in which the change occurs.
ii. In words, describe the environments that condition the alveolar tap.
iii. Give the phonemic transcription for the words *captain* and *atom*.

3.9 The following data are from Spanish. Focus on the segments [b d g β ð ɣ].
[β] represents a voiced bilabial fricative;
[ð] represents a voiced interdental fricative;

[ɣ] represents a voiced velar fricative.

[gato]	cat
[dato]	data
[tato]	I touch
[goma]	eraser
[baka]	cow
[aβako]	abacus
[deðo]	finger
[aðentro]	inside
[aɣatʃar]	bend over
[aðmitir]	admit
[grjeta]	crack
[aɣrjetar]	to crack
[eðukar]	to educate
[eðað]	age
[drama]	drama
[umbeso]	a kiss
[undaðo]	a die (singular form of "dice")
[kluβ]	club
[elboton]	the button
[aβnormal]	abnormal
[eɣresaðo]	graduate
[unaβlusa]	a blouse
[burdo]	coarse
[sombra]	shadow
[jerba]	grass

i.   List the environments in which [b d g β ð ɣ] occur.

ii.   Determine whether [b d g] are phonemes or if they are allophones of one phoneme. State your evidence.

iii.   Determine whether there are overlapping environments between [b] and [β], [d] and [ð], and [g] and [ɣ]. Explain what this shows regarding the status of these pairs of segments.

iv.   Write the rule that explains the change to [β], [ð], and [ɣ]. Be as general as possible.

3.10 The following data are from Arabic (thanks to Ms. Albandary Aldossari for the data). The relevant data come from the addition of the article *the* to nouns. In the first column you find the word without the article, and in the third the article is attached to the beginning of the word. Focus on the form the article takes in each case.

[kalb]	dog	[ʔalkalb]	the dog
[qɪsm]	section	[ʔalqism]	the section
[fikra]	idea	[ʔalfikra]	the idea
[waraqa]	paper	[ʔalwaraqa]	the paper
[madrasah]	school	[ʔalmadrasah]	the school
[bɪnt]	girl	[ʔalbɪnt]	the girl
[kitaab]	book	[ʔalkitaab]	the book
[d͡ʒejb]	pocket	[ʔald͡ʒejb]	the pocket
[ʔakil]	food	[ʔalʔakil]	the food
[hilaal]	crescent	[ʔalhilaal]	the crescent
[su:q]	market	[ʔassu:q]	the market
[dʕoah]	invitation	[ʔaddʕoah]	the invitation

[samaaʔ]	sky	[ʔassamaaʔ]	the sky
[ʃadʒara]	tree	[ʔaʃʃadʒara]	the tree
[talib]	scholar	[ʔattalib]	the scholar
[dirasah]	study	[ʔaddirasah]	the study
[taʕliim]	learning	[ʔattaʕliim]	the learning
[durub]	road	[ʔaddurub]	the road
[salaam]	peace	[ʔassalaam]	the peace
[ziːarah]	visitation	[ʔazziːarah]	the visitation
[rasmah]	drawing	[ʔarrasmah]	the drawing
[naar]	fire	[ʔannaar]	the fire
[tafsir]	interpretation	[ʔattafsir]	the interpretation
[nuur]	light	[ʔannur]	the light
[tʃaaluutʃ]	tool	[ʔatʃtʃaaluutʃ]	the tool
[taʕbiːr]	expression	[ʔattaʕbiːr]	the expression
[risalah]	letter	[ʔarrisalah]	the letter
[zawaal]	demise	[ʔazzaawaal]	the demise
[sahaab]	clouds	[ʔassahaab]	the clouds

i.   List the environments in which the definite article takes the form [ʔal] and those in which it takes different forms.

ii. What feature in the first segment of the noun determines the change from [ʔal] to the other forms?

iii. Indicate what form the definite article would take for [beet] *house* and [ʃahar] *moon*.

3.11 Nahuatl is a language spoken in Mexico. Its syllable structure is quite simple: it does not permit either branching codas or branching onsets, but it does permit branching rhymes. Consider the following data.

[koton]	shirt
[kwahtɬa]	fields
[nawatɬ]	Nahuatl
[tɬaul]	corn

i.   Considering the rules about Nahualt syllable structure, determine whether [tɬ] constitutes one segment [tɬ] or two [tɬ].

ii. Draw the structures for the syllables in [nawatɬ].

iii. Nahuatl borrows many words from Spanish. A Spanish speaker from Spain would syllabify the word *atlas* as [at.las]. How would a Nahuatl speaker probably syllabify the word in Nahuatl?

3.12 **Part A**

Consider [i] and [y] in French (/y/ is a high, front, rounded vowel). Are they phonemes or allophones? What is the evidence for your answer?

[li]	bed
[ly]	read
[si]	if
[su]	known
[ri]	laughs
[ry]	street

Part B

Now consider the allophones of /t/ [t] and [t͡s], and the allophones of /d/: [d] and [d͡z], in Canadian French.

[tuʒur]	always
[ete]	summer
[mõd]	world
[dɔrmir]	sleep
[sede]	yield
[dɑ̃se]	dance
[tas]	cup
[put͡sin]	poutine
[pət͡si]	small
[t͡sire]	take out
[d͡zifisil]	difficult
[d͡zi]	says
[rid͡zicyl]	ridiculous

i. List the environments in which we find [t] or [d].
ii. List the environments in which we find [t͡s] and [d͡z].
iii. Do the environments for [t] and [t͡s], [d] and [d͡z] overlap or are they in complementary distribution?
iv. In words, describe the rule that explains the realization of the allophones.
v. Diagram the realization of the allophones of [t] and [d], including the conditioning environments.

3.13 Below you will find a list of non-existing words.

[pɹatu]
[bɹza]
[lastɹ]
[ɹestɹup]

i. Decide which are possible words in English.
ii. For the impossible words, determine which constraint on the structure of syllables is violated.

3.14 For each of the following pairs of phonemes, name the single feature that distinguishes them.

i.	/i/	/u/
ii.	/z/	/ð/
iii.	/d/	/n/
iv.	/ð/	/θ/
v.	/ə/	/ʌ/
vi.	/u/	/ʊ/
vii.	/k/	/g/
viii.	/l/	/r/
ix.	/d͡ʒ/	/t͡ʃ/
x.	/u/	/o/

3.15 Write the phonemic representations of the following words. Then briefly describe the rule of English that accounts for the phonetic form.

i.	[pʰæ̃n]	pan
ii.	[pɹɑːd]	prod
iii.	[ˈɹajɾɪŋ]	riding
iv.	[kʰɪŋ]	king

REFERENCES

Ladefoged, P., & Maddieson, I. (1996). *The sounds of the world's languages*. Malden, MA: Blackwell.

Odden, D. (2013). *Introducing phonology* (2nd Edition). Cambridge: Cambridge University Press.

Piggott, G. (1992). Variability in feature dependency: The case of nasality. *Natural Language and Linguistic Theory*, *10*(1), 33–77.

Quesada Castillo, F. (2006). *Quechua de Cajamarca: Fonología, morfología, sintaxis*. Lima: Editorial Mantaro.

Tranel, B. (1987). *The sounds of French: an introduction*. Cambridge: Cambridge University Press.

PART 3

STRUCTURE AND MEANING

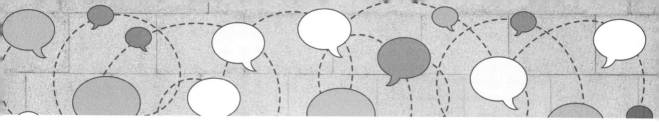

4 Morphology

Word Structure

Joyce Bruhn de Garavito

OVERVIEW

In this chapter, you will develop an understanding of how words are formed. Our objectives are to:

- learn how words may be made up of smaller units called morphemes;
- recognize the difference between types of morphemes;
- examine the rules that govern the ordering of morphemes;
- practice representing the structure of words via trees;
- understand how words may be created or adapted; and
- observe how languages may differ in how they build words.

4.1 What is Morphology?

Morphology is the study of words, how they are formed, and how they relate to other words. For example, in (1), the word *books* is built by bringing together the word *book* and the plural marker *–s*. We find the same plural marker on other words such as *cats*, *tables*, and *girls*. However, we do not find the plural marker on words such as *over*, *with*, or *gone*. Words such as *books*, *cats*, *tables*, and *girls* relate to each other because they belong to a class of words that behaves in a similar fashion.

In the same way, we can turn words such as *slow*, *violent*, and *clear* into other types of words by adding *–ly*, as seen in (2), but we cannot add this ending to words such as *book*. This shows that words like *slow*, *violent*, and *clear* do not belong to the same class of words as the ones found those in (1).

(1) a. book + –s = books
    b. cat + –s = cats
    c. table + –s = tables
    d. girl + –s = girls
    e. over + –s = *overs

* (ungrammatical) in a language.

(2)   a. slow + –ly = slowly

     b. violent + –ly = violently

     c. clear + –ly = clearly

     d. book + –ly = *bookly

4.1.1   What Is a Word?

The **word** is one of the most important units of language. We see it as a unit that carries meaning. When we are learning a second language we often have trouble getting our meaning across, and we feel this is so because we cannot find the words. Our belief about the importance of the relationship between words and meaning leads us to try to memorize lists of vocabulary items that will help us communicate in the new language. In fact, many foreign language textbooks begin each chapter with a list of words that are to be practiced and acquired.

Our understanding of what a word represents is closely related to our association with literacy and dictionaries. We think of words as units that refer to concepts or elements that can be defined and when we don't know the exact meaning of a word, we look it up.

We also believe words can be written independently from each other, with a space on each side. We actively use far fewer words than we know the meaning of, and we probably write a greater variety of words than we use in conversation. We also admire people who know a lot of (long) words. However, most of us would be hard put to define the concept **word**.

PAUSE AND REFLECT 4.1

Consider the following words. Which ones would you expect to find as separate entries in the dictionary? Why?

i. play, walk, go
ii. plays, walks, goes

iii. big, strong, happy
iv. bigger, stronger, happier
v.   rapid, slow, kind
vi. rapidly, slowly, kindly

Now consult a dictionary to see if you were right.

4.1.2   Words and Patterns

You are probably thinking that it is obvious why *walks*, *plays*, and *goes* are not generally in the dictionary: because they form a pattern that is applicable to almost any verb in English. Furthermore, *walk*, *walks*, *walked* all refer to the same action. The endings of these verbs do not change the meaning, they add additional information regarding the person and the tense. In fact, if we were to invent a new verb, for

LINGUISTICS TIDBITS: WORDS IN OTHER LANGUAGES
A word in one language may represent a sentence or a phrase in another language. For example, in Nahuatl (an indigenous language spoken by around a million speakers in Mexico), *nitlaulnemakas* is a single word that translates into English *I will buy corn*. In Inuktitut (a language spoken in Northern Canada by around 50,000 speakers), the word *supuurutiviniqauti* means *ashtray*. However, if we break the word down into parts the resulting translation is the phrase *that which contains the remains of that which is used to blow* (Allen and Crago, 1996). In a similar fashion, the English verb *kick* may be expressed by a whole phrase in French, *donner un coup de pied*, and in Spanish, *dar una patada*.

example the verb *flad*, English speakers would automatically say *flads* for the third person and *fladded* for the past, and they would expect each form to share the basic interpretation of *flad*. However, an irregular past tense form such as *went* may be included in the dictionary because it does not follow a pattern, it is one of a kind.

The difficulty of defining a word is also noticeable if we think about other types of words, words such as *the*, *a*, and *this*. These never appear alone in a sentence unless, as in this paragraph, they are being used in citation form. They do not seem to have meaning in and of themselves. Like the verb endings mentioned above, they add meaning to a phrase: *the book* is typically used in a context in which both the speaker and the hearer know which book is being talked about, *a book* is used when the object is first referred to, *this book* is used if the book is close to the speaker.

4.1.3 The Lexeme

One way around the problem of defining the term *word* is to generalize. Linguists propose an abstract way of representing what all the forms of a word such as *walk* have in common. We refer to this abstract representation as a **lexeme**, and it is generally written in upper-case letters. For example, the lexeme WALK can be realized in speech by different concrete forms: *walk*, *walks*, *walked*. All these forms have a common core of meaning, something along the lines of "using your legs to move".

4.2 Simple and Complex Words

Simple words consist of one unit and can stand on their own, for example *donkey*, *hat*, *man*. **Complex words** are made up of more than one unit. For example, the word *donkeys* is made up of *donkey* and the plural marker *–s*, *walked* is made up of *walk* and the past form *–ed*. So we can identify *husband* as a simple word, but *ex-husband* as a complex word.

4.2.1 Morphemes

Morphemes are the smallest units of language which carry meaning. In some cases the smallest unit can be a simple word, such as *walk*, *book*, or *carrot*. We consider words such as these as **free morphemes**, because they can appear on their own. A **bound morpheme** is one that must attach to another morpheme. For example, the ending *–ed*, which attaches to regular verbs in English, is a bound morpheme that has the meaning [+past]. The morpheme –s, when attached to English nouns, carries the meaning [+plural]. The morpheme –able is added to verbs in English, turning them into adjectives that indicate a property. *Comparable* means that something has the property of being compared.

4.2.2 Roots, Affixes, and Bases

Complex words are often made up of a root and one or more affixes. We call the morphemes *walk*, *donkey*, and *husband* **roots**. The root carries the main meaning of the word and cannot be divided into further parts. It generally belongs to a lexical category such as *noun, verb, adjective, adverb,* or *preposition*. Lexical categories will be examined in detail in Chapter 5 Syntax, but Table 4.1 provides a short roadmap.

PAUSE AND REFLECT 4.2

Underline the root morpheme in the following words.

i.   considering
ii. impossible
iii. hospitalize

iv. hospitalization
v. bottomless
vi. thinks

TABLE 4.1 The Categories of Words

Category	General meaning	Examples
Nouns (N)	refer to people, places, animals, and things	teacher, boy, dog, house, table
Verbs (V)	denote actions or states	walk, find, think, know, build
Adjectives (A)	denote properties or features	short, happy, red, busy
Prepositions (P)	express relations in space and time	on, over, with, until, after, before
Adverbs (Adv)	modify verbs or adjectives	nearly, well, very, often

We refer to the elements that have been added to a root as *affixes*. An **affix** is an element that cannot appear as a stand-alone word. It is always a bound morpheme. In the examples in (3) we have separated the root from the affix with a hyphen. The affix is in bold and underlined.

(3) a. window–**s**
     b. play–**s**
     c. play–**ed**
     d. play–**ing**
     e. curious–**ly**
     f. fear–**less**
     g. real–**ize**

Affixes may be attached to words that already have one or more affixes. Consider the word *hospitalizations*. As you can see in (4), we have added three different affixes to the root, *hospital*.

(4) a. hospital
     b. hospital–ize
     c. hospital–iz–ation
     d. hospital–iz–ation–s

The **base** is any form to which affixes are attached. It can consist of a single morpheme or a root, or a root with one or more affixes. For example, *hospital* is the base for *hospitals* and for *hospitalize*. In turn, *hospitalize* constitutes the base for *hospitalization*. Note that *hospital* is a free standing word so it is also an example of a free morpheme. Furthermore, it is the root of all the words that we form from it.

EYES ON WORLD LANGUAGES: FREE FORMS AND BASES IN OTHER LANGUAGES

In English there are many words that consist of only one morpheme, that is, they are free. This is not always the case in other languages. For example, in Nahuatl (Mexico), a verb can never be produced on its own, it is always the base for one or more affixes. The same thing applies to most of the nouns and verbs in Spanish. The well-known –o and –a endings that we associate with masculine and feminine gender are affixes that are attached to a base, which happens to be the root. In the following examples, *cas–*, the root/base that means "house", and *libr–* "book", are not free morphemes because they need the gender endings. In the same way, verb roots such as *habl–*, which is the root/base that means "speak" and *com–* "eat", are not free, they must always be attached to an affix.

i.   cas–a "house"
ii. libr–o "book"
iii. habl–a–r "to speak"; habl–a–ste "you spoke"
iv. com–e–r "to eat"; com–e–mos "we eat"

PAUSE AND REFLECT 4.3

Underline the affixes in the following words.

i.   repainting
ii. incomparable
iii. constructions
iv. finalizing

v.   discontinued
vi. lovable
vii. displaced

4.2.3 Affixes: Suffixes and Prefixes

Affixes can be attached to the beginning or the end of a base. When an affix is attached at the end it is referred to as a **suffix**. When it is attached at the beginning it is called a **prefix**. Table 4.2 shows some examples of English suffixes and Table 4.3 provides some examples of prefixes.

EYES ON WORLD LANGUAGES: CIRCUMFIXES AND INFIXES

In some languages, an affix attaches to both the beginning and end of a word, constituting a bound morpheme with two parts. It wraps around the word. We refer to this type of affix as a **circumfix**. The best known example is the German past participle. For instance, the past participle of the verb *machen* "to make" is *ge–mach–t*. The root is *–mach–*, and the circumfix is *ge—t*.

Other languages have infixes. An **infix** is an affix that is inserted inside the root. For example, in Malagasy (Madagascar), we find the infix *–in–* that creates passive verbs:

baby "carrying on the back"	b–in–aby "carried on the back"
dimby "replacement"	d–in–imby "replaced"
folaka "break"	f–in–olaka "broken, tamed"
toraka "act of throwing"	t–in–oraka "thrown"

Beware of confusing an affix that lies between the root and another affix with a real infix. For example, *–iz* in *hospital–iz–ation* is not an infix because it has not been inserted inside the root *hospital*. See Appendix 1 at the end of this chapter for some ideas on how to analyze morphological structure in other languages.

TABLE 4.2 Examples of Suffixes in English

general	general-ize	general-iz-ation	general-iz-ation-s
thought	thought-ful	thought-ful-ness	
nation	nation-al	nation-al-ity	
small	small-ish		

TABLE 4.3 Examples of Prefixes in English

button	un-button
obey	dis-obey
husband	ex-husband
understand	mis-understand

PAUSE AND REFLECT 4.4

Consider the bolded segments in the words below. For each, place checkmarks under the appropriate classification. If the segment is neither of the first four options mark *none*. The first word has been done for you.

	Root	Base	Affix Prefix	Suffix	None
characterization		√			
impossible					
p**ool**					
inter**nation**al					
shy**ness**					
con**cept**					
dis**cover**					
remember					

4.2.4 The Internal Structure of Words

There are rules for attaching affixes of any type to a base. For example, we cannot add the suffix –*ation* to adjectives or nouns, as shown in the examples in (5), which are all ungrammatical. We first have to turn the adjective or noun into a verb, as shown in (6).

(5) a. *general–ation
     b. *grammatical–ation
     c. *category–ation

(6) a. general → general-ize →general–iz–ation
     b. grammatical → grammatical–ize → grammatical–iz–ation
     c. category → categor–ize → categor–iz–ation

Examples such as (5) and (6) are evidence that we have morphological mental **rules** and that words have internal structure. We know the rules for attaching the different affixes and we can apply them to new or invented words. For example, if we invent an adjective such as *furil*, we know we must convert it into a verb, *furil–ize*, before we can use it as a noun, *furil–iz–ation*.

Linguists represent the internal structure of words using trees. A morphological tree indicates the lexical category of the root, the order in which affixes are added, and the lexical category of the final and intermediate products. We illustrate this process in (7). The lexical categories are indicated as follows: N stands for noun; V for verb; A for adjective; P for preposition; Adv for adverb. We use *af* to represent any type of affix.

(7) a.   generalize

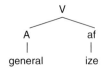

b.   generalization

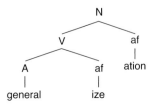

c.   unbutton

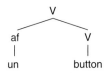

PAUSE AND REFLECT 4.5

Draw the trees that represent the structure of the following words:

i.   mower   vi.   blacken
ii.   remarry   vii. untie
iii. inconsiderate   viii. reinvention
iv.   teach   ix.   preheat
v.   seriousness   x.   antiwar

4.2.5 Problems for our Definition of a Morpheme

We have defined a morpheme as the smallest unit of meaning. The association between the morpheme and meaning generally works. For example, it is easy to recognize that the words *hoot*, *foot*, and *root* are all words made up of one morpheme. We cannot divide them into smaller units because no native speaker will assign meaning to *–oot*. In contrast, in the case of *boots*, *beds*, and *houses*, the final *–s* is a bound morpheme because in all these cases and thousands more, it is interpreted to mean "more than one" (i.e., plural). We can also state a rule that says that the plural morpheme *–s* in English always attaches to a noun.

However, consider the following words: *mulberry, cranberry, raspberry,* among others. All of these include the morpheme *berry,* which clearly has meaning in English. However, the apparent roots *mul, cran,* and *ras(p)*[1] do not mean anything on their own. They acquire meaning only when linked to the morpheme *berry.* They are therefore problematic for our definition. We consider these morphemes, often referred to as *cranberry morphemes,* a special case of bound roots.

A similar problem arises with verbs such as *receive, conceive, deceive,* and verbs such as *commit, permit, submit, transmit,* among others. Historically, these words were made up of two morphemes, but in modern English, the original meaning has been lost. We therefore consider them monomorphemic, that is, constituted of only one morpheme.

4.2.6 Allomorphs

Some morphemes can be realized in different ways depending on the phonological context. The different forms that a morpheme may take are called **allomorphs**. The morpheme for the English indefinite article *a* is a good example. As shown in (8), we pronounce it as *a* when it precedes a word that starts with a consonant and as *an* when it precedes a word that starts with a vowel. In other words, the indefinite article morpheme has two allomorphs, and which is chosen depends on the sound that follows it.

(8) a. a table; a chair; a small elephant

b. an airplane; an apple; an elegant tie

The English plural is another good example. Although we have represented the affix that indicates plural as *–s,* it can be pronounced differently depending on the ending of the base it is attached to, as shown in (9). We use slashes around the plural (/s/, /z/, or /əz/) to indicate that we are transcribing phonemically. This is because we are interested in the way the plural morpheme is realized in each context.

(9) a. top/s/, rat/s/, rack/s/, ruff/s/

b. gum/z/, fad/z/, bog/z/, bell/z/, table/z/

c. judg/əz/, church/əz/, bush/əz/, bus/əz/

The bases in (9a) end in /p/, /t/, /k/, and /f/. Recall from Chapter 2 Phonetics that these sounds are all voiceless. Compare these with the endings in (9b): /m/, /d/, /g/, /l/ are all voiced. Using these examples, and many others, we can conclude that the plural morpheme is voiced (/z/) when following a voiced phoneme and voiceless (/s/) when following a voiceless phoneme.

The examples in (9c) are slightly more complicated. An additional segment, /ə/, is inserted to break up a consonant cluster that is not allowed in English within a syllable: *judg/z/, *church/s/, *bush/s/, *bus/s/. This typically occurs when the base ends in a strident. Recall that the segments /s/, /z/, /ʃ/, /ʒ/, /t͡ʃ/, and /d͡ʒ/ are [+strident].

---

[1] English does include the word *rasp,* but its meaning is not related to our understanding of the word *raspberry.*

To summarize, the plural morpheme in English has three allomorphs: /s/, /z/, and /əz/ and which of these is chosen depends on the phonological context, in this case the nature of the preceding sound.

A third example of an English morpheme with several allomorphs is the prefix *in–* which means "not". Consider the examples in (10).

(10) a. /in/experienced, /in/accurate, /in/accessible
b. /in/tolerable, /in/definite, /in/sufficient
c. /im/probable, /im/polite, /im/measurable
d. /iŋ/comprehensible, /iŋ/compatible, /iŋ/glorious
e. /il/legal, /ir/regular

The examples in (10a) and (10b) show the most common pronounciation of /in/. However, (10c) shows that it is realized as /im/ preceding a labial and (10d) shows that it is realized as /iŋ/ when the base begins with a velar such as /g/ or /k/. The examples in (10e) show that the prefix *in–* is realized as /il/ and /ir/ when preceding /l/ and /r/. So we see that the allomorphs of the morpheme *in–* are /in/, /im/, /iŋ/, /il/, and /ir/.

PAUSE AND REFLECT 4.6

Consider the third person singular *–s* that attaches to verbs in English. Pronounce the examples in (i) carefully and you will realize that there are different allomorphs for the third person singular, as we saw above for the plural *–s*. Can you describe the phonological context for each one?

i. a. chop/s/, put/s/, break/s/, puff/s/
b. come/z/, grab/z/, mention/z/, fade/z/, see/z/
c. miss/əz/, judg/əz/, munch/əz/

4.2.7 Morphophonology

As we have seen, allomorphs are variants of a morpheme which are usually determined by the phonological environment. The study of this interaction between phonology and morphology is referred to as **morphophonology**. On the one hand, phonology is involved. The morpheme for the plural is pronounced in a different way depending on the phonological properties of the preceding segment. On the other hand, morphology is also involved as the change happens specifically at morpheme boundaries. For example, we determined that a noun ending in a vowel requires the plural allomorph /z/. However, there is no phonological rule in English that says that vowels must be followed by the phoneme /z/, they are frequently followed by /s/: *mistress, bus, race*.

4.3 **Derivational and Inflectional Morphology**

So far, we have treated all affixes the same. However, morphemes such as the plural *–s*, the third person *–s*, the past tense *–ed*, and the progressive *–ing* differ in important ways from morphemes such as *–ize* in *hospitalize* or *–ity* in *probability*. The morphemes that indicate properties such as plural, progressive, or past tense do not change the lexical category or the meaning of the base, they simply make it more precise by specifying number or tense. *Walk, walks, walked,* and *walking* belong to the same lexeme, WALK. They all maintain the same meaning, the use of legs for movement, and they belong to the same category, the verb.

Word formation processes that add grammatical information and do not change the meaning and/or the category of the root are referred to as **inflection** and the morphemes that participate in inflectional processes are referred to as **inflectional morphemes**.

In contrast, we speak of **derivation** when the addition of an affix changes the meaning and/or the category of the base. In other words, derivation creates new lexemes. For example, *hospital* is a noun that refers to a place. The addition of the affix *–ize* not only changes a noun into a verb, it also means something different. It no longer refers to a place but rather the action of admitting a person to a hospital. Morphemes that change the meaning and/or category of a base are referred to as **derivational morphemes**.

PAUSE AND REFLECT 4.7

In the following list, certain morphemes are in bold. Determine whether they are derivational or inflectional.

i. distrac**tion**
ii. **mis**communication**s**

iii. realize**s**
iv. (I am) read**ing**
v. institution**al-ize-s**

4.3.1   Derivational Morphology

As we saw above, derivational morphemes such as *–ize* and *–(a)tion* change the meaning and very often the lexical category of the base they are attached to. However, there are regularities as to the type of base a particular morpheme may attach to and the kind of category change that results. Some of these regularities, as they apply to suffixes, are listed in Tables 4.4–4.10. Note that the addition of morphemes may lead to changes in the spelling of either the base or the affix.

TABLE 4.4 Examples of Suffixes: Nouns → Adjectives

Suffix	Examples
–(u)al	cause → caus-al dialect → dialect-al habit → habit-ual verb → verb-al
–ful	faith → faith-ful help → help-ful hope → hope-ful mind → mind-ful

TABLE 4.4 (*cont.*)

Suffix	Examples
–(i)al	nation → nation-al actuary → actuari-al ministry → minister-ial category → categori-al
–ic	alcohol → alcohol-ic pessimist → pessimist-ic climax → climact-ic dogma → dogma-tic
–less	mercy → merci-less name → name-less clue → clue-less flaw → flaw-less
–ous	nerve → nerv-ous virtue → virtu-ous clamor → clamor-ous prodigy → prodigi-ous

TABLE 4.5 Examples of Suffixes: Noun → Verb

Suffix	Examples
–ize	hospital → hospital-ize magnet → magnet-ize material → material-ize character → character-ize

TABLE 4.6 Examples of Suffixes: Nouns → Nouns (No change in category)

Suffix	Examples
–ship	friend → friend-ship author → author-ship censor → censor-ship companion → companion-ship

TABLE 4.7 Examples of Suffixes: Verbs → Nouns

Suffix	Examples
–al	refuse → refus-al acquit → acquitt-al dismiss → dismiss-al recite → recit-al
–ance	continue → continu-ance observe → observ-ance appear → appear-ance admit → admitt-ance
–ant	contest → contest-ant attend → attend-ant defend → defend-ant assist → assist-ant
–(at)ion	confirm → confirm-ation recollect → recollect-ion accuse → accus-ation protect → protect-ion
–er	teach → teach-er paint → paint-er sing → sing-er produce → produc-er
–ment	commit → commit-ment atone → atone-ment announce → announce-ment disappoint → disappoint-ment

TABLE 4.8 Examples of Suffixes: Verbs → Adjectives

Suffix	Examples
–able	read → read-able compare → compar-able adore → ador-able debate → debat-able
–ive	invent → invent-ive instruct → instruct-ive oppress → oppress-ive abuse → abus-ive

TABLE 4.9 Examples of Suffixes: Adjectives → Verbs

Suffix	Examples
–en	white → whit-en mad → madd-en awake → awak-en soft → soft-en
–ize	equal → equal-ize central → central-ize vocal → vocal-ize real → real-ize

TABLE 4.10 Examples of Suffixes: Adjectives → Nouns

Suffix	Examples
–ity	modern → modern-ity eccentric → eccentric-ity active → activ-ity actual → actual-ity
–ness	small → small-ness faithful → faithful-ness stubborn → stubborn-ness empty → empti-ness

In Tables 4.11–4.13, we list some of the prefixes used in English. Note that they change the meaning but not the category of the base.

TABLE 4.11 Examples of Prefixes: Nouns → Nouns

Prefix	Examples
anti–	government → anti-government climax→ anti-climax aggression → anti-aggression aircraft → anti-aircraft
ex–	husband → ex-husband minister → ex-minister member → ex-member dictator → ex-dictator
super–	strength → super-strength achiever → super-achiever abundance → super-abundance billionaire → super-billionnaire

TABLE 4.12 Examples of Prefixes: Adjectives → Adjectives

Prefix	Examples
in/im–	complete → in-complete possible → im-possible tolerant → in-tolerant determinate → in-determinate
un–	biased → un-biased caring → un-caring attractive → un-attractive important → un-important
super–	cheap → super-cheap rich → super-rich interesting → super-interesting busy → super-busy

TABLE 4.13 Examples of Prefixes: Verbs → Verbs

Prefix	Examples
de–	caffeinate → de-caffeinate escalate → de-escalate clutter → de-clutter list → de-list
dis–	like → dis-like appear → dis-appear agree → dis-agree connect → dis-connect
mis–	interpret → mis-interpret diagnose → mis-diagnose manage → mis-manage align → mis-align
re–	make → re-make do → re-do live → re-live finish → re-finish
un–	do → un-do balance → un-balance fasten → un-fasten seal → un-seal

Although we have listed many derivational morphemes and the types of words they can attach to, not all combinations exist or are possible. In other words, some combinations are more productive than others. For example, the prefix *un–*, although quite productive, is not used with all adjectives. We may say *unhappy* but we do not refer to someone as *unsad*, or we may use *unavailable* but not *unaccessible*. Often these cases are due to an accidental gap in English. In other cases, the restrictions may be quite specific, often involving the phonological make-up of words or their history.

Regarding meaning, sometimes derivation maintains a certain transparency: a *worker* is someone who works, a *swimmer* is someone who swims. However, a *bumper* is not someone who bumps, it is a part of a car, and a *cashier* is someone who works at a cash register, not someone who cashes.

PAUSE AND REFLECT 4.8

Over time, the meaning of complex words can stabilize in such a way that the original derivation is lost. For example, *ostracize*, meaning to exclude someone from a group, is derived from the Greek word *ostrakon*, which was a pot-shard that ancient Greeks used to vote with to banish someone from the city. For most of us, this derivation is lost.

Consider the following words and decide whether the present meaning is transparent, that is, whether we still see a relation between the derived word and the root, or whether it has been lost.

i.   patronize
ii. lionize
iii. pasteurize
iv. authorize
v.   legalize
vi. idolize

As we have seen, morphemes have different allomorphs, and this may apply to roots as well. For example, /d/ may alternate with /s/ in derivations such as *defend* → *defens-ive*, *offend* → *offens-ive*; or the sound /k/ may alternate with /s/ in cases such as *eccentric* (pronounced /ɛksɛntrɪk/) → eccentric-ity (pronounced /ɛksɛntrɪs-ɪti/).

Sometimes it may be difficult to determine what the category of the root is. For example, *list* and *clutter*, roots for *delist* and *declutter*, could be either nouns or verbs. However, it is clear that *de–* generally attaches to verbs and the result is a verb (**this is a declutter*; **I lost my delist*).

PAUSE AND REFLECT 4.9

Recall that derivational morphology changes the meaning and very often the category of a word. Inflectional morphology adds grammatical information. Consider the following list of words. Which underlined segments are morphemes and which are not? Of the morphemes, which are derivational and which are inflectional?

i.   mast**er**
ii.   think**er**
iii. bigg**er**
iv.   **in**capable
v.   **in**dicate
vi.   think**s**
vii. viru**s**
viii. John**'s**

Conversion

Conversion is the process that changes the lexical category of a word without the addition of derivational affixes. Because conversion leads to changes quite similar to those produced by derivational morphology, it is assumed that conversion is a form of derivation. Conversion is often accompanied by sound changes. For example, among the examples of conversion in Table 4.14, we find the word *house*, a noun that is pronounced as /haws/, and *house*, a verb, pronounced /hawz/. The most common change relates to stress placement. For example, the noun *ímpact* is stressed on the first syllable, while the verb *impáct* is stressed on the last.

PAUSE AND REFLECT 4.10

The following words can belong to two lexical categories. Keeping conversion in mind, for each one, invent two sentences that show the different uses.

   i. board
  ii. doubt
 iii. clear
 iv. sin
  v. model

TABLE 4.14 Examples of Conversion in English

I bought an antique **table**. (Noun)	We have to **table** a motion. (Verb)
I already read that **book**. (Noun)	I am going to **book** an appointment. (Verb)
That **house** is for sale. (Noun)	The building will **house** 20 people. (Verb)
He made quite an **impact**. (Noun)	This will **impact** all of us. (Verb)
I always **run** in the morning. (Verb)	He has had a long **run** as PM. (Noun)
You should **drink** more water. (Verb)	Let's have a **drink**. (Noun)
I will not **drive** home. (Verb)	It was a long **drive**. (Noun)
This party is really **dull**. (Adjective)	Boredom **dulls** the senses. (Verb)
The pool is **round**. (Adjective)	The car **rounded** the bend at speed. (Verb)
The street is **wet** after the rain. (Adjective)	You have to **wet** the paper first. (Verb)

Reduplication

Reduplication is the morphological process by which part of a word or the entire word is repeated, leading to a change in meaning and/or lexical category of the base word. The process is systematic and productive, that is, it is not the equivalent of saying the same word over and over again, as in *go, go, go*. In many languages reduplication serves to indicate grammatical functions such as plurality or intensity.

Reduplication may be **partial**, in which part of the base is repeated, or it may be **total**, the repetition of the entire base. In (11), we see examples of total reduplication in Nukuoro (Polynesian region) and (12) shows examples of partial reduplication in Ilocano (Philippines). Data are from Rubino (2005, p. 14).

(11) a. gohu   dark   gohu–gohu   getting dark
     b. vai   water   vai–vai   watery
     c. gada   smile   gada–gada   laugh
     d. ahi   fire   ahi–ahi   evening

(12) a. kaldíng   goat   kal–kaldíng   goats
     b. ag-bása   read   ag–bas–bása   reading
     c. dakkél   big   dak–dakkél   bigger

> **LINGUISTICS TIDBITS: REDUPLICATION**
>
> English often uses reduplication for fun. Here are some examples. Chick-flick; chock-a-block; helter-skelter; hocus-pocus; itsy-bitsy; lovey-dovey; meatloaf-smeatloaf; mumbo-jumbo. Can you think of others?

4.3.2   Inflectional Morphology

In most languages, there are free morphemes that are used to express grammatical relations, including pronouns such as *I* and *you*, determiners such as *this*, *the*, and *a*, among others. However, grammatical information can also be expressed with bound morphemes. As we briefly saw above, inflectional morphemes add grammatical information, they do not change the lexical category or the meaning of the base. Inflectional morphology often interacts with syntax, as we will see in Chapter 5 Syntax.

In comparison with other languages, English includes a relatively small number of bound inflectional morphemes. Table 4.15 shows a complete list of these inflectional morphemes and includes examples of irregular forms, that is, forms that do not follow a clear pattern.

TABLE 4.15 Inflectional Morphemes in English

Category	Meaning	Examples
Nouns		
Plural	More than one	Regular: book, book**s** table, table**s** house, house**s**
		Irregular: sheep (singular), sheep (plural) goose, geese child, children phenomenon, phenomena

TABLE 4.15 (*cont.*)

Category	Meaning	Examples
Possessive (attaches to noun phrases)	Ownership/ pertaining to	the book**'s** cover children**'s** books boys**'** hats
Adjectives		
Comparative	Comparison	Regular: tall**er** small**er** quiet**er**
		Irregular: more important less qualified
Superlative	Highest or very high degree of a property	Regular: tall**est** small**est** quiet**est**
		Irregular: The most important The least qualified
Verbs		
3rd person singular present	Agrees with third person subjects (he, she, it, etc.)	Regular: He speak**s** It rain**s** John smile**s**
		Modals (can, will, should) do not show agreement
Past tense	Indicates an action or state in the past	Regular: play, play**ed** jump, jump**ed** create, creat**ed**
		Irregular: bring, brought cost, cost run, ran
Past participle	Completed action. Generally follows the verbs *be* and *have*	Regular: wait, wait**ed** fall, fall**en**

TABLE 4.15 (*cont.*)

Category	Meaning	Examples
		Irregular: drink, drunk put, put bring, brought
Present participle	Ongoing action, generally follows the verb *be*	walk, walk**ing** run, runn**ing** come, com**ing**

EYES ON WORLD LANGUAGES: SEMITIC LANGUAGES

Morphology in Semitic languages such as Hebrew and Arabic is quite different from non-Semitic languages such as English because the typical root of verbs and nouns consists of three consonants. The various derivational and inflectional morphemes consist of different patterns of vowels that are inserted in the root, as shown in (i).

(i) a. k t b (root, the meaning is related to writing)
   b. **ka**ta**ba** "he wrote"
   c. u**kt**ub "write!"
   d. **ki**ta**ab** "book"

Psycholinguistic research has shown that speakers of Arabic store the consonantal roots as separate from the affixes (Prunet, Béland, & Idrissi, 2000). See Appendix 1 for some ideas on how to analyze morphological structure in other languages. Below, you can see how this type of word formation is represented for *kataba*.

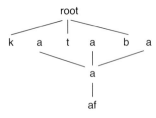

Irregular Forms: Internal Change and Suppletion

So far we have mainly focused on regular inflection. However, in English, as in other languages, there are many "exceptions". In fact, in many instances, the most frequent words in a language are the ones that have irregular forms.

In English, many irregular verbs follow a pattern of their own, as shown in Table 4.16. These verbs undergo a process in which one segment, which does not constitute a

TABLE 4.16 Internal Change in English Inflection

Present, past, and past participle of verbs	Plural of nouns
begin, began, begun	goose, geese
drive, drove, driven	tooth, teeth
choose, chose, chosen	mouse, mice

morpheme on its own, is substituted for another segment. The process is referred to as **internal change**. Internal change also affects a few nouns also shown in Table 4.16.

Though some irregular forms used to be quite productive in Old English, they have become real exceptions in Modern English. Examples are the plural of *child, children,* and the plural of *ox, oxen.*

In some instances, grammatical changes, such as present to past or singular to plural, may take place although there is no change to the form of the word. Compare *I always* **put** *my slippers under the bed*, with *Last night I* **put** *my slippers on the bed.* In a similar fashion, the plural of *sheep* is *sheep,* and the plural of *fish* is *fish.*

Suppletion refers to those cases in which a morpheme is completely replaced by a different one. In English the verbs *go* and *be* form their past tenses by way of suppletion: *go – went*; *be – was/were.*

4.3.3 Complex Word Formation: Some Additional Examples

As we have seen, a word may be made up of a root and several affixes. Derivational affixes are always attached before inflectional affixes. That is, derivation always precedes inflection. Below you will find several examples of complex word derivations. As you saw in (7), when representing word formation, we abbreviated affixes as *af.* From now on, we will label affixes as either *af* (for derivational affixes) or *inf* (for inflectional affixes). See Appendix 2 for further instructions on how to represent the structure of complex words with trees.

(13) a. hospitalize

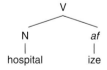

b. hospitalized

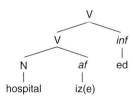

c.   hospitalization

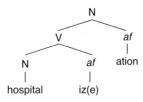

In (14) we illustrate the derivation of a word with a prefix. There are two possible ways of representing the word *incomparable,* but only one of them turns out to be accurate, as we show below.

(14) a.   incomparable

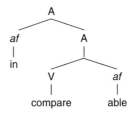

b.   incomparable

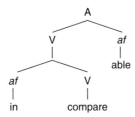

In (14a), we first attached the suffix *–able* to the base *compare,* turning a verb into an adjective. As we know from our discussion on derivational morphology, *–able* attaches to verbs and therefore *comparable* is well formed. We then attach *in–* to the adjective base *comparable,* giving us *incomparable.* This is also well formed because *in–* attaches to adjectives.

In (14b) we first attached the prefix *in–* to the verb *compare.* As shown in (15), however, *in–* only attaches to adjectives, not to verbs. Therefore, the first step in the derivation of *incomparable* (14b) does not represent a process allowed by the grammar of English.

(15) a. in-comparable, in-attentive, in-credible
       *in-compare, *in-attend, *in-credit

Now consider the form *immaturity,* which also has two possible derivations, as shown in (16). Recall that /im/ is an allomorph of *in–.*

(16) a.   immaturity

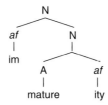

b.   immaturity

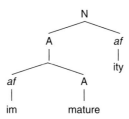

In (16a), we first combined the adjective *mature* with the affix *–ity*, forming the word *maturity*. Referring back to Table 4.10, you can see that this is an acceptable combination in English, as *–ity* attaches to adjectives such as *mature*, to produce nouns. However, if we now try to attach the prefix *in–* to the noun *maturity* the result is unacceptable. This prefix *in–* can only attach to adjectives, as shown in (17a), but not to nouns, as shown in (17b). Therefore (16a) is not well formed.

(17) a.   indefensible, inconclusive, inadmissible
b.   *indefense, *inconclusion, *inadmission

In (16b), we combined the prefix *in–* with the adjective *mature*, violating no rules. The result is an adjective, *immature*. To the adjective *immature* we may attach the suffix *–ity* that converts it into the noun *immaturity*. The only correct representation for the internal structure of *immaturity* is therefore (16b).

PAUSE AND REFLECT 4.11

Use trees to represent the structure of the following words. Hint: consult Tables 4.4–4.13 and 4.15 for help.

i.   reestablishes
ii.   humanity
iii.   underperformed
iv.   unpredictability
v.   intensity
vi.   kingship
vii.   privatization
viii. understands

4.3.4   Inflection and Derivation

Derivational and inflectional morphemes are compared in Table 4.17.

TABLE 4.17 Derivational vs. Inflectional Morphemes

Derivational morphemes	Inflectional morphemes
Often change the category of the base.	Never change the category of the base.
Often change the meaning of the root.	Never change the meaning of the root.
Are attached before inflectional morphemes.	Are attached at the end of all other morphological processes.
Obey many restrictions regarding order of attachment and bases to which they may attach.	Are very productive, applying across the board when conditions are met (with irregularities).

4.3.5 Points to Remember

- Words can be simple or complex.
  - Simple words do not have any internal parts.
  - Complex words are made up of several parts, very often a root and one or more affixes.
  - The root is the main source of meaning and belongs to a lexical category.
- A morpheme is the smallest unit of meaning.
  - A simple word is a morpheme.
  - Complex words are made up of two or more morphemes.
  - Roots and affixes are morphemes.
- The base is the form to which we attach an affix.
  - The base may consist of just a root.
  - The base may be the root plus one or more affixes.
- In English, affixes can be attached at the beginning or the end of the base. In some languages, an affix may be placed between the beginning and end of the base. In other languages, a morpheme can consist of two parts, one at the beginning and one at the end of the base.
  - An affix added to the beginning of a base is referred to as a prefix.
  - An affix added to the end of a base is referred to as a suffix.
  - An affix inserted inside the root is referred to as an infix.
  - An affix consisting of two parts is referred to as a circumfix.
- Bound morphemes (affixes) are of two types: derivational morphemes and inflectional morphemes.
  - Derivational morphemes change the meaning and/or category of the base.
  - Inflectional morphemes add grammatical information to the base without changing the meaning or the category.

4.4 Compounds

Consider the words in (18). They are not made up of a root and an affix, but rather by two free morphemes brought together.

(18) greenhouse, blackboard, steamboat, fire truck, bath towel

Compounds are words made up of the combination of two or more words. Compounding is very productive in many languages, including English.

The spelling of English compounds can be quite variable. As the examples in (19) show, compounds can be spelled as one word (19a), as two separate words (19b), or with a hyphen (19c). In fact, as your spell checker may show, in many cases there is no agreement on the spelling, as in the examples in (19d).

(19) a. bluebird, steamboat, sawdust
b. fire truck, bath towel, oil well
c. absent-minded, freeze-dry, close-up
d. childcare, child-care; clearinghouse, clearing-house; copayment, co-payment.

English allows combinations of words from different lexical categories when producing compounds. For example, *bluebird* is made up of an adjective, *blue*, and a noun, *bird*. *Doghouse* includes two nouns, *sleepwalk* has two verbs, *homesick* consists of a noun and a verb. Further examples of possible combinations are shown in Table 4.18. The word that determines the category of the compound is the **head**. In English, the head of most compounds is the rightmost word, as the examples presented in Table 4.18 show. The exceptions involve prepositions, which are generally not heads whatever side they appear on.

TABLE 4.18 Different Types of Compounds in English

Noun + Noun → Noun
voicemail
fire drill
steamboat
teapot
Adjective + Adjective → Adjective
red hot
bittersweet
deep blue

TABLE 4.18 (*cont.*)

pale pink

Verb + Verb → Verb

stir fry

spell check

sleepwalk

freeze-dry

Adjective + Noun → Noun

greenhouse

blackboard

wetsuit

wild flower

Verb + Noun → Noun

pickpocket

playground

think tank

pushcart

Noun + Verb → Verb

headhunt

brain wash

babysit

soundproof

Adjective + Verb → Verb

whitewash

dry clean

fast forward

slow cook

Examples involving prepositions

overdose (verb)

TABLE 4.18 (*cont.*)

afterlife (noun)
within (preposition)
undercooked (adjective)
underdeveloped (adjective)
takeover (noun)

PAUSE AND REFLECT 4.12

Use some of the following words to create around ten compounds in English. Compounds may include two or more words. You may add derivational morphology. Decide what category the compound belongs to.

i. nouns: box, camp, tail, class, guest, shelf, team, house, fire, knife, beaver, ground, sound, motion, stream, cream, response, action, screen, TV

ii. verbs: play, cut, wash, scrub, drop, load, develop, write,

iii. adjectives: green, slow, high, wide, white, black, sour, fast, light

iv. prepositions: under, up, down, on

4.4.1 Pronunciation of Compounds

Although there is some variation, the pronunciation of certain types of compounds is systematic. For example, compounds that are nouns or verbs generally take primary stress on the first word (see Chapter 3 Phonology regarding stress), as you can see in Table 4.19. In the case of compound adjectives, it is generally the rightmost adjective (the head) that takes primary stress. The position of stress is useful for distinguishing between true compounds and other combinations. In Table 4.19, the stressed syllable is indicated in upper-case letters.

TABLE 4.19 Stress in Non-compound and Compound Words

Non-compound	Compound
dark ROOM	DARKroom
mobile CHILD	MOBile phone
summer WEAther	SUMMer camp
brain DEfect	BRAIN wash
stir toGEther	STIR fry
FAvorite GREEN	dark GREEN
WONderful BLUE	light BLUE

4.4.2 Meaning of Compounds

In most of the examples we have seen that the meaning of a compound is quite transparent and is usually determined by the head. For example, a *steamboat* is a type of boat with the property that it is powered by steam. To *roller-skate* is the action of skating, *sky blue* refers to a type of blue. Compounds whose meaning is derived from the meaning of the head are **endocentric**. In contrast, **exocentric compounds** are those whose meaning cannot be inferred from that of the head. For example, a *pickpocket* is not a type of pocket, it is a person that steals in a certain way. In the same way *sawbones* does not refer to a type of bone, but rather to a doctor. Linguists are still debating whether these compounds don't have a head, or the head is outside of the compound.

PAUSE AND REFLECT 4.13

Determine which of the following compounds are exocentric and which are endocentric. If they can be both, explain how.

i. beaver tail (Canadian pastry)
ii. campground
iii. bookworm
iv. snowsuit
v. skyscraper

4.4.3 The Structure of Compounds

Like derived words, compounds also exhibit internal structure (see Appendix 2 for further instructions on how to represent the structure of complex words with trees). Evidence for this comes from ambiguities in some compounds. For example, a *big dog walker* could refer to someone who walks big dogs, or to someone big who walks dogs. A *small car repair shop* could refer to a shop that repairs small cars or to a small shop that repairs cars. The ambiguity of *small car repair shop* can be captured by comparing the trees in (20c) and (21c).

(20) a. car repair

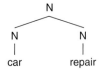

b. car repair shop

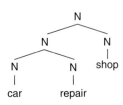

c.   small car repair shop (a small shop that repairs cars)

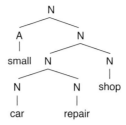

(21) a.   small car

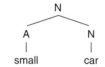

b.   small car repair

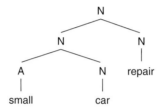

c.   small car repair shop (a shop that repairs small cars)

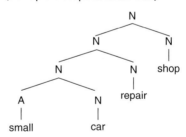

In (22) we include further examples of the structure of compounds.

(22) a.   voicemail

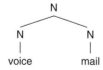

b.   bittersweet

c. spell check

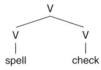

d. wetsuit

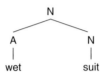

e. brain wash

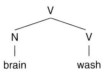

f. slow cook

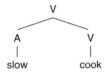

g. overdose

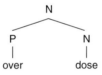

LINGUISTICS TIDBITS: CALQUES

A calque is an expression that is borrowed into another language by translating it word-for-word. This often happens with compounds. For example, the word *skyscraper* has been translated as a calque into French as *gratte-ciel* and into Spanish as *rasca-cielos*. The order (scrape sky) is different from English (sky scrape) because the head of most compounds in these languages is on the left.

In the same way, *flea market* has been translated word-for-word from the French *marché-aux-puces* and *new wave* from the French *Nouvelle Vague*.

4.4.4 Compounding and Derivation

Compounding can also combine with derivation, for example in *worldwide development, high school teacher, institutional racism*, among many others. The internal structure of the derivation and compounding of these words is shown in examples (23)–(25).

(23) a. development (derivation)

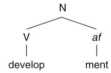

b. worldwide development (compounding)

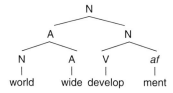

(24) a. teacher (derivation)

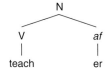

b. high school teacher (compounding)

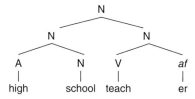

(25) a. institutional (derivation)

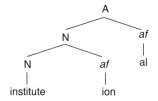

b. racism (derivation)

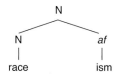

c. institutional racism (compounding)

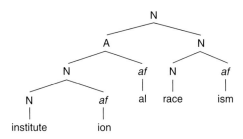

PAUSE AND REFLECT 4.14

Draw the trees that represent the following compounds.

i. inflectional affixation
ii. flower bed
iii. conditional release
iv. developmental impairment
v. rapid response fire vehicle

4.4.5   Compounding and Inflection

With a few exceptions, inflection in English is generally added to the head of compounds, that is, the rightmost element. Compare *oak leaves* and **oaks leaf*; *stir fried* and **stirred fry*; *oil wells* and **oils well*; *spell checked* and **spelled check*. Interestingly, irregular plurals in the first element of a compound are sometimes permitted: *teeth marks*; *mice infested*; *men bashing* (examples from Berent & Pinker, 2007).

There are some words that behave as exceptions in English, that is, they require that inflection appear on the first member of the compound. However, there is no agreement among the general public. Some English speakers prefer *governor generals of Canada*, others prefer *governors general of Canada*; some say *sergeant majors*, others say *sergeants major*. Most people, however, would say *commanders in chief*.

Consider the examples in Table 4.20. As you see, irregular plurals are often regularized in exocentric compounds, in contrast to endocentric compounds.

Besides inflection, compounds can occasionally include function words such as *of* and *the*, as shown in the examples in (26). These are all exocentric.

(26)   a.   run-of-the-mill (idea)
       b.   state-of-the-art (technology)

4.4.6   Compounds in Other Languages

Compounding is one of the most frequent ways of creating new words in language. However, compounding

---

LINGUISTICS TIDBITS: THE WORD *MOUSE*

The word *mouse* is used to refer to a rodent or to a device used to move a cursor across a computer screen. The plural of the first meaning is *mice*, the plural of the second is often, though not always, *mouses* (although some people find this so strange they avoid pluralizing the device). This is evidence that when the meaning of a word is extended to other uses it often regularizes.

Interestingly, the word *mouse* has been directly translated (i.e., it is a *calque*) into more than 30 languages to describe the device: *souris* (French); *ratón* (Spanish); *maus* (German); *rato* (Portuguese); *fare* (Turkish).

TABLE 4.20 Irregular Plurals in Endocentric and Exocentric Compounds

Endocentric	Exocentric
baby tooth, baby teeth	saber-tooth, saber-tooths
good life, good lives	still life, still lifes
bare foot, bare feet	tenderfoot, tenderfoots

in other languages may follow rules that differ from those of English (see Appendix 1 for some ideas on how to analyze morphological structure in other languages). We will briefly mention some examples of these differences.

1. **Headedness.** We have seen that in English, the head of compounds is the rightmost word. This is not the case in all languages, as the left-headed examples of [Noun Noun] compounds in Spanish (27), French (28), and Persian (29) show.

(27) a. hombre rana
    man frog
    "frogman"
  b. baloncesto
    ball basket
    "basketball"
  c. bocacalle
    mouthstreet
    "street intersection"

(28) a. pause-café
    pause coffee
    "coffee break"
  b. timbre poste
    stamp mail
    "postage stamp"

(29) a. ab sib
    water apple
    "apple juice"
  b. tut farangi
    berry foreign
    "strawberry"
  c. mahi shur
    fish salted
    "salted fish"

2. **Productivity.** The number of compounds in English made from combinations of two or more nouns seems unlimited. This is not the case in other languages. In French and Spanish, nouns that are made of [Verb Noun] combinations are much more productive. Some examples are shown in (30) for Spanish and (31) for French. In these languages, [Noun Noun] compounds often include function words such as *of*, as shown in (32) for Spanish and (33) for French. These more complex compounds are more productive than simple [Noun Noun] compounds.

(30) a. sacacorchos
       extract corks
       "corkscrew"
   b. parabrisas
       stop wind
       "windshield"
   c. cascanueces
       crack nuts
       "nut cracker"

(31) a. sèche-cheveux
       dry hair
       "hair dryer"
   b. tire bouchon
       extract cork
       "corkscrew"
   c. chasse neige
       hunt snow
       "snow plow"

(32) a. leche de chocolate
       milk of chocolate
       "chocolate milk"
   b. zapatos de tacón alto
       shoes of heel high
       "high heel shoes"
   c. pozo de petróleo
       well of oil
       "oil well"

(33) a. hôtel de ville
       hall of town
       "town hall"
   b. pomme de terre
       apple of earth
       "potato"
   c. arc-en-ciel
       arch in sky
       "rainbow"

3. ***Endocentric or exocentric?*** In some languages, compounds are frequently exocentric. Examples from French include *rendez-vous* (go you) "appointment", *passe-partout* (pass everywhere) "master key", and *mange tout* (eat everything) "snow pea".

4. ***Inflection.*** Generally, in English, inflection is added to the rightmost element, with some exceptions. In other languages, this is not the case. The plural of compounds in French is notoriously difficult to learn. In some cases, the plural and the singular are the same form, as in (34a), in others, the plural is attached to both nouns (34b), or only to the first noun (34c), or the second noun (34d).

(34) a. un pot-au-feu,   deux pot-au-feu
        a pot on fire,   two pot on fire
        "a beef stew"   "two beef stews"
    b. un chou-fleur   deux choux-fleurs
        a cabbage flower   two cabbages flowers
        "a cauliflower"   "two cauliflowers"
    c. une pause café   deux pauses café
        a break coffee   two breaks coffee
        "a coffee break"   "two coffee breaks"
    d. un couvre-lit   deux couvre-lits
        a cover bed   two cover beds
        "a bedspread"   "two bedspreads"

EYES ON WORLD LANGUAGES: THE STRUCTURE OF SOME FRENCH COMPOUNDS

The head in French [Noun Noun] compounds is on the left. We infer this because the gender of the compound is always the gender of the leftmost word. Compare (i) and (ii).

i. *pause* (feminine) "break"
    café (masculine) "coffee"
    pause-café (feminine) "coffee break"

ii chou (masculine) "cabbage"
    fleur (feminine) "flower"
    chou fleur (masculine) "cauliflower"

The representation of the structure of these compounds is shown in (iii) and (iv).

iii. pause café

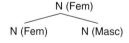

N (Fem)
N (Fem)   N (Masc)

iv. chou fleur

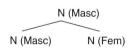

N (Masc)
N (Masc)   N (Fem)

4.4.7   Points to Remember about Compounds

- Compounds are made up of two or more words.
- You cannot rely on the spelling of words to determine whether they are compounds.
- Pronunciation can be a reliable guide in determining the status of compounds.
- Compounding can be combined with derivation.
- Inflection is generally attached to the head of the compound.
- Compounding, like derivation, is structural.

4.5   Other Word Formation Processes

Acronyms are words formed from the initials of several words. When possible, these words are pronounced as they are spelled. Examples are UNICEF (United Nations International Children's Emergency Fund), NAFTA (North America Free Trade Agreement), and NASA (North America Space Agency). When the initials cannot be pronounced, they may be spelled out, as we do with RCMP (Royal Canadian Mounted Police), BBC (British Broadcasting Corporation), PM (Prime Minister), MP (Member of Parliament), CEO (Chief Executive Officer), and IPA (International Phonetic Alphabet or India Pale Ale). Spelling out the initials is called **initialism**.

Some acronyms become words on their own, such as *laser* (light amplification by stimulated emission of radiation). Acronyms and initialisms are frequently used in digital communications, LOL (Laugh Out Loud), SLAP (Sounds Like a Plan), FYI (For Your Information), among many others.

Clipping consists of shortening longer words or phrases. Some of these abbreviated words become part of the standard lexicon or of the lexicon of certain groups of users. Examples include *prof* for professor, *psych* for psychology, *math* for mathematics, *flu* for influenza, and *meds* for medications.

Backformations are the result of mistaken morphological analysis on the part of speakers. Generally, what appears to be a derivational morpheme is removed, creating a new word. Over time, these new words become part of the lexicon, and the erroneous analysis is maintained. Examples include *televise* from *television*, *translate* from *translation*, *burgle* and *burglarize* from *burglar*, and *euthanize* from *euthanasia*.

EYES ON WORLD LANGUAGES: REANALYSIS: ORANGES, APRONS, AND ALLIGATORS

Many jokes are based on people mishearing what is said. In a famous case of misinterpretation, a child confused a line in a song, *and laid him on the green*, for *and Lady Mondegreen*. For this reason many of these errors, which linguists refer to as reanalysis, are often popularly referred to as *mondegreens*.

In some cases, mondegreens have become standard lexical items. One historical source of confusion in English are the two forms of the indefinite article, *a* (as in *a dog*) and *an* (as in *an*

EYES ON WORLD LANGUAGES (*cont.*)

apple). As we saw in Chapter 3 Phonology, when pronouncing words such as *an apple*, the final /n/ of the article typically attaches to the beginning of the following word. This happened with the word *orange*. Oranges come from the middle east so the word *orange* is derived from the Arabic word *narange*, but reanalysis led people to change *a narange* to *an orange*. In the same way, the French *napperon* (a small cloth) gave us *an apron*; and the Spanish *el lagarto* "the lizard" gave us "alligator".

Blends, like compounds, are formed by the combination of two or more words. However, unlike compounds, parts of the words are deleted. Examples include *motel* from *motor* and *hotel*, *brunch* from *breakfast* and *lunch*, *simulcast* from *simultaneous* and *broadcast*, *chocoholic* from *chocolate* and *alcoholic*, and *spam* from *spiced* and *ham*.

Borrowing consists of the integration of foreign words into a language. It is said that almost 30 percent of words in English have been borrowed from French due to contact between the two nations through history. With modern communication systems, borrowing in most of the world's languages has increased. Presently, other languages are borrowing from English, but English has also borrowed extensively from other languages. Table 4.21 shows a few of the many borrowings into English.

TABLE 4.21 Borrowings into English from Other Languages

Borrowed word	Source language
cigar	Spanish
tamale	Spanish
bonsai	Japanese
manga	Japanese
bangle	Hindi
balalaika	Russian
balaclava	Russian
igloo	Inuktitut
kayak	Inuktitut
canoe	Taino (Amerindian language) via Spanish
chocolate	Nahuatl (Amerindian language)
algebra	Arabic
alcohol	Arabic
pizza	Italian

LINGUISTICS TIDBITS: DOUBLE BORROWING FROM FRENCH

French Normans invaded England in 1066, and French became the language of power. Many words came into English from French, including many words related to administration and commerce.

Norman French is not the same as what we now know as standard French. As a consequence, words that had been borrowed from Norman French were occasionally borrowed a second time from the French of Paris. This explains why English includes words such as *warranty* and *warden*, from Norman French, and the Paris equivalents *guarantee* and *guardian*.

Coinage creates new words without resorting to any of the word formation processes we have seen. Brand names are often an important source of new words: *Velcro*, *Kleenex*, *Aspirin*, and *Google*. Other sources of new words come from science (*quark*) and literature (*muggle*, *jabberwocky*).

In many languages, words are created to mimic the sounds that an object or animal makes. For example, *Zipper* represents the object that sounds like *zip* when you pull it up; *zoom* is the sound of something flying by; and *tick tock* is the sound of a clock. These are examples of **onomatopoeia**. In almost all languages, common onomatopoeias include the sounds animals make. However, as these are only mimicking the sound, there are distinct cultural differences. Some examples are given below.

- Rooster: cock-a-doodle-doo (English), quiquiriquí (Spanish), chicchirichi (Italian), kikeriki (German), cocorico (French), kukuriku (Hebrew), koko koko (Korean).
- Frog: ribbit (English), cra cra (Italian), croá croá (Spanish), quak (German), gegul gegul (Korean).
- Dog: woof woof (English), gwau gwau (Spanish), bup bup (Catalan), txau txau and zaunk zaunk (Basque), bau bau (Italian), haw haw (Arabic).
- Cat: miaw (English), yaong (Korean), mèu (Catalan), naw naw (Arabic).

PAUSE AND REFLECT 4.15

Complete the following table with the missing items. Try not to use examples that have been used previously in this chapter.

Word formation process	Example
blend	
	tweet tweet
	burrito
initialism	
acronym	
	bike
backformation	
	nylon
	host (an event)

Finally, **cliticization** is the process of attaching a **clitic** to a host word. A clitic is a word-like element that must attach to a host (e.g., the object pronouns in French, such as *Je le vois* "I see it" and the possessive – '*s* in English as in John'*s* ball). To read more about clitics, read 'Delving Deeper' in Chapter 4's resources on the website to accompany this book at www.cambridge.org/introducing-linguistics.

SUMMARY

We often think of words as the basic units of language. However, words can be quite complex, often consisting of different parts. We call the minimal units of meaning morphemes. A morpheme can be the equivalent of a word (*cat*, *dog*), or it can be a part of the word that contributes meaning, giving rise to complex words (*unbelievable*, *variability*, *music boxes*).

Depending on the context, a morpheme may vary its shape. The different forms a morpheme can take are called allomorphs. For example, the indefinite article in English can be produced as *a* or *an*, depending on whether the following word begins with a vowel (*a dog*, *an apple*).

We distinguish root morphemes, which contribute the main meaning of the word, from affixes. Affixes are bound morphemes that are added on to the beginning (prefix), middle (infix), or end (suffix) of a word. For example, the word *unbeatable* is made up of the root *beat*, the prefix *un–*, and the suffix *–able*. The form to which an affix is added is called the base.

We also distinguish between derivational and inflectional affixes. Derivational affixes usually change the meaning and/or category of the base (*un–able*). Inflectional affixes add grammatical information such as number, gender, class, tense, etc. (*book–s*, *play–ed*).

Words can also be constructed by the combination of two or more roots or words. This process is called compounding (*bookshelf*, *desktop*).

Building words, either by inflection, derivation, or compounding, is a systematic process that obeys different rules. For example, inflection is added after derivation and compounding (*teach–er–s*, **teach–s–er; desktop–s*, *deskstop). Furthermore, different affixes impose constraints on the type of bases they may attach to (*modern–ize–ation*, **modern–ation*). The structure of words is represented with trees (see Appendix 2).

Besides derivation and compounding there are many ways of adding words to a language: acronyms (*UNICEF*); blends (*motel*); clipping (*math*); backformations (*televise*); borrowing (*burrito*); coinage (*to google*); onomatopoeia (*cluck cluck*). Although words in different languages may vary in interesting ways, the processes for building words are universal.

Appendix 1

Identifying Roots and Bound Morphemes in Other Languages

One of the main tasks of linguists is to identify the morphemes of different languages, both languages they are familiar with and languages they are beginning to research.

The main objective of an initial morphological analysis is to find sound–meaning correspondences. In order to do this we compare and contrast patterns of sounds that recur and that can be associated with recurring meanings.

We will use Spanish verbs as an example. In (i) you will find a list of verbs and their translations. This set of data is quite small and has been chosen to help you. In real life situations the data might run to thousands of words and would not be arranged for our convenience. In fact, in recent years, digital technology has been shown to be quite helpful in this type of analysis.

i a. hablabas   "you used to speak"
   b. estudiabas "you used to study"
   c. celebrabas "you used to celebrate"
   d. practicabas "you used to practice"

In (i) we find a string of sounds that is repeated, *abas*, and two meanings that recur: "you" and "used to". Our initial hypothesis is that –*abas* means "you used to". But can this string of sounds be broken down more? We need more data (ii) which we can contrast with (i).

ii. a. hablaba   "he/she used to speak"
    b. estudiaba "he/she used to study"
    c. celebraba "he/she used to celebrate"
    d. practicaba "he/she used to practice"
    e. hablas   "you speak"
    f. estudias   "you study"
    g. habla   "he/she speaks"
    h. estudia   "he/she studies"

The data in (ii.a–d) shows that the third person (he/she) of these verbs, while maintaining the –*aba* ending and the meaning "used to", no longer ends in –*s*. Our hypothesis at this point is that –*s* indicates second person, "you". This is confirmed in (ii.e and ii.f) in which the second person –*s* recurs and so does the meaning of you, now in the present tense. The examples in (ii.g and ii.h) show that when the meaning is not "second person" (you) the –*s* is not present. Our hypotheses, based on these data, are the following:

Roots:

- habl– "speak"
- estudi– "study"

- celebr– "celebrate"
- practic– "practice"

Affixes:

- –aba "used to"
- –s "second person"

As you can see, both the roots and the affixes of verbs in Spanish are bound morphemes. Further data might lead us to change our hypotheses.

We have used English translations to determine meaning. This is very often not possible because:

- Languages may use morphemes to express meaning distinctions that English does not make. For example, languages such as Spanish and Italian may include morphemes to indicate gender on all nouns, something that English does not do. Verbs in these languages must also include morphemes to distinguish between completed and incomplete actions, a distinction not found in the verbal morphology of English.
- English may make morphological distinctions that other languages do not make. For example, Chinese, Japanese, and Serbian do not include functional morphemes such as the English articles *the* and *a*.
- The order of morphemes may vary across languages. For example, Romanian morphology includes definite articles, but they are attached at the end of the noun. As you know, articles in English precede nouns and are not allowed.

Appendix 2

How to Build Trees that Represent the Structure of Complex Words

- It is important to keep in mind that derivation will always precede inflection.
- In the case of derivation, the first step is to determine the root of the word. This will form the base for building the construction. As an example we will use the word *inadvisability*. The root of the word is *advise*.
- We then determine the bound morphemes (affixes). Two we recognize easily: *in–* and *–ity*.
- We still do not know what *–abil* represents. Our next step should be to look at other words in the language that sound like inadvisability. Among them we find the following:
  - available → availability
  - desirable → desirability
  - readable → readability
  - variable → variability

- We notice that the change from *–able* to *–abil* is consistent. From the data we conclude that the bound morpheme *–able* has two allomorphs: *–able* and *–abil*. *–abil* appears in the base when the following affix is *–ity*.
- Recall what we know about the three affixes we have found in *inadvisability*.
  - *in–* attaches to adjectives, and the result is an adjective.
  - *–able/abil* attaches to verbs and converts them to adjectives.
  - *–ity* attaches to adjectives and converts them to nouns.
- From our knowledge of the three affixes we determine that:
  - We cannot attach *in–* to the root, *advise*, which is a verb.
  - We cannot attach *in–* to the base, *advisability*, because it is a noun.
  - Therefore, first we must convert the verb to an adjective, then attach the prefix to this adjectival base, and finally convert the whole to a noun by the attachment of the suffix *–ity*. This process is illustrated in the following tree:

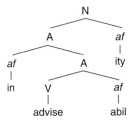

EXERCISES

4.1   Consider the following list of words and underline all the bound morphemes.

   i.   unsuccessful
   ii.   sub-arctic
   iii.   luminosity
   iv.   happen
   v.   claims
   vi.   strangely
   vii.   overcompensation
   viii.   unending
   ix.   mistreatment
   x.   unicellular
   xi.   unhappiest
   xii.   fell
   xiii.   Brazilians
   xiv.   impetuosity
   xv.   loving

4.2   The following are complex words. Indicate the base to which the underlined and bolded morpheme is attached.

   i.   unevent**ful**
   ii.   **in**determinate
   iii.   reconsider**ed**
   iv.   **un**fashionable
   v.   **re**covered

4.3 Match the word combinations in A with the corresponding descriptive statements in B.

A	B
a. spoon feed	1. endocentric compound noun
b. elegant shoes	2. compound adjective
c. over ripe	3. compound verb
d. egg-head	4. non-compound
e. computer screen	5. exocentric compound noun

4.4 Match the bolded morphemes in A with the appropriate description in B.

A	B
a. **hippopotamus**	1. prefix
b. **mis**represented	2. base
c. good – **better**	3. inflectional morpheme
d. **unattractive**ness	4. root and base
e. nice – nic**er**	5. suppletion
f. **teach**er	6. free morpheme

4.5 Draw the trees that represent the structure of each of the following items.

i.   explorations
ii. unreliable
iii. abnormality
iv. house-sitter
v.   domino effect
vi. bathroom towel rack (two interpretations, two trees)

4.6 Match the words in A with the appropriate designation in B. In each case, think of another example of the same morphological phenomenon.

A	B
a. BCE (Before Common Era)	1. backformation
b. bottle (N) → bottle (a liquid)	2. blend
c. bulldozer → bulldoze	3. onomatopoeia
d. picture + element → pixel	4. initialism
e. baa, baa	5. clipping
f. applications → APPS	6. conversion

4.7 Consider the following words from classical Greek and then answer the following questions. The Greek alphabet has been transcribed into the Roman alphabet (that we use in English). Aspiration and vowel length have been simplified.

   In classical Greek and Latin, words change shape according to their function in the sentence. This is called case. In the first column of the table we find the form these words take when they represent the subject of the sentence. This is referred to as *nominative* case. In the second column we find the *genitive* case, the form used to indicate possession. In the third column we find the *dative* case, that is used to express *from* and *to*, among other things. Finally, the accusative case is used as the object of a verb, as in *I saw the **meeting place***.

Nominative case	Genitive case	Dative case	Accusative	Nominative plural
agora "meeting place"	agoras "of the meeting place"	agorai "to the meeting place"	agoran "meeting place"	agorai "meeting places"
elaia "olive tree"	elaias "of the olive tree"	elaiai "to the olive tree"	elaian "olive tree"	elaiai "olive trees"

Nominative case	Genitive case	Dative case	Accusative	Nominative plural
doxa "opinion"	doxes "of opinion"	doxei "for opinion"	doxan "opinion"	doxai "opinions"
axantha "thorn"	axanthes "of the thorn"	axanthei "for the thorn"	axanthan "thorn"	axanthai "thorn"

a. Based on the data, which is the root of the words for *meeting place, olive tree, opinion*, and *thorn*?
b. Which is the affix that indicates nominative case? Does it have allomorphs? If so, which are they?
c. Which is the morpheme that indicates nominative case in the plural? Does it have allomorphs?
d. Which is the affix that indicates genitive case? Does it have allomorphs? If so, which are they?
e. Which is the affix that indicates dative case? Does it have allomorphs? If so, which are they?
f. Which is the affix that indicates accusative case? Does it have allomorphs? If so, which are they?

4.8 The following data come from Papiamentu, a language spoken in Aruba, Bonaire, and Curaçao, in the Caribbean. This is a Creole language (see Chapter 7 The Classification of Languages).

i.   Mi ta lesa e buki.   "I am reading the book."
ii.   Mi tabata lesa e buki.   "I was reading the book."
iii. Mi a lesa e buki.   "I read the book." (past)
iv.   Lo mi lesa e buki.   "I will read the book."
v.   E ta lesa e buki.   "He is reading the book."
vi.   E tabata lesa e buki.   "He was reading the book."
vii. Nan a lesa e buki.   "They read the book."(past)
viii. Lo nan lesa un buki.   "They will read a book."
ix.   Lo nan lesa buki.   "They read books."
x.   E tin buki.   "He has a book."

Additional vocabulary: bai, "go; leave"; traha, "to work"; e corant, "the newspaper"; un sombré, "a hat"; aki, "here"; bo, "you".
   Answer the following questions:

a. Does Papiamentu include a great many inflectional morphemes?
b. How does Papiamentu express tense (past, present, future) and aspect (ongoing, completed) differences found in English?
c. What is the order of morphemes that express verbal tenses and aspect? Is there an exception?
d. Based on the data, does Papiamentu distinguish gender and number on nouns?
e. Translate the following sentences into Papiamentu:
   • They have hats.
   • You were working here.
   • He has left.
   • He will read a newspaper.

4.9 The following data are from Nahuatl, a language spoken in Mexico. These data come from the region of Tlaxcala, in central Mexico.

i.   nichoka   "I cry"
ii.   tichoka   "you cry"
iii. choka   "he/she cries"
iv.   nichokas   "I will cry"
v.   otichoka   "you cried"
vi.   nihualla   "I come"
vii. tihualla   "you come"
viii. hualla   "he/she comes"
ix.   ohualla   "he/she came"
x.   tihuallas   "you will come"

Answer the following questions:

a. What is the root for *cry* and *come* in Nahuatl?
b. What is the affix that indicates first person (I), second person (you), and third person (he/she)? Are these prefixes or suffixes?
c. What is the affix that indicates past in Nahuatl? Is it a prefix or a suffix?
d. What is the affix that indicates future in Nahuatl? Is it a prefix or a suffix?

4.10 This exercise is a continuation of the data set in Exercise 4.9. The verbs we saw above, *come* and *cry*, are intransitive, that is, they do not take an object. You do not *come something* or *cry something* (though we do have expressions such as *cry me a river*). The following data from Nahuatl contains verbs that do have an object. We say they are transitive.

i.	nikpia kalli.	"I have a house."
ii.	tikpia kalli.	"You have a house."
iii.	kipia kalli.	"He/she has a house."
iv.	niknemaka tlaol.	"I sell corn."
v.	kinemaka tlaol.	"He/she sells corn."
vi.	tikchihua tlaskal.	"You eat tortillas."
vii.	nikchihuas tlaskal.	"I will eat tortillas."
viii.	kichihuas tlaskal.	"He/she will eat tortillas."

Answer the following questions:

a. What are the roots for "have", "sell", and "eat"? Is there a morpheme that indicates these verbs are transitive? If so, is it a prefix or a suffix? Does it have more than one allomorph?
b. What is the relative order of the different prefixes in Nahuatl?
c. Translate into Nahuatl:
   You will sell tortillas.
   I had corn.

4.11 Consider the following sentences from Turkish. Turkish does not have any articles (the, a) although we may use them in the translations.

It is important to consider the vowels in Turkish. Recall from Chapter 3 Phonology that front vowels include /i/, /e/, /ü/, and /ö/. Back vowels are /a/, /u/, and /o/.

i.	elim	"hand"
ii.	elimde	"in the hand"
iii.	evde	"in the house"
iv.	gözde	"in the eye"
v.	süt	"milk"
vi.	sütte	"in milk"
vii.	seste	"in the voice"
viii.	lokanta	"a restaurant"
ix.	lokantada	"in a restaurant"
x.	randevuda	"in an appointment"
xi.	kitap	"a book"
xii.	kitapta	"in the book"
xiii.	koltukta	"in the armchair"

Answer the following questions:

a. What are the roots for the preceding words?
b. For each root, determine whether the last phoneme is voiced or voiceless.
c. For each root, determine whether the vowel in the last syllable is a front vowel or a back vowel.
d. What are the allomorphs for the bound morpheme that means *in* or *at*?
e. Can you describe the context for each allomorph?

4.12 We have described the morpheme *–er* as a derivational suffix that serves to indicate a person who does X: *golfer* is a person who plays golf, *worker* is a person who works, etc. But this is not the only meaning. Explain in your own words the different meanings of the suffix *–er* in the following words.

   i.   pencil sharpener, lawnmower
   ii.   breather, disclaimer
   iii. diner, sleeper
   iv.   New Yorker, Quebecker

4.13 Arabic has two genders, masculine (MASC) and feminine (FEM). Nouns and adjectives also indicate case (see the Greek examples in Exercise 4.7), but we will not focus on case distinctions. POSS stands for possessor (genitive case), and LOC stands for locative (place).

   i.   Ahmedu   muhanndisun.
         Ahmed-MASC SING   *engineer-MASC SING*
         "Ahmed is an engineer."

   ii.   Mohammadu   tabibun.
         Mohammad-MASC SING   *doctor-MASC SING*
         "Mohammad is a doctor."

   iii. Fatima   tabibatun.
         Fatima-FEM SING   *doctor-FEM SING*
         "Fatima is a doctor."

   iv.   Ghalia   talibatun.
         Ghalia-FEM SING   *student-FEM SING*
         "Ghalia is a student."

   v.   Altalibun   fii   almanzeli.
         the student-MASC SING   *in*   *the house-LOC*
         "The male student is in the house."

   vi.   Altalibatun   fii   almaddrasati.
         the student-FEM SING   *in*   *the school-LOC*
         "The female student is in the school."

   vii. Kalbu   Ahmedin   fii   almanzeli.
         dog-MASC SING   *Ahmed-POSS*   *in*   *the house-LOC*
         "A dog of Ahmed is in the house."

   viii. Alwardaatun   jameelahtun.
         the flower-FEM SING   *beautiful-FEM SING*
         "The flower is beautiful."

   ix.   Ibnatun   Ahmedin   fii   manzeli.
         daughter-FEM SING   *Ahmed-POSS*   *in*   *a house-LOC*
         "The daughter of Ahmed is in the house."

   x.   Ibnu   tabibin   fii   almaddrasati.
         son-MASC SING   *doctor-POSS*   *in*   *the school-LOC*
         "A son of a doctor is in the school."

xi. Murshidun   min   wezaraht   altaaleemi   fii almaddrasati.
     advisor-MASC SING   *from*   *ministry*   *the education* *in the school-LOC*
     "A male advisor from the ministry of education is in the school."

xii. Murshidatun   fii   maddrasati.
      advisor-FEM SING   *in*   *a school-LOC*
      "A female advisor is in the school."

xiii. Fii   alsyaarati   tifllun.
       in   *the-car-LOC* *child-MASC SING*
       "In the car is a child."

xiv. Altifllun   fii   almanzeli.
      The child-MASC SING *in*   *the house-LOC*
      "The child is in the house."

Answer the following questions:

a. What morpheme represents the definite article (*the*) in Arabic? Is it a prefix or a suffix? How would you translate *the dog* into Arabic?

b. What morpheme represents the indefinite article (*a*) in Arabic? How would you say *a female student*?

c. What morpheme is used to indicate masculine singular on common nouns (not names) in Arabic? Are there allomorphs?

d. What morpheme is used to indicate feminine singular on common nouns in Arabic? Are there allomorphs?

e. What morpheme is used to indicate location on the noun after the preposition *fii* 'in'?

f. How do you decide what gender and number to use on adjectives?

g. How do you express the possessor in Arabic?

h. How do you express the present of the verb *be* in Arabic?

4.14 Consider the following data from Spanish. Spanish nouns have two genders, masculine and feminine, and also number, singular and plural. The masculine singular article is *el* "the", the feminine singular is *la*, the plural masculine is *los*, and the plural feminine is *las*.

Masculine	Feminine
el libro, los libros "the book(s)" el abuelo, los abuelos "the grandfather(s)" el momento, los momentos "the moment(s)"	la libreta, las libretas "the notebook(s)" la abuela, las abuelas "the grandmother(s)" la casa, las casas "the house(s)"
el café, los cafés "the coffee shop(s)" el puente, los puentes "the bridge(s)" el hombre, los hombres "the man/men"	la calle, las calles "the street(s)" la clase, las clases "the classroom(s)" la torre, las torres "the tower(s)"
el corazón, los corazones "the heart(s)" el dolor, los dolores "the pain(s)" el ratón, los ratones "the mouse/mice"	la mujer, las mujeres "the woman/women" la ciudad, las ciudades "city/cities" la razón, las razones "the reason(s)"

Answer the following questions:

a. What is the morpheme that indicates plural on the noun? Is there more than one allomorph? What determines the form of the allomorph?

b. Is there a morpheme that indicates masculine gender? Is there a morpheme that indicates feminine gender? Do these morphemes apply to all nouns in Spanish?

4.15 Spanish speakers frequently use diminutives of nouns and other lexical categories. A diminutive usually indicates that an element is smaller than normal but this is not always the case. Compare the following data with that given in Exercise 4.14. It consists of the diminutive forms for the same nouns.

Masculine	Feminine
el librito "the little book" el abuelito "the grandfather" el momentito "the short moment"	la libretita "the small notebook" la abuelita "the grandmother" la casita "the little house"
el cafecito "the little coffee shop" el puentecito "the small bridge" el hombrecito "the little man"	la callecita "the little street" la clasecita "the little classroom" la torrecita "the small tower"
el corazoncito "the little heart" el dolorcito "the little pain" el ratoncito "the little mouse"	la mujercita "the little woman" la ciudadcita "the little city" la razóncita "the little reason"

a. What is the morpheme that converts a noun to a diminutive in Spanish? Is there more than one allomorph? What determines the shape of the allomorph?
b. Indicate which are the affixes present in the words *corazoncito* and *abuelita* based on the data.
c. When assigning the diminutive, how do speakers choose between the –o and the –a ending? Can they simply copy the endings from the base? If not, what must they know?

REFERENCES

Allen, S., & Crago, M. (1996). Early passive acquisition in Inuktitut. *Journal of Child Language, 23*(1), 129–155.

Berent, I., & Pinker, S. (2007). The dislike of regular plurals in compounds: Phonological familiarity or morphological constraint? *The Mental Lexicon, 2*(2), 129–181.

Booij, G. (2012). *The grammar of words: An introduction to linguistic morphology*. Oxford: Oxford University Press.

Harris, J. (1991). The exponence of gender in Spanish. *Linguistic Inquiry, 22*(1), 27–62.

Ledgeway, A., & Maiden, M. (2016). *The Oxford guide to the Romance languages*. Oxford: Oxford University Press.

Pinker, S. (1994). *The language instinct: How the mind creates language*. New York, NY: Morrow.

Prunet, J., Béland, R., & Idrissi, A. (2000). The mental representation of semitic words. *Linguistic Inquiry, 31*(4), 609–648.

Roberge, Y. (1990). *The syntactic recoverability of null arguments*. Kingston and Montreal: McGill-Queen's University Press.

Rubino, C. (2005). Reduplication: Form, function and distribution. In B. Hurch & V. Mattes (Eds.), *Studies on reduplication* (pp. 11–30). Berlin: De Gruyter.

We give special thanks to our informants: Yasaman Rafat for Persian; Yahia Kharrat and Deema Aldahan for Arabic; Ileana Paul for data on infixes.

5 Syntax

Phrase and Sentence Structure
Joyce Bruhn de Garavito

OVERVIEW

In this chapter, you will develop an understanding of how sentences are built. You will:

- notice that the strings of words that make up sentences are organized in particular ways we call structure;
- explore how the structure of sentences relates to meaning;
- learn about the units that constitute the building blocks of structure;
- examine how the different units interact with each other;
- practice representing the structure of sentences via tree diagrams; and
- observe the nature of evidence in syntactic theory.

5.1 What Is Syntax?

Syntax can be defined in two ways:

(a) The part of our mental grammar (knowledge) that represents how sentences and phrases are built;

(b) A branch of linguistics that describes our knowledge of how sentences are put together.

We refer to knowledge of language as **competence**. This contrasts with **performance**, which is our use of language in different situations. This chapter will focus mainly on our syntactic competence.

Sentences are made up of units that we refer to as phrases or constituents. The meaning of sentences depends in great part on how phrases combine and how they relate to each other. In other words, the meaning of a sentence is more than the meaning of individual words that appear in it.

Phrases are single words or groups of words that are combined to form larger units, sentences. For example, the words *monkeys, parrots, the, see,* and *the* can be combined to form the phrases in (1), and these can be combined to form the sentences in (2a) and (2b). However, your intuition as a speaker of English will tell you that the combinations of words found in (2c) and (2d) are not possible. As in previous chapters, we indicate that they are not possible with an asterisk (often referred to as a star) at the beginning of the sentence.

(1) the monkeys; the parrots; see the parrots.

(2) a. The monkeys see the parrots.
b. The parrots see the monkeys.
c. *Parrots the monkeys the see.
d. *see the monkeys the parrots.

Sentences or phrases that speakers feel are possible in a particular language, because they are well formed according to their intuition, are referred to as **grammatical** sentences. Sentences or phrases that speakers feel are impossible in a particular language are considered **ungrammatical**. Linguists rely quite a bit on native speakers' intuition to determine grammaticality. This is because our intuition reflects our competence, that is, our knowledge of the principles and rules of syntax. For example, all speakers of English would agree that the phrase *monkeys the* is ungrammatical in English. However, a word-for-word translation into Romanian would constitute a grammatical sequence.

5.1.1 Grammaticality and Prescriptive Grammar

We must always be careful to distinguish between ungrammatical or impossible sentences in a language, and sentences or phrases that we are told are not "correct" according to some social standard. Compare the two sentences below and decide whether they are grammatical or ungrammatical according to your intuition. Would you judge one, both, or neither as ungrammatical?

(3) a. To boldly go where no one has gone before.
b. To boldly went where no one has gone before.

It is probable that you find (3a) to be acceptable, while (3b) is not, and should be starred marked with an asterisk. And yet, there are those who consider (3a) ungrammatical, not because their intuition tells them so, but because tradition tells us that there is a rule in English that says an infinitive, such as *to go*, should not be split up by words such as *boldly*. The grammars that are based on rules such as these are referred to as **prescriptive grammars**. Prescriptive rules are useful in certain contexts but are not the topic of this chapter.

5.1.2 Structure

Structure refers to the arrangement of parts or elements in a whole, parts or elements that are put together in a particular way. For example, we speak of the structure of a building, that is, a building is constructed with beams and columns that are arranged in a certain way so that the building does not collapse. Do words need to be arranged

PAUSE AND REFLECT 5.1

Compare the sentences below and decide whether they are grammatical or ungrammatical. Some of them raise very interesting questions for linguistics. Have you been taught that any of these sentences are unacceptable, and yet you commonly use such expressions?

i.   It is me.
ii. It is I.

iii. Me and John went to the movies.
iv. Do you can come to the party?
v.   I wanna go.
vi. You know something?
vii. He doesn't like I.
viii. He don't know nothing.

in a particular way in order for grammaticality not to break down? The words in sentences follow each other in a linear fashion, both in speech and in writing. Do we form sentences by simply stringing words together like pearls in a necklace? Or do the words combine into structural units that are part of larger units?

There is evidence that words combine into structural units, although we may not be consciously aware of it. For example, if there were no structure, we would have no explanation for why (2c) and (2d) are ungrammatical. Furthermore, if linear order is all that matters, we should be able to pause at any point in the utterance. However, as the sentences in (4) show, we have strong intuition that sentences can only be broken up in particular ways. In (4a) the pauses, represented by slashes, seem natural, while you probably feel that pausing as in (4b) would be a strange way to speak. This is evidence that words are not just jumbled together but that there is an underlying structure in the mind of the speaker (and hearer). This underlying structure is what syntax describes.

(4) The parrots see the monkeys.
     a. The parrots / see / the monkeys.
     b. *the / parrots see / the / monkeys.

5.1.3 Ambiguous Sentences or Phrases

Further support for the importance of underlying structure is found in the relationship between meaning and structure. There is an important link between the interpretation of a sentence or phrase and the way the words or phrases relate to each other. This becomes very clear in the case of **ambiguous** phrases or sentences. Ambiguous phrases or sentences are those that are open to more than one meaning. A very famous example comes from the classic comedian Groucho Marx (1890–1977): *This morning I shot an elephant in my pajamas.* The most logical interpretation is that the person is wearing pajamas, but the comedian continues: *How he got into my pajamas I don't know.* In other words, his interpretation is that *an elephant in my pajamas* forms a unit, while the most common interpretation is that *in my pajamas* goes with *I*, not with elephant.

Consider the example in (5).

(5) Black triangles and circles.

In (5) we may interpret the word *black* as applying to both triangles and circles as in Figure 5.1, or only to the triangles, as illustrated in Figure 5.2.

We show the close connection between words and phrases by enclosing them in brackets, as shown in (6a) and (6b), or with tree diagrams. In (6a), *black* is saying something about both shapes (it describes both), so we link the two together in one pair of brackets. In (6b), in contrast, *black* describes only *triangles* and therefore the two words constitute a phrase, enclosed in brackets, excluding the word *circles*.

(6) a. [Black [triangles and circles]]
     b. [[Black triangles] and circles]

LINGUISTICS TIDBITS: EVIDENCE FOR STRUCTURE

Linguists make up sentences, both grammatical and ungrammatical, to test for knowledge of structure. We will continue to do this in this chapter. However, evidence for structure can come from many other sources, including slips of the tongue, child language, second language learners, bilinguals, or the speech of people with brain injury. Linguists also take into consideration different modes of expression, such as oral and written forms.

Tree diagrams are easier than brackets to interpret. Therefore, in the remainder of this chapter we will focus on learning to represent sentence and phrase structure with tree diagrams, similar to those used in Chapter 4 Morphology. To summarize this section, sentences and phrases are not made up simply by stringing words together. Instead, there is an underlying structure, or a basic template, without which humans would not be able to interpret and construct language. The underlying structure is what we refer to as the syntax of the sentence or phrase.

Figure 5.1 Black triangles and black circles

Figure 5.2 Black triangles and non-black circles

5.2 Classification of Words

The words that allow us to build phrases and sentences are classified into two main categories: lexical and functional. Words that belong to **lexical categories** are generally quite easy to define because they have descriptive content. For example, it is quite easy to explain what the word *house* means, or the word *play*. If asked, we would say something like *a house is a building where people live* and *play is an activity carried out for fun*.

The sets of lexical categories are considered **open classes** because new words can be added to the community's or to the speakers' lexicon, and old words can disappear. For example, the word *snollygoster*, a noun that was used in the past to refer to an unprincipled person, has dropped out of most people's active vocabulary (although maybe we should consider reinstating it), while at the same time we have added new words such as *bromance* or *agritourism*.

Functional categories, on the other hand, do not generally have intrinsic meaning. Instead, they add grammatical precision to what we say. For example, among the functional categories we find articles such as *a* and *the*. The use of the definite article *the* in a phrase such as *the house* leads the hearer to understand that I am referring to a house previously mentioned. In contrast, the use of the indefinite article indicates I am speaking of one of several possible houses. Functional categories such as *the* and *a* form **closed classes**, because we do not often add new words of this type to a language's lexicon.

EYES ON WORLD LANGUAGES: WORDS AND SENTENCES

English uses words to create phrases, which in turn make up sentences. However, as we saw in Chapter 4 Morphology, the difference between a word, a phrase, and a sentence is not always as clear-cut in other languages as it is in English. In many languages, a whole sentence can be represented by a very complex word. For example, in Inuktitut, the language spoken by around 39,000 Inuit in Northern Canada, *Inuktitusuunguvit* means *Do you speak Inuktitut?* In the same way, in Nahuatl, a language spoken in Mexico (around 1.5 million people), *nitlaulnemaka* means *I sell corn*. Both of these languages are polysynthetic, which means that what appears to be a single word may actually consist of a combination of several smaller words and affixes.

5.2.1   Classification of Lexical Categories

Lexical words are divided into five main classes: nouns, verbs, adjectives, adverbs, and prepositions. You are probably familiar with most of these. Table 5.1 gives examples of each type.

TABLE 5.1 Lexical Categories with Examples

Noun (N)	Louisa, turtle, woman, student, water, beauty, health, interest
Verb (V)	listen, sharpen, buy, arrive, give, greet, send, put, ask
Adjective (A)	big, short, happy, irresistible, responsible, slow, careless, blue
Preposition (P)	on, in, near, up, down, with, above, below
Adverb (Adv)	happily, responsibly, slowly, always, sometimes, now, possibly, yesterday

In most cases, we can decide intuitively how to classify the members of the lexical categories. For example, people agree that *dog* belongs to the set of nouns while *listen* is a verb. However, how can we be sure that our classification is correct? As in all other areas of linguistics, we look for evidence. Evidence for word classes is generally found in three main areas: semantics (meaning), morphology (inflection and derivation), and syntax (distribution).

Evidence from Meaning

Nouns (N) are said to denote entities (persons, places, animals, things, etc.); verbs (V) denote events or actions; adjectives (A) designate properties of nouns; adverbs (Adv) often denote properties of verbs such as manner, frequency, or time; and prepositions (P) often refer to location and direction. However, meaning is the least reliable type of evidence for classifying words. For example, a word such as *destruction* is classified as a noun although it denotes an event. An adverb such as *yesterday* does not modify a verb but rather tells us when a complete event took place. Verbs such as *seem* or *resemble* do not appear to denote actions. We therefore rely more on morphological or distributional (syntactic) evidence to determine the category of a word.

Evidence from Morphology

Remember from Chapter 4 Morphology that inflectional morphology adds grammatical features to words without changing the lexical category. Table 5.2 shows the use of inflectional morphology as evidence for the category of a word in English.

Morphology is not always reliable as evidence for the lexical category of a word either. Mass nouns cannot be easily pluralized unless a very particular meaning is implied (e.g., *the snows of Kilimanjaro*). Many adjectives cannot take the comparative or superlative endings (*beautifuller*, *specialer*), and we have to be careful to recognize verbs with an irregular past tense.

PAUSE AND REFLECT 5.2

In English, nouns can often become verbs, sometimes, but not always, with small changes in pronunciation or stress, as we saw in Chapter 4 Morphology. Using inflectional morphology, can you demonstrate the category of the following words?

i.   table (as in *on the table* vs. *table a motion*)
ii. chair (as in *the chair in the corner* vs. *chair the meeting*)
iii. worm (as in *it's a worm* vs. *worm your way*)

TABLE 5.2 Types of Inflection that Characterize Different Word Classes in English

Word class	Inflection	Examples
Noun	plural –s possessive 's	houses, hats, chairs, rivers Joanne's, the Prime Minister's
Verb	third person singular –s past tense –ed present progressive –ing	plays, looks, walks, munches played, looked, walked, munched playing, looking, walking, munching
Adjective	comparative –er superlative –est	bigger, nicer, prettier, braver biggest, nicest, prettiest, bravest
Adverb	None	quickly, nicely, bravely, kindly yesterday, always, often
Preposition	None	up, on, in, under, with

Evidence from Syntax

Word classes may differ in the types of elements they may combine with, that is, their syntactic distribution. For example, you expect to find a noun with an article, as we saw above (*the house, a house*), but this is not true of a verb (**the walked*), an adjective (**the pretty*), or an adverb (**the quickly*). Table 5.3 provides some examples of how evidence from syntactic distribution can be used to determine the category of words.

The best way to determine the category of a word is to use the three kinds of tests: semantics, morphology, and syntactic distribution. Syntactic distribution is the most reliable.

TABLE 5.3 Syntactic Distribution of Word Classes with Some Examples

Noun (N)	a/the _____ my _____ this _____	a house, the water my garden, his sister this cat, that parrot
Verb (V)	may _____ should _____ can _____ have _____	may go should think can help have practiced
Adjective (A)	very _____ the _____ + noun	very good the big problem
Adverb (Adv)	very _____ _____verb _____	very quickly frequently eat (frequently)
Preposition (P)	right _____ _____ noun phrase	right down right up the street down an alley over this table on my desk

5.2.2 Classification of Functional Categories

Functional categories consist of words or features that have no clear descriptive content and whose primary role is to fulfill a grammatical function. In other words, they are used in language to satisfy grammatical needs. We refer here to these as *functional words*, but these words in one language may be represented by bound morphemes in another. For example, in English, an action that is repeated in the past may be expressed with the function words *used to*. In French, the suffix that indicates imperfect tense is used to express the same idea, as seen in (7).

(7) Jean étudi**ait** beaucoup.
     Jean study-imp a lot
     "Jean used to study a lot."

Table 5.4 lists the categories of function words, the types of elements that are included in each category, and some examples.

TABLE 5.4 Functional Categories

Category	Types of words it contains	Examples of use
Determiner (D)	the, a, this, that, these, those, my, your, his, her, our, their	the monkey; an animal this exercise; those books my dog; their sister
Quantifier (Quant)	all, some, many, each	all the children some people many instructors
Pronouns (Pro)	I, you, he, she, we, they, me, you, him, her, us, them one, mine, yours, his, hers, ours, theirs, this, that, these, those (when standing alone)	She is working. I saw him. I bought a blue one. Did you bring yours? This is very expensive.
Conjunctions (Conj)	and, or, but	John and I got married. Do you prefer the house or the apartment? I went but I did not stay.
Complementizers (C)	that, if, whether	I know that you are wrong. If he comes, invite him in. He doesn't know whether to go or stay.
Auxiliaries (Aux)	have, do, be	He has broken his promise. Do you like this song? We are getting ready.
Modals (M)	can, could, will, would, shall, should, may, might, must	We will go to the party. Would you please help? Should I finish now? I may decide later.

PAUSE AND REFLECT 5.3

Consider each of the words in the following sentences. First, determine whether they belong to a lexical or a functional category, and then name the category. In the case of lexical categories, use morphological and syntactic tests to show that your classification is correct.

i. The children are playing with their toys.
ii. Milk tastes good.
iii. She wants some help.

5.2.3 Features

A syntactic **feature** is a way of representing an abstract grammatical property. Function words and inflectional morphemes (see Chapter 4 Morphology) are often considered the concrete expression of abstract features such as number, gender, person, tense, aspect, etc. Consider the feature [number]. In English it is expressed by the morpheme [–s/–es], which is added to the end of nouns. The feature **[number]** is important to syntax as it may affect agreement with the verb, as can be seen in the distinction between *the dog barks* and *the dogs bark*. The form of the verb *bark* changes depending on whether we are talking about one dog or several.

In a similar fashion, in many languages such as French, German, and Arabic, nouns exhibit the feature **[gender]** (masculine, feminine, neuter), which is important to the syntax because other words in the phrase have to adopt the same gender and number, as shown in examples (8a) and (8b) for French. In (8a) the feminine form of the article *la* and the feminine form of the adjective *ronde* must be used because *table* is a feminine noun. In (8b), the plural form of the article *les* and the masculine plural form of the adjective *ronds* are used because the noun *trou* is masculine and appears in plural form.

(8) a. La   table   ronde
         the-*FEM SING*   table-*FEM SING*   round-*FEM SING*
     b. Les   trous   ronds
         the-*MASC PL*   holes-*MASC PL*   round-*MASC PL*

The feature [tense] plays a central role in syntax because it anchors the event in time. Tense specifies the timeframe that applies to the action or state expressed by the sentence. In English and many other languages the main tenses are [past], [future], and [present]. Tense can be expressed by inflection of the verb (9) or by adding free morphemes such as the auxiliaries *do*, *be*, and *have* (10), or modals such as *will*, *can*, and *shall*, as seen in (11).

(9) a. She walk**s** to work every day.
     b. I play**ed** the guitar at the party.

(10) a. He doe**s** not dance very well.
     b. Harry **is** prepar**ing** lunch.
     c. I **have** brok**en** my toe.

(11) a. Lucy **will** visit her parents next month.

    b. Helen **can** help us tomorrow.

    c. I **shall** not go there.

EYES ON WORLD LANGUAGES: VARIATION IN WORD CATEGORIES ACROSS LANGUAGES

Languages vary a great deal regarding what classes are included in their lexicon. Although it has been argued that all languages have verbs and nouns, believe it or not, some languages either do not include adjectives or have very few: Nahuatl, spoken in Mexico by about a million and a half speakers; Siouan language family, spoken by Indigenous people of the Great Plains of North America, about 21,000 speakers; and Chinese; among others. Furthermore, there is a lot of variation in the expression of spatial or temporal relations. In English we use prepositions (**in** the house), in Korean and Japanese these words follow the noun phrase, in which case they are referred to as postpositions (the house **in**). In some languages we find both prepositions and postpositions (German), and in some others these relations are expressed by way of affixes (Hungarian). Many languages do not have the equivalent of the English articles *a* and *the* (Latin, Russian, Japanese) although most languages have the equivalent of demonstratives such as *this* and *that*. Languages such as Chinese have very little inflexion on the verb, so it is not certain whether they have tense. Many languages have no gender, not even in pronouns (Nahuatl, language spoken in Mexico; Anishinaabe, language spoken in Canada and the northern United States by the Ojibway), and some do not distinguish number on the noun either (Chinese, Japanese) or do so only with nouns that refer to living things (Nahuatl). Finally, it is surprising in how many languages it is possible to omit the verb *to be* (Turkish, Korean, Arabic)!

5.3 Constituents

The term **constituent** refers to a word or group of words that function as a unit in a syntactic structure. It is synonymous with phrase. Meaning is derived not only from word order but also from how the constituents relate to one another. In the examples given in (12) we see how the constituents can be combined to form larger constituents. We have written each constituent in brackets. In addition to placing constituents in brackets, another way to represent them is with tree diagrams, as we will see below.

(12) a. [the monkeys]

    b. [see [the monkeys]]

    c. [the parrots]

    d. [[The parrots] [see [the monkeys]]]

5.3.1 Identifying Constituents

The following tests are useful in determining with some certainty whether a word or string of words form a constituent.

    Substitution test: the grammatical replacement of a string of words with a single word or expression such as *do so* constitutes evidence that the string forms a constituent. For example, in (13a), *the child's mother* can be replaced by *she*, as seen in (13b); in

(14a), *a great picture of the mountains* can be substituted by the pronoun *it*, as shown in (14b); in (15a) *go to the party* is substituted by *do so* (15b); and *under the bed* (16a) can be substituted by *here* (16b). In all these cases we are dealing with constituents. However, we find nothing to replace the string *always buy* in (17), evidence it is not a constituent.

(13) a. The child's mother bought the teacher a gift.
   b. *She* bought the teacher a gift.

(14) a. I took a great picture of the mountains.
   b. I took *it*.

(15) a. My friends will go to the party.
   b. My friends will *do so* too.

(16) a. I hid the surprise under the bed.
   b. I hid the surprise *there*.

(17) a. I always buy an apple.
   b. *I *do so* a pear.

Movement of a string of words to a different position in the sentence is also evidence that the string is a constituent. We call this the **movement test**. In (18b) we have moved *the gift* to the beginning of the sentence. In (19b) we have moved *during lunchtime*. This shows both are constituents. However, as we see by the ungrammaticality of (19c), *tomorrow during* is not.

(18) a. She bought flowers and a gift. She gave the gift to the teacher.
   b. *The gift,* she gave to the teacher.

(19) a. I will go to the movies tomorrow during lunchtime.
   b. *During lunchtime* I will go to the movies tomorrow.
   c. **Tomorrow during* I will go to the movies lunchtime.

EYES ON WORLD LANGUAGES: MOVEMENT OF CONSTITUENTS

English has a relatively fixed word order. Other languages, however, move constituents very frequently. Some languages are considered free word order languages because of this property. Consider the following examples from Mohawk, an Iroquoian language spoken in parts of Canada and the United States. The word order is very free, as the examples (from Baker, 1996) show.

i.   Wa'ketshʌri-' kíkʌ káhure'
     I found   this gun
     "I found this gun."
ii. kíkʌ káhure' wa'ketshʌri-'
     this gun   I found
     "I found this gun."
iii. Ne kíkʌ   wa'ketshʌri-' ne káhure'
     NE this   I found   NE gun
     "I found this gun."

The **question and answer test** is another way of finding evidence for a constituent. The short answer to a question is almost always a constituent. This is because constituents can often stand alone, as illustrated in (20). Strings that do not form a constituent cannot do so.

(20) a. Where did you put the book I lent you?
       On the shelf.
     b. Who broke the window?
       The children who live on the corner.
     c. Who broke the window?
       *The children who live on.

Linking two words or strings of words by conjunctions such as *and* or *but* constitutes a good test for constituency. This is so because it is not possible to link two elements that do not have the same structure. We call this the **coordination test**. For example, we cannot link a verb phrase and a noun phrase (21c), but we can link two verb phrases (21a) or two noun phrases, (21b).

(21) a. Luisa will *buy a present* and *visit the museum*.
     b. Paul will buy *a gift* and *a scarf* during lunchtime.
     c. *The child* and *went to the store*.

On a final note, not all tests can be used for all types of constituents. However, if proceeding correctly, none of the tests should work with a random string of words.

PAUSE AND REFLECT 5.4

Use at least one of the tests we have discussed to show whether the underlined words below form a constituent.

i.   My mother will <u>buy a pie for dinner</u>.
ii. <u>The cat that lives next door</u> drank my dog's water.

iii. <u>The neighbors bought</u> a new car.
iv. William ordered a drink <u>before the meal</u>.
v.   I gave a biscuit <u>to the parrot yesterday</u>.

5.3.2 The Heart of Constituent Structure: The Head

The **head** is the word that determines the properties of a constituent. For example, if I say *little monkeys*, you know that I am talking about some animals, *monkeys*, that happen to be small in size. *Monkeys* is the head of [*little monkeys*]. Because the head is a noun, we call the constituent *little monkeys* a noun phrase (NP). *Little* indicates additional information about the *monkeys* and because of that we say *little* modifies the head *monkeys*.

Every constituent must have a head, and only one. The head of a verb phrase (VP), for example [*see* [*the monkeys*]], is a verb. Adjectival phrases (AP) are headed by an adjective, for example the adjective *big* as in [*very* [*big*]], adverbial phrases (AdvP) by an adverb, for example [*very* [*frequently*]], and prepositional phrases (PP) by a preposition, as in [*on* [*the table*]].

Remember that a constituent may be made up of only one word. For example, in *I always eat bananas for breakfast*, the word *always* is the head of an AdvP, which forms a constituent.

We provide more examples of the types of phrases headed by lexical categories in Table 5.5.

TABLE 5.5 Examples of Different Types of Phrases

Phrase type	Examples with the head underlined
Noun Phrase (NP)	• the <u>mouse</u> that ate the cheese • <u>children</u> • a green <u>apple</u>
Verb Phrase (VP)	• <u>drink</u> my juice • <u>walk</u> along the beach. • <u>run</u>
Adjectival Phrase (AP)	• quite <u>interesting</u> • <u>blue</u> • <u>proud</u> of his accomplishments
Adverbial Phrase (AdvP)	• quite <u>often</u> • <u>usually</u> • very <u>calmly</u>
Prepositional Phrase (PP)	• <u>in</u> the box • <u>with</u> my friends from school • <u>over</u> my head

---

PAUSE AND REFLECT 5.5

Below you will find different constituents underlined. Identify the type of constituent (e.g., NP, VP, etc.) and the head.

i. The dog eats <u>old bones</u>.
ii. The <u>man with the yellow hat</u> gave me that.
iii. I <u>often</u> go to the movies.
iv. It is <u>quite ripe</u>.
v. The parrot <u>wants a treat</u>.

5.4 Arguments

The term **argument** refers to the number of participants in the event described by the sentence. The two main arguments of verbs are subjects and complements. For example, to use the verb *buy* in a sentence we need to express two participants: the entity that buys (i.e., the subject) and the thing that is bought (i.e., the complement). We say that the verb *buy* requires two arguments.

5.4.1 Subjects

The **subject** of a sentence in English can be recognized because it agrees with the verb and generally precedes it in statements. For example, in (22a), the verb ends in third person –s because the subject is third person. The subject *she* also appears before the verb.

All tensed verbs have a subject, that is, they require a subject argument. Compare the grammatical sentence in (22a) with the ungrammatical (22b). *Walks* cannot be interpreted correctly in English without a subject, that is, we must indicate who is doing the walking.

(22) a. **She** walks to school.
 b. *Walks to school.

Subjects may play different roles in the sentence: the agent (doer of the action), the experiencer (the entity that experiences an emotion), etc. In Chapter 6 Semantics, we will further discuss the different roles assigned to arguments.

EYES ON WORLD LANGUAGES: SUBJECTS IN OTHER LANGUAGES

In English, the overt presence of subjects is obligatory in most contexts, but this is not the case for all languages. Compare the Italian (i) and Spanish (ii) sentences with the equivalent French (iii) and English sentences (iv).

i. Ha telefonato / Lui ha telefonato. (Italian)
 has called   he has called

ii. Ha llamado / Ella ha llamado. (Spanish)
 has called   she has called

iii. *A téléphoné / Il a téléphoné. (French)
 has called   he has called

iv. *Has called/ she has called.

In Italian and Spanish, you may omit the subject pronoun *he/she* or you may include it, both possibilities are grammatical (i)–(ii). This is not the case for French or English (iii)–(iv). However, this does not mean that in Spanish and Italian subjects are not necessary. In fact, there is evidence that subjects are universally obligatory. We assume that in languages like Italian and Spanish, when no overt subject is present, there nevertheless exists a covert (not pronounced) form of the subject pronoun that we call *pro* (short for pronoun). These languages are referred to as pro-drop or null-subject languages.

5.4.2 Complements

A **complement** is an argument that is required by the head, often a verb, in order to complete its meaning. Verbs are traditionally divided into two classes, transitive and intransitive, according to whether they require a complement or not.

Intransitive verbs are those that do not require a complement. They only require one argument, the subject. The verbs *walk*, *laugh*, and *swim* are intransitive. As you can see in (23), no additional information is required to complete the actions of these verbs, though we may optionally add information such as *where* or *when* the action takes place.

(23) a. My sister swims.
       b. My sister swims in the pool every Saturday.

Unlike intransitive verbs, **transitive** verbs require a complement. The complement of a verb is typically the entity that is affected by the action of the verb. For example, a sentence with the verb *to buy* needs to include information about what is bought to be complete. Compare (24a), with a complement, with (24b), without. Other transitive verbs include *take*, *sell*, *see*, and *prepare*.

(24) a. My sister bought **a pair of shoes**.
       b. *My sister bought.

Prepositions in phrases such as *on the table* are also said to require complements, in this case *the table* is the complement of the preposition *on*. Adjectives and adverbs never take complements. Some nouns and adjectives may occasionally take complements.

There are also some verbs that are **ditransitive**, they require the subject and two other arguments. Examples are the verbs *put* and *give*, illustrated in (25).

(25) a. I put the book on the table.
       b. *I put the book.
       c. I gave him a puppy.
       d. *I gave him.

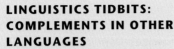

Subcategorization

Verbs and prepositions are types of heads that may require the presence of a complement to complete their meaning, as we have seen above. Knowledge of the different complements that are required by a head is part of our mental lexicon. For example, our knowledge of the verbs *buy* and *find* includes the information that these verbs are transitive, while knowledge of the verb *walk* includes the fact that no complement is necessary. This information is referred to as **subcategorization**. We say the verbs *find* and *buy* subcategorize for a complement.

5.4.3   Adjuncts

So far, we have examined subjects and complements, both of which constitute arguments of a verb or preposition. However, we frequently add information that is not required when we build a phrase: when the action takes place, where it takes place, why it takes place, etc. The phrases that are not required but that add extra information or modify the head are called **adjuncts**. In (26) we illustrate a sentence with both arguments (in bold) and adjuncts (underlined). Note that, unlike arguments, the sentence is still grammatical if we omit the adjunct (26b). It is not grammatical if we omit either the complement (26c) or the subject (26d).

(26) a. **The repairman** fixed **the fridge** <u>yesterday</u> <u>at lunchtime</u> <u>in his shop</u>.
   b. **The repairman** fixed **the fridge**.
   c. *__The repairman__ fixed yesterday at lunchtime in his shop.
   d. *Fixed **the fridge** yesterday at lunchtime in his shop

Nouns may also be modified by the presence of adjuncts, as shown in (27). Both *red* and *in the garage* are adjuncts and can be omitted. Omitting the head noun makes the phrase ungrammatical.

(27) a. The <u>red</u> car <u>in the garage</u> (is mine).
   b. The car (is mine).
   c. *The red in the garage (is mine).

In the following sentences, determine which underlined phrases are complements and which adjuncts. Provide evidence for your identification by showing whether omission of the phrase makes the sentence ungrammatical.

   i. Yesterday, I chose <u>the paint for the bedroom</u>.
   ii. I want the cake <u>with pink frosting</u>.
   iii. Ursula repaired <u>her bike</u> <u>in the garage</u>.
   iv. She brought <u>her pyjamas</u> <u>for the sleepover</u>.
   v. I ran <u>along the beach</u> <u>with my brother</u>.

5.5 Merge: Forming Phrases and Sentences

The syntactic operations called merge and move are the two main processes used for building phrases and sentences. In this section we focus on merge.

Merge is an operation that consists of combining two elements to form another. Because we always combine or merge two elements, the structures will always be at most **binary**, that is, we maintain a maximum of two branches at each level. As we have already seen in Chapter 3 Phonology and Chapter 4 Morphology, binary branching serves as a powerful explanation for many linguistic facts.

5.5.1 Building Phrases: A Template

In order to help us understand how the process of building phrases works, linguists try to represent structures visually, generally through the use of brackets and tree diagrams to represent the internal structure of syllables (Chapter 3 Phonology) and words (Chapter 4 Morphology). In our exploration of syntax, we will do the same to show the structure of phrases and sentences.

Tree diagrams should include the following information:

- the order of the constituents, which should match the linear order of the sentence as it is said or heard;
- the category of the head and of the phrase associated with it; and
- the structural relation between the different elements, including the subject, complements, and adjuncts.

In (28), we illustrate the template that is used to represent phrases.

(28) The template for phrases

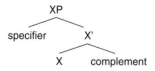

The symbol X represents a generalization that stands for any type of head (noun, verb, adjective, preposition, etc.). As the category of a phrase is determined by the head, we say that the head X projects a phrase XP. For example, a noun (N) projects a noun phrase (NP), a verb (V) projects a verb phrase (VP), an adjective (A) projects an adjective phrase (AP), and a preposition (P) projects a prepositional phrase (PP).

Besides the head and the phrase it projects, we also use an intermediate level, X' (X-bar). For this reason we refer to the visualization in (28) as the X-bar template, which is the result of the merge operation.

As we have seen, every phrase needs a head. We also know that the presence of a complement depends on the subcategorization of the head: a transitive verb requires a complement, an intransitive one typically does not; a preposition generally requires a complement; a noun seldom requires one, and adverbs never do.

The **specifier** gets its name because it narrows down, specifies, the interpretation of the head. As you can see in the template tree diagram, the specifier is always immediately below the XP and to the left of X'. Not all phrases have specifiers. Subjects always occupy the specifier position.

A final definition: when two elements are merged together on the same level we say they are **sisters**. In the template, the complement is the sister of the head X. In fact, complements, and only complements, are sisters of a head. The importance of this will become apparent later in the chapter.

Recursion

The X-bar template illustrated above allows us to show you one of the key properties of language: recursion. **Recursion** consists of **embedding**, that is, nesting a structure within another structure of the same type. For example, a sentence or clause can be contained within another clause, as shown in (29).

(29) The mouse that ate the cheese that was on the table ran away.

In (29) we have a main clause, *the mouse ran away*, with a sentence nested inside, *that ate the cheese that was on the table*. Within the sentence *that ate the cheese that was on the table* there is another nested sentence: *that was on the table*. If humans did not have memory limitations, we could go on forever.

The template allows us to represent recursion very easily. We simply use the same template over and over again to build complex structures.

5.5.2   Practicing the X-bar Template

Consider the simple phrase *apples*, as in *The cook bought apples*. We know that *apples* is a noun, therefore it must project an NP. In this sentence, it does not have a complement, nor does it have a specifier. The structure is represented in (30a).

(30) a. The cook bought <u>apples.</u>

Now consider the phrase [*bought* [*apples*]] (30b). The verb *bought* is the head of a VP. It is a transitive verb, and *apples* is the complement. Therefore the NP *apples* is represented as the sister of the head (i.e., the verb *bought*).

b.   The cook <u>bought apples</u>.

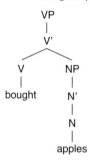

The subject of *the cook bought apples* is *the cook*. Unlike the NP *apples*, the phrase *the cook* includes the determiner *the*. We know that determiners (D) such as *the* are functional items. Like all other categories, determiners project a phrase which we call a determiner phrase (DP). The complement of D is always an NP, in this case the NP *cook*. The structure of the DP [*the* [*cook*]] is illustrated in (30c).

c.   <u>The cook</u> bought apples.

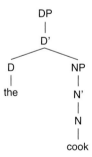

5.5.3 The Template and the Sentence

We have seen that every phrase is the projection of a head. This should apply to the sentence as well. We assume that the sentence is the projection of the feature [tense] (T). In other words, the head of a sentence is T because it is tense that links together the subject of the sentence and the verb phrase. If the head of the sentence is T and the sentence is the projection of T, the sentence is a **Tensed Phrase**, TP. The template as applied to the sentence is illustrated in (31). You can think of TP as being equal to *sentence*.

(31) The template for a sentence.

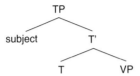

The template shows that the VP is the complement (sister of) T. The subject, like the subject of all sentences, occupies the specifier position of T.

In (32) we apply what we have seen so far to illustrate the structure of the sentence *The cook bought apples*. Note that we have placed the feature tense as [+past] or [–past] under T.

(32) The cook bought apples.

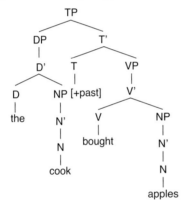

In (33) we give another example of a sentence represented in a tree diagram, this time using the simple present of an intransitive verb.

(33) My friend walks.

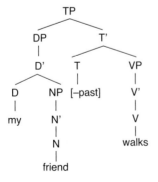

Represent the structure of the following sentences with a tree diagram, following the suggested steps. See Appendix 1 for a detailed example of building a syntactic tree.

i. That kid ate my muffin.
    • First, build the phrase for *muffin*. The noun *muffin* projects an NP.
    • Merge the NP *muffin* as the complement (sister) of the D *my*. Recall that possessives are determiners. Project the full DP.

• Merge the DP *my muffin* as the complement (sister) of the verb *ate*. Project the VP.
• Merge the VP *ate my muffin* with T. Project the sentence (TP).
• Merge the **subject** DP *that kid* in the specifier of T.

ii. The student reads a book.
    • Follow the same steps for (ii) as you did for (i).

Tense

The **tense** node (T) not only includes the features [+past] and [–past], but also all modals and auxiliaries. Recall from Table 5.4 that the modals include *will, may, can, would, could*, etc. The auxiliaries in English are the verbs *to have* and *to be* when they are followed by a main verb. In (34) we represent a sentence with the modal *will*. We use triangles in place of the fully expanded representation of a phrase, mainly to save space. We will do this with the subject DP *the children*.

(34) The children will ride a donkey.

• The NP *donkey* is projected.

• The NP *donkey* merges with the determiner *a*. The determiner is the head of the DP.

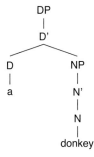

• The DP *a donkey* is the complement of the verb *ride*. The verb *ride* is the head of the VP *ride a donkey*.

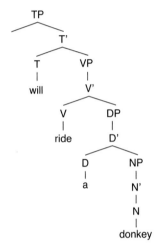

- The VP merges with *will*, the head that is in T. T projects a TP (the sentence).

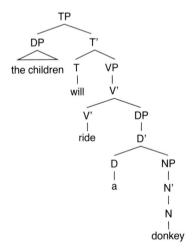

- The subject *the children* is merged as the specifier of T.

Representing Adjuncts in the VP

Recall that adjuncts are phrases that are not required by a head. They add additional information such as time and place. Typically, prepositional phrases, adverb phrases, and adjective phrases are adjuncts. It is important to note that adjuncts may appear on either side of a head. For example, in (35a), the adjunct *always* precedes the verb, but in (35b) the adjunct *in the garden* follows it.

(35) a. I **always** buy popcorn.
     b. I can walk **in the garden**.

We use the following templates to represent adjuncts. You may have more than one adjunct in a phrase. This can be easily accommodated by adding X-bar levels (36).

(36) a. adjunct branching to the right.

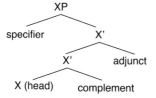

b. adjunct branching to the left.

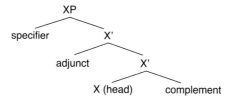

The templates in (36) illustrate the fact that complements, which are required elements, are represented as sisters to the head. Adjuncts, on the other hand, are separated from it by an additional X'. In this way, we represent the fact that adjuncts are optional. In (37) we show the tree diagram of a sentence with an intransitive verb and an adjunct.

(37) I could walk in the garden.

- First, merge the DP [*the* [*garden*]].

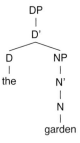

- *the garden* is the complement of the preposition *in*. The preposition is the head of the prepositional phrase [*in* [*the garden*].

- The verb *walk* is the head of the VP. *In the garden* constitutes an adjunct within the VP.

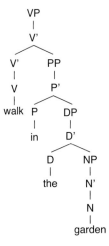

- The verb merges with T, which projects the sentence, TP.

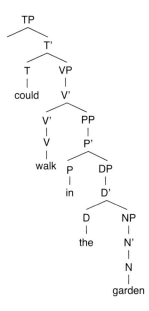

- Merge the subject in the specifier of T.

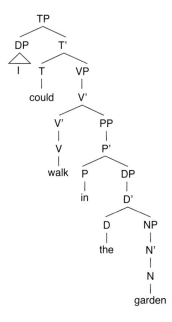

In (38) we illustrate an adjunct that precedes the verb.

(38) That child always screams.

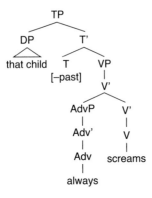

Keep in mind that complements are always sisters to the head X, adjuncts are sisters to X'.

PAUSE AND REFLECT 5.10

Are trees (i)–(iii) true representations of the sentences? If there are errors, correct them. Focus on the difference between complements and adjuncts.

i. Philip plays with his friends.

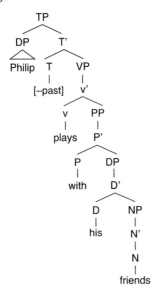

ii. I changed the channel.

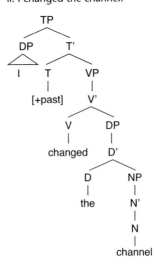

iii. Rebecca always comes late.

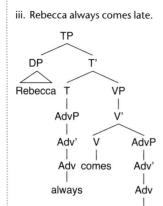

Representing Adjuncts in the DP

Recall that, in most cases, additional material in the DP will be constituted by adjuncts, given that nouns rarely have complements. Similar to adjuncts in the VP, the adjunct to a noun will be attached as the sister of N'. N' levels allow us to separate the adjunct from the head noun. In (39), we illustrate the most common type of adjunct in the NP, an adjective, and in (40), a PP.

(39) my best friend

- The AP, *best*, is merged as the sister of N'. The NP is projected.

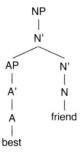

- The NP *best friend* is merged as the sister of D, *my*, and the DP is projected.

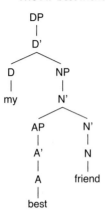

(40) the car in the garage

- We first build the DP *the garage*. The DP *the garage* merges as the complement (sister of) the preposition *in* to form the PP *in the garage*.

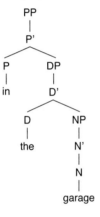

- The adjunct merges with the noun *car*. It is very important that we do not represent the adjunct as sister to N because this position is reserved for complements.

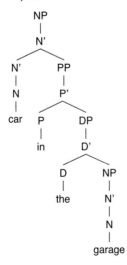

- We merge the NP *the car in the garage* with D, the head of the DP.

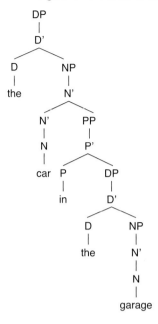

PAUSE AND REFLECT 5.11

Draw the tree diagrams that represent the following sentences and phrases. Remember to distinguish between complements and adjuncts.

i.   The cat died yesterday. (Use triangles for DPs)

ii. Lucy has almost finished her homework. (Use triangles for DPs)

iii. my old sweater

iv. The man with the yellow hat.

Points to Remember: Building and Understanding Tree Diagrams

- All phrases have a head, and only one.
- All heads project an X' level and an XP level.
- Heads may belong to lexical categories (N, V, P, A, Adv), or to functional categories (T, D).
- The sentence is the projection of the tense head T. In other words, every sentence is represented as TP.
- The subject of the sentence is the DP found in the specifier of T, the branch immediately to the left of T', right under TP.
- A complement is an argument that is required in order to complete the meaning of the head.
- Complements are always represented as sisters to the head. In English they are merged to the right of the head.
- An adjunct is never projected as the sister to the head.

- Adjuncts are elements that are not required by the head but add additional information. Removing adjuncts does not affect the grammaticality of the sentence.
- Adjuncts are sisters to an X-Bar (X′) projection. This means that they may be merged on the left or the right of the head.
- Nouns often take APs or PPs as adjuncts.
- Verbs often take AdvPs or PPs as adjuncts.

PAUSE AND REFLECT 5.12

The template that we have described above works well for sentences in English. What about other languages? Consider the Japanese sentences below. Japanese has particles such as *ga* and *o* that indicate the function of the phrase, but you can ignore them here, just focus on the word order.

(i) a. Arisu-san ga terebi o mimasu.
        Alice   television watch

        "Alice watches television."

    b. *Arisu-san ga mimasu terebi o.
        Alice   watches television

(ii) a. Jon-san ga hon o yomimasu.
        John   book read

        "John reads a book."

    b. *Jon-san ga yomimasu hon o.
        John   reads   book

(iii) a. Suzuki-san ga zasshi o yomimasu.
        Suzuki   magazine read

        "Mr. Suzuki reads a magazine."

    b. *Suzuki-san ga yomimasu zasshi o.
        Suzuki   read   magazine

What is the difference in the order of the constituents between Japanese and English? How would you change the template of the VP to accommodate Japanese? Draw a tree for the VP of the Japanese sentence (i,a). As there are no articles in Japanese you can simply project an NP, not a DP.

5.6 Recursion and Embedding of Sentences

Recall that recursion is the embedding of structures within other structures. In this section we will look at how recursion may apply to sentences. When sentences are nested inside each other we refer to them as **clauses**, with the term *sentence* used for the whole.

5.6.1 Embedded Clauses Introduced by a Complementizer

The complements we have looked at so far consist mainly of DPs. However, sentences can also constitute clauses, and in many cases adjuncts as well. We refer to these as **embedded clauses**, because they are dependent on another (main) clause.

In Table 5.4 we saw that the most frequent complementizers in English are *if, whether,* and *that.* These serve to introduce embedded clauses, as illustrated in (41). Note that the complementizer *that* can often be omitted. When it is omitted in speech or writing we cross it out on the tree diagram to indicate it is present but not pronounced.

(41) a. He said that he needed a drink. (He said he needed a drink.)
b. I wonder whether Lucy has left.

Consider (41a). The verb *say* is transitive, *that he needed a drink* is the complement. We can replace *that he needed a drink* by a pronoun: *He said it.*

The tree diagram in (42) represents the embedded clause *he needed a drink.* You have probably realized it is a TP, like all other tensed clauses.

(42) He needed a drink.

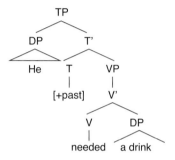

So far we have not built structure above TP. However, we now have to include the complementizer (C), *that.* As expected, C is the head of a complementizer phrase, CP. The structure of CP is illustrated in (43). TP is the complement of C. Below we will see that this structure is also useful to represent questions.

(43) Structure of CP

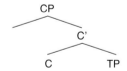

With this additional structure we can complete the representation of the sentences in (41) with the trees in (44) and (45). We assume CP is always present, although it may not be clear yet why we need it in the first part of the two.

(44) He said that he needed a drink.

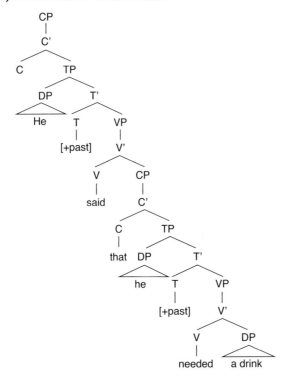

(45) I wonder whether Lucy has left.

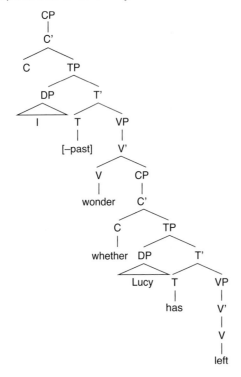

PAUSE AND REFLECT 5.13

Draw the trees to represent the following statements. You can use triangles for all DPs and AdvPs. Note that the verb *go* is intransitive. Therefore, in (iii) the clause *if you go* is not a complement but an adjunct.

i.   Raul thinks that his brother generally wins.
ii. I believe Tracy bought that house yesterday.
iii. I will go if you go.

5.7 Move: Changing Position while Keeping Structure

We build sentences and phrases by merging two elements to form another. However, a second operation, move, is necessary to account for certain structures, including questions.

Move is an operation that displaces a constituent (a head or an entire phrase) from one position in the structure to another, typically higher, position. In English, movement generally takes place to the left. The position to which the constituent moves is referred to as a **landing site**.

In current linguistic approaches, there has to be a reason for the Move operation to take place. In other words, linguists have to justify why they think something moves. We will only be touching briefly on the possible reasons for movement, but it is important to keep in mind that a justification is needed.

5.7.1 Types of Movement

There are two types of movement:

- **Head movement** refers to the displacement of a head such as T, V, or N. As we have seen, in English, French, Spanish, and many other languages, the landing site is to a higher position (i.e., on the left).
- **Phrase movement** refers to the displacement of an entire phrase such as the DP.

Both types of movement can be found in the formation of questions.

5.7.2. Inversion in *Yes/No* Questions: An Example of Head Movement

Compare the sets of sentences in (46) and (47). You will notice that in (46a) and (47a) the modal and auxiliary follow the subject. This is evidence that they are in the T position, as we would expect. In questions such as (46b) and (47b), however, the modal and auxiliary precede the subject. The X-bar template for TP is the same in both cases. The only possible explanation for the word order is that the auxiliary or modal has moved. The movement of the modal/auxiliary is referred to as **inversion**.

(46) a. The teacher <u>has</u> left.
　　　b. <u>Has</u> the teacher left?

(47) a. The painters <u>will</u> finish.
　　　b. <u>Will</u> the painters finish?

When a head or phrase moves, it leaves a trace or **copy** of itself behind. This copy is not pronounced in standard speech. Recall that, in tree diagrams, we cross out a complementizer that is not pronounced. In the same way, we represent the fact that the copy of a moved element is not pronounced by crossing it out. Maintaining the copy ensures, among other things, that the structure we have already built is preserved. The move operation changes the location of the head or phrase that has moved, but it cannot change categories or reduce structure. For example, to produce a sentence such as (46b) we begin with (46a) and move the auxiliary *has* to the beginning of the sentence leaving a copy behind, as shown in (48).

(48) Has the teacher ~~has~~ left?

Structure above TP

Inversion in questions indicates movement of the auxiliary or modal to a position above the core sentence, TP. We know of a good candidate for this position: C, the head of the complementizer phrase (CP). You cannot find both a complementizer and an auxiliary together in C, as shown in (49). This is evidence that the auxiliary has indeed landed there. We call this movement **T-to-C movement** for ease of recall.

(49) a. I wonder whether the teacher has left.
b. *I wonder whether has the teacher left.

Linguists assume C contains features that tell us whether a sentence is a statement or a question. We will indicate this feature with the symbol [+Q] for questions or [–Q] for statements. The feature [+Q] acts like a magnet, attracting the auxiliary or modal to C. As mentioned above, we assume CP is always present, whether we are dealing with a question or not, although very often it is not included in tree diagrams to save space. The updated template for the structure of a statement/question is illustrated in (50).

(50)

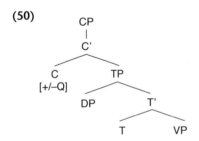

Building Statements and Questions: An Update

In (51) we illustrate an example of a statement. Because the feature in C is [–Q], no movement of T takes place.

(51) She has left.

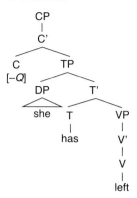

In (52) we illustrate a question. The feature [+Q] has attracted T to it, and the two join in C.

(52) Has she left?

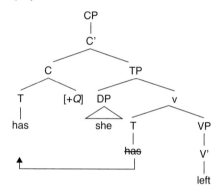

In (52), the auxiliary *has* moves to C. However, T still remains in the position it first merged in, with a copy of the auxiliary that is not pronounced. We have therefore crossed it out in the tree.

Yes/No Questions when No Auxiliary or Modal Is Present

We have seen that, when forming questions, a modal or auxiliary in T moves up to C. We also know that T may simply be occupied by tense features such as [+/–past]. In these cases there is no auxiliary or modal for T-to-C movement. English has an interesting solution to the problem of getting the abstract tense features to C. It inserts a dummy verb, the verb *do*, to move T and the features it contains to C. In fact, we sometimes use this **dummy *do*** in statements for emphasis (*The girls do play in the park*). Movement of T-to- C with dummy *do* is illustrated in the examples in

---

LINGUISTICS TIDBITS: PRONOUNCING TWO COPIES OF T

Children sometimes make questions by repeating an auxiliary in both the C and the T positions. In other words, they pronounce both copies of T: the one that has moved to C and the hidden copy that remains in T. Below you will find some examples from Lightbown & Spada (2013) and Radford (2004):

i.   <u>Is</u> the teddy <u>is</u> tired?
ii. <u>Do</u> I <u>can</u> have a cookie?
iii. <u>Can</u> its wheels <u>can</u> spin?
iv. <u>Did</u> the kitchen light <u>did</u> flash?

Adult second language learners sometimes do this too, as the following example from Lightbown & Spada (2013) shows:

i.   <u>Does</u> in this picture there <u>is</u> four astronauts?

(53). In (53a), we show a simple statement. In (53b), we see the movement necessary to produce a question. In (53c) we illustrate the structure.

(53) a. The girls play in the park.
   b. Do the girls play in the park?

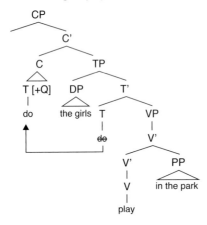

PAUSE AND REFLECT 5.14

Draw the trees that represent the structure of the following sentences. You may use triangles for the DPs.

i. Does the minister understand the problem?
ii. Are the children practicing their scales?
iii. Should I go?

Points to Remember about Building *Yes/No* Questions

- Above the core sentence, TP, we find an additional structure, CP.
- TP is the complement of C. It merges with C, the head of CP. TP is the sister of C.
- C contains abstract features that tell us whether the structure represents a statement [–Q] or a question [+Q].
- If the features point to a question, C attracts T, and the contents of T move to C.
- Every Move operation leaves behind a copy of the moved element. We indicate the copy that is not pronounced by crossing it out on the tree.

5.7.3 *Wh*-questions

Wh-questions are those that include an interrogative word or words: *what, who, where, when, why, how, how many, how much, etc.* All question words represent a phrase, as the answer to the questions in (54) show. Although these phrases fulfill many grammatical functions such as subject, complement, or adjunct, we will refer to all such question phrases as QP. In other words, *who* in (54a) and *when* in (54b) both represent QPs: *who* is the subject of the sentence, *when* is an adjunct. QPs can represent a phrase made up of one word (*who, when*), or several words (*what colour, at what time, how many*). We will always use triangles with QPs.

(54) a. <u>Who</u> will you see?

   I will see <u>the man with red hair</u>.

b. <u>When</u> did Louise buy the book?

   She bought it <u>yesterday afternoon</u>.

In many languages, including English, it is possible to sometimes leave the QP in its original position, for example to express surprise, as shown in (55).

(55) a. You saw <u>who</u>?

b. You bought the book <u>when</u>?

Nevertheless, it is much more frequent to move the QP to the front of the sentence, as shown in (54). In these cases, where does the QP move? It cannot move into C. In the first place, QP is a phrase and C is a head. In the second place, *wh*-questions in English, like *yes/no* questions, include T-to-C movement. In (54a), the modal *will* precedes the subject *you*, in (54b) we find dummy *do*. Therefore, C is occupied by the features of T in most *wh*-questions as well. There is, however, a position in CP that is not occupied in *yes/no* questions, the specifier of C. It is to this position that QPs move. Phrases typically occupy specifier positions. In the next section we will see how this is visualized step-by-step in a tree.

EYES ON WORLD LANGUAGES: POSITION OF QP

In English, QP moves to the front of the sentence, but this is not the case in all languages. In many languages, the question phrase stays in the original position in which it is merged, whether as subject, complement, or adjunct. French is a good example of this, as shown in (i). French also permits many other question structures that are the bane of second language learners.

(i) a Tu vois qui?
        "You see who?"
     b Qui tu vois?
        "Who do you see?"

Languages such as Chinese, Japanese, Korean, and Turkish also leave the question word in the position where English leaves a copy. Examples in (ii) are from Turkish.

(ii) a. Meri elmalar yer.
          Mary apples eats

          "Mary eats apples."

      b. Meri ne yer?
          Mary what eats

          "What does Mary eat?"

Note that there is neither inversion nor movement of *what* to the beginning in these examples. For more about how this works in French, read 'Delving Deeper' in Chapter 5's resources on the website to accompany this book at www.cambridge.org/introducing-linguistics.

Building *Wh*-questions Step-by-step

Let's take a look at how to represent the structure of a question as in (56).

(56) Who will you see?

- To begin building this question, QP is merged as the complement of the verb *see*. We know it is the complement because the verb *see* is a transitive verb and thus requires a complement. Furthermore, when we answer the question, the answer will be the complement of *see* (*I will see <u>the principal</u>*). Finally, as we saw above, it is possible to pronounce the QP in the position of the complement of the verb (*you will see who?*).

a. see who

- As usual, we merge the VP as the complement of T, and project T'.

b. will see who

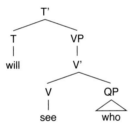

- TP is projected, and the subject is merged as the specifier of T.

c. you will see who

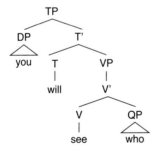

- C is merged with TP. TP is the complement (sister) of C. C has the feature [+Q] that marks the structure as a question.

d. you will see who?

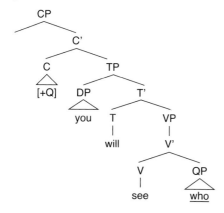

- Inversion applies, and T moves to C, leaving a hidden copy behind. We indicate the copy by crossing it out.

e. will you see who?

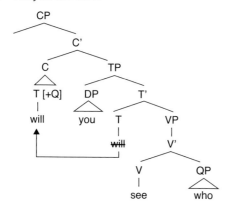

- Finally, the QP *who* moves to the specifier of C. The QP leaves behind a copy of itself that is not pronounced. We indicate this by crossing it out inside the VP.

f. Who will you see?

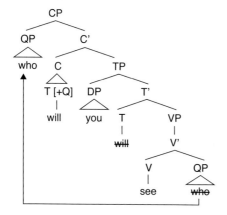

Subject *Wh*-questions

Consider the two questions in (57). They are different in an interesting way.

(57) a. Who did Sarah meet?

b. Who met Sarah?

In (57a) the QP *who* represents the complement of *meet*. There is no modal or auxiliary present so we use the dummy *do* to carry the tense features to C. In (57b), in contrast, *who* represents the subject of the sentence. We notice that there is no inversion, T does not move to C, as the absence of the dummy verb *do* shows. The question word, in contrast, does move to the front of the sentence. The structure for (57b) is illustrated in (58). The lack of movement of T to C in these cases is particular to English.

(58) Who met Sarah?

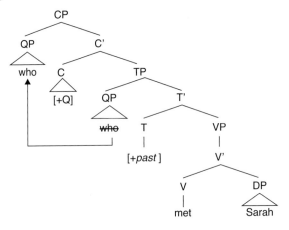

Embedded *Wh*-questions

Some verbs may subcategorize for *wh*-questions (i.e., require them) as complements. Examples are found in (59) and (60), in which the complements are in square brackets. The verbs *ask* and *wonder* subcategorize for a question in complement position (or a DP). In other words, they subcategorize for an embedded clause that is interpreted as a question.

(59) I asked [who Lucy loves].

(60) The salesman wondered [what the client wanted].

Note that in these embedded structures, the QP moves to the front of the embedded CP, in the same way the QP does when the question stands alone. However, we do not find T-to-C movement. In other words, there is no inversion of modals and auxiliaries and we do not use dummy *do*. The structure of (59) is illustrated in (61), which is similar to what we have been practicing.

- The QP *who* is merged as the complement of the verb *loves*. The VP is projected.
- The VP merges with T, which projects TP. In T we find the tense features.
- The subject *Lucy* then merges in the specifier of T.
- C, with the feature [+Q], is merged, indicating the clause is a question.
- QP *who* moves into the specifier of C, leaving behind a copy. There is, however, no movement of T to C.
- The whole embedded CP then merges with the main clause *I asked*.

(61) I asked who Lucy loves.

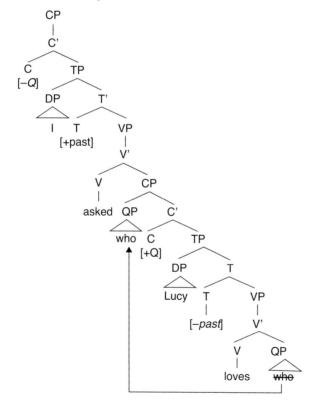

Points to Remember about Building *Wh*-questions

- Inversion applies in *wh*-questions just as it applies in *yes/no* questions. In other words, T moves to C.
- As in *yes/no* questions, if there is a modal or auxiliary in T, the modal or auxiliary will move to C, leaving a copy behind. If there is no modal or auxiliary in T, we must use *do* to carry the features of T.
- There are exceptions to T-to-C movement: (a) when QP represents the subject of the sentence and (b) in embedded questions.
- The QP may be represented by one word (who, what, where, etc.) or by many (how many books, what color, whose essay).
- QPs in English are merged as subjects, complements, or adjuncts, but they generally move to the beginning of the structure, into the specifier of C.
- QPs in some languages may remain in the position where they merge.

PAUSE AND REFLECT 5.16

Build the trees to represent the following questions. Before you attempt to do so, try to determine what the role of the question word is, for example, whether it is a subject, a complement, or an adjunct. The QP *when* will always represent an adjunct. Also remember that *how many balls* constitutes a QP that has moved from the complement position. Do not attempt to break it down into parts. Use triangles for DPs.

  i. Why did the clowns attend the parade?
 ii. Who found the wallet?
iii. How many balls did the golfer lose?
 iv. Craig wondered who Lucy had seen.

5.7.4 Passive: An Instance of DP Movement

Consider the sentences in (62).

(62) a. The police arrested Mr. Jones.
b. Mr. Jones was arrested (by the police).

Both (a) and (b) have similar meaning, but (62a) is an **active sentence** while (62b) is a **passive sentence**. In English, the passive is formed with the auxiliary *be* and the past participle of the main verb (i.e., *gone, eaten, broken*). In example (62b), the past participle is *arrested*.

Linguists assume that the active and the passive forms of a sentence are related to each other, which serves to explain the similarity in meaning. The active is the basic structure, and by moving different phrases we obtain the passive.

Two things happen in the passive:

- The agent of the action has lost importance. In fact, the agent can be omitted. As you saw in example (62b), we can simply say *Mr. Jones was arrested*.
- The complement of the verb has been promoted, it is now the subject of the sentence.

In (62b) we know that the phrase *Mr. Jones* is originally the complement of the verb because *arrest* is a transitive verb. Omitting the complement makes the sentence ungrammatical, as seen in (63). The complement must move to subject position to form the passive.

(63) *The police arrested.

The movement of the complement DP is illustrated in the tree diagram in (64). As usual, we cross out the complement to indicate it is not pronounced.

(64) Mr. Jones was arrested.

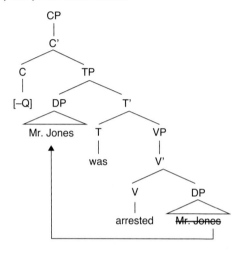

EYES ON WORLD LANGUAGES: PASSIVES IN OTHER LANGUAGES

In English, passives involve the verb *be* and the past participle of the main verb, as in *was arrested* in Example (64). In other languages, the formation of the passive may be quite different. For example, in the Inuktitut example below (from Allen & Crago 1996), the complement becomes a subject, but instead of an auxiliary verb and a main verb, the morphology of the main verb is changed to indicate that the sentence is passive. The use of the passive is much more frequent in Inuktitut, and is learned very early by young children, unlike the English passive that is quite difficult to acquire and is used more rarely.

a.   **Jaaniup iqaluk nirijanga.**
     Johnny fish   ate
     "Johnny ate fish."

b.   **Iqaluk Jaanimut   nirijaujuq**
     fish   Johnny-by   eat-passive
     "The fish was eaten by Johnny."

5.8 We All Speak the Same Language

In spite of the differences you may find between the languages you speak and other languages, there are a great many commonalities that all languages share. This leads many linguists to argue that these commonalities are evidence for a set of principles that are part of a **Universal Grammar (UG)**. For example, all languages have recursion, the ability to apply X-bar structure, heads of phrases, and distinctions between complements and adjuncts. UG is therefore part of the mind/brain of all human beings. We say it is part of our competence. **Competence** is the underlying structure, while **performance** is the use of that structure to produce or understand speech.

Why then do we not understand each other? The simplest reason is that languages do not differ very much in their syntax, rather the differences lie in the lexicon. This is rather obvious, in English we say *table*, in German we say *Tisch*, in Spanish we say *mesa*. But it is more complicated than this, because features such as *tense* or *gender* and functional categories such as *determiner* or *modal* are also considered part of the lexicon, and they may or may not be included in a particular language.

Differences in the lexicon have enormous effects on the syntax. For example, the feature [+/–Q] may or may not attract QP to the specifier of C.

Overarching differences between languages, often associated with functional features or categories, are referred to as **parameters**. Some of the parameters we have learned about in this chapter include:

- The pro-drop or null subject parameter.
  - ○ Languages may permit null subjects (Spanish, Chinese, Arabic).
  - ○ Languages may not permit null subjects (German, English).
- The *wh*-movement parameter.
  - ○ QP stays in the position where it originally merged (Chinese, Japanese, French).
  - ○ QP moves to the specifier of C, at the beginning of the clause (English, German, French).
- The verb inversion parameter.
  - ○ T moves to C in questions (English, Spanish, Portuguese).
  - ○ T stays in place in questions (Chinese, Japanese, Nahuatl).
- The determiner parameter.
  - ○ Language includes articles (English, Arabic, German).
  - ○ Language does not include articles (Chinese, Inuktitut, Mohawk).

SUMMARY

Sentences are not simply a collection of words set out in a string. There is an underlying structure that determines the relation between words, phrases, and clauses. We represent these relations in tree diagrams which try to capture generalities that help explain not just one language but many.

There are two operations used to build syntactic structures: Merge, which combines two elements to form a third; and move, which displaces an element from the position in which it was first merged in to another position. When elements are moved they leave behind a copy which is not pronounced. This way structure is always preserved.

All phrases, including the sentence itself, have a head, the word that determines the category of the phrase. The head of the sentence is Tense (T), therefore the sentence is a tense phrase, TP. Above TP we find CP, with features that determine the type of sentence we are building: a question or a statement.

Besides a head, phrases may have complements and specifiers. The specifier is merged right below the phrase in question (XP), immediately to the left. Subjects are merged in specifier positions.

Complements are elements that are required by the head to complete its meaning. They are merged as sisters to the head. Adjuncts representing additional information are merged further away, as sisters to X'.

After merge, elements may move to satisfy some requirement. There are two kinds of movement: head movement and phrase movement. Examples of phrase movement are question formation and passives. In questions, QPs in English move to the left edge of the sentence, the specifier of C. In passives, the complement of the verb moves to the specifier of T, the subject position. Examples of head movement include movement of T and its features to C in some questions in English and movement of V to T in languages such as French. With simple operations such as merge and move we are able to explain the structure of sentences in all languages.

Appendix

How to Build the Trees that Represent Syntactic Structures

Before beginning to build a tree, try to understand the relations between the different phrases and words. For example, determine what the subject is, the verb phrase, the complements, and the adjuncts. Although we generally build the tree from the bottom up, it is important to see with your mind's eye what the general structure is. We will practice with a simple sentence.

i.   I will wash these dishes in the morning.

You probably see already that the subject is *I*, there is a modal *will*, and the main verb is *wash*. The verb is transitive and, as expected, it has a complement, *these dishes*. There is also an adjunct in the verb phrase, *in the morning*.

We will start with the adjunct *in the morning*.

- First, we determine the category of the rightmost word: it is a noun. Therefore, it will project a NP.

- We then merge the second rightmost word *the*. It is a determiner, so it will project a DP. The NP is the sister of D because it is the complement of D.

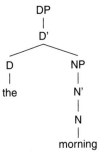

- To complete the adjunct phrase, we merge the final element, *in*. We identify it as a preposition. We build a prepositional phrase: *in the morning*.

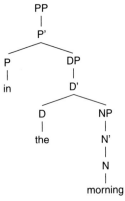

We will now use the operation merge in the same way to build the complement *these dishes*.

- The last word of this phrase is the noun *dishes*.

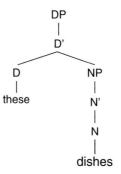

- We then merge the determiner *these*.

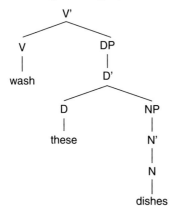

   We are now ready to merge the next word, *wash*. We determine it is a verb that will project a VP. It has a complement, and an adjunct that we have already built. V will merge first with the complement, and then with the adjunct.

- We merge V and project V'.

- We project another V′ to be able to merge the adjunct. We then build the VP.

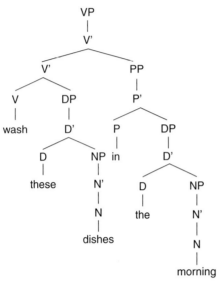

- We now have to merge the modal, *will*. It will merge as the head of T, which will be present in every clause. Recall the VP is the complement of T. T will project T′.

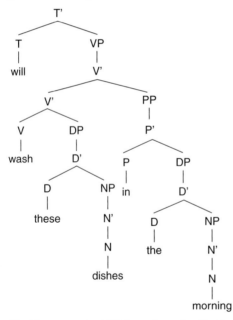

- Finally, we project TP (=sentence) with the specifier. The subject pronoun *I*, which we have identified as a DP, will be merged in the specifier. We also add CP, which carries the feature [–Q].

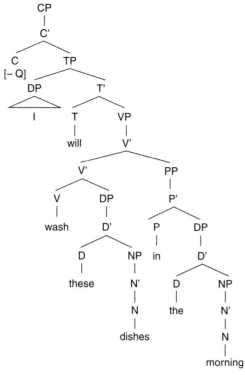

In order to practice the Move operation, we will turn our statement into a question.

ii.   What will you wash?

- We have to determine what the function of the QP is in the sentence: it is the complement of the verb *wash*. We therefore first merge the QP with the verb and project the VP.

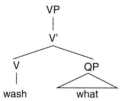

- *Will* is the head in T. We merge it with its complement, the VP *wash what*.

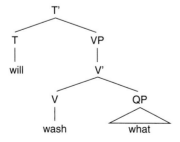

- We complete the sentence projecting TP, and merging the DP subject *you* in the specifier.

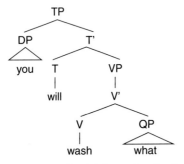

- We merge C, which carries the feature [+Q] that indicates it is a question.

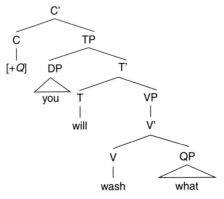

- The feature [+Q] causes inversion, that is, it attracts T to C. This is an instance of head movement. A copy is left behind in T.

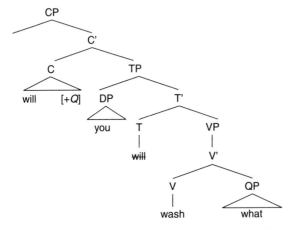

- In English, the QP also moves to CP in questions, leaving a copy behind. Copies are not pronounced.

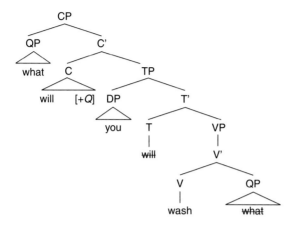

EXERCISES

5.1 What information is represented in syntactic tree diagrams?

5.2 Determine the category of each of the following words.

orchard	distraction	apply	over	absolutely
could	his	sell	seem	beside

5.3 Are the following verbs transitive or intransitive?

drink	swim	ask	dance	implement

5.4 Do the underlined words form a constituent? If the answer is yes, use at least one constituency test to show this is the case, and indicate what type of constituent it is and which is the head. If the sentence is ambiguous, answer for each possible interpretation.

 i.   I have to look <u>after my dog</u> next week.
 ii.   We could <u>have the picnic in the kitchen</u>.
 iii. Martha <u>is actively trying</u> to destroy the career of the minister.
 iv.   John decided <u>to quit last month</u>.
 v.   I may <u>be mistaken</u>.
 vi.   I ate <u>the cheese on the counter</u>.
 vii. <u>The house that we inspected</u> was sold.
 viii. I left <u>the money for the rent in the kitchen</u>.

5.5 Imagine you are teaching syntax. How would you convince a student that a moved element leaves a copy behind?

5.6 Where are the underlined elements first merged: as the head of C, T, V; in the specifier of C, T, V; or as a complement of C, T, V? If movement is involved, what is the landing cite?

    i.   I <u>will</u> pay you tomorrow.
    ii.   <u>The window</u> was broken (by the kids).
    iii.   <u>The boy</u> ate all the pancakes.
    iv.   <u>What</u> did Mary buy?
    v.   I <u>put</u> the books on the table.
    vi.   What <u>can</u> you do in the library?

5.7 Draw trees for the following phrases.

    i.   the yellow road
    ii.   the building on the left
    iii.   the cat in the red hat
    iv.   to the park
    v.   very big
    vi.   beside the tall ship
    vii.   the table by the door
    viii. run fast
    ix.   always practice your syntax
    x.   the pink flowers in the basket

5.8 Draw trees for the following sentences. Use triangles for DPs, PPs, APs, and AdvPs.

    i.   My sister is climbing a tree.
    ii.   You drove the car down the hill.
    iii.   Ryan Gosling won the Oscar.
    iv.   Helen came to the party late.
    v.   Erika does not like her neighbors. (Consult Chapter 5's 'Delving Deeper' on the website to accompany this book at www.cambridge.org/introducing-linguistics for information about negation).
    vi.   The students should learn the dates.
    vii.   Those kids are running on the road.
    viii. I will arrive at noon.
    ix.   She is always dancing.
    x.   We could not finish the exercises. (Consult Chapter 5's 'Delving Deeper' on the website to accompany this book at www.cambridge.org/introducing-linguistics for information about negation).

5.9 Draw trees for the following sentences. Use triangles for DPs, PPs, APs, and AdvPs.

    i.   I know who cheated.
    ii.   The man said he could speak German.
    iii.   The dishes were washed early.
    iv.   When did her sister win the prize?
    v.   Has he decided whether he loves Mary?
    vi.   Which book did you misplace?
    vii.   Who did you see at the supermarket?
    viii. Who came to the party?

5.10 Draw trees for the following sentences in different languages. First you must determine whether the language is like English, in which objects follow verbs, or the reverse, like Japanese.

    i.   Meri elmalar yedi.   (Turkish)
         Mary apples ate
         "Mary ate apples."

ii.	Meri yürüdü.	(Turkish)
	Mary walked	
	"Mary walked."	
iii.	Ich habe ein Buch gelesen.	(German)
	I have a book read	
	"I have read a book."	
iv.	Was wird Ingrid tun?	(German)
	what will Ingrid do	
	"What will Ingrid do?"	
v.	Mi ta lesa e buki.	(Papiamentu)
	I am read a book	
	"I am reading a book."	
vi.	Wo gege pingchang he pijiu.	(Chinese, from Yuan, 2001)
	my brother usually drinks wine	
	"My brother usually drinks wine."	

5.11 The following sentence is ambiguous. Draw two trees to express the interpretations.

    i.   He kept the vase in the cabinet.

5.12 For most speakers, the contraction of *want to* into *wanna* is acceptable in most situations. There are exceptions, however, as the examples below show. Try to explain why contraction is possible in (i–b) but it is not possible in (ii–b). Focus on the fact that moved elements leave a copy behind.

    (i)   a.   What do you want to win?

          b.   What do you wanna win?

    (ii)   a.   Who do you want to win the race?

          b.   *Who do you wanna win the race?

5.13 In section 5.8 you read about a few parameters that distinguish between languages. Go through these parameters and give a grammatical and an ungrammatical example that shows how English stands with regards to each parameter. To start you off we supply examples for the first one:

Null Subject Parameter: English Requires Subjects

    i.   John wants a chocolate bar.
    ii.   *wants a chocolate bar.

5.14 Consider the following ungrammatical sentences. Using your knowledge of structure, explain in each case why the sentence is incorrect.

    i.   *Child eats a lot of junk food.
    ii.   *Who John saw?
    iii. *Rudolph eats quickly his salad.
    iv. *I don't know John came when.
    v.   *Bought Mary a new car.

5.15 In English it is possible for a sentence to include both a modal and an auxiliary. Be creative and find a way to represent the structure of the sentence in (i). You will have to add a phrase we have not used so far in this textbook. Hint: It is AuxP.

i.   I could have eaten a horse.

REFERENCES

Allen, S., & Crago, M. (1996). Early passive acquisition in Inuktitut. *Journal of Child Language, 23*(1), 129–155.

Baker, M. (1996). *The polysynthesis parameter.* Oxford: Oxford University Press.

Lightbown, P., & Spada, N. (2013). *How languages are learned* (4th Edition). Oxford: Oxford University Press.

Radford, A. (2004). *Minimalist syntax: Exploring the structure of English.* Cambridge: Cambridge University Press.

Yuan, B. (2001). The status of thematic verbs in the second language acquisition of Chinese: Against inevitability of thematic-verb raising in second language acquisition. *Second Language Research, 17*(3), 248–272.

6 Semantics

Language and Meaning
Roumyana Slabakova

OVERVIEW

In this chapter, you will develop an understanding of the linguistic field of semantics, the study of meaning in language. Semantics describes how speakers/writers encode meaning and how listeners/readers comprehend it. In this chapter, we aim to:

- **compare and contrast different types of meaning in language;**
- **explore how meaning is captured in words and how words are related to each other based on meaning;**
- **describe how we put together word meanings to come up with phrase meaning;**
- **look at how phrases are combined to create sentence meaning; and**
- **examine some theoretical approaches to studying meaning in language.**

6.1 What Is Semantics?

The subject of **semantics** is the systematic study of the meaning of linguistic expressions. Every linguistic expression, be it morphemes, words, phrases, sentences, even text, has its own meaning.

Linguistic meanings are also put together into larger units following semantic rules. The term which linguists use for this process is "semantic composition", and we will discuss various tenets of this process in the chapter.

6.1.1 Semantic Rules

Before we go on, it is important to appreciate that meaning comes to us, language users, without explicitly thinking about it: it comes automatically, effortlessly, and immediately when we hear a sentence. Also immediately, we recognize when a sentence is perfectly put together grammatically, but makes no sense whatsoever. The famous sentence by Noam Chomsky comes to mind: *Colorless green ideas sleep furiously* (Chomsky, 1957, p. 15). The sentence breaks so many unwritten semantic rules: ideas don't have color, an object cannot be green and colorless at the same time, ideas don't sleep, and even if they do, can that happen furiously? Consider that no one has taught you the semantic rules that are broken in this sentence. How do you know them? You do because a great many semantic rules are universal, that is, they come to us from our general knowledge of language, as well as knowledge of the world around us, without the need for teaching or even thinking.

PAUSE AND REFLECT 6.1

There is a famous poem by William Carlos Williams (1923). You may have already seen it.

The Red Wheelbarrow by William Carlos Williams

so much depends upon
a red wheel barrow
glazed with rain water
beside the white chickens

Does this poem break any semantic rules of putting words together in a meaningful way? Discuss how the phrases fit together. What makes the overall meaning of the poem so elusive, so difficult to pinpoint?

6.1.2   Types of Meaning

Different linguistic expressions have meanings of their own, and it helps to keep those apart when we talk about semantics. Words, or lexical items, are stored in our mental lexicon. So, first, we have **lexical meaning**, the meaning encoded in the words or parts of words. Lexical meanings can combine, too. Consider *water* and *fall*, two words that we know and can use separately. When they combine in the compound noun *waterfall*, the meaning is different (see Chapter 4 Morphology). Linguists say that the compound lexical meaning is *composed* from the meanings of the ingredient words. There are rules for this composition that we know without thinking: for example, *chocolate cake* is a kind of cake, and not a kind of chocolate. This rule becomes even clearer when we consider *birthday cake*. We shall see more of these rules in Section 6.2.

Still at the level of morphemes and words, we have to appreciate the contribution of **grammatical**, or functional morphemes to meaning. As a very simple example, take the past tense morpheme in English. The sentences *Jane work-s in the library* and *Jane work-ed in the library* do not mean the same thing. The first sentence describes a habitual situation coinciding with the present moment while the second sentence captures a situation that was true at some time in the past. This meaning difference is imparted by the –s and –ed tense endings.

Next, think of the meaning of plural and how we mark it in English. The meaning *more than one* is different from idiosyncratic lexical meanings, because it can apply to many lexical items: *ball–balls, child–children*, etc. Note that usually the plural member of the singular–plural opposition is marked with an additional morpheme. A different marking exists in Majang, an Eastern Sudanic language spoken by around 33,000

**LINGUISTICS TIDBITS 6.1:
RELATIONAL ADJECTIVES**
Let's take the adjectives *large* and *small*. They can only be interpreted in relation to some standard given by the rest of the phrase. *A small elephant* is a much larger animal than *a large butterfly*. When we say *a small elephant*, we intuitively reason that this animal is small in comparison to a typically sized elephant, and not in comparison to butterflies.

people in Ethiopia. In this language, the collective form of the noun is unmarked: *ŋɛɛti* "lice", contrasting with the marked singular *ŋɛɛti-n* "louse", but the grammatical meaning remains largely the same (Pereltsvaig, 2012, p. 109). No sentence can be interpreted without taking grammatical meaning into consideration. Tense and aspect, gender and number, definite and indefinite are some examples of grammatical meanings.

Phrasal or sentence semantics describes the patterns and rules for building more elaborate meanings, up to the level of sentence meanings. For example, we can add the demonstrative pronoun *this* to the compound noun *waterfall* and get the noun phrase *this waterfall*. We can also expand the noun phrase by adding an adjective, as in *this beautiful waterfall*. It is interesting to note that some words change meaning depending on the phrase they are in.

When we combine lexical items and grammatical morphemes to make a complete sentence, word order is very important. Think of how many different phrases or sentences we can compose from the mix of words and morphemes that follows within the curly brackets {*the, that, fat, cat, rat, chased*}, using some of them twice.

(1) a. That fat cat chased the rat.
     b. The cat that chased the fat rat.
     c. The rat chased that fat cat.

PAUSE AND REFLECT 6.2

Can you go on? The meaning of example (1a) is very different from that of (1c). What has changed, if we are using the exact same words?

The word order is all-important. In English, for example, the first noun phrase (*the fat cat* in (1a)) tells us who the doer of the action is; the noun phrase after the verb is usually the creature or thing affected by the action. Let's take another example, this time from French (Dekydtspotter & Sprouse, 2001):

(2) *Qui de célèbre fumait au bistro dans les années 70?*
     Who of famous smoked in the bar in the years 70?
     "Which famous person smoked in bars in the 70s?"

(3) *Qui fumait de célèbre au bistro dans les années 70?*
     Who smoked of famous in the bar in the years 70s?
     "Which famous person smoked in bars in the 70s?"

If you look at the examples (2) and (3) carefully, you will see small changes in the word order. In (2) the interrogative phrase *qui de célèbre* "which famous person" appears together, while in (3) it is split in two by the verb form *fumait* "smoked". The question in (2) is ambiguous as it can be answered with a present and a past celebrity, that is, someone who was famous in the 70s but now may be forgotten, such as actress Farrah Fawcett, as well as someone who is famous now but was not so famous in the 70s, such as journalist and TV celebrity Oprah Winfrey. (A person such as the singer Leonard Cohen who was famous in the 70s and is still famous today would be a good answer, too.) I am sure you can substitute other current and past celebrities' names. Importantly, the question in (3) does not have the two interpretations that (2) has: it can only be answered with a past celebrity. This very subtle change in meaning is signaled by nothing else but the discontinuous interrogative.

Finally, although we will not discuss pragmatic meaning much in this chapter (see Chapter 10 Pragmatics), we have to distinguish it from phrasal and sentence meaning. Pragmatic meaning depends on knowledge of the world and the situation surrounding the conversation. If I am discussing what type of restaurant to go to with my friend, and I say *Do you like sushi?* she is likely to interpret this as an encouragement to go to a Japanese place. But if a doctor asks the same question of his pregnant patient, he may want to discuss which type of raw fish is safe for her to eat during pregnancy. Furthermore, if I am considering how to lose weight and talking about it with my friend, his mentioning sushi could mean that he is suggesting a fish-rich diet. These are only three of the many possible sentence interpretations that would depend on the interlocutors, the question under discussion, where the sentence is uttered, and under what circumstances. Pragmatics enriches the interpretation resulting from the mapping of lexical meanings and structure by putting it all in context. Can you think of some other, context-dependent meanings of the same question *Do you like sushi?*

Think of another type of pragmatic meaning supplied by the context: the **deictic meaning**. Deixis comes from the Greek word for the here and now. If you hear the sentence *She is here*, you will interpret it to mean that a context-identified person of female gender is in the vicinity of the speaker. The exact location of *here* is not specified by the words of this sentence, but the language faculty tells you how to consult your non-linguistic knowledge to find that location. You can think of this instruction as the meaning of *here*, which is fixed based on the observable context and situation every time it is used. Other deictic expressions include *yesterday, today, tomorrow, now*, the pronouns *I* and *you*, and even the past tense itself, which is linked to the moment of speaking.

Sometimes sentence meaning is open to more than one interpretation, as in the case of a famous 1953 murder trial in Britain. Bentley was a young man who was on trial for his involvement in a police officer's murder. Bentley didn't pull the trigger himself, but when his accomplice was cornered by the ill-fated officer, Bentley was heard to yell, *Let him have it!* Bentley's defense attorney argued that command was intended to mean, *Let him have the gun*, while Crown prosecutors insisted it was an idiomatic instruction to shoot the officer. Both interpretations are possible, but the judge preferred the prosecution's interpretation, and Bentley was sentenced to death.

PAUSE AND REFLECT 6.3

Which word is the source of ambiguity in the Bentley murder case? Does pragmatics play a role in the interpretation?

PAUSE AND REFLECT 6.4

Imagine that you ask someone *what is the meaning of life?* and his/her response is *I don't know, the internet is down.* What is the type of meaning here? Is it any of the meanings we discussed above? How so, or why not?

To sum up, in this section we distinguished between lexical, grammatical, phrasal, and sentence meaning (the true object of the description of semantics), and pragmatic meaning. We also described deictic meaning, which depends on the time and place of the utterance.

6.2 Meaning of Words

6.2.1 Denotation and Connotation, Reference, and Sense

When thinking about meaning, most people think of the meaning of lexical items. This makes a lot of sense. One of the first things children acquiring their native language do is learn a list of words, starting with concrete nouns such as *mummy, cup, water*, etc., and build on them. Adult second language learners have the advantage of a native mental lexicon, so they associate the new language lexical meanings with the native ones. If I tell you that *mesa* in Spanish means "table", you access your English lexical item, situated in a vast network of other lexical items, to align the new form with that meaning (especially if you are a beginner in Spanish).

The **denotation** of a word or a phrase is its literal, dictionary meaning. Another way to think of it is as the associated concept that the word triggers in the mind of most speakers of a language. When a *chair* is mentioned, most people imagine a standard-issue piece of furniture to sit on, concentrating mostly on its function. Look at the chairs in Figure 6.1. Which one of them contains the prototypical chair, in your view?

Furthermore, there may be some emotional and cultural meaning associated with a word, known as **connotation**. Denotation and connotation are two aspects of the same linguistic sign. Discuss possible connotations related to the chairs in Figure 6.1. The name *Hollywood* refers to a neighborhood of Los Angeles where the film industry is concentrated. But its connotation is one of glamor and glitz, celebrity and dreams of stardom. A *dove* is a type of bird, but it is associated with peace and gentleness.

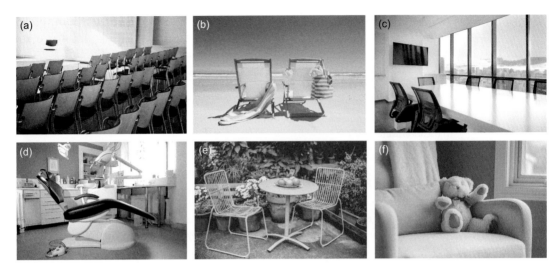

Figure 6.1 Chairs

Politician has a negative connotation of a scheming, insincere person. Let's take as another example: the words *house* and *home*. These words have very similar denotations, a house denotes a building while a home denotes a place where people live. For many people, *home* has the additional connotation of a sense of belonging and comfort, while *house* conveys little more than a structure. That is why, when you are talking to a real estate agent who is trying to sell you a house, she or he will be talking of selling you *a home*.

EYES ON WORLD LANGUAGES: DENOTATION AND CONNOTATION

The connotation of a word depends on cultural context and personal associations. The example of the difference between *house* and *home* may not be easily translatable to other languages. For example, Bulgarian, a Slavic language, has the two lexical items: [kəʃta] "house" and [dɔm] "home", while Russian only has [dɔm] for both meanings and their additional connotations. Try to think of languages that you know and check whether this particular pair exists. Think of other examples where very similar denotations would have different connotations.

The relationship between the next two terms used to define meaning is a bit more complex and subtle. The German philosopher Gottlob Frege proposed that the meaning of an expression is called **sense**, and if the expression refers to something or someone, it has **reference**. Reference is that part of meaning through which a speaker indicates which person or object in the outside world is being pointed to or talked about. When I say *My daughter lives in San Francisco*, I *refer* to a person and a city. Talking of sense, we are dealing with meaning relationships inside language; talking of reference, we are dealing with relationships between language and the world. The linguistic expression *my daughter* has a sense, that is, meaning; it also refers to a real person out there in the world that you can meet or see. She is not part of language, although the *expression* with which I refer to her has a linguistic sense.

To clarify sense and reference further, think of the following question. Who would be the referent of the phrase *the present Prime Minister of Canada* if someone pronounced this phrase in 1992? Is it the same person we refer to now? We can think of one sense with several possible referents. The reference of an expression may vary according to the circumstances (time, place, etc.) and even the topic of the conversation. In the same way, I sometimes designate my daughter by other means, calling her *my baby,* or if I am talking with my son, *your sister.* Since we are talking about the same person, there is one referent with many senses, depending on the relationship of the interlocutor and my mood. Virtually every object or person can have several senses. Think of Bruce Wayne and Batman, Clark Kent and Superman!

Names (e.g., Leonard Cohen, Oprah Winfrey) are referential; they have little or no sense. The term *father,* which has the sense A MALE PARENT, refers to anyone who falls under this description. When capitalized, Father can refer to a contextually identified male parent, for example, the speaker's father. As a rule, all dictionary definitions define sense, not reference. Verbs, much like nouns, have sense, not reference. When used in a concrete utterance, verbs together with the other words point to a state or event, so they assume reference.

6.2.2   Componential Analysis

Componential analysis of word meaning is an approach that equates a word's meaning with a number of smaller components called semantic features. Word meanings are defined in terms of necessary and sufficient features (the features are necessary in that no entity which does not possess the full set is a member of the category; and they are sufficient in that possession of all the features guarantees membership). Here are some examples:

(4)   Semantic feature composition for *man, boy, woman, girl*

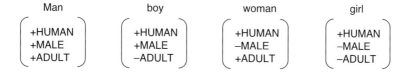

Man	boy	woman	girl
+HUMAN	+HUMAN	+HUMAN	+HUMAN
+MALE	+MALE	−MALE	−MALE
+ADULT	−ADULT	+ADULT	−ADULT

Componential analysis is effective when representing similarities and differences among words with related meanings. It allows us to group entities into natural classes (similar to phonology); e.g., *man* and *woman* fall together in a class defined by the features [+HUMAN, +ADULT]. Such binary features are very useful when describing semantic categories of nouns, e.g., [±COMMON], [±COUNT], etc. or verbs, e.g., [±STATIVE],

[±TELIC], etc. In general, componential analysis is convenient in defining sense relations such as synonymy and antonymy (see Section 6.2.3).

However, its use is limited when we need to define semantic fields that do not lend themselves to binary description, such as color terms, a set of eating utensils, cars, etc.

6.2.3 Synonymy, Antonymy, Hyponymy, Polysemy, and Homonymy

All these terms are considered to be sense relations, that is, the senses of words are related to each other based on certain mappings such as partial overlap, identity, etc. They are called paradigmatic semantic relations between words and they are relevant to the organization of our mental lexicon. Words whose senses are closely related are usually retrieved faster together, or the appearance of one helps the faster retrieval of the other.

Before we embark on this discussion, though, let us look at the sense terms themselves: Synonymy, antonymy, hyponymy, polysemy, and homonymy. These are clearly of Greek origin, and it will be helpful to think of the meanings of the roots and prefixes that make up these terms. This morphological analysis will help you to remember their definitions. The roots are *–nym–* "name", *–phon–* "sound", *–graph–* "writing", and *–sem–* "meaning".

PAUSE AND REFLECT 6.5

Define the meanings of the prefixes *homo-, poly-, ant(i)-, hyp(o)-, and syn-*. They are common derivational morphemes of many English words.

Let's start with **synonyms**. These are words or expressions that have the same or partially the same sense. Although their meanings may overlap, they are rarely exactly the same. If you think about it, this makes sense. Why would a language have two words with exactly the same meaning? Perfect synonyms are hard to find, but here are some examples: *stubborn* and *obstinate*, *freedom* and *liberty*. However, even complete synonyms cannot be used interchangeably, as you will realize when you try to use *freedom* and *liberty* in sentences and then switch them around. One can *take* or *have the liberty*, but one *has* or is *given the freedom* to do something. If you hear the sentence *I am not at freedom to disclose the names …*, you know that something subtle is wrong with it, and the correct expression is *I am not at liberty to disclose the names …*

Next, think of the synonyms *answer*, *response*, and *reply*; do they overlap completely in meaning and usage? When we say *question and …*, the word that follows is not *reply*. We can enrich our mental lexicons by studying lists of synonyms, such as *intelligent, smart, bright, brilliant, sharp*, etc.

It is possible for synonyms to belong to different dialects or varieties within a language, such as *truck* and *lorry*, *elevator* and *lift*, *fall* and *autumn* in North American and

British English. Synonyms are also distinguished on the basis of register, or degree of formality: although *child* and *kid* have similar senses, *kid* belongs to the informal register.

Antonyms are words or phrases expressing opposite senses. Again, this relation is better considered with examples. There are binary antonyms, such as *true* and *false*, where another state of affairs outside of these two is impossible to consider. That which is not true is false. Another way to view this relationship is to say that a word is a binary antonym of another word if it entails the negative of the first word (see Section 6.3.4 on entailment). However, *hot* is not the only antonym of *cold*, because there is also *warm*. These are degree adjectives and their relationship is on a scale.

Now, recall the semantic features we exemplified in (4), specifically [±MALE], [±ADULT]. We can use them to distribute the words *man, woman, boy*, and *girl* into antonym pairs based on those features: *man* and *woman* are opposites with respect to which feature? How about *bachelor, spinster, husband*, and *wife*? What is the second semantic feature that we need in order to distinguish *bachelor* from *husband*? Are the terms *synonym* and *antonym* opposite in meaning, hence antonyms?

Hyponymy is the relationship where the meaning of one word is a subset, or included in the meaning of the other. Some classic examples come from biology, where *animal, bovine*, and *cow* are each a hyponym of the previous one. A bovine is a type of animal, a cow is a type of bovine. *Oak, beech*, and *sycamore* are kinds of tree, so they are hyponyms of *tree*. Arrange *daisy, plant*, and *flower* on a hyponym scale as we saw above. When thinking about hyponymy, one should be careful to consider complete, not partial, inclusion of the sense of the words.

The next two terms, polysemy and homonymy, describe word relations that are a matter of degree. A word is **polysemous** if it has more than one sense, or meaning. Very often, the senses are closely related. For example, *mouth* of a river and *mouth* of a human being may be included in the dictionary as two different senses, but a proficient speaker of English can see the relation between them. This is also the case with the two meanings of *ceiling* as (a) the top-most part of a room and (b) the upper limit. English verbs are exceptionally polysemous: how many meanings of the verb *run* can you think of? Consider just three phrases: *run a computer program, run the risk*, and *run a department*. Is there a similarity among their meanings that is due to the verb *run*? Linguists argue that a lot of verbs change meaning slightly based on the object that they combine with.

When the two or more meanings of a word are considered sufficiently different, such as *bank* of a river and *bank* as in the financial institution, they are considered **homonyms**, or two different names. In the dictionary, these words will have separate entries and the overlap in form (both sound and orthography!) is a matter of mere accident or coincidence. Of course, sometimes it is difficult to judge whether two senses are related or not. Some examples include *train*, *port*, and *fall*. In such cases, the trusted lexicographer, the author of the dictionary, is your best friend.

PAUSE AND REFLECT 6.6

Think of the two meanings of "doctor" when someone says "So what if I doctored the documents? I am a doctor." Are the two uses related? Does it matter that one is a verb and the other a noun? Is *doctor* polysemous or are we dealing with two homonyms? Discuss whether polysemy occurs when a verb is turned into a noun, and vice versa.

To recapitulate, in this section we saw that sense relations between words and expressions can go in a positive direction, as in adding related meanings (synonyms, hyponyms, polysemous words) or in a negative direction, creating opposing pairs (antonyms, homonyms). It is easier to learn and retain words in memory if we can relate them in systematic ways. It is very likely that lexical entries are organized along semantic network lines in our mental lexicons.

LINGUISTIC TIDBITS: HOMOPHONES AND HOMOGRAPHS

Besides homonyms, names completely overlapping in form but not in meaning, we also distinguish homophones and homographs. Checking the Latin roots given in the beginning of this section, can you define homophones and homographs? Give some examples.

6.2.4 Verb Meaning and Subcategorization

Verbs are the most important words in a language and are crucial ingredients in the sentences they participate in. Why is that? Verbs carry a lot of grammatical information, impose a number of requirements and constitute the hub around which the other phrases in the sentence revolve. What do we know when we know a verb in our native or second or additional language? Apart from knowing its form and idiosyncratic meaning, we know how many arguments it needs to combine with in order to produce an acceptable verbal phrase, and then an acceptable sentence. Arguments represent the indispensable participants in the situation denoted by the verb, without which the verb phrase will be unacceptable. Let's take the verb *put* as in (5a).

(5) a. Jane put <u>the cake in the fridge</u>.
     b. *Jane put the cake.
     c. *Jane put in the fridge.
     d. *Jane put.

The sentence in (5a) describes a placing action with three participants (underlined). When a speaker of English knows the verb *put*, she knows that it needs to combine with three arguments (noun phrases and prepositional phrases). One argument is the doer of the action, *Jane*; the second argument is the thing affected by the action or changing location, *the cake*; and the third argument is the location, *in the fridge*. None of these arguments can be omitted; otherwise the sentence would sound strange. Linguists call sentences in (5b)–(5d) ungrammatical, and designate them with a star before the example. All three arguments are necessary to describe the situation adequately: this is ensured by the requirements of the verb *put*.

You can think of these requirements as syntactic requirements: the verb wants to combine with a certain number of arguments as syntactic constituents in the sentence. However, verbs impose some semantic requirements on their arguments, as well. Consider the sentence in (6).

(6)   #Jane put the lake/the sky in the fridge.

This sentence is not syntactically odd because the verb has three arguments, but still does not make sense. It is odd because the affected argument is not puttable: you can't put a lake or the sky anywhere. Such requirements are called semantic requirements or restrictions. Note that the unacceptable sentence is marked with a # hashtag symbol this time, indicating lack of semantic wellformedness.

Let's return to verbal syntactic requirements. These are known as subcategorization, a pretty long term that is actually not as complicated as it sounds (see Chapter 5 Syntax). It just means that a verb needs to combine, or a verb subcategorizes for, a number of arguments, as we saw above. Verbs such as *put* that need three arguments (including the subject) are called **ditransitive verbs**. Other examples include *send* and *place*. Those verbs that need two arguments, in other words they are unacceptable without an object, are **transitive**. Most English verbs fall into that category; examples include *drink, eat, allege*, and many, many others. Note that the argument of *allege* can be a whole clause such as *He alleges that he was framed*. Verbs that take only one argument, the subject, are known as **intransitive**. Some examples are *smile, sneeze*, and *fall*.

We shall make a further distinction among intransitive verbs, because not all intransitive verbs are created equal. The division into **unaccusative** and **unergative** verbs is very often made in syntax, because these classes of verbs have distinct syntactic behavior.[1] However, we are mentioning them here because they have distinct meaning as well. With unaccusative verbs, the one argument is affected by the action, frequently in an adverse way. For example, *fall* is an unaccusative verb, as the participant is not in control of the action, falling just happens to him or her. On the other hand, *smile* is unergative because the participant can initiate this action. We shall come back to this distinction between intransitive verbs when we discuss thematic roles in Section 6.3.6.

PAUSE AND REFLECT 6.7

Can you come up with more examples of unaccusative and unergative classes of intransitive verbs?

---

[1] The terms "unaccusative" and "unergative" are difficult to remember because their names are based on theory-internal analyses. However, nothing hinges on these names for now, and you can call them intransitive verbs class A and class B. The point is that they are systematically different.

Sometimes arguments can be implied and not overtly mentioned in the sentence, but we can uncover their denotation from the verb's meaning and from knowledge of the world. Take the examples in (7).

(7) a. She is expecting her guests at 8.
     b. She is expecting.
     c. I have eaten/I just ate.

What does (7b) mean? Although *expect*, a transitive verb as shown in (7a), is left without an object, we know that the sentence in (7b) involves an implied object, *a baby*. It cannot mean anything else, such as *she is expecting a ship/piece of news*. Implied objects make up part of the whole message, although we don't hear them.

PAUSE AND REFLECT 6.8

Think about how we know the meaning of implied objects. Consider the sentence in (7c). What can the silent but implied object refer to?

Discussing subcategorization brings us to the important realization that verb meanings and their arguments, hence their syntactic behavior, are intimately related. I shall exemplify this further by discussing the four **aspectual classes of verbs** proposed by the philosopher Zeno Vendler. This distinction applies to verbs and their participant argument, so to verb phrases. The four classes shown in (8) are universal, that is, they are distinguishable in all languages of the world. In English, their meanings are related to the form and shape of the object argument (the affected participant).

(8) Aspectual classes of verb phrases:
     a. States: *resemble someone, be white, be tired*
     b. Activities: *eat sushi, drink cider, swim in the pool*
     c. Accomplishments: *eat ten pieces of sushi, drink a bottle of cider, swim to the other bank*
     d. Achievements: *realize, knock, reach the summit*

The class of states includes verbs denoting a situation without change: *I resemble my father* is not a dynamic situation. The other three classes are known as dynamic verb classes, in opposition to states. Activities are situations in which some action is going on, but there is no inherent endpoint to it. *He swam in the pool for an hour* is a sentence with an activity verb phrase, because the action is presented as ongoing during a time interval. One can swim in the pool for an hour without reaching an endpoint: the action can be terminated but not completed.

Accomplishments, on the other hand, have an endpoint specified by their internal argument, the object or prepositional phrase. Compare activities to accomplishments with the verb *swim* as in (8c). Swimming to the other bank of the river is different from swimming in the pool, since completion of the accomplishment entails an endpoint: the reaching of the other bank. On the other hand, the activity has no completion; it can only be stopped, not finished. Finally, achievements (*realize, knock, reach the summit*) are just like accomplishments in having an inherent endpoint, but reaching that endpoint is instantaneous.

Now, we have just demonstrated that the aspectual classes of verbs have different types of meanings (roughly captured by their names). But the number and shape of their arguments differ as well.

Activities either have no arguments, or have arguments which *cannot* be counted or measured. Accomplishments have arguments that *can* be counted or measured. We can check this by transforming one class into the other. *I eat sushi* is a statement of what I normally eat, or like to eat. If we change the uncountable object *sushi* into a countable one, the verb phrase becomes an accomplishment, as in *I ate ten pieces of sushi last night*. Completed, not terminated.

EYES ON WORLD LANGUAGES: RUSSIAN ACTIVITIES AND ACCOMPLISHMENTS

We said that the shape of the object and whether it is countable or measurable determines whether a verb phrase denotes an accomplishment or an achievement. However, in Slavic languages such as Russian, a prefix on the verb signals the same information. Compare *pisat' pis'mo* "to write a letter" and *na-pisat' pis'mo* "to complete writing a letter". The verb forms differ while the objects are the same.

To sum up, we have seen that the meaning of verbs can be reflected in the arguments they subcategorize for. It can also be determined by the number and shape of the arguments they take in a specific verb phrase. The verbs are the hubs around which the arguments and the whole sentence meaning revolve.

6.2.5 Conceptual System: Fuzzy Concepts, Metaphor, and Metonymy

We tend to think that the concepts expressed by words and phrases have precise denotations with clear-cut boundaries which distinguish them from other concepts. But not all concepts are so straightforward. Some notions do not have clear-cut boundaries; they are what we call *fuzzy* concepts. Many linguists believe that this type of fuzziness is pervasive in the human conceptual system. Recall that we mentioned gradable adjectives when we were talking about antonyms: *hot* is not the exact antonym of *cold*. There are such graded concepts in terms of typical representative.

The classical example is *bird*. What is included in the concept of *bird*? The term can have a number of hyponyms. Some cognitive linguists have argued that there are species of birds more typical of the concept, such as a robin or a hawk, while other birds such as ostrich and penguin are not as *bird-like*. This idea that concepts can be gradable and have more typical and less typical representatives gave rise to the idea of **proto-type** and **periphery** of a concept. To continue with the bird example, one could say that the robin is a prototypical bird while the penguin is not. Cognitive linguists believe that the existence of fuzzy concepts and of graded membership in concepts provides important insights into the nature of the human conceptual system.

PAUSE AND REFLECT 6.9

Looking back at Figure 6.1, which chairs are more prototypical? Why do you think this is the case?

This approach to concepts allows the linguistic phenomenon of **metaphor**: the understanding of one concept in terms of another. A metaphor applies an expression to an object, person, or event to which it is not really applicable. The use of the metaphor reveals the two seemingly incompatible objects to have some similar characteristics. You have heard the (clichéd) metaphors *Time is money*, *the apple of my eye*, and *to drown in* (e.g., *gold/tomatoes/invitations*). A wonderful metaphor due to Albert Camus is: *Within me there lay an invincible summer.* The literal meanings of these expressions are briefly considered by speakers, but because they do not make much sense, they are abandoned in favor of the figurative meanings.

Note that the principle of compositionality, that the meaning of a sentence is made up of the meanings of its ingredient words, has to be relaxed in the comprehension of metaphors. The traditional view has been that metaphors are exceptions of compositionality which belong to poetic language. Cognitive linguists Lakoff and Johnson changed this perception, arguing that metaphors are actually pervasive in language precisely because concepts have fuzzy boundaries that can be pushed by context (Lakoff & Johnson, 1980).

PAUSE AND REFLECT 6.10

In order to understand metaphors, linguistic knowledge combines with knowledge of the world as well as culture. Read the poem by American poet Sylvia Plath (published in 1959), which she wrote when she was pregnant, and consider the metaphors in it. Which metaphor of herself gives you the idea that she is talking of her pregnant state? When the playful tone changes in the second part of the poem, what do these other metaphors suggest?

Metaphors by Sylvia Plath

I'm a riddle in nine syllables, An elephant, a ponderous house,
A melon strolling on two tendrils. O red fruit, ivory, fine timbers!
This loaf's big with its yeasty rising. Money's new-minted in this fat purse.
I'm a means, a stage, a cow in calf. I've eaten a bag of green apples, Boarded the train there's no getting off.

Metonymy is similar to metaphor in that it replaces the name of an object, or person, or event, with the name of something else with which it is closely associated. A very frequent example is a place name for the people who work there or for the institution housed in them: *The Oval Office, the Prime Minister's office, 10 Downing Street, Bay Street, Brussels. A pink slip, red tape, boots on the ground, the bench, the Ivy League, and the suits* are all metonymies readily available in our English mental lexicon. Substitutions of an author for the work (*He bought an early Degas*), and a place name for the product (*We drank an excellent Côte du Rhône last night*) are also conventional metonymies. Think about what the difference is between metaphor and metonymy.

In addition to the conventional ready-made metonymies, unconventional or novel ones can be made on the fly. They include expressions we have never heard before and are highly dependent on the situation in which they are uttered. A classic example is the following type of sentence heard in a diner, as one waiter addresses another: *The ham sandwich in the corner wants another coffee.* Clearly, they are talking about a person who has ordered or is eating a ham sandwich, not about a talking and coffee-drinking sandwich.

PAUSE AND REFLECT 6.11

Try to paraphrase the following sentence: *Tell the exit row what to do in case of an accident.* What does *the exit row* refer to? Where could this sentence be uttered and by whom?

There is evidence that, in trying to understand metonymy, we pass through a check of the literal meaning, and since that does not yield a plausible meaning, the figurative one is reached. That second pass through meaning takes more time, which is measurable in psycholinguistic experiments. However, such experiments demonstrate additional processing time for unconventional metonymies only. This suggests that conventional metonymies make up part of the mental lexicon and are processed as fast as other set expressions.

In sum, metaphors and metonymy are the embodiment of the creativity of language. All speakers of a language can comprehend them because they can push the boundaries of concepts and apply them in a novel and creative way.

6.3 Meaning of Sentences

6.3.1 Sentence, Proposition, and Utterance

What do we know when we know the meaning of sentences? At this point, we must make a very important three-way distinction. We will distinguish between a sentence, a proposition, and an utterance. We shall reserve the term **sentence** for the linguistic expression, the mental structure that is part of a speaker's knowledge of language

(Chapter 5 Syntax). Sentences, are not part of the outside world, they are abstractions that live in the speaker's mind/brain. A **proposition**, on the other hand, is a logical expression, not a linguistic expression; it is a statement describing a state of affairs in the world, that may be true of the world or false. You can think of the proposition as roughly the content of the sentence. When we speak a language, we can match the linguistic expression (a sentence) with the appropriate content (a proposition).

Finally, an **utterance** is the concrete use of a linguistic expression in a context. One sentence may be uttered many times, and its meaning may change slightly depending on the context, the interlocutors, the time, the place, and so forth. *You are bad!* for example, may mean that the hearer is a morally reprehensible person, or that she is not good at something, or even that she is good at something (in some varieties of English *bad* is a synonym of *good*).

Semanticists consider the meaning of the proposition to be its truth value. For every utterance that we hear and comprehend, we can work out its proposition and whether it is true or false. Imagine that you hear the sentence *Hamburg is the capital of Germany*, you immediately know that the proposition expressed by this sentence is false. A sentence conveying a true proposition is *Berlin is the capital of Germany*. Some sentences happen to be always true, such as *Steel is a metal* and *Trees produce oxygen through photosynthesis*. For most other sentences (e.g., *Josephine is sick*), we really don't know their truth value *a priori*, but we know what the world has to be like in order for the sentence to be true.

An interesting consequence of this division of labor between sentences, propositions, and utterances is that sentences do not really carry truth value. Technically speaking, it is improper to say that a sentence is true or false. Only propositions carry truth value. So, saying something like, *The proposition expressed by sentence A is true,* is to use truth-value in a precise way; whereas, to say, *Sentence A is true,* would be technically inappropriate, but still a useful shortcut. As long as we understand this division of labor, we can take shortcuts.

6.3.2 Compositionality, Word Order, and Structural Ambiguity

How is the overall sentence meaning (the proposition) derived in the course of utterance comprehension? Every semantic theory must explain how the words and syntactic expressions in a language come to be paired with their meaning. A first, and very reasonable, guess might be that the meaning of a sentence is composed of the meanings of its words. If we know the referents of *John* and *Mary* and the situation they were in, we can give the sentence *John kissed Mary* a truth value, let's say it is true.

If lexical meanings are all there is to **compositionality**, though, we would predict that a sentence which has the same words will have the same meaning. Let's put this prediction to the test. Does *Mary kissed John* denote the same event as *John kissed Mary?* Certainly not, so this simple view of compositionality is discredited. What else can contribute to meaning formation? As our little experiment shows, the order in which the words appear in the sentence is also important, at least for languages like English.

We could say that the meaning of the sentence combines the meanings of its words as a function of their order. A preliminary definition of compositionality can be seen in (9).

(9) The meaning of a sentence is a function of the meaning of words, taking their order into account.

That cannot be the whole story, however, for languages like Russian and Polish, which mark the names *John* and *Mary* with different case endings in their equivalent sentences, and then move them around rather freely. For example, *John-SUBJECT Mary-OBJECT kissed* is a possible word order, but the mirror word order is perfectly possible, too. It appears that the grammatical function marking morphemes, the case endings, are important, too. And so are the other grammatical morphemes, in this case the past tense ending *–ed*. Our definition then, has to take a more general form:

(10) The meaning of a sentence is a function of the meaning of its grammatical and lexical morphemes, taking their order into account.

Finally, structure also plays a very important role in figuring out the meanings of sentences. We can illustrate this by looking at a structurally ambiguous sentence, one in which the words and the grammatical morphemes and the word order are the same, but which still has two different meanings. Here is one such sentence:

(11) Lisa ate the cake in the kitchen.
    a. Lisa engaged in a cake-eating event in the kitchen.
    b. Lisa ate the cake which was in the kitchen (but left the one in the living room untouched).

The two paraphrases given in (11) disambiguate the sentence. We can think of this case involving one sentence mapping onto two distinct propositions. It seems that the difference in meaning comes from the prepositional phrase (PP) *in the kitchen* and what sentence constituent it modifies. In (11a) it modifies the eating event; in (11b) it modifies the cake itself. Linguists diagram these two meanings (propositions), representing modification as attachment: the modifier attaching itself as a sister of the modified phrase, as in (12).

(12) a. Lisa ate [the cake] [in the kitchen].

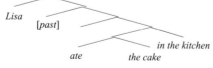

    b. Lisa ate [the cake in the kitchen].

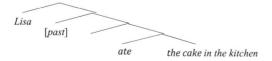

You should look at these sentence structures, represented by trees (Chapter 5 Syntax) from the bottom up. The trees give you an idea of how meaning is composed by merging together words, morphemes, and phrases one-by-one, until at the end we reach the top node, the sentence. Notice where [$_{PP}$ in the kitchen] is attached in the structure. In (12a) representing interpretation (11a), the PP attaches as a sister of the verbal phrase [$_{VP}$ ate the cake], which it modifies. There was an event of cake-eating, and it happened in the kitchen. In (12b), on the other hand, [$_{PP}$ in the kitchen] is sister to the object [$_{NP}$ the cake], and so this time the PP says something about the cake itself (where it was). The whole phrase [$_{NP}$ the cake in the kitchen] gets to become a unit together (a DP) before it combines with the verb *ate*.

I could give each node in these trees a syntactic label. By not providing labels, I want to draw your attention to the fact that we are talking about meaning, not syntactic structure. But in reality, meaning and syntactic structure are very closely mapped, as this ambiguity example demonstrates. We have one sentence and two structures aligned with two propositions.

PAUSE AND REFLECT 6.12

Give two interpretations for the ambiguous sentence *Jane saw the guy with the binoculars.*

Let's see how we are doing with our definition of compositionality. There is one more iteration that we need to provide, and that is given in (13).

(13) The meaning of a sentence is a function of the meaning of its grammatical and lexical morphemes, taking their order and syntactic structure into account.

A challenge to this idea is provided by construction grammar, arguing that the meaning of the whole is not a compositional function of the meaning of the parts put together locally and one-by-one. Instead, constructions themselves have meanings. One such construction is [(Someone) verb–ed their way into (some place)]: *John danced his way into the hallway* or *James hugged and kissed his way into middle management.* We will return to this in section 6.4.2.

6.3.3 Tense, Aspect, and Mood

In the previous section, we briefly mentioned that sentence meaning depends on grammatical morphemes, among other factors. Let us expand on this a little. Among the most important and most meaningful grammatical morphemes across languages of the world are those signaling **Tense**, **Aspect**, and **Mood**.[2] The linguist Bernard

---

[2] The discussion in this subsection follows the chapter on tense and aspect in the *World atlas of language structures* (WALS), http://wals.info/chapter/s7. You can read more on this topic on the original website.

Comrie (1985, p. 6) discussed tense and aspect as related concepts, as indeed they are. He considered tense to be the grammaticalization of location in time (past, present, future) and aspect as an expression of "internal temporal constituency" (of events, processes etc.). What is meant by internal constituency? If we are talking about a complete event, we are viewing it from the outside as a complete whole. If we are considering an ongoing event or a habitual series of events, we think of both as open-ended and being in progress. Figure 6.2 may help you visualize this. The complete aspect is also known as perfective aspect, while the ongoing or habitual is known as imperfective aspect.

Perfective aspect: [**Beginning ... Progress ... End**]
(**e.g.,** *I ate an apple* or *I will read a book tomorrow*)
Imperfective aspect: ... **Progress** ...
(**e.g.,** *I was eating an apple when he came* **or** *I will be reading a book when he comes*)
or ... **Event ... Event ... Event** ...
(**e.g.,** *I (used to) visit my grandma on Tuesdays.*)

Figure 6.2. Graphic representation of perfective and imperfective aspect

The two grammatical categories, tense and aspect, are indeed conceptually very close because both deal with time. However, they are not the same. Note how we have both past and future tenses in the examples in Figure 6.2, which cut across perfective and imperfective aspects.

At the same time, tense and aspect may be mutually dependent, or interwoven in some grammatical systems. The first example of such a dependency would be the fact that perfective events are usually past events. This relationship probably has a cognitive basis, as we cannot think of something as completed if we have not already experienced all of it in the past, including its endpoint. In Mandarin Chinese, for example, which lacks a tense morpheme, the morpheme *le* marks complete (perfective) aspect and strongly implies that the event is in the past. Verbs that typically denote states and activities and ongoing (imperfective) aspect, on the other hand, tend to be interpreted as referring to the present.

EYES ON WORLD LANGUAGES: BULGARIAN ASPECT

Not all languages express tense and aspect with parallel forms. For example, Bulgarian does not have a separate verbal form for the progressive aspect. Bulgarian verbs in the present tense are ambiguous between a habitual and an ongoing interpretation. Note that the verb form in *Četa edna kniga* "I am reading a book right now" and *Četa mnogo* "I read a lot" are exactly the same. The two possible interpretations are disambiguated by the object and the context.

Mood is not exactly related to time, although it is often one of the categories expressed on the verb, just as tense and aspect. It conveys the speaker's attitude about the truth value of what the sentence describes. This may sound a little complicated, but it's simple enough: In the **indicative mood**, for instance, the speaker is sure that something is the case, so she asserts it. We use the indicative to make factual statements and to ask questions. It is the most commonly used among the types of mood. A speaker uses the **imperative mood** when she desires that something should happen. Imperative sentences are either commands or requests. In English, the **subjunctive mood** is used to explore hypothetical, conditional, or imaginary situations, and it is rare. One example is the use of *were* with first person singular: *If I were you*, or *If I were in your shoes …*

PAUSE AND REFLECT 6.13

The sentence *He demanded that she be fired* is also an expression of the subjunctive mood. Can you describe which verbal form in the sentence signals the subjunctive? What is another way of expressing the same proposition?

EYES ON WORLD LANGUAGES: SPANISH SUBJUNCTIVE

Languages such as Spanish and French have many more extensive subjunctive paradigms than English does. Subjunctive forms appear in the subordinate clause when the main clause expresses a hypothetical situation, doubt, emotion, command, advice or begging, permission of prohibition, and wishes. One example of the present subjunctive is *Yo espero que tú hables español* "I hope that you speak Spanish."

In summary, tense, aspect, and mood are grammatical meanings frequently expressed on the verb. They relate to the time of the utterance, how the speaker wants to represent the internal structure of the event or state, and how she feels about the truth value of the sentence.

6.3.4   Truth Conditions, Entailment, Contradiction, and Presupposition

Recall that the meaning of a sentence, or its proposition, is its truth value. We also said that when we know the meaning of a sentence, we know what it would take for the sentence to be true. We could express this idea in a slightly different way: we know the meaning of a proposition if we know its truth conditions. The truth conditions of a sentence S specify when S is true and when it is not. For example, consider the truth conditions for *The tree outside my window is in bloom*. We say that the sentence is true if and only if (written *iff*) the tree is in bloom right now. We say that the sentence is false if it has only green leaves but no blooms or if the tree was blooming a week ago but is not blooming now.

You might think that the truth conditions of a sentence look trivial. But they are not! Imagine that there is another language (the language of emojis, if that were a natural language) which contains an expression like that in Figure 6.3.

Figure 6.3 A made-up language using emojis. From: 2018 Apple MacOS Emojis.

You meet some native speakers of this language and ask them what the sentence means, and find out that it is true if the tree outside my window is blooming, but false otherwise. Now you know the meaning of the sentence: it means the same thing as our English example sentence The tree outside my window is in bloom. If two sentences have the same truth conditions, then they mean the same thing.

Once we have figured out the meaning of a proposition, we can consider some meaning relations between propositions. **Entailment** is one such relationship: it holds when the truth of sentence A requires/necessitates the truth of sentence B. Whenever A is true, B is also true, and speakers have intuitions about that. Sentence (14a) entails (14b), (14c), and (14d). It does not entail, however, (14e).

(14) a. Homer drew apples and oranges.
b. Homer drew something.
c. Homer drew apples.
d. Homer drew oranges.
e. Homer is an artist.

PAUSE AND REFLECT 6.14

Discuss the entailment relationships exemplified in (14) in more detail. Why is (14e) not entailed by (14a)?

In what follows, we will mark propositions with capital letters (e.g., A., B., C., etc.). Entailments can take the form of *if … then …* conditions as exemplified in (15). It cannot be the case that Sampson does not eat grass.

(15) If A. All horses eat grass, and B. Sampson is a horse, then it must necessarily be true that C. Sampson eats grass.

Contradiction is another relation between propositions, in a sense the opposite of entailment. Sentence A contradicts sentence B if and whenever A is true B is false. Let's take proposition A. *Joshua is married to John,* a contradictory statement would be

B. *Joshua is single*, because if A is true B is necessarily false. Some more examples, then. *Joshua owns a green jacket* entails *Joshua owns a jacket* but is contradicted by *Joshua does not own a jacket*. *Catriona reached the summit at 3 o'clock* contradicts *Catriona reached the summit at 4 o'clock*. To practice, come up with a statement of your own, and see what entailments and contradictions you can formulate. It's not as easy as you think.

Sometimes a sentence is neither true nor false. The sentence *The Queen of the United States is bald* can only have a truth value, true or false, if such a person exists. This condition is called a **presupposition**. In the example *The tree outside my window is in bloom*, there is a presupposition that there is some tree or other outside my window, and even that I live in a house with windows. The truth conditions of presupposition are as follows:

(16) 1. When A is true, B is true; and
       2. When A is false, B is still true; and
       3. When B is false, A is neither true nor false.

Let's see how that works for the example. When A. *The tree outside my window is in bloom* is true, B. *There is a tree outside my window* is true. When A. *The tree outside my window is in bloom* is false, B. *There is a tree outside my window* can still be true. However, if B. *There is a tree outside my window* is false, A is neither true nor false because if there is no tree, the issue of its blooming is of no consequence. Here are some more examples: *Bill stopped smoking* presupposes that *Bill* used to smoke. *My husband is a doctor* presupposes *I am married*, and so on.

6.3.5 Implicature

There is another very interesting relationship between propositions that is discussed in another branch of linguistics, that is, pragmatics.[3] **Implicature** is a technical term coined by the philosopher H. P. Grice, referring to what is suggested in an utterance, even though not explicitly expressed nor strictly entailed by the utterance. Another way of thinking of implicature is as the act of implying one thing by saying something else. Implicatures can be part of sentence meaning, and very often, although not always, they depend on conversational context. To understand implicature, consider the simple example of an everyday conversation in (17).

(17) John: Are you coming to the party tonight?
       Mary: I have to work.

Mary's reply does not contain a direct statement of *Yes* or *No* to John's question; still the meaning is more than clear, it is a No. How do we understand this? Knowledge of common forms of implicature is acquired along with one's native language at an early age. It is arguably universal, that is, part of all human languages. Implicature serves a variety of goals beyond communication such as maintaining good social relations, misleading

[3] The presentation in this section follows the *Stanford encyclopedia of philosophy* (http://plato .stanford.edu/entries/implicature/).

without lying, suggesting rather than stating where the latter would be awkward, saving face, etc. An interesting subset of implicature is **scalar implicature**. It involves quantifiers such as *<some, most, all>*, which are arranged on a scale from the weakest to the strongest term. The natural numbers are another scale. Uttering a sentence with the weaker term implies that the stronger terms in the same scale are not true. For example, (18a) strongly implies (18b).

(18) a. Some professors are smart.

b. Not all professors are smart.

The calculation goes like this. The logical meaning of *some* is *some and possibly all*. But if the speaker of (18a) wanted to say that all professors are smart, she would have used the stronger member of the scale, *all*. Since she didn't, she must intend to imply that only the weaker member of the scale is the case, as in (18b).

An important conceptual and methodological issue in semantics is how to distinguish senses and entailments from conventional conversational implicatures. One test that is often used is cancelability. Since implicatures are only suggestions, they can be continued with a contradictory statement. This is not the case with entailments.

(19) a. Some professors are smart. In fact, it may be true that all professors are smart.

b. (All) Professors are smart. #In fact, it may be true that not all professors are smart.

(19a) is a concealed implication that *Not all professors are smart*. Its acceptable continuation in (19a) cancels the implicature with a contradictory statement: *Some and indeed all*. On the other hand, the first statement in (19b) containing the strongest member of the scale cannot be followed by a contradictory statement. Thus cancelability is a test for implicature.

A related issue is the degree to which sentence meaning determines what is said. Grice developed an influential theory to explain and predict conversational implicatures, and describe how they arise and are understood. He proposed the **Cooperative Principle** and described four maxims specifying how speakers behave in a cooperative way. They are given below, following Grice, (1975, p. 26–30).

(20) Cooperative Principle. Contribute what is required by the jointly accepted purpose of the conversation.

Maxim of Quality: Make your contribution true; do not convey what you believe to be false or unjustified.

Maxim of Quantity: Be as informative as is required.

Maxim of Relation: Be relevant.

Maxim of Manner: Be perspicuous; avoid obscurity and ambiguity; strive for brevity and order.

The Maxim of Relevance, for example, explains how we understand what Mary means in (17). She would have violated relevance if she did not make her contribution relevant to John's question.

> **PAUSE AND REFLECT 6.15**
>
> Think of the following exchange between a child and an adult:
>
> Adult: What did you get for your birthday?
> Child: A present.
>
> Does this answer obey the Maxim of Quality? How about the Maxims of Quantity and Relation?

Scalar implicature as in (18) is explained by the Maxim of Quantity. Assuming that the accepted purpose of the conversation requires the speaker to say whether or not professors are smart, a speaker who said "Some professors are smart" would be flouting the Maxim of Quantity if she believed that all professors are smart but didn't say it.

6.3.6 Thematic Roles

The sentence meaning, or proposition, is dependent on the meaning of the verb and its arguments, even the adjuncts. In this section, we will look at these relations more closely. In order to describe and use this information theoretically, linguists unify them in classes called **thematic roles**, or **theta roles**. (21) shows some labels with examples. Keep in mind that the lists may vary somewhat across the literature. The underlined phrases are carriers of the theta role before each sentence:

(21) a. Agent: _John_ ate the cake.
       Instrument: _The key_ opened the car.
       Cause: _The wind_ blew out the candle.
   b. Experiencer: _Mary_ enjoyed the movie. The article annoyed _Mary_.
   c. Beneficiary/Recipient: Joe baked _Julie_ a cake.
       Path: The river flowed _towards the sea_.
       Source: The river sprang _from the mountains_.
       Goal: Jane sent the package _to Chicago_.
       Theme: John ate _the cake_. Jane sent _the package_ to Chicago.
       Location: I met Joan _at the market_.
       Measure: The book cost _twelve dollars_.

The theta roles in (21a), Agent, Instrument, and Cause, bring about a state of affairs. Without them, the event would not come to pass. The lines between them can be fuzzy, but it is accepted that Agents have to be conscious and sentient in a way that Causes and Instruments are not. It follows, then, that states (_I resemble my father_) are not associated with Agents, because they are not dynamic situations. What is the theta role of the pronoun _I_ in _I resemble my father_? Linguists are still arguing about this one.

The role experiencer in (21b) represents arguments that undergo some sort of emotional, cognitive, or sensory experience. The next grouping of theta roles in (21c) have much in common and can be very close in meaning. For example, the Recipient could be a kind of Goal. The labels of this group are pretty self-explanatory. The important one, and a bit of a catch-all theta role is the Theme (some linguists call it the Patient). A Theme refers to the argument that is changing location, undergoing movement of any sort (even metaphorical movement), or undergoing a change of state. Another, more general definition is that the Theme is the affected participant in the action.

An interesting set of linguistic facts in English affects the double object–dative argument construction. The linguist Georgia Green noticed that it is acceptable to say (22a) as well as (22b). They are equivalent in truth value; that is, we have two sentences reflecting the same proposition.

(22) a. I sent a package to Becky.   Agent–Verb–Theme–Goal
        b. I sent Betty a package.   Agent–Verb–Recipient–Theme
        c. I sent the package to Chicago. Agent–Verb–Theme–Goal
        d. #/? I sent Chicago the package. Agent–Verb–Recipient–Theme

The Recipient theta role carrier has to be sentient (a person), because they have to be fully in possession of the Theme at the end of the event. The Recipient is not a Goal. To see how this works, consider (22c) and (22d). In these sentences, *Chicago* the city is a plausible Goal but not an acceptable Recipient, since a city cannot be in possession of a package. However, if *Chicago* stands for a branch office of a company, for example, which would be a metonymy in itself, (22d) becomes much more acceptable. It has been noticed that the theta roles can be grouped together based on what kind of grammatical function, subject or object or indirect/prepositional object, they are likely to land in. Most verbs allow certain mappings between grammatical relations and thematic roles. If you look at the list in (21a), these three theta roles are likely to surface as subjects; those in (21c) are more likely to be represented by objects; and experiencer in (21b) can be both. For each verb, the lexicon specifies a theta grid: the theta role that can be associated with their subject, object, etc., as shown in (23).

(23) put V: <AGENT, THEME, LOCATION>
        Fred$_{AGENT}$ put the glass$_{THEME}$ on the counter$_{LOCATION}$

Verbs can be organized in classes on the basis of a common theta grid, as in (24).

(24) <AGENT, THEME, RECIPIENT> *give, lend, supply, pay, donate, contribute*
        <RECIPIENT, THEME, SOURCE> *receive, accept, borrow, buy, purchase, rent, hire*

There is evidence that such classes of verbs are useful in language acquisition: once a certain class becomes part of the grammar, it is easier to add newly acquired verbs to it.

PAUSE AND REFLECT 6.16

The Experiencer theta role, as exemplified in (21d), is special. Experiencers are the arguments of a class of verbs known as psych verbs, because they denote feelings and psychological events (*annoy, frighten, delight*). This class of verbs is divided into two: Experiencer Subject verbs (*Mary enjoyed the movie*) and Experiencer Object verbs (*The article annoyed Mary*). Can you identify which of these classes the verbs *frighten, fear, please,* and *delight* belong to?

Linguists have wondered what semantic basis we have for characterizing thematic roles, especially in view of their varied and somewhat fluid membership. The semanticist David Dowty came up with the idea that thematic roles are not semantic primitives but can be defined by a number of primitive features, leading to different degrees of membership of so-called **proto-roles**. This idea should remind you of the lexical features we discussed earlier in this chapter. Let's take the Agent proto-role. It is made up of a) volitional involvement in the event or state, b) sentience (and/or perception), c) causing an event or change of state in another participant, and d) movement (relative to the position of another participant). The Agent theta role, then, has all these primitive semantic features as in _Mary opened the door_, while an Experiencer is less of a proto-Agent because it lacks volition (_Mary fears conflict_).

In summary, thematic roles are useful descriptions of the relationship between the verb and its arguments. They also help divide verbs into semantic classes with similar theta grids. Note that the list of theta roles is finite, hence the semantic verb classes are easily learnable.

6.4   Approaches to the Study of Semantics

As you have gathered by now, meaning-making is not only a complicated business, but is in fact the main goal of linguistic communication. It is very natural then, as in all branches of science, that there are different approaches to the study of semantics. In the following sections, we will review the main ideas of two of these approaches.

6.4.1   Formal Semantics

Formal semantics is predicated on the idea that the natural world exists, and it is open to human cognition. However, the world exists outside of the human beings that perceive it. If you are in a green park, and you close your eyes so that you no longer see the grass and the trees, the park continues to exist. This view is in contrast with a more subjective view of the world. Ultimately, these distinctions are rooted in philosophical views of the world. The study of semantics and the study of philosophy are closely related.

Linguists rarely employed formal semantics until the mathematician and philosopher Richard Montague showed how English (or any natural language) could be treated like the formal artificial languages of the logician. His idea was that natural languages can be described as _interpreted_ formal systems, using the methods of the so-called model-theoretic semantics. This type of semantics assigns to sentences interpretations that themselves are not language; in particular, interpretations that have to do with whether they are true or false. What do we need to know in order to determine whether a sentence is true or false? Two things are necessary: (1) we must know what the sentence means and (2) we must pair the sentence with some situation out there in the real world and see whether it corresponds to the sentence meaning (Think of _New York is the capital_ *of the United States.*) The word *formal* in the name *formal semantics* refers to sentence–world relations being maximally explicit and precise.

Starting from the idea that the meaning of a sentence consists of its truth-conditions, the meanings of other expressions (words, phrases, clauses) are analyzed in terms of their contribution to the truth-conditions of the sentences in which they occur. In formal semantics, truth-conditions are expressed relative to various parameters or models of the world – a proposition (expressed by a formula) may be true at a given time, in a given possible world, relative to a certain context that fixes speaker, addressee, etc., and relative to a certain assignment of meanings to its lexical expressions and of particular values assigned to its variables.

In formal semantics, we operate with constants (individuals), variables, predicates (such as verbs), and formulas. I will give you intuitive examples of these. Imagine someone describing an unrequited love situation that Ann loves Barry but he doesn't love her back. We can express this situation using the constants *a, b* and the predicate *Love* producing the formula *Love (a, b),* which will be true for the situation described. However, the formula *Love (b, a)* is going to be sadly false. Next, consider variables. Variables are like pronouns *he* and *him*: we cannot understand a sentence such as *He read "War and Peace"* until we know which individual in the outside world *he* refers to (*Peter, my father, your boss*, etc.). This information is given to us by the discourse or it may be common knowledge between the speaker and hearer.

This very perfunctory introduction to formulas is intended to give you a brief taste of formal semantics. It is a fascinating branch of linguistics that depends on formalisms because it endeavors to capture in the most precise way the mapping between form and meaning in its relation to the outside world.

> ### LINGUISTICS TIDBITS: BOUND VARIABLES
>
> Consider now another example: *Every farmer who has a donkey beats it.* Is the pronoun *it* referring to an individual donkey, say Poncho? After all, the pronoun *it* is singular? No, *it* refers to every individual donkey that belongs to a farmer, and if there are many farmers, there are also many donkeys. We call such a pronoun *a bound variable.*

6.4.2 Cognitive Semantics

Cognitive semantics, on the other hand, holds that language is part of a more general human cognitive ability; it describes the world as people conceive it. Implicit in this definition is that there is some difference between this conceptual world and the real world. Cognitive semantics is part of cognitive linguistics. A tenet of this framework is the rejection of language as a special innate capacity. The cognitive semantics approach rejects the traditional separation of linguistics into modules of the grammar such as phonology, morphology, syntax, pragmatics, etc.

Cognitive semanticists hold that grammar manifests a conception of the world held in a (regional) culture, and that cultural differences give rise to differences between grammars. They also maintain that knowledge of language is contextual and personal. A word meaning is an extension of our bodily and cultural experiences. For example, the notion of *restaurant* is associated with a series of concepts, like *food*, *service*, *waiters*, *tables*, and *eating*. These rich associations can be very personal; thus they cannot be captured by an analysis in terms of features, necessary and sufficient conditions, etc. Yet they still seem to be intimately related to the understanding of *restaurant*, making part of its connotation (see Section 6.2.1).

Cognitive semantics studies much of the area traditionally devoted to lexical connotations as well as areas within pragmatics and its interface with semantics. Metaphor and metonymy, which we discussed in Section 6.2.5, are prime real estate for cognitive semanticists, as is prototype theory, cognitive models of mental spaces. Construction Grammar (as developed by Kay, Fillmore, and Lakoff in the 1980s) is often classified within cognitive linguistics.

A classical analysis due to George Lakoff is that of *there*-constructions as in *There is a fly in my soup*. Another well-known analysis, due to Adele Goldberg, is of the resultative construction as in *Mary wiped the table clean*. The main idea is that the meaning of the whole comes from the construction itself, not from the meaning of the ingredient constituents compositionally. Within this approach, any linguistic pattern is recognized as a construction as long as some aspect of its form or function is not strictly predictable from its component parts. In this way, there is no rigid distinction between words, phrases, and sentences: their form–meaning mappings are considered to be on a continuum.

SUMMARY

In this chapter, we discussed the study of meaning in language. Meaning exchange is the main goal of communication: we do not speak with our interlocutors to hear the beautiful sounds of language but to exchange messages with them. The study of meaning-making considers how speakers/writers encode it and how listeners/readers comprehend it. We compared and contrasted different types of meaning in language; we explored how meaning is reflected in words and how words are inter-connected in semantic fields based on meaning. We also described how we put together word meanings to come up with phrase meaning, and how we take structure into account to get to sentence meaning.

Sentence interpretation is intimately connected to the sentence syntax and the grammatical meanings of its functional morphology. Finally, we looked at some theoretical approaches to studying meaning in language, the main philosophical difference between them being whether reality is considered to be objective or subjective. Computing meaning in everyday communication may come from our language faculty enriched with general cognitive mechanisms and our knowledge of the world.

EXERCISES

A few more activities and resources can be found in 'Delving Deeper' in Chapter 6's resources on the website to accompany this book at www.cambridge.org/introducing-linguistics

6.1   Technically speaking, the mental lexicon contains morphemes, not just words. Recall that morphemes are the smallest meaning-bearing units of language (Chapter 4 Morphology). Your English mental lexicon contains entries like these, where meanings are given in small caps:

a.   dog = DOMESTIC CANINE
b.   –s = PLURAL
c.   pave = COVER WITH STONE, TILES, OR OTHER HARD MATERIAL
d.   –ment = SUFFIX CREATING NOUNS
e.   –ing = ACTION IN PROGRESS, etc.

Keeping in mind the lexical and grammatical meanings we discussed in the chapter, it is easy to see which are the lexical and which are the grammatical morphemes above. *Dog* and *pave* are certainly lexical morphemes, because they have idiosyncratic meanings of their own, such that no other word has exactly the same meaning. But how about the derivational morpheme *–ment,* which we can use to create the noun *pave–ment*? The grammatical meaning it carries is related to the category of word it creates: nouns. Some other derivational morphemes include *–er, –ness*, etc. From the point of view of semantics, how many meanings can we identify in derivational morphemes? Which meanings?

6.2   Order the words in these lists from those having the most negative to those with the most positive connotations:

Group 1:   thin, slim, lanky, skinny, gaunt, slender
Group 2:   aggressive, assertive, domineering, dynamic, pushy, forceful
Group 3:   shrewd, egghead, bright, clever, brilliant, cunning, smart, intelligent, brainy

6.3   Provide the componential analysis for *horse, stallion, mare, colt, filly.*

6.4   Think of a list of FOUR homophones in English.

6.5   Suppose John has two sons, Bill and Henry; one nephew, Pete; and one grandson, Dave. When we refer to John as such, there is no additional sense in this word. *John* is the arbitrary name given to the referent. However, consider the following phrases:

Bill's father
Henry's father
Pete's uncle
Dave's grandfather

Each phrase refers either to John (X's father) or to John himself. Pete may have more than one uncle and Dave has a second grandfather. Thus the first two phrases are unambiguous while the second two are ambiguous. In the latter cases, the addressee does not know which of the possible referents is the intended referent except when clear from the context. The four phrases listed above represent a different sense of the intended referent, John. Virtually every object can have several senses. Compose other sets of phrases that illustrate this phenomenon. Make sure you provide both unambiguous and ambiguous phrases.

6.6   Consider the following sentences:

(1) Alvin kissed Elvina passionately.
    a.   Alvin kissed Elvina.
    b.   Alvin kissed Elvina many times.

    c. Alvin did not kiss Elvina.
    d. Elvina was kissed by Alvin.
    e. Alvin touched Elvina with his lips.
    f. Elvina kissed Alvin.
    g. Elvina was kissed.

Try to work out the entailment and contradiction relations between them. To start, let's say that (1) entails (1a). Now, you do the rest.

6.7 The sentence in (1) presupposes the sentence in (2):
(1) The mayor of Liverpool is bald.
(2) The mayor of Liverpool exists.

Give the presuppositions for the following sentences:

  (3) Bill stopped smoking.
  (4) Someone is reading a book. Hint: the answer is not presupposition.
  (5) Ken knows that it's raining.
  (6) My cousin lives in California with her family.
  (7) The professor's husband is at the lecture.
  (8) Mary didn't see the chicken with two heads.
  (9) What Bill lost wasn't his laptop.
 (10) John regrets that he stopped doing linguistics before he left Cambridge.

6.8 Divide the following intransitive verbs into unaccusative and unergative, based on the semantic principle discussed in the chapter.

    Fall, enter, smile, arrive, dance, walk, blush, talk, freeze

Then check your judgements using the following three syntactic diagnostics.

  (1) Unaccusative verbs do not allow a cognate object, an object which shares the same lexical root with the verb, while unergatives do:
    a. He danced a merry dance.   b. *She fell a nasty fall.
  (2) Unergative verbs typically do not allow prenominal modifiers:
    a. *the recently laughed boy   b. the recently arrived man
  (3) Unaccusatives allow resultative secondary predicates (they are bolded below), while unergatives do not. In a., the meaning is that the popsicles froze until they were solid.
    a. The popsicles froze **solid**.   b. *John ate **sick**.

6.9 Identify the grammatical mood used in the following sentences (indicative, imperative, or subjunctive):

  (1) Let's eat those brownies.
  (2) My sister works for the Mayor of London.
  (3) My sister insists that everyone be on time.
  (4) Pretend that you cannot see him.
  (5) My mom taught me that one should always be on time.
  (6) The doctor demanded that the drunk patient leave the premises.
  (7) The manager suggested to John that he should pull himself together.
  (8) Take out the trash, Martin, please.
  (9) Identify two salient features of this car.
 (10) The leadership suggested that our team implement a budget cut in June.

6.10 Identify the relationship between these groups of words, choosing among homonymy, homography, homophony, synonymy, antonymy, hyponymy, and polysemy.

Example: *violin – fiddle.*
"Violin and fiddle are synonyms*"*

   (1) *bank – bank*
   (2) *doe – dough*
   (3) *good – good*
   (4) *learn – teach*
   (5) *afraid – scared*
   (6) *float – sink*
   (7) *bow – bow*
   (8) *beverage – tea – coffee*
   (9) *evil – bad – wicked*
(10) *hammer – tool*
(11) *seal – seal*
(12) *rein – rein*
(13) *to – two – too*
(14) *mole – mole*

6.11 Identify the thematic roles of the underlined phrases.

   (1) Fred threw <u>the rock.</u>
   (2) They ran f<u>rom the police.</u>
   (3) <u>Jill</u> saw <u>the car.</u>
   (4) Marina studied hard <u>for her mother.</u>
   (5) <u>Jake</u> ate the soup.
   (6) Fred opened the phone <u>with a paper clip.</u>
   (7) His portrait hangs <u>above the mantelpiece.</u>
   (8) Lee walked <u>to his office.</u>
   (9) Martin mowed <u>the lawn.</u>
(10)   The concert pianist pleased <u>the audience.</u>

6.12 Discuss the interpretation of the following ambiguous sentences as shown in the chapter:

   (1) Jennifer saw the man with the binoculars.
   (2) Mona spotted the kitten with one eye.
   (3) One morning I shot an elephant in my pyjamas.

This is the first sentence in this video from a Groucho Marx movie: https://www.youtube.com/watch?v=NfN_gcjGoJo

6.13 Discuss the literal meaning and the implied meaning of the sentences:

   (1) Everybody went to the party.
   (2) There is nothing to eat in the house.
   (3) Some stories he tells are true.

6.14 In the chapter, we identified the sentence meaning as its truth value. This is a formal semantics definition. How would this definition change within cognitive semantics?

6.15 Where do word meanings come from? How about sentence meanings?

REFERENCES

Chomsky, N. (1957). *Syntactic structures*. The Hague/ Paris: Mouton.

Comrie, B. (1985). *Tense*. Cambridge: Cambridge University Press.

Dekydtspotter, L., & Sprouse, R. (2001). Mental design and (second) language epistemology: Adjectival restrictions of wh-quantifier and tense in English-French interlanguage. *Second Language Research, 17*, 1–35.

Green, G. (1974). *Semantics and syntactic regularity*. Bloomington, IN: Indiana University Press.

Grice, H. (1975). Logic and conversation. In P. Cole & J. Morgan (Eds.), *Studies in syntax and semantics III: Speech acts* (pp. 183–198). New York, NY: Academic Press.

Lakoff, G., & Johnson, M. (1980). *Metaphors we live by*. Chicago, IL: Chicago University Press.

Pereltsvaig, A. (2012). *Languages of the world*. Cambridge: Cambridge University Press.

PART 4

LANGUAGE TYPOLOGIES AND CHANGE

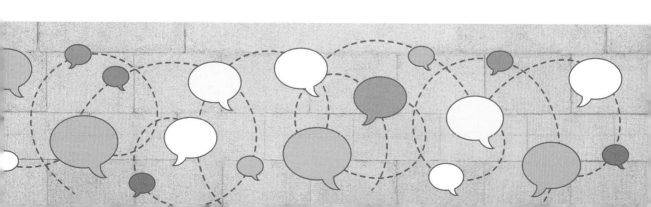

7 The Classification of Languages

Asya Pereltsvaig

OVERVIEW

In this chapter, you will develop an understanding of language classification, both in terms of historical relationships among languages and linguistic typology. Our objectives are to:

- explore how languages can be grouped into families;
- learn the basics of the comparative reconstruction method;
- gain knowledge about linguistic typology;
- examine three ways in which languages can differ and hence be classified; and
- look at some theoretical approaches to studying linguistic typology.

7.1 How Can Languages Be Classified?

There are approximately 7,000 languages spoken in the world today. Despite differences in vocabularies, sound systems, and grammars, these languages exhibit certain similarities that allow us to classify them in different ways.

Linguists have developed two ways of classifying language: by historical relation to other languages and by their linguistic properties. The first way of classifying languages is based on historical relationships among languages: languages are said to belong to a **language family** if they developed from a shared ancestral language. This way of classifying languages is often called **genetic classification** but it must be remembered that historical relationships among languages need not match genetic (that is, biological) relationships among people who speak them. For example, most speakers of English today are not genetic descendants of Angles, Saxons, and Jutes, but English is nonetheless a linguistic descendant of Anglo-Saxon.

The second way of classifying languages, referred to as **linguistic typology**, examines a wide range of linguistic properties, such as sound inventory, ways of building words out of morphemes, word order, and so on, and groups languages that share

LINGUISTICS TIDBITS: THE BEGINNINGS OF GENETIC CLASSIFICATION OF LANGUAGES

Did you know that genetic classification of languages was one of the first subjects of linguistic scholarship?

- First attempts to relate languages to their putative shared ancestors began as early as the eighteenth century.
- The earliest accounts were based mostly on the Bible, such as the story of Japhet, Shem, and Ham, the three sons of Noah in the Book of Genesis.
- By the late 1700s, philologists (which is what historical linguists were then called) discovered historical links among Indo-European languages such as Latin, Ancient Greek, and Sanskrit, as well as between Romani (the language of the Gypsies) and languages of northern India.
- By the mid-1800s, the comparative method was fleshed out and enough of the presumed ancestral Indo-European language was reconstructed to write an entire story in it.

similar traits. Importantly, languages that are historically related need not share typological traits and vice versa.

7.1.1 Language vs. Dialect

Before we proceed to discuss different ways in which languages can be classified, we need to clarify what a language is and what makes a language distinct from a dialect. Ordinary speakers of languages like English or French tend to think that dialects (or *patois*, as they are called in French) are unwritten, substandard ways of speaking a given language. In this sense, people who speak Geordie (in the Newcastle-upon-Tyne area in northeastern England) or African American Vernacular English (typically African-American speakers) speak an English dialect, but people who speak a *general British English* or a *general American English* speak a language but not a dialect. This is not how linguists look at this distinction, however, since most of the world's languages are neither written nor have an accepted standard. We will discuss more about language varieties in Chapter 9 Sociolinguistics.

Another popular view of the distinction between a language and a dialect can be summarized by a quip by Yiddish linguist Max Weinreich: "A language is a dialect with an army and a navy." However, he said this now-famous quote to explain why Yiddish had been for a long time considered a dialect of German, despite substantial differences between Yiddish and any form of German. In fact, many of these differences are due to the influence of Slavic languages, with which Yiddish was in contact for about half a millennium. Because Yiddish has never been a language of any state ("with an army and a navy"), Weinreich reasoned that it is not viewed *by the general public* as a language in its own right. For a linguist such as Weinreich, Yiddish is clearly a distinct language.

PAUSE AND REFLECT 7.1

What other languages besides Yiddish can you think of which lack "an army and a navy" yet are distinctive enough to be called a separate language? Which languages do you know that either acquired or lost their own "army and navy", as Weinreich put it, in the course of history?

For linguists, dialects need not be unwritten, substandard, or stateless. In fact, from a linguist's perspective, everyone speaks some dialect or another. So where then do we draw a line between a language and a dialect? The boundary is determined by **mutual intelligibility**: if speakers of two varieties can understand each other, we often say that they speak dialects of the same language, and if they cannot, they speak different languages.

Mutual intelligibility is a spectrum rather than an all-or-nothing concept. Thus, speakers of fairly distinctive dialects may have difficulties understanding each other. For example, speakers of American or Canadian dialects of English typically have a hard time understanding Yorkshire or Glaswegian dialects. Furthermore, mutual intelligibility is not always truly mutual. For instance, speakers of Québecois French generally can understand French speakers from France better than the other way around.

The results produced by the mutual intelligibility test are not always in accord with how speakers themselves perceive their ways of speaking. For example, many Serbs and Croats would claim that they speak different languages – mostly for reasons of nationalism – while mutual intelligibility between Serbian and Croatian is fairly high, and so linguists would typically consider them dialects of the same language, Serbo-Croatian. In reality, the dialectal picture in the former Yugoslavian region is more complicated than that, so there are several distinctive dialects there, which do not match the geopolitical borders between Serbia, Croatia, and Bosnia.

Even linguists may disagree among themselves as to whether to call certain varieties *dialects* or *languages*. Depending on the phenomenon of interest, Danish, Norwegian, and Swedish may be considered dialects of the same language, Mainland Scandinavian – mutual intelligibility among them is very high. Yet, when certain phenomena that work very differently in Danish, Norwegian, and Swedish are being examined, linguists might refer to these as three distinct languages.

EYES ON WORLD LANGUAGES: LANGUAGE OR DIALECT?

Many language varieties around the world are considered *languages* by their speakers yet would be defined as a *dialect* by most linguists. For example, speakers of Judeo-Tat, a language originally spoken by Mountain Jews in Dagestan and Azerbaijan (most of them now live in Israel), consider it a distinct language. Yet it is linguistically very close – and mutually intelligible – with Muslim Tat. So for linguists, Judeo-Tat and Muslim Tat are dialects of the same language. Religion and politics are also the reason why speakers of Hindi and Urdu consider them distinct languages.

The reverse is also true: for reasons of politics and ideology, speakers – and state policies – may consider two ways of speaking to be *dialects* whereas linguists would treat them as distinct languages. An example of that is presented by Mandarin and Cantonese (and other Chinese varieties), which the Chinese government considers to be dialects of the same language, *Chinese*. Since the two use essentially the same writing system, *in writing*, Mandarin and Cantonese are fairly mutually intelligible, yet *in spoken form*, Mandarin and Cantonese speakers cannot understand each other. Since linguists treat spoken language as primary over the written form, they take Mandarin and Cantonese to be different languages.

7.2 The Genetic Classification of Languages

Let's start by considering the sentence *The green iguana jumped onto a leaf* rendered in three languages: Spanish, Italian, and French:

(1) Spanish: La   iguana   verde   saltó   sobre   una   hoja.
            the   *iguana* *green* *jumped*   *onto* *a*   *leaf*
    Italian: L'   iguana   verde   è   saltato   su   una   foglia.
            the   *iguana* *green* *is*   *jumped* *onto* *a*   *leaf*
    French: L'   iguane   vert   a   sauté   sur   une   feuille.
            the   *iguana* *green* *has*   *jumped* *onto* *a*   *leaf*

What has probably *jumped* at you is how similar these sentences are across the three languages. Among the most conspicuous similarities are the likeness between their nouns for *iguana*, adjectives for *green*, and verbs for *jump*. Perhaps less noticeable, but no less important, are similarities in functional words such as the definite articles (*la* in Spanish, *l'* in Italian and French), indefinite articles (*una* in Spanish and Italian, *une* in French), and prepositions (*sobre* in Spanish, *su* in Italian, *sur* in French). Some other similarities are less obvious: for instance, Italian *foglia* and French *feuille* sound similar, but their Spanish counterpart, *hoja*, seems rather different. However, as it turns out, *hoja* is historically related to its Italian and French counterparts, but several independent historical sound changes, such as /f/ turning into /h/ and then disappearing entirely in pronunciation, obscure their historical relatedness. Nor do the similarities end with individual words: word order in this sentence is also parallel across the three languages.

PAUSE AND REFLECT 7.2

As can be seen from the translations of (1) into other languages, each of the words (ignoring for the moment the word *iguana*, to which we will return shortly) could be expressed by several different sound combinations. Note also the differences in the order of *iguana* and *green*, and the lack of indefinite articles in Hebrew and of both definite and indefinite articles in Russian.

It is therefore highly unlikely that systematic similarities between Spanish, Italian, and French, shown in (1), are accidental. What then could be the reason for these similarities?

Russian: Zelënaja   iguana   prygnula   na   list.
            green   *iguana*   *jumped*   *onto*   *leaf*
Hebrew: Ha-iguana   ha-yeruka   kaftsa   'al   'ele.
            the-iguana *the-green*   *jumped*   *onto*   *leaf*
Hungarian: A   zöld   leguán   felugrott   egy   levél.
            the *green* *iguana*   *jumped*   *a*   *leaf*

LINGUISTICS TIDBITS: ROMANCE, ROMANIAN, AND ROMANI

- While some people may indeed associate Romance languages such as Italian or French with romance, the term comes from *Rome*, the capital of the Latin-speaking world in antiquity.
- The name of the Romanian language also comes from *Rome*: present-day Romania largely overlaps with the historic Roman province of Dacia.
- Romani, the language of the Roma people (or "*the Gypsies*") has nothing to do with Rome, ancient or modern. It comes from the Romani word *roma*, meaning "people", which also serves as their self-designation.

Whenever we observe non-accidental similarities across languages, such as the ones illustrated in (1), two hypotheses can be entertained:

- Similar words or other linguistic traits are borrowed from one language into the others, or by all the languages in question from some other language; or
- Similar words or other linguistic traits are inherited by the languages in question from their common ancestor.

In the case of Spanish, Italian, and French considered here, some of the similarities are accounted for by borrowing and other similarities by shared inheritance. For instance, the word for *iguana* has been borrowed into Spanish, Italian, and French, as well as into Russian, Hebrew, and Hungarian, as we saw in Pause and Reflect 7.2, from one of the Native South American languages in the Arawak family. In contrast, similar words for *green*, *jump*, and *leaf* have all been inherited from a common ancestor, Latin. The existence of such a shared ancestor is the reason that Spanish, Italian, and French are grouped into one language family, Romance.

7.2.1 Proving Language Relatedness

To show that certain languages are related due to a shared ancestor, we must identify the existence of similarities between them that are too numerous and systematic to be accidental. Moreover, such similarities should not be explainable through borrowing from one language into another. Before we can deal with the borrowing issue, let's consider what *numerous and systematic similarities* entails. The easiest place to look for such similarities is in the lexicon. However, not all words of a language are a good indication of its belonging to a particular language family. In fact, words for cultural concepts such as foods, religious beliefs and practices, or technological innovations are very often borrowed from one language into another. For example, English has borrowed *spaghetti* from Italian and *sushi* from Japanese, *kosher* from Yiddish, and *sputnik* from Russian. The words for *iguana* in the languages illustrated above are loanwords from Taino, an Arawak language historically spoken in the Caribbean.

Linguists therefore look for words from the so-called **basic vocabulary**, which includes words for kinship terms (e.g., *mother*, *brother*), basic body parts (e.g., *head*, *heart*), low numbers (e.g., *three*, *five*), pronouns (e.g., *I*, *you*), etc. Such words can on occasion be borrowed also – for example, English borrowed pronouns *they, them, their* from Old Norse – but compared to *cultural vocabulary*, borrowing of basic vocabulary is considerably rarer. Therefore, numerous similar words across certain languages within their basic vocabularies is good evidence for these languages belonging to the same language family.

It is important to note that *similar words* does not mean words that are identical. In fact, in most cases, words that are similar across languages because they descend from the same ancestral form (known as **cognates**) are not identical. Such subtle yet systematic differences come about because each language in a language family undergoes its own sound changes (see Chapter 8 Historical Linguistics to read more on sound change).

Let's go back to the three Romance languages considered above and their words for *leaf*:

(2) Spanish: hoja
Italian: foglia
French: feuille

All three words developed from a shared ancestral form, the Latin *folia*. In the case of Spanish, the initial /f/ was replaced first by /h/ (which is still evident in spelling) and then dropped in pronunciation altogether, leaving us with ['oxa]. This process is evident in other words inherited from Latin, such as *hijo* "son" (pronounced ['ixo]), which corresponds to French *fils* and Italian *figlio*. Another sound change exhibited by the Spanish *hoja* is the change from the palatalized /lj/ into voiceless velar fricative /x/ (also evident in *hijo* "son").

EYES ON WORLD LANGUAGES: LADINO

The sound changes that Spanish underwent in the course of its history, with their intermediate stages, can be seen through another language that shares an ancestor with Modern Spanish – Ladino. Sometimes called Judeo-Spanish, Judezmo, or Hakitia, Ladino is a language of Sephardic Jews who were exiled from Spain in 1492. The majority of these exiles resettled in either the Ottoman Empire or North Africa (chiefly, Morocco) and continued to speak the language based on fifteenth-century Castilian Spanish. As is often the case with the languages of immigrants and settlers, Ladino has preserved many traits that have long disappeared from Modern Spanish.

Consider, for example, the word for *son*, which is pronounced ['fiʒo], ['hiʒo], ['iʒo] in different dialects of Ladino. The first, most conservative form contains [f] inherited by shared ancestry of Spanish and Ladino from Latin. The second form shows the intermediate stage in the development of this sound in Spanish, when it was pronounced [h] (which is also reflected in the spelling of Modern Spanish). The third, most innovative form is closest to the corresponding word in Modern Spanish, where the initial consonant has been deleted.

Note also the pronunciation of the second consonant [ʒ] in the word *son* in Ladino. It is pronounced the same as the first sound of the French *jour* "day" or the last consonant of the English *garage*. It is therefore unlike both the Latin source, [lj], and the Modern Spanish form [x]. In fact, the Ladino pronunciation once again reveals the intermediate stage in the sound change that happened in Spanish, from [lj] to [dʒ] to [ʒ] to [x], which is otherwise only noticeable in spelling.

French, on the other hand, underwent different changes, including the deletion of final /a/ (which is still retained in Spanish and Italian), the change of /lj/ to /j/, the fronting of the stressed /o/ into /ø/. As a result, the Spanish and the French words are quite different both from each other and from the Italian word, which is the closest to the original Latin form.

The systematic nature of sound correspondences across languages within the same family is further illustrated in Table 7.1. The /k/ in Sardinian corresponds to /tʃ/ in Italian, /ts/ in Romansh (a Romance language spoken in eastern Switzerland), /s/ in French, and /θ/ in European Spanish.

TABLE 7.1 Sound Correspondences in Some Romance Languages

	Sardinian	Italian	Romansh	French	(European) Spanish
one hundred	/kɛntu/	/tʃɛnto/	/tsjɛnt/	/sã/	/θjen/
sky	/kɛlu/	/tʃelo/	/tsil/	/sjɛl/	/θjelo/
stag	/kɛrbu/	/tʃɛrvo/	/tsɛrf/	/sɛʀ/	/θjerbo/

Besides comparing individual words across languages, hypothesized language relatedness can also be shown by comparing grammatical patterns across languages. For example, in both Homer's *Iliad*, written in Ancient Greek, and the *Rigveda*, written in Sanskrit, we find the phrase meaning "imperishable fame" in (3).

(3)   Ancient Greek: /kléos/   /ápʰtʰiton/
Sanskrit: /ʃrávah/   /ákṣitam/

Notice in (3) that in both languages, the word order is the same: the adjective *imperishable* follows the noun *fame* (unlike in English, where the order is reversed). Moreover, both Ancient Greek and Sanskrit had a grammatical gender system (in particular, the word *fame* was neuter in both languages) and a case system; in both languages, neuter nouns like *fame* did not distinguish nominative and accusative case forms. The specific endings, such as the neuter nominative/accusative singular ending on *imperishable* (*–on* vs. *–am*), were similar in the two languages.

Based on similarities such as these, British philologist and Chief Justice of India Sir William Jones (1746–1794) noted in a famous speech at the Royal Asiatic Society:

> The Sanskrit language, whatever be its antiquity, is of a wonderful structure; more perfect than the Greek, more copious than the Latin, and more exquisitely refined than either, yet bearing to both of them a stronger affinity, both in the roots of verbs and in the forms of grammar, than could possibly have been produced by accident; so strong, indeed, that no philologer could examine them all three, without believing them to have sprung from some common source, which, perhaps, no longer exists.

This observation laid the ground for establishing the existence of the Indo-European language family, which includes English, Spanish, Greek, Irish, Russian, and Hindi, as well as many other languages in Europe, the Middle East, and northern and central India. Today, this is the most wide-spread language family, with some 45 percent of the world's population speaking one of the Indo-European languages as their mother tongue.

7.2.2   Reconstructing Ancestral Languages

Following on the work of eighteenth century British philologists, early nineteenth century German scholars such as Franz Bopp (1791–1867) and August Schleicher (1821–1868) fleshed out what became known as the **comparative reconstruction method**, whereby words and structures are compared across related languages in order to reconstruct their shared ancestor. Such a reconstructed ancestral language is typically called a **proto-language**, (e.g., *proto-X*, where X is the name of the language family). Thus, the reconstructed ancestor of all Indo-European languages is called **Proto-Indo-European** (PIE).

We will fully discuss and practice language reconstruction in Chapter 8 Historical Linguistics but since it is highly relevant to this chapter, we will briefly introduce it here. Such reconstructions of ancestral languages are needed because in most cases, these ancestral languages are not known to us through written records. Some ancestral languages were spoken before writing existed (see Chapter 11 Writing Systems), while others were spoken more recently by illiterate groups. Only a few ancestral languages survived in the written record, most notably Latin, the ancestor of the Romance languages, and Old Norse, the ancestor of present-day Scandinavian languages (Icelandic, Faroese, Swedish, Danish, and Norwegian).

Although in previous chapters, we have used the asterisk to represent that something is ungrammatical, in our chapter in addition to Chapter 8 Historical Linguistics, we use the * to show reconstructed forms that are gleaned from written records. For example, the reconstructed form in PIE for the word *two* is **dwóh*.

PAUSE AND REFLECT 7.3

Some languages, like PIE, are entirely reconstructed, and hence all PIE forms must be preceded by an asterisk. Latin, in contrast, is known to us from numerous written sources, yet on occasion you might see a Latin form preceded by an asterisk to mark it as a reconstruction rather than a recorded form. Why would anyone bother to reconstruct Latin, which has left plentiful written documents?

Let's now consider more closely how ancestral languages can be reconstructed from forms found in their descendant languages. First, we need to collect presumed cognates, that is words that are similar in sound and meaning and which we assume to have derived from a common ancestral word. For purposes of illustration, let's consider cognate words for *goat* from four Romance languages: Italian, Spanish, Portuguese, and French, shown in Table 7.2. Those words are aligned so that patterns of similarities can be more easily observed. For the purposes of this illustration, we will focus on the first four sounds only.

PAUSE AND REFLECT 7.4

As you can see from Table 7.2, the first sound is /k/ in Italian, Spanish, and Portuguese, corresponding to /ʃ/ in French. The second sound is likewise the same in Italian, Spanish, and Portuguese, /a/, corresponding to /ɛ/ in French. In the third slot, we have /p/ in Italian, /b/ in Spanish and Portuguese, and /v/ in French. What were the sounds in those positions in the ancestral language (which you now know to be Latin)?

TABLE 7.2 More Sound Correspondences in Romance languages

Language	"goat"	#1	#2	#3	#4	Etc.
Italian	/kapra/	k	a	p	r	…
Spanish	/kabra/	k	a	b	r	…
Portuguese	/kabra/	k	a	b	r	…
French	/ʃɛvrə/	ʃ	ɛ	v	r	…
ancestral		?	?	?	?	…

In answering the question in Pause and Reflect 7.4, you might have decided to go with the "majority vote", picking whatever sound is found in that position in most languages: /k/ in the first position, /a/ in the second, etc. This approach is quite reasonable: since languages inherit forms and patterns from their ancestor, more languages would show the conservative, unchanged form rather than a new one. For example, having inherited /k/ from Latin, most languages in the sample did not change it, with only French palatalizing it into /ʃ/. Similarly, most languages would be postulated to have inherited and maintained /a/ in the second position with French again being the only innovator.

While this majority-based approach to reconstruction works some of the time, it falls apart in other instances. Consider the third slot in these words for *goat*: did the ancestral language have /p/, /b/, or /v/? The majority approach predicts /b/ since two out of four languages, Spanish and Portuguese, have /b/ in this position. If this were correct, the Latin word for *goat* would have been *cabra*, however, we know that is incorrect: think of the zodiac sign, whose name derives from this Latin word: it is *Capricorn*, not *Cabricorn* (here, the asterisk indicates our incorrect reconstruction). Now you can see that reconstructing Latin – and then comparing it to the forms that are either recorded in written documents or are known through later (learned) loanwords – has its merit. Through such reconstruction-and-comparison we discover that the majority approach to reconstruction is not always valid.

But do we have a better way to reconstruct ancestral forms, especially where no comparison with known forms is possible? Through decades of examining sound changes at different time periods and around the world, linguists have noted that certain changes tend to happen in language after language, while the reverse changes are either very rare or unheard of. For example, it was noted that voiceless consonants tend to become voiced between two voiced sounds, especially vowels and /r/. This process is known as *rendaku* in Japanese, giving us *origami* (literally "folding paper"), from *ori* "folding" and **k**ami "paper", as well as *nigiri-zushi* "type of sushi roll" and *yu-**d**ofu* "simmered tofu". In these compound words, the first sound of the second part of the compound becomes voiced due to its position between two vowels.

The very same process turned the voiceless /p/ in the Latin *capra* into a voiced /b/ in Spanish and Portuguese, while an additional process further made it into a fricative in French. The reverse sound change, whereby a voiced consonant turns voiceless between vowels or /r/, is unheard of. Reconstructing ancestral forms by considering which sound changes are common, and which ones are rare or unknown, is known as the **directionality approach**.

Let us now go back to the words in Table 7.1. Which sound do you think should be in the initial position of these words? Since each language exhibits a different sound – /k/ in Sardinian, /tʃ/ in Italian, /ts/ in Romansch, /s/ in French, and /θ/ in European Spanish – the majority approach gives us no clear winner. The directionality approach, on the other hand, is more promising: it has been noted that velar sounds tend to become fronted before front vowels. This process which you read about in Chapter 2 Phonetics, known as **palatalization**, was observed in the history of English, giving us *church* rather than *kirk*, as in related Germanic languages. The same process of palatalization also happened in Slavic languages, as reflected by such present-day Russian alternations as *čelove**k*** "man" – *čelove**č**ek* "little man".

> **LINGUISTICS TIDBITS: DUNKIRK, KIRKBYMOORSIDE, AND KIRKCALDY**
>
> The three words in the title of this box all contain -*kirk*, but in each case, it comes from a different source. The -*kirk* in *Dunkirk* comes from the West Flemish word for "church", which unlike its English counterpart did not undergo palatalization. (West Flemish is a Germanic language spoken in Belgium and the Netherlands.) The *kirk*- in *Kirkbymoorside* is of Scandinavian origin and also means "church". (The -*by* in this placename is another Viking word, meaning "town".) But the *kirk*- in *Kirkcaldy* is of Celtic origin and means "fortress".

The reverse of palatalization – namely a change from alveolar or palato-alveolar into velar sounds, especially before front vowels – has not been observed across many languages. Based on this generalization, we can postulate that the ancestral Proto-Romance (i.e., Latin) had /k/ in the beginning of the words in Table 7.1, which was retained in Sardinian, while all the other languages innovated by turning the velar /k/ into a palato-alveolar /tʃ/, an alveolar /ts/ or /s/, or even an interdental /θ/.

Thus, by comparing forms in descendant languages, piece-by-piece, we can reconstruct their shared ancestors, sometimes – as in the case of PIE – enough to write an entire story in the language. For example, August Schleicher wrote a story in PIE about a sheep and a horse, which is shown in a more recent rendition in Figure 7.1.

h₂áu̯ei̯ h₁i̯osméi̯ h₂ul̥h₁náh₂ né h₁ést, só h₁éku̯oms derḱt. só gʷr̥h₂úm u̯óǵʰom u̯eǵʰed; só méǵh₂m̥ bʰórom; só dʰǵʰémonm̥ h₂ṓḱu bʰered. h₂óu̯is h₁ékʷoi̯bʰi̯os u̯eu̯ked: "dʰǵʰémonm̥ spéḱi̯oh₂ h₁éku̯oms-kʷe h₂áǵeti, ḱér moi̯ agʰnutor". h₁éku̯ōs tu u̯eu̯kond: "ḱludʰí, h₂ou̯ei̯! tód spéḱi̯omes, n̥sméi̯ agʰnutór ḱér: dʰǵʰémō, pótis, sē h₂áu̯i̯es h₂ul̥h₁náh₂ gʷʰérmom u̯éstrom u̯ept, h₂áu̯i̯bʰi̯os tu h₂ul̥h₁náh₂ né h₁esti. tód ḱeḱlu̯u̯ṓs h₂óu̯is h₂aǵróm bʰuged.

Figure 7.1 August Schleicher's PIE story. Translation: A sheep that had no wool saw horses, one of them pulling a heavy wagon, one carrying a big load, and one carrying a man quickly. The sheep said to the horses: "My heart pains me, seeing a man driving horses." The horses said: "Listen, sheep, our hearts pain us when we see this: a man, the master, makes the wool of the sheep into a warm garment for himself. And the sheep has no wool." Having heard this, the sheep fled into the plain (Beekes, 2011, p. 287).

7.2.3 Language Families within Language Families

Our discussion so far has focused on two language families: Romance and Indo-European. However, these two language families are not independent but rather, the Romance language family is a subset of a larger Indo-European language family. Unlike biologists, who label various levels on the Tree of Life differently (kingdom, order, family, genus), linguists use the same term *language family* for groupings at different levels of the Language Family Tree. To continue with our example, Spanish and Portuguese form the Ibero-Romance language family within a larger Western Romance language family (which also includes Catalan and French), within a larger Italo-Romance language family (which also includes Italian), within a larger Romance family, within a larger Indo-European language family.

Similarly, Swedish, Danish, and Norwegian constitute the Mainland Scandinavian language family, within a larger Scandinavian (or North Germanic) language family (which also includes Icelandic and Faroese), within a larger Germanic family (which also includes German, Dutch, Yiddish, and English), within a larger Indo-European family. Using a little creativity, language families can be thought of as Russian *matryoshka*-dolls, as shown in Figure 7.2.

7.2.4 Language Families around the World

Most of the languages mentioned so far in this chapter belong to the Indo-European language family; the only two exceptions are Hebrew and Hungarian, mentioned in Pause and Reflect 7.2. These two languages belong to Semitic and Finno-Ugric language families, respectively.

The Semitic language family also includes such languages as Arabic, Amharic, and Tigrinya (the latter two are major languages of Ethiopia). The Semitic family constitutes a branch of a larger language family called Afroasiatic, which also includes Berber, Chadic, Cushitic, Omotic, and Egyptian language families (the latter includes only one language, Coptic), all spoken in northern Africa.

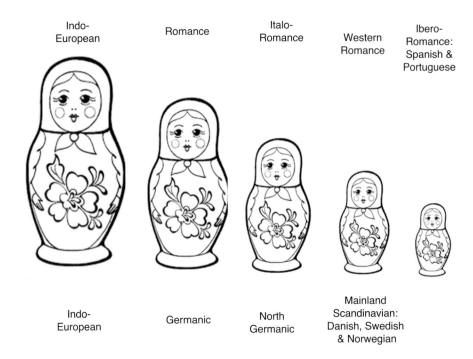

Indo-
European

Romance

Italo-
Romance

Western
Romance

Ibero-
Romance:
Spanish &
Portuguese

Indo-
European

Germanic

North
Germanic

Mainland
Scandinavian:
Danish, Swedish
& Norwegian

Figure 7.2 Language families within language families

PAUSE AND REFLECT 7.5

Can you think of any other examples of *matryoshka*-doll-like language classifications involving familiar languages?

The best-known members of the Finno-Ugric language family, besides Hungarian, are Finnish and Estonian, but the family also includes a number of smaller languages spoken by various groups primarily in northern Russia. The closest linguistic relatives of Hungarian, found in the Ugric branch of the Finno-Ugric family, are Khanty and Mansi, spoken by two semi-nomadic reindeer-herding groups east of the Ural Mountains. The Finno-Ugric family is often grouped with a smaller family of languages called Samoyedic, likewise spoken in Western Siberia, into a larger Uralic family.

Many other languages in Siberia have been grouped together into a putative Altaic language family, although it remains highly controversial. Its constituent branches – Turkic, Mongolic, and Tungusic – are, however, well established. Languages of the Turkic family are spoken in a large swath of territory extending from Turkey to the Sakha Republic (a constituent part of the Russian Federation in Eastern Siberia). The Mongolic language family includes Mongolian, as well as a number of smaller languages in the same region. Tungusic languages are also spoken by reindeer-herding nomads of Eastern Siberia.

Other well-established language families include:

- Dravidian languages in southern India (including Malayalam, Tamil, and Kannada);
- Kartvelian languages in southern Caucasus (including Georgian, Laz, and several smaller languages);
- Niger-Congo languages, the largest language family in terms of the number of languages (with over 1,500 languages) spoken in Western, Central, and southern Africa;
- Sino-Tibetan languages, including Mandarin, Cantonese and other "Chinese languages", as well as Tibetan languages;
- Austronesian languages, the second largest language family (with over 1,200 languages), spoken by aboriginal Taiwanese groups in the Philippines, Madagascar, and throughout Polynesia; and
- Athabaskan languages, spoken in western North America – a family that includes several languages spoken in the Canadian provinces of British Columbia, Alberta, Saskatchewan, Manitoba, and in the Northwest Territories.

While many known languages have been classified into language families, several languages simply cannot be grouped as such. These languages are known as **isolates**. Unlike other languages, which have *siblings* and *cousins*, isolates are – to the best of our current understanding – *orphan* languages, with no known relatives. Two well-known isolates are Basque and Burushaski, both of which are spoken in geographically isolated, mountainous regions. Such terrain indeed promotes linguistic diversity and the survival of last known members of language families.

As our understanding of various languages and their history develops, the overall genetic classification of languages and labeling of some of them as isolates may change. For example, recent work by Edward Vajda has shown that an indigenous Western Siberian language called Ket, formerly considered to be an isolate, is distantly related to Athabaskan languages in North America.

Classification of indigenous languages, both in North and South America, was first proposed by American linguist Joseph Greenberg. Yet, many controversies surrounding the classification of these languages are still standing.

EYES ON WORLD LANGUAGES: INDIGENOUS LANGUAGES IN NORTH AMERICA

There are hundreds of indigenous languages spoken in North America with the vast majority of them in different degrees of endangerment. Efforts are underway to record, maintain, and revive some of these languages. Often, indigenous languages in North America are classified into several language families:

- Algonquian: Abenaki, Algonquin, Atikamekw, Blackfoot, Cree (different varieties), Malecite-Passamaquoddy, Micmac, Montagnais, Munsee, Naskapi, Ojibwa (different varieties), Ottawa, Potawatomi;

- Athabaskan: Babine, Beaver, Carrier, Chilcotin, Dene, Dogrib, Gwich'in, Han, Kaska, Sarsi, Sekani, Slavey (different varieties), Tagish, Tahltan, Tanana, Tutchone (different varieties);
- Eskimo-Aleut: Inuinnaqtun, Inuktitut (different varieties);
- Haida: Northern Haida, Southern Haida;
- Iroquoian: Cayuga, Mohawk, Oneida, Onondaga, Tuscarora, Wyandot;
- Salish: Bella Coola, Comox, Halkomelem, Lillooet, Okanagan, Straits Salish, Sechelt, Shuswap, Squamish, Thompson;
- Siouan: Assiniboine, Dakota, Lakota, Stoney;
- Tsimshian: Gitxsan, Nisga'a, Tsimshian;
- Wakashan: Ditidaht, Haisla, Heiltsuk, Kwakiutl, Nuu-chah-nulth.

Kutenai is considered an isolate, whereas Michif cannot be classified into a particular language family because it is a mixed language deriving not from one ancestral language but from two: it combines nouns and nominal bound morphemes from French with verbs and verbal bound morphemes from Cree.

7.2.5   Language Families: How Far Back Can We Go?

If we think of Romance and Germanic as families (or as they are sometimes called *branches*) within a larger Indo-European language family, you might wonder whether the Indo-European family itself is a part of some even larger language family. This is a valid question, and many scholars have argued over this issue for decades. Still, it remains a heated controversy to this day. Joseph Greenberg proposed that Indo-European is a branch of a large family called Eurasiatic, which would also include Uralic and Altaic language families. More recently, Allan Bomhard proposed that Eurasiatic is a branch of an even bigger language family, called Nostratic. This Nostratic mega-family would also include Afro-Asiatic, Kartvelian, and Dravidian language families. The Nostratic hypothesis goes back to Danish linguist Holger Pedersen, who put it forward in the early twentieth century. In the 1960s, the Nostratic proposal was further expanded by two Soviet scholars, Vladislav Illich-Svitych and Aharon Dolgopolsky.

Today, these hypotheses are endorsed by a minority of linguists, including American scholar Merritt Ruhlen for the Eurasiatic hypothesis, and several Russian linguists for the Nostratic hypothesis. However, neither theory gained much traction within the larger field of historical linguistics, the primary reason being that most linguists think that comparative reconstruction can only be taken so far.

Still, a number of far-reaching – and very controversial – hypotheses have been put forward over the years, including:

- The Sino-Caucasian hypothesis, proposed by Sergei Starostin, relates Chinese and languages of the North Caucasus region;
- The Dene-Caucasian hypothesis, which places the putative Sino-Caucasian language family as a branch of a larger family to include Athabaskan languages, and two languages currently considered to be isolates: Basque and Burushaski;

- The Sino-Austric hypothesis, which relates Chinese and Tibetan languages with Austroasiatic languages (including Vietnamese and Khmer), Austronesian languages (such as Filipino, Malagasy, and Hawaiian), as well as Thai and Hmong-Mien languages; and
- The Borean hypothesis, which includes all of the above language families.

7.3   The Typological Classification of Languages

Besides their genetic relatedness to other languages, languages can also be classified by their linguistic features. Since languages differ on many aspects at various levels – phonology, morphology, syntax, semantics – numerous typological classifications have been devised. Below, we will consider three such classifications that fall into the domains of morphology, syntax, and semantics.

7.3.1   Morphological Types

The first typological classification to be considered here involves the ways in which languages build words out of morphemes. There are three major types of languages with respect to the way their morphology operates: isolating, agglutinative, and fusional.

In an **isolating language** (not to be confused with an isolate language), words typically consist of one or two morphemes, and grammatical meanings such as number or tense are expressed not by affixes attached to nouns or verbs, but by separate words. An example of a language with (mostly) isolating morphology is Mandarin Chinese. In Mandarin, plurality is not expressed by an affix on the noun, but by a separate word. As you can see in example (4), Mandarin has marked plural with the (unbound) word ji^3 (note that the superscripted numbers indicate tones on the preceding vowels).

(4) na⁴er⁵   you³   ji³   zhi¹   gou³
     there   have   several CLASSIFIER dog
     "There are dogs there."

In an additional twist, the presence of the plural word requires yet another word, called a **classifier**, which makes the noun itself countable. Classifiers are somewhat like words such as *grain* in *a grain of sand* in English, which are sometimes called *massifiers*. Yet Mandarin *massifiers* and *classifiers* behave differently and therefore cannot be subsumed under the same category.

In an **agglutinative language**, words typically consist of multiple morphemes. Each grammatical morpheme in such a language carries only one meaning, with meanings like number and case being expressed by separate morphemes. Table 7.3 provides some examples from Tatar, a language spoken by 5.3 million people in the Volga Region of Russia (for the sake of presentation, the morphemes are separated by hyphens):

As can be seen from Table 7.3, nominative does not have a specific marker, while genitive is marked by –nıŋ, and dative by –ga. Plural number is expressed by the suffix –lar,

TABLE 7.3 Some of the Case-Number Forms of *bala* "child" in Tatar

Case	Singular	Plural
Nominative ("child")	bala	bala-lar
Genitive ("of child")	bala-nıŋ	bala-lar-nıŋ
Dative ("to child")	bala-ga	bala-lar-ga

which attaches before the case marker. (There is no definite marker in Tatar, so *bala-lar* can be translated as either "children" or "the children".)

Furthermore, possession is also expressed by a separate suffix, which must follow the number suffix and precede the case suffix. For example, "our children" is *bala-lar-ıbız* and "of our children" is *bala-lar-ıbız-nıŋ*.

PAUSE AND REFLECT 7.6

Given what you have just read about Tatar morphology, how would you say the genitive plural of *alma* "apple" ("of the apples")? How about the dative singular of *mašina* "car" ("to the car")? And what about the dative plural of the possessed noun, "to our cars"?

Finally, the third major morphological type of language is **fusional**. In such a language, several grammatical meanings can be expressed by a single, *fused* morpheme. Compare, for example, how *of the children* is expressed in Tatar (an agglutinative language) and in Russian (a fusional language). Note that neither language expresses definiteness or indefiniteness, but the two grammatical meanings that are expressed in both languages – number and case – are expressed differently: by a three-morpheme Tatar word *bala-lar-nıŋ* vs. a two-morpheme Russian word *det-ej*. The first morpheme in each word is the root *child*, but the difference in the number of morphemes comes from the fact that in Tatar the plural number and the genitive case are expressed by two separate morphemes, –lar and –nıŋ, respectively, whereas in Russian, both concepts are expressed simultaneously by a single morpheme, –ej.

But differences between agglutinative and fusional languages do not end there. In Tatar, the plural is always –lar and the genitive is always –nıŋ (except for adjustments due to vowel harmony, which are ubiquitous in the language and do not concern these specific morphemes). In Russian, in contrast, the genitive plural may be expressed by the suffix *–ej*, as in the example above, or by *–ov*, as in *kot–ov* "of (male) cats", or by a zero morpheme, as in *sobak–0* (where "0" indicates a zero morpheme) meaning "of dogs". The choice idiosyncratically depends on the noun itself. If you want to speak Russian, you must learn which nouns go with *–ej*, *–ov*, or no morpheme at all, and the same for all other number/case combinations.

In a fusional language, a root may affect the form of the suffix, but sometimes the suffix can affect the form of the root too. For example, in Russian, the suffix *–n*, which forms adjectives out of nouns, affects the pronunciation of the last consonant in the root. In particular, it turns the /k/ in *ru**k**–* "hand" into [tʃ] in *ručnoj*, the /g/ in *sne**g**–* "snow" into [ʒ] (as in the middle of the English *measure*) in *snežnyj*, and the /x/ in *pu**x**–* "down" into [ʃ] in *pušnoj*. As is evident from words like ***kn**iga* "book", ***gn**u* "gnu", and ***xn**a* "henna", the combinations of /k/, /g/, and /x/ with the following /n/ are not themselves a problem, and it is the adjective-forming suffix that determines these changes.

PAUSE AND REFLECT 7.7

What process does the alternation of [k] *ruk–* [tʃ] *ručnoj* illustrate? If this process is triggered by the suffix *–n*, as suggested in the text, what makes this particular instance of the more general process odd?

To recap:

- In an isolating language, grammatical meanings are expressed by separate words rather than morphemes;
- In an agglutinative language, grammatical meanings are each expressed by separate morphemes, which attach to the root sequentially and do not affect the form of other grammatical affixes or of the root;
- In a fusional language, several grammatical meanings can be expressed jointly by a single morpheme, with both grammatical affixes and roots affecting the choice and pronunciation of each other.

7.3.2 Word Orders

Perhaps one of the most conspicuous differences among languages is their syntax. Recall from our discussion in Section 7.2 above, that adjectives may precede or follow the noun they modify. For example, in English, adjectives precede the nouns they modify as in *a white house*, while in Spanish, adjectives typically follow the nouns they modify as in *una casa blanca*, literally "a house white". In French, adjectives may either follow or precede the nouns, sometimes with a difference in meaning: *un grand homme*, literally "a big man", refers to a man great in significance, whereas *un homme grand* means someone large in stature. Napoleon may have been *un grand homme*, but not *un homme grand*.

In fact, languages within the Romance family differ as to the placement of adjectives with respect to nouns, with French and Walloon (a Romance language spoken in Belgium) allowing the most pre-nominal adjectives and Sardinian and Sicilian going exclusively for the noun-adjectives order. This trait of French and Walloon, rather unusual for their language family, is said to be a result of an influence from Germanic languages such as Old Frankish and Old Flemish.

Let's now consider nouns modified by multiple adjectives, as in *a nice English woman*. The reverse order, *an English nice woman*, appears to be degraded (without emphasis, it sounds like *bad English*, which is marked here by an asterisk). Curiously, it appears that all languages in which adjectives precede the noun exhibit the same order, with the so-called *evaluative* adjectives preceding an adjective of origin or nationality. In languages where adjectives follow the nouns, however, either order is possible, depending on the language. For example, in Irish, evaluative adjectives *precede* those of origin or nationality as in (5a) whereas in Hebrew, evaluative adjectives *follow* those of origin or nationality like in (5b).

(5)	a.	an fear	deas	Eireannach	(Irish)
		the man	nice	Irish	
		"the nice Irish man"			
	b.	ha-baxur	ha-'isra'eli	ha-nexmad	(Hebrew)
		DEF-guy	DEF-Israeli	DEF-nice	
		"the nice Israeli guy"			

PAUSE AND REFLECT 7.8

Consider how noun phrases with multiple adjectives (e.g., evaluative adjectives and adjectives of origin or nationality) work in French, a language where some adjectives precede the noun and others follow it. If you speak French, consider your own intuitions. If you do not speak French, ask a speaker if you can find one. You can also Google different hypothesized patterns using adjectives from the examples in the text – which patterns do you find and how many hits do you get?

For the rest of this section, we will consider the order of the major sentence constituents: subject (S), object (O), and verb (V). Hypothetically, these three elements can appear in any of the six orders: SOV, SVO, VSO, VOS, OSV, and OVS. As it turns out, each of these logical orders is used in the world's languages, as illustrated in (6).

(6)   Tatar (a Turkic language, spoken in Russia, SOV):

Marat	kızıl	alma-nı	ašadı.
Marat	red	apple-ACC	ate
S	O		V

"Marat ate a red apple" or "Marat ate the red apple."

Italian (a Romance language, spoken in Italy, SVO):

Gianni ha	mangiato	la	pasta.
Gianni has	eaten	the	pasta
S	V	O	

"Gianni has eaten the pasta."

Welsh (a Celtic language, spoken in Wales, VSO):

Ddarllenodd	Emrys mo	'r	llyfr.
read	Emrys not	the	book
V	S	O	

"Emrys hasn't read the book."

Malagasy (an Austronesian language, spoken on Madagascar, VOS):

Manasa	ny	lamba	Rakoto.
washes	the	clothes	Rakoto
V	O		S

"Rakoto washes the clothes."

Apurinã (a Southern Maipurean language, spoken in Amazonia, OSV):

anana	nota	apa
pineapple	I	fetch
O	S	V

"I fetch a pineapple."

Hixkaryana (a Carib language, spoken in Amazonia, OVS):

toto	yonoye	kamara
person	ate	jaguar
O	V	S

"The jaguar ate the man."

Although all of the six word order possibilities in (6) can be found in the languages of the world, they are not distributed evenly across languages. The most frequent order is SOV, found in about 45 percent of the world's languages, including Japanese, Korean, Hindi, Tamil, Georgian, and Basque. Second comes SVO, which is only slightly less common than SOV and is found in about 42 percent of the world's languages, including Mandarin, Hausa, Indonesian, and of course English. Since the majority (about 87 percent) of the world's languages exhibit one of two subject-initial orders, the other four possible orders are considerably rarer. The third most frequent order is VSO, which is found in only 9 per cent of languages, including Biblical Hebrew and Classical Arabic, Irish and Scottish Gaelic, Filipino, and Tuareg (a Berber language). Next comes VOS, which is found, for example, in Malagasy and several Arawakan languages indigenous to South America. This order is exhibited by only 3 percent of the world's languages. Object-initial orders, OSV and OVS, are the least common and found in only a handful of languages.

Many languages, however, show variable word order: depending on the context, a different order of subject, object, and verb may be suitable. An example of such a language is Russian, shown in (7), where all six logically possible orders are possible. The chosen order depends on what has been the subject of conversation thus far: typically, elements already brought up in a given conversation are placed early in the sentence, while the final position is reserved for new information.

(7)   Russian (a Slavic language, spoken in Russia, "free order"?):

Vanya	vodk-u	vypil.
Vanya	vodka-ACC	drank
S	O	V

Vanya	vypil	vodk-u.
Vanya	drank	vodka-ACC
S	V	O

Vypil	Vanya	vodk-u.
drank	Vanya	vodka-ACC
V	S	O

Vypil	vodk-u	Vanya.
drank	vodka-ACC	Vanya
V	O	S

Vodk-u	Vanya	vypil.
vodka-ACC	Vanya	drank
O	S	V

Vodk-u	vypil	Vanya.
vodka-ACC	drank	Vanya
O	V	S

all: "Vanya drank vodka."

One possible approach in dealing with free-word-order languages like Russian is to place them outside the word order typology. However, there are reasons to believe that this is not the right way to handle word order in Russian. As was noted by Russian

PAUSE AND REFLECT 7.9

When relying on word order, how can one classify a language like Russian, where depending on the context of the conversation, any of the six orders may be

chosen? Where does it fit into the word order typology? Should such *free word order* languages be considered a separate type? Explain why.

linguist Roman Jakobson (Jakobson, 1936/1984), when a sentence contains a subject and an object that are both nouns but because of a quirk of Russian morphology, do not distinguish nominative and accusative forms (thus making it impossible to tell from the form of the nouns which is the subject and which is the object), speakers of Russian understand such sentences as having the SVO order, and not OVS. We see this type of example in (8).

(8) Mat'   ljubit   doč'.
     mother.NOM/ACC   loves   daughter.NOM/ACC
     "Mother loves daughter", *not* "Daughter loves mother."

The preference for SVO even when a sentence could be interpreted as OVS as in (8) has been confirmed by experimental work conducted by Irina Sekerina (1997). In her experiment, Russian speakers were asked to choose one of two pictures that best represented a given sentence. For instance, the experimental sentence (9) was accompanied by two pictures: one of a bus overtaking a trolley and the other of a trolley overtaking a bus. The participants overwhelmingly chose the pictures that illustrated the SVO order even though the sentence could have been interpreted as OVS.

(9) Avtobus   obognal   trollejbus.
     bus.NOM/ACC   overtook   trolley.NOM/ACC
     "The bus overtook the trolley", *not* "The trolley overtook the bus."

On the basis of such studies, it has been concluded that Russian is inherently an SVO order, with the apparent variability of word order being due to the case marking, which helps figure out which is the subject and which is the object. To read more on how to deal with free order languages using Russian as an example, see 'Delving Deeper' in Chapter 7's resources located on the website to accompany this book at www.cambridge.org/introducing-linguistics.

Indigenous languages spoken in North America exhibit a variety of word order types, with many languages exhibiting the VSO order (e.g., Lillooet, Upriver Halkomelem, Nisgha, Bella Coola, Coast Tsimshian, Squamish, Musqueam, Heiltsuk, and Kyuquot), and many others alternating between the VSO and VOS orders (e.g., Nuuchahnulth, Eastern Ojibwa, Shuswap, Kutenai, and Thompson) or between the VSO and SVO orders (e.g., Kwakw'ala). Some languages indigenous to Canada exhibit the SOV order (e.g., Sarcee, Chipewyan, Haida, and Slave). In Cayuga, a Northern Iroquoian language spoken in Ontario and New York, the object may either follow or precede the verb depending on whether the speaker has a specific entity in mind, as you can see in (10) (adapted from Mithun, 1992, p. 28).

(10) katsihwá'   kihsa:s
Hammer   I.seek
O   V

"I'm looking for a hammer." (Said in a shop, with no particular hammer in mind.)

to:	ti'	nika:nô:'	nê:kyê	katsihwá'
how	then	so.it.costs	this	hammer
		V		O

"How much does this hammer cost?" (Indicating a specific hammer.)

Several other languages show no dominant word order at all (e.g., Blackfoot, Passamaquoddy-Maliseet, Plains Cree, Wyandot).

7.3.3 The Typology of Complex Events

So far, we have considered two linguistic typologies: one concerning the ways morphemes are combined into words and the other concerning the ways words are put together into phrases and sentences. In this section, we will consider a third typology that classifies languages according to a semantic phenomenon: how they express manner and direction of movement. Let's start with contrasting English and a Romance language such as French.

In English, when a sentence expresses both the manner and the direction of motion, the manner may be expressed by the verb, with the direction expressed by an adverb (e.g., *back*) or prepositional phrase (e.g., *into the room*). Look at the sentence in (11).

(11) John jogged [MANNER] back [DIRECTION].
Mary waltzed [MANNER] into the room [DIRECTION].

In contrast, in French the verb expresses direction, and the manner must be expressed by a prepositional phrase (e.g., *au petit trot* "at a jog") or some other means outside the verb as you can see in (12).

(12) Nous   sommes   revenus [DIRECTION]   au petit trot [MANNER].
we   are   returned   at.the jog
"We came back at a jog."

The same contrast is also true for when the manner concerns not the motion itself but the manner in which some agent causes the motion of another object. In English, the manner of the agent causing a motion event can be expressed in the verb, but in French it cannot be (the ungrammaticality of the examples is indicated here and below with an asterisk). The corresponding grammatical sentence in French involves a verb that does not express manner as noted in (13).

(13) English:
John shook [MANNER] the dice onto the table [DIRECTION].

French:

| *Jean | a | secoué [MANNER] | les | dès | sur | la | table [DIRECTION]. |
| John | has | shaken | the | dice | on | the | table |

intended: "John shook the dice onto the table."

| Jean | a | jeté | les | dès | sur | la | table [DIRECTION]. |
| John | has | thrown | the | dice | on | the | table |

"John threw the dice onto the table."

Furthermore, in addition to descriptions of motion, which can be understood as change of location, the same contrast is found in descriptions of change of state brought about in a specific manner. If you take a look at the examples in (14), you will see again that in English, the manner in which the change of state was brought about can be expressed in the verb, while in French it cannot.

(14) English:
John sponged [MANNER] the table clean [CHANGE].

French:

| Jean | a | nettoyé [CHANGE] | la | table avec | une | éponge [MANNER]. |
| John | has | cleaned | the | table with | a | sponge |

"John cleaned the table with a sponge."

Note that there is an asymmetry between the two types of languages: English-type languages can typically express what French-type languages can as was shown in (14). But French-type languages are not able to structure expressions in the same way as English-type languages can.

In a series of typological works, Leonard Talmy suggested classifying languages according to whether they encode direction or change in the verb (as in French), or in what he called a **satellite** – for example, an adverb, a prepositional phrase, a participle, or a gerund – as in English. He thus distinguished between **V(erb)-framed** and **S(atellite)-framed languages** (Talmy, 1985, 2000). The list of S-framed languages includes, besides English, other Germanic languages (e.g., German, Dutch, Icelandic, Swedish, and Yiddish), Slavic languages (e.g., Polish and Serbo-Croatian), Finno-Ugric languages (e.g., Finnish and Hungarian), as well as Latin. The list of V-framed languages includes various Romance languages (e.g., French as seen above, Spanish, Portuguese, Catalan, Galician), as well as Basque, Turkish, and Arabic. Interestingly, sign languages such as American Sign Language (ASL) and Sign Language of the Netherlands also belong to the V-framed type.

Subsequently, Talmy's typology has been extended by adding a third type of language, referred to as **equipollently-framed languages**, where direction and manner are expressed by equivalent grammatical forms. In some equipollently framed languages, including those in Niger-Congo, Hmong-Mien, Sino-Tibetan, Tai-Kadai, Mon-Khmer, and Austronesian families, both direction and manner are expressed by verbs in a serial verb construction, as in the Korean example in (15) (adapted from Choi & Arunachalam, 2013):

(15) Korean:

Jaein-i	wungtengi-rul	ttwuie [MANNER]	nem-esse [DIRECTION].
Jane-NOM	puddle-ACC	jump	(go)over-PAST.

"Jane jumped over the puddle."

In other equipollently-framed languages, particularly those found in North America (Algonquian, Athabaskan, Hokan, and Klamath-Takelman language families), direction and manner can be expressed in the same complex verb, as in example (16) from Chinookan (adapted from DeLancey, 2009):

(16) Chinookan:

i-	tc-	i-	u-	łáda-[MANNER]	tcu [DIRECTION]
PAST-	he-	him-	DIR-	drag-	down

"he dragged him down"

Experimental studies (cf., Cifuentes-Férez & Gentner, 2006) have shown that the V-framed/S-framed typology not only determines what structures are available in that particular language, but it also affects how speakers of that language interpret novel verbs. Read the example in (17) with the newly-introduced verb *ransined*.

(17) *So she decided to keep walking up the river and look for a bridge. After a while she noticed the river had become shallow and not so dangerous. So she took off her shoes and socks, rolled up her jeans and **ransined** the river. That night she was very happy to be back among friends again.*

Speakers of an S-framed language such as English are more likely to infer a manner interpretation than a direction interpretation, whereas speakers of a V-framed language like Spanish prefer the reverse interpretation.

7.4 Linguistic Typology and Change

In Section 7.3.3, we said that Romance languages belong to the type of V-framed languages, while their ancestral language, Latin, was an S-framed language. This means that historically Romance languages underwent a shift from S-framed to V-framed pattern. This is not the only example of a language switching its typological classification. According to Malka Rappaport Hovav, Hebrew underwent the opposite change: from V-framed Biblical Hebrew to S-framed Modern Hebrew. As shown in the following example, in Biblical Hebrew, manner and direction of motion could not be expressed in one clause; instead, they were expressed by separate coordinated clauses (sharing a subject) as shown in (18).

(18) Biblical Hebrew:

way-	yirkav [MANNER]	yehu	way-	yelɛk̲ [DIRECTION]	yizrə?ɛl-	ah.
and-	rode	Jehu	and-	went	Jezreel-	LOC

"Yehu rode and went to Jezreel." (Kings II 9:16)

Note that this structure is different from the Korean example in (15). In Korean, the two verbs form a serial verb construction whereby the tense marker (in this case, *–ess*) is shared by the two verbs. In the Biblical Hebrew example in (18), there are two conjoined clauses containing two verbs, each of which is marked for tense independently.

In contrast, you can see in (19) that in Modern Hebrew, like in English, the verb can express the manner of motion, while direction is expressed by a prepositional phrase.

(19) Modern Hebrew:

yehu raxav [MANNER]	lə- yizra?el [DIRECTION].
Jehu rode	to-Jezreel

"Yehu rode to Jezreel."

PAUSE AND REFLECT 7.10

Consider the Hebrew examples in (18) and (19). Do you notice any other typological change in the transition from Biblical to Modern Hebrew?

Just as languages can shift from V-framed to S-framed pattern and vice versa, they can also shift their allegiance with respect to other typological classifications as well. For example, you might have noticed that the Biblical Hebrew example in (18) exhibited a different order of subject and verb from that found in the Modern Hebrew sentence in (19). In Biblical Hebrew, subjects followed verbs (and objects followed subjects, in VSO order), whereas in Modern Hebrew, subjects precede verbs (while objects still follow the verb, in SVO order). You can also see the difference in word order in (20).

(20) Biblical Hebrew (VSO):

way-	yacav	'avimele<u>k</u>	'et	kol-	ha-	ʔam.
and-	warned	Avimelech	ACC	all-	the-	people

"So Avimelech warned all the people." (Genesis 26:11)

Modern Hebrew (SVO):

Dani	'axal	'et	ha-	falafel.
Dani	ate	ACC	the-	falafel

"Dani ate the falafel."

In fact, English also switched its default word order. In Old English, the default order was SOV as can be seen most clearly from subordinate clauses. But by the Middle English period, the order switched to SVO, also observable in Modern English. Compare these two formations in (21).

(21) Old English (SOV):

þæt	heora	cyng	fulwihte	onfon	wolde
that	their	king	baptism	receive	would

"that their king would receive baptism" (Anglo-Saxon Chronicle, 878CE)

Middle English (SVO):

Thyn	Astolabie	hath	a	ring	to	putten	on	the	thombe
your	astrolabe	has	a	ring	to	put	on	the	thumb

"Your astrolabe has a ring to put on the thumb."

It is thought that the change in word order in the history of English was brought about by another typological change, namely the loss of inflectional morphology. With grammatical relations, such as subject and object, no longer clearly expressed morphologically, word order became the way to convey such information. However, already in the Old English period, nouns did not distinguish nominative (subject) and accusative (object) forms. For example, "stone" was *stan* in both nominative and accusative, and its plural form was *stanas*, for both nominative and accusative. Recall from Section 7.3.2 in our discussion of the word order in Russian that in this language, in sentences where subjects and objects are not clearly marked as nominative or accusative, the word order is understood to be SVO. Clearly, the same thing did not apply to Old English.

Still, Old English had some distinguishable case forms. For example, the dative (indirect object) singular "stone" was *stane*, and the genitive (possessive) singular "stone's" was *stanes*. The genitive plural "stones'" form was *stana* and the dative plural "stones" was *stanum*. By the Middle English period, the only distinguishable form in the singular was the genitive *stanes* (nominative, accusative, and dative were all *stan*). In the plural, case marking was effectively lost, with all cases now expressed by the same form, *stanes*, which was the same as the genitive singular. With the loss of morphological dative case, its function shifted to the preposition *to*.

PAUSE AND REFLECT 7.11

Think about how tense is expressed in Modern English, in terms of morphological models discussed in Section 7.3.1. You will notice that past tense and future tense are expressed very differently. One of them is expressed through an auxiliary verb, whereas for the other the marker attaches directly to the verb. Now consider how past and future tenses are expressed in Romance languages such as French, Spanish, or Italian. Based on the fact that English and Romance languages share a common ancestor (i.e., Indo-European), which tense in Modern English would you take to be an innovation?

At the same time, English also experienced a loss of verbal inflection, with tense morphology more often being interpreted through auxiliary verbs. Because of this and other evidence, English can be said to gradually move from being a fusional language to an isolating type (as we talked about in Section 7.3.1). The same type of shift has been happening in other Indo-European languages as well. PIE is reconstructed as having a purely fusional model, while its present-day descendants have all developed some degree of isolating morphology. English and French (as well as other Romance languages) have moved further along this path, as compared to Slavic languages like Russian or Baltic languages like Lithuanian.

Isolating languages do not stand still either (in fact, no language can ever remain totally unchanged). Thus, Early Chinese is reconstructed as being predominantly isolating with elements of fusion (not unlike Modern English), while Classical Chinese was a purely isolating language, and Modern Chinese (e.g., Mandarin) has developed some agglutinative morphology. For example, in (22), aspectual markers *–le* and *–guo* (expressing different types of perfective aspect) attach to the verb in an agglutinative fashion.

(22) *le* (perfective)

tā	kàn-**le**	sān chăng qiú sài
he	watched-PERF	three ballgames

"He watched three ballgames."

guo (experiential perfective)

tā	kàn-**guo**	sān chăng qiú sài
he	watched-EXP.PERF	three ballgames

"He has watched three ballgames."

Similarly, languages in other families have experienced a change in morphological type. For example, Proto-Dravidian was mostly agglutinative with elements of isolating morphology, whereas modern Dravidian languages developed into agglutinative languages with elements of fusional morphology. Similarly, Proto-Australian (the ancestor of various aboriginal Australian languages) is reconstructed as mostly agglutinative with elements of isolating morphology. However, its descendants in the Pama-Nyungan family have turned into purely agglutinative or mostly agglutinative languages with elements of fusional morphology. The non-Pama-Nyungan descendants of Proto-Australian have moved even further down the path towards fusional languages. Finno-Ugric languages have also moved from a mostly agglutinative to a mostly fusional model.

Why do languages change in terms of their morphological type? Simply put, it is because no morphological type is perfect. In an agglutinative language, words end up being very long since they are composed of multiple morphemes which each express a single grammatical meaning. Because of a universal linguistic tendency to contract (which produces such English words as *I'd*, *he'll*, and *aren't*), over time grammatical morphemes that frequently find themselves next to each other in an agglutinative formation start to *rub* and *wear* against each other, gradually fusing together.

For example, recall from our discussion above that Tatar is mostly an agglutinative language where case is marked through suffixes that attach to noun roots. Specifically, the dative case suffix is *–ga*, as in *bala–ga* "to {a/the} child". The same dative suffix can be seen in some pronominal forms, such as *bez–gä* "to us" (from *bez* "we") and *sez–gä* "to you (plural)" (from *sez* "you (plural)"). The change from the back vowel in *–ga* to the front vowel in *–gä* is due to vowel harmony, which applies across affixes in the language, and is therefore irrelevant to us here. But in other pronominal forms, for example in the first and second person singular, the /g/ of the suffix fuses with the final /n/ of the pronoun root, producing a velar nasal [ŋ] as in (23).

(23) Tatar:
min + ga = miŋa
"I" + DAT = "to me"

sin + ga = siŋa
"you (singular)" + DAT = "to you (singular)"

But a fusional model is not stable either as it involves a lot of morphophonological alternations and multiple morphemes with the same meaning. Over time, this complicated morphophonological system may be lost, giving rise to an isolating system. Yet, an isolating model is also complicated, but in a unique way. Many grammatical words (auxiliaries, prepositions, etc.) are needed, and such grammatical words are typically refashioned from lexical words (e.g., auxiliaries are often created out of lexical verbs, while prepositions may be created out of nouns or verbs). As a result, in an isolating language, many roots serve a double or even triple purpose, meaning that an extensive homophony exists in such a language. Over time, auxiliaries that find themselves next to verbs and prepositions (or postpositions) which are next to nouns, tend to undergo **grammaticalization**, a process by which free-standing words turn into affixes. You will read more about this in Chapter 8 Historical Linguistics.

While languages can switch from one typological class to another because of histori-cal changes, it is crucial to note that languages cannot switch from one language family into another. If a language has roots in one language family, it cannot be later reassigned to another language family, no matter how much influence languages from that other language family exert on it. For example, the roots of English are in the Germanic fam-ily, and although several Romance languages, especially French and Latin, have exerted a significant influence over English, it can never be considered a Romance language.

7.5 Typological Universals and the Parametric Theory of Language

So far, we have seen several ways in which languages differ from one another and which provide the basis for various typological classifications such as morphological struc-ture, word order patterns, and the expression of complex motion events. However, we also mentioned that some typological traits tend to occur together. In this section, we will examine how such correlations of typological traits have been analyzed by two theoretical approaches: the so-called Greenbergian Universals (named after American typologist Joseph Greenberg) and the Parametric Theory (most commonly associated with Noam Chomsky).

In this chapter, you learned that languages can be classified according to their default order of subjects, objects, and verbs. To simplify the discussion, let's focus on the order of objects and verbs. There are two possible orders: VO (instantiated in SVO, VSO, and VOS languages) and OV (instantiated in SOV, OVS, and OSV languages). It has been noted that VO languages, especially those with VSO order, have prepositions (e.g., English: *in the room*), while OV languages have **postpositions**, that is, "prepositions" that follow rather than precede their noun phrase complement (e.g., *the room in*, if English permit-ted this). The umbrella term for both prepositions and postpositions is **adpositions**.

For example, Welsh, as we saw in (6), has VSO order and has prepositions such as *i* "to". Sentence (24) shows another example of Welsh.

(24) Welsh:

Mi	roddes	i	lyfr	da	**i**	dad	Eleri	ddoe.
PTCP	give.1SG.PAST	I	book	good	to	father	Eleri	yesterday
	V	S	O		Preposition			

"I gave Eleri's father a good book yesterday."

Besides Welsh, this correlation is observed in Breton (another Celtic/Indo-European language), Modern Standard Arabic (Semitic), and Fijian (Austronesian), to name just a few languages.

In contrast, Tatar – an SOV language, as was illustrated in (6) above – has postpositions as noted in (25).

(25) Tatar:

keček	arkasenda
dog	because.of

"because of the dog"

The observation that VO languages have prepositions and OV languages have postpositions is motivation for two of Greenberg's Universals shown in (26).

(26) Greenberg's Universal 3:
Languages with dominant VSO order are always prepositional.

Greenberg's Universal 4:
With overwhelmingly greater than chance frequency, languages with normal SOV order are postpositional.

While we won't discuss Greenberg's Universal 1 and 2, you can see that Universal 4 is formulated as a tendency and not an absolute. Many languages indeed fit this pattern: SOV and postpositions. The list includes Udmurt (Finno-Ugric), Telugu (Dravidian), Basque and Burushaski (both isolates), Hindi and Armenian (both Indo-European), Georgian (Kartvelian), Amharic (Semitic), and Japanese (Japonic), to name just a few. However, there are also exceptions to this, especially among languages with OV order and prepositions. *The world atlas of language structures online* (http://wals.info) offers a sample of 437 languages for which these two traits are known, of which 427 (98 percent) pattern in accordance with Universal 4. Yet, ten languages including Farsi/Persian (Indo-European), Tigré (Semitic), and Mangarrayi (a Gunwingguan language, spoken in Australia) have the opposite pattern: OV order and prepositions. This is illustrated for Persian in (27).

(27) Persian:

man	seeb	mikhoram
I	apple	eat.1.SG.PRESENT
S	O	V

"I am eating an apple."

dar	mâh-e	septâmbr
in	month-of	September

"in September"

One important conclusion to be drawn from correlations such as those described by Universals 3 and 4, is that traits such as these – and even their co-occurrence in a pair of languages – cannot be taken as evidence for genetic relationships between these languages. Such patterns "come as a package", and are therefore considered to be overt realizations of a single underlying rule, which linguists call a parameter, that is, a point of variation across languages that have more than one reflection in surface phenomena. Look back at Chapter 5 Syntax to review our discussion on Universal Grammar and parameters.

The parameter of which Universals 3 and 4 are overt reflections is called Headedness Parameter (or Head Directionality Parameter) as it controls the order of a head, such as a verb or an adposition, and its complement, namely the object (which is a complement of the verb) or the noun phrase (NP) complement of an adposition. Looking at (28), you can see that the Headedness Parameter is binary in that it allows for only two options.

(28) Left-headed: Right-headed:
     Head-Complement   Complement-Head
     V O   O V
     P (preposition) NP   NP P (postposition)

The left-headed option is realized, for example, in English, Spanish, Russian, Chichewa, Fijian, Welsh, and Breton. Other languages are right-headed such as Udmurt, Telugu, Hindi, Basque, Japanese, Tatar, Turkish, Korean, Georgian, Amharic, and many others.

The Parametric Theory is quite powerful in that it has been used to account not only for typological variation – and more importantly, for correlations between certain typological traits – but also for first language acquisition by children and second language acquisition for adults, as well as how languages change over time.

SUMMARY

In this chapter, we have examined how the world's languages, past and present, can be classified. Languages, and their dialects, can be grouped together based on shared descent into language families. Among the best-known such families are the Germanic family (which includes English), the Romance family (which includes French), and the Slavic family (which includes Russian). These three families and many other additional families together form the Indo-European family, which includes over 400 languages. Many of the world's languages have been classified with their "relatives" in this fashion, although some languages remain – and may forever remain – isolates, that is languages without near relatives.

While familial (or genetic) classification of languages is based on historical connections of shared descent, typological classifications look at shared properties among languages. For example, some languages exhibit isolating morphology, others are agglutinative or fusional. While some languages have the SVO order (like English or French), others employ SOV, VSO, VOS, OSV, or OVS. Languages also contrast in the ways they express certain meanings, such as complex motion events. For instance, in some languages, like English, the manner of motion is expressed in the main verb (e.g., *crawl*, *run*, *fly*, *waltz*, etc.), whereas in other languages, like French, the manner cannot be expressed by the verb but rather must be encoded in adverbs, prepositional phrases, or gerunds.

While languages may switch from one typological category to another, genetic classifications remain unchanging throughout time. For example, English used to be an SOV language until around the time of the Norman invasion, but since then, it has become an SVO language. Yet, it was and still is a Germanic language, regardless of the (mostly lexical) influence of Norman French.

EXERCISES

7.1 Summarize the differences between genetic and typological classifications of languages. Think of such factors as the basis for classification, how historical changes affect classifications, the number of alternative genetic and typological classifications, and so on.

7.2 What is the difference between a language and a dialect? For every definition of language-vs.-dialect, explain why that definition works for some people and what the problems with that definition are.

7.3 Is Canadian English a dialect or a language? Explain why.

7.4 If we are trying to determine relatedness of English and French, which of the two lists below would offer us better evidence of the genetic relationship between the two languages, List A or List B? Explain why.

List A		List B	
English	French	English	French
heart	cœur	castle	château
worm	ver	army	armée
father	père	veil	voile
sun	soleil	pork	porc
three	trois	veal	veau

7.5 The next few questions are based on the data in the Table below. Based solely on the words for "three", which languages would you group together into one language family? Which languages do not have cognate words for "three" with those in that language family? Do any of the languages that do not fit into the one big language family have cognate words for "three" between them? Explain your answers.

Language	"three"	"father"	"five"	"bread"	"onion"
Albanian	tre	baba	pesë	bukë	qepë
Basque	hiru	aita	bost	ogia	tipula
Croatian	tri	otac	pet	kruh	luk
Czech	tři	otec	pět	chléb	cibule

Language	"three"	"father"	"five"	"bread"	"onion"
Danish	tre	far	fem	brød	løg
Dutch	drie	vader	vijf	brood	ui
English	three	father	five	bread	onion
Estonian	kolm	isa	viis	leib	sibul
Finnish	kolme	isä	viisi	leipä	sipuli
French	trois	père	cinq	pain	oignon
German	drei	Vater	fünf	Brot	Zwiebel
Greek	tría	patéras	pénte	psomí	kremmýdi
Hungarian	három	apa	öt	kenyér	hagyma
Icelandic	þrjú [θrju]	faðir	fimm	brauð	laukur
Italian	tre	padre	cinque	pane	cipolla
Latvian	trīs	tēvs	pieci	maize	sīpols
Lithuanian	trys	tévas	penki	duona	svogūnas
Maltese	tlieta	missier	ħames	ħobż	basla
Norwegian	tre	far	fem	brød	løk
Polish	trzy	ojciec	pięć	chleb	cebula
Romanian	trei	tată	cinci	pâine	ceapă
Russian	tri	otets	pjat'	xleb	luk
Spanish	tres	padre	cinco	pan	cebolla
Ukrainian	tri	bat'ko	pjat'	xlib	tsibulja
Yiddish	dray	tate	finf	broyt	tsibele

7.6 Now consider words for *father* and *five* in the Table in Exercise 7.5. Which languages share similar forms for these words? Which languages do not? Do these words support the division you have drawn in 7.5 between languages that belong to one large family and those that do not? Based on these two words, can you subdivide the family you established based on *three* into several branches? Do any languages in this family not fit into any branches you have established? Explain your answers.

7.7 Now consider the words for *bread* and *onion* in the Table in Exercise 7.5. Do they support the division you have drawn between languages that belong to one large language family and those that do not? Do these words support the subdivision into branches of that large language family that you have established so far? Why or why not? Which of the five words in the table appears to be most problematic in terms of offering evidence of language relatedness? Explain why.

7.8 Draw a diagram to represent family relationships among the languages in the Table in Exercise 7.5. Remember that language families may be branches (or subsets) of larger language families. Explain your answer.

7.9 Consider the forms in the following table for words *whole* and *gray* in several Slavic languages. (Old Novgorod is the Slavic variety attested in birch bark documents dating from the eleventh to fifteenth centuries, found in or near the city of Great Novgorod in northern Russia.) How would you reconstruct the first sound in each root for the shared common ancestor of these languages, Proto-Slavic? What would the reconstructed consonant be in each case, based on the majority approach? And based on the directionality approach?

Language	"whole"	"gray"
Polish	tsał-	szar- [ʃar]
Bulgarian	tsjal-	n/a
Ukrainian	tsil-	sir-
Old Novgorod	kɛl-	xer-

7.10 Consider the pronunciation of the first sound in the following six words from several Romance languages. What would be your reconstruction for the first sound in each of the three pairs of words for the shared common ancestor, Latin? Which of these words and which languages exhibit innovations?

Spanish	Portuguese	Catalan	Occitan	Italian	Romanian	Sardinian	Gloss
kampo	**k**ãpu	**k**am	**k**amp	**k**ampo	**k**imp	**k**ampu	field
kanta	**k**anta	**k**antə	**k**anta	**k**anta	**k**intə	**k**anta	sings
sjelo	**s**ew	**s**ɛl	**s**ɛl	**tʃ**ɛlo	**tʃ**er	**k**elu	heaven
sjervo	**s**ɛrvu	**s**ɛrvul	**s**ɛrv	**tʃ**ervo	**tʃ**ɛrb	**k**erbu	deer
seko	**s**eku	**s**ɛk	**s**ek	**s**ek:o	**s**ek	**s**ik:u	dry
sol	**s**ol	**s**ol	**s**ol	**s**ole	**s**oare	**s**ole	sun

7.11 Consider the following Swahili forms:

a-	li-	wa-	andika
he/she-	PAST-	them-	write

"He/she wrote them."

u-	li-	tu-	uliza
you(SG)-	PAST-	us-	ask

"You (sg.) asked us."

wa-	li-	m-	piga
they-	PAST-	him/her-	hit

"They hit him/her."

m-	li-	m-	piga
you(PL)-	PAST-	him/her-	hit

"You (pl.) hit him/her."

ni-	li-	m-	busu
I-	PAST-	him/her	kiss

"I kissed him/her."

What morphological type – isolating, agglutinative, or fusional – does Swahili exhibit? Explain your answer.

7.12 Using data from *The world atlas of language structures online*, Feature 81A (http://wals.info/feature/81A#2/18.0/152.8), discuss whether there is a correlation between word order typology and physical environment (type of terrain, altitude, latitude, climate, and the like).

7.13 Using data from *The world atlas of language structures online*, Feature 81A (http://wals.info/feature/81A#2/18.0/152.8), discuss whether there is a correlation between word order typology and genetic classification of languages into language families.

7.14 Using interactive feature combination functionality from *The world atlas of language structures online*, Features 81A (http://wals.info/feature/81A#2/18.0/152.8) and 87A, (http://wals.info/feature/87A#2/18.0/152.8) discuss whether there is a correlation between the order of subject, object, and verb and the order of adjectives and nouns.

7.15 Consider the following data from the perspective of V-framed/S-framed classification. For each example, underline the expression of manner and double underline the expression of direction. Determine whether a given language is V-framed or S-framed.

Italian:

L'	uomo	attraversò	la	strada	correndo.
the	man	crossed	the	street	running

"The man crossed the street running."

Russian:

Pulja   vletela   v   komnatu.
bullet   in.flew   into   room
"The bullet flew into the room."

Japanese:

John-wa   arui-te   gakkoo-ni   itta.
John-TOPIC   walking(GERUND)   school-at   went
"John went to school walking." (adapted from Inagaki, 2002, p. 6)

7.16 Consider the following data from a corpus of written Tatar. How are complex motion events expressed in this language? How are they different from those in English?
(LOC = locative case, ABL = ablative case, CONV = converb/gerund, PST = past tense)

(1) Tön   urtasın-da   ber   jak-tan   bik   zur   ber   koš   oči-p   kil-de.
        night   middle-LOC   one   side-ABL   very   big   one   bird   fly-CONV arrive-PST
        "In the middle of the night a very big bird flew from somewhere."

(2) Dä   Maugli   jögere-p   kit-te.
        and   Mowgli   run-CONV   leave-PST
        "And Mowgli ran away."

(3) Malaj,   kurk-ıp,   jögere-p   kit-te.
        boy   be.afraid- run-   leave-PST
                   CONV   CONV
        "The boy, being afraid, ran away."

(4) Kara   jılan   ilgä   šuıšı-p   čık-tı.
        black   snake   to.outside   crawl-CONV exit-PST
        "The black snake crawled outside."

REFERENCES

Beekes, R. (2011). *Comparative Indo-European linguistics: An introduction* (2nd Edition). Amsterdam: Benjamins.

Choi, Y., & Arunachalam, S. (2013). Learning manner and path verbs from the Serial Verb Construction in Korean. In S. Baiz, N. Goldman, & R. Hawkes (Eds.), *Proceedings of the 37th Annual Boston University Conference on Language Development* (pp. 62–73). Somerville, MA: Cascadilla.

Cifuentes-Férez, P., & Gentner, D. (2006). Naming motion events in Spanish and English. *Cognitive Linguistics, 17*(4), 443–462.

DeLancey, S. (2009). Bipartite verbs in languages of western North America: In time and space in languages of various typology. In *Proceedings of the XXV International Conference Dulson Readings*. Tomsk: Tomsk State Pedagogical University.

Inagaki, S. (2002). Japanese learners' acquisition of English manner-of-motion verbs with locational/directional PPs. *Second Language Research, 18*(1), 3–27.

Jakobson, R. (1936/1984). Beitrag zur Allgemeinen Kasuslehre: Gesamtbedeutungen der Russischen Kasus. In L. Waugh & M. Halle (Eds.), *Russian and Slavic grammar: Studies by Roman Jakobson* (pp. 59–103). Berlin: Mouton.

Mithun, M. (1992). Is basic word order universal? In D. Payne (Ed.), *Pragmatics of word order flexibility* (pp. 15–62). Amsterdam: Benjamins.

Sekerina, I. (1997). Scrambling and configurationality: Evidence from Russian syntactic processing. In W. Browne, E. Dornisch, N. Kondrashova, & D. Zec (Eds.), *Annual Workshop on Formal Approaches to Slavic Linguistics* (pp. 435–463). Ann Arbor, MI: Michigan Slavic Publications.

Talmy, L. (1985). Lexicalization patterns: Semantic structure in lexical forms. In T. Shopen (Ed.), *Language typology and syntactic description: Volume 3: Grammatical categories and the lexicon* (pp. 57–149). Cambridge: Cambridge University Press.

Talmy, L. (2000). *Toward a cognitive semantics.* Cambridge, MA: MIT Press.

8 Historical Linguistics

Laura Grestenberger

OVERVIEW

In this chapter your will learn about historical linguistics, the subfield of linguistics that studies language change and **past language stages**. You will:

- acquire an understanding of the development of languages across time;
- learn about the changes that occur in their phonology, morphology, syntax, and lexicon;
- compare present language stages to past language stages;
- learn about the reasons for language change;
- gain knowledge of the reconstruction of unattested languages; and
- study and apply the methods of comparative reconstruction.

8.1 What Is Historical Linguistics?

Historical linguistics studies **past language stages** (dead languages) and **language change** over time. Languages are constantly changing, and historical linguists study how and why this happens. Historical linguistics

- studies languages that are no longer spoken, like Old English or Old French;
- examines changes between two language stages, for example, the changes from Old English to Middle English and from Middle English to Modern English;
- reconstructs even earlier language stages based on historical evidence.

You may have noticed that the variety of English you speak (your personal **idiolect**) is subtly different from the English of your grandparents. Over time, such miniscule changes accumulate and lead to quite profound differences between past and present stages of a language – just compare your idiolect of today's English to that of William Shakespeare around 1600 CE, or to that of the Old English poem *Beowulf* (ca. 800 CE).

There is a common notion that language change is somehow inherently "bad", a sign of deterioration, or just general sloppiness. Unfortunate and misguided as these notions are, they go back quite a long way. For example, the Latin *Appendix Probi* from the third century CE contains a list of "wrong" pronunciation of Latin words, and the prescribed (correct) way of pronouncing them. Some examples of entries from this list are in (1):

(1) *Appendix Probi*
  a. *speculum non speclum* "say speculum, not speclum"   (Italian *specchio* "mirror")
  b. *calida non calda* "say calida, not calda"   (Italian *caldo* "hot")
  c. *auris non oricla* "say auris, not oricla"   (French *oreille* "ear")

Also in the third century CE, Latin was well on its way to developing into the Romance languages (Spanish, Portuguese, French, Italian, Romanian, etc.). But the *Appendix Probi* proves that some speakers were quite unhappy about this development and tried to correct: "Don't say *speclum*, say *speculum!*" They had a **prescriptive** approach to the use of the Latin language, whereas historical linguists prefer a **descriptive** approach. That is, as historical linguists we want to *describe* how speakers use language and how their grammars change over time, rather than forcing them to use an arbitrary correct standard language. Go back to Chapter 1 Introducing Linguistics and Chapter 5 Syntax to read more about prescriptive and descriptive grammar. You will also read more in Chapter 9 Sociolinguistics.

PAUSE AND REFLECT 8.1

Think about the way your first language(s) differ(s) from that/those of your friends, parents, and grandparents. What differences in its phonology, morphology, syntax, and lexicon can you think of? What differences do you notice between formal and informal/colloquial speech, and between different regional varieties?

8.2 Language Change

8.2.1 I-language and E-language

Languages change constantly and there is nothing we can do about it. The English or French spoken in Montreal nowadays is very different from the English of Shakespeare or the French of Voltaire. Notions like *the English language* or *the French language* are sociopolitical concepts that characterize the linguistic conventions and language use of different speech communities. Linguists refer to these entities as **E-language**, where *E* stands for *external* to the individual. On the other hand, we refer to the knowledge of language or **mental grammar** of an individual as **I-language**, where *I* stands for the *internal* knowledge state of an individual. Language in this sense is part of the cognitive capacities of an individual's brain.

When we study language change, we must keep in mind that *language* can refer to these two very distinct notions – the habits of a speech community, and the knowledge state in the brains of each member of that speech community. In the following, we will use *language* in the I-language sense – the mental grammar of an individual.

8.2.2 Synchrony and Diachrony

A core concern in historical linguistics is how languages develop over time. This is known as the diachronic approach (Greek *diá* "through, across", *khrónos* "time"). **Diachronic linguistics** studies the changes in speakers' grammars across time (between a given stage X and stage Y), the **diachrony** of a language is its development over time. **Synchronic** linguistics, on the other hand, studies the properties of speakers' grammars at a given linguistic stage (Greek *sýn* "with, together" + *khrónos* "time"). Historical linguists often work on the interaction of synchrony and diachrony. These two ways of studying language are illustrated in Figure 8.1.

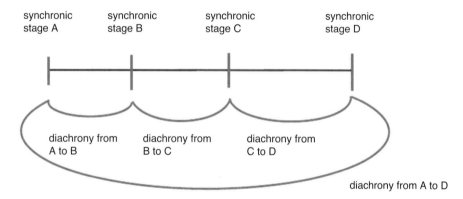

Figure 8.1 Synchrony and diachrony

In this illustration, each vertical bar stands for a synchronic language stage, called A, B, C, and D. You can think of these as the mental grammars of four different individuals: Person A speaks (a variety of) Old English, Person B speaks Middle English, Person C speaks early Modern English, and Person D speaks contemporary Yorkshire English. Under a synchronic approach to these four stages, a linguist would study the properties of each of these four stages without referring to the stages that came before or after. On the other hand, the arcs between the vertical bars illustrate the diachrony between two given stages. Under a diachronic approach, a linguist would study the changes between A and B (Old English and Middle English), or between B and C (Middle English to Early Modern English), or between A and D (Old English to contemporary Yorkshire English). Of course, such a diachronic approach presupposes an understanding of the relevant synchronic properties of the two stages under study and of the intermediate stages.

8.2.3 Correspondence between Grammars

How do we decide whether two grammars (i.e., languages) are diachronically related? To answer this, we determine whether there are correspondences between the two grammars.

- **Correspondence**: A linguistic form X (a phoneme, morpheme, or word) in Grammar G_1 diachronically corresponds to a linguistic form Y in Grammar G_2 if X can be related to Y through one or more changes which transformed X into Y.

  The example in (2) illustrates a simple diachronic correspondence.

(2) Old English /mu:s/ > Modern English /maws/ "mouse"

The symbol > means "changes into". For instance, form X in G_1 (in this case Old English) changes into form Y in G_2 (in this case Modern English). As a result of this change, the Modern English word *mouse* /maws/ corresponds to the Old English word /mu:s/. The two forms are related through a change that transformed the Old English long high back vowel /u:/ into the Modern English diphthong /aw/ while the other sounds stayed the same. This change was regular, it happened to all Old English long high back vowels on the way to Modern English. By observing regular correspondences such as this one, we establish that Modern English is in a **lineal descent** relationship with Old English. Lineal descent means that the grammar G_2 (Modern English) corresponds diachronically to the grammar of G_1 (Old English) through a series of intermediate changes. Figure 8.2 illustrates a simplified lineal descent relationship (Hale, 2007). There are also **non-lineal descent** relationships, which we'll explore in Section 8. 7.2.

Figure 8.2 Lineal descent relationship between G_1 and G_2

8.2.4 Change and Diffusion

Now that we have established how grammars are related over time, we can sharpen our definition of language change. Remember that G_1 and G_2 represent two different I-languages which can be related across time through a series of intermediate steps. These intermediate steps happen piecemeal, as grammars are transmitted from one generation to the next. Change means that the transmission of a given grammar during language acquisition is flawed with respect to some feature of that grammar. In other words, language change is **imperfect transmission**.

- **Imperfect transmission**: "Change results when transmission is flawed with respect to some feature. When transmission is not flawed (with respect to some feature), there has been no change in the strict sense." (Hale, 2007, p. 36)

Under this view, language change takes hold as soon as children acquire a grammar G_2 that is different from the input grammar G_1 with respect to some feature(s). Imperfect transmission happens when children misanalyze some aspect(s) of the input data they receive and end up constructing a slightly different grammar than the input grammar(s).

This view of language change leads to a paradox: If change happens piecemeal and grammar-by-grammar through transmission errors during first language acquisition, why do we have the impression that language change affects whole speech communities? After all, the changes from Old English to Middle English to Modern English (and their respective varieties) affected large speech communities, not just individuals. The solution is to distinguish carefully between **change** and **diffusion**. Change means that a language learner maps a string of input (Primary Linguistic Data, PLD) to a grammar G_2 that is different from the grammar G_1 that generated the input. This is known as misanalysis or **imperfect transmission**. Diffusion, on the other hand, is the spread of a change in an individual speaker's grammar throughout a linguistic community. In other words, change is flawed transmission, diffusion is successful transmission.

Another way to differentiate change and diffusion is by returning to the distinction between I-language and E-language discussed above. Change affects the I-language of an individual, while diffusion is an E-language phenomenon that affects a linguistic community. Diffusion can and must be studied using the tools of sociolinguistic analysis (see Chapter 9 Sociolinguistics). On the other hand, change in the narrow sense must be studied with the analytical tools used in theoretical linguistics to understand language as a faculty of the human brain.

So, what do historical linguists study? Change or diffusion? The answer must be: both. When we deal with past language stages, we only have access to features of grammars that were successfully transmitted and are documented in one way or another. Grammars (or features thereof) that are not documented (directly or indirectly) cannot, by definition, be studied. Our knowledge of change (in the I-language sense) therefore always depends on successful transmission (diffusion). However, we should be careful to distinguish between the two, as they depend on very different mechanisms.

8.2.5 What Can Change?

Language change is usually divided into four separate domains, corresponding to the domains of grammar that you have studied in previous chapters.

- **Phonological change** or **sound change** affects the phonological system of a given language. An example is the change from Old English /mu:s/ to Modern English /maws/ *mouse*, in which a long vowel was turned into a diphthong. This change was **regular**: it applied to all instances of the affected sound (i.e., Old English /hu:s/

became Modern English /h**aw**s/ *house*, etc.). The precise mechanisms of this will be discussed in Section 8.3.

- **Morphological change** alters a language's inventory of functional items, usually inflectional and derivational morphemes. For example, the Modern English adjectival/adverbial suffix *–ly* (in *friend–ly*, *easi–ly*, etc.) is related to Modern English *like* and the Old English noun *līc* "body", from which it developed into a derivational suffix. We will discuss morphological change in Section 8.4.

- **Syntactic change** primarily affects the word order and distribution of functional and lexical items in a given language. Common syntactic changes include changes in the distribution and movement properties of verbs, negation markers, interrogatives ("*wh*-words"), and pronouns. Syntactic change is discussed in Section 8.5.

- **Semantic change** can occur to **lexical categories**, such as the change in meaning of English *dog*, which used to have a more specific meaning than it does nowadays (it used to refer to a specific breed of dog, cp. German *Dogge* "mastiff"), or to **functional categories** like personal and demonstrative pronouns, modal verbs, and adverbs. For example, third person pronouns such as English *he*, *she*, and *they* have almost always developed diachronically from anaphoric demonstratives (*this one* or *that one*). Semantic change is discussed in Section 8.6.

As you have probably noticed in the examples above, these different domains of language change tend to interact with each other. While it is useful to discuss these domains separately, most research in historical linguistics spans two or more of these domains for any given topic, making it a truly interdisciplinary field.

8.3 Phonological Change

8.3.1 Sound Laws and the Neogrammarian Hypothesis

In studying the changes in the phonological systems between different language stages, historical linguists rely on the **Neogrammarian hypothesis**, the observation that sound change is regular and exceptionless (it applies whenever the phonetic environment that triggers the change is found).

LINGUISTICS TIDBITS: THE NEOGRAMMARIANS

The Neogrammarian hypothesis is named after a group of nineteenth-century linguists from Germany who held what was considered quite a radical view at the time: that sound change follows general and law-like principles similar to the general laws of physics. The German term *Junggrammatiker* translates more accurately as "young grammarians", a reference to both their age and the vigor with which they renewed the field.

(3) The Neogrammarian hypothesis: "Sound change is regular and operates without exceptions" (Hock, 1991, p. 34)

What is a **sound law**? It is a phonological change that occurs between two grammars which are in a lineal descent relationship or, more informally, two stages of a given language. Sound laws can be described using phonological rules like the ones you studied in Chapter 3 Phonology. Take a look at (4) to see how we express a sound law.

(4)   A template for sound laws:
    a. A > B
        "A turns into B" or "A becomes B"
    b. A > B/_C
        "A turns into B before C"

We have already seen a sound law like (4a) above: The change of Old English /u:/ to Modern English /aw/. This was an across-the-board change: it happened to all instances of Old English /u:/, independent of the environment they were in. That is, this change did not depend on a particular phonetic context. Moreover, this change was part of a broader one that affected the entire vowel system of English in the fifteenth century, at the end of the Middle English period. This change is known as the **Great Vowel Shift**. The stage of this shift that turned the long high vowels /u:/ and /i:/ into the diphthongs /aw/ and /aj/ is called **diphthongization**, illustrated in Table 8.1.

PAUSE AND REFLECT 8.2

Look at the Middle English words below. Based on the sound change rule you just learned (diphthongization of high vowels), what are the predicted Modern English versions of these words after the Great Vowel Shift took place? Note that final –ə is also lost on the way to Modern English.

- /bi:tə/
- /pru:d/
- /lu:s/
- /li:k/
- /u:t/

While the Great Vowel Shift applied independently of a particular context, most sound changes are context-sensitive: they apply only in certain sound environments. Rule (4b) illustrates the format of such sound laws. A common instance of context-sensitive sound changes are **palatalization** changes, in which non-palatal consonants (usually velar or dental stops) develop a front (palatal) co-articulation or affrication before front vowels. Such a change happened in Old English: the Old English velars /k/ and /ɣ/ became the postalveolar affricate /ʧ/ and the palatal glide /j/, respectively, before front

TABLE 8.1 Diphthongization in the History of English

Middle English	Modern English	Meaning	Middle English	Modern English	Meaning
/mu:s/	/maws/	mouse	/mi:s/	/majs/	mice
/hu:s/	/haws/	house	/ri:də/	/rajd/	ride
/hlu:d/	/lawd/	loud	/ti:mə/	/tajm/	time
/ku:/	/kaw/	cow	/hwi:t/	/wajt/	white

vowels. Before back vowels and consonants, these sounds did not change. The effects of this change are still seen in Modern English – it's the reason you say *cool* and *climb* with a /k/ and *glad* with a /g/, but *church* and **ch**eek with a /ʧ/ and *yard* with a /j/. Table 8.2 illustrates the difference between palatalized and non-palatalized velars in Modern English and their earlier predecessors before palatalization took place (Old English /ɣ/ later became /g/; to simplify things, the latter is used in the following discussion).

The velars in the Old English column on the left in Table 8.2 are before front vowels (Old English /ea/ and /eo/ are diphthongs whose first element is [+front]), while the velars in the Old English column on the right are before back vowels or before consonants. Old English /k/ and /g/ correspond to Modern English /ʧ/ and /j/ before front vowels, but to /k/ and /g/ everywhere else. We will talk more about this in Section 8.8.4 but for now, we can formalize this as a diachronic rule of the type A > B/_C as shown in (5).

(5) Old English *k, g* > ʧ, j/_V[+front]

Note that the **phonetic environment** is crucial to the operation of this rule – if the velars are not before a front vowel, the rule does not apply. A more abstract way of writing a palatalization rule is in (6).

(6) C[+velar] > C[+palatal]/_V[+front]
"a velar consonant becomes palatal before a front vowel."

This rule is very general – as the Old English case shows, palatalization affects different sounds in different ways (e.g., /k/ becomes an affricate, but /g/ becomes a glide).

PAUSE AND REFLECT 8.3

Look at the Old English words below. Based on the sound change rules you just learned (palatalization, diphthongization), what are the predicted Modern English versions of these words? Assume that the final –*an* of the first two words is lost; further hints are given below.

- /ke:osan/ (the sequence *e:o* developed into Modern English /u/, /s/ became /z/)

- /gieldan/ (the sequence *ie* developed into Modern English /i/)
- /gold/
- /kɪn/
- /ki:ld/

TABLE 8.2 Palatalization in the History of English

Palatalization		No palatalization	
Early Old English	Modern English	Early Old English	Modern English
cirice /kirike/	church /ʧərʧ/	*climban* /klimban/, later /kl:imban/	climb /klajm/
cīdan /ki:dan/	chide /ʧajd/	*cōl* /ko:l/	cool /ku:l/
geard /geard/	yard /jard/	*gōs* /go:s/	goose /gu:s/
geolu /geolu/	yellow /jɛlo/	*glæd* /glæd/	glad /glæd/

While the template for sound laws we used above is similar to that used by phonologists for synchronic phonological rules, it is important to note that our diachronic sound change rules have a different status than synchronic phonological rules. Synchronic rules (e.g., *oral vowels are pronounced as nasal vowels before a nasal stop* in English) are part of a speaker's mental grammar. Sound laws, or diachronic phonological rules, describe the start and end points of a change, or sequence of changes, between two different grammars at two different diachronic stages.

8.3.2 Rule Ordering

An important observation in studying sound change is that sound laws are *ordered* with respect to one another. Consider our English sound laws above, diphthongization and palatalization. Dipthongization turns the high front vowel /i:/ into the diphthong /aj/, whose first element /a/ is [-front] (it also turns /u:/ into /aw/, but this is not relevant to the palatalization rule). Palatalization, on the other hand, takes place before [+front] vowels, but not before [-front] vowels. We can now determine whether palatalization happened before or after diphthongization. If it happened *before* diphthongization, we'd expect velars to be palatalized before an Old English /i:/ before that /i:/ turns into /aj/. If palatalization happened *after* diphthongization, we would not expect velars to become palatalized before an Old English /i:/, since this sound would turn into /aj/ before the palatalization rule took place. Table 8.3 illustrates these two options for the Old English word *cīdan* /ki:dan/ "chide".

In Ordering A, palatalization takes place *before* diphthongization, so we get /ki:dan/ > /tʃi:dan/ > /tʃajdan/. Since both palatalization and diphthongization take place, we expect the Modern English word to be /tʃajd/, and this is correct (*chide*; the Old English ending *–an* is lost). What happens if we change the order, as in Ordering B above? If the input is the same and diphthongization happens first, we get /ki:dan/ > /kajdan/. While this seems to work, we now cannot apply the second rule, palatalization. Palatalization happens before front vowels, but the initial /k/ of /kajdan/ is now before /a/, which is not a front vowel. Since the environment for palatalization is no longer there, the palatalization rule is not applicable in this ordering. The expected Modern English form is /kajd/ (which would probably be spelled *kide*), which does not exist. We have shown that the ordering must have been Ordering A, with palatalization happening before diphthongization. The ordering of two changes with respect to each other is called their **relative chronology**.

TABLE 8.3 Rule Ordering

Ordering A	1. Palatalization	2. Diphthongization	Expected Modern English
Input: /ki:dan/	/tʃi:dan/	/tʃajdan/	/tʃajd/✓
Ordering B	1. Diphthongization	2. Palatalization	Expected Modern English
Input: /ki:dan/	/kajdan/	n/a?	/kajd/✗

PAUSE AND REFLECT 8.4

Consider the following data (Hale & Kissock, 2013) from Hawaiian and its ancestor, Proto-Polynesian in the table below.

Proto-Polynesian	Hawaiian	English
ʔau	au	"current"
peka	peʔa	"bat"
ʔumu	umu	"oven, earthen"
ika	iʔa	"fish"
waʔe	wae	"leg"

- Which sound changes took place from Proto-Polynesian to Hawaiian?
- How are these sound changes ordered with respect to one another? Give a rule ordering/relative chronology and explain why it's the correct one.

8.3.3   Why Is Sound Change Regular?

The Neogrammarian hypothesis is one of the fundamental insights of historical linguistics, without which we would be unable to test sound laws and work on **comparative reconstruction**. But why *is* sound change regular?

We have seen above that sound changes usually depend on a particular phonetic environment (there are also across-the-board changes, as in the Great Vowel Shift, whose explanations are trickier). The fact that sound change is regular is precisely *because* it occurs only in a particular phonetic environment. That is, it is *conditioned* by some phonetic property of that environment. Consider the palatalization of Old English /g/ discussed above. /g/ is a voiced velar stop, but before front vowels, it became a palatal glide, /j/. Why did this happen? /j/ is pronounced closer to the front of the mouth than /g/, it is more "front".

With respect to the manner of articulation, a glide is fairly similar to a front vowel in terms of the closure of the articulators. What happened, therefore, is that the stop /g/ **assimilated** to the following front vowel by taking on or adapting to some of its phonetic properties, notably place and manner of articulation. This is an **anticipatory** change, since the sound that undergoes the change seems to anticipate some of the properties of the following sound. More precisely, the change happens because, as children acquire their first language, they misanalyze the [+front] feature of the vowel as belonging to the preceding consonant.

If sound change is phonetically conditioned, this explains why it is regular and exceptionless. It occurs because the sounds undergoing the change pick up some feature(s) of the conditioning environment (or rather, because language learners unconsciously assign some feature of that environment to the sound in question). If the conditioning environment is absent, the change does not occur. For example, in the word *cool* /kul/, the sound following the velar is [+back], rather than [+front]. We therefore do not expect to see the fronting of the velar associated with palatalization, since there is nothing in the phonetic environment that would trigger such a fronting. This explains why the velars in the right column of Table 8.2 stayed the same in Old English while the ones in the left column became more "front" in their articulation.

8.3.4 Common Types of Sound Changes

In this section, some common types of sound changes are briefly introduced. Many of these are also articulatory processes you have already studied in Chapter 2 Phonetics.

Assimilation: a segment takes on some or all phonetic features of a preceding or following segment (it becomes more similar to a preceding or following segment). Assimilation is an umbrella term for several types of changes which involve *feature spreading*. **Palatalization**, for example, is a type of assimilation: a consonant takes on the phonetic feature [+front] from the following segment (a front vowel). Another common type of assimilation is consonant assimilation in clusters: when two consonants are adjacent to each other, they tend to assimilate in voicing, place, or manner of articulation. If a sound assimilates to a following sound, like in (7), it's called a **regressive** (or **anticipatory**) assimilation. Assimilation to a preceding sound is called **progressive** assimilation.

(7)   Latin *septem* "seven" > Italian *sette*

Another common type of assimilation is nasalization, which is usually regressive, meaning that a nasal consonant influences another sound before it.

Nasalization: an oral vowel becomes nasalized before (or, more rarely, after) a nasal stop. Nasalization took place in the history of French. In Old French, vowels were nasalized before nasal stops, as can be seen in (8).

(8)   a. Latin *bonus* "good" > French *bon* /bɔ̃/
       b. Latin *līnum* "flax" > French *lin* /lɛ̃/ (contrast this vowel with the non-nasal vowel in *laid* /lɛ/ "ugly")

While the French writing system obscures this change a bit, the nasal stop has been lost completely in the words in (8), and only the nasalization on the preceding vowel tells us that it was once there.

Other types of sound change involve the loss of a segment. If this occurs in the middle of the word, it is called **syncope** (Greek *synkopē* "cutting short"). The loss of a segment at the end of a word is called **apocope** (Greek *apokopē* "cutting off").

Syncope: a segment (usually an unstressed or weakly-stressed vowel) is lost in the middle of a word. Syncope has applied in English words like *family* and *laboratory*, which (in North American English) are usually pronounced /ˈfæmli/ (two syllables) and /ˈlæbrətɔri/ (four syllables), respectively. Syncope also occurred in many of the Romance languages as they developed from Latin, as in example (9).

(9)   Latin *popul*us "people" > French *peu*p*le*, Spanish *pueblo*

Apocope: a segment (usually an unstressed or weakly-stressed vowel) is lost at the end of a word. Apocope occurred in the history of English, where final consonants and unstressed final vowels were lost. Take, for instance, Old English *climb**an*** (two syllables) > Modern English *climb* (one syllable), or *mōn**a*** (two syllables) > *moon* (one syllable). Apocope also occurred in the development of the Modern Indic languages such as Hindi, Bengali, and Gujarati from Sanskrit (as it moved through Middle Indic), as can be seen in (10).

(10) a. Sanskrit *e:k**ah*** "one" > Hindi *e:k*
      b. Sanskrit *sapt**a*** "seven" > Hindi *sa:t*

Syncope and apocope usually target vowels. When a consonant is lost, on the other hand, a preceding vowel is often lengthened, as if to compensate for the loss of a segment. This is called **compensatory lengthening**. Compensatory lengthening is when a vowel is lengthened when a following consonant is lost.

Compensatory lengthening occurred in varieties of English that lost /r/ in codas (so called "non-rhotic" (i.e., r-less) varieties of English that you might hear in the Northeast of the United States and in the UK). In these varieties, *farm* is pronounced as /fa:m/ and *car* is pronounced as /ka:/. You may have noticed that compensatory lengthening also took place in the Hindi example in (10b). (11) shows more examples from Hindi. Note that the nasal in (11b) triggered nasalization before it was lost with compensatory lengthening.

(11) a. Sanskrit *bh**ak**tam* "cooked rice" > Hindi *bha:t*
      b. Sanskrit *paɳʧa* "five" > Hindi *pã:ʧ*

Merger: a phonemic contrast between two segments is lost and they merge as one and the same segment. In some varieties of North American English, the vowels /ɛ/ and /ɪ/ merge before nasals, so that the words *pen* and *pin* have the same vowel. Consonants can also merge. In Tocharian, inherited voiceless, voiced, and voiced aspirated labial stops were merged as voiceless labial stops, illustrated in (12).

(12) a. Proto-Indo-European **ph₂tér* "father" > B *p*acer
      b. Proto-Indo-European **dʰubrós* "deep" > Tocharian B *ta**p**re*
      c. Proto-Indo-European ***b**ʰer* "carry" > Tocharian B *p*är

Monophthongization: a diphthong becomes a monophthong. We've already encountered diphthongization, by which a monophthong (usually a long vowel) becomes a diphthong, like in Old English /m**u**ːs/ > Modern English /m**aw**s/. The reverse happens in monophthongization, for example in Modern Greek in (13).

(13) a. Classical Greek grap^h**ei** "he/she writes" > Modern Greek graf**i**

     b. Classical Greek erk^hom**ai** "I come, go" > Modern Greek erxom**e**

PAUSE AND REFLECT 8.5

Analyze and classify the sound changes you observe in the following examples (some may not fall under any of the categories discussed above). Note that in most words, more than one change has taken place.

  i Proto-Semitic *damiqum "good" > Akkadian damqum
  ii Latin fabulāre "to speak" > Spanish hablar /ablar/
  iii Latin aurum "gold" > French /ɔr/
  iv Sanskrit agni "fire" > Pāli aggi
  v Proto-Algonquian *eθkwe- "woman" > Ojibwe ikkwe-

8.4 Morphological Change

8.4.1 Types of Morphological Change

Morphological change affects word structure, particularly inflectional and derivational morphology. We can distinguish between changes that result in the *loss* of morphological material (e.g., case endings on nouns or agreement markers on verbs) and changes that result in the *development* of new morphological material. Another useful distinction, which we will look at next, is between **deductive change** (rule extension) and **abductive change** (creation of a new morphological rule).

8.4.2 Deductive Change

Deductive change means extending an already existing morphological rule or pattern to an environment where it did not previously apply. **Analogy** is a very common form of deductive change and involves the generalization of a formal relationship from one form (or set of forms) to another form (or set of forms). Simply put, analogy makes words more similar to one another. **Proportional analogy** copies a relationship between one set of forms to another set of forms and can be formalized as follows (based on Campbell, 1998):

- Proportional analogy: **a : b = c : x**

"a is to b as c is to x, where x is … " (x = the new, **analogical form**)

In proportional analogy, a part (or all) of the relation between a and b (in terms of phonological and/or morphological features) is copied to the relation between c and x, where c shares some salient features with a. For example, the past tense of English *dive* used to be *dived*, but this was replaced by *dove* in analogy with past tense forms like *strove*, *drove*, etc., through proportional analogy (see Table 8.4).

TABLE 8.4 Proportional Analogy

Present		Past
strive	:	strove
ride	:	rode
drive	:	drove
dive	:	dove

Note that proportional analogy extends *unproductive* morphology to new contexts (the synchronically productive way of forming the simple past tense is by adding the suffix /–(ə)d/ to a verb).

Another morphological change that is usually analyzed as analogy extends *productive* morphology to a new context. For example, this happened to the plural of the word *cow*. In Old English, the singular was *cū* /ku:/, while the plural was *cȳ* /ki:/ (in fact, this form lives on in Scottish English *kye* /kaj/). This plural was later changed to *kīne* /ki:n/ in Middle English by adding the plural marker –*n(e)* (an archaic plural ending also seen in *childr–en* and *ox–en*), so that the Early Middle English pair was singular /ku:/, plural /ki:n/. After the Great Vowel Shift, these forms should have become Modern English /kaw/, plural /kajn/. Look back at Table 8.1 for the development of long high vowels during the Great Vowel Shift. Instead, Modern English has /kaw/, plural /kawz/. We already know that /ki:n/ cannot have turned into /kawz/ by regular sound change: Early Middle English /i:/ should have turned into /aj/, not /aw/, and Middle English /n/ did not become Modern English /z/. What is the morphological explanation for this?

First, we need to understand the status of regular plural forms such as *cows*, *dogs*, *hats*, and *linguists* vs. irregular plural forms such as *feet*, *mice*, *children*, and *cacti*. The irregular forms need to be stored in your mental lexicon since they cannot be generated by a productive morphological rule. The regular plural forms, on the other hand, do not need to be stored in the lexicon. They can be generated by applying the productive rule of plural formation to any singular noun – even nouns that you've never heard before, like *zlorp* or *wug*, whose plural forms must be *zlorps* /zlorps/ and *wugs* /wəgz/.

So how do we lose irregular plurals like *cacti* or Middle English /ki:n/? All that needs to happen is that speakers fail to store the irregular plural form in their mental lexicon. This may happen because they are never actually exposed to them, because they don't hear them often enough, or because they assign them a new meaning (so that *kīne* comes to mean "cattle", for example). Now, a speaker who has never heard the rare and highly irregular plural *cacti* will probably pronounce the plural of *cactus* as *cactuses* (which is what many English speakers actually say). The same seems to have happened to Middle English /ki:n/, which was replaced by the regular form /kawz/ because English speakers at some point failed to store the irregular form, for one of the reasons mentioned above. Although this type of change is usually called analogy, it does not depend on a relation of similarity between two forms in the way that proportional analogy does.

PAUSE AND REFLECT 8.6

i Regular plurals in Standard French are identical to the singular, e.g., /ʃa/ *cat*, plural /ʃa/; /mɛʁ/ *mother*, plural /mɛʁ/, etc. There are also a few irregular nouns in which the plural differs from the singular, for example, the word for *horse*, /ʃval/, whose plural is /ʃvo/. However, in some varieties of Quebec French, the plural of *horse* is /ʃval/. What kind of morphological change is this and why do you think it happened?

ii Form the English plurals of the words *octopus* and *rhinoceros* and ask your friends to do the same. How many variants do you get? Why is the plural of these words difficult?

8.4.3 Abductive Change

Abductive change means creating a new (morphological) rule based on a misanalysis of the available data during first language acquisition. Like in Section 8.4.2, *misanalysis* means that children learning language interpret a given pattern in their input differently than the previous generation, resulting in a slightly different grammar than that of their predecessors. The changes usually subsumed under the term *grammaticalization* can be characterized as abductive changes. As briefly mentioned in Chapter 7 The Classification of Languages, grammaticalization means that lexical items (nouns, verbs, adjectives) develop into functional items (for example, classifiers, determiners, auxiliaries, modal verbs, etc.); while functional syntactic categories (auxiliaries, determiners, complementizers, etc.) tend to become reduced to affixal material (inflectional endings on nouns and verbs, etc.).

Grammaticalization (Hopper & Traugott, 2003, p. xv): "The process whereby lexical items and constructions come in certain linguistic contexts to serve grammatical functions, and, once grammaticalized, continue to develop new grammatical functions." In other words, grammaticalization makes lexical items more abstract and functional. In turn, this creates new functional items, especially inflectional and derivational morphology. As the linguist Talmy Givón put it, "today's morphology is yesterday's syntax".

Grammaticalization usually involves several steps:

- **Phonological reduction**: functional elements are weakly stressed or unstressed compared to lexical elements. If a lexical element becomes unstressed, this can lead to its reanalysis as a functional element and further phonological reduction.
- **Semantic bleaching**: a lexical item loses part or all of its meaning (functional categories usually have more abstract and restricted meaning than lexical categories).

- **Loss of syntactic freedom** or **cliticization**: functional elements are highly restricted in their distribution and are often clitics (unstressed elements which are dependent on a preceding or following stressed word) or affixes. If a lexical item undergoes grammaticalization, it usually becomes syntactically restricted to certain environments.

One example of grammaticalization is the development of the Modern English adjectival/adverbial suffix *–ly* (in *friend–ly*, *easi–ly*, etc.) from the Old English noun *līc* "body" (< Proto-Germanic **līk(a)-* "body, shape"). This noun lost phonological content (it underwent phonological reduction), semantic content, and syntactic freedom as it was developing into an adjectival (and adverbial) suffix. This change started in compounds like Old English *freond–līc* "friend–like, friend–shaped" > Modern English *friend–ly* through a **reanalysis** of the second part of the compound. Reanalysis means that speakers assign a structure to a string (of words or morphemes) that is different than that of the previous generation of speakers. This process was called *misanalysis* above, implying that speakers miss the target grammar G_1 (cp. the discussion of **flawed transmission**). In this case, the noun *shape* in the second part of the compound in (14a) must have been reanalyzed as an adjective (14b) at some point (we know that this happened independently to the English word *like*).

(14)   Reanalysis
   a. $[freond]_N–[līc]_N$ (early Old English)
   b. $[freond]_N–[līc]_A$ (late Old English)
   c. $[[friend]_N–ly]_A$ (Modern English)

Note that nothing has changed on the surface yet: (14a) and (14b) look exactly alike, but the subscript letters indicated different underlying structures ("noun" vs. "adjective"). From (14b) to (14c), another reanalysis took place: while [–*līc*] in (14b) could still stand by itself in a clause, –*ly* in (14c) is an affix and must attach to something else, as indicated by the bracketing.

PAUSE AND REFLECT 8.7

You can test the grammaticalization diagnostics yourself by comparing the Modern English suffix –*ly* to its distant predecessor, the Old English noun *līc*:

- –*ly* is phonologically reduced: the regular development of Old English *līc* is Modern English /lajk/, as in *like*;
- –*ly* is semantically bleached: while you can easily describe the meaning or referent of most nouns

(except maybe very abstract ones), the only way to describe the meaning of –*ly* is by making reference to its adjectival (or adverbial) function;

- –*ly* is morphosyntactically restricted: while (Old English and Modern English) nouns can occur on their own and in different positions in a sentence, affixes like –*ly* must attach to a base.

Reanalysis depends on the possibility of more than one analysis of a given construction. Another example is the development of auxiliaries from main (i.e., lexical) verbs. English has two future auxiliaries, as seen in (15).

(15) English future auxiliaries
a. I'**m going to** see Cora tomorrow
b. I'**ll** see Cora tomorrow

Both (15a) and (15b) refer to a single event: the event of seeing Cora, which will take place in the future. *Going to* and *will* are auxiliaries that express the future tense. However, *go* is also a lexical verb that refers to a particular type of motion. Does it refer to motion in (15a)? The answer is no: you do not need to be physically walking towards Cora in order for (15a) to be true. This indicates that semantic bleaching has taken place: the lexical verb *go* has lost its meaning as a verb of motion and instead expresses the functional category *future* in its use as an auxiliary – but note that *go* is still a verb of motion in sentences like *I'm going to the store*.

This suggests that English has (at least) two verbs *go*: 1. *go* verb of motion, "walk, move, advance", and 2. *go* AUX, future auxiliary. The development of the second one from the first one is an instance of grammaticalization through **reanalysis** of the underlying structure of sentences like (15a). This is illustrated in the following example:

(16) Grammaticalization of *going to*:
a. [I am [going$_V$]$_{VP}$ [to [see$_V$ Cora]$_{VP}$]$_{TP}$]$_{TP}$
b. [I am going$_T$ to [see$_V$ Cora]$_{VP}$]$_{TP}$

(16a) is a *biclausal* structure, meaning that there are two separate events: the event of going and the event of seeing Cora. You might utter this sentence as you are walking towards Cora. In (16b), on the other hand, there is only one event: the event of seeing Cora, which takes place in the future. That is, (16b) is *monoclausal*: there is only one event, expressed by the verb *see*. *Going* has been reanalyzed as a functional category expressing future tense. Functional categories expressing tense are usually thought to head a functional **tense phrase** (**TP**) above the verb phrase. Once again, **rebracketing** has taken place: the underlying structure of (16b) is different from that of (16a), even though they are the same on the surface.

PAUSE AND REFLECT 8.8

Apply the grammaticalization diagnostics discussed above to the English *go*-auxiliary. We have already seen that semantic bleaching has applied. What about the other diagnostics? Specifically, note that:

i In many varieties of English, *going to* is reduced to *gonna*: *I'm gonna see Cora tomorrow* (while it's ungrammatical to say **I'm gonna the store*)

ii Is *going to/gonna* as restricted in its distribution as the suffix *–ly* discussed above? How does it differ? In which context(s) is it found?

8.5 Syntactic Change

8.5.1 Parameters of Syntactic Change

While morphological change can affect individual lexical items (e.g., the words *līc-* "body" or *go* as we saw in Section 8.4), syntactic change affects structure at the phrase and sentence level, usually across the board. For instance, the change of object-verb (OV) to verb-object (VO) word order affects *all* instances of verbs and their objects, not just one particular verb and one particular object.

When we study syntactic change, the **Principles and Parameters** approach has been especially successful. **Principles** are abstract properties of grammars that are shared by all languages – they are part of Universal Grammar (UG), as you may recall from our discussions in Chapter 5 (Syntax) and Chapter 7 (The Classification of Languages). Basically, principles are what all languages have in common, whereas **parameters** are the possible options that these general principles offer. Parameter settings are what distinguish languages from one another (at the syntactic level – languages are of course also distinct in terms of their phonology, morphology, and lexicon).

To read more about language universals and language change read 'Delving Deeper' in Chapter 8's resources on the website to accompany this book at www.cambridge.org/introducing-linguistics. Let's now take a look at one particular parameter and its change in the history of English: null subjects.

8.5.2 Null Subjects

Consider the examples in (17), which illustrate variation in the expression of subject pronouns in Italian, French, and English. In standard Italian (as in many other languages around the world), subject pronouns such as *he, she, it, they*, etc., can remain unexpressed (indicated by the symbol "Ø".

(17) a. Ø parla   italiano   (Italian)
         speak.3sg.pres   *Italian*
         "He/she speaks   Italian"
     b. * Ø Parle italien   (French)
     c. * Ø Speaks Italian   (English)

The sentence in (17a) is grammatical in Italian and can mean either "she speaks Italian" or "he speaks Italian", depending on context, even though the word for *he* or *she* is *dropped*. This phenomenon is known as **pro-drop** (for pronoun dropping). Spanish, Italian, Mandarin Chinese, Greek, Navajo, Japanese, and Arabic, among others, are pro-drop languages, while English, French, and German are not. That is, in these languages, dropping a subject pronoun makes a sentence ungrammatical, as illustrated in (17b) for French and in (17c) for English. Roberts (2007, p. 25) formalizes this as the "null-subject parameter":

- **The null-subject parameter** (Roberts, 2007, p. 25): *Does every finite clause require an overt subject?*

YES: non-null-subject languages (French, English …)
NO: null-subject languages (Italian, Spanish, Greek, Japanese, Navajo …)

As you saw in Chapter 5 Syntax, parameters are like switches that can be turned on or off for any given language. If the null-subject switch is turned on, the result is a language in which all pronominal subjects are overtly expressed (like in English). If the null-subject switch is turned off, the result is a language like Italian in which pronominal subjects can be dropped. However, the parameter setting can change over time and this is indeed what we see with the null-subject parameter in the history of English. Old English (or at least some varieties thereof) was a subject pro-drop language, as you can see in the Old English sentences with null subjects in (18) and (19) (from Van Gelderen, 2013).

(18) Nu   scylun   hergan   hefaenricaes   uard.
Now   Ø   must   praise   heaven.kingdom's   guard
"Now **we** must praise the lord of the heavenly kingdom."

(19) Nearwe   ___   genyddon   on   norðwegas.
Anxiously   Ø   hastened.*3pl*   on   north.ways
"Anxiously, **they** hastened north."

The sentences in (18) and (19) are ungrammatical with null subjects in Modern English, so the parameter must have switched from NO to YES at some point. How might this have happened? Note that the definition of the parameter does not *exclude* the possibility of overt subject pronouns. In fact, Old English also used overt subject pronouns (as do all other null-subject languages, under varying circumstances). You can see the use of overt subjects in Old English in (20) and (21) (Van Gelderen, 2013).

(20) hi   cwædon him   betweonan þæt **hi**   woldon bugan to þæra apostola geferrædene
They said   them between   that **they** would   bend   to the   apostles' fellowship
"They said between themselves that they wanted to join the fellowship of the apostles."

(21) Nolde   **ic**   sweord   beran …
not.would   **I**   sword   bear
"I would not bear a sword … "

It is conceivable that the null-subject parameter switched from NO to YES because some children who were acquiring Old English as their first language had more sentences with subject pronouns like (20) and (21) in their input than sentences like (18) and (19) without subject pronouns.

PAUSE AND REFLECT 8.9

Compare the following Old English sentences from the Anglo-Saxon Chronicle to their Modern English counterparts. Which syntactic changes do you see? Pay attention to word order changes, especially the position of subject, object, verbs, participles, etc.

(i) *And*   *hi*   *hæfdon*   *heora*   *cyning*   *aworþanne* …
     And   they   had   their   king   overthrown …
     "and they had overthrown their king …"

(ii) *Her*   *for*   *se*   *ilca*   *here*   *innan*   *Myrce*   *to*   *Snotingham* …
     Here   went   the   same   army   inside   Mercia   to   Nottingham …
     "Here (in that year) the same army went inside Mercia to Nottingham …"

8.6 Semantic Change

Semantic change affects meaning over time. Traditionally, historical linguists distinguish between semantic change in **lexical categories** (nouns, lexical verbs, adjectives) and semantic change in **functional categories** (complementizers, determiners, auxiliary verbs). You will read about both of these in this section.

8.6.1 Semantic Change in Lexical Categories

A common change in lexical categories (nouns, verbs, adjectives) is that a given word comes to refer to either a *subset* or a *superset* of its original denotation. If it comes to refer to a superset, the change is called semantic broadening. If it refers to a subset, the change is called semantic narrowing.

- **Semantic broadening**: a word refers to a superset (i.e., a broader set) than its previous meaning. Examples include English *dog*, which originally referred to a specific breed of dog (cp. German *Dogge* "mastiff") and now refers to the superset *dogs*.
- **Semantic narrowing**: a word refers to a subset (i.e., a narrower set) than its previous meaning. For example, the word *deer* originally meant "animal" (cp. German *Tier* "animal"), but its meaning narrowed to refer to only a particular type of animal.

Semantic change of lexical items often builds on the **metaphorical** use of nouns, verbs, and adjectives. A **metaphor**, or figure of speech, draws a comparison between two related concepts. The metaphorical use of a lexical category can become its primary function over time, which is called **metaphorical extension**. Here are some examples:

- *to grasp*: to understand
- *to break up*: to end a romantic relationship
- *dope*: awesome, great
- *river bed*: the bottom of a stream or river, *not* an actual bed that contains a river

Examples of metaphorical use of language can be multiplied almost indefinitely and constitute a major source of *lexical* semantic change.

Another common type of lexical change concerns the connotation of words (refer back to Chapter 6 Semantics about connotation and denotion). Words (or rather, the concepts or entities they refer to) can have a socially, culturally, or subjectively conditioned positive or negative connotation. For example, the word *cat* may have a negative connotation to somebody with a cat allergy. If the positive or negative connotation becomes part of the core meaning of a word over time, we speak of amelioration (positive connotation) or pejoration (negative connotation).

Amelioration means that a word acquires a positive connotation as part of its meaning. For example, the word *knight* goes back to Old English *cniht* "servant, young boy" and acquired the meaning "nobleman" via "military servant".

Pejoration means that a word acquires a negative connotation as part of its meaning. For example, the word *villain* originally meant "villager" (it was borrowed from Old French *vilain* "peasant") and underwent a pejoration that's typical for terms referring to the countryside-dwelling population. The word *attitude* is currently undergoing a pejoration from its meaning "state of mind, opinion" to the meaning "uncooperative and antagonistic behavior", as in "don't give me that attitude!". Words that refer to women also tend to undergo pejoration over time, such as *hussy* from Middle English *husewif* "housewife" or German *Weib* "unpleasant woman" from Old High German *wīp* "woman".

Semantic changes of words are interesting because "they tell us a lot about past cultural and social history, and probably also about certain pervasive social attitudes" (Hock, 1991, p. 303). However, they tell us less about *grammar* change, for which we need to look to changes in functional categories.

LINGUISTICS TIDBITS: LEXICAL CHANGE

Semantic change in lexical items can be quite dramatic: the Albanian word for "sister", *motër*, comes from the reconstructed Proto-Indo-European word **mā́tēr* (from even older **méh₂tēr*), which means "mother" in all other related languages: Greek *métēr*, Latin *māter*, Sanskrit *mātár-*, English *mother* (from Old English *mōdor*), etc. Such drastic changes in the meaning of core vocabulary are rare, however. In the Albanian case, it was probably triggered by a change in family structure, in which older sisters took care of their younger siblings.

PAUSE AND REFLECT 8.10

Briefly explain the semantic change (broadening, narrowing, metaphorical extension, amelioration, or pejoration) demonstrated in the examples below.

i   English *silly*: from Middle English *sely* "blissful, blessed", Old English *gesǽlig* "happy, prosperous".
ii German *Du Bauer*! "you peasant!", one of the gravest insults in the variety of German spoken by the city-dwelling author of this chapter.
iii English *head* in *head of state*, Italian *capo* "head" in *capofamiglia* "head of the family".
iv English *bird*: from Old English *brid(d)* "young bird".
v   English *wife* (related to Modern High German *Weib* "unpleasant woman") comes from Old English *wīf* "woman".

8.6.2 Semantic Change in Functional Categories

Semantic change in functional categories such as demonstratives, auxiliaries, and pronouns is closely connected to morphological and syntactic change and to the many changes you read about in Section 8.4.3. Functional categories often change their meaning by grammaticalizing implicatures, entailments, or presuppositions of their original meaning. For example, it is common for demonstrative pronouns like *this (one)* and *that (one)* to develop into third person pronouns like *he*, *she*, and *it*.

Such demonstrative pronouns originally track *contrastive* third person discourse topics and entail non-contrastive or general third person topics. This entailment then becomes grammaticalized as the more general pronominal use. This happened to the Latin demonstrative pronouns *ille* and *illa* "that (one)" that we see in French *il* and *elle*. The French subject pronouns *il* and *elle* no longer mean "that (one)", as seen in (22).

(22) a. Latin: *ille venit* "THAT ONE is coming"
b. French: *il vient* "he comes"

Lexical items (nouns, verbs, adjectives), on the other hand, can acquire functional semantics over time. Such development is often found with container nouns like *cup, glass, sack, bottle*, which refer to items that can *contain* a substance. These tend to develop into measure nouns and refer to a quantity or *measure* of a substance through the grammaticalization of an entailment. Consider the phrase *a glass of water*. This phrase denotes a container, *glass*, which contains a substance, *water*. But it also entails a quantity or measure, namely the quantity of water that fits into a glass. This is exemplified in (23). Note that the # symbol means that something is syntactically well-formed, but semantically ill-formed.

(23) a. *A glass of water* <u>smashed</u> *on the floor* (but: #*water smashed on the floor*)
b. *A glass of water* <u>spilled</u> *on the floor* (but: #*a glass spilled on the floor*)

(23a) is an example of the container reading (*smash* refers to the container *glass*), while (23b) is an example of the quantity reading (*spill* refers to the substance *water*). The container interpretation entails the quantity, and this entailment can become grammaticalized. For example, in some varieties of English it is possible to use measure nouns to determine quantities in recipes without using the preposition *of*, as in *two cups water, one cup rice*, etc. In this context, *cup* only refers to a quantity, not a container (you're not going to throw an actual cup filled with rice into a pot of water to make dinner).

PAUSE AND REFLECT 8.11

Modern Mandarin Chinese has a negation marker *méi* "not" that is used to negate sentences with the existential verb *yǒu* "there is, exists", as in (i). In Old Chinese, this verb meant "to die", as in (ii), transcribed into Modern Mandarin Chinese. The examples are modified from van Gelderen (2008).

(i) wǒ   <u>méi</u>   yǒu   shū.
     I   NEG   exist   book
     "I don't have a book."

(ii) *Yáo*   *Shùn*   *jì*   <u>*mò*</u>
      Yao   Shun   since   died
      "Since Yao and Shun died, …"

Describe the semantic change that happened to this verb – why do you think it changed into a negation marker?

8.7 The Comparative Method and Language Reconstruction

8.7.1 Attested and Unattested Languages

So far we have discussed changes between two different attested language stages that are in a descent relationship. **Attested** means that we have some sort of historical record of a past language stage, usually manuscripts or other written evidence. What about unattested language stages of which there is no historical record whatsoever? You have already encountered the symbol * (the asterisk) in Chapter 7 Classification of Languages. This indicates that a linguistic form is reconstructed rather than directly attested. The **reconstruction** of past language stages is one of the main subfields of historical linguistics. In this section, we will briefly elaborate on those principles.

Why do we have to reconstruct past language stages? The answer lies in the fact that our knowledge of the past is often incomplete because of a lack of sources (this is true in other fields as well, not just in linguistics). Historical linguists usually study languages that are no longer spoken – dead languages, or, more precisely, **non-informant languages**. This means that there are no native speaker informants to consult for grammaticality judgements. These languages are only accessible through **historical records**.

EYES ON WORLD LANGUAGES: HISTORICAL RECORDS AND LANGUAGE ATTESTATION

The records and artifacts that historical linguists work with vary widely from language to language. Here are some examples:

- Rock inscriptions: the Behistun inscription in Old Persian, sixth century BCE;
- Parchment (animal hides): the Gothic *Codex Argenteus*, sixth century CE;

EYES ON WORLD LANGUAGES: (*cont.*)

- Tree bark: Old Russian Novgorod manuscripts, ca. eleventh to fifteenth centuries CE;
- Animal bones: Old Chinese, ca. 1000 BCE;
- Papyrus or paper: Old Egyptian, from ca. 2500 BCE;
- Clay tablets: Sumerian, from ca. 3000 BCE; Akkadian, from ca. 2,500 BCE;
- Wax cylinder recordings: Yurok (Algic), California, 1900 CE.

  Historical linguists also study contemporary languages that are still spoken. For example, the Australian linguist Claire Bowern works on the reconstruction of indigenous languages of Australia and has carried out extensive fieldwork on these languages.

  The study and evaluation of written texts and their origin is called **philology**. The philological analysis of a given text usually goes hand-in-hand with its linguistic analysis.

8.7.2   Comparative Reconstruction and Non-lineal Descent

Because our records of past language stages are often incomplete, historical linguists must fill in the gaps using **comparative reconstruction**. Comparative reconstruction relies on the **comparative method**, which was developed in the nineteenth century by establishing **genetic relationship**s between languages that belong to the same language family through regular **sound correspondences**. As you read in Chapter 7 The Classification of Languages, languages that are genetically related share a common ancestor, or **proto-language**. There are no written records of these proto-languages; they were reconstructed based on the attested languages that descended from them.

To understand how this works, the notion of **non-lineal descent** becomes relevant. We have defined lineal descent in Section 8.2.3 as a diachronic relationship between two grammars G_1 and G_2 in which G_2 is directly descended from G_1. However, historical linguists often deal with situations in which forms in G_1 correspond to forms in G_2 even though G_2 is not directly descended from G_1. That is, G_1 and G_2 are genetically related because they share a common ancestor, but neither is directly descended from the other. This is a form of **non-lineal descent**, which means that there is a regular correspondence between features of G_1 and G_2 that are *not* due to a lineal descent relationship $G_1 > G_2$ (Hale, 2007). Non-lineal descent is illustrated in Figure 8.3.

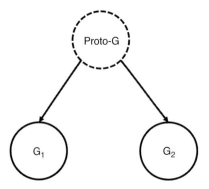

Figure 8.3 Non-lineal descent

In these situations, historical linguists reconstruct a grammar, *Proto-G* from which G_1 and G_2 are lineally descended. You can read about language families in 'Delving Deeper' in Chapter 8's resources on the website to accompany this book at www.cambridge.org/introducing-linguistics.

8.7.3 The Comparative Method

In this section, we will work through a case study to illustrate the comparative method in action. Campbell (1998) proposes the following steps for applying the comparative method (there are more, but these will suffice to get us started):

- Assemble cognates;
- Establish sound correspondences;
- Reconstruct the proto-sound; and
- Determine the status of similar (partially overlapping) correspondence sets.

LINGUISTICS TIDBITS: SOME USEFUL ETYMOLOGIES

- The word **toe** is related to the word **dic**tator (Latin **dictāre** "to assert") and the names of the Indian states of Uttar Pradesh and Andhra **Pradesh** (Sanskrit **deśá-** "region, country"). They all go back to a reconstructed root *deiḱ "to show, point to".
- The word *lady* is from Old English *hlǽf-dige*, literally "loaf-shaper" (the person responsible for kneading dough).
- French *cher*, *chère* "dear", Irish *cara* "friend", English *whore*, and Sanskrit *kāma-* "love" (as in the famous *Kāmasūtra*) all go back to the reconstructed root *kā (< *keh²) "to love, desire".

We will start by establishing **correspondence sets** (refer back to Section 8.2.3) based on **cognates**. Cognates (Latin *co-gnātus* "sharing ancestors, kindred, related") are words that share the same **etymology**, meaning that they go back to the same (reconstructed) word in the proto-language. We usually start by assembling basic vocabulary (kinship terms, numerals, body part terms, etc.) and searching it for **regular correspondences** between sounds to establish whether or not the words are indeed cognates.

There is a common misconception that the etymology of a word somehow reveals its *true* meaning. But the past meaning of a given word is no more *true* than the current or future meaning of that word. Rather, the etymology of a word sheds light on past stages of its development, some of which may be relevant to understanding its present form and meaning.

Table 8.5 illustrates sound correspondences between cognate words in Sanskrit, Greek, and Latin, using the IPA for a more accurate rendering of the relevant sounds (refer back to Chapter 2 Phonetics). You can ignore the bracketed material.

TABLE 8.5 Sound Correspondences in Sanskrit, Greek, and Latin

Sanskrit	Greek	Latin	Meaning
/saɽ-/	/hal-/	/sal-/	to jump
/saɽp-/	/hɛrp-/	/sɛrp-/	to crawl
/svaɽ/	/hɛːl[ios]/	/soːl/	sun
/sapta/	/hɛpta/	/sɛptɛm/	seven

Comparing the words in Table 8.5, you will notice that an initial /s/ in Sanskrit and Latin always corresponds to an /h/ in Greek. This correspondence can be summarized as follows (taking into account that we only have evidence for a word-initial correspondence at this point):

(24) Sanskrit /#s/ = Latin /#s/ = Greek /#h/

If languages share regular sound correspondences such as this one, they must be genetically related. Historical linguists use regular correspondences like (24) to reconstruct the proto-language from which these languages descended. Because sound change is regular, the two different sounds in (24) go back to just one single sound in the ancestral language (Proto-Indo-European, in this case, which you also read about in Chapter 7: The Classification of Languages).

So how do we decide what this *proto-sound* was? We can start with the assumption that this sound had the phonetic features [–voice, +continuant] (a voiceless fricative), since these phonetic features are shared by all correspondents in (24). That is, we start by determining the common phonetic features found in our correspondence set (we could assume that both sounds developed out of an entirely different sound, but unless we have evidence for it, such an assumption would be uneconomical).

However, the two sounds /s/ and /h/ differ with respect to place of articulation: /s/ is an alveolar, coronal fricative while /h/ is glottal. We therefore have to decide which of these was the place of articulation of the proto-sound. You have already encountered arguments against using the *majority wins* principle in Chapter 7 Classification of Languages because this principle depends on accidents in the transmission (or nontransmission) of recorded languages. Therefore, we need independent principles based on the typology of phonetically natural sound changes. *Phonetically natural* means that a sound change occurs because of the phonetic properties of the sounds involved and their phonetic environment. In this case, it is more phonetically natural for a sound to lose its original place feature and become glottal (note that *glottal* is technically not a place of articulation for consonants, but the absence of any restriction in the oral cavity) than the other way around. Countless instances of the change /s/ > /h/ in different languages attest to this, while the change in the opposite direction is never found. In general, it is more natural to lose a feature than to gain one out of the blue. So, our proto-sound was [–voice, +alveolar, +continuant], and we reconstruct *s for Proto-Indo-European (see Figure 8.4).

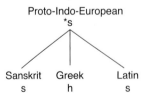

Figure 8.4 Reconstruction of Proto-Indo-European *s in word-initial position

We have now reconstructed our first Proto-Indo-European sound by working through the first three of Campbell's steps. Looking back at Table 8.5, we notice another correspondence: Sanskrit /ṛ/ sometimes corresponds to /r/ in Greek and Latin, and sometimes to /l/. A few additional examples are given in Table 8.6.

This is an **overlapping correspondence set** (cf. Campbell's step 4 above). Such sets are very common in comparative reconstruction. They can come about in two ways: 1) due to a phonemic **split** triggered by a particular phonetic environment, or 2) due to a **merger** of two phonemes into one. We can exclude 1) because there is no uniform phonetic environment that could be responsible for a split: Greek and Latin /r/ and /l/ both occur word-initially, word-medially before and after consonants, word- or syllable-finally, and before and after front, back, high, and low vowels. That is, unlike the palatalization and intervocalic voicing examples that you have already seen, there does not seem to be any common factor in the phonetic environment in these examples that could have triggered a split into two segments /r/ and /l/. We therefore assume that Proto-Indo-European had two phonemes *r and *l, which were merged as /r/ on the way to Sanskrit (this /r/ later became retroflex, but this was not a phonemic change). Table 8.7 illustrates the reconstructed proto-forms for some of the words in Tables 8.5 and 8.6.

Regular correspondences such as these confirm that the words in Table 8.7 are indeed cognates. Specifically, a form F_1 in language L_1 and a form F_2 in language L_2 are cognate

TABLE 8.6 More Sound Correspondences in Sanskrit, Greek, and Latin

Sanskrit	Greek	Latin	Meaning
/tṛajah/	/treːs/	/treːs/	three
/kṛawis-/	/krɛas/	/kruor/	bloody flesh, gore
/ṛink-/	/limp-/	/linkʷ-/	to abandon, leave behind
/ṛoːʧ-/	/lɛwk-/	/luːk-/	(be) bright, light

TABLE 8.7 More Sound Correspondences in Sanskrit, Greek, and Latin

Sanskrit	Greek	Latin	Meaning	Proto-Indo-European
/saṛ-/	/hal-/	/sal-/	to jump	*sal-
/saṛp-/	/hɛrp-/	/sɛrp-/	to crawl	*serp-
/tṛajah/	/treːs/	/treːs/	three	*trejes
/ṛink-/	/limp-/	/linkʷ-/	to leave	*linkʷ-
/sapta/	/hɛpta/	/sɛptɛm/	seven	*septm̥

if they go back to the same proto-form *F in the reconstructed proto-language *L, where *L is the ancestor of L₁ and L₂.

PAUSE AND REFLECT 8.12

Below is a correspondence set from the Semitic languages Akkadian (ancient East Semitic), Classical Arabic, Biblical Hebrew (both Central Semitic), and Ge'ez (ancient South Semitic). Reconstruct the bolded sound for Proto-Semitic and draw a tree like the one in Figure 8.4. Give arguments for your reconstruction and explain why *majority wins* is not a helpful principle in this case.

	Akkadian	Arabic	Hebrew	Ge'ez	Meaning
i.	appu	ʔanf	ʔap	ʔanf	nose
ii.	pe:mtu	faħm	peħa:m	fəħm	charcoal
iii.	upnu	ħufnat-	ħopnayim	həfn	hollow of the hand

PAUSE AND REFLECT 8.13

Old English, Old High German, Middle Dutch (Old Dutch isn't well attested), and Yiddish belong to the Western branch of the Germanic languages and go back to Proto-West Germanic. Using the cognate sets below, reconstruct the Proto-West-Germanic words for *foot, apple, bath*, and *fife*, using the methods discussed above. You may have to use the *majority wins* principle, but keep in mind that this principle can be problematic.

	Old English	Old High German	Middle Dutch	Yiddish	Meaning
i.	/foːt/	/fuos/	/vuət/	/fʊs/	foot
ii.	/æpel/	/apfəl/	/ɑpel/	/ɛpəl/	apple
iii.	/bæð/	/bad/	/bat/	/bɔd/	bath (house)
iv.	/fiːf/	/fimf/	/viːf/	/finf/	five

SUMMARY

In this chapter, we have introduced the core concepts of historical linguistics as the field that studies language change and past language stages. We have discussed the differences between change and diffusion, synchrony and diachrony, and ways of determining correspondences between different diachronic language stages. Change affects all aspects of language (in the sense of "grammar", or knowledge of language), and we have discussed phonological, morphological, syntactic, and semantic change.

A crucial insight in the study of language change and correspondence between languages is the observation that sound change is regular (the Neogrammarian Hypothesis). This regularity makes it possible to establish sound correspondences, interrelationships between languages descended from the same proto-language, and reconstructed proto-languages themselves. Throughout this chapter, we have seen that the different components of mental grammars are interconnected when it comes to language change. This is especially evident in grammaticalization changes, which usually combine changes in the phonology, syntax, and semantics of a given lexical or functional item, making historical linguistics a strongly interdisciplinary field.

Finally, we have seen that language change, despite its bewildering variety of manifestations, is constrained by universal properties of the language faculty. Understanding what is constant and invariant about human language and what is subject to variation and change is one of the most exciting challenges of modern linguistic theory. The goal of historical linguistics is to provide a theory of language change that captures those aspects that are variable.

EXERCISES

8.1 Explain the following terms and their relevance to the study of language change:

   i   Synchrony vs. diachrony;
   ii The Neogrammarian Hypothesis;
   iii The comparative method;
   iv Imperfect transmission;
   v Language reconstruction;
   vi Deductive change.

8.2 "Languages change constantly"; "the language faculty has not changed since it developed in humans": there is apparent tension between these two statements. Discuss how this tension arises, using the terms **I-language**, **E-language**, **universals**, and the **Uniformitarian Principle**.

8.3 The core tenet of the Neogrammarian Hypothesis is that sound change is regular. However, the actual texts that historical linguists work with tend to be full of irregularities and exceptions. For example, the Old English consonant cluster /sk/ became /ʃ/ during the time of the palatalization changes discussed in Section 8.3.1, as in the following examples:

Old English	Modern English
/sk(e)ort/	/ʃɔrt/ short
/skeakan/	/ʃek/ shake
/skeotan/	/ʃut/ shoot

However, there are also plenty of English words which do start with /sk/, such as *skirt* /skərt/, *scar* /skar/, and *school* /skul/. Even worse, there are apparent doublets, words which seem to have both the palatalized and the non-palatalized variant: *skirt* and *shirt* are both from Proto-Germanic **skurta-* "short garment", and *scar* is related to *share* (both go back to a root **sker-* that meant "to cut (off)"). While the /sk/-variants at first glance look like exceptions to the Neogrammarian hypothesis, we know that they were actually borrowed from Old Norse into English at the time of the early Danish settlement in England in the eighth and ninth centuries CE. Old Norse was a Germanic language closely related to Old English and did not undergo palatalization of /sk/. Discuss why such loan words are not counterexamples to the Neogrammarian hypothesis while considering the Linguistics Tidbits box on taboo words in Section 8.3.3. What problems might loan words pose for historical linguists? How could we identify them?

8.4   The following data illustrate some of the sound changes from Sanskrit (Indo-Iranian) to Pāli, a Middle Indic language that descended from Sanskrit (data based on Oberlies 2001). The symbol 'ɴ' stands for a uvular nasal.

	Sanskrit	Pāli	Meaning
1.	sapta	satta	seven
2.	a:tman-	attan-	self, soul
3.	pa:tra-	patta-	bowl
4.	saktʰi-	sattʰi-	thigh
5.	saɴrakta-	sa:ratta-	impassioned
6.	siɴha-	si:ha-	lion
7.	ra:trau	ratto	at night
8.	magna-	magga-	immersed
9.	paitrika-	pettika-	paternal
10.	pu:rɳa-	puɳɳa-	full
11.	ʃaikṣa-	sekʰa-	to be trained
12.	udbalika-	ubbalika-	tax-free
13.	ali:ka-	alika-	lie
14.	aurasa-	orasa-	own; legitimate son
15.	viɴʃati	vi:sati	twenty
16.	marma-	mamma-	vulnerable point, joint

i   Make a list of sound changes from Sanskrit to Pāli and classify them according to the types of changes discussed in Section 8.3.4. Generalize as much as possible (i.e., "Voiceless stops become voiced stops" instead of "p > b, t > d, k > g", etc.). Formalize as much as possible (i.e., "C[–voice] > C[+voice]" instead of "voiceless stops become voiced stops").

ii   Do any of the rules need to be ordered with respect to one another? Explain why.

iii   What are the expected Pāli outcomes of the hypothetical Sanskrit words *ʃaɴha-*, *aukta-*, and *ru:tra*? You can figure out the expected outcomes by applying the relevant sound laws you found.

8.5   The following data illustrate some of the sound changes between Mycenaean Greek (attested ca. 1400–1100 BCE) and Classical Greek (Attic–Ionic, fifth century BCE). Note that kʷ, gʷ, kʷʰ are labialized (or rounded) velars, similar to the initial sound in **qu**een.

	Mycenaean Greek	Classical Greek	Meaning
1.	wanaks	anaks	king
2.	wetos	etos	year
3.	kʷetra-	tetra-	four (in compounds)
4.	-okʷs	-ops	-eyed (in compounds)
5.	hekʰonsi	hekʰo:si	they have
6.	pansi	pa:si	all (dat.pl.)
7.	-kʷe	te	and
8.	-kʷʰonta:s	-pʰonte:s	-slayer (in compounds)
9.	diwjos	dios	of Zeus
10.	korwa:	ko:re:	girl
11.	pʰarwos	pʰa:ros	cloth
12.	kʷrijato	priato	he/she bought
13.	ma:te:r	me:te:r	mother
14.	kʷʰe:r-	tʰe:r-	wild animal

i   List all the sound changes that you can find in this data set. Some changes crucially depend on the phonetic environment (especially those affecting the labialized velars). Be as general as possible (e.g., "voiceless stops become voiceless fricatives between vowels"). The rules should be as formalized as possible (e.g., A > B/_C).

ii   For each change, explain what type of change it is, referring to the types of common sound changes discussed in Section 8.3.

iii   Are there any changes that need to be *ordered* with respect to each other? Which ones, and why?

8.6   The following table illustrates some of the changes that took place between Proto-East-Bodish (PEB; Tibeto-Burman family) and the East Bodish languages Dzala, Kurtöp, Bumthap, and Khengkha. The data are adapted from Hyslop (2014).

	PEB	Dzala	Kurtöp	Bumthap	Khengkha	Meaning
1.	*kak	ke:ʔ	ka:	kak	ka:	blood
2.	*lak	la:	ja:	jak	ja:	nose
3.	*kram	rɛm	rám	-	kram	otter
4.	*lok	lok	jo:	jok	jo	to pour
5.	*tʰek	tʰe	tʰe:	tʰek	tʰek	one
6.	*laŋa	lɛŋe	jaŋa	jaŋa	jaŋa	five
7.	*ta	te	ta	ta	ta	horse
8.	*kʰrat	tʰet	kʰrat	kʰrat	tʰat	waist

i   Make a list of sound changes from PEB to each of the East Bodish languages (PEB to Dzala, PEB to Kurtöp, etc.). Generalize and formalize as much as possible and try to classify each change according to the types of sound changes discussed in Section 8.3.4 (hint: some of the changes in this set were not explicitly discussed).

ii   The reconstruction of Proto-East-Bodish is relatively recent (see Hyslop, 2014), and some details remain to be worked out. You will notice that not all changes can easily be captured by a general rule or sound law. List the irregularities or exceptions you find.

iii   Which language is the most conservative or archaic? This means that it is closer to the proto-language than the other languages. Look for the language with the least amount of sound changes that differentiate it from the proto-language.

8.7   The following data illustrate cognates between Latin, Greek, and Sanskrit, which go back to the reconstructed ancestor language Proto-Indo-European (the data are in IPA). You will notice that there is an overlapping correspondence set in these data: The Sanskrit vowel *a* corresponds to the vowels *e*, *a*, and *o* in Greek and Latin (the relevant vowels are bolded; ignore the other vowels and the material in square brackets):

	Latin	Greek	Sanskrit	Meaning
1.	**e**st	**e**sti	**a**sti	is
2.	**o**kto	**o**kto:	**a**ʂṭa:	eight
3.	**a**ger	**a**gros	**a**dʒrah	field
4.	f**e**ro:	pʰ**e**ro:	bh**a**ra:[mi]	I carry
5.	-**o**sj**o** (Old Latin)	-**o**jo	-**a**sja	suffix of the gen.sg.masc.
6.	n**o**kt-	nukt- (from *n**o**kt-)	n**a**kt-	night
7.	n**e**b[ula]	n**e**pʰ[ele:]	n**a**bh[as-]	fog, mist
8.	**a**k[us]	**a**k[ros]	**a**ʃ[ri-]	sharp(ness), point(ed)
9.	kʷ**o**d	p**o**(-)	k**a**d	what, which … ?
10.	-kʷ**e**	-t**e**	-tʃ**a**	and (enclitic)

i   There are two ways of dealing with this set: 1) reconstruct *a for all words based on Sanskrit and assume a **split** into e, a, o in Greek and Latin, or 2) reconstruct *e, *a, *o based on Greek and Latin and assume a **merger** of these vowels in Sanskrit. Which solution is better?
- Hint 1: a split must be *conditioned* by the phonetic environment. Is there a conditioning factor for a split?
- Hint 2: The data in 9 and 10 are crucial. Why?

ii   Reconstruct the Proto-Indo-European words for 1–10 as accurately as possible (ignoring the bracketed material). You will not always be able to decide with absolute certainty, but make use of the principles discussed in Section 8.7 as much as possible (especially Campbell's steps of applying the comparative method).

- To figure out the last two, recall the development of *kʷ in Greek from Exercise 8.5.

8.8   Below is a list of cognate words in the Polynesian languages Hawaiian, Maori, Samoan, and Tongan (from Hale & Kissock, 2013) which go back to the reconstructed ancestor language Proto-Polynesian. Your task is to reconstruct these words in Proto-Polynesian and make a list of relevant sound changes (with rule ordering) from Proto-Polynesian to the daughter languages (Hawaiian, Maori, Samoan, Tongan). You'll find some hints below.

	Hawaiian	Maori	Samoan	Tongan	Translation
1.	niu	niu	niu	niu	coconut
2.	pua	pua	pua	pua	flower
3.	pe?a	peka	pe?a	peka	bat
4.	muli	muri	muli	mui	behind
5.	kani	taŋi	taŋi	taŋi	cry
6.	au	au	au	?au	current
7.	kuna	tuna	tuna	tuna	eel species
8.	walu	waru	walu	walu	eight
9.	i?a	ika	i?a	ika	fish
10.	kae	tae	tae	ta?e	excrement
11.	lau	rau	lau	lau	leaf
12.	?uku	kutu	?utu	kutu	louse
13.	umu	umu	umu	?umu	oven, earthen
14.	walu	waru	walu	wau	scratch
15.	kapu	tapu	tapu	tapu	taboo
16.	ako	ato	ato	?ato	thatch, roof
17.	lua	rua	lua	ua	two
18.	lua	rua	lua	lua	vomit

i   List the reconstructed words. You may want to start with words which are identical in all four languages – in these cases you can assume that nothing has changed since Proto-Polynesian was spoken.

ii   You will see some overlapping correspondence sets (e.g., n – ŋ – ŋ – ŋ vs. n – n – n – n in 7 vs. 9, respectively). Make a list of these sets and compare with Section 8.7 for hints on how to deal with them.

iii   List all the sound changes in each language. Some of the changes will need to be ordered. Look up rule ordering in Section 8.3.2. You can also look back at Pause and Reflect 8.4, which you can use as a starting point for unlocking the changes in the stops (hint: start with the correspondence sets ?– k – ? – k (e.g., 3) and Ø – Ø – Ø – ? (e.g., 6)).

8.9   In some varieties of English, the verb *bring* has acquired a past tense form *brang* and a participle *brung* (if you don't believe it, google the traditional folk song *the Hangman's Song* but not the Led Zeppelin version). Compare this change to the morphological changes discussed in Section 8.4 and explain what kind of change it is and how it came about.

8.10 Latin used the feminine noun *mēns* (genitive *mentis*) "mind" in adverbial phrases such as the following:

a) *clār-ā*   *mente*
    clear-FEM.ABL   mind.FEM.ABL
    "of/with a clear mind, clear-mindedly"

ABL stands for ablative case, a noun case marker that means "of" or "from". This construction gave rise to the French adverbial suffix *–ment* (e.g., *claire–ment* "clearly", *clair* masc./*claire* fem. "clear"; *franche–ment* "frankly", *franc* masc./*franche* fem. "frank", etc.), as in:

b) *elle*   *parle*   **franchement**   *à*   *son*   *père*
    she   speaks   frankly   to   her   father

   i   Using the grammaticalization diagnostics discussed in Section 8.4.3, explain how the French adverbial su fix developed from its Latin ancestor.

   ii Why are the wrench adverbs made from the feminine rather than masculine form of the adjective (*franchement*, not *francment)?

8.11 Latin has a preposition *ante* "before" (e.g., *ante eum* "before him"), which corresponds to the Ancient Greek preposition *antí* "against, instead of, opposed to" (e.g., *antì gámoio* "instead of a wedding"). In Hittite, an Indo-European language spoken in Anatolia in the second millennium BCE, we find a noun *ḫant-* "forehead, front" (the *ḫ* stands for a velar or glottal fricative). It is generally assumed that the Hittite word is related to the Latin and Greek prepositions.

   i   Describe the semantic and morphological differences that set the Hittite word apart from the Greek and Latin words.

   ii Which function/meaning is the original one, the Hittite one or the Latin and Greek ones? Explain why, and describe how it changed into the other meaning.

8.12 English, French, and many other languages use the verb *to be* (the copula) to link or equate a noun with another noun or with an adjective, as in *Lisa **is** tall/an artist*. In many other languages (e.g., Russian, Turkish, Arabic), the copula can be dropped and remains unexpressed. In Old Chinese, for example, there was no copula in clauses such as in (a) (examples from Li & Thompson, 1977, cited after Lohndal, 2009; the element glossed "DCL" is a declarative or emphatic particle).

(a) Wáng-Tái   wù   zhě   yě.
     Wang-Tai   outstanding   person   DCL
     "Wang-Tai is an outstanding person."

Note that there is nothing glossed as "be" in (a). Modern Mandarin Chinese, on the other hand, uses the copula *shì* in copular sentences, as in (b).

(b) nèi-ge   rén   **shì**   xuéshēng.
     that-CLASS   man   **COP/'BE'**   student
     "That man is a student."

Where does *shì* come from? In Old Chinese, it was a demonstrative pronoun, as shown in (c) and (d).

(c) fū-zǐ   zhì   yù   **shì**   bāng   yě.
     Confucius   arrive   at   **this**   nation   DCL
     "Confucius arrived at this nation."

(d) Jì   yù   qí   shēng   yòu   yù   qí   sǐ   **shí**   huò   yě.
     already   wish   him   live   also   wish   him   die   **this**   indecision   DCL
     "Wishing him to live while wishing him to die, that is indecision."

Using the concept of reanalysis discussed in Section 8.4.3, explain how *shì* developed from a demonstrative pronoun into a copula. The anaphoric use of *shì* in sentence (d) is crucial – think about what possible misanalysis of this sentence could have changed the function of *shì* from the perspective of a language acquirer.

8.13 Consider the following Middle English sentences, especially the bolded parts (from Ringe & Eska, 2013):

a.   … spoile him of his riches by sondrie frauds, which he **perceiueth not**.
b.   Quene Ester **looked never** with swich an eye.
c.   How great and greuous tribulations **suffered the Holy Appostyls** … ?

These sentences are ungrammatical in Modern English. Here are the relevant Modern English correspondences:

d.   … which he **did not perceive**.
e.   Queen E. **never looked** with …
f.   … **did the holy apostles suffer?**

i   Which syntactic changes do you observe between Middle English and Modern English with respect to the position of the lexical verb?
ii   What is the function of the verb *do/did* in the examples above?
iii   Try to formulate a parameter that could capture the changes between Middle English and Modern English (see Section 8.5 on parameter change). How might the parameter setting have changed over time?

8.14 Study the following Old French sentences in (a)–(c), taken from Roberts (2007).

a) | Si | chaï | en | grant | povreté. |
      | thus | fell.1sg | into | great | poverty |
      "Thus I fell into great poverty." (*Perceval*, 441)

b) | Si | en | orent | moult | grant | merveille. |
      | thus | of.it | had.3pl | very | great | marvel |
      "So they wondered very greatly at it." (Literally "So they had great marvel of it", *Merlin*, 1.)

c) | Tresqu'en | la | mer | cunquist | la | tere | altaigne. |
      | until | the | sea | conquered.3sg | the | land | high |
      "He conquered the high land all the way to the sea." (*Roland*, 3)

i   Based on these examples, was Old French a pro-drop language?
ii   Compare the Old French sentences to the Modern French sentences in (d) and (e). What change(s) do you notice with respect to the subject pronouns?

d) | Je | tombais | dans | la | pauvreté / * | tombais | dans | la | pauvreté |
      | I | fell | into | the | poverty | fell | into | the | poverty |

e) | Donc | ils | en | avaient | parlé / * | donc | en | avaient | parlé |
      | then | they | of.it | had.3pl | spoken / | then | of.it | had.3pl | spoken |

8.15 Classify the following changes into metaphorical extension, amelioration, pejoration, semantic broadening, and semantic narrowing.

(i)   German *aufheben* "to lift up" > "to revoke, repeal something"
(ii)   Latin *christianum* "Christian" > French *crétin* "stupid person"
(iii)   Latin *testa* "pot; brick, shard" > French *tête* "head"

(iv) French *chevalier* "horse rider" > "knight"
(v)   German *satt* "full, satiated" > "fed up, angry"
(vi) Proto-Indo-European *luHs-* "louse" > Tocharian B *luwo* "animal"
(vii) French *maîtresse* "lady, female ruler" > "lover, paramour"
(viii English *cool* "cold" > "cold; calm, distant; hip, chic"

REFERENCES

Campbell, L. (1998). *Historical linguistics: An introduction* (2nd Edition). Cambridge, MA: MIT Press.

Hale, M. (2007). *Historical linguistics: Theory and method*. Malden, MA: Wiley-Blackwell.

Hale, M., & Kissock, M. (2013). *Introduction to linguistic science*. Montreal: Concordia University.

Hock, H. (1991). *Principles of historical linguistics* (2nd Edition). Berlin: de Gruyter.

Hopper, P., & Traugott, E. (2003). *Grammaticalization* (2nd Edition). Cambridge: Cambridge University Press.

Hyslop, G. (2014). A preliminary reconstruction of East Bodish. In T. Owen-Smith and N. Hill (Eds.), *Trans-Himalayan linguistics*, pp. 155–180. Berlin: de Gruyter.

Labov, W., Ash, S., & Boberg, C. (2006). *The atlas of North American English: Phonetics, phonology, and sound change*. Berlin: de Gruyter.

Li, C., & Thompson, S. (1977). A mechanism for the development of copula morphemes. In C. Li (Ed.), *Mechanisms of syntactic change* (pp. 419–444). Austin, TX: University of Texas Press.

Lohndal, T. (2009). The copula cycle. In E. Van Gelderen (Ed.), *Cyclical change* (pp. 209–242). Amsterdam: Benjamins.

Oberlies, T. (2001). *Pāli: A grammar of the language of the Theravāda Tipiṭaka*. Berlin: de Gruyter.

Ringe, D., & Eska, J. (2013). *Historical linguistics: Toward a twenty-first century reintegration*. Cambridge: Cambridge University Press.

Roberts, I. (2007). *Diachronic syntax*. Oxford: Oxford University Press.

Van Gelderen, E. (2008). Negative cycles. *Linguistic Typology, 12*, 195–243.

Van Gelderen, E. (2013). Null subjects in old English. *Linguistic Inquiry, 44*, 271–285.

PART 5

LANGUAGE AND SOCIAL ASPECTS

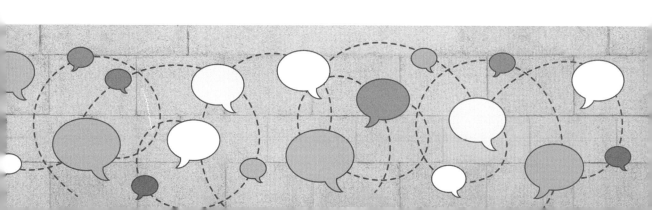

9 Sociolinguistics

Language in Society

Terry Nadasdi

OVERVIEW

The goal of the present chapter is to familiarize you with key concepts and findings in sociolinguistics. More specifically, you will:

- **learn about language and society;**
- **acquire concepts needed to study variation in the use of language;**
- **discover factors relevant for how different people speak;**
- **discover factors relevant for how individuals vary their speech;** and
- **explore variation in bilingual societies.**

9.1 What Is Sociolinguistics?

The branch of linguistics which seeks to examine and explain the everyday **variation** that characterizes human languages is **sociolinguistics**. Linguistic variation not only refers to the fact that many different languages in the world are spoken by humans, but also refers to the variation within a given language and even within speech communities of that language. In other words, linguistic variation happens at many levels: between languages, within a language, and within individuals who speak those languages.

We don't always express the same information in the same way. You probably already have noticed just by being human that how people speak is based on factors like:

- where they are from (regional variation);
- who they are (age, gender, socioeconomic status, etc.);
- the situation they are in (formal, informal);
- their linguistic profile (bilingual, monolingual).

Sociolinguistics studies the (often quantitative) relationships that exist between different linguistic forms, and social and situational categories. Another way to understand what sociolinguistics investigates is to contrast it with other approaches to language, like structural and prescriptive perspectives.

Structural approaches are interested in the invariable properties of language (i.e., what is and isn't possible in a given language). For example, a structural analysis of English would point out that determiners come before nouns in English as in *the girls* but they do not come after nouns as in **girls the*. Structural perspectives would also point out that the vowel /y/ exists in French (e.g., *vu*) but not in English.

Approaches to language which are **prescriptive** are interested in *good* (standard) and *bad* (non-standard) language, but ignore what people actually do when using language. You may recall our discussion of prescriptive grammar in Chapter 1 Introducing Linguistics. For example, prescriptive studies would encourage people to say *He and I left* and to avoid *Me and him left*, regardless of the fact that both are spoken by native speakers of English. Prescriptive linguistics doesn't study how people talk, it tells them how they *should* talk according to some subjective norm.

Unlike structural and prescriptive approaches to linguistics, sociolinguistics, as we have described above, examines the different forms of language people use to express the same information when speaking. For example, a sociolinguist, upon observing the two structures *He and I left* and *Me and him left* would establish their relative frequency among a given population and correlate these two structures with social factors (e.g., education, age, etc.). The data used by sociolinguistics usually comes from interviews or observations of people participating in natural conversations. Sociolinguists also examine language use in bilingual societies and study their linguistic distributions and characteristics. Unlike prescriptive linguistics, sociolinguistics is **descriptive** in nature (refer back to Chapter 1 Introducing Linguistics to read more about descriptive and prescriptive grammar).

In the next section, we examine several concepts that are used in all sociolinguistic studies. These key terms will help you understand this line of research and will even allow you to more critically think about the language(s) you hear in society each day. As you familiarize yourself with sociolinguistic concepts, pay attention to the language that surrounds you and you'll notice that language variation isn't just a topic but rather something you participate in daily.

After reading this chapter, you will understand how distinct groups of people speak and the different ways they change their manner of speaking according to social factors. If you speak more than one language, you are probably aware of some of the phenomena that sociolinguists study in bilingual communities (like code-switching). This chapter will also help you to understand what bilinguals do when using two languages.

PAUSE AND REFLECT 9.1

Imagine that you heard someone speaking, but could not see them (e.g., they were talking on the radio). What would their manner of speech reveal about them?

For example, could you guess their age or sex? What other information might you be able to gather just from hearing them speak?

9.2 Key Terms in Language Variation

Let's first consider a few key concepts that sociolinguists use to study and describe language variation. These are:

- a linguistic variable (an alternation);
- a linguistic variant (a linguistic form involved in the alternation);
- the variable domain (where the variants are *interchangeable*);
- standard language; and
- non-standard language.

We will describe these concepts in more detail in the next sections.

9.2.1 Variables and Variants

Let's begin our discussion on sociolinguistic variables and variants by taking a look at an example. What do you call a piece of furniture that seats three people? Canadian English has three words for this object: a) *couch*; b) *sofa*; c) *chesterfield*. American English uses *davenport* instead of *chesterfield*. What's important to note is that while these are different **forms**, they mean exactly the same thing. Our choice of one versus the others doesn't depend on the meaning we are trying to convey (unlike our choice between *table* and *chair*). It would therefore make no sense to ask *Did you buy a couch or a sofa?* Let's therefore define a **linguistic variable** as an instance of variation between forms that mean the same thing and a **linguistic variant** as a form participating in this variation. We illustrate the *couch-sofa-chesterfield/davenport* variants in Figure 9.1.

In a way, one goal of sociolinguistics is to dispel the myth that the alternation between variants of a variable is random. Rather, there are patterns we can find if we pay attention to sociolinguistic factors. The sociolinguist is a language detective of sorts who looks at the evidence and determines what is going on when language is used in conversation. If we consider the *couch-sofa-chesterfield/davenport* variants, we can identify several differences that are social. For example, *chesterfield* is fairly rare in Canadian English and is used primarily by older speakers. It is believed to originate from England after a former Earl of Chesterfield. In the United States, *davenport* was the name of a series of sofas produced by the Massachusetts furniture manufacturer Davenport and Company. The company went defunct in 1974 and as a result, the use of the word has also all but

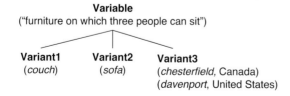

Figure 9.1 Linguistic variable and variants

vanished with the older population. It also appears that *sofa* is more prestigious than *couch* since *sofa* tends to be the one used in advertising and is found more often with positive adjectives like *beautiful new* versus *dirty old*. Does one sound better to you? Try some Internet searches to confirm this.

PAUSE AND REFLECT 9.2

Can you think of items in your kitchen that constitute linguistic variables? Remember, they must mean the same thing (so *fork* and *spoon* would not be an example).

The *couch-sofa-chesterfield/davenport* example we used to present the notion of a **linguistic variable** is lexical because it involves the alternation between words. However, sociolinguistic variation is by no means limited to the alternation between synonyms. Many variables studied by sociolinguists involve grammatical variation (e.g., *me and him* vs. *he and I* as the subject of a verb; *turn the light off* vs. *turn off the light*) or pronunciation variation (e.g., saying *–ing* as /n/ or /ŋ/ in a word like *working;* the word *pasta* as either /pɑstə/ or /pæstə/).

Not all sociolinguistic variables can be expressed by more than one variant. For example, speakers of English only have one option when it comes to expressing the variable *table*. Here, there is a complete overlap between variant and variable and, as such, it doesn't matter where you are from or who you are, we all choose the same word to refer to a table.

PAUSE AND REFLECT 9.3

Do you know people who use the word *chesterfield* or *davenport*? What are their social characteristics?

EYES ON WORLD LANGUAGES: VARIATION IN SPANISH

Language variation is by no means limited to the English-speaking world. In fact, every language provides examples of variation wth words, sounds, and even grammar. For example, in Spanish, examples of regional variation are plentiful. The word for avocado is *aguacate* in most Spanish-speaking regions, while it is referred to as *palta* in some South American countries like Argentina, Chile, Peru, and Uruguay.

Variation is also found at the sound level in Spanish. For example, the pronunciation of *–s* in syllable- and word-final position tends to be pronounced as /s/ in standard Spanish, or aspirated /h/, or completely deleted in other areas such as in the Caribbean and many coastal regions in Latin America.

Many examples of grammatical variation can also be noted. One example is the existence of two forms of a past subjunctive. While you may hear some speakers say *si fueras* "if you were", others may say *si fueses* instead. This grammatical variation not only appears between different varieties of Spanish, as you can imagine, but you may also hear the same speaker show this variation.

9.2.2   The Variable Domain

Another important notion to review as we introduce language variation is the **variable domain** (also called the variable context). Before quantifying the distribution of variants (and correlating them with social factors), we must first focus on a situation in which all variants are possible. Let's imagine you want to study the variation between *going to* and its contracted variant *gonna*. You can't simply count the number of each variant used by speakers according to age, sex, etc. That's because you must first exclude cases that are not part of the variable domain (i.e., the context where competition between variants is possible). Consider the examples in (1)–(4).

(1)   I'm going to leave.

(2)   I'm gonna leave.

(3)   That's where I'm going to.

(4)   *That's where I'm gonna.

In the examples in (1)–(4), you may notice a problem. The two variants only compete when indicating the future tense (i.e., when followed by a verb like *leave*). Only the non-contracted variant can be used when describing physical movement as in the examples (3) and (4). There's no point finding out the social characteristics of the person who said (3) since it is the only option available for all speakers of English.

Let's consider another variable: *trash* vs. *garbage*. These are definitely interchangeable in many contexts, but not all. You can say *I need to take out the trash* or *I need to take out the garbage*. This is because the domain for this variable involves cases where both variants function as a noun. However, only *trash* can be used as a verb. In other words, you can say *They might trash the apartment*, but you cannot say *They might garbage the apartment*. So, cases that fall outside the variable domain for both variants are not to be counted in quantitative analyses looking at language variation. The first step in any analysis of variation is therefore to clearly identify the **variable domain**.

EYES ON WORLD LANGUAGES: WORDS FOR *CAR* IN FRENCH

The number of variants for a given notion is very different from language to language. Consider the English word *car*. We really only have one word for this specific concept in English. Note that words like *vehicle* don't count since they are more general and don't mean the same thing (for example, *vehicle* could refer to a truck, a van, a bus, or a motorcycle).

French, on the other hand, has a tremendous range of variants for this specific notion (in both Canada and in France), for example: *auto, automobile, voiture, bagnole, caisse, tire, char, machine*. The first three words are used in both Europe and Canada, the words *bagnole, caisse,* and *tire* are found primarily in Europe, while the last two are limited to the French of Canada.

Not surprisingly, these words don't have the same social value. For example, in Canada, the word *voiture* tends to be the standard variant, the word *auto* is relatively neutral, while the word *char* seems to be typical of informal settings. Finally, the word *machine* is associated with older speakers in Canada. So, while these are all different ways of saying the same thing, their usage depends on social and geographic factors.

9.2.3   Standard and Non-standard Speech Varieties

In many cases of sociolinguistic variation, the variable involves an alternation between a **standard** variant and a **non-standard** one. Let's take a moment to explain what these terms mean. The standard variety (e.g., standard English, standard French, etc.) is characterized by the following features:

- typical of formal situations;
- promoted in educational institutions;
- strongly associated with the written language;
- described in reference books (grammars, styles guides, etc.).

Standard varieties are learned ways of speaking and require extensive exposure to the standard, usually via access to education. For example, standard English is not really learned naturally in the home as a first language.

Standard speech is often characterized as the *correct* way of speaking. However, this is simply a subjective viewpoint and there is nothing inherently *correct* about the linguistic forms that society looks up to. Forms that are now frowned upon were once part of the standard and vice versa. For example, before the French Revolution, diphthongs were considered prestigious, such that the word for "me", *moi*, was pronounced *moé* by the aristocracy. However, following the revolution, this pronunciation was avoided and no longer associated with the people in power.

In many cases, the standard variety fails to make important linguistic distinctions. Consider, for example, the standard English pronominal system. The word *you* does not distinguish number (singular or plural) or formality (informal or formal). But, many languages, like French, German, and Spanish have (at least) two forms of "you" (e.g., French *tu/vous*) to distinguish the singular and the plural (i.e., when speaking directly to one person or more than one person). In English, this gap is filled by non-standard forms like *you guys* and *y'all*. However, these non-standard variants are often considered *incorrect* by many since their use is not promoted by standard English grammar guides.

In other cases, the non-standard form is frowned upon because it departs from written English. For example, the pronunciation of *–ing* as *–in* (*work'**n*** instead of *work**ing***) is viewed as less correct because of the relationship between writing and the standard. Although there are a great many differences between spoken and written English (e.g., words like *knight* and *thought* don't represent how these words are pronounced), there is often pressure to speak how we write when possible. There's nothing particularly logical about this (after all, written language's first purpose was to represent spoken language, not the other way around). Our attitudes about correct and incorrect language are simply related to the relationship between power and education. Indeed, the grammar of the standard variety often defies logic. This is evident in the English pronominal system which distinguishes first person subject/object pronouns, but not second person ones (e.g., ***I** am, for **me*** vs. ***you** are, for **you***).

While standard variants are not linguistically better than non-standard ones, they are important to master because they tend to be favored in public interactions and provide social and economic advantages.

PAUSE AND REFLECT 9.4

Which seems more standard: *between you and I* or *between you and me*?

To summarize, among many other things, sociolinguists:

- identify linguistic variables in a given community;
- quantify the distribution of variants (standard vs. non-standard); and
- examine correlations between variants and relevant factors in order to find patterns in variation.

In the following sections, we will expand the categories of information relevant for variation and consider how sociolinguists study the way we speak.

9.3 Variation between Individuals and Subgroups

You already realize by now that different people speak in different ways. But what are the social factors that contribute to these differences? In this section, we will look at the key factors examined by sociolinguists. These are:

- region;
- socioeconomic status;
- gender; and
- age.

9.3.1 Region

Of course, English speakers from various geographic regions speak differently. For example, most people in England do not pronounce the -*r* at the end of words while most (but not all) speakers from North America do. If we are going to study variation in English, we need to identify the rules for a particular (relatively cohesive) group or society. Sociolinguists prefer to study the speech of individuals who form part of the same **speech community** and/or focus on variation within a circumscribed geographic area (e.g., a city). People of the same speech community tend to have some contact with one another (either directly or indirectly through media, the Internet, etc.) and have similar views on what counts as prestigious ways of speaking.

So, for example, it would make little sense to group all English speakers in the same speech community since they do not interact with one another and often don't share the same views of the prestige of a given form. For example, **r-dropping** (e.g., *cah* instead of *car*) is considered prestigious in England, but can be somewhat stigmatized in some parts of the United States (where its use is often heard in the Northeast). In research on language variation, sociolinguists recognize the importance of first identifying the precise group of speakers in the region they are examining.

PAUSE AND REFLECT 9.5

Within the United Kingdom, there are many different accents. How many different "British" accents are you familiar with? What are the positive/negative connotations that you have for these different accents?

So why do people from different regions speak the same language but in a different way? Believe it or not, it has nothing to do with geography. It has to do with historic settlement patterns and isolation from/contact with other groups (only in this sense can it be said to be related to geography).

Consider French spoken in Quebec and Acadia. While both areas speak a regional variety of French, they are very different in terms of pronunciation and vocabulary. Again, this is attributed to settlement patterns and isolation. First of all, both regions were populated by immigrants from different parts of France (Quebec French can be traced to northwestern France; Acadian French can be traced to central western France). Second, speakers from these two regions have had little contact with one another for many centuries. It's even more complicated than that since social histories and institutional support for French has been quite different in the two regions.

Canadian English and American English: Some Examples of Regional Differences

Have you ever heard of Canadians being mistaken for Americans because of how they talk? This is a common experience for Canadians travelling abroad. Part of the reason for this is that Canadian English can be traced to the English spoken during the eighteenth century within the Thirteen Colonies (which today includes an area containing several states along the Northeast coast). The people who formed the base for Canadian English, the Loyalists, fled this area during the American Revolution and established key cities like Toronto and Kingston.

While other groups arrived at later dates, the loyalists had by far the strongest influence (Chambers, 1998). Their way of speaking was then transported to other parts of Canada. This is why it is not really possible to hear notable differences between a person from Vancouver and someone from Toronto, or in fact, someone from Seattle. The minimal variation found across the English-speaking provinces is further bolstered by the fact that Canadians are a more socially homogeneous group (most are urban, middle-class, and formally educated). This is not the case for American English which shows a great deal of regional and social variation.

There are some differences in pronunciation between Canadians and Americans (see Canadian Raising Chapter 3 Phonology). One also finds general vocabulary differences. Some of the most striking ones are shown in Table 9.1.

TABLE 9.1 Canadian and American Vocabulary Differences

Type	American English	Canadian English
Education example	fourth grade	grade four
Pronunciation of the letter z	zee	zed
Food example	candy bar	chocolate bar
Clothes example	stocking cap	tuque
Drink example	soda (not all varieties)	pop

Across the English-speaking world, there are varieties that differ in interesting ways, either because the regions where they are spoken have remained isolated, because of cultural factors (different foods, animals, ways of interacting with others), for historical reasons or because of immigration patterns. You may have heard of *kangaroos* and *koalas* from Australia, but you may not be familiar with expressions such as *fair dinkum* "genuine" or *gander* "take a look"; you may know that people from Scotland may speak Gaelic besides English, but you may not be familiar with the use of *aye* for "yes", *bairn* for "baby", or *sláinte* used when making a toast. In North America, Appalachian English is famous for reputedly having maintained phonological, syntactic and lexical properties from 16th century English. Another North American example comes from Newfoundland, a province of Canada, whose variety is greatly influenced by the large number of Irish immigrants that settled there. Traditional Newfoundland English is distinct from other Canadian varieties in its pronunciation (like the use of *d* for *th* in the word *mother*), vocabulary (e.g., *nippers* "mosquitos"; *a sleevin* "an untrustworthy person"; *a bedlammer* "a young boy")[1] and grammar (e.g., the use of after to indicate the past perfect tense as in *I'm after doing my homework* for *I have done my homework*). Many more examples could be added including English spoken in South East Asian and African countries, but this gives you an idea of the extent to which English may vary in all domains.

In contrast, through the media, you are probably aware of American varieties of English: North vs. South, East Coast vs. West Coast vs. the Midwest, r-less vs. r-full

---

[1] We thank Dr. Steve Chalk for this example.

varieties, and many others. Notable is the presence of African-American English, with its complex grammar, and Hispanic English, that, when the situation demands it, often includes rule-governed code switching between English and Spanish. Although we have very briefly discussed here two varieties of English, you can read about others in Chapter 18 English Varieties Outside of North America.

PAUSE AND REFLECT 9.6

How do you refer to the country to the immediate south of Canada? The States? The US? The United States? America? Can you think of why some speakers may avoid using the term *America*?

9.3.2 Socioeconomic Status

Part of the answer to the pattern we find in variation concerns a person's position/status in society, which is referred to as their **socioeconomic status**. A person's socioeconomic status is usually established by considering the following factors:

- Educational level (e.g., high school, undergraduate, graduate);
- Income range (e.g., in the low, mid, or high range);
- Occupation type (e.g., unskilled worker, skilled worker, professional).

Although it may be sensitive to talk about socioeconomic status, it nonetheless affects how people use language. In order to come up with a system to place individuals in a given socioeconomic status, let's assign the numbers 1–3 for the information above (with three being the highest). Using this system, an individual with a graduate degree, earning what is considered to be a high salary in that speech community, and having a professional career would have a score of 9 and would be considered part of the highest socioeconomic status. We could then have three classes (0–3; 4–6; 7–9) and examine the distribution of variants across categories in our analysis of variation according to socioeconomic status.

In most speech communities, people of different socioeconomic status share many linguistic features. However, there tend to be quantitative differences in terms of the number of standard features that are found (with relatively more standard features in the higher class).

In some communities, using socioeconomic status is not all that appropriate. For example, in a small rural community or in a small fishing village, people tend to have the same level of education and income, and similar types of professions. However, that does not mean that variation can't be found in these sparsely populated areas.

Let's consider an example from the French spoken on Prince Edward Island (PEI). French speakers arrived in PEI following the expulsion of Acadians from Nova Scotia around 1755. As such, the French of PEI has contained many traditional Acadian French features not found in standard French. One striking example is the first-person plural (i.e., *we*) form of verbs. Standard French uses the pronoun *nous* followed by a verb ending in *–ons*, whereas traditional Acadian uses *je* followed by a verb ending in *–ons* as can be seen in (6).

(6) English: **we** *speak*
Standard Written French: **nous** *parlons*
Traditional Acadian French: **je** *parlons*

Like the language of all persecuted people, the traditional Acadian form is viewed as non-standard and has disappeared from the speech of many Acadians, especially among residents who have been exposed to standard French.

TABLE 9.2 Use of *je–ons* and *nous–ons* in Abram-Village and Saint-Louis, PEI

Abram-Village, PEI	je–ons	nous–ons
	18 percent	82 percent
Saint-Louis, PEI	76 percent	24 percent

Have all Acadians in PEI given up the traditional form? The answer to this is social in nature: Acadians in PEI who no longer use the *je–ons* form are under pressure from standard French. You can get a sense of this by looking at the statistics from two small Acadian communities in Table 9.2.

The difference in the use of *je–ons* and *nous–ons* in Table 9.2 is striking. One would expect speakers of the same socioeconomic status from two small communities (both of which have a population under 300) on the same island to speak the same way. However, there are some key differences to which we can attribute these different speech patterns. These concern the role of French within each community. Specifically, standard French is important in Abram-Village where there is institutional support for it and where people use it in some public interactions. This is not the case in Saint-Louis where non-standard French is found (and valued) primarily in the home.

Sociolinguists can interpret the difference between the use of *je–ons* in Abram-Village and Saint-Louis through the **social network** approach. A social network includes individuals with whom speakers interact on a regular basis. Those with strong, local connections tend to make greater use of non-standard features; those with few local connections tend to use standard variants more frequently. The way people speak is a reflection of their values and the particular forms they use can be viewed as acts of identity.

PAUSE AND REFLECT 9.7

Your social network is made up of those individuals you interact with on a regular basis. Make a list of the people you speak to every week. Does anyone in your network tend to speak less formally than you? Try to explain your answer.

We see therefore that our social analysis must be tailored to the individual society in question to make sense of the distribution of standard and non-standard speech variants.

9.3.3 Gender

Many sociolinguistic studies examine potential differences in the way men and women speak. An often reported finding is that women tend to use standard speech variants more frequently than do men (see Eckert & McConnell-Ginet, 2013). Consider, for example, the pronunciation of words ending in *–ing* as in *talking*. The *–ing* can be pronounced as /ɪŋ/ (like in **sing**) or as /n/ (like in **sin**) to be either *talking* or *talkin'*. Studies have noted that women pronounce the standard variant /ɪŋ/ more often than men.

In general, the variant typical of the highest socioeconomic group is found more frequently in the speech of women than in that of men. This tendency has also been noted in other languages. For example, francophone men tend to delete the consonant /l/ more often than do francophone women (e.g., in the word *elle* "she").

> **LINGUISTICS TIDBITS: MALE AND FEMALE VOICE RANGE**
>
> It's not always possible to distinguish a male voice from a female voice. The range for females is from 100 to 525 Hz, while the male range is between 65 and 260 Hz. This means that a voice between 100 and 260 Hz could be classified as male or female.

Although these are only a few examples of the differences between male and female speech, many other variants have been identified and studied in several (North American and European) communities. Consistent in these findings is that women show a preference for standard variants over non-standard variants.

Studying language variation by looking at gender in isolation makes little sense because other factors (e.g., socioeconomic status, educational level, etc.) are simultaneously relevant and interacting. For example, the gender difference is much more pronounced in the speech of the lower-middle class than of the working class. And, it is by no means the case that women always favor the standard prestige variant.

In terms of conversational styles, research has documented the following trends (see Eckert & McConnell-Ginet, 2013):

- women are better at turn taking (that is, they interrupt less often and wait their turn to speak);
- women make greater use of supportive utterances like *MMhum, yes*, etc. while someone else is speaking;
- women tend to change the topic less often than do men;
- women tend to ask more questions than men.

So far, do these differences support the saying "men are from Mars, women are from Venus", which is also the title of a best-selling book by John Gray (1992)? While we cannot deny these striking differences exist, we probably should not go so far as to say they are from different planets. So then, to what might we the differences found between men and women's speech? It seems unlikely that it has anything to do with biology. If it did, we would expect far greater differences and it would be difficult to explain the fact that many men and women do not adhere to the documented patterns.

The explanation must have to do with the structures and expectations of the societies in which we use language. In other words, the difference between male and female speech is largely a result of socialization. Various explanations have been proposed to account for this. The main ones are that women tend to prefer standard variants since it grants them prestige/power in a society where they unfortunately (still) have a subordinated role to men. Regardless, it seems obvious that this is a **learned behavior** and not a biologically rooted one.

Perhaps a more important point to make, however, is that for the most part, men and women speak the same way. It is unfortunate that social science research tends to favor reporting and explaining findings that show differences, not similarities. This is really a matter of choice. Focusing only on differences between men and women's speech gives the false impression that men and women are mostly different when, in fact, they are mostly the same in the way they use language.

PAUSE AND REFLECT 9.8

We mentioned the book *Men are from Mars, Women are from Venus* (Gray, 1992). While this is a clever title to capture the differences between male and female speech, try to create another book title for one that would illustrate their similarities while subtly showing their distinctness?

The Linguistic Representation of Females and Males

Sociolinguists are not only interested in comparing male and female speech but also in the way language refers to men and women. There are many examples to suggest that language makes reference to men and women in a way that reflects a male-dominated, sexist society.

One example of sexist language can be seen in terms of address. For example, it is still common for women to reveal their marital status by using *Miss* or *Mrs.* No such imposition has ever existed for males. The use of *Ms.* exists to provide a more equal system of addressing females, but resistance to this continues. Changing a surname upon getting married is another example of an identity being defined in terms of a spouse.

Our vocabulary is also reflective of the gender imbalance. For example, words traditionally associated with females often have negative connotations (e.g., *She's a*

LINGUISTICS TIDBITS: EXPLETIVES

You will also find gender imbalance in other languages. In Mexican Spanish, some expletives with *madre* (mother) are negative while others formed with *padre* are positive. For example, *¡qué padre!* means "how cool!" but saying something like *me vale madre* means loosely "I don't give a crap." One exception in Mexican Spanish seems to be *a toda madre* which roughly means "totally awesome."

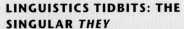

LINGUISTICS TIDBITS: THE SINGULAR *THEY*

Standard English has long condemned the use of *singular they* to refer to someone whose gender is unknown as in (i).

(i)   Everyone on the team should play **their** best.

A long time ago, it was claimed that *they* and *their* could only be used to refer to plural nouns (although oddly enough, standard English doesn't seem to mind the fact that *you* can be singular or plural). Traditionally, English would have preferred a sentence like (ii).

(ii)   Everyone on the team should play his or her best.

Over the years, *singular they* has introduced itself into the mainstream as a gender-neutral pronoun for generic referents. In fact, the prestigious *Washington Post* recently has adopted singular *they* into their style guide.

real witch), while those associated with males are viewed less negatively (e.g., *He's a real wizard*). This is even seen in the fact that words for male animals have positive or neutral connotations whereas those that refer to females tend to be negative. Compare, for example, the connotation word pairs like *dog/bitch* and *bull/cow* in spoken English.

The gender bias is also clear in grammar. For example, in English, many people still use male-centered pronouns to refer to both men and women. We see this in the use of so-called **andro-centric generics**. These are cases where a male pronoun is used by default to refer to individuals whose gender is not known. For example, *the candidate should submit **his** résumé*. This usage has real-world, exclusionist implications. For example, when job advertisements use such language, female applicants are much less likely to apply. Clearly, these are not truly generic.

English is not the only language to show this bias. For example, according to the rules of standard French and many other languages, the male-centric pronoun *ils* ("they", masculine plural) should be used to refer to a group that contains both males and females, even if *they* refers to one male and 99 females.

Given the negative ways women are referred to and represented in our language, it is not surprising that efforts have been made to reform some of these practices. One current example concerns the Canadian National Anthem that has recently been changed from *in all thy sons command* to *in all of us command*. While people are often resistant to changes to language, efforts to make the language we use more inclusive are needed and are slowly happening.

PAUSE AND REFLECT 9.9

Are you in favor of the changes to Canada's National Anthem? In what ways do you agree/disagree with them? Make a list of positive and negative effects of this change.

9.3.4   Age

As you read in Chapter 8 Historical Linguistics, all languages change over time. This change, though, is usually quite subtle. Despite the major changes that have taken place throughout the history of English, people are largely unaware of such changes as they are happening. Sociolinguists study change as it creeps through society. There are two ways that sociolinguists can study changes in progress:

- Apparent-time studies; and
- Real-time studies.

An **apparent-time study** compares the speech of people of different ages. Do you speak the same way as your parents or your grandparents? The comparison of generational differences provides an interesting window on language change, without having to wait several decades. Consider the variable mentioned above that involves the variants *couch*, *sofa*, and *chesterfield/davenport*. One study that considered this variable in Canadian English (Chambers, 1998) found strong, apparent-time evidence that *chesterfield* was disappearing from Canadian English despite that fact that it used to be the most common. Specifically, the study found that while people over 80 years old still used *chesterfield* around 73 percent of the time, teenagers made very little use of it. This latter group only used the variant *chesterfield* 6 percent of the time and showed a strong preference for the *couch* variant, which it used 85 percent of the time. Such a result is evidence of a change in Canadian English and suggests that the word *chesterfield* will soon disappear. We would expect the same for *davenport* in the United States.

A **real-time** study considers speakers of the same age, but from different points in time, for example, a real-time study would compare the speech of adolescents in 1980 with adolescents in 2000. If a difference between the two is found, one can safely conclude that the particular aspect of language being examined has changed (been modified, added, or disappeared).

Let's consider an example of a real-time study of language change (Sammons, Nadasdi, & Mougeon, 2015). The project in question considers change in the French spoken in Cornwall, Ontario. Two databases (or corpora) were used, one from 1978 and one from 2005. Each of the databases included interviews with high school students from the same community. The variable in question was the manner in which one says *I went* in Canadian French. The standard variant is *je suis allé*. However, this is not the one typically used by speakers of Canadian French who prefer the variant *j'ai été*. This certainly was the case for adolescents in Cornwall in 1978, but what about 2005? Consider the results in Table 9.3.

TABLE 9.3 Frequency of "I went" in the French of Cornwall, Ontario Adolescents

"I went"	1978	2005
J'ai été	86 percent	37 percent
Je suis allé	14 percent	48 percent
J'ai allé	0	15 percent

You can see in Table 9.3 that in 1978, the most common way for adolescents in Cornwall to say *I went* was the same as that of French speakers in Quebec. However, a real-time change found in the databases has taken place over the 28-year span. Now, it is the more standard *je suis allé* that is the most frequent. Furthermore, a new variant, *j'ai allé* is now being used 15 percent of the time. The reasons for these changes are varied and include lack of exposure to the traditional variant and the influence of standard French via the educational system (since these speakers use French almost exclusively in a school setting). Now that years have gone by since the 2005 database interviews, how do you think the distribution might look today?

9.4 Variation within Individuals

While much of the variation examined by sociolinguists takes place between people of different social categories, variation is also found within the speech of an individual. None of us always speaks *exactly* the same at all times. The two main factors to consider when studying language variation at the individual level are **speech style** and **linguistic context**. We will go into more detail about each of these in the following.

9.4.1 Speech Style/Register

One important factor that influences the different ways an individual speaks is the situation in which he/she is using language. In formal situations, people shift to a more standard way of speaking while in informal ones, they are more likely to decrease their use of standard variants. We refer to these types of formalities as the **speech style** or **register**. But what precisely makes a situation *formal*? Here are some contributing factors:

- **Topic**: serious topics like religion, politics, and even linguistics give rise to a formal speech style;
- **Place**: in public institutions (like schools, places of business), people shift to a more standard way of speaking;
- **Interlocutor**: people tend to use a more formal style when speaking to people with whom they are less familiar.

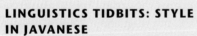

LINGUISTICS TIDBITS: STYLE IN JAVANESE

The notion of style in Javanese, a language spoken by around 82 million people in Indonesia, is far more complex than in English. Javanese distinguishes three very different styles that are characterized by their own pronunciation, vocabulary, and grammatical features. The particular style is determined by social factors such as whether you know the person you are speaking to and whether you are of the same social standing.

While style is often divided into formal vs. informal, it is more accurate to talk about a range of levels. We illustrate an example of this spectrum in Figure 9.3.

Highly informal > informal > neutral > formal > highly formal

Figure 9.3 A spectrum of speech styles/registers

The frequency and types of standard variants that an individual uses will depend, in part, on the specific level of formality of the situation in which language is used. The reason for this kind of shifting is related to the importance we attribute to how we are viewed in public interactions. In more formal settings, we focus less on the message and more on how we are speaking since most people want to show that they are knowledgeable of the standard variety. In more informal settings, the information conveyed is more important.

PAUSE AND REFLECT 9.10

People tend to use more standard speech forms when they know someone is paying attention to how they are speaking. Why do you think this happens?

9.4.2 Linguistic Factors

As you have been reading throughout the chapter, sociolinguists are interested in explaining the patterns of language variation. They do not accept the notion that variation *just happens*. Part of our ability to reject the notion that variation is random depends on finding the relevant social factors, as discussed above. However, that is only part of the puzzle. Some factors that are relevant for our quest to find the pattern in variation are linguistic in nature. By **linguistic factors**, we mean linguistic elements that vary from utterance to utterance. Let's consider a widely-studied variant, the presence or absence of /ɹ/.

While many English speakers pronounce /ɹ/ in all contexts, some American speakers display variation when a vowel directly precedes it. For example, the word *car* will sometimes be pronounced as /kaɹ/ and sometimes the /ɹ/ is deleted to sound like /ka/. Of course, as you may have already guessed from reading this chapter, there are several relevant social factors that explain why this variation occurs. For example, we might find /ɹ/ deletion more prominent among the working class.

But our understanding of the presence or absence of /ɹ/ would be incomplete if we didn't pay attention to the linguistic contexts which permit one but not the other. In other words, we must look at the surrounding sounds to see what linguistic factors determine

LINGUISTICS TIDBITS: WORD-FINAL /ɹ/

The dropping of the sound /ɹ/ in word-final position used to be a prestigious variant in American English up until around 1950. This prestige continued in the southern states for many decades. However, today /ɹ/ is used by most people in the higher socioeconomic groups, even in the south. This reality is usually misrepresented in movies where all southern characters drop the /ɹ/ sounds.

whether the /ɹ/ is pronounced or deleted. Consider where the /ɹ/ occurs in the words *fourth* and *floor*. A good linguistic detective would notice that the variable appears in different linguistic contexts. In *fourth*, the variable occurs in the middle of a word, before a consonant. In *floor*, it occurs at the end of the word.

From the words *floor* and *fourth*, you can see that the sociolinguistic variable under consideration (i.e., /ɹ/ in this case) may not always be in the same sound environment. Does this linguistic context affect whether the /ɹ/ is pronounced or deleted? As the American sociolinguistic William Labov noted in his pioneering study, the likelihood of deleting the /ɹ/ is not the same in both contexts. Deletion is more likely to occur at the end of a word (e.g., /flɔ/) rather than when /ɹ/ comes before another consonant (e.g., /fɔɹθ/). As such, we must pay attention to both social and linguistic information when looking for patterns in language variation.

Let's consider another example, this time from French. In both European and Canadian French, there are two ways to express the future. Just as in English, these expressions have the equivalents of *going to* and *will*. The two variants are the **periphrastic future** (7) and the **inflected future** (8).

(7)   The periphrastic future: *aller* + infinitive, e.g., *je **vais** partir* "I'm going to leave"

(8)   The inflected future: infinitive + future ending, e.g., *je part**irai*** "I will leave"

While the examples in French in (7) and (8) imply leaving sometime in the future, the frequency of their use is not at all the same. The periphrastic future is much more common in Canadian French, being used around 80 percent of the time. However, there is one linguistic context where this is not the case. In negative sentences, the use of the inflected future skyrockets from 20 percent to 99 percent. So, the negative sentence as in (9) is almost always constructed using the inflected future.

(9)   *Je partirai **pas** avec vous* "I will not leave with you."

As was the case with the /ɹ/ deletion we saw above, we see once again that any analysis of variation must consider both social and linguistic factors (this time, negation).

PAUSE AND REFLECT 9.11

One common variable that has been studied in English is the deletion of the consonants /t/ and /d/. Consider the following sequences:

- The las<u>t</u> person;
- The las<u>t</u> event;

- She work<u>ed</u> too hard.

In what linguistic contexts do you think that /t/ is most likely to be deleted? What is the variable domain for /t/–/d/ deletion?

9.5 Variation in Bilingual Communities

Did you know that monolingualism is actually the exception, not the norm? Over half the world speaks at least two languages. So it should come as no surprise that variation in bilingual communities has been the object of many sociolinguistic studies. This body of work has taken two basic forms: a) investigating the distribution and characterization of languages in the same speech community; and b) a linguistic analysis of a sociolinguistic variable found in a bilingual's discourse (often compared to monolinguals). Below, we will talk about these two veins of research.

9.5.1 Language Distribution

Studies that consider the distribution of two (or more) languages in a society remind us that the term *bilingualism* is somewhat misleading since it suggests a situation of equality/duality. In effect, this is rarely the case both linguistically and, especially, socially. In reality, bilingualism is all too often about linguistic dominance. In almost all bilingual communities, there is one powerful, socially revered language and one or more subordinate languages. The powerful language tends to be the one used in public interactions (e.g., education, courts, business, etc.). A good example of this would be the distribution of English and Spanish in the United States. While there are millions of Spanish speakers in the United States, official business is mostly done in English.

In the United States, English is the de-facto national language that is used in the majority of public interactions. But Spanish is spoken by 40 million people in the United States – roughly 13 percent of the population – and has been spoken there for centuries. However, it is often confined to the home and within cultural/community interactions. In other words, this means that while it is common in the United States for an English-only speaker to hold positions of economic and political power, Spanish speakers must learn English if they are to enjoy social advancement.

In Canada, the bilingual situation is different since institutional support exists at the federal level for both English and French. However, even in Canada, English is clearly the dominant language in all provinces outside of Quebec (French is the official language in Quebec; English and French are both official languages in New Brunswick). On the other hand, indigenous languages are very much under threat of disappearing. Currently, only one in four indigenous Canadians report being

> **LINGUISTICS TIDBITS: IS THE UNITED STATES A BILINGUAL COUNTRY?**
>
> People sometimes incorrectly assume that many (or most) Americans speak Spanish. But can a country be *bilingual* if it doesn't even have one official language? The United States' federal government has no official language. However, in what some call the *English-only movement*, 30 of the 50 states have passed laws allowing only English official status. Only the last two states to join the Union (both in 1959) have more than one official language. Hawai'i recognizes English and Hawaiian and Alaska has English and twenty indigenous languages.

able to speak an indigenous language. Furthermore, while there are some 50 different indigenous languages still spoken in Canada, the vast majority of them have very few speakers (some in single digits) and sadly may soon disappear.

In situations where subordinated minority languages receive little or no institutional support, there is a danger of the language disappearing. Sociolinguists refer to this as **language shift** or **language death**. Examples of languages that have died are Beothuk (an aboriginal language once spoken in Newfoundland) and Manx (a Gaelic language once spoken on the Isle of Man).

Below is a list of signs that suggest a language may be undergoing shift.

- It is not used in a wide variety of social situations.
- Its speakers become more proficient in the majority language than in their first language.
- Its speakers are not able to express themselves in both formal and informal ways.
- It is not used in the workplace.
- It is viewed negatively by its own speakers.
- It is not learned by the next generation.
- It is not learned by immigrants or their children.
- It does not have legislative power (i.e., its use in public interactions is not protected by laws).

Since language death happens for social reasons, not linguistic ones, improving a language's status within society is key to its survival and maintenance. So how does one go about improving the status of a language? We address this issue in the following section.

PAUSE AND REFLECT 9.12

Imagine you have been given the responsibility of reviving a language that has died. What kinds of things would you do to ensure that your revival efforts were successful?

9.5.2 Language Planning for Minority Languages

It should be noted that language shift is by no means irreversible. Furthermore, languages that have disappeared may once again flourish if the appropriate measures are taken. This was the case for Irish and most notably for Hebrew, a language that had not been spoken for centuries but is now the language of some five million people (although this is a rare example).

Language planning for a minority language involves two kinds of planning: **corpus planning** and **status planning**. Corpus planning involves the creation of resources and documentation in the language and status planning makes efforts to create positive connotations for the language. Let's consider the language planning efforts used to strengthen the place of French in Quebec to get an idea of the common steps taken.

EYES ON WORLD LANGUAGES: THE REVITALIZATION OF HEBREW

While languages die, it is not impossible to revive them (though this is a rare occurrence). The best example of a language being brought back to life is Hebrew. It ceased to be spoken in everyday conversation for close to 2,000 years (though it continued to be used in prayers and religious texts). The renaissance of Hebrew is the result of a collection of events over several centuries. The first contributions to its revival began in the late eighteenth century, at which time a small number of authors began producing texts in Hebrew. It also received a significant boost from Eliezer Ben-Yehuda's efforts to modernize the Hebrew lexicon in the late nineteenth century. Not only did he produce new words, he also spoke it to his child and encouraged others to do the same.

This alone would not have been enough though. Its current widespread use (Hebrew is spoken by approximately five million people) can be attributed in great part to the rise in Jewish nationalism during the nineteenth century and to its use in new settlements of immigrants to Israel. The creation of Hebrew schools also played an important role since this allowed the language to spread to new generations. The history of Modern Hebrew clearly shows the importance of social factors for successful revitalization of a language.

A Language Planning Example: Quebec

French presence in Quebec dates back to the arrival of Cartier in 1534, though permanent settlements were not established until the first part of the seventeenth century. Various attempts to recognize the status of French in Quebec (and Canada) can be found throughout the eighteenth, nineteenth, and twentieth centuries. For example, French civil law has been recognized since the Quebec Act of 1774 and the official status of French was established by the British North America Act in 1867. This latter act replaced the Union Act of 1840 which included English as the official language in what would someday become Canada.

In spite of early recognition, francophones have struggled for centuries to have their language recognized in all spheres of Canadian and Québecois society. Prior to the 1960s, French had a very low social status and francophones did not enjoy the same economic advantages as anglophones, even in Quebec. Immigrants to Quebec learned English to reap the economic benefits associated with the language.

The same was true of francophones in Quebec since fluency in English greatly increased one's chances of finding a well-paid job. At the same time, anglophones remained monolingual without suffering negative economic consequences. The low status of French (and francophones) within the borders of Quebec eventually gave rise to a socio-political movement known as the Quiet Revolution that resulted in significant changes to the use of French in education and the workplace.

The first important step in improving the status of French in Quebec was the creation of the *Office de la langue française* in 1961. Since 2002, it is called the *Office québécois de la langue française* (OQLF). The mandate of the OQLF is to ensure that French is the language of work, communication, and business in Quebec. This is achieved in part by the development of documentation and terminology for businesses and by addressing complaints concerning the inability to be served in French.

The status of French was further bolstered by a series of legislative measures such as Bill 22 (1973), which made French the sole official language of Quebec. Still, it was not until the passage of Bill 101 (1977) that the status of French began to improve in tangible ways. Bill 101 accomplished this in at least two important ways:

LINGUISTICS TIDBITS: SIGNAGE IN CATALONIA, SPAIN

Controversy around what language business signs should be in is not unique to Quebec and Canada. Similar policies also exist for Catalan, a language spoken by some four million people in north eastern Spain. Locally, businesses can be fined if their signs are displayed only in Spanish. Such legislation is in place to ensure that Catalan speakers can be served in their language. This piece of Catalonian legislation, however, is not supported by the central government of Spain.

- French became the language of education for all citizens (except those with an anglophone parent/sibling educated in English in Canada); and
- French became the language of business by requiring all signs to be posted only in French and requiring that businesses function in French at all levels.

The positive effects of Bill 101's provisions have been confirmed by several studies (e.g., Bouchard & Bourhis, 2002). We see from this legislative step and others that it is indeed possible to improve the place of a language in a society and, in so doing, ensure its future.

PAUSE AND REFLECT 9.13

One important measure taken in Quebec concerns the use of French in commercial signs. Do you think it is fair for the provincial government to legislate the language use on signs? What is the justification for this?

9.5.3 Linguistic Analysis of a Bilingual's Languages

There is a common misconception that people who speak a minority language (e.g., Spanish in the United States or French in Canadian provinces outside of Quebec) in some way speak a poorer version of its standard variety. The reason for this is that the minority variety of a language is often compared to the standard version of the language or a version as spoken in another country where it has institutional support.

Since it is rare for minority speakers to receive education in their first language, they necessarily speak a non-standard version that is of course different from the standard one used and promoted in schools and institutions. However, these varieties remain fully functional and allow speakers to make the same distinctions as majority language speakers.

This is not to say that one doesn't find the occasional influence from the dominant language. For example, you may hear *je suis peur* for "I am afraid", among some speakers of French in Ontario (as opposed to *j'ai peur*, the version used by most francophones). Still, such influence is often overstated. Less than five percent of the vocabulary used by francophones in the Ottawa region can be attributed to English.

9.5.4   Code-switching

One relatively common practice that is found in bilingual communities is **code-switching**. We can define this phenomenon as the use of elements from two (or more) linguistic systems during the same conversation. Consider the sentence in (10) in which a bilingual speaker of Acadian French starts in English and finishes in French.

(10) *I guess qu'on peut pas le faire* ("I guess we can't do it").

The example of code-switching in (10) demonstrates switching over to another language within the same sentence. Commonly, we see that code-switching is not an infiltration of one language in another, but rather a back-and-forth movement between two separate languages. There are different ways of categorizing code-switching, depending on where in the conversation the switch takes place. It can occur between speakers, or within the discourse of one speaker. Here too, we can identify different types of switches. For example, they can be between sentences or within a single sentence. Generally, switches between sentences are more common than switches within a sentence.

Code-switching Is a Rule-governed Skill

The average person is unlikely to be aware that bilinguals do not usually code-switch because of an inability or lack of words in one of their languages. In fact, code-switching is a skill that is found almost exclusively in bilinguals who are highly proficient in both languages. It is unfortunate that such behavior is often referred to negatively with labels like *franglais* or *Spanglish*. This gives the false impression that code-switching represents a bad version of either language. It is true that learners of a second language will revert back to their first language when they are unable to express something in the language they are learning. However, this should not be viewed as code-switching but rather as **code-abandonment**.

In reality, speakers who code-switch move seamlessly between the two languages and do so for a variety of reasons. It's not always possible to explain the reason for every switch, but they are often related to changes in topic and situation. This is in part related to the relative role of the two languages in society. If the topic or situation becomes more formal, a change to the socially powerful language may occur. If the topic or situation is related to friends and family, then some switching to the local language may take place. Still, in many cases, code-switching is simply the reflection of a bilingual's identity.

Sociolinguists point out that code-switching is a rule-governed activity. There are cases where switching is likely and possible, there are other cases where code-switching never happens. In other words, it is by no means an *anything goes* phenomenon. Let's consider some restrictions on code-switching. First, code-switching never takes place within a word. So, for example, an English/Spanish bilingual would never produce a sequence like *runeando* where the first part of the word is in English and the second part is in Spanish. Secondly, code-switching only occurs when the two languages follow the same grammatical structure. For example, French places object pronouns before the verb, while English places them after (e.g., *Je **le** veux* "I want **it**"). As such, you would not find a switch like **Je want it* or *I le veux*. In other words, code-switching reflects an adult bilingual's grammatical knowledge of both languages and seems to adhere to predictable rules.

Code-switching vs. Borrowing

As we said above, code-switching can occur within or between sentences. It is common for only one word to be switched. This poses somewhat of a problem since languages commonly borrow words from other languages. However, this is very different from code-switching. **Borrowing** is something a language does; code-switching is something a bilingual speaker does. Speakers who use a borrowed word like *cliché* don't necessarily speak the language of the borrowed word. On the other hand, speakers who code-switch *do* speak both languages and at such a level of proficiency that they can smoothly and effortlessly switch back and forth between language systems.

The main difference is that borrowings have been integrated into the new system. By **integrated**, we mean a foreign word adheres to the rules of the language that has borrowed it. For example, a French borrowing that is used in English uses English sounds, not French ones. Consider the English expression *déjà vu*. In French, the vowel in *vu* is very different from the one used by anglophones when using this expression.

PAUSE AND REFLECT 9.14

Consider the following excerpt from an old Andrews Sisters' song: "He's in the army now, blow'n *reveille*, he's the Boogy-Woogy bugle boy from Company B." When they used the French-origin word *reveille*, did they code-switch? How do you know?

It is interesting to note that borrowed words often change meaning when compared to the source language. This is true of the expression *déjà vu* since it has a very general meaning in French, while it refers to a very specific sensation in English.

In some cases, the borrowed word has a more general meaning. Consider the borrowing *Le fon* found in Canadian French. The English adjective *fun* refers to something that creates a sense of joy and amusement, often accompanied by smiles and laughter. In Canadian French however, it is more general and simply means "enjoyable" or "nice". For example, if you say *C'est un restaurant le fon*, it would mean "it's a nice/interesting, or enjoyable restaurant." Compare that to *It's a fun restaurant*. In English, you might expect balloons, games, or something that makes you smile or laugh. Table 9.4 summarizes some distinctions between code-switching and borrowing.

TABLE 9.4 Differences between Code-switching and Borrowing

Code-switching	Borrowing	Example of borrowing
Situation-dependent	Never situation-dependent	n/a
Change in phonology	Phonological integration	reveille, placard
Not morphologically integrated	Morphological integration	courts, chalets
Never change in meaning from source	Possible meaning change (generalization, restriction)	le fon, chum, foqué
Can indicate solidarity (metaphorical)	Never metaphorical	n/a
Non-recurrent	Recurrent, common dictionary	patio

9.5.5 Pidgins and Creoles

We saw that when languages come in contact with one another, it is common for speakers of the less powerful group to shift their speaking preference to the language of the dominant group. This is what happened in Ireland when the Gaelic speakers lost their language after subsequent generations. It is also what happened to millions of indigenous speakers in North America. For example, while there were some five million speakers of various indigenous languages in the 1500s, there are only around half a million today. Furthermore, most individuals of indigenous heritage are now monolingual speakers of English.

Still, language shift or maintenance is not the only possible outcome that we can examine in sociolinguistics. In some cases, the two groups develop a third language that is influenced largely by the vocabulary of the dominant group, by the grammar of the subordinate (indigenous) group, and by language acquisition principles universal to all languages. Languages that arise in this fashion are known as **pidgins**. When they first emerge, pidgins are relatively simple, unstable systems in terms of sounds, words, and grammar and they are used primarily for trade between speakers of two different languages. For example, two people come together to accomplish a task of some kind, yet neither speaks the other language. The result is often a compromise whereby they create a form of communication that they can understand between them in order to reach their common goals.

Often, a pidgin becomes widely spoken in a given society and may eventually be learned as a first language. Pidgins learned as a child's first language are known as **creoles**. Creoles are full-fledged linguistic systems that are much more stable than their pidgin form. In this sense, creoles are like any other human language. What sets them apart, however, is the role played by innate language learning principles. When children learn their first language, it is the result of the input to which they are exposed (i.e., the words and sentences they hear from their parents and others with whom they come into contact) among other things. When the input to which a child is exposed is an unstable, minimal system like a pidgin, the brain's language learning system fills in the gaps.

This is one of the reasons why creoles involving different language groups tend to share many grammatical features. For example, most creoles tend to mark negation by placing *no* before the verb. Another common feature is the absence of the linking verb *be*, for example, the Haitian Creole translation of "I am happy" would be *mwen kontan* (literally "me happy"). Still, creoles aren't the only language without linking *be* (it isn't found in Russian or Japanese either).

PAUSE AND REFLECT 9.15

An English-based creole will share some vocabulary with English though its grammatical system will be quite different. Do an Internet search of Hawaiian Creole and see if there are words you can understand.

9.5.6 Variation in Second Language Acquisition

The study of sociolinguistic variation is not limited to a person's first language. There exists one strand of sociolinguistics that focuses on variation in the speech of second language learners. Of course, one kind of variation we find is between native speaker usage and forms that are not used by native speakers (i.e., errors). For example, one might consider the social and linguistic factors that are relevant for people learning how to use plural–*s* with English nouns. By taking a variety of factors into account, the researcher can help dispel the notion that variation of this type is random.

A more recent sociolinguistic approach to second language variation examines the sociolinguistic competence of language learners. This approach seeks to determine the extent to which learners have mastered the natural variation between formal and informal ways of speaking, which is something all native speakers do. The reasoning behind this approach is that mastery of a language includes not only linguistic rules, but also the ability to use a range of variants.

For example, a learner of French should know that in written French, negative sentences are made by putting *ne* before the verb and *pas* after, as in *Je **ne** sais **pas*** "I do not know". However, advanced learners should also be aware that francophones rarely use the *ne* when speaking. Indeed, sociolinguistic studies in Europe and Canada have found that native speakers delete *ne* around 95 percent of the time when participating in a conversation (e.g., Ashby, 1981). However, this stylistic difference is not usually reflected in the speech of second language learners. Table 9.5 provides examples of differences in the way francophones and learners of French make use of informal features when speaking.

TABLE 9.5 Comparison of Informal Features between Francophones and French Immersion Students when Speaking

Linguistic variable	Francophones	French immersion students
on vs. *nous* ("we")	99 percent	56 percent
ne deletion	99.6 percent	28 percent
schwa deletion (e.g., *sam'di*)	73 percent	15 percent
/l/ deletion (e.g., *i'faut* "it's necessary")	96.4 percent	2 percent

Sociolinguistic studies (e.g., Mougeon, Nadasdi, & Rehner, 2010) have pointed out the narrow range of variants used by learners. But they have also drawn attention to the fact that, like in native speaker discourse, the variation in the speech of second language learners is conditioned by linguistic and social factors. For example, English first language speakers are more likely to delete *ne* than are speakers of Spanish (a language that uses a negative marker before verbs). Furthermore, deletion is more common with negation words like *jamais* ("never") and *rien* ("nothing") than with *pas*. We see then that there are many parallels between variation in both first language and second language speakers and ongoing research promises to uncover more.

SUMMARY

In this chapter, we have provided an overview of the key terms and topics considered in sociolinguistics. We noted that while there is no *single way* of approaching sociolinguistics, we see that all approaches share great interest in language variation. All areas of sociolinguists are interested in the fact that humans don't speak the same way all the time. We saw this in our discussion of linguistic variables (i.e., different ways of saying the same thing). The extent to which a person uses a given variant depends on different social categories such as gender, age, and socioeconomic status. It also depends on style/register (or levels of formality) and on elements present in the linguistic context (i.e., the linguistic forms that surround the variant when used in speech).

Sociolinguists are also keen to draw attention to imbalances and injustices in the use of language(s). These imbalances take place within a given language as we saw in our discussion of gender and also across languages like we saw in bilingual communities. Too often, the variants used by subordinate groups are negatively viewed, or at least seen as inferior to the dominant language. This, of course, is rooted in misinformed preconceptions and has nothing to do with linguistics. Finally, we saw that the study of variation is not limited to first language learners, but that the same approaches can be applied to situations of second language acquisition.

EXERCISES

9.1 State if the following are examples of linguistic variables and explain why.

- i)   spaghetti/linguini/fettuccini
- ii) USB key/thumb/drive
- iii) tap/faucet/hose

9.2 Are *no* and *nope* variants of the same variable? Are there contexts in which they are not inerchangeable?

9.3 What is the variable domain for the alternation between *soda* and *pop*? Provide examples where only one of the variants is possible.

9.4 How many variants are there for the pronunciation of the word *decal*? What are they?

9.5 What factors are relevant for the notion of speech style?

9.6 Many women still change their name at marriage. Do you think this practice has negative consequences for women in society? Do you think there are social differences between women who do and do not change their name?

9.7 What is the name given to a study that measures language change by comparing speakers of different generations?

9.8 Consider the pronunciations of the word *coyote* (with or without *ee* at the end). Ask people which one they use and determine if there is a pattern.

9.9 Make a list of words/expressions your grandparents use but that you would not use.

9.10 List three things the Quebec government did to improve the status of French in Quebec.

9.11 Consider the use of *maître d'* in the following sentence: *My uncle works as the **maître d'** of a French restaurant.* Is this an example of borrowing or code-switching? Explain your response.

9.12   Is the following a likely example of code-switching: *the house grande*?

9.13   What is the main difference between a pidgin and a creole?

9.14   Which form would be more common in the speech of a second language speaker who learned English exclusively in school: *I want to leave* or *I wanna leave*. Explain your response.

REFERENCES

Ashby, W. (1981). The loss of the negative particle *ne* in French: A syntactic change in progress. *Language, 57*, 674–687.

Bouchard, P., & Bourhis, R. (Eds.) (2002). Special volume of the *Revue d'aménagement linguistique: L'aménagement linguistique au Québec*: 25 ans d'application de la Charte de la langue française. Québec: Les Publications du Québec.

Chambers, J. (1998). *English: Canadian varieties*. In J. Edwards (Ed.), *Language in Canada* (pp. 252–272). Cambridge: Cambridge University Press.

Downes, W. (1998). *Language and society* (2nd Edition). Cambridge: Cambridge University Press.

Eckert, P., & McConnell-Ginet, S. (2013). *Language and gender*. Cambridge: Cambridge University Press.

Gray, J. (1992). *Men are from Mars, women are from Venus: A practical guide for improving communication and getting what you want in your relationships*. New York, NY: HarperCollins.

Labov, W. (1972). *Sociolinguistic patterns*. Philadelphia, PA: University of Pennsylvania Press.

Mougeon, R., Nadasdi, T., & Rehner, K. (2010). *The sociolinguistic competence of immersion students*. Bristol: Multilingual Matters.

Poplack, S. (1989). The care and handling of a mega-corpus. In R. Fasold & D. Schiffrin (Eds.), *Language change and variation* (pp. 411–451). Amsterdam: Benjamins.

Sammons, O., Nadasdi, T., & Mougeon, R. (2015). "Moving" through the past: Thirty years of avoir été in Ontario French. *Journal of French Language Studies, 25*(3), 397–422.

10 Pragmatics and Discourse Analysis

Maite Taboada

OVERVIEW

In this chapter, you will develop an understanding of the study of linguistic phenomena above the sentence level. Our objectives are to:

- **define and explain the difference between pragmatics and discourse analysis;**
- **explore how pragmatic aspects of language are captured by the Cooperative Principle;**
- **learn about why and how texts are coherent** and
- **understand different genres and styles of discourse.**

10.1 What Are Pragmatics and Discourse Analysis?

Textbooks, courses, and introductions to this area of linguistics often group together pragmatics and discourse analysis. While they share an interest in the study of language in context, there are some differences in how each subdiscipline approaches language, and what types of phenomena are considered.

Pragmatics is concerned with the study of meaning in context, as a companion subfield to semantics, which studies meaning in words and expressions, but without reflecting on how context contributes to meaning. Pragmatics is closely related to research in philosophy of language, with an interest in how language accomplishes actions. For instance, one of the most influential books in this field is titled *How to do things with words* (Austin, 1962).

Discourse analysis embraces all aspects of language use and the interaction of language and context. In this sense, it is more encompassing, capturing several theoretical approaches and methodological frameworks. This often includes an interest in the context and the social aspects that affect the production and interpretation of discourse. Because of this interest in context, large and small, it intersects with some of the research in corpus linguistics. Because of the interest in social aspects of language, it also overlaps with sociolinguistics.

Both pragmatics and discourse analysis study language above the sentence level. In other words, analysis that goes beyond the structural analysis of words and phrases. When we talk about being *above the sentence level*, we refer to things like:

- how sentences are put together to form **coherent texts**;
- how conversation participants manage to take **turns** without much overlap and without uncomfortable pauses;
- how the same sentence or piece of discourse can be **interpreted** differently in different contexts; and
- what **linguistic characteristics** distinguish different types of texts.

The study of language in context overlaps with other areas in the social sciences, such as sociology or psychology. Because of this, the research methodologies used in pragmatics and discourse analysis are diverse. Listed below is a range of the methodologies employed (Jucker, 2009):

- Some researchers use **introspection**, that is, reflection on how language is used based on personal experience. They are sometimes referred to as *armchair linguists*.
- Some researchers employ methods from **corpus linguistics**, searching through large amounts of data, sometimes online, or sometimes collected and selected according to specific criteria (a set of television scripts, or all the editorials published by a newspaper in a given year).
- Other researchers use elicitation methods commonly found in sociology and psychology, where researchers ask participants to produce language in certain circumstances, or simply to engage in conversation. In pragmatics and discourse analysis, and in many areas of research, this type of research is called **field research**.

Finally, you will notice that pragmatics and discourse analysis are related to meaning, the topic of focus in Chapter 6 Semantics. In fact, there are a few places later in this chapter, such as our discussion on the Cooperative Principle, in which we will remind you of this. We hope that it will serve to reinforce your understanding of these concepts.

We will use the word **text** to refer to both spoken and written language. Pragmatics and discourse analysis deal with all types of language in context, and we tend to use the word *text* to refer to all of them: a prepared speech, a tweet, a university lecture, a book, or a text message.

PAUSE AND REFLECT 10.1

You want to find out the structure of exchanges between a professor and a student in language x. Which methodology do you think would be most helpful? Do you think you would need ethical approval?

10.2 Pragmatics

10.2.1 Speech Acts

Speech acts are utterances that accomplish something in the world. Speech Act Theory captures the basic principle that we use language to do things. Sometimes the *thing* done is directly a result of the words said. For example, see (1),[1] a statement from the Canadian Government using the words *we apologize*. By saying those words, the act of apologizing was performed. This is a **performative speech act** (more specifically, an **apology**).

(1) […] the Government of Canada now recognizes that it was wrong to forcibly remove children from their homes and we apologize for having done this.

EYES ON WORLD LANGUAGES: SPEECH ACTS ACROSS LANGUAGES

A frequent concern in the study of speech acts is how to organize them into classes, and how many there are. This becomes an even more important issue when translating speech acts and their intention across languages. The linguist Anna Wierzbicka (Wierzbicka, 1987) proposed a dictionary of English speech act verbs that contains about 250 entries. Each verb is described in plain and simple language, so that its meaning is clear, and translation into other languages is possible. For instance, this is the definition of the verb *suggest* (p. 187):

I say: I think it would be a good thing if you did X
I say this because I want to cause you to think about it
I don't know if you will do it
I don't want to say that I want you to do it

Other work in speech acts has examined how people express the same speech act in different languages. Blum-Kulka et al. (1989) investigated how to express requests and apologies in English, French, Danish, German, and Hebrew. The researchers provided speakers of those languages with a situation and asked participants to fill in the blanks. In the example below, the answer tells us how to express an apology.

A: I hope you brought the book I lent you.
B: _____.
A: Okay, but please remember it next week.

Most speech acts are not as dramatic as performatives. They simply try to achieve a goal, but they may or may not succeed. The tweet in (2)[2] is a **request** speech act. It asks the reader to do something, to vote in an online poll to suggest a musical guest for the show *Saturday Night Live*. The reader may not vote at all or they may vote for somebody else. The request is not a performative speech act; it simply conveys the writer's intention.

(2) PLEASE GO AND VOTE FOR LANA DEL REY ON THIS POLL.

Other examples of speech acts include greet, answer, inform, claim, agree, suggest, warn, threaten, congratulate, or thank.

---

[1] https://www.rcaanc-cirnac.gc.ca/eng/1100100015657/1571589032314.
[2] https://twitter.com/iMxggy/status/843515331805102082. Reproduced as posted.

Speech acts may be clearly stated and recognizable in the way that the speaker formulates them, or they may be **indirect**, left to the hearer or reader to infer.

PAUSE AND REFLECT 10.2

The following is an exchange copied from a cartoon, a conversation between a mother and a daughter. Think about how this is a good example of indirect speech acts. The mother asks what seems like a genuine question, but the question is really meant to prompt the daughter to pick up her jacket, so it is a command, not a question. The mother elaborates on this in her second turn: "When I say X, I really mean Y."

MOTHER: Whose jacket is this?

DAUGHTER: Your mind must be starting to go, Mum. Don't you remember you bought it for me a month ago?

MOTHER: When I say "Whose jacket is this?" I really mean "Come here and hang it up."

DAUGHTER: How about when you say "Answer the door"? Do you really mean "Pass the potatoes"?

MOTHER: What do you suppose I mean when I say, "Watch your step, kiddo"?

Sometimes, the intention behind a speech act is moderated, or cancelled, with an expression, as is the case with the expression *just sayin'* in (3).[3]

(3)   You look awful in that. Just sayin'.

PAUSE AND REFLECT 10.3

Given what you have read so far about speech acts, ask someone from another culture how they would apologize if they are trying to get through a crowded bus. Is that different from what you would say or do?

LINGUISTICS TIDBITS: SPEECH ACTS IN DIALOGUE SYSTEMS

Humans can sometimes have trouble understanding the intention behind a speech act. It is much more difficult for **dialogue systems** or **voice-activated** systems, automated software like Siri, Cortana, Google Home, or Alexa, which tries to understand what we say and respond adequately. Much of the research in these systems is devoted to figuring out how humans are likely to state requests or questions, and what the most appropriate answer is. Machines also need information about the most likely way a conversation can develop, and what the correct politeness levels are, such as how to address a human. Linguists are often employed by tech companies to help solve these issues.

10.2.2   Conversation Analysis

Conversation Analysis is an area of pragmatics that deals with how we take turns in conversation and how this dialogue is structured. The object of analysis in this case is always spontaneous conversation, because the goal is to discover how it is naturally structured.

Studies of spontaneous conversation have yielded a rich set of insights about how we open and close conversations, how we take turns so naturally, yet so systematically, and how we interrupt, correct, and in general organize conversations. The analysis explains why there is a minimal amount of overlap in most casual conversations while at the same time silence between turns is rare. Speakers perform a complicated set of calculations for deciding whether they can take the turn and at which point.

---

[3]   http://languagelog.ldc.upenn.edu/nll/?p=3692 .

Perhaps the most important discovery of conversation analysis is the set of rules for turn-taking. Sacks et al. (1974) propose that conversations are made up of **turn-constructional units**, that is, units of conversation that make up turns. The potential end of each of those is called a **transition-relevant place**. At each of those potential ends, speakers follow a deceptively simple set of rules for deciding whether to take the turn:

1. At a transition-relevant place:
    a. Current speaker selects next.
    b. Current speaker self-selects.
    c. Current speaker may continue talking; another speaker may self-select.

2. Rule 1 applies at each next transition-relevant place.

The rules simply state that somebody who is talking may give the turn to somebody else, may continue talking, or may continue talking but be interrupted. If you think of recent conversations that you have had, you will see that one or all of those cases occurred. The self-selection may be more or less aggressive (raising your hand in class; opening your mouth to signal you want to speak; or speaking more loudly than the other person if they are still talking). All of these are just variants of self-selection strategies, depending on the situation, the level of formality, or the familiarity among the participants (see the discussion of register in 10.3.1 for a more detailed account of how the context of situation affects language).

EYES ON WORLD LANGUAGES: TURN-TAKING ACROSS LANGUAGES

If you speak another language, or if you have witnessed conversations in other languages, you may have compared the speed of the conversation and the amount of silence between turns. Cultural stereotypes often characterize conversations in certain languages as faster or slower and more or less polite (which usually means with less or more overlap). Researchers studying conversations in multiple languages have found a surprising amount of uniformity. The 200 milliseconds pause is universally valid: most silences in conversation are about that length. Any longer, and the pause is noticeable to the participants. Using a sample of ten languages from around the world, a group of researchers (Stivers et al., 2009) found that, indeed, there is minimal overlap and minimal gap between turns across a very varied set of languages. They did find some cultural differences (also noted by Tannen, 2012 and others), but the variation is often no more than a quarter of a second from the overall mean. It looks like our structure for conversation is universal across languages and cultures.

How we decide that there is a potential transition-relevance place is the result of a complex set of signals embedded in the language and the context. The language provides syntactic and prosodic information about what is likely to be the end of the clause and intonation unit. Gesture and eye contact have a very important place in signaling that the current speaker wants to pass the turn or keep it. Think of very regulated turn-taking situations, like debates with a moderator and strict time limits. The participants are aware of when their turn starts and ends. In casual conversation, the debate is completely unmoderated, but speakers still take turns in an orderly fashion in the vast majority of conversations.

The most remarkable aspect of conversation is that silence between turns is very rare and very short (about 200 milliseconds) and that overlap is also rare. You may be surprised to read that overlap is rare if you are used to rapid-fire conversations among friends. Your impression may be that you have quite a bit of overlap, but we know from large studies of conversation that it is a small fraction of the conversation. In fact, you may remember more overlap than there is because it is so salient when it actually happens. Consider the following example, from Levinson (1983, p. 320). When C asks a question and the answer is a perceivably long silence (2 seconds), C assumes that the answer is no.

(4) C: So I was wondering would you be in your office on Monday (.) by any chance?
     (2.0 seconds)
     C: Probably not.

LINGUISTICS TIDBITS: SILENCE BETWEEN TURNS

Participants in a conversation do not wait to hear the end of the current turn to start to speak. As we have seen from research in conversation analysis, the amount of silence between turns is on average 200 milliseconds. We also know, from the literature on language processing, that it takes about 600 milliseconds from the time we formulate a sentence to the time it is uttered (see Chapter 14 Psycholinguistics). That is simply the reaction time that our brain needs. It is clear, then, that we start to plan our utterance before the other person has finished speaking (Levinson & Torreira, 2015). This is an amazing feat of planning and multi-tasking. As Stephen Levinson puts it: "When you take into account the complexity of what's going into these short turns, you start to realize that this is an elite behavior. [...] Dolphins can swim amazingly fast, and eagles can fly as high as a jet, but this is our trick" (Yong, 2016).

10.2.3 Presuppositions and Implicatures

In Chapter 6 Semantics, you read about presupposition and implicatures. Recall that a **presupposition** is what the speaker assumes to be true. It is taken for granted for a speech act to make sense. For example, if I say *Why did you cheat on the exam?*, there is a presupposition that you, in fact, cheated.

In some cases, we mean more than we say, which leads to **implicatures**. In both semantics and pragmatics, an implicature is intended by the speaker to be made by the hearer. The sentence *Some students did very well in the exam* implies that not all of them did.

PAUSE AND REFLECT 10.4

Which of the following contains a presupposition? Which one contains an implicature?

(i) The age of prosperity and peace has ended.

(ii) [In a letter of recommendation] This student attended all the classes, and all her assignments had her name and student ID on them.

10.2.4   The Cooperative Principle

Another overlapping concept you should remember from Chapter 6 Semantics is our discussion on the Cooperative Principle. Let's briefly review what it means for pragmatics. The philosopher H. P. Grice stated that, beneath all our communication underlies a principle that we are cooperative with each other. This does not mean that we always are; simply that we assume that as a principle for communication it makes sense. He named this the **Cooperative Principle** and broke it down into four maxims: Quantity, Quality, Relevance, and Manner.

- Quantity: Make your contribution as informative as required, and not more.
- Quality: Try to make your contribution one that is true. (Do not lie, do not say something you are not sure about.)
- Relevance: Make your contribution relevant.
- Manner: Avoid obscurity. Avoid ambiguity. Be brief. Be orderly.

In real life, speakers assume the maxims are always at work, but that violations are common. In (5), Speaker B is violating the Quantity maxim. They are not being fully informative, because they are not answering the question about the dog's location. They are, on the other hand, being truthful (Quality).

(5)   A: Where's the dog?
B: Not here.

10.2.5   Politeness and Impoliteness

Politeness Theory and Impoliteness Theory address how we manage our social identities and those of others through language. Politeness Theory (Brown & Levinson, 1987 [1978]) proposed that our interactions are driven by two basic needs: the need to do as we please, and the need to be appreciated by others. These are referred to as **negative face** and **positive face**. For example, our desire to maintain negative face leads us to take things without asking (think of how children do this). Our desire to be appreciated, however, that is, our positive face, results in a polite request (with the level of politeness determined by the situation, the relative power difference between the participants, and other circumstances).

As examples, consider the following requests by a student, asking their professor to reconsider a course grade. In all cases, the request may cause a problem for the professor's negative face. The professor would like to give a certain grade, and be free to do so. It is also a problem for the student's negative face, as the student would presumably like to have the higher grade without having to ask for it. They all represent different strategies for how to deal with this situation. In the first case, example (6), the student simply asks, stating the reasons. This has the advantage that it is direct. The following two examples work with positive face. In (7), the student addresses the professor's positive face. The student knows that positive face is important in social negotiations and mentions the professor's fairness. In example (8), however, it is the student's positive face that is brought up, by pointing out that they are a good and diligent student. These examples all illustrate how we manage our social identities and how we make use of language to mitigate potentially difficult speech acts.

(6) I need a higher grade in this course to get into my program.

(7) I know that you are fair and don't make exceptions, but I was wondering if you would consider revising my grade.

(8) As you know, I have participated actively in the course. I was wondering if you could revise my grade for the course.

Politeness Theory is grounded in the Cooperative Principle, and assumes speakers are generally cooperative. Impoliteness Theory, on the other hand, studies situations where lack of politeness is the dominant principle. It deals with language use that can be interpreted as intentionally confrontational, rude, or aggressive (Culpeper, 2011). The speaker is well aware that their words will be an attack on the hearer's positive or negative face; they say them anyway.

Impoliteness can take many forms, from insults and criticism to challenges, condescension, or threats. For instance, (9) is a challenging question that has no easy answer and is best interpreted as a complaint; (10) is condescending. Examples are from Culpeper (2009).

(9) Why do you make my life impossible?

(10) You're being childish.

PAUSE AND REFLECT 10.5

Imagine that you are waiting at a store for the cashier to serve you, but the individual is on the phone. State a polite and an impolite way to complain.

In summary, speech acts form the core of the study of pragmatics, with different emphases: indirect use, how they work under the Cooperative Principle, and how they are interpreted as part of politeness and impoliteness strategies. Conversation Analysis is the part of pragmatics that studies conversational behavior: how turns are structured and how speakers take turns.

10.3 Discourse Analysis

10.3.1 Genre and Register

If you are presented with a small piece of text (spoken or written), you can usually guess what the text is about, where it may have been said, printed, or typed, and who the likely participants are. This is knowledge of genres, of the function and structure of types of text that we are exposed to and participate in. It is also knowledge of registers, that is, of the likely choices of words and expressions most appropriate in each context. We use this knowledge in everyday life, involving knowledge of the interaction of culture, context, and language. The study of that interaction is one of the most fundamental aspects of discourse analysis.

Genres or text types are configurations of texts that have specific function in their context. For instance, the function or goal of a university lecture is to inform about content related to the course (perhaps including administrative details such as assignments). The function of a job interview is to evaluate a candidate. Because of their function, they develop in specific ways, with a recognizable structure. Genres also have clearly differentiating linguistic characteristics. For example, think of a news report. Its typical structure consists of an opening paragraph and a description of newsworthy events, maybe with quotes from relevant sources. Linguistically, it tends to contain short, telegraphic information in the headline. It also contains text written in full sentences in the story itself, with verbs of action to retell the event (who and what) and verbs of saying to report on what sources describe. There are often many adjuncts, in the form of prepositional phrases, adverbs, or clauses to explain the circumstances of the event (where, how, why).

PAUSE AND REFLECT 10.6

What do you think are some of the characteristics of the genre *text messaging with a good friend*?

There are many classifications of genres. One basic distinction is between descriptive, narrative, expository, and argumentative. More fine-grained classifications contain labels such as stories, history reports, explanations, and procedures (Martin & Rose, 2008). A great deal of research has been devoted to academic text types, and in particular research articles (Swales, 1990).

The Reading to Learn initiative in Australia[4] has articulated a classification of the types of genres school students are exposed to and supposed to master as they go through their school years. The articulation makes it clear what each of the genres is, in terms of purpose and stages, so that students who may be less familiar with certain genres can understand and use them in the right context. The initiative has a clear goal of social integration, spelling out the function and structure of texts to which some children may not have been exposed.

Figure 10.1 presents a classification of different genres based on their main function (telling stories, informing, describing procedures, or evaluating). The text in bold is the label typically given to a genre in the school curriculum.

---

[4] http://www.readingtolearn.com.au/.

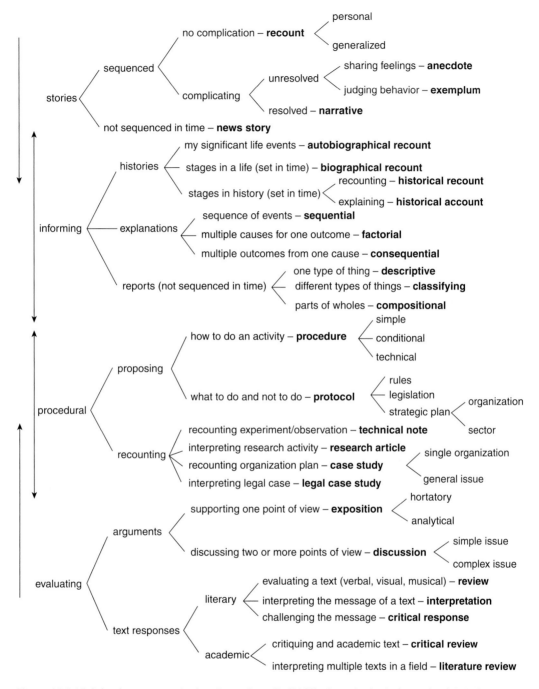

Figure 10.1 High-level genre organization. From: Rose, D. (2012). Genre in the Sydney school. In J. Gee & M. Handford (Eds.), *The Routledge handbook of discourse analysis* (pp. 209–225). London, UK: Routledge. Reproduced by permission of Taylor & Francis Group.

Genres are classified based on function and stages. For instance, the function of narrative is often to entertain, whereas news stories inform. Narratives are time-structured (they are told following the sequence of events) and usually have the following stages: Orientation – Complication – Resolution. News stories do not need to be told in linear time (the story may open with a traffic accident, not with the causes of the accident) and are composed of Lead – Key Events / (Quotes). The order of Main Events and Quotes is variable, and Quotes may not always be present.

EYES ON WORLD LANGUAGES: NEW LANGUAGE, NEW GENRES

Learning a new language involves, in part, also learning a new set of genres and how they are likely to develop in that language. This is why it is difficult to be completely fluent in a new culture, even if we are quite fluent in the language itself. Every genre in the new language will have slightly different goals and stages. For instance, Zhu (2005) studied three different business genres in English and Chinese and found that there are subtle differences. Chinese sales letters have, in addition to the usual goals of offering a product, also a goal of establishing a long-term relationship between the company and the (potential) client, which does not seem to be present in the English letters that Zhu analyzed. As a consequence, the Chinese letters tend to contain greeting and introductory stages which help establish rapport between the company and the client.

LINGUISTICS TIDBITS: NEW SITUATION, NEW GENRES

Just like learning a new language involves learning a new set of genres, a new context means a new set of genres. This is particularly prominent in the academic context. We have seen the large range of genres present in the elementary and secondary school curriculum (Figure 10.1). In the post-secondary context, those genres are taken for granted and expanded on. If students have not received sufficient explicit instruction in their secondary education, they may not be able to understand and produce academic genres. Explicit instruction is necessary to be fully fluent in academic language. One common saying among writing and academic writing specialists is *Nobody is born speaking academic English*.

Instructors in post-secondary institutions are noticing a shift in the genres that students are familiar with. We know that students are very comfortable with many forms of online language and social media conventions (see Linguistics Tidbits: Online Genres). We are also increasingly noticing that students struggle with email, a form of communication that instructors take for granted and one in which we are very fluent. Email etiquette guidelines are often shared at the beginning of the academic year, to ensure students are familiar with the structure and conventions of this genre. The advice from an *Inside Higher Ed* article[5] includes the following:

- Use a subject line;
- Use a salutation and signature;
- Use standard punctuation, capitalization, spelling, and grammar.

---

[5] http://www.insidehighered.com/views/2015/04/16/advice-students-so-they-dont-sound-silly-emails-essay .

These instructions point to instructors thinking of email as a form of letter writing. Letters have salutations and signatures and use formal writing style. Email in the post-secondary context is, indeed, a type of formal letter writing, involving social distance between the student and the instructor. Some students probably think of it as a form of electronic communication, which tends to occur between people with low social distance and is mostly informal. If students are not usually exposed to email as a formal text type, then they have to learn to use it in the way that instructors expect. These instructions also assume that politeness is at work and that conversational maxims are functioning. Instructors expect students to protect the instructor's negative face. The instructor does not want to receive email that they do not understand well, for instance without a subject line. The instructor is also helping the student increase their positive face. By showing that they follow the conventions of the genre, the student shows that they are a good student and understand academic communication.

PAUSE AND REFLECT 10.7

You have to send an email to a student but you don't know the individual's gender because the name is unfamiliar to you. How do you solve this issue?

LINGUISTICS TIDBITS: ONLINE GENRES

Online communication has given us a wealth of new genres. Starting with bulletin boards and chat rooms, and continuing with blogs, Facebook posts, tweets, or comments on news articles, our linguistic repertoire has clearly increased. Linguists are actively studying the characteristics of these new genres, often combining purely linguistic analyses with studies of their visual nature, because online communication is **multimodal**, that is, it uses different modes of communication in addition to just printed words, such as emoticons, emoji, images, video, or interesting layout. Memes are a great example of multimodal communication.

The concept of genre is closely connected to another aspect of language use in context, **register**, which you read about in Chapter 9 Sociolinguistics. Whereas genre is concerned with the functions of texts in the culture and how they are structured, register ties more directly to the relationship between context of situation and language. The register of a text refers to what we are talking about (the **field**), the relationship between the participants (the **tenor**), and the channel of communication (the **mode**).

We say that register ties more directly to language because those aspects influence choices of language. The field will affect the lexical items most likely to appear in a text. For instance, a biology textbook may include words such as *adaptation*, *molecule*, or *zygote*. A conversation between two students getting ready for soccer practice may contain *game*, *cleats*, or *coach*. The tenor has an influence on choices of forms of address. A person may be addressed by his/her first name at home and with a formal title (e.g., Dr.) in an email from a student. Some languages have different forms of the second person pronoun (*you*), depending on the relationship between the participants of the conversation, such as *tu* or *vous* in French. The mode of communication influences language choices depending on the way we are communicating. A textbook implies a great spatial and temporal distance between the participants, since it is read at a different location and in a different time than it was written. That distance means that pronouns need to be used judiciously, so that their referent is clear and that the connections between ideas are explicit, so that they can be recognized by the reader.

PAUSE AND REFLECT 10.8

What words would you expect to find in an advertisement for perfume? For a laundry detergent?

In summary, register captures how language reflects the specific situation in which the text is produced. Genre describes how texts are structured according to the functions that they have in a particular culture, or in cultures in general.

The relationship between genre and register can be viewed as one of influence (see Figure 10.2). The genre of a text reflects its goal and organizational structure. The genre has an influence on the register, but it is the register that more closely relates to linguistic choices. Those choices have to do with the register's field, tenor, and mode.

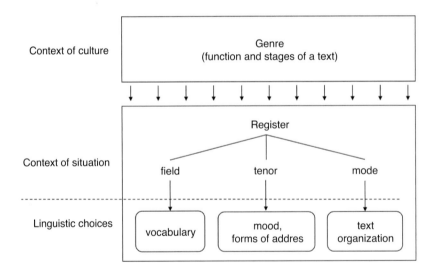

Figure 10.2 Relationship of genre and register and influence on linguistic choices

10.3.2 Coherence and Cohesion

We began the chapter by stating that text refers to both spoken and written language. One of the main concerns of discourse analysis is to define the concept of text. In other words, we are interested in why we refer to something as a good text, or a well-written text, as opposed to an instance of language that is not as clear or does not work as well in the context.

You may be surprised to find out that the word *text* shares a common origin with the words *texture* and *textile*. If you think of the fabric that makes up whatever clothing you are wearing or own, you'll see that it has texture. It is an instance of a textile. Now think about, or find online a picture of a loom, the traditional instrument for producing textiles. A loom works by weaving together strands of material (cotton, linen, wool, silk, or synthetic threads) in two directions. The loom holds together vertical threads, through which horizontal threads are weaved.

Now let us carry that image to the metaphor of a text. You can think of a text as weaving together different strands. On the one hand, you have the **entities** (the people and things) involved in the text. On the other hand, you have the ways in which those people and things are linked together in the text, through **propositions**. Propositions are the ideas conveyed in the text, usually contained in a clause or simple sentence. The two strands, entities and propositions, give the text some **texture**, that is, they make it a well-formed text, **coherent text** (Halliday & Hasan, 1976).

Let us examine the following two mini-texts. Neither seems to be well-formed, that is, coherent. In (11), there are many entities repeated across the sentences: *night* in the first sentence is picked up in the second one. Anyone who has read the Harry Potter books will link *owl* in the second sentence to both *Harry Potter* and *owl* in the third sentence. And so on. The text, however, is not coherent because the propositions do not make sense together. The ideas in the sentences do not flow well from one to another, although there are entities linked together in the text. It has one aspect of coherence (entities), but not the other (propositions).

(11) I went home very late last night. At night, owls come out and hunt. Harry Potter uses an owl to have his mail delivered. The mail was very erratic over the Christmas holidays. The holidays were too short, and short indeed is this paragraph.

In the second mini-text shown in (12), we have another linking of entities, because our human experience tells us that *dark clouds* and *rain* are related to each other. Usually, one leads to the other. The problem in this case is that the link is made with the conjunction or **discourse marker** *however*. The two propositions are linked, but with the wrong kind of link. The conjunction *however* is usually used to link two things that are somehow contradictory, that is, you don't expect the second thing from the first one. The example would have worked if it were formulated as *There were dark clouds in the sky today. However, it didn't rain*. In this case, both entities and propositions are connected well; it is the item used to link them that does not work in this context.

(12) There were dark clouds in the sky today. However, it rained.

These two aspects of discourse are what make it coherent. The linking of entities is often referred to as **cohesion** and we tend to reserve the term **coherence** in a narrower sense to the linking of propositions. Let's look more closely at what we mean by coherence and cohesion.

10.3.3   Coherence and Cohesion in Different Genres

You intuitively know that some forms of language are more acceptable in some contexts than others. The lack of space and short attention spans in online contexts naturally invite abbreviations, and you may write *RT* on Twitter, *TBT* on Facebook or Instagram, and *BTW* in a text message. But you also know that those, as most abbreviations, are not as appropriate in a homework assignment or a *résumé*.

Similarly, the coherence and cohesion of your text depend on the genre. Recall that, in this chapter, *text* means any discourse in context, whether written or spoken. You will choose different words to refer to the same entity, depending on the situation. You will also use more or less explicit links between propositions, depending on the genre and the context. When you talk to a friend, you may not need to clearly indicate how your thoughts are connected to each other. A journalist for written media, on the other hand, may feel that they have to use discourse markers to clearly point to the connections in their articles.

Compare (13) and (14). The first one is from a *Globe and Mail* article about the Canadian federal budget.[6] It contains references to entities using words from the formal end of the spectrum (*prevalence, résumé, unfounded*). It also links two of the main ideas with the conjunction *however*. Example (14) is a tweet by Kate McInturff on the same budget. The vocabulary itself is not very different. The phrase *sexual assault* is used in both. The connection between propositions is similar: although the Government is doing something, it is not doing enough (no new funds), or not the right things (innovation, but not on sexual assault). The connection in the tweet is implicit, left to the reader to interpret. The difference in length, range of vocabulary, and types of connections can be attributed to the difference in text types.

(13)   The budget noted that "improved data is necessary to better understand the prevalence and impact of sexual assault in Canada." However, it did not commit new funds for Statistics Canada to resume collecting national numbers on unfounded cases through the Uniform Crime Reporting Survey – a recommendation made earlier this week in a parliamentary report on violence against young women and girls.

(14)   Innovation budget? Innovate this: women now more likely to be victims of violent crime than men. Sexual assault rates unchanged. **#Budget2017**

10.3.4   Stylistics and Corpus Analysis in Discourse

The analysis of discourse often involves analyzing differences across text types, as discussed in the previous sections. It can also be enlightening about differences across individual writers. A related field of study, stylistics, is devoted to describing how different people write, and how writing, even by the same individual, changes from text type to text type. Although stylistics often refers to the study of literary text (McIntyre & Busse,

---

[6] http://www.theglobeandmail.com/news/politics/federal-budget-2017-unfounded-violence-gender/article34388068/.

2010), its methods can be applied to any type of text. The methodology consists of gathering sample texts and analyzing the linguistic characteristics that make the writing or the author distinctive. Biber & Conrad (2009) describe stylistic analysis as the study of linguistic features that are chosen because of aesthetic or personal preferences; think of how some people prefer to say *I helped him move* over *I helped him **to** move*. The choice is often individual, although, over time, it may spread, with one option becoming more popular, and lead to language change.

PAUSE AND REFLECT 10.9

Some people believe you can tell the difference between an essay written by a woman and one written by a man. Do you agree? Why or why not?

   In order to study such choices and changes over time and across individuals, discourse analysts often make use of **corpus analysis**, a methodology which includes a large and representative amount of language data (a **corpus**). Studies of discourse from a corpus point of view include analyses of academic writing, news text, or conversation, and often focus on stylistic variation (Semino & Short, 2004).

SUMMARY

Pragmatics and discourse analysis deal with language in context, with how speakers communicate through speech acts and rely on the Cooperative Principle, and how texts (spoken or written) are coherent, in other words, they have texture. The texture that we perceive all texts to have is the result of a combination of factors, from the lexical items used to refer to entities to the connections between propositions.

   Discourse analysis studies language in context. By context, we mean the context of culture in which it takes place, and the specific context of situation. The context of culture influences the types of genres a culture develops and how they are structured. The context of situation influences the specific register configuration, which is a combination of field, tenor, and mode, that is, the specific content, the relationships among participants, and the mode of communication.

   Pragmatics and discourse analysis are wide-ranging areas of research, given the many contexts and many types of interactions in which we use language to communicate.

EXERCISES

10.1 In each of the following, decide whether the inference in parenthesis is a presupposition or an implicature (Peccei, 1999, p. 30).

   i.   A: I am going to Paris next week.
         B: That's great! My boyfriend lives in Paris. (I have a boyfriend).

ii.   A: (Laughs)
      B: Why are you laughing at me? (You are laughing at me).
iii. A: Why is she eating those?
      B: Her father didn't give her lunch. (She didn't have lunch).
iv.   A: Is Mike engaged?
      B: He bought a ring. (Mike is engaged).
v.   A: You look pleased.
      B: I managed to pass the exam. (I tried to pass the exam).
vi.   A: Did you finish that report?
      B: I started it. (I didn't finish the report).

10.2   Misleading advertising unfortunately happens often. Below are some completely unsubstantiated claims about various products (Peccei, 1999, p. 23). For each one, write a 1-2-sentence advertisement that slips in the claim via a presupposition.

i.   Zonko cures insomnia.
ii.   HappyHavens Inn has beautiful views.
iii. Kissgood eliminates bad breath.
iv.   No-Ant kills ants.
v.   Crook & Sons Inc. employ skilled workers.
vi.   Dogs love Yappy dog food.
vii. Dentists use Grin toothpaste.

10.3   Examine the following conversation that a user is having with Amazon's Alexa, an intelligent personal assistant. Label each turn with a speech act. Potential speech acts are: request (an action, a clarification, a confirmation), ask, answer, acknowledge, inform, apologize, correct.

USER: Alexa, call Domino's.
ALEXA: What would you like to order?
USER: Large ham and pineapple.
ALEXA: You would like a large pizza with thyme and pineapple. Is that correct?
USER: No.
ALEXA: Sorry, what was it again?
USER: Large HAM and pineapple.
ALEXA: You would like a large pizza with ham and pineapple. Is that correct?
USER: Yes.
ALEXA: I've added it to your order. Anything else?
USER: No.
ALEXA: I have one large pizza with ham and pineapple for a total of one item. Is that correct?
USER: Yes.
ALEXA: Your order is complete. It will cost $18.97.

10.4   Direct and indirect speech acts. Consider the following speech acts and decide whether they are instances of direct or indirect speech acts. Label the speech act. The first is provided as an illustration.

i.   I'm moving this weekend and I don't know if I can do it all by myself.
      Possible answer: Indirect request. The speaker is asking for help moving, but is not using a direct request.
ii.   (Instructor to students) You may want to format your paper in double space so that I can write comments.
iii   (German President Frank-Walter Steinmeier in an act commemorating the eightieth anniversary of the start of World War II in Poland[7]) "I bow before the Polish victims of German tyranny. And I ask for your forgiveness."
iv.   (Car driver to cyclist after car forces cyclist off the road) I'm sorry!

[7] From: https://www.politico.eu/article/german-president-asks-for-polish-forgiveness-at-world-war-ii-commemoration/ .

10.5   Pragmatics in translation. Compare a text and its translation. Are there aspects of pragmatics that make the translation difficult? Think of potential implicatures, of how speech acts are conveyed, and how politeness levels may have to be different.

10.6   Flouting of Cooperative Principle maxims in comedy is common. There are many examples of this, but consider the following exchange in the film *Pink panther strikes again* (1976).[8] One of Grice's Maxims has been violated here. Which one? Discuss.

(A man arrives in a hotel and requests a room. While the manager is preparing some paperwork, the man notices a dog.)

HOTEL GUEST: Does your dog bite?
HOTEL MANAGER: (shakes head) No.

(Hotel guest leans over to pet dog. Dog bites his hand.)

HOTEL GUEST: (looks at manager, angrily) I thought you said your dog did not bite!
HOTEL MANAGER: That is not my dog.

10.7   If you speak more than one language or have tried to learn a second language, compare genres and registers that you know in both languages. Are there any differences in how they are structured and what types of linguistic features are likely to appear in each?

10.8   Think of your favorite social media platform or if you don't have a favorite, one that you are familiar with. Describe a sample text/post in terms of genre and register:

i   What is the purpose of the post?
ii   Does it have stages? Since most social media posts are short, sometimes they don't have clearly delineated stages. Sometimes you can find different parts.
iii What are the field, tenor, and mode for the text?
iv   What are the most significant linguistic characteristics?
v   Is there multimodal content? How is it related to the text?

10.9   Use the questions from the previous exercise to analyze the following tweet from the Canadian Prime Minister's Office.[9]

CanadianPM ✓
@CanadianPM

It's back-to-school season! Learn how the #CanadaChildBenefit can provide you with more money to help pay for things like school supplies: ow.ly /Sw1D50vLsnm

BEST OF LUCK IN THE NEW SCHOOL YEAR!

0:03   3.6K views

11:03 AM · Aug 27, 2019 · Twitter Media Studio

29 Retweets   **112** Likes

---

[8]   Information on the film: https://en.wikipedia.org/wiki/The_Pink_Panther_Strikes_Again. Clip: https://www.youtube.com/watch?v=ui442IDw16o.
[9]   https://twitter.com/CanadianPM/status/1166411029733105665?s=20.

10.10 The text below is an online review of the film *Logan*.[10] In the text, underline every instance of an entity and observe what type of word is used (noun, pronoun, other forms). Think of the connections between propositions, and whether they are clearly indicated by a conjunction or discourse marker.

> James Mangold crafts an action adventure, not a superhero movie, with Logan. This is a good thing. The story drives its way to easily over 2 hours and it does feel that long. The pacing is slow, and while it works in this film's favor leaving the characters to excel with drama, it slows a bit much at times. Yes, Logan is story driven, but it also needs its share of action. The violence is brutal and backed up with a lot of F-bombs in the dialogue. Definitely an R-rated picture in its own right. Hugh Jackman and Patrick Stewart are all over this picture. They shoulder the load leaving everyone else in the dust. Dafne Keen does have her moments despite minimal dialogue. Logan hits the spot as a violent action adventure. Beware the adamantium.

10.11 Take a piece of writing that you have done recently. This could be a paper or assignment, an email message, or an online post. Make sure it is at least 150 words in length. Then do the same analysis as for the previous exercise. Considering what you know now about connections between entities and propositions in discourse, would you write it differently?

REFERENCES

Austin, J. (1962). *How to do things with words*. Harvard, MA: Harvard University Press.

Biber, D., & Conrad, S. (2009). *Register, genre, and style*. Cambridge: Cambridge University Press.

Blum-Kulka, S., House, J., & Kasper, G. (Eds.) (1989). *Cross-cultural pragmatics: Requests and apologies*. Norwood, NJ: Ablex.

Brown, P., & Levinson, S. (1987/1978). *Politeness: Some universals in language usage*. Cambridge: Cambridge University Press.

Culpeper, J. (2009). *Impoliteness: Using and understanding the language of offence*. Retrieved May 11, 2018, from: http://www.lancaster.ac.uk/fass/projects/impoliteness/ .

Culpeper, J. (2011). *Impoliteness: Using language to cause offence*. Cambridge: Cambridge University Press.

Halliday, M., & Hasan, R. (1976). *Cohesion in English*. London: Longman.

Jucker, A. (2009). Speech act research between armchair, field, and laboratory. *Journal of Pragmatics*, *41*(8), 1611–1635.

Levinson, S. (1983). *Pragmatics*. Cambridge: Cambridge University Press.

Levinson, S., & Torreira, F. (2015). Timing in turn-taking and its implications for processing models of language. *Frontiers in Psychology*, *6*(731).

Martin, J., & Rose, D. (2003). *Working with discourse*. London: Continuum.

Martin, J., & Rose, D. (2008). *Genre relations: Mapping culture*. London: Equinox.

McIntyre, D., & Busse, B. (Eds.) (2010). *Language and style: In honour of Mick Short*. Houndmills: Palgrave Macmillan.

Peccei, J. (1999). *Pragmatics*. London: Routledge.

Rose, D. (2012). Genre in the Sydney school. In J. Gee & M. Handford (Eds.), *The Routledge handbook of discourse analysis* (pp. 209–225). London: Routledge.

Sacks, H., Schegloff, E., & Jefferson, G. (1974). A simplest systematics for the organization of turn-taking in conversation. *Language*, *50*, 696–735.

Semino, E., & Short, M. (2004). *Corpus stylistics: Speech, writing and thought presentation in a corpus of English writing*. London: Taylor & Francis.

---

[10] https://www.rottentomatoes.com/m/logan_2017.

Stivers, T., Enfield, N., Brown, P., Englert, C., Hayashi, M. ..., & Levinson, S. (2009). Universals and cultural variation in turn-taking in conversation. *Proceedings of the National Academy of Sciences, 106*(26), 10587–10592.

Swales, J. (1990). *Genre analysis: English in academic and research settings*. Cambridge: Cambridge University Press.

Tannen, D. (2012). Turn-taking and intercultural discourse and communication. In C. Bratt Paulston, S. Kiesling, & E. Rangel (Eds.), *Handbook of intercultural discourse and communication* (pp. 135–157). Hoboken, NJ: Wiley.

Wierzbicka, A. (1987). *English speech act verbs: A semantic dictionary*. Sydney: Academic Press.

Yong, E. (2016). The incredible thing we do during conversations. *The Atlantic*. Retreived from: https://www.theatlantic.com/science/archive/2016/01/the-incredible-thing-we-do-during-conversations/422439 .

Zhu, Y. (2005). *Written communication across cultures: A sociocognitive perspective on business genres*. Amsterdam: Benjamins.

FURTHER READING

The following are two excellent introductions to Pragmatics and Discourse Analysis.

- Flowerdew, J. (2013). *Discourse in English language education*. New York, NY: Routledge.
- Paltridge, B. (2012). *Discourse analysis* (2nd Edition). London: Continuum.

The Linguistic Society of America has a YouTube channel with videos in this area: https://www.youtube.com/user/LingSocAm

Stanford encyclopedia of philosophy, entry on Pragmatics: https://plato.stanford.edu/entries/pragmatics/

11 Writing Systems

Peter T. Daniels and John W. Schwieter

OVERVIEW

In this chapter, you will develop an understanding of the study of writing systems. Our objectives are to:

- consider what writing is and the ways it is used;
- discover how writing systems (alphabets, syllabaries, etc.) relate to the languages they record;
- explore how writing systems developed over time and space;
- recognize how language and writing are essentially different; and
- learn about reading written script.

11.1 What Is a Writing System?

You've already learned that the main interest of linguistics is spoken language rather than written language. A side effect of this attitude is that the written registers and especially the writing systems of modern languages have been neglected or disregarded entirely. In recent decades, this neglect has begun to be remedied.

Writing is a system of more or less permanent marks used to represent an utterance in such a way that it can be recovered more or less exactly without the intervention of the utterer. Because the person who writes does not have to be present, writing constitutes one of the most important inventions in human history, allowing us to communicate across space and time.

In order to fully understand what writing *is*, let's first look at what it *does*. One of the most important purposes of writing is to represent spoken language, as in narration or instruction. But a look at what history has preserved suggests that this hasn't always been the case. The earliest surviving examples of written documents do not carry myths or scriptures, the sorts of things we associate with ancient civilizations. Instead, they are economic records and lists of words, queries to the gods, or elaborate calendrical calculations.

It might be beneficial to consider what writing *is not*. Books about writing often begin with a chapter about *forerunners of writing* or *pre-writing*. These describe symbol systems that convey meaning but not by representing languages. One kind is **ideograms**, symbols that represent things or concepts (i.e., ideas). Among these are **petroglyphs** scratched or carved into rocks or cliffs – found in suitable climates around the world – and mnemonic records that help a storyteller recall the key points of a narrative. Ideograms can be **pictograms,** which are simplified, stylized pictures, or **iconic symbols** that by their appearance suggest what they represent. They could even be **aniconic symbols** that are associated with meanings arbitrarily. A cover term for visual communication not representing language is **semasiography**.

> **PAUSE AND REFLECT 11.1**
>
> Would you classify emojis used in text messages as petroglyphs, pictograms, iconic symbols, or aniconic symbols?

11.2 How Does Writing Relate to Language?

The English alphabet and Chinese characters represent only the two most familiar ways that writing represents language. Let's take a brief look at all of the ways.

11.2.1 Alphabets

The most widely spoken languages in the Western World, including English, French, German, Italian, and Spanish, are written with varieties of the Roman **alphabet**. An alphabet consists (at first approximation) of characters, or *letters*, which ideally each represent a consonant or a vowel. Most of the time, those consonants and vowels are phonemes of the language (see Chapter 3 Phonology).

Unlike languages such as Italian and Spanish, English and French are less than ideal examples of languages with written alphabets because their spelling was largely fixed centuries ago, while the languages continued to change. For example, the French verb *parler* "to speak" is conjugated, in writing, as *parle* "I speak", *parles* "you speak", and *parlent* "they speak". However, these forms are now all pronounced the same, although centuries ago, they were each pronounced differently. Similarly, *peak, peek,* and *pique* are all pronounced the same, but they reflect the different origins of the three words.

> **PAUSE AND REFLECT 11.2**
>
> Languages that have received alphabets more recently, or that have undergone *"spelling reform"*, are more likely to have each letter represent just one phoneme, and just one way to spell each phoneme. Czech and Finnish are examples of such languages. In English, morphemes that are pronounced differently may be spelled the same: *hymn* [hɪm], *hymnal* ['hɪmnəl]. Should *hymn* be spelled without the *n*?

After the Roman alphabet, the Cyrillic alphabet is the second most widely used. It is most associated with Russian, but during the time of the Soviet Union, Cyrillic was adapted for many indigenous Caucasian, Iranian, and Turkic languages. However, this didn't happen for Armenian and Georgian, which had long had distinctive alphabets of their own. Take a look at the differences in alphabets in (1)–(4).

(1) Российская Федерация   *Rossijskaja Federacija*   [rɐˈsʲijskəjə fʲɪdʲɪˈratsijə]   "Russian Federation"

(2) Аԥсны Аҳәынҭқарра   *Apʼsʼny Aχ°ynt̪karra*   [apʰsʼnɨ ahʷəntkarra]   "Republic of Abkhazia"

(3) Հայաստան   *Hayastan*   [hɑjasˈtan]   "Armenia"

(4) საქართველო   *Sakartvelo*   [sɑkʰartʰvɛlo]   "Georgia"

(5) ᏣᎳᎩᎯ ᎠᏰᎵ   *Tsalagihi Ayeli*   [tsalakihi ajeli]   "Cherokee Nation"

PAUSE AND REFLECT 11.3

From time-to-time, calls are heard to impose spelling reform in English so that each letter equals a single sound, and each sound has just one spelling. Who would have the authority to do that? Is it a clever idea? Should we spell *house* and *houses* as *house* and *houzez* instead? To read more about the advantages of writing systems and spelling reform, visit 'Delving Deeper' on Chapter 11's resources on the website to accompany this book at www.cambridge.org/introducing linguistics.

11.2.2 Syllabaries

In the modern world, a handful of writing systems use characters that represent syllables consisting of either a vowel (V) or a consonant + vowel (CV). In a **syllabary**, there is no resemblance between the characters that begin with the same consonant or end with the same vowel. Japanese has the best-known syllabary – actually, a pair of syllabaries with complementary uses – but serving alongside Chinese-origin characters.

A notable syllabary used in the world today is the Cherokee, which was devised around 1821 by Sequoyah (English name: George Gist) for his people. Members of the Cherokee nation now mostly live in Oklahoma, where both language and syllabary are learned by young children. An example is in (5).

PAUSE AND REFLECT 11.4

Originally devised for a Cree community near the Hudson Bay in 1841 by a Methodist missionary, James Evans, syllabics has been expanded and adapted for numerous Indigenous languages, including representatives of the three major indigenous language families – Algonquian (e.g., Cree, Ojibwe), Athapaskan (e.g., Chipewyan), and Eskimo-Aleut (e.g., Inuktitut). Given this example of one word in Northern Ojibwe, do you think syllabics should be called a syllabary? ⟨Angle brackets⟩ enclose letter-by-letter transliterations of scripts into Roman equivalents.

⟨ᐸᑕᓂᑕᐊᓂᔑᓇᐯᒧᐠ⟩
(pa-ta-ni-ta-a-ni-shi-na-pe-mok)
baataa-nitaa-anishinaabemong
[baːhtaːnihtaːʔanihʃinaːbeːmong]
"being.able.to.speak.Ojibwe"

What can you say about the characters that represent the same consonant followed by different vowels?

11.2.3 Abjads

Two of the world's major writing systems, Hebrew and Arabic, use letters that represent, for the most part, consonants only. These writing systems are called **abjads**. All the abjads happen to be written from right to left. Ordinarily, they leave the vowels unexpressed (Arabic uses the consonant letters *w* and *y* for all the long vowels *ū* and *ī*, Hebrew for some of them), but for special purposes, such as writing the Bible or Qur'ān, and in young children's books, ways of writing the vowels without disturbing the series of consonants have been invented. They are dashes, curves, and dots placed above, below, and even inside letters, as can be seen in (6) and (7).

(6) מדינת ישראל   <mdynt   *Medīnat*   [medi'nat   "State of
     מְדִינַת יִשְׂרָאֵל   yśr'l>   *Yisrā'el*   jisʁa'ʔel]   Israel"

(7) جمهورية مصر العربية   <jmhwryᵗ   *Jumhūrīyat* [dʒumhu:'ri:jat "Arab Republic
     جُمْهُوْرِيَّة مِصْرَ اَلْعَرَبِيَّة   mṣr 'l'rbyᵗ> *Miṣr   misˤr   of Egypt"
                                        al-'Arabīyah* alˤara'bi:ja:]

> **PAUSE AND REFLECT 11.5**
>
> Cn y mk sns f ths qstn f nn f th vwls r rprsntd? Cn y mk sns ʒf ths qstn ʒf th ʒntl vwls ʒr ʒndctd?

11.2.4 Morphosyllabaries

A **morphosyllabary** is a writing system in which each character represents a syllable while also distinguishing the meaning of the morpheme it represents from those of homophones, that is, words or morphemes that sound the same but have different meaning.

If Chinese characters were ideograms, they would represent ideas, and in principle they could represent those ideas independently of the language they were expressed in. In turn, that would mean that the characters could be used for recording any language. This was a popular view when Europeans first got an inkling of the nature of Chinese writing, perhaps as far back as the travel narratives of Marco Polo in the thirteenth century – but it's clear that they can't.

What, then, *do* Chinese characters represent? They represent morphemes of the language (refer back to Chapter 4 Morphology). In Chinese, nearly every morpheme is a single syllable, so each character also represents a syllable. One way to think of it is that Chinese writing is a syllabary, but with homophones distinguished. Example (8) shows two pairs of homophones. It doesn't show four homophones, because the tones marked above the vowels make as much difference as the vowels and consonants themselves.

(8) 妈   *mā*   "mom"
     抹   *mā*   "wipe"
     马   *mǎ*   "horse"
     码   *mǎ*   "yard"

Why isn't Chinese considered a *syllabary*? Example 9 shows a few reasons why Chinese is not syllabic. You'll often hear it said that Chinese has 50,000 characters. That's not true. That is the number of characters in the largest dictionary ever compiled (including every variant that was ever invented, every character that might have been used just once). You only need to know about 3,000 characters for everyday use, and specialists might know as many as 5,000 characters.

(9) 马表   *mǎbiǎo*   "stopwatch"
     马上   *mǎshàng*   "immediately"
     马桶   *mǎtǒng*   "lavatory"
     码头   *mǎtóu*   "dock"

No language gets along with just 3,000–5,000 words. Even a pocket Chinese–English dictionary may have as many as 20,000 entries. Those are what we think of as Chinese words. Most Chinese words aren't a single syllable or morpheme, but two or sometimes three syllables. And that's why we name the Chinese type of writing system *morphosyllabic* and not *logosyllabic*.

PAUSE AND REFLECT 11.6

In a Chinese–English dictionary, we find that 表 *biǎo* means "table, watch, meter, surface, outside"; 上 *shàng* is "on, atop, up"; 桶 *tòng* is "barrel, tub"; and 头 *tóu* is "head". Does putting those senses together with 马 "horse" or 码 "yard" yield the meanings of the words in (9)? Can you explain the data?

Even 3,000 different characters seem like an awful lot to learn and remember. Although English has a similar number of irregularly spelled words, at least we have just 26 letters, and those letters usually tell us how to pronounce a word. But Chinese characters just look like bunches of squiggles, don't they? No, they don't. They aren't 3,000 arbitrarily different little drawings. Look back at the four characters in (8). The simplest is 马 *mǎ* "horse". But if you look closely, you'll see the same shape in two of the other three characters, at the right side of 妈 *mā* "mom" and 码 *mǎ* "yard". This shape is present in these words to indicate the pronunciation of the character. This is why it is called the **phonetic component** of the character. The characters were standardized some 2,000 years ago, and because language is always changing, the phonetic components often aren't as precise as in (8).

The left halves of these two **compound characters** in (8) give a clue to the meaning of the morpheme represented by the character. In 妈 *mā* "mom", the left part is 女

nü "woman", and in 码 *mǎ* "yard" the left part is 石 *shí* "stone". The pronunciations *nü* and *shí* play no part in recognizing and interpreting the characters (just as the meaning *horse* doesn't, either). This part of a character is called the **semantic component** or the **radical**.

More than 80 percent of all Chinese characters in use are compound. Most often the phonetic component is on the right and the radical on the left, but all sorts of other arrangements are also found. The remaining 20 percent of Chinese characters are simple, like 马, 上, 女, and 石, plus just a very few examples of characters made of several components used only for their meaning, as in 林 *lín* "bushy" and 森 *sēn* "forest", which are simply made of 木 *mù* "tree". The phonetic component of a compound character, however, is not so limited. Almost any character can be pressed into service for that purpose.

EYES ON WORLD LANGUAGES: DICTIONARIES IN CHINESE

Traditional Chinese dictionaries are organized by the radicals (the semantic components). Traditionally, there were 214 of them. The radicals are given in the order of the number of brushstrokes used in writing them, from one, as in 一 *yī* "one", to 14, as in 鼻 *bí* "nose". One of the characters listed under the radical 一 is 三 *sān* "three". (But 二 *èr* "two" counts as a radical itself.) A character listed under the radical 鼻 is 鼾, which appears in the word 鼾声 *hānshēng* "snoring". Under each radical, the characters are listed in the order of the total number of brushstrokes used in writing the phonetic component. For instance, 林 *lín* "bushy", with four additional strokes, comes before 格 *gé* "grid", with six. In *gé* you can see 女 *nü* "woman" above 口 *kǒu* "mouth" (which is the radical in many characters having to do with speech), which make 各 *gè* "each".

11.2.5 Abugidas

In two parts of the world, South and Southeast Asia and the Horn of Africa, writing systems are used where each simple letter represents a consonant plus a basic vowel (usually *a*). The other vowels are written by adding marks to the simple letters in a consistent way.

In the Indic scripts, a sequence of two or more consonants is written by joining together the letters for the successive consonants (sometimes you can't recognize the components of the compound characters). In the Ethiopic script, however, letters don't join together. Instead, to indicate that two consonants are adjacent, the letter-form that represents the consonant plus a high central vowel is also used to write a consonant that doesn't have a vowel after it. Some of the letters of the Amharic (Ethiopic) writing system are shown in (10) with all the vowel possibilities. In (11), you can see the country's name in Amharic.

(10)

υ	*ha*	ሁ	*hu*	ሂ	*hi*	ሃ	*hā*	ሄ	*he*	υ	*hi*	ሆ	*ho*
ለ	*la*	ሉ	*lu*	ሊ	*li*	ላ	*lā*	ሌ	*le*	ል	*li*	ሎ	*lo*
ሐ	*ḥa*	ሑ	*ḥu*	ሒ	*ḥi*	ሓ	*ḥā*	ሔ	*ḥe*	ሕ	*ḥi*	ሖ	*ḥo*
መ	*ma*	ሙ	*mu*	ሚ	*mi*	ማ	*mā*	ሜ	*me*	ም	*mi*	ሞ	*mo*
ሠ	*sha*	ሡ	*shu*	ሢ	*shi*	ሣ	*shā*	ሤ	*she*	ሥ	*shi*	ሦ	*sho*

(11)   የኢትዮጵያ፡ ፌዴራላዊ፡ ዲሞክራሲያዊ፡ ሪፐብሊክ፡
ya'Itiyoṗṗiyā Federālāwi Demokirāsiyāwi Ripabilik
"Federal Democratic Republic of Ethiopia"

11.3 Where Did Writing Come From and How Has It Changed?

Chinese writing is the only one of the three original writing systems that has remained in continued use since the invention of writing around 5,000 years ago. But the first was Mesopotamian cuneiform writing, and only recently recognized was the third, an ancestor of Mayan writing.

Let's look at these three original writing systems in chronological order to see how two of them gave rise to contemporary writing systems.

PAUSE AND REFLECT 11.7

The units of an alphabet using Roman script are called *letters*; units of Chinese writing are called *characters*; units of cuneiform writing are called *signs*; and units of Mayan writing are called *glyphs*. The units of Egyptian writing, which we'll come to later, are called *hieroglyphs*. Is this confusing? Should one of these terms prevail over the others, or should perhaps a new term be devised?

11.3.1 The First Writing Systems

Perhaps as early as 3400 BCE, people began living in groups larger than the villages where everyone knew everyone else – and everyone else's business. This was the outcome of the development of agriculture in several places around the world in which people could provide enough food to support more than just their immediate circle.

When so many people are interacting with many unseen people, some sort of communication more permanent than speech becomes helpful. Various solutions were used in various places, such as keeping tallies, or drawing pictograms that could remind the viewer of known events, or recording numbers with elaborate arrays of knotted cords. We are now in a position to explain why, in just three places around the world, the solution turned out to be writing as we defined it earlier.

Mesopotamian Cuneiform
Tokens

One of the first regions where writing developed was Mesopotamia, which at the time was not the barren desert of most of present-day Iraq. Instead, it was ripe with vast irrigation system that could provide for major cities. Small formed clay objects (which have come to be known as **tokens**), of the order of 1 cm in size, could lie behind **cuneiform** writing. These tokens have been found at archeological sites going back several thousand years before the beginnings of writing, ranging from Anatolia (modern Turkey) to the Iranian plateau (modern Iran).

Some of the tokens are simple shapes such as spheres, tetrahedra, disks, and crescents. Many have simple designs incised on them, such as X. They may have been used as tallies for keeping track of livestock or goods exchanged between people, but we have no way of knowing.

It has been suggested that the images incised in clay from which the first cuneiform signs soon developed were imitations of tokens and the meanings of the tokens carried over to the meanings of the signs that (sort of) resembled them. Unfortunately for this theory, it turns out that the tokens that look like some of the common signs that aren't pictograms, such as the sign for *sheep*, are not common at all among the thousands that have been recorded. It's possible, though, that the early *numerals* used with cuneiform writing reflect earlier tokens.

Pictograms

The first known documents in the world have survived because they were written on clay. Clay could be extracted from riverbanks and divided into small, manageable lumps. When moist, these lumps could be shaped into a flat top surface and a slightly rounded bottom surface with enough thickness to hold them together. Pictograms could be etched into the surfaces with a pointed tool (e.g., a shaped reed).

What did the pictograms stand for? Initially they stood for the objects they represented: things like man, woman, sheep, and mountain. But they *also* stood for the names of those objects – for *words*. These words happened to be in the Sumerian language. The Sumerian scribes soon realized that they could use the *sounds* of these words for writing words that named things that it wasn't easy to create pictograms of. In an English rebus game, we can use a picture of an eye to represent the word *I*. In a similar fashion, in Sumerian, a pictogram of an arrow, *ti*, could be used to represent the word *ti* "life".

This system worked for all sorts of words in Sumerian. How was that possible? It's fairly easy to draw a pictogram of an abalone or an albatross, but those pictograms wouldn't be particularly useful in writing any other English word for which it is hard to come up with a pictogram. Sumerian, though, was different. *Almost every morpheme in Sumerian is a single syllable*, which means that lots of morphemes sounded the same. Signs for morphemes whose meanings were easy to picture could be reused for morphemes whose meanings weren't.

Individual signs could also be used for related words: A pictogram of legs could also be used for *walk*. Signs could even get alterations that weren't pictographic: a pictogram of a head with extra marks near the chin was used for *mouth*, and if you added a reduced pictogram of a bowl, the meaning changed to *eat*. There were two ways to clarify the meanings of signs: **semantic determinatives** and **phonetic complements**. A determinative is a sign indicating a category (e.g., birds, people, wooden things) written before (occasionally after) another sign. A phonetic complement is a sign that copied one of the sounds in the intended word.

LINGUISTICS TIDBITS: EARLY SUMERIAN
For the first several hundred years when Sumerian was written, only the semantically-significant part of a word would be written. Grammatical suffixes were simply omitted, and if complete sentences were intended, it was up to the reader to determine the relations between the words.

At this early stage, what exactly was being written? Just two things: economic records (records of exchanges of goods, lists of rations distributed to individuals, etc.); and lists of signs. In order to write their language, scribes had to learn the hundreds of signs used in writing, and from the very earliest times, lists of signs in categories (professions, animals, etc.) were compiled and copied. These same lists were greatly expanded and still being copied and memorized more than 3,000 years later until the very end of the use of cuneiform.

Cuneiform Signs

Soon after Sumerian writing began, curved lines were replaced by wedge-shaped indentations. They were produced by touching the corner of a square-ended reed stylus to the surface of the clay, leaving a horizontal, vertical, or angled wedge-shaped mark. A wedge is a *cuneus* in Latin, so the writing was dubbed *cuneiform*.

At first, the designs made with the wedges resembled the earlier drawings, but they were soon regularized into simpler or more complex patterns that followed certain design principles. Over the next many centuries, the signs became simpler and more regular and used fewer wedges.

For several centuries, Sumerian orthography didn't change much. But then – perhaps around 2500 BCE – another language came onto the scene: the Semitic language Akkadian. Scribes happily began writing Akkadian with cuneiform signs. They used the signs for the most part only for their sound values, and they had no problem writing all their grammatical prefixes and suffixes. It was after this time that scribes writing Sumerian also included the grammatical suffixes in their texts. Figure 11.1 shows

Figure 11.1 The Flood Tablet

Mesopotamian rulers loved to display accounts of their mighty deeds on their statues, on the walls of cliffs and palaces, and in clay documents that could be considerably larger than those used in ordinary communication. The tablets used for preserving literary compositions, such as the Gilgamesh Epic, were also large. In fact, *The Laws of Hammurapi* were neatly incised all around a near-cylindrical stone stela (a slab or stone carved with inscriptions) taller than a person.

the eleventh tablet (of 12) of the Gilgamesh Epic, also called the Flood Tablet, considered by some the most famous cuneiform text. The tablet tells a story of how the gods sent a flood to destroy earth but one man was told to make a boat to survive. The story resembles the great flood described in the Bible.

Akkadian scribes did use a few signs for their meaning rather than their sound. They were pronounced in Akkadian, though, and not in Sumerian. We call these non-phonetic signs **logograms**. In later times, and in some genres (scientific texts, magical texts, etc., where secrecy might have been a motivation), logograms became more frequent.

As the successive empires of the cuneiform world expanded their territories, cuneiform writing came to be used for a variety of neighboring languages, the most important being Hittite, Elamite, Hurrian, and Urartian. Hittite is an Indo-European language. The other three, like Sumerian, aren't clearly related to any other known languages, though Hurrian and Urartian are related to each other.

The decipherment of cuneiform was a lengthy process. In numerous long articles between 1846 and 1852, Edward Hincks explained his ongoing discoveries. A crucial one dealt not with Akkadian or Sumerian, but with a long inscription in the language now called Urartian. He observed that it consisted of numerous paragraphs that all began the same way. This suggested that he was looking at the annals of a king. But the various copies of what seemed to be the same formula weren't completely identical: some were a little longer than others. The pattern he discovered is shown in Figure 11.2.

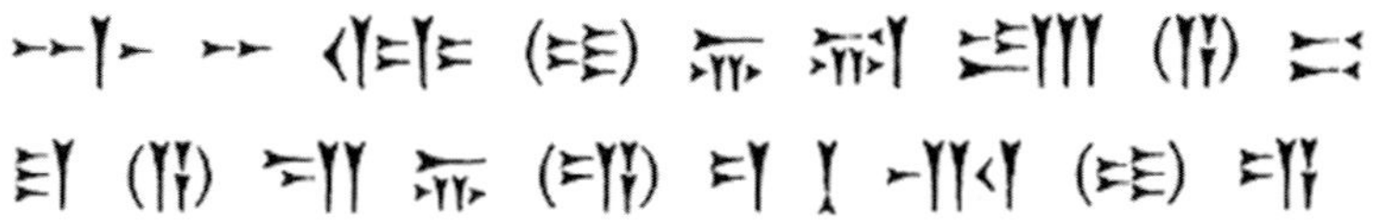

Figure 11.2 Patterns in cuneiform script observed by Hincks (1848)

PAUSE AND REFLECT 11.8

Although the example of cuneiform in Figure 11.2 does not show it, there are other examples of cuneiform in which some symbols appeared within parentheses (𒁹𒁹) in some places in the paragraph but not in others. What do you think the signs in parentheses represented?

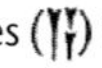

Chinese Writing

In contrast to Sumerian, we know very little about the origins of Chinese writing. The earliest texts found in the archeological record are the Oracle Bone Inscriptions from about 1250 BCE. These inscriptions were a way of interacting with the supernatural. The diviner incised a query into a flat bone – either a plastron (a tortoise shell as in Figure 11.3) or the scapula of an ox. The inscribed object was then placed in a fire and the surface cracked in the heat. The cracks were interpreted and the response from the Beyond was added as another inscription on the same piece.

About half the characters used in writing the Oracle Bone Inscriptions can now be read, because scholars can trace the shapes back over the thousand or so years before the system was organized into its present appearance. The characters were similar to today's: a radical and a phonetic symbol combined into a single character. A larger proportion of characters were of simple rather than this compound form, though. In a few Modern Chinese characters, if you know the meaning that the character represents, you can detect what may have been its pictographic origin. However, just by looking at their shapes, you usually can't.

Although not much is known about the origin of Chinese writing – does this sound familiar? – as with Sumerian, almost every morpheme in Chinese is a single syllable. This means that lots of words sounded the same. Characters for words whose meanings

Figure 11.3 An Oracle Bone Inscription on a tortoise plastron

were easy to deduce could be reused for words whose meanings weren't. But Chinese scribes, unlike Sumerian scribes, combined semantic determinatives and phonetic complements into individual characters. Thus, there were more individual characters to learn, but a message required fewer characters.

PAUSE AND REFLECT 11.9

Why do you think early Chinese writing occurred? It's possible, of course, that the only communication that Chinese scribes were interested in was communication with the spirits. What could be another reason for writing to have been born? Hint: This could be an answer for the origin of all writing.

What could the earliest-written Chinese language have sounded like? The phonetic components don't give us much precise guidance about the pronunciation of the characters today, but they did when the system was reorganized, beginning about 200 BCE, and codified about 100 CE. Chinese today includes eight different languages, such as Mandarin and Cantonese. Speakers of one cannot understand speakers of another even though they share a common ancestor. Just as you saw in Chapter 8 Historical Linguistics, we can use comparative reconstruction to give us an idea of earlier stages of Chinese sound.

Traditional Chinese Characters

Chinese poetry needed to rhyme. Poets often had to rely on extensive, elaborate charts known as rhyme tables. The characters beginning with one consonant – the **initial** – were arrayed in each table. The columns across the table showed characters that ended with all the rest of the characters – the **final** – namely the vowel, the closing consonant, and the tone (see Figure 11.4).

When modern scholars reconstruct a possible pronunciation of a character for the era of Chinese that a particular rhyme table was drawn up in, they can then apply those reconstructions across a whole table. Comparing different versions of the tables from various time periods gives an idea of how the standard (poetic) language changed over time.

These comparisons are possible and verifiable in medieval dictionaries and in inscriptions carved on monuments. This is because the shapes of the characters have barely changed in 2,000 years (similarly, we have no trouble reading Latin inscriptions from ancient Rome). Differences in handwriting come from different eras, and writing with a pen gives a different appearance from traditional writing with a brush, but there is nothing as different as Cyrillic is from Roman.

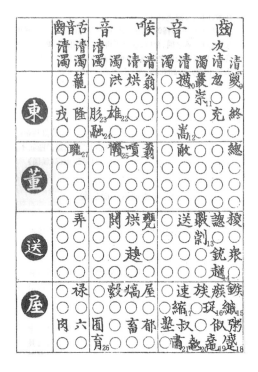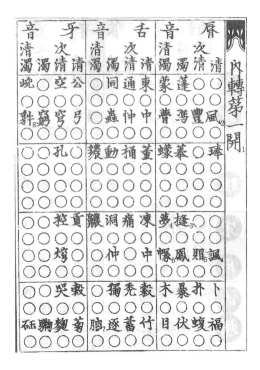

Figure 11.4 A Chinese rhyme table, this example compiled ca. 1000 CE and printed in Japan in 1564

Simplified Chinese Characters

Until the 1950s, traditional Chinese characters constituted the only form of writing. However, after the Chinese communist revolution, scholars were consulted about easing the burden of learning to read and write the more than 3,000 different characters that were needed for basic literacy. Some proposed doing away with characters entirely and replacing them with a phonetic writing system.

The eventual outcome of these proposals was *pinyin*, an idiosyncratic adaptation of the Roman alphabet, which is used for street signs and such in places where Westerners are likely to visit. It is also used in first-grade classes to help with learning the first characters but not afterward, and Chinese-speakers for the most part aren't comfortable with it.

It was understood that entirely abandoning characters would mean cutting off future generations of Chinese people from their literary heritage. The solution eventually adopted was to replace about 2,000 frequently used characters with simplified versions. Many of these simplifications could be found as abbreviations in handwriting or were current in Japanese writing, but they had never been part of Standard Chinese. Traditional characters are still used in Hong Kong, Taiwan, and Singapore.

PAUSE AND REFLECT 11.10

All the Chinese characters used in this chapter are Simplified, and all the Chinese–English dictionaries in bookstores these days use Simplified. Compare the Simplified "horse" 马 *mǎ* with the Traditional "horse" 馬 *mǎ*. Each form serves as a radical as well as a phonetic in its own system. Is 马 easier to write? Is it easier to read? What about "head" 头 *tóu*, Traditional 頭 *tóu* "head", which consists of the radical 頁 *yè* "head" and the phonetic 豆 *dòu* "beans"? The character 豆 *dòu* "beans" is unaltered in Simplified. In Simplified, 头 *tóu* "head" is assigned to the radical 丶, which in Traditional was a character *zhǔ* "dot" but now has no independent existence; nor is the residue an existing character. Is the loss of these kinds of relationships between characters compensated by simplicity of writing?

Mesoamerican Writing

The writing systems of Mesoamerica – a cultural area stretching from north of modern-day Mexico City eastward and southward to the Yucatan Peninsula and the neighboring nations of Guatemala and Belize – have only recently begun to be understood. The only one that survived the Spanish Conquest, for a short time anyway, recorded Aztec, the language ancestral to modern Nahuatl with around 1.5 million speakers who live mainly in central Mexico.

Aztec manuscripts used signs for place names and personal names that seem to have been mnemonic-pictographic. It's not entirely clear whether they were used phonetically before Aztec scribes could have become familiar with Spanish alphabetic writing.

LINGUISTICS TIDBITS: OLMEC SCRIPT

Mayan was probably not the first Mesoamerican language to be written. Scant examples have been found of quite a few other things that appear to be writing and that involve shapes resembling Mayan glyphs, but whether the languages they may represent have any modern descendants is unclear, and any readings assigned to them are conjectural. The earliest inscriptions now known, whose script may have been ancestral to all the others, are from the Olmec civilization, from the late second millennium BCE, but even Olmec script may have developed from some other. We can barely guess what the earliest texts might have recorded. But two guesses are that they recorded either commercial transactions – or calendrical calculations.

Almost all Mayan and Aztec manuscripts were considered heathen heresy and destroyed by the Spanish Conquistadors. No one tried to learn how to interpret these Mayan manuscripts in those times except for Bishop Diego Landa, who asked a scribe to write an alphabet in Mayan glyphs with an interpretation as letters of the Spanish alphabet. This document lay ignored in the archives in Spain for hundreds of years. Only in 1952 did the Russian scholar Yuri Knorosov realize that the *alphabet* was actually syllabograms – the Spanish names of the letters of the alphabet. In some of the pictograms, he could recognize items whose names in modern Mayan languages began with the syllables indicated on Landa's document. It took almost 30 years to make sense of the language underlying the texts.

What has emerged about the Mayan writing system is its unimagined complexity. For any given syllable (or

THE PALENQUE CROSS.

Figure 11.5 Ancient Mayan hieroglyphics in Palenque, Mexico

concept, in the case of numerals), there might be a glyph depicting an object whose name sounds like what the pictogram represents, or an abbreviated version of the same image, or a carefully individuated human or animal head, or even a full human figure.

Mayan orthography is strikingly like Sumerian. In both, a noun or verb base is written with either a logogram or a phonetic character. It may be accompanied by phonetic complements, before or after, and grammatical affixes are indicated with additional glyphs. But all the glyphs fit into a square – and glyphs are read in horizontal pairs of glyphs (left before right), with the next pair of glyphs beneath them, making columns of two. A new column then appears to the right. Take a look at what we mean in Figure 11.5 in which there are three columns of two pairs in each side. The labels on elements of the drawing in the middle are arranged more freely.

What made it possible for logograms to be used phonetically? *Many morphemes* in Mayan languages are *single syllables*, which means that lots of words sounded the same. Characters for words whose meanings were easy to picture could be reused for words whose meanings weren't. Numbers, though, were usually written clearly: up to four dots for the units, accompanied by bars for *five*. The numerical notation was less difficult to interpret, and by the end of the nineteenth century, it was clear that an expansive calendrical system was in use, involving cycles of tens of thousands of years.

EYES ON WORLD LANGUAGES: CHEROKEE AND CREE WRITING

You may have noticed a similarity between Mesopotamian cuneiform, Chinese writing, and Mesoamerican writing: Each used primarily monosyllabic morphemes. Is that a coincidence? Perhaps not. Writing was not invented in places with urban development where other types of languages were spoken: Indo-European in India, Semitic along the eastern Mediterranean coast, Quechua in Incan Peru.

Recall from Section 11.2.2 that Cherokee writing has different shapes for every syllabogram and Cree writing has the same shape for each consonant-syllable. The four different vowels are indicated by rotating and reflecting that shape, as shown in (i). Sequoyah, the inventor of Cherokee writing, did not know anything about writing any language, except that writing existed. Evans, the inventor of Syllabics, spoke and read English and also knew about early versions of phonetic shorthand.

(i)

	Cherokee	Cree		Cherokee	Cree		Cherokee	Cree
e	Ꭱ	ᐁ	*te*	Ꮦ	ᑌ	*ne*	Ꮑ	ᓀ
i	Ꭲ	ᐃ	*ti*	Ꮨ	ᑎ	*ni*	Ꮒ	ᓂ
o	Ꭳ	ᐅ	*to*	Ꮩ	ᑐ	*no*	Ꮓ	ᓄ
a	Ꭰ	ᐊ	*ta*	Ꮤ	ᑕ	*na*	Ꮎ	ᓇ

Whenever someone who can't read any script, but who knows that writing exists, invents a script (it has happened at least a dozen times around the world over the last two centuries), they start by dividing the words of their language into syllables. This is because syllables are the shortest stretch of speech that people who haven't been taught to read *with an alphabet* are able to identify.

It's reasonable to think that ancient peoples with no writing to be inspired by, who wrote one-syllable pictograms, were able to recognize syllables when they reappeared in words other than the ones represented by the pictures. In other words, the pictograms could be reused for their sound value alone. And thus, new writing systems were born.

11.3.2 The First Developments

The history of writing is filled with Sequoyahs and Evanses. In most cases, though, we don't know their names. On three occasions, these inventors made fascinating and fortuitous "*mistakes*" in adapting other people's ideas about writing for their own language's use.

Egyptian Hieroglyphs

Histories of writing commonly list Egyptian as another independent invention of writing. But if the idea of the importance of single-syllable morphemes to the process is correct, Egyptian hieroglyphs could not have been an original invention out of nothing. Egyptian is not a monosyllabic language, as seen in (12). In these examples, the first column shows what the hieroglyphs tell us and the second column is an educated guess about what the words sounded like.

(12)

sḏm=j	/sajjami/	"I hear"
sḏm.kw	/sajimku/	"I was heard"
sḏm	/sajâmu/	"to hear"
sḏm	/sâjim/	"hearer"
sḏm.w	?	"(not) to hear"

Egyptian hieroglyphs do not write any vowels at all. Each hieroglyph stands for one, two, or three consonants. A small number of hieroglyphs are used for only a single morpheme – that is, their consonants aren't reused in representing any other morpheme – and they are considered logograms.

PAUSE AND REFLECT 11.11

Egyptian writing uses phonetic complements (signs that copy one or more of the sounds in the intended word) and semantic determinatives (signs that indicate the semantic category of the word) much more than cuneiform does. Why do you think this was?

The earliest examples of Egyptian hieroglyphic writing date a little later than the earliest examples of Sumerian writing. Archeologists have found that there was commerce between Egypt and Sumer at that time. Maybe an Egyptian merchant saw a Sumerian merchant keeping accounts and asked what was going on. The Sumerian merchant explained that you draw a little picture for each word you want to say. They didn't realize that when a Sumerian wrote a word, it sounded pretty much the same every time, but when an Egyptian wrote a word, the vowels in the middle could be different in different situations: Egyptian grammar works by changing the vowels as well as by adding prefixes and suffixes. When an Egyptian wrote a word the same way each time, it was only the consonants that stayed the same, so each hieroglyph was seen as standing for just one, two, or three consonants, and they could be reused for writing anything at all. This was the first "*mistake*" in the history of writing.

Where did the shapes of Egyptian hieroglyphs come from? It seems that the idea of using pictograms – or perhaps ideograms – in keeping records already existed before the writing system was introduced. Several **labels** (i.e., tags of ivory with one or two drawings incised or painted on them) have recently been found, with a hole so they could be tied to packages. The packages have long since disappeared. The best guess is that the labels identified people and places (perhaps sellers, buyers, or sources of the package). Thus, scribes may have had a model for the signs they were creating on the Sumerian principle.

Uniquely, Egyptian hieroglyphs maintained their artistic shapes over the more than 3,000 years they were in use. Except in extravagant circumstances, they weren't well suited for writing in ink on papyrus paper. Almost from the very beginning, alongside the hieroglyphs (Greek for "sacred writing") a cursive form of them developed, which the Greeks named *hieratic* ("sacred", because they misunderstood its use). Each artistic hieroglyph had a hieratic equivalent.

Much later, around 1000 BCE, a third script was introduced. The Greeks called it *demotic* ("popular"). It was used not for the standard variety of the language, but for a variety closer to the Egyptian that was spoken at the time. Its characters no longer had a one-to-one correspondence with hieroglyphs.

The Rosetta Stone, discovered in 1799, provides the same text written in Greek and two forms of Egyptian: hieroglyphic and demotic. It had already been suggested that groups of hieroglyphs enclosed in an oval tablet called, a *cartouche*, represented royal names. A young man named Jean-François Champollion by 1822 had thrown off the misconception, dating all the way back to the ancient Greek historians, that Egyptian writing was ideographic and concealed great mysteries. He recognized that if he could find hieroglyphs in *cartouches* in the Egyptian in corresponding places to where kings were named in the Greek, he could see at least how Greek, if not native, names were phonetically spelled. You can see the Egyptian hieroglyphics at the top of the Rosetta Stone, demotic writing in the middle, and Greek at the bottom in Figure 11.6.

Figure 11.6 The Rosetta Stone

Unfortunately, as you can see in Figure 11.6, some of the top of the Rosetta Stone is broken away, and the only preserved *cartouches* – in the middle of the sixth line, at the left of the last line, and at the right of the third from last line – correspond to mentions of King *Ptolemy* in the Greek (see Figure 11.7a). The English polymath Thomas Young sent Champollion a copy of an inscription, by then in England, mentioning *Cleopatra* in hieroglyphs and in Greek (Figure 11.7b)

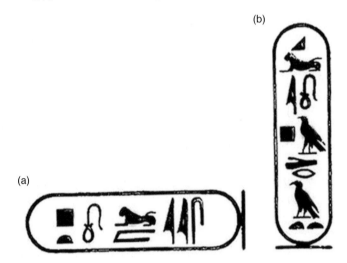

Figure 11.7 Mention of King Ptolemy (11.7a) and Cleopatra (11.7b) on the Rosetta Stone.

PAUSE AND REFLECT 11.12

Why do you think the name in Figure 11.7a did not help decipher the hieroglyphics? Why did the name in Figure 11.7b make it possible for Champollion to begin the decipherment?

EYES ON WORLD LANGUAGES: THE "AEGEAN" SYLLABARIES

Between early in the second millennium BCE and early in the first millennium BCE, several syllabaries appeared on Crete, in Anatolia, and on Cyprus. The best-known is Cretan Linear B. The name means that the characters are linear – drawn with lines rather than pictographic – and that it was the second linear script (B) used on the island. It was discovered by archeologists around the turn of the twentieth century. Subsequently, examples were found on the Greek mainland, associated with the Mycenaean civilization beginning around 1550 BCE. Linear B was deciphered by Michael Ventris in 1953, who showed it represented a type of Greek. Another script found on the island, Linear A, has never been deciphered. Can you imagine how much culture and knowledge is lost when a script cannot be read?

In Anatolia, alongside cuneiform Hittite, a hieroglyphic syllabary was used for what proved to be the related language Luvian. Ideographic uses of the signs go back to the second millennium BCE, but later on, the signs were true writing. Many of the signs are syllabic, but there are quite a few logograms.

On Cyprus, between about 800 and 200 BCE, the Cypriote syllabary was used to write Greek – in preference to the Greek alphabet, which had spread throughout the rest of the Mediterranean with Greek merchants.

Both Crete and Cyprus have yielded texts in several other scripts that have not been satisfactorily deciphered: some because there is insufficient material, some because there are no clues to what they might mean. Decipherers don't always need to know a related language in order to succeed.

You can try an exercise on decipherment of Linear B in 'Delving Deeper' in Chapter 11's recourses on the website to accompany this chapter at www.cambridge.org/introducing-linguistics

The Original Abjad

The few inscriptions in what is called Proto-Sinaitic writing come from a turquoise-mining area in the southern Sinai Peninsula. They date to the Twelfth Dynasty of Egypt, around 1800 BCE, and use fewer than 30 letters, many of them recognizable pictograms. Most of the inscriptions can be interpreted as invocations, in Phoenician, Hebrew, and their relatives, *ləba'alat* "to the Lady," the goddess Hathor (who is invoked in adjacent Egyptian inscriptions).

This interpretation is possible because the pictograms represent items with familiar names. The first consonant of each name is the sound assigned to the letter, and those names are still used as the names of the Hebrew letters. The location and circumstances of these inscriptions make it seem improbable that they represent the starting point of so many of today's writing systems, but no similar inscriptions have yet been found from an earlier time.

How might this abjad have come about? It may have happened like this: A Semitic-speaker observed the Egyptians keeping records and reading them aloud. This seemed like a useful skill, so the Semitic-speaker inquired of a friendly Egyptian how the writing worked. The Egyptian explained that each hieroglyph represented sounds of the language: sometimes the first sound of the word it represented. Maybe the Semitic-speaker didn't know much Egyptian, or maybe the Egyptian scribe didn't reveal which words went with which symbols. Either way, the Semitic-speaker went through the language, trying to find names beginning with all the sounds it contained, and chose pictures from the ones already known to represent a sound. Only a small number of letters were needed for writing all the consonants, instead of several hundred hieroglyphs. This was the second *"mistake"* in the history of writing.

A small number of brief inscriptions from subsequent centuries have been found in the Levant, which over time were simplified from their original pictographic qualities. This small group of inscriptions has come to be called Proto-Canaanite, because many of them came from the area known as Canaan. Eventually, before 1000 BCE, the Phoenicians, whose homeland was in present-day Lebanon, were using a 22-letter abjad, with highly simplified, linear shapes. As great navigators, the Phoenicians established settlements throughout the Mediterranean, in Sicily, Sardinia, Tunisia, the French Riviera, and even the Spanish coast.

Around 500 BCE–500 CE, in southern Arabia – present-day Yemen and Oman – another West Semitic descendant of Proto-Sinaitic appears, with 29 letters. It was found on monumental walls as inscriptions and, in cursive form, on batons of cypress wood.

The Original Alphabet

Somewhere in a territory where Phoenician merchants traded, the Phoenicians came into contact with traveling Greek merchants. Once again, we see a familiar story: a Greek merchant asked a Phoenician friend about the records of transactions that were being made. The Phoenician recited the 22 letters by name. The Greek grasped the idea of using the letter to represent the first sound in the letter's name.

And this is where the problem arose: Phoenician had six consonants that Greek doesn't have. Because of this, the Greek merchant didn't hear that the Phoenician was saying something significant at the beginning of [ʔalp], or [heh], or [u̯au̯], or [ħeːt], or [i̯od], or [ʕɔjn]. As a result, the Greek heard the first sounds as [a], [e], [u], [eː], [i], and [o] respectively. With that, the Greek alphabet was born. This was the third *"mistake"* in the history of writing. The letter for ō came along later, and they never did get one for ā.

11.3.3   The Subsequent Developments

Out of the original abjad descended further abjads as well as abugidas. Likewise, out of the original alphabet descended further alphabets. Let's describe these derived writing systems.

The Derived Abjads

Ugaritic

Before there was a 22-letter Phoenician abjad, the Proto-Canaanite had about 27 letters. A shocking discovery in 1929 revolutionized the study of Semitic languages and of the Hebrew Bible. A major city named Ugarit, which dated to the thirteenth century BCE, was uncovered just inland from the Syrian coast. It was a major international trading center, for documents in at least half a dozen languages have been found, including Sumerian, Akkadian, Hurrian, and Egyptian.

Most important, however, is the Ugaritic language itself. Ugaritic uses the 27 letters of Proto-Canaanite but it writes them with letters made of wedge-impressions like those we saw in Mesopotamian cuneiform. The shapes of the Ugaritic letters do not resemble any similar-sounding cuneiform syllabograms. However, some resemblances with the earlier pictograms of Proto-Canaanite can be noted.

The importance of Ugaritic was two-fold. As soon as the script was deciphered, it was realized that some of the largest tablets bore literary compositions similar to poetic passages in the Bible. Its importance for the history of writing, however, lies in a unique property. Instead of one letter for the glottal stop /ʔ/ it has three, which record the glottal stop when it is followed by *a*, *i*, or *u*. These letters do not represent vowels but rather simply show which vowels are inside or at the ends of words that happen to include /ʔ/. The city of Ugarit was destroyed in 1185 BCE. Who knows what could have happened in the history of writing if the use of the voweled /ʔ/ had become known in other abjads?

Phoenician and Aramaic

The Phoenician language must have had fewer consonants than Ugaritic, because five of the available letters were discarded. Its 22 letters were passed on to Hebrew and to the related language, Aramaic. Hebrew scribes maintained the inherited Phoenician forms pretty well, but Aramaic scribes began to write more quickly. The corners of the letters tended to get rounded off, displaying more efficient writing called **cursive**.

A more significant innovation from Aramaic scribes, though, was that they began to use a few of the consonant letters to indicate the presence of vowels. Over the centuries, most long /ī/ and /ē/ came to be written with the letter for *y*, and most long /ō/ and /ū/ came to be written with the letter for *w*. At the end of a word, but not in the middle, /ā/ was written with the letter for *h*, and eventually with the letter for *ʔ*. When letters are used this way in abjads, they're called **matres lectionis**, which is Latin for "mothers of reading", a translation of what Medieval Hebrew grammarians called them.

Hebrew scribes began using *matres lectionis* not long after Aramaic scribes did, though they didn't begin to use them as fully as the Aramaic scribes did until after many of their intelligentsia had been deported to the city of Babylon in 587 BCE. There, they and their descendants remained for some 70 years, immersed in the Mesopotamian culture that was written in the, by then, dead language Akkadian. Akkadians left their mark on Hebrew literature, speaking (like the people around them) Aramaic, and using an Aramaic form of their script.

The only surviving variety of Phoenician script proper is the Samaritan, which is used for both Hebrew and Aramaic texts by the dwindling Samaritan community.

The Square Hebrew script – the one still seen in both Jewish texts and secular Israel – is only one among many forms of Aramaic script that flourished throughout ancient Southwest Asia between about 500 BCE and 500 CE. Some of them took cursiveness so far that the letters are connected to each other. The pen is rarely raised from the paper within a word. A surviving example is the Syriac script, which is used for the literature of many Eastern Christian churches. A variety of Syriac script is used for writing the literature of Modern Aramaic.

The most successful Aramaic script is that for Arabic, which began to emerge from the Nabataean variety of Aramaic writing around the fourth century CE. Nabataean was the Aramaic written language of the Arab people of Petra in modern Jordan. Arabic is one of the most cursive scripts that has ever developed, and the art of calligraphy flourished throughout the Islamic world (see Figure 11.8). Arabic script has been adapted for many languages of the Muslim world, including the other two literary languages of Islam, Persian, and Ottoman Turkish.

Until around the middle of the first millennium CE, abjads, usually with *matres lectionis*, sufficed for all the languages that used them. Soon after, scholars took steps to preserve the correct pronunciation of the sacred scriptures, first in Syriac, followed by Hebrew, and then Arabic. This was needed because the scripts were written in older or geographically different dialects from those being spoken at the time.

Figure 11.8 Arabic calligraphy for *As-salaam* ('peace/tranquility')

Syriac, Hebrew, and Arabic scholars devised ways of showing vowels without altering the written texts. There was some influence from the earlier to the later systems, and all relied on dots, Hebrew adding dashes, and Arabic adding curls. To this day, those vowel marks are hardly ever used outside the sacred texts (and instructional materials).

Across Northern Asia

With the demise of Akkadian as the spoken and diplomatic language of the ancient empires, Aramaic took its place. Aramaic accompanied the Persian Empire from the southern frontier of Egypt to the western edges of India. Its script came to be used for a series of Iranian languages over the centuries. Often the script followed religion, as Mani, the prolific founder of Manichaeism, displayed his scriptures in several languages.

The last of the Iranian languages in that sequence was Sogdian. Sogdiana is at the far northeastern extreme of the succession of Iranian empires that ruled until and beyond the coming of Islam in the seventh century. That put them in contact with the Uyghurs, a Turkic people who adapted the Sogdian abjad for their own use. In fact, they turned it vertical so that it was written downward in columns that followed left to right.

Under Genghis Khan, the Uyghur abjad was adapted in turn, for Mongolian. With the fall of communism in 1991, an attempt was made to revive the classic Mongolian script in Mongolia after some decades of Cyrillic, which had been imposed in 1946, but this attempt failed. It is said to still be used in Inner Mongolia, within the People's Republic of China.

One last adaptation took place in 1599, when the Mongolian script became the basis of the Manchu script, which served the language of the last imperial dynasty of China, though the language itself has become extinct.

The Derived Alphabets

Returning to our discussion of the original alphabets, Greek seafarers brought their alphabet to locations around the Mediterranean. In Anatolia, it was altered in a variety of ways to serve languages related to Hittite: Phrygian, Lydian, Lycian, Carian.

In Italy, the alphabet was adopted essentially without change for Etruscan. It even included the letters corresponding to B, C (Γ), and D (Δ) even though the Etruscan language had no voiced stops and thus no need for these letters. Several other Italic languages, ones that are closely related to Latin, also adapted the Etruscan alphabet, and reuse of B, Γ, and Δ for the voiced stops shows that they were also familiar with Greek.

PAUSE AND REFLECT 11.13

The Greek language had numerous dialects, and different Greek communities added letters in different ways. The variety used to this day was established by law in Athens in 401 BCE. It had lost three of the Phoenician letters but tacked five more on, ending up with 24. Can you think why this may have been?

The Roman West

Much about the Etruscans and their language remains obscure. However, we know quite a bit about their alphabet. We have no trouble pronouncing the thousands of inscriptions they left in their tombs and on their possessions – but all but a handful are trivial: the names of the deceased or the owner, the names of the divinities depicted on the tomb murals or the engraved pictures. We can read Etruscan because they used a Greek alphabet – and passed their alphabet on to their rivals and successors, the Latins with their capital at Rome.

The Romans received from the Etruscans not only their alphabet, but much of their religion. Even so, the Romans must have acquired some knowledge of Greek writing early on because they used the Etruscan letters for the voiced stops ⟨B⟩ and ⟨D⟩ to write them in Latin. For a reason we do not know, Etruscan spelled *k* three different ways: ⟨K⟩ before *a*, ⟨C⟩ before *e* or *i*, and ⟨Q⟩ before *o* or *u*. Latin took over this last practice, where it made sense because ⟨QV⟩ represented /kʷ/, the labiovelar consonant inherited from Indo-European.

In the third century BCE, a new letter ⟨G⟩ was invented for the voiced velar stop. In the first century BCE, ⟨Y⟩ and ⟨Z⟩ were borrowed from the Greek alphabet solely for writing Greek loanwords, and the Latin alphabet was complete with 23 letters. It didn't have ⟨J⟩, ⟨U⟩, or ⟨W⟩. Etruscan, like early Greek, had been written from right to left. From almost the earliest moment, though, Latin was written left to right.

LINGUISTICS TIDBITS: INFLUENCE FROM NORMAN ORTHOGRAPHY

The Norman Conquest in 1066 brought Norman scribes with Norman orthographic habits. This included adopting the Latin device using ⟨PH⟩ and ⟨TH⟩ for Greek's ⟨Φ⟩ and ⟨Θ⟩: ⟨ch sh th wh⟩. However, ⟨i j⟩ didn't represent different sounds; nor did ⟨u v⟩. Using one of each pair for the consonant sound, the other for the vowel, began only in France in the sixteenth century and didn't come to English until later in the seventeenth century.

English

The Romans showed no interest in the languages of the peoples they conquered. They neither wrote them down nor transcribed examples. Latin remained the language of religion and scholarship for centuries afterward, but from time-to-time, local scholars began to write their own languages using local forms of the Roman alphabet. In England, the local language first appeared in the late seventh century as **glosses** – explanatory translations of individual words and phrases – in Latin texts. By the late ninth century, King Alfred was writing in Old English. The earliest texts identifiable as ancestral to French and German were the Oaths of Strasbourg of 842.

Old English scribes devised their own methods of writing English sounds not found in Latin, including letters for the interdental ⟨þ⟩ and ⟨ð⟩ (either one could be used for either [θ] or [ð] because they were not yet different phonemes in the language). Scribes also created a few other letters for a brief time along with the ⟨w⟩, and **digraphs**, which are combinations of two letters, such as ⟨sc⟩ for [ʃ].

The principles of English spelling became more regularized with the beginning of English printing in 1475 under the reign of King Edward IV. If books were to be distributed and read throughout the realm, it would be a good idea if everyone who wanted to read them could learn a fairly standard way of spelling, even if people in different areas pronounced the same words somewhat differently. Some local spelling practices were also incorporated into the system as people throughout the kingdom came to cosmopolitan London. For nearly the next 200 years, though, uniformity was not a goal. It took Samuel Johnson and his great dictionary of 1755 to truly establish and impose a standard spelling.

In the United States, Noah Webster took advantage of the intellectual upheaval during the War of Independence (1775–1783) to introduce a number of spelling changes in the interest of creating a new *American language*. Most of his proposals went nowhere, but a few, such as *–or* for *–our* and *–er* for *–re*, became standard in the United States, and *–ic* for *–ick* was adopted everywhere.

France had the advantage, from the spelling reform point of view, of having an *Académie*, or an official governing body that has the authority to decree how words would be spelled. Both Spain and Italy also have academies of language.

PAUSE AND REFLECT 11.14

Canadian French differs noticeably from European French. Would it be a good idea to reform *Québecois* spelling to reflect the differences?

Elsewhere in Western Europe

In English, we've seen the addition of digraphs and letters, and in French, the adoption of diacritics or special symbols on letters (refer back to Chapter 2 Phonetics). These three types of additions also occurred in other languages when the Roman alphabet was adapted in Christianized countries. For example, Spanish uses *ñ* for [ɲ] and *ll* for [ʎ], whereas Italian uses *gn* and *gl*, respectively. Slavic languages like Polish and Czech also use both digraphs and diacritics to record their vast array of sibilants. Hungarian marks its front rounded vowels with umlauts (*ü* and *ö*) and its long vowels with an acute accent (*ú* and *ó*). It combines the two diacritics to mark long front rounded vowels (*ű* and *ő*). Maltese, a language derived from Arabic with much Italian influence, uses *ħ* for [ħ].

In two pre-Christian or partially pagan lands of northwestern Europe, scripts were based on the Roman alphabet but adapted to local materials. In Denmark and Scandinavia, and later in England, inscriptions, often of magical content, were incised on wood, giving their letters, called *runes*, their straight-line, angular shapes. These writings recorded Germanic languages. In Ireland and Scotland, notches cut into the angled edges of standing stones, with lines extending on one or both sides, wrote brief, usually memorial, inscriptions in Irish and occasionally Pictish *ogham*.

The Christian East

With the division of the Roman Empire into the Latin-speaking West and the Greek-speaking East, the Christian Church followed suit and doctrinal differences arose that ended in a major split. Eastern churches began to translate their scriptures and to compose new writings in local languages. As a result, several alphabets based on Greek came about, in the following order:

- The Coptic alphabet for the language descended from Egyptian. It simply adds several letters to the end of the Greek alphabet, their shapes coming from demotic Egyptian characters.

- The Gothic alphabet for the only East Germanic language came about, which was used in the area of present-day Moldova; some of the additions suggest the influence of the Roman alphabet.

- The Glagolitic and Cyrillic alphabets for Old Church Slavonic (Old Bulgarian) emerged. Glagolitic was used for church materials until the nineteenth century and is still occasionally seen, while Cyrillic is best known from Russian and Orthodox lands of Eastern Europe and also serves many languages from the former Soviet Union.

LINGUISTICS TIDBITS: ONE MAN, THREE ALPHABETS

Legend tells us that in the early fifth century one man, the Armenian cleric Saint Mesrop Mashtots, created three alphabets that use the principles, but not the shapes, of the Greek alphabet. These were for Armenian, Georgian, and the little-known Udi. While it's unlikely that one person actually created all three alphabets (they use three different techniques for adding new letters to the alphabet, for instance), the legend acknowledges their essential similarities.

The Abugidas
Kharoṣṭhi and Brahmi

We said above that the Persian Empire brought the Aramaic abjad as far as India around 500 BCE. At that time, writing was unknown in India, yet there was an extensive sacred poetic literature, the Vedas, that had been handed down orally for as long as a thousand years. The spoken language, a form of Sanskrit, had changed over that time, but the Vedic language was analyzed and described in formulaic poetic language that was also passed down orally. The analyses and descriptions were grammatical compositions. The grammarians who created and studied them understood the sound-structure of the language even below the level of the syllable.

The earliest surviving texts written in a script of India come from the time of Emperor Aśoka, in the middle of the third century BCE. They use an abugida, now known as Kharoṣṭhi, and the shapes of the consonants show that they were inspired by the Aramaic abjad. Each letter represents a consonant and the *a* that follows it. The other vowels are shown with marks of various shapes added to the consonant, one each for *i*, *e*, *o*, and *u*. These vowel marks are called **matras**.

How could this first abugida have come about? By the time the Indian grammarians were becoming aware of Aramaic writing, *matres lectionis* were liberally used in Aramaic and Iranian texts. But within a word, *a* almost never received a *mater*. Thus, for the astute Indian grammarians, the letters appeared to stand, usually, for a consonant plus *a*, but when the other vowels appeared, they were often explicitly marked. It fell to them, or to one of them whose name we do not know, to systematize the writing system. The task was made easier because the syllables of the first Indic language to be written were almost always open, CV. The matras represent them admirably.

For a long time, the only language written with Kharoṣṭhi was Gandhara Prakrit. Later, Kharoṣṭhi was occasionally used for other languages spoken along the Silk Road linking China to the Mediterranean. Emperor Aśoka placed his inscriptions all over his realm, using local varieties of Prakrits.

Besides Kharosthi, the oldest writing system developed in India is Brahmi. In Brahmi (see Figure 11.9), the letter shapes were geometrically regularized, and an additional set of vowel marks was devised so that long vowels were distinguished from short vowels. Furthermore, separate, full-size letters were added for vowels that appeared at the beginning of a word, and a distinctive way was found to show a consonant cluster inside a word.

The vowel marks in Brahmi's descendants are unusual in that some of them come before, above, or below the consonant letter. But no matter where they are placed, they always represent the vowel that comes *after* the consonant. The way of showing a consonant cluster within a word was with a single symbol. Usually the parts of the (usually two) consonants remain recognizable in the combinations, but sometimes

Figure 11.9 A Brahmi inscription, one of many installed by Emperor Aśoka throughout India © Creative Commons Attribution-Share Alike 3.0. From: https://en.wikipedia.org/wiki/Brahmi_script#/media/File:Brahmi_pillar_inscription_in_Sarnath.jpg

they don't. The part of a consonant symbol used for connecting to another symbol is called a **conjunct**. Each individual unit of consonant(s) and matra (if any) is called an **akshara**.

LINGUISTICS TIDBITS: WRITING (AND CURRENCY) IN MODERN INDIA

Well over 300 languages are spoken in India today. These belong to four major language families. Hindi and English are the most widely used. Fifteen other languages are "scheduled" and have special status. Every Indian banknote has a panel on the back stating the denomination in each of the languages. Take a look below and you will note that the languages on the currency are listed alphabetically by their names in English.

Across Southern Asia and the Arabian Sea

For the first several centuries of writing in India, it was most unusual to write in Sanskrit. Most religious and scientific texts were preserved in memory to be passed on from generation to generation. The various Prakrits developed into the regional Indic languages, and Brahmi developed regional variations. Where there was little need for written communication between various peoples, there was little need for their writing to develop or be standardized together. There weren't even standardized varieties of writings within each state or realm.

Only with the British Raj, beginning in the eighteenth century, were some languages standardized and regularized into distinct typefaces. The most familiar one these days is Devanagari, the script of Hindi and several other languages of northern India and the one usually used for Sanskrit in Western scholarship. In southern India, Dravidian languages also acquired written forms, beginning with Old Tamil and eventually adding three other varieties.

When scholars in India began to write down their holy texts, the Hindus recorded them in the old Vedic and the newer Sanskrit. The Buddhists wrote in a script that the Prakrits called Pali, and a southern variety of script, perhaps originating in Sri Lanka, was associated with it.

During the "Indianization" of Southeast Asia, much of the contact with the mainland came by sea to the south, and over the centuries, scripts used first for writing Sanskrit developed into the modern Thai, Lao, and Khmer (Cambodian) scripts. They also developed into Burmese as well as numerous varieties that survive only in ancient inscriptions.

Island Southeast Asia, too – Indonesia and the Philippines – participated in the process, and in addition, north Indian Gujurati merchants apparently brought their cursive abugida to the more eastern areas, where the aksharas were greatly simplified. Their numbers were reduced as well, because Austronesian languages have considerably fewer consonants.

The South Arabian abjad had made its way across the Bab el-Mandab to northern Ethiopia around 300 BCE and served in royal inscriptions for several centuries. A curious thing happened about 350 CE, in the middle of the reign of King Ezana. At the moment his inscriptions show that he had converted to Christianity, the abjad turned into an abugida: the vowels (except *a*) began to be written with the diacritics we discussed above.

Tibet

Writing came to Tibet via a variety of Devanagari from Nepal, during the eighth century CE. Tibet, like India, had a grammatical tradition. The Tibetan grammarians understood that their language worked differently from Sanskrit. Like Chinese, to which it is distantly related, Tibetan uses monosyllabic morphemes (but uses consonantal prefixes and suffixes). Tibetan grammarians therefore abandoned the use of conjuncts, because the several consonants in a compound akshara could belong to different syllables. Instead, a dot was placed at the upper right of each syllable, and consonant clusters are shown by writing consonant letters before, after, above, and below a core consonant letter, plus a matra if the vowel is *e*, *i*, *o*, or *u*. You can see an example in (13).

(13) In བསྒྲུབས་ *bsgrubs* "established", the radical is ག *g*. Before it is བ *b*; above it is ས *s*; below it are ◌ྲ which is the combining form of ར *r*, and the vowel ◌ུ *u*; and after it are another *b* and *s*.

PAUSE AND REFLECT 11.15

The Classical Tibetan word *bsgrubs* shown in Example (13) is pronounced [ɖ̀ùp] in modern Lhasa Tibetan. In nearby Bhutan, the script associated with the classical Tibetan scriptures is considered too sacred for everyday use, and today, a Tibetan-based script is being developed to write a Bhutanese language. Would it be a good idea for the Tibetans to introduce a far-reaching script reform, or even to write their modern language with a completely different script? Keep in mind the religious and political ramifications of the question.

There was an offshoot of Tibetan that wasn't particularly significant in itself but proved important in the subsequent development of writing. Recall that Genghis Khan had caused a Mongolian abjad to be created for his empire's language. His heir Kublai Khan, however, decided that a script was needed for writing all the languages of the empire, including Mongolian, Sanskrit, and Chinese.

He commissioned a Tibetan monk to create such a script, and the result was an abugida. The shapes are like the Tibetan letters but more squared. The vowels were not in the form of matras, but were separate letters (except for *a*), a bit smaller than the consonants, and each was written below the consonant it follows. The script was called Phags pa, named for the monk who invented it, and was written in columns, top to bottom, from left to right.

Phags pa was used only from 1269 to 1368 and mostly for Chinese. The Chinese texts written with it are useful in determining the pronunciation of the language at that time. But knowledge of Phags pa remained alive among scholars.

11.3.4   Hybrid Systems

From time-to-time, scripts have been devised that combine characteristics of more than one type.

Korean

Knowledge of Phags pa may have played a crucial role when King Sejong of Korea in the fifteenth century wanted to give his people a writing system that was easier to learn and use than the Chinese script that had been adopted by Korean scholars. He also wanted to bring Buddhism to Korea.

King Sejong's committee studied Chinese phonology. But they went beyond the theory of sound and realized that the consonant parts in the coda of their syllables could be identified with the set of onset consonants. Therefore, they assigned letters to those consonants, regardless of where they appeared in a syllable.

Perhaps knowledge of the final consonants came from familiarity with Buddhist Sanskrit texts written with Phags pa. The five basic shapes of Korean consonant letters closely resemble the corresponding Phags pa letters. And those are all the shapes they needed because the rest of the consonant letters were created by modifying the basic shapes, as seen in (14).

(14) ㅅ[s]   ㅈ[ʧ]   ㅊ[ʧʰ]   ㅆ[s']   ㅉ[ʧ']

The five basic shapes were said to be based on the shapes of the vocal organs that form the sounds, so that the *s* letter represents the front lower teeth. Several of the comparisons are pretty far-fetched. More than likely, only one or two of the letters resembled the organ or articulators that produced it but explanations for the others were extrapolated from them. The three basic vowel components symbolize philosophical concepts of heaven, earth, and man.

In acknowledgment of the Chinese intellectual past, Korean letters are combined into syllable-sized groups. King Sejong's alphabet, now known as *han'gul*, surprisingly found little acceptance until late in the nineteenth century. When it was finally adopted, it was used in combination with Chinese characters read as Korean morphemes. In the second half of the twentieth century, the use of Chinese characters was essentially phased out (entirely, in North Korea). The only characters many speakers of Modern Korean can write are those used in their own name.

Japanese

To a considerable extent, Chinese culture reached Japan by Korean mediation, but Japanese modified Chinese writing much earlier and more successfully than Korean. At first, Japanese morphemes were written with Chinese characters (called **kanji** in Japanese), but so were a multitude of loanwords from Chinese. Unlike Chinese, Japanese shows grammatical functions with inflections, and when Japanese is written without these inflections, it is very difficult to understand.

Early on in Japan's acquisition of Chinese literacy, it began to use some of the characters only for their syllabic values and not for their meaning. Over time, the shapes of these characters became simplified, and they were codified into a set of (originally) 50 syllables, to represent each of the five vowels alone or with the nine consonants. In principle, the Japanese language could be written syllabically only, and for some purposes it is, but about 2,000 characters remain in common use. And almost every one of them can represent either a native Japanese word or a Chinese loanword.

There's yet another complication to Japanese writing: there are two different sets of syllable characters. One set, called *hiragana*, is used for the grammatical bits of words; and the consonants that start suffixes indicate the ending consonant of the main morpheme of the word. The other set, known as *katakana*, is used like italics in English: for emphasis and for loanwords from languages other than Chinese. In Figure 11.10 you can see the differences in shape between the hiragana and katakana.

	Hiragana						Katakana				
	-a	-i	-u	-e	-o		-a	-i	-u	-e	-o
–	あ	い	う	え	お	–	ア	イ	ウ	エ	オ
k-	か	き	く	け	こ	k-	カ	キ	ク	ケ	コ
s-	さ	し	す	せ	そ	s-	サ	シ	ス	セ	ソ
t-	た	ち	つ	て	と	t-	タ	チ	ツ	テ	ト
n-	な	に	ぬ	ね	の	n-	ナ	ニ	ヌ	ネ	ノ
h-	は	ひ	ふ	へ	ほ	h-	ハ	ヒ	フ	ヘ	ホ
m-	ま	み	む	め	も	m-	マ	ミ	ム	メ	モ
y-	や		ゆ		よ	y-	ヤ		ユ		ヨ
r-	ら	り	る	れ	り	r-	ラ	リ	ル	レ	ロ
w-	わ	ゐ		ゑ	を	w-	ワ	ヰ		ヱ	ヲ

Figure 11.10 Basic hiragana and katakana letters

LINGUISTICS TIDBITS: BEING CREATIVE WITH SCRIPT
Occasionally, texts have been devised that use each letter once and (sort of) make sense. The best known is a Japanese poem *Iroha* which contains each of the 50 syllables just once. This poem is used for *alphabetic order* when the phonetic grid seen in Figure 11.10 is not.

Iranian

A very interesting family of writing systems is that used for Iranian languages between the fall of the Persian Empire around 325 BCE and the arrival of Islam in the seventh century CE. They inherited the Aramaic abjad along with Aramaic as the imperial administrative language. With time, the administrators came to use their native Iranian languages more and more in their official work, but they never stopped writing Aramaic words.

We can see from consistent mistakes in ancient texts, and sometimes from the grammatical affixes, that even though the texts look like they were written in Aramaic, the administrators were actually writing Iranian words but spelling them as Aramaic words. The practice was basically the same as Akkadian using Sumerian logograms or Japanese using Chinese characters, as you read earlier.

The Aramaic origins of the curious spellings were soon forgotten, and dictionaries were compiled showing about a thousand such spellings that remained in use through the time of Pahlavi, which was and is used for Zoroastrian writings. Some of the letters grew increasingly similar in shape. Nothing was done about this, and there were eventually only 14 different lettershapes to represent at least 23 different sounds.

Having few letters corresponding to many sounds must have been recognized as a problem as early as the third or fourth century CE. Zoroastrian scholars recognized that they could no longer rely on oral transmission of their scriptures, the Avesta, some of which probably date back to around 1500 BCE. For the texts they devised a phonetic alphabet, the Avestan, that, almost uniquely, recorded sound details at a more precise level than the phonemes of the language.

We know that Zoroastrian scholars were familiar with the Greek alphabet because they borrowed the letter ε (epsilon) for a similar sound and included a very full complement of vowel letters. Unfortunately, because the alphabet is subphonemic, modern scholars cannot always be sure of exactly what details were being recorded.

EYES ON WORLD LANGUAGES: ALPHABETICAL ORDER IN LANGUAGES

Clay tablets from Ugarit written around 1200 BCE show that scribal students learned their letters in the same order we use today, allowing for letters that were subtracted and added along the way. Many explanations have been offered for the order of the letters but none of them is convincing.

But what we do know is that letter orders aren't just to help remember all the letters. They are also tools for ordering lists and labeling sequences. Letters were also used as actual numbers in many places, both before sets of numerals were imported from India, and even afterward. Usually the first nine letters represent 1–9, the second nine represent the tens 10–90, and so on.

In South Arabia, the letter order was entirely different from the Northwest Semitic order we still use, and is just as inexplicable. The Ethiopic letter order is similar but not identical to the South Arabian.

The Arabic order, though, *can* be explained. The first few letters are ا *ā*, ب *b*, ت *t*, ث *θ*, ج *dʒ* (*j* < *g*), ح *ħ*, خ *x*, د *d*, ذ *ð*, ر *r*, ز *z*. You can see the framework of *a b g d (h w) z* – and that the letters that are the same shape but have different dottings are brought together. But when the letters are used as numerals, the number value refers to the ancient position, so that *b* is "2" but *t* is "400". The ancient order is also known in Ethiopic. The Arabic name for the ancient order is *abjad*. The

11.4   How Is Writing Not Like Spoken and Signed Languages?

At the turn of the twentieth century, the field of linguistics saw a shift away from the traditional view that the only languages worth studying were those that had long written pedigrees and that standard forms were all that mattered, because with the discovery of complex languages (e.g., in Africa and North America) that had never had written forms, it became evident that non-written languages had as much to tell us as texts by Homer, Confucius, Zoroaster, Virgil, or Shakespeare. With this newly found interest in languages that were only spoken, writing became seen as secondary, a mere aid like audio recordings in the study of language.

A reaction eventually set in, and the properties of written language began to be studied. The most basic, easily overlooked point is that spoken utterances are temporary, surviving only in memory and then usually for their content and rarely for the exact expressions used. Written texts, on the other hand, are static and can be referred to again and again. Therefore, written language can be more complex than spoken language. Some scholars have gone so far as to mistakenly claim that a language is not *complete* until it is written.

Writing is not like language for biological reasons. The human language faculty is a product of evolution, and no human infants can avoid learning the language(s) spoken around them. No child, however, can learn to read or write simply by watching others read or write. Explicit instruction is required. So writing doesn't have to be described or even structured the same as language, and some tools used for analyzing language don't work so well for writing.

PAUSE AND REFLECT 11.16

Think back to when you were learning to write. What techniques did your teachers use to help you learn to write letters and words?

As you read in previous chapters, every language includes an inventory of phonemes, which do not carry meaning but are used to form morphemes that do. Every string of speech is made up entirely of morphemes. This *double articulation* or *duality of patterning* is an unconscious way brains have of organizing the world – it doesn't apply only to language. But writing isn't an unconscious, built-in feature of the mind. Rather, all writing systems were consciously devised and often are deliberately modified.

Below are some important points that remind us that writing is not the same as spoken and signed languages.

- Unlike languages, writing systems do not all operate the same. Different writing systems relate to the sound systems they record in different ways (see Section 11.2).
- Language is constantly changing. Writing, on the other hand, generally obeys tradition and does not readily respond to changes. Simplification in some areas of language is accompanied by complication in other areas, as a language's overall efficiency tends to remain the same. But a script's efficiency is greatest when it is devised. It tends to deteriorate thereafter.
- Because writing is learned and studied rather than acquired automatically like spoken language, there's no particular pressure on writing systems to be easy to learn. Whether someone is born into a scribal family, as seems to have been the case in Mesopotamia at least, or whether they have to go to school until they're at least 14 years old so that society can attain the elusive goal of universal literacy, as in most of the Developed World, they're required to master their society's writing system no matter how little or how much time it might take. For a variety of reasons, if there is no counterpressure, writing systems can grow more and more complex, until some significant change in society prompts an alteration to or even replacement of a writing system.
- Writing systems can be altered by fiat. Kemal Atatürk could not have ordered the minority peoples of Turkey to stop speaking their languages and use only Turkish, but he could decree that the Turkish language would be written with a Roman alphabet rather than an Arabic one beginning in 1928. Noah Webster could not successfully tell Americans to not split infinitives (e.g., not to say *To boldly go where no one has gone before*), say, but he could successfully recommend that they drop the *u* from words like *colour*.

11.5   Reading Written Scripts

Throughout this textbook, you have probably simply scanned across the text, easily interpreting what it communicates. That is called **fluent reading**.[1] But it's not an inborn ability. It's a learned skill, and typically people in North America are about four years old when they start being taught to read. They learn the basic symbols of their writing system – letters of the alphabet or abjad, C*a* characters of the abugida, CV characters of the syllabary, or morpheme-characters (a few at a time) of the logosyllabary.

---

[1] We gratefully acknowledge the invaluable contribution of David L. Share at Haifa University to this section.

11.5.1   Reading Development and Practice

As we learn to read writing systems, we need to sound out each word by identifying and putting together the symbols that constitute it. But with practice, we begin to recognize morphemes as wholes. These two processes – **identification** of new words and rapid **recognition** of familiar words – form a sequence in learning to read. However, identification is never abandoned: it must come into play at least whenever an unfamiliar or infrequent word is met, sounding it out to discover the intended meaning.

This distinction is also captured by psycholinguists' dual-route theory of reading processing. The theory predicts that when we read, words and their meanings are accessed via a phonological (indirect) route and via a separate direct route. You will read about dual-route theory in Chapter 14 Psycholinguistics.

One technique psychologists use in investigating reading is computer screens that flash a sequence of letters on the screen for a few hundred milliseconds. This speed is so fast that the participant isn't consciously aware of seeing anything, yet long enough for it to be processed. In 'Delving Deeper' in Chapter 11's resources on the website to accompany this book, you will find information about how reading works in the brain (www.cambridge.org/introducing-linguistics). Chapter 14 Psycholinguistics will also present information about language processing and reading.

SUMMARY

The study of writing systems has only recently become a part of linguistics. Until the 1980s, writing was studied almost entirely in terms of how one script developed out of another, and almost no attention was paid to how writing systems relate to language. It was assumed that there were logographies, syllabographies, and alphabets, and naturally the alphabet was best – because it stood at the evolutionary end of the historical development.

Now some scholars see things differently. Attention to how scripts relate to languages (not just to shapes of characters), has changed over time. The shift from the Euro-American mindset has begun to provide new insights into how writing could have come about and how it relates to both individuals and societies. These investigations have only just begun, and there is much more work to be done.

EXERCISES

11.1   List 25 words in English that are not pronounced as they are spelled (examples: *one, thought*).

11.2   What do the words you listed in Exercise 11.1 have in common?

> *[Shavian script passage]*
>
> Lɛntju:ləs n Mɛtələs kʌm ıntʊ
> ð skwɛə frɔm ð wɛst saıd wıð ə
> lıtəl retınju: v sɜːvənts. bəʊθ aː
> jʌŋ kɔːtıəz, drɛst ın ð
> ıkstrɛmıtı v fæʃən. Lɛntju:ləs ız
> slɛndə, fɛə-hɛəd, ɛpısiːn.
> Mɛtələs ız mænlı, kəmpæktlı
> bılt, ɒlıv skınd, nɒt ə tɔːkə.

For Exercises 11.3–11.6, refer to the passage below from George Bernard Shaw's (1962) *Androcles and the Lion*. During his lifetime Shaw was interested in developing a script that would simplify English spelling, making it more phonetic. He left funding for this task in his will. The script that was developed was then used in the publication of Shaw's play.

11.3   Given the transliteration into IPA, can you understand and state what it says?

11.4   Make a chart of the readings of as many "Shavian" letters as you can. Note that there are 48 letters in the system but not all are used in the passage.

11.5   What principles are involved in assigning the shapes of letters to sounds? Pay special attention to 𐑤 and 𐑦.

11.6   If you have difficulties understanding the passage, what does that say about the usefulness of phonetically-based script reform?

11.7   What follows is part of the Bible verse Genesis 4:7 in the original Hebrew and as interpreted into Jewish Palestinian Aramaic (Targum Onqelos) in Fassberg (2015, p. 77). The script reads from right to left. Identify the *matres lectionis* in the two passages. Hint: locate all the alephs, waws, and yods in the two texts and check in the transcriptions that they're not serving as consonants.

זבר תאטח חתפל ביתית אל סאו תאש ביתית־סא אולה ...

hā-lō ʾim tēṭîḇ śəʾēṯ wəʾim lō ṯēṭîḇ lap-pɛṯaḥ ḥaṭṭāṯ rōḇēṣ …

"Surely, if you do right, there is uplift. But if you do not do right, sin couches at the door."

ריטנ האטח אניד סוייל דדבוע ביתות אל סאו דל קיבתשי דדבוע ביתות סא אלה ...

hə-lā ʾim tōṭîḇ ʿūḇāḏāḵ yištəḇēq lāḵ wəʾim lā tōṭîḇ ʿūḇāḏāḵ lə-yōm dīnā ḥiṭʾā nəṭîr …

"Will it not be that if you improve your deeds, it will be pardoned for you, but if you do not improve your deeds, sin is kept for the Day of Judgment … "

For Exercises 11.8–11.10, refer to the Korean writing below. In the Korean alphabet, consonants and vowels have different-looking letters, and the letters for each syllable are grouped into a block of two, three, or sometimes four letters. Here are three ways of writing the Korean word *nimkum-i* "lord-NOMINATIVE":

님금이
님금미
님그미

11.8   Six different letters are used. Determine the sound represented by each one. (Hint: One of the six represents no sound.)

11.9   The three spellings were used at different times over the history of Korean. Which do you think came first, second, and last, and why?

11.10   Guess how the four consonant letters you identified are supposed to represent the vocal organs involved in making their sounds.

For Exercises 11.11–11.14, refer to the names Mahātmā Gāndhī, Jawāharlāl Nehru, and Indirā Gāndhī written with several of the scripts of India, Bangladesh, and Sri Lanka. All the scripts read from left to right. (Note that Bengali and Oriya do not have characters for *wa* and substitute *o* for the syllable.)

Mahātmā Gāndhī	*Jawāharlāl Nehru*	*Indirā Gāndhī*	
মহাত্মা গান্ধী	জওহরলাল নেহরু	ইন্দিরা গান্ধী	(Bengali)
મહાત્મા ગાંધી	જવાહરલાલ નેહરુ	ઇન્દિરા ગાંધી	(Gujarati)
महात्मा गांधी	जवाहर लाल नेहरु	इंदिरा गांधी	(Hindi)
ಮಹಾತ್ಮ ಗಾಂಧಿ	ಜವಾಹರಲಾಲ್ ನೆಹರು	ಇಂದಿರಾ ಗಾಂಧಿ	(Kannada)
മഹാത്മാ ഗാന്ധി	ജവഹര്‍ലാല്‍ നെഹ്‌റു	ഇന്ദിരാ ഗാന്ധി	(Malayalam)
ମହାତ୍ମା ଗାଁଧୀ	ଜଓହରଲାଲ ନେହରୁ	ଇନ୍ଦିରା ଗାଁଧୀ	(Oriya)
ਮਹਾਤਮਾ ਗਾਂਧੀ	ਜਵਾਹਰ ਲਾਲ ਨਹਿਰੂ	ਇਨਿਰਾ ਗਾਂਧੀ	(Punjabi)
මහත්මා ගාන්ධි	ජවහර්ලාල් නේරු	ඉන්දිරා ගාන්ධි	(Sinhala)
மகாத்மா காந்தி	ஜவகர்லால் நேரு	இந்திரா காந்தி	(Tamil)
మహత్మ గాంధి	జవహర్ లాల్ నెప్రూ	ఇందిరా గాంధి	(Telugu)

11.11   Make a chart of the symbols for each sound used in the different scripts.

11.12   All these scripts developed out of a common ancestral script that was in use nearly 2,000 years ago. Comparing the shapes of the letters, try to determine which scripts are more closely related to each other.

11.13   How do the historical relationships between the scripts compare with the linguistic relationships between the languages involved?

11.14   Which one of these scripts appears to operate somewhat differently from all the others?

11.15   In the table below, there are 16 Chinese characters with the pronunciations and the meanings of the morphemes they represent. The diacritics on the vowels represent the four different lexical tones that are part of the morphemes. Determine a plausible pronunciation represented by the phonetic component seen in each column and a plausible meaning for the morpheme represented by the semantic component (or radical) seen in each row.

	丁			工			堯			番		
人 (亻)	仃	*dīng*	left alone	仜	*hōng*	paunch	僥	*jiāo*	lucky	僠	*bō*	(a name)
手 (扌)	打	*dǎ*	strike	扛	*káng*	carry	撓	*náo*	scratch	播	*bō*	strew
水 (氵)	汀	*tīng*	spit of land	江	*jiāng*	river	澆	*jiāo*	sprinkle	潘	*pān*	ricewater
糸 (糹)	紅	*zhēng*	——	紅	*hóng*	red	繞	*rào*	——	繙	*fān*	translate

REFERENCES

Fassberg, S. (2015). Judeo-Aramaic. In A. Rubin & L. Kahn (Eds.), *Handbook of Jewish languages* (pp. 64–117). Leiden: Brill.

Hincks, E. (1848). On the Inscriptions at Van. *Journal of the Royal Asiatic Society*, 9, 387–449.

Shaw, G. (1962). *Androcles and the lion: Shaw alphabet edition*. Harmondsworth: Penguin.

PART 6

LANGUAGE ACQUISITION

12 First Language Acquisition

John W. Schwieter

OVERVIEW

In this chapter, you will develop an understanding of first language (L1) acquisition and will:

- explore how phonology, vocabulary, morphology, syntax, and communicative development occur in an L1;
- discuss how internal factors such as a critical period for language acquisition, innate knowledge, and general cognition affect L1 acquisition;
- study how external factors such as input and experience, feedback and recasts, and cultural and social factors affect L1 acquisition;
- learn about L1 acquisition among atypical populations such as children in situations of deafness or blindness or who may have intellectual disabilities, autism spectrum disorders, or a developmental language disorder;
- consider the effects of acquiring two L1s from birth; and
- review some approaches to studying L1 acquisition.

12.1 What Is First Language Acquisition?

Do you remember learning language as a baby? Do you recall anyone explicitly teaching it to you? Chances are you probably answered *no* to both. **L1 acquisition** is the study of infants' and children's development of language from birth. It is a rather quick process, happening over the first six years or so of life. It is amazing to think that newborn infants who neither speak nor understand any language are soon able to express complex ideas – and sometimes in more than one L1, as we will also discuss later in this chapter.

Parents always get excited when hearing their baby's first word. But they may not realize that the baby has been using language before this first word, just not in the conventional sense. In fact, the sounds and babbling they make communicate what they need. But when you stop to think about it, the fact that a baby shows signs of language should not be surprising at all – it should be expected. Humans are wired for language, even those with visual, hearing, cognitive, or neurological disorders. So, while the development of an L1 is complex, this complexity is available to all of us and comes naturally. Nonetheless, hearing babies say their first word seems to be exciting even though it simply validates their *being a human*.

PAUSE AND REFLECT 12.1

Have you ever been present to hear a baby's first word? If not, try to find someone who has and ask them how it felt.

Before we begin, you may be wondering what methods can be used to study language in babies (after all, it isn't the same to test babies and adults). To learn a little about this, read 'Delving Deeper' in Chapter 12's resources on the website to accompany this book at www.cambridge.org/introducing-linguistics

12.2 Phonological Development

One of the first things – if not *the* first – a baby does is cry. This is a natural response to being introduced to a new environment far different from the comfortable womb. But crying also suggests that infants communicate well before their *first word*. Let's take a look at how sound develops in an L1.

12.2.1 Pre-speech Vocal Development

Infants are listening to the speech around them from the moment they are born. In a matter of days, they are able to distinguish between human and non-human sounds

---

PAUSE AND REFLECT 12.2

We study L1 acquisition in infants using several observational and recording techniques. You may not have thought about some of the natural behaviors that can tell us about language acquisition. Researchers can measure things like changes in heart rate to estimate whether infants are responding to certain language features. What do you think are some other things that infants do naturally that we can use to test their response to language?

---

and can even tell the difference between the language(s) spoken by their parents and other languages. In just a couple of weeks, infants are able to recognize their parents' voices and to hear the difference between individual sounds like /p/ vs. /b/.

During the first months, infants move through several stages of **pre-speech vocal development**. Pre-speech refers to sounds such as crying, burping, and babbling that allow infants to explore their vocal abilities and familiarize themselves with processes they will later use to speak. These sounds vibrate vocal cords and move air through the vocal apparatus. Below are five important stages of pre-speech vocal development (Stark, 1986).

- **Reflexive vocalizations**. These earliest vocalizations include crying and **vegetative sounds** such as breathing, sucking, or sneezing and occur from 0–6 weeks of age.
- **Cooing and laughter**. Infants use **cooing** sounds at around six to eight weeks of age and laughter by four months. The first cooing sounds resemble one long vowel but after several months, cooing changes to include a series of vowel-like sounds strung together but separated by breaths.
- **Vocal play**. From four to seven-and-a-half months of age, infants engage in **vocal play** to test their speech abilities by using different consonant- and vowel-like sounds. They produce primarily flat or falling pitch contours because rising pitch would require the infants to raise subglottal pressure to increase vocal fold length or tension – movements which infants are not able to control yet. Other examples of sounds made during this stage are squeals, growls, and friction-like noises.
- **Reduplicated babbling**. From six to ten months of age, infants begin to emit true syllables that are usually produced in series of the same consonant and vowel combinations (e.g., [bababa] or [gugugugu]).
- **Non-reduplicated babbling**. Infants combine vowels and consonants into syllable strings without reduplicating them by the time they are nine to 14 months of age (e.g., [gapaga]). By this time, they may use **invented words** to consistently refer to an object (e.g., calling their favorite toy a [kiki]). By around 12 months, infants are usually able to produce various stress and intonation patterns including rising pitch contours.

> **LINGUISTICS TIDBITS: STARTING TO *SOUND LIKE* THE L1**
>
> Infants begin to show signs that their speech is acquiring properties specific to their L1 at some point during babbling stages. In fact, all of the sounds they made up until this point could have easily been made regardless of the L1 they were learning. In contrast, nine- to ten-month-olds learning French produce more pre-voiced stops (which exist in French but not English) in their babbling than English-learning infants at the same age. For instance, children learning French have a shorter time lag between the voiceless stop /t/ and the following sound while children learning English have a longer time lag. By eight months they also begin to lose the ability to perceive contrasts not present in their L1.

12.2.2 Natural Order of Sound Acquisition

By the end of the babbling stage, infants are able to perceive and produce many vowels and consonants. However, they have not yet learned all the sounds in their L1. In fact, in one study on 12-month-olds acquiring L1 English, about 90 percent of the sounds produced included only 11 consonants: /h, w, j, p, b, m, t, d, n, k, g/ (Locke & Pearson, 1992). Studies have shown that throughout the pre-speech vocal development stage and well beyond, there is a predictable order in which L1 sounds are acquired. Interestingly, this mirrors the frequency of their distribution among world languages.

Although there is variation, we can make a few generalizations about which sounds are acquired before (>) others:

- vowels > consonants
- nasals and stops > glides > liquids > fricatives > affricates
- labials > velars > alveolars > palatals > interdentals

TABLE 12.1 Typical Early Sound Inventories

Age 2

Stops	Nasals	Glides	Liquids	Fricatives	Affricates
p b	m	w		f	
t d	n			s	
k g				h	
?					

Age 4

Stops	Nasals	Glides	Liquids	Fricatives	Affricates
p b	m	j	l	f	t͡ʃ d͡ʒ
t d	n	w		s z	
k g	ŋ			ʃ	
?				h	

Ages 6–8

Stops	Nasals	Glides	Liquids	Fricatives	Affricates
p b	m	j	l	f v	t͡ʃ d͡ʒ
t d	n	w	ɹ	θ ð	
k g	ŋ			s z	
?				ʃ ʒ	
				h	

Table 12.1 shows the typical sound inventory for children at ages two, four, and six to eight acquiring English as an L1.

12.2.3 Articulatory Processes

As children establish their sound inventory, they adjust their speech according to the limitations of their abilities. Children use **articulatory processes** to systematically alter their speech so that it fits within their current sound repertoire and production abilities. For example, a two-year-old who has not yet acquired /ʃ/ may simplify /wɪʃ/ to be /wɪs/ while a four-year-old may say it correctly. Interestingly enough, the same two-year-old would be able to hear and distinguish the differences between /ʃ/ and /s/ as can be seen in (1):

(1) Adult: Do you want to make a wish?
     Child: Yes, wis!

Example (1) shows that the perception of sounds comes before their production so it is not surprising that a child may say both /ʃ/ and /s/ as [s]. Some articulatory processes like the substitution of /ʃ/ for /s/ apply to individual sounds whereas others occur to the entire word. Below we describe common articulatory processes that children may use to assist their speech until they have greater articulatory control.

Substitution

Children may use **substitution** to simply replace one sound with another, but not as a result of a neighboring sound. Commonly, these articulatory processes are classified as stopping, fronting, gliding, and denasalization.

- **Stopping** is when a fricative becomes a stop as in [s → t] or [z → d].
- **Fronting** is the moving forward of the place of articulation of a sound such as [velar → dental] or [alveopalatal → alveolar].
- **Gliding** is the result of a liquid changing to a glide as in [l → j] or [r → w].
- **Denasalization** is when a nasal consonant is replaced by a non-nasal consonant as in [n → d] or [m → b].

While these last two examples may look like stopping because the two sounds become a stop, we only refer to stopping as changing from a fricative, not from a nasal. Table 12.2 provides examples of substitution.

TABLE 12.2 Some Examples of Substitution in Early Child Speech

Stopping: a fricative becomes a stop

[s] → [t]	soup	[sup] → [tup]
[z] → [d]	zoo	[zu] → [du]
[ʃ] → [t]	shoe	[ʃu] → [tu]
[θ] → [t]	thanks	[θæŋks] → [tæŋ]
[ð] → [d]	there	[ðɛɹ] → [dɛ]

Fronting: a sound becomes a more-forward sound

[g] → [d]	goat	[got] → [dot]
[k] → [t]	car	[kʰɑɹ] → [tɑ]
[ʃ] → [s]	show	[ʃow] → [sow]
[t͡ʃ] → [t]	cheek	[t͡ʃik] → [tik]
[d͡ʒ] → [d]	jump	[d͡ʒʌmp] → [dʌp]

TABLE 12.2 (*cont.*)

Gliding: a liquid becomes a glide

[l] → [w]	laugh	[læf] → [wæf]
[l] → [j]	lion	[lajɛn] → [jajɛn]
[ɹ] → [w]	run	[ɹʌn] → [wʌn]

Denasalization: a nasal becomes a non-nasal

| [n] → [d] | nose | [nowz] → [dowz] |
| [m] → [b] | bedroom | [bɛdɹum] → [bɛwub] |

Assimilation

When sounds are influenced by neighboring sounds, we refer to this as **assimilation**. Because children seem to prefer maintaining similar sounds within a word, they may change one sound to match another. This tendency is not all that surprising given that much of their babbling consists of repeated syllables [bababa] and sequences of related sounds like stops [gapala]. When a vowel or consonant becomes more like or the same as another vowel or consonant in the word, we call this **vowel** or **consonant harmony**, respectively. For example, instead of [dædi] as *daddy*, a child may say [didi] so that both vowels are the same. Or rather than [dɑgi] as *doggy*, he/she may say [gɑgi] so that both consonants match.

Vowel and consonant harmony do not have to result in identical sounds, but the result is normally similar in terms of natural class (stops, fricatives) or place of articulation (bilabial, velar). For example, instead of [dʌk] as *duck*, a child may say [gʌk] since /g/ and /k/ are both velar stops whereas /d/ is an alveolar stop.

Finally, we may also find examples of **reduplication** in which syllables are repeated as in [baba] for *bottle*. It is usually the first syllable that is reduplicated although this could depend on whether the syllable is stressed or unstressed, as we will see in the next section. Table 12.3 includes examples of vowel and consonant harmony and reduplication.

Deletion and Simplification of Syllables

Syllables carry primary stress (ˈ), secondary stress (ˌ), or no stress within words (Chapter 3 Phonology). As children acquire their L1, it is likely that they notice sounds in stressed environments more than sounds in unstressed environments. Because of this, they are also more likely to maintain sounds in stressed syllables when they speak. However, **syllable deletion** may occur to weaker, unstressed syllables as in [ˈbʌ.ɹəɪ.ˌflaj] → [bʌfaj]. We also find that children often delete consonants in word-final position. This is more than likely because they have not yet acquired that particular consonant like /ɹ/ as in [kʰɑɹ] → [kɑ] or because it is simply easier to say as in [lʊk] → [lʊ]. Examples of deletion of word-final consonants and unstressed syllables are provided in Table 12.4.

TABLE 12.3 Some Examples of Types of Assimilation in Early Child Speech

Vowel harmony

kitty = [kɪti] → [kɪki]

zebra = [zibɹə] → [zibi]

mommy = [mɑmi] → [mɑmɑ] or [mimi]

Consonant harmony

tub = [tʌb] → [bʌb]

look = [lʊk] → [kʊk]

desk = [dɛsk] → [dɛd]

Reduplication

rabbit = [ɹæbɪt] → [wæwæ]

apple = [æpəl] → [æpæp]

hello = [hɛlo] → [jojo]

TABLE 12.4 Some Examples of Deletion in Early Child Speech

Word-final consonants

thought = [θɑt] → [tɑ] *

boat = [bot] → [bo]

cat = [kæt] → [kæ]

bed = [bɛd] → [bɛ]

bus = [bʌs] → [bʌ]

Unstressed syllables

butterfly = [ˈbʌ.ɹəɹ.ˌflaj] → [bʌfaj]

potato = [pə.ˈte.to] → [ˈte.to]

banana = [bə.ˈnæ.nə] → [ˈnæ.nə]

* This example also illustrates stopping since the fricative [θ] becomes the stop [t]. It is common that more than one articulatory process appears in words.

Children may also break up consonants that occur in clusters. An example of this **syllable simplification** is [slow] → [low] and the result usually brings syllable structure closer to the universally-favored CV pattern. Table 12.5 shows examples of syllable simplification.

TABLE 12.5 Some Examples of Syllable Simplification in Early Child Speech

Syllable simplification

[s] may be deleted when occurring *before stops or nasals*

spoon = [spun] → [pun]

stop = [stɑp] → [tɑp]

skate = [sket] → [ket]

small = [smɑl] → [mɑl]

snake = [snek] → [nek]

Liquids may be deleted when occurring *after stops or fricatives*

plane = [plen] → [pen]

pretend = [pɹətɛnd] → [pətɛn]

try = [taj] → [taj]

clean = [kin] → [kin]

cry = [kɹaj] → [kaj]

black = [blæk] → [bæk]

bread = [bɹɛd] → [bɛd]

dry = [dɹaj] → [daj]

glad = [glæd] → [gæd]

great = [gɹet] → [get]

fly = [flaj] → [faj]

afraid = [əfɹed] → [əfed]

slip = [slɪp] → [sɪp]

Nasals may be deleted when occurring *before stops or fricatives*

[mp] → [p] = [bʌmp] → [bʌp]

[nt] → [t] = [ɛləfɛnt] → [ɛləfɛt]

LINGUISTICS TIDBITS: LEARNING LIKE A SPONGE

It is not a language-specific phenomenon that children learn language like a sponge. They can understand their first word as early as five months, say their first word by ten to 15 months, reach their 50-word milestone by 18 months, and break through their 100-word milestone by 20–22 months. By 22–24 months, vocabulary development is so fast that it is difficult to predict the number of words known by certain months.

The sound system continues to develop up until seven or eight years of age, although some children may complete this sooner. The acquisition of sound is extremely important for vocabulary learning, as we will discuss in the next section. For example, the difference between /kæt/ and /bæt/ is only the first sound, yet this difference is large enough to change the meaning. The ability, then, to discriminate between /k/ and /b/ is essential to learning words. Let's take a closer look at word learning.

12.3　Vocabulary Development

12.3.1　From the First Word to the 50-word Milestone

As we mentioned earlier, a child's first word at around 12 months can be a significant milestone for L1 acquisition. It has, after all, taken about a year for him/her to get to this point. This speed of vocabulary learning sluggishly continues and by between 15–24 months, a child may only know around 50 words. For obvious reasons, these first 50 words commonly include foods, family members, pets, animals, toys, vehicles, and clothing. To illustrate similarities and differences among the first words learned, we provide Table 12.6 which shows the first ten words acquired by four children.

TABLE 12.6 The First 10 Words Acquired by Four Children (Harris, Barrett, Jones, & Brookes, 1988)

Child 1	Child 2	Child 3	Child 4
ball	bee	bye-bye	baby
boo	down	car	brum
buzz	go	choo-choo	bye-bye
go	hello	doggy	hello
moo	here	moo	here
more	Jacqui	mummy	shoes
mummy	more	no	teddy
quack	mummy	shoe	there
teddy	no	teddy	woof
there	wee	there	yes

EYES ON WORLD LANGUAGES: EARLY VOCABULARY DEVELOPMENT IN ENGLISH, CANTONESE, AND MANDARIN

Tardif *et al.* (2008) compared the first words learned by children in three different languages. The researchers studied a large sample of nearly 1,000 infants to make their comparisons. These eight- to 16-month-old infants included three groups: 264 infants in the United States learning English, 336 in Beijing learning Mandarin, and 367 in Hong Kong learning Cantonese.

Caregivers recorded the infants' first words and striking similarities were found between the three groups: six of the top 20 words were the same for all three language groups and many other words were the same for two of the languages. Compare these words in the table below.

English	Cantonese	Mandarin
Daddy (54)	Daddy (54)	Mommy (87)
Mommy (50)	Aah (60)	Daddy (85)
BaaBaa (33)	Mommy (57)	Grandma – Paternal (40)
Bye (25)	YumYum (36)	Grandpa – Paternal (17)
Hi (24)	Sister – Older (21)	Hello?/Wei? (14)
UhOh (20)	UhOh (Aiyou) (20)	Hit (12)
Grr (16)	Hit (18)	Uncle – Paternal (11)
Bottle (13)	Hello?/Wei (13)	Grab/Grasp (9)
YumYum (13)	Milk (13)	Auntie – Maternal (8)
Dog (12)	Naughty (8)	Bye (8)
No (12)	Brother – Older (7)	UhOh (Aiyou) (7)
WoofWoof (11)	Grandma – Maternal (6)	Ya/Wow (7)
Vroom (11)	Grandma – Paternal (6)	Sister – Older (7)
Kitty (10)	Bye (5)	WoofWoof (7)
Ball (10)	Bread (5)	Brother – Older (6)
Baby (7)	Auntie – Maternal (4)	Hug/Hold (6)
Duck (6)	Ball (4)	Light (4)
Cat (5)	Grandpa – Paternal (4)	Grandma – Maternal (3)
Ouch (5)	Car (3)	Egg (3)
Banana (3)	WoofWoof (2)	Vroom (3)

While many similarities were found for the three groups' first 20 words learned, the same was not the case when comparing their total vocabulary knowledge beyond those 20 words. The types of words (nouns, adjectives, etc.) that made up the complete word inventory of the three groups were quite different. For example, for children learning English, *people terms* make up 30 percent of their total vocabulary whereas they make up 78 percent for children learning Mandarin and 43 percent for those learning Cantonese.

Tardif *et al.* show that even though there can be general trends in vocabulary acquisition across languages, these may be limited to the first handful of words. There appear to be factors such as parental input and cultural characteristics that strongly affect children's early word-learning.

Although it is difficult to predict which *exact* words are among the first 50 a child acquires in English, we can be more certain of the distribution of the types of words learned. For example, research shows that about half of the first 50 words refer to names of people, animals, and things. Following this, there will be a fairly even distribution of words expressing: action/events; adjectives/modifiers; and personal/social things. We provide an example based on this distribution in Table 12.7.

TABLE 12.7 Distribution of the First 50 Words Acquired in English

People, animals, and things (25)

apple	book	cat	gloves	mummy
baby	bottle	cookie	hat	shoe
ball	bread	daddy	horse	toast
blanket	cake	dog	juice	truck
boat	car	duck	milk	water

Actions/events (9)

down	give	put	sit	up
eat	go	see	stop	

Adjectives/modifiers (9)

all-gone	dirty	hot	nice	this
cold	here	more	there	

Personal/social things (7)

bye-bye	hi	please	thank-you
hey	no	yes	

12.3.2 Word Spurts

When children have learned their first 50 words or so, many go through a **word spurt period** in which the rate of acquiring new words exponentially increases. By the time they are six years old, they will know approximately 14,000 words. Also around age six, they may start a second word spurt which involves faster vocabulary learning than the first spurt. This could be triggered by having started formal education. Figure 12.1 shows an example timeline for word learning.

Researchers had once believed that the brain needed to develop to a certain point to be able to enter a word spurt stage. Later studies have shown that this may not be quite true. In fact, recent research has shown that the brain has been learning words

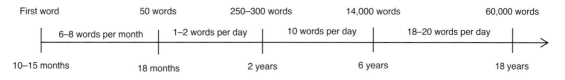

Figure 12.1 Approximate timeline and rate of word learning

throughout infancy but this word learning has been occurring simultaneously. It is believed that once infants come to understand a few dozen words, they also begin to understand the basic functions of language. Rather than brain development, this understanding seems to prompt a word spurt.

Some children do not go through a spurt at all and instead show an even rate of vocabulary development. Figure 12.2 displays an example of the rate and development of vocabulary for four children. Notice that although three of the children started their word spurt between 16–22 months, one of them did not enter a spurt at all.

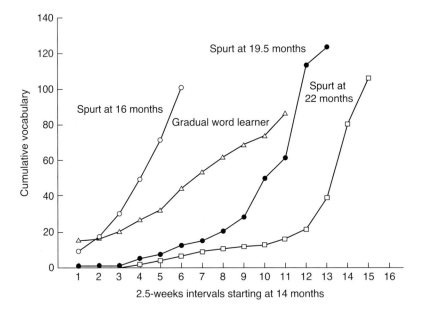

Figure 12.2 Word spurts and gradual vocabulary development

12.3.3   The Mental Lexicon and Meaning

As children learn words, they develop a **mental lexicon**, which we define as a mental dictionary which contains information on words: their sounds, meanings, and structural properties. When you stop to think about it, when an infant acquires a new word, say *bottle*, this learning comes with not only the sounds to comprehend and produce the word, but also the meaning of the word. All of this information forms part of the mental lexicon. As L1 acquisition continues, the mental lexicon gets richer and the entry for *bottle* will also contain information on its morphological characteristics, like being able to add –*s* to make *bottles* and its syntactic information, like being able to say *the bottle* but not *bottle the*.

PAUSE AND REFLECT 12.5

Learning the meaning of a word may be easier said than done. When an adult points to a cat eating and says *cat*, how does the child know that the adult is talking about the actual cat, the action of eating, or even the color of the cat? To make things even more difficult, what if the adult sometimes calls the cat a *kitty* and other times by its name, *Griselda*? What do you think is key for the child to learn what a *cat* really is?

Two common types of mistakes that children make involve overextending and underextending the meaning of words. **Overextension errors** are the overly broad uses of a word such that it is more general or inclusive than it should be. Returning to our cat example, a child who overextends the meaning of *cat* may call each four-legged animal he/she encounters a *cat*. Errors of overextension are commonly due to physical similarities.

Underextension errors are the overly restricted uses of a word such that it is less inclusive than it should be. A child who underextends the word *cat* may not call his/her grandmother's long-haired white cat a *cat* because it looks nothing like *Griselda* who is a short-haired, grey and brown tabby. Both overextension and underextension types of errors are primarily due to the fact that the child is still unsure of the features that actually constitute a cat as opposed to similar, yet unknown objects like a rabbit or squirrel. Table 12.8 shows examples of both types of errors.

TABLE 12.8 Overextension and Underextension errors

Target word	Overextension errors	Underextension errors
apple	cherry, onion, pear	only red apples
ball	balloon, egg, stone	only baseballs
book	magazine, newspaper, paper	only picture books
cookie	cracker, dessert, snack	only chocolate cookies
dog	cows, horses, sheep	only poodles
car	bus, train, truck	only the family car

PAUSE AND REFLECT 12.6

Take a moment to consider additional examples of overextension and underextension. Ask a few people what types of mistakes they have heard children make and figure out if they too represent overextension and underextension errors.

12.4 Morphological Development

Soon after the first words, we begin to see the development of word structure. Once again, we know quite a bit about the development of word formation by taking a look at some of the errors children make. You may have heard a child say something like *mouses* instead of *mice*, or *throwed* instead of *threw*. Why do you think they do this? Have they heard this from adults before? These errors are evidence that children overgeneralize rules of word formation that they have acquired. Below we will look at some issues related to the development of L1 morphology.

12.4.1 Overgeneralization

As children learn words, they also come to understand things like the –*s* on the end of *toys* refers to more than one toy and that the –*ed* on the end of *walked* refers to the action of walking in the past. They then use this knowledge to also make other nouns plural and past and as we saw in our examples of *mouses* and *throwed*, this does not always result in grammatical structures. Even so, these errors show us that children are acquiring an underlying grammar which allows them to create new structures that they have never heard before based on the rules of this acquired grammar. **Overgeneralization errors** occur from the broad application of a rule in cases where it doesn't apply.

Interestingly, because of the frequent exposure to common irregular words such as *men* and *fell*, children may begin using these words correctly only to later start saying them incorrectly. This may occur because when they unconsciously realize that an –*s* can make a noun plural and an –*ed* can situate a verb in the past – usually around the age of two-and-a-half years old – children may overgeneralize this rule throughout their language.

At the same time as children are overgeneralizing these rules, they may also blend the correct form (that they may have even once used) such as *men* and *fell* with the overgeneralized form such as *mans* and *falled* and things like *mens* and *felled*. From this, researchers argue that morphemes are first learned on a case-by-case basis (*men, fell, broke*). Following this, children will likely overgeneralize rules (*mans, falled, breaked*) before finally mastering the exceptions to those rules (*men, fell, broke*).

How do we know that a child has acquired a morphological rule? One way is to have children produce or comprehend the application of the rule in a context that they have never heard before. For instance, in Jean Berko's (1958) classic **wug test**, children are introduced to made-up animals and actions. For example, they first see a picture and are told *this is a wug*. Right after, they see another picture in which they are asked to pluralize the new word (see Figure 12.3).

The spoken form of the plural morpheme –*s* depends on the sound that comes directly before it (Chapter 3 Phonology). We can test whether or not a child has acquired this rule by seeing if he/she is able to say the three different sounds of the plural in English.

THIS IS A WUG.

NOW THERE IS ANOTHER ONE.

THERE ARE TWO OF THEM.

THERE ARE TWO _____.

Figure 12.3 Example from the Wug test. From: Berko, J. (1958). The child's learning of English morphology. *Word, 14*, 150–177. Reproduced by permission of Taylor & Francis Group. Taylor & Francis Ltd, http://www.tandfonline.com.

LINGUISTICS TIDBITS: SIGN LANGUAGE MORPHOLOGY

You may not have considered that a signed language is actually quite rich in morphology. In fact, sign languages, like spoken languages, have free and bound morphemes, grammatical morphemes, derivational and inflectional morphemes, and morphological rules that allow users to combine signs in order to form other signed words.

For example, American Sign Language, mostly used in Canada and the United States, marks inflectional morphology by modifying movements of the hands and the spatial contours of the body where the sign is articulated. Don't forget that sign languages, as we will discuss below, are full-fledged and sophisticated linguistic systems.

Compare the following plural pronunciations of the nonsense animals *gutch*, *wug*, and *heaf* from Berko's study:

gutches [gʊtʃ͡əz]
wugs [wʌgz]
heafs [hifs̲]

In Berko's study, children were able to apply the appropriate plural [əz], [z], or [s] to words that they had never seen or heard before. This suggested that they had learned the rule that the plural morpheme –s depends on the sound that comes before it: It becomes [əz] before sibilants; [z] before other voiced sounds; and [s] before other voiceless sounds.

12.4.2 Natural Order of Morpheme Acquisition

An important contribution from morphology in L1 acquisition is the observation that there is a natural order of acquisition for morphemes. For instance, you may have

heard a child say "Me eat*ing*" before using "I <u>am</u> eating." Research has shown that the
–*ing* morpheme is acquired before the auxiliary *to be*. The first pioneering work on this
comes from a longitudinal study of three children learning L1 English by Roger Brown
(1973). Among these children, there was a consistent order of acquisition for 14 grammatical morphemes (i.e., bound morphemes and functional categories like auxiliaries
and determiners). This order can be seen in Table 12.9. Many studies after Brown's work
have found similar support.

TABLE 12.9 Order of Acquisition of 14 Grammatical Morphemes

Grammatical morpheme	Example utterance
1. present progressive –ing	Me play<u>ing</u>.
2. in	<u>In</u> bed.
3. on	<u>On</u> table.
4. plural –s	Have toy<u>s</u>. Get carrot<u>s</u>.
5. past irregular	He <u>came</u> here. You <u>went</u>.
6. possessive –'s	Baby<u>'s</u> toy.
7. uncontractible copula	I <u>am</u> happy.
8. articles	I have <u>the</u> ball. I see <u>a</u> dog.
9. past regular –ed	She climb<u>ed</u>.
10. third-person regular –s	Grandma read<u>s</u>.
11. third-person irregular	Daddy <u>has</u> the ball. He <u>does</u>.
12. uncontractible auxiliary	Baby <u>is</u> playing.
13. contractible copula	I<u>'m</u> happy.
14. contractible auxiliary	The baby<u>'s</u> eating.

Strangely enough, the frequency with which adults use bound morphemes and functional categories does not quite match the developmental sequence shown by children.
So if children do not acquire these morphemes according to how often they hear them,
what can explain the order? A few examples and possible explanations are seen in Table
12.10. From these examples, it appears that children acquire morphemes which are
more noticeable, consistent, and/or meaningful before morphemes that are less noticeable, more irregular, and/or carry little meaning.

TABLE 12.10 Examples and Possible Explanations of a Natural Order of Morpheme Acquisition

Example	Possible explanation
–ing > the	• Morphemes in word-final position may be noticed and remembered more often.
–ing > –ed	• Morphemes that form a syllable (swi.m–ing) may be learnt faster than those that do not (a–chiev<u>ed</u>). • Morphemes that always sound the same (swimm<u>ing</u>, drink<u>ing</u>, read-<u>ing</u>) may be learnt faster than those with more than one sound variation (chas<u>ed</u> = [–t], achiev<u>ed</u> = [–d] ; scold<u>ed</u> = [–əd]).
–s > –ed	• Morphemes that have more regular forms (swim<u>s</u>, drink<u>s</u>, read<u>s</u>) may be learnt faster than those with more irregular forms (swam, drank, read).
plural –s > third person singular –s	• Morphemes that have more expressive meanings (the –s in book<u>s</u> creates more than one book) may be learnt faster than those that do not (the –s in "Mary read<u>s</u> a book" does not much affect meaning).

12.4.3   Derivation and Compounding

In addition to grammatical morphemes, children also learn about word formation processes such as derivation and compounding. As we discussed in Chapter 4 Morphology, **derivational morphemes** are meaningful units that are added to a word to make a new word that has either changed categories (e.g., from a verb to a noun) or meaning. For instance, adding *–er* to the end of the verb *give* creates the noun *giver* and adding *re–* to the beginning of the verb *do* creates a verb of a different meaning *redo*. Some of the first derivational morphemes that children learn are *–er*, *–ie* or *–y*, *–ing*, and *–ness* as in the words *sing<u>er</u>, dogg<u>ie</u>, pupp<u>y</u>, runn<u>ing</u>,* and *happ<u>iness</u>*.

As children unconsciously learn derivational rules, they may overgeneralize these rules in incorrect contexts. For example, children who have learned that some verbs can be derived from nouns (e.g., the invention of the microwave gives us the verb *to microwave*) may say things like *Mommy broomed it up* instead of *Mommy swept it up* and *Daddy giggled me* instead of *Daddy made me giggle*.

Like derivational rules, children learn about **compounding**, the process of combining two or more words to create a new word. Examples of compound words that children hear and learn include *baseball, football, peppermint, butterflies,* and *playthings*. Once again, though, we may hear amusing overgeneralizations as in *garden-man* (gardener), *sick-woman* (nurse), *doggy-doctor* (veterinarian), and *glass-eyes* (glasses).

PAUSE AND REFLECT 12.7

Can you think of some more examples of derivational and compounding overgeneralizations that we may expect from a child learning English?

12.5   Syntactic Development

During vocabulary and morphology development, children also begin to learn about how words can come together to create multiple-word phrases. In this section we look at some of the milestones related to the development of L1 phrase and sentence structure. We should note that the linguistic domains that we have discussed so far do not occur one-after-the-other, but rather they overlap. In fact, phonology and morphology can take years to master. So in some way, we are actually taking a step back in time from where we left off in the previous section since the first stage we discuss below begins anywhere from 12 to 18 months of age.

12.5.1   The One-word Stage

When you think about it, we see the development of L1 syntax when children use a single word in cases where adults would say several words. We call this the **one-word stage**. These single words are called **holophrases**. For example, at around 12 to 18 months, a child may say, *juice* to make a request for more juice to be served. Perhaps this is not surprising because they do not yet know the syntax to construct the full sentence *I want juice* let alone *Can I have some juice?*

Other holophrase examples include: *Daddy* for *I want daddy*; *Up* for *Pick me up*; and *Gone* for *The cereal is gone*. Research has shown, however, that children do not choose which word to be the holophrase randomly. The word is the most meaningful word in the adult equivalent.

12.5.2   The Two-word Stage

A few months after speaking in one-word utterances, by around 24 months of age, children enter a **two-word stage**. Some of the first two-word utterances may in fact be two holophrases from the one-word stage such as *juice gone*. Soon after this, though, they will begin to create other two-word utterances that are syntactically ordered correctly, meaningful, and context-appropriate.

Examples of utterances in the two-word stage can be seen in Table 12.11. The table also shows that we can characterize the examples by several **relational meanings**. Relational meaning refers to the semantic relationship between the referents of the two words in question. Roger Brown (1973) showed that children use eight different relational meanings in the two-word stage.

TABLE 12.11 Examples of Two-word Utterances

Child utterance	Intended meaning	Relational meaning
Daddy shirt	Daddy is putting on a shirt.	agent + action
bounce ball	I bounced the ball.	action + theme
doggy water	The doggy has water.	agent + theme
Mommy bed	Mommy is on the bed.	agent + location

TABLE 12.11 (*cont.*)

Child utterance	Intended meaning	Relational meaning
sweater chair	The sweater is on the chair.	entity + location
Billy sock	Billy's sock.	possessor + possession
kitty grey	The kitty is grey.	entity + attribute
this telephone	This telephone.	demonstrative + entity

12.5.3   The Telegraphic Stage

You may have been expecting a three-word stage to come next. However, a few months after children have been combining two words, they begin putting together three, four, or more words. They now begin to show signs that they are acquiring phrase structure. In other words, they start to correctly put more than two words together in a way that is syntactically correct. For example, they know that in *Daddy like Mommy, Daddy* is the subject whereas in *Mommy like Daddy, Mommy* is the subject.

In this **telegraphic stage**, the speech of children sounds telegraphic because of its choppiness. We can usually expect a lack of bound morphemes and non-lexical categories such as determiners and auxiliaries. Also, the structure of the utterances in the telegraphic stage seems to progress from imperatives, declarative statements, to later include negations and questions. Once children enter the telegraphic stage, language development greatly speeds up.

What words make up these telegraphic utterances? Research has shown that children use nouns, verbs, and adjectives before they use grammatical morphemes. Recall that grammatical morphemes are words or word endings that mark grammatical relations. These include articles, prepositions, auxiliaries, and noun and verb endings like the plural –*s* and the third person –*s*. More than likely, grammatical morphemes are produced later than nouns, verbs, and adjectives because they are not essential to meaning. However, recent research has shown that young children may use these functional morphemes to infer the category of a word. For example, a word preceded by *the* is likely a noun.

As shown in Table 12.12, it has taken a child about two-and-a-half years to get to this point.

TABLE 12.12 Main Stages of L1 Syntactic Development

Stage	Age in years	Example	Description
one-word	1–1½	Truck! (for asking that a toy truck be given to him/her).	Children speak in single-word, holographic utterances with no structure.
two-word	1½–2	Mommy busy.	Children begin to put two words together.
tele-graphic	2–2½	He good boy. Sissy eat cracker.	Children show signs of acquiring word order even though inflection and functional words may be missing.

EYES ON WORLD LANGUAGES: MORPHOLOGICAL DEVELOPMENT

Some languages such as Catalan, German, Italian, Spanish, and Swahili have rich **inflectional morphology**. For example, in these languages, verbs must be inflected for number and person to agree with the subject. So whereas English may conjugate *walk* the same for *I*, *they*, *we*, and *you*, these other languages would use a different verb form for each. While this may seem complicated, research shows that children learning these languages as an L1 actually develop this inflectional morphology very early.

Languages like German, Hungarian, Russian, and Turkish also have **case morphology**. In these languages, nouns are marked with morphemes depending on their grammatical function. For example, if a noun acts as a direct object, it will be marked differently than if it is an indirect object. In Hungarian, this is marked with the morphemes *–et* and *–nak*, respectively:

A	fiú	egy	könyv<u>et</u>		adott	a	lany<u>nak</u>.
the	*boy*	*a*	*book(direct object)*		*gave*	*the*	*girl(indirect object)*
"The boy gave a book to the girl."							

Like languages with complex inflectional morphology, those with extensive case systems may look hard for L1 learners but are acquired easily and early. What seems to be most important is not that Hungarian has 18 different distinctions among roles of nouns, but rather that it has regular patterns rather than irregular exceptions. Predictable patterns in morphology are not complicated for L1 learners to acquire.

In sum, research suggests that for L1 learners of rich inflectional and case morphology, word formation is a larger component of L1 acquisition. Other languages such as English and French may be more extensive in the area of phonology or syntax.

12.5.4 Advanced Development

By this time, children have a substantial amount of language competence in place. In the months following the telegraphic stage – starting from two-and-a-half to three years of age – children showcase their ability to produce and understand complex structures such as negation, questions, passive constructions, and pronominals and reflexives.

In English, making a sentence negative does not consist of simply adding the words *no* or *not*. Look at sentences (1)–(3) and think of the complexity of the use and placement of negation for children.

(1) Grandpa does not have milk.
(2) Grandpa doesn't have milk.
(3) Grandpa has no milk.

Children start forming negation by adding *no* to the beginning, and sometimes to the end, of sentences. Generally, these sentences do not include the subject, as seen in (4).

(4) No have milk.

Following this, they begin placing negation closer to where it should be placed. Negation may now be marked inside the sentence correctly but the sentence still remains syntactically incorrect as in (5).

(5) Grandpa not have milk.

Finally, once children have acquired auxiliaries such as *do, can, should*, among others, they begin forming negation as adults would shown in (6).

(6) Grandpa does not have milk.

Examples from these three stages of negation development can be seen in Table 12.13.

TABLE 12.13 Main Stages of L1 Syntactic Development

Stage	Example
Sentence-external negation	*No have towel. *Wear hat no. *No the table clean.
Sentence-internal negation without auxiliaries	*I no get treat. *See no cat. *Shirt no clean.
Sentence-internal negation with auxiliaries	*I didn't ate it. Billy won't play. Kitty has no food.

Like negation, to form a question, an auxiliary must be used. But before auxiliaries are acquired, children have no other option than to rely on rising intonation, a typical characteristic of questions in English, as in (7)–(9).

(7) Jack play ball?
(8) I good boy?
(9) Daddy happy?

Interestingly, even though children have not yet acquired auxiliaries, research has shown that they are able to apply movement operations with *wh*-phrases (*who, what, when, where, why*, and *how*). As we saw in Chapter 5 Syntax, in English, auxiliaries and *wh*-phrases move to the complementizer phrase at the beginning of the sentence. So although a *wh*-phrase as in (10) is generated at the end of the sentence, children actually never say it that way. Rather, when they ask questions, we see that they have acquired *wh*-movement as in (11).

(10) Sally doing what?
(11) What Sally doing ~~what~~?

We are not sure, though, if children already know how to preform move operations before learning *wh*-words (i.e., it forms part of their UG) or whether the acquisition of the move operation comes with learning the elements that undergo movement. Read 'Delving Deeper' in Chapter 12's resources to learn more about syntactic parameters on the website to accompany this book at www.cambridge.org/introducing-linguistics

The passive construction is another advanced structure children acquire, although not until around three-and-a-half years of age. Compare the sentences in (12) and (13).

(12)   The French built the house.

(13)   The house was built by the French.

Sentences in the passive voice like (13) are less common in English than sentences in the active voice like (12). Many researchers argue that because the active voice is more common, children come to expect that the first noun is often the subject of the sentence. In fact, research shows that the comprehension of the passive voice remains quite difficult for children throughout grade school. Some studies show that five-year-old children only comprehend the passive construction a third of the time. By seven years of age, they still may only correctly understand the passive two-thirds of the time.

12.6   Communicative Development

Beyond the phrase and sentence level, we find discourse and communication. Now that we have learned about the development of grammatical areas of an L1, we will discuss how children develop the communicative functions of their L1.

12.6.1   Conversational Skill Development

The conversational skills of children are different from those of adults. In many ways, children's conversations are seen as less successful than adults' and some researchers have even claimed that children's conversations are not all that communicative. In fact, Piaget's (1926) theory of **childhood egocentrism** argues that although children engage in a conversation, what they actually say has little to do with the previous statement spoken by their conversation partner. These non-relevant statements have been referred to as **collective monologues**. Piaget argued that these monologues may form part of children's conversational development during pre-school years because they find it difficult, if not impossible, to place themselves in the point of view of their listeners.

PAUSE AND REFLECT 12.8

Have you ever noticed that children seem to talk to themselves often? Why do you think they do this?

We all talk to ourselves, perhaps more so when doing difficult tasks or when others are not around. Researchers have consistently shown that younger children are more likely to talk to themselves (and for different reasons) than older children or adults. Their use of **private speech** is their way of practicing language. Believe it or not, some research has even shown that children produce longer and more complex private speech than the speech they use with adults. Evidence of children engaging in private speech does not mean that they need to practice or work hard at language. On the contrary, we call this practice **language play**, a normal part of L1 conversational skill development in which children use activities such as rhyming and making puns to manipulate and test-out language.

To briefly sum up, let's take a moment to list some of the milestones of L1 acquisition during the first four years (Hoff, 2014, p. 6). The ages below are approximate.

Phonological

- During the first months, babies play with their vocal abilities and coo. This is followed by babbling.
- Nearing two years old, babies have reorganized and consolidated phonological representations.
- Around three years old, their phonetic inventory is likely complete but their phonological awareness continues to grow.

Lexical

- Babies are able to recognize their own name months before saying their first word.
- By 18 months, a baby can produce around 50 words and enters a word spurt stage.
- Between two to three years old, they know around 500 words.
- From three years on, their knowledge of derivational morphology helps increase vocabulary.

Grammatical

- From around 18–24 months old, babies enter a two-word stage.
- Shortly after this, they begin increasing length of word combinations.
- They learn to add grammatical morphemes, form negative sentences, and form questions from two to three years of age.
- Complex utterances with multiple clauses will continue to develop.

Communicative

- In the months leading up to their first birthday, babies show intentional communication.
- From 12–24 months, their range of distinguishable communicative purposes grows.
- From two to three years of age, their conversational initiative and responsiveness grow.
- Narrative skills will continue to develop.

If you read 'Delving Deeper' in Chapter 12's resources on the website to accompany this book at www.cambridge.org/introducing-linguistics, you can read about the development of higher-level knowledge of making requests, narrative, sociolinguistic, pragmatic, and politeness language skills. You can also read about developing different linguistic registers (e.g., formal vs. informal) and what we have learned about it through observing the inner-speech produced by children (e.g., talking aloud to oneself when playing).

12.7   Factors Affecting First Language Acquisition

So far, we have studied how sounds, words, structure, and communication develop in an L1. But we know that not all infants develop language in the same way. Let's take a look at some of the factors – both internal and external to the learner – that contribute to and affect L1 acquisition.

12.7.1   External Factors
Input and Exposure

It may go without saying that infants have to be exposed to language in order to acquire it. But how much language exposure and input is needed? While we cannot measure the exact amount required, it is obvious that humans must be getting enough input since they end up acquiring an L1. Even so, some research suggests that children who are exposed to larger amounts of input from birth come to know nearly twice as many words by 30 months compared to children exposed to smaller amounts of input.

Rather than studying the amount of exposure, researchers have focused on the nature of the input that leads to L1 acquisition. This line of inquiry has asked questions such as what are some of the characteristics of L1 input that shape language acquisition? When adults speak to infants, they may unconsciously make adjustments in their speech, using what some have called **child-directed speech** or caregiver speech. This simplified way of speaking many times resembles the child's speech level. Caregiver speech can adjust sounds, words, structures, and even conversational patterns (see Table 12.14).

TABLE 12.14 Examples of Child-directed Speech

Domain	Example	Description
Phonological	See ... the ... kiiiiiitty?	Use of higher pitch, exaggerated pitch changes, elongated vowels, and long pauses between phonemes.
Lexical	horsey, dolly, potty	Use of diminutive for horse, doll, and toilet.
	da-da, moo-moo, choo-choo	Use of duplication for dad, cow, and train.
Grammatical	You want train?	Phrases and sentences sometimes lack functional words.
	Beddy-bye	Simplification of a sentence to a holophrase.
Communicative	You like that candy, don't you?	Conversations with children are mostly about the present instead of the past or future.
	Are you wearing your favorite shirt?	Topics that may interest children more include talking about members of the family, food, animals, parts of the body, and clothing.

PAUSE AND REFLECT 12.9

Do you think that if babies did not hear simplified language such as in *baby like his din-din?* instead of "Did you enjoy dinner?" the infant would still easily learn his/her L1? Why or why not?

LINGUISTICS TIDBITS: CHILD-DIRECTED SPEECH ACROSS CULTURES

Adults interact with and speak to babies in different ways across cultures. For example, in the Kaluli tribe of Papua New Guinea, adults speak to children the same way they speak to other adults and in some Samoan tribes, adults do not speak to children at all until they reach a certain age. In both cases, the lack of child-directed speech does not hurt L1 acquisition. This may be because they make up for it in societal ways like involving children in daily activities.

Feedback and Recasts

Feedback from adults about correct and incorrect language use may have some, but usually very little, effect on L1 acquisition. Feedback typically involves the modification of language as a basis for improvement and development. However, correcting children's language errors may not be as effective as adults think. Take a look at the following conversation from the work of David McNeill in the mid-1960s between the child and his mother.

CHILD: Want other one shoe, Mommy.
MOTHER: You mean, you want *the other shoe*
CHILD: Yes, I want other one shoe, please.
MOTHER: Can you say "the other shoe?"
CHILD: Other … one … shoe

MOTHER: No, say *the other*
CHILD: The other
MOTHER: *Shoe*
CHILD: Shoe
MOTHER: The other … shoe
CHILD: The other … shoe. Now you give me the other one shoe?

Examples such as the above conversation suggest that children may not realize what they are doing wrong and are unable to provide the correct form even when having it pointed out to them. Because adults are typically more in tune with the meaning of what children say rather than with the grammaticality of their speech, corrective feedback like the above does not dominate conversation exchanges between adults and children. In fact, adults are probably quite forgiving of speech errors in children because they expect them to make language errors and may even find them cute and amusing.

Adults may also provide indirect feedback through **recasts** in which they repeat and adjust the form and/or content of a child's incorrect utterances. While adults may feel as though recasts help children's language development, research actually shows that they may have little effect. For instance, if a child says *I hungry* and an adult provides a recast by saying *yes, you* are *hungry*, there has really been no correction of the missing first-person *am*. But if the child says *she playing*, and the adult responds *yes, she* is *playing*, an accurate correction has been made. This could be why studies have shown that children exposed to more recasts seem to learn just as fast as children who receive fewer recasts. We will return to discuss recasts in Chapter 13 Second Language Acquisition where they seem to be more effective when given to an adult.

12.7.2 Internal and Biological Factors

Innate Knowledge

The idea that infants are born with the innate and unique ability for language acquisition is referred to as the **innateness hypothesis**. This idea is primarily based on **Universal Grammar (UG)**, a theory in language acquisition which argues that there is a set of inborn principles that are universal to all languages. This innate template for language can be understood as a blueprint for language acquisition which helps children to construct an L1 grammar.

According to these theories, all languages conform to **principles** (i.e., rules) of UG. For instance, in Chapter 5 Syntax, we noted that all phrases contain a head and may contain a complement but they do not occur in the same order across languages. UG allows for **parameters** to be set which provide options permitted by the language being learned. So children do not have to acquire the fact that phrases contain heads and complements, but rather they must learn from the language around them whether their language is head-first or head-last. Table 12.15 provides some examples in which children either set their parameters to match one of the two options provided in UG.

TABLE 12.15 Parameter Setting for the Head-Complement Principle

Parameter setting	Example
Order = Head + complement	
English	read the book
Swedish	köpt en bok bought the book "bought the book"
Order = Complement + head	
Japanese	ringo-o tabe-ru apple-ACC eat-NONPAST "eat an apple"
Korean	ku chayk ilke that book read "read that book"

PAUSE AND REFLECT 12.10

As you may have read in 'Delving Deeper' in the resources of Chapter 5 Syntax on the book's accompanying website (www.cambridge.org/introducing-linguistics), in some languages the main verb moves out of the verb phrase into T and from there may move to C in questions. We refer to this as the Verb Movement parameter. Consider the sentences below. What do you think is the setting of this parameter for each language? What evidence do you think children find for the setting of this parameter in question formation? Explain.

English:	*See$_i$ you the book?			
Dutch:	Ziet$_i$	u	het	boek?
	see	you	the	book
	"Do you see the book?"			
French:	Vois$_i$-tu		le	livre?
	see-you		the	book
	"Do you see the book?"			

Age of Exposure to Language

Have you ever stopped to wonder what would have happened if you had not been exposed to language from birth? Do you think you would have eventually learned your L1? Or do you think this would have depended on just how late your exposure was? Research supports the idea that there is a sensitive period during which time an L1 must be learned. The **critical period hypothesis** argues that the first years of infants' lives are a vital time during which they must acquire their L1. If this exposure to input does not occur during this time, they will not be able to achieve complete command of the L1, no matter how much training they receive. The linguistic domains that seem to be most sensitive to this are morphology and syntax.

The critical period hypothesis was first proposed by neurosurgeons Wilder Penfield and Lamar Roberts in their book *Speech and brain mechanisms* (1959). Penfield significantly expanded brain surgery methods and techniques. The critical period hypothesis gained linguists' attention with Eric Lenneberg's book *Biological foundations of language* (1967). Lenneberg argued that there are age constraints on the time during which an L1 can be acquired. His theories suggest that L1 acquisition relies on the brain's ability to change, also known as **neuroplasticity**, and that after the critical period it becomes rather unresponsive to language acquisition.

What type of evidence do we have for the critical period hypothesis given that most infants receive language input from birth? Even infants born deaf have exposure to language during the critical period since they learn sign language and read lips. In fact, it would be unethical to withhold language from an infant by isolating him/her completely. Some researchers have called this *the forbidden experiment* because of the immoral and extreme deprivation of ordinary human contact it would require. However, there are a few cases – some quite sad – which seem to support the critical period hypothesis for L1 acquisition.

Although extremely rare, there are some cases of **feral children** who have lived isolated from human contact from a very young age. These children usually have very little to no experience with human interaction, care, behavior, or language. One well-documented case is that of Victor, who appeared around 1800 in Aveyron, France after apparently living in the woods for most of his life.

When he was found, Victor was about 12 years old, he ran mostly on all fours, and ate roots, nuts, and raw vegetables. He was only able to make sounds but nothing that resembled human language. A physician, Jean-Marc Itard, took the child in and was eventually able to teach him some socially appropriate behaviors. In terms of language, Victor was never able to learn more than a handful of words. Some recent research suggests however, that in addition to missing the critical period, Victor may have been autistic (Wolff, 2004). Having both an intellectual disability and not being exposed to language when it was most critical made L1 acquisition nearly impossible for Victor.

PAUSE AND REFLECT 12.11

Take a moment to look for other cases of feral children on the Internet. You may be surprised how many cases have been documented, even in the twenty-first century.

Genie is perhaps the most widely referenced case of support for the critical period for L1 acquisition. Child protective services in California in 1970 took into their custody a 13-year-old girl who had been subjected to a life of physical and mental abuse and lack of language input. When she was rescued, her case gained the attention of linguists. Genie was immediately admitted to a hospital where her language training first began. In their ground-breaking study, linguist Susan Curtiss – who wrote her doctoral dissertation on Genie – and colleagues (1974) chillingly report:

> When we first encountered [Genie], she was 13 years and 7 months old—a painfully thin child who appeared six to seven years old. When hospitalized for malnutrition, Genie could not stand erect or chew food; she was not toilet trained; and she did not speak, cry, or produce any vocal sounds (p. 529).

The fact that Genie was completely isolated from language and social interaction had unfortunate and detrimental effects on her ability to learn language. Even so, after just months of language training, she was successful at learning an extensive amount of vocabulary. In fact, after about four years of training, Genie had learned enough vocabulary knowledge to resemble that of a four- or five-year-old. She had also learned to use and understand nonverbal communication skills (e.g., pointing, nodding or shaking one's head). However, even after years of training, her social behaviors remained atypical (e.g., ignoring speech addressed to her), perhaps due to lack of early socialization experiences in life.

Unlike vocabulary and meaning, for Genie, morphology and syntax development was extremely difficult in both production and comprehension. By the end of the language training, when she spoke, her utterances were mostly telegraphic and contained very few grammatical morphemes. In comprehension, Genie was unable to understand passive constructions (*the ball is bounced by John*) and she even had difficulties understanding how time can be marked by morphemes (*Jane plays* vs. *Jane played*).

Returning to the neuroplasticity of the brain, some of Curtiss' (1977) research suggested that once Genie began training, language may have been a right-hemisphere activity. During the critical period, brain functions and cognitive processes find *their hemisphere home* and then tend to be more dominant in that hemisphere. For instance, during typical L1 acquisition, language seems to be more dominant in the left hemisphere than in the right.

This **lateralization** of brain function for language was not the same for Genie because she had been exposed to language too late to be acquired as a primarily left-hemisphere function. After the critical period, Genie appeared to be acquiring language using the right hemisphere which is notoriously known for being poorer at language than the left hemisphere. Research on patients who have had to relearn language after having a hemispherectomy, a procedure in which one of the two hemispheres of the brain is surgically removed or disabled, confirms that learning a language without the left hemisphere results in similar grammatical limitations to Genie's.

PAUSE AND REFLECT 12.12

Biologists have found that zebra finches raised in complete isolation will not sing the same song as zebra finches living in the wild. In fact, those that have been completely isolated and cut off from other finches are only able to acquire and sing very simple songs. Interestingly when two of these isolated finches were paired and had offspring of their own, not only did this next generation imitate its parents' simple song, but it also systematically improved the song. By the fourth or fifth generation, the song was very similar to and as complex as that of finches brought up in the wild. Do you think that the same would happen for humans?

In the 1980s, the case of Chelsea was found to support the critical period hypothesis. Chelsea was misdiagnosed as mentally disabled as an infant and was not properly diagnosed as deaf until decades later. By the time she was fitted with hearing aids at age 31 and was finally able to hear language for the first time, the critical period had long since passed. Nonetheless, after years of intense language therapy, Chelsea was able to learn about 2,000 vocabulary words but like Genie, her grammatical skills were significantly impaired. The development of word order for Chelsea was most resistant to training, making it almost impossible to learn. Many of her sentences came out as *The man is car the going* and *Wearing hat the girl*.

Cases such as Victor, Genie, and Chelsea suggest that early exposure to an L1 is vital to language acquisition. They also provide support for a critical period, a biological window of time during which the brain is prepared to learn language. After this period, L1 acquisition is painstakingly difficult, no matter how much or intense the language training.

12.8 Atypical Language Development

We began the chapter by looking at how an L1 develops for the majority of individuals. We then discussed a few special cases in which lack of exposure to an L1 resulted in detrimental effects on language acquisition. Let us now discuss how L1 acquisition happens in the context of conditions such as deafness, blindness, cognitive disabilities, autism spectrum disorders, and developmental language disorders.

12.8.1 Deafness

Babies who are born deaf and acquire sign language from birth have similar L1 developmental trends as hearing babies. For instance, deaf babies also coo and babble at around the same time as hearing infants. In fact, they may babble with their hands. But instead of their *first word*, they have their *first sign*. You may be surprised to know that their first sign usually comes before hearing babies' first word. This is even found among hearing babies who are learning both sign and spoken language. This may be due to the fact that control of the hands may develop before control of the oral and laryngeal muscles. Deaf babies also go through a holophrastic stage where they use one sign for an entire sentence (e.g., *Juice!* instead of *Give me some juice*) and a telegraphic stage in which they produce ungrammatical signs such as missing functional elements (e.g., **Daddy go out* instead of *Daddy is going out*).

However, only about 10 percent of deaf children are raised in deaf households where they are exposed to sign language. For the other 90 percent who are raised in hearing households, it is common that they receive training in **oralist** and **total communication methods**. In the oralist method, deaf children are intensively trained to produce speech and read lips. The total communication approach draws on the oralist method but adds the combination of some signs and gestures. These training procedures significantly improve oral language among deaf infants – without which such oral abilities would not be acquirable. However, we find further support for a critical period for L1 acquisition when comparing children who learned sign from infancy to that of children who were first exposed to sign later in childhood or in adulthood. Studies have shown that children who have learned L1 sign from infancy outperform those who have learned L1 sign later (e.g., those who began training at age four) on grammar abilities and overall proficiency.

EYES ON WORLD LANGUAGES: THE MULTITUDE OF SIGN LANGUAGES

Just like spoken languages, there are many sign languages used throughout the world. In fact, it is estimated that there are more than 300 sign languages, with more appearing each year as a result of creolization. Some linguists argue that there are six major families of sign languages: French Sign, British Sign, Arab Sign, Japanese Sign, German Sign, and Swedish Sign. The largest family is French Sign which includes American Sign Language, Quebec Sign Language, and over 50 others.

Other sign languages are considered to be language isolates because they have no demonstrable genealogical relationship with other languages. For instance, in 1978 when the Nicaraguan government opened its first public school for the deaf, the children who initially went to school there did not share a common sign language. However, after daily contact, a new sign language, Nicaraguan Sign Language (NSL) developed. Today, NSL has evolved to be a full language and has provided an interesting opportunity to study *the birth of a new language*.

12.8.2   Blindness

For the most part, the development of an L1 is remarkably unaffected by blindness. However, there are a few interesting differences between blind and sighted children that deserve discussing. In fact, we see subtle differences, mostly in sound and vocabulary development. When it comes to phonology, blind children make more errors pronouncing sounds that have highly visible articulation like bilabials (e.g., /b/, /m/) and dentals (e.g., /f/, /v/) compared to sighted children. This would suggest that there is a correlation between lip configuration and sound development.

In terms of vocabulary, sighted children have more words for objects that can be seen but not touched (e.g., moon, red). However, blind children may have more words to describe objects associated with sound change (e.g., piano, bird). Blind children rarely overgeneralize the meaning of words, suggesting that visual information plays a role in establishing categories (e.g., *animals*) and extending those categories to include new objects.

12.8.3   Intellectual Disabilities

L1 development seems to be fairly independent from other types of cognitive development. However, studies have shown that while a child who has deficiencies in general cognitive abilities may have highly developed language, another child with normal cognitive abilities may have grammatical difficulties and say things like *I eat three cracker*.

In other cases, an individual is considered to have an **intellectual disability** if their general IQ is two or more standard deviations below the mean for the population. Infants who are born with an intellectual disability are likely to have limitations in their ability to function without assistance in their daily lives. These types of intellectual disabilities are commonly associated with significant impairment to language development. We will look at a few of these below.

Down Syndrome

Occurring in approximately one in 1,000 newborns, **Down syndrome** is a chromosomal abnormality that causes moderate to severe mental retardation and a delay of language development. These effects span all domains of L1 acquisition as can be seen in Table 12.16.

TABLE 12.16 Effects of Down Syndrome on L1 Development

Domain	Description
Phonological	Babbling is delayed by about 2 months.
	Articulatory processes such as consonant cluster simplification proceed throughout childhood and adulthood.
	Overall pronunciation may be difficult to understand.
Lexical	First word appears at around 24 months – a year after typically developing children.
	By age six, the productive vocabulary is similar in size to that of an average three-year-old.
	Communicative gestures may be produced to compensate for limited vocabulary.
Grammatical	Most affected domain of language.
	Delay in grammatical development such that it may take 12 years to accomplish what most children accomplish in 30 months.
	After adolescence, some research shows a plateau in syntactic development while other research shows a slow continuation.
Communicative and pragmatic	Strongest domain of language.
	At six months, children with Down syndrome vocalize and engage in more eye contact than typical children.
	Down syndrome affects secondary intersubjectivity, or the ability to engage with somebody about a third party.

Williams Syndrome

Williams syndrome is a rare neurodevelopmental disorder which causes mild to moderate intellectual disability in one in 7,500 to one in 20,000 births. Although individuals with Williams syndrome have below-average general intelligence and severely impaired visuospatial skills, they are quite strong with verbal abilities. Nonetheless, they develop their L1 much later than other children, with the first word not occurring until as late as 36 months.

As adolescents, individuals with Williams syndrome use emotional and descriptive speech that includes advanced and unusual vocabulary and strange idioms. Even so, a closer look at their language shows quite a few deficits. For instance, because lexical development precedes cognitive development in children with Williams syndrome, it is not uncommon that they learn a word before being able to point to the object that represents that word. Some problems in morphology and syntax have been reported for children with Williams syndrome even though they largely display language skills that are superior to their cognitive skills. However, L1 acquisition is delayed due to cognitive disabilities, making language development follow a different speed and trajectory than most children.

Individuals with Williams syndrome have:

- *strengths* in vocabulary and phonological skills;
- *expected abilities* in morphology and syntax that are in line with their overall intellectual abilities; and
- *weaknesses* in pragmatics and conversation.

Pragmatic and conversational skills are often affected among individuals with Williams syndrome, likely because these individuals also face social difficulties where interaction is involved. Like some individuals with Down syndrome, people with Williams syndrome and autism spectrum disorders (see 12.8.4) may be comfortable engaging in social interactions, although they may also be overly affectionate.

12.8.4 Autism Spectrum Disorders

Affecting about one in 166 children, **autism spectrum disorders** include a group of severe developmental disorders which typically include impaired social development, delayed language development, and a strong preference for routine and sameness. One of the most common characteristics related to language development among children with autism is that they appear to show impairment in visual attention skills, do not orient well to their own names, try to avoid social interaction, and rarely, if ever, use gestures or facial expressions in their communication.

In severe cases of autism, language development may be affected so much that an individual may appear to have poor or no language skills at all. They may have primarily **echolalic speech** that includes meaningless repetition of a word or several words previously spoken by another speaker. Highly functioning individuals with autism have fewer language impairments, although L1 development is still affected. For instance, while some may have articulation problems probably due to poor oral-motor skills, almost all individuals with autism may have difficulties with prosody and pitch, volume, and voice quality.

It is with communication, rather than linguistic competence, where we see the most obvious impairments to language for children with autism. They may show little interest in taking part in a conversation and when they do, they may confuse speaker roles within the discourse or make pronoun reversal errors (e.g., they might interpret or *say I see you* as *You see me*). Autism also may affect the ability to interpret indirect requests, to explain something beyond simple identification, or to describe ongoing events.

PAUSE AND REFLECT 12.13

Why do you think that it might be difficult for a non-autistic listener to have a successful conversation with an individual with autism?

12.8.5 Developmental Language Disorders

An impairment which is restricted to language and is not accompanied by another cognitive, social, or sensory condition is known as developmental language disorder (DLD) (previously known as Specific Language Impairment). This includes about one in 14 individuals, although in milder cases, language impairment may be hardly detectible to an untrained listener. Children are usually classified as having DLD if their language skills are below those of age-matched children but not because of other explanations such as autism or hearing loss. A developmental delay is the most obvious characteristic of children with DLD.

Some researchers estimate that children with DLD have productive language abilities about one year behind typical children and receptive language abilities about six months behind. Interestingly, some domains of language development are delayed even more so than others. For example, children with DLD may have more difficulties acquiring grammatical morphology than vocabulary.

There seems to be a genetic basis that shows that problems with L1 acquisition run in families. Neurobiological research using brain imaging has shown that children with DLD often do not have the typical larger areas in the left hemisphere that are normally responsible for language. Their brains also seem to respond differently to mismatched stimuli, suggesting that they have speech perception deficiencies.

12.9   Bilingual First Language Acquisition

Many but not all adults who speak two languages have grown up in bilingual households or communities. We commonly refer to this type of language acquisition as **simultaneous language acquisition**. Researchers believe that children know they are learning two L1s quite early. In fact, studies such as Genesee & Nicoladis (2007) have shown that bilingual children quickly develop awareness of which people in their environment know which language.

Most research on simultaneous language acquisition stems from cognitive science and because of this, we will return to discuss it in Chapter 14 Psycholinguistics. For now, let's look at a few important issues related to simultaneous language acquisition.

12.9.1   Cross-linguistic Interference

Often parents are concerned with whether or not speaking to their children in more than one language will imply cross-linguistic interference and be cognitively harmful or cause confusion given the complexities of learning two languages at the same time. They sometimes worry that learning two languages would be simply too difficult to add to their child's development and that it would trigger learning and cognitive handicaps when it came to the time for the child to begin school. As a matter of fact, up until the 1950s, experimental studies in cognitive psychology provided support for these worries: Research consistently found that bilingual children performed worse on verbal and mental ability tests.

However, after significant scrutiny from researchers, this account was discounted due to the fact that these studies had serious methodological flaws. As better measures were designed and employed, it became apparent that bilingual children actually *outperformed* their monolingual counterparts on a variety of tasks such as mental reasoning, metalinguistic awareness, and verbal and nonverbal intelligence tests.

12.9.2   Effects on Overall Language Development

As we mentioned, children who grow up speaking two languages realize that they are developing two different language systems. However, we often see interesting effects of bilingualism on the course and rate of overall language development. Related to the course of language development, research shows that learning two L1s from birth mirrors the developmental patterns found in monolinguals. Although it is not true that a bilingual is two monolingual speakers in one, we should note that being exposed early to two or more L1s allows for learners to have a similar course of development as those who learn only one L1.

Even with similar developmental trends, there are some notable differences between children who grow up learning two L1s and monolingual children when it comes to the rate of acquisition. Children learning two L1s will ultimately come to dominate each of the two languages (although one is always likely to be more dominant that the other). However, they may slightly lag behind monolingual children in vocabulary and grammatical development when measured in each language separately (Bialystok & Feng, 2011). Interestingly, when including vocabularies from both L1s in the measure, bilingual children's vocabulary knowledge resembles – and oftentimes is greater than – that of monolingual children. In the left graph of Figure 12.4, you can see what we might expect the number of words to be for monolingual and bilingual children at ages 22, 25, and 30 months. The graph on the right of Figure 12.4 adds together bilinguals' words from both languages.

Even beyond 30 months of age, bilinguals may show some lag in the rate of vocabulary learning well into the later school years. In fact, there have been differences in vocabulary size between bilinguals (in one language) and monolinguals (in that same language) for every age tested in previous research. It is probably because vocabulary learning does not have an end point. This smaller vocabulary size is probably not noticeable in everyday speech but when specifically measured, we find differences. The lag for bilingual children's grammatical development seems to disappear and catch up with monolinguals by around age ten.

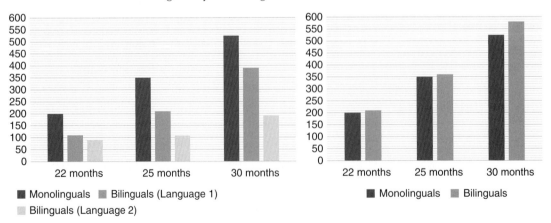

Figure 12.4 Typical number of words in monolingual and bilingual children's vocabulary

12.9.3   Effects on Cognition

Some researchers exploring psycholinguistic aspects of bilingual acquisition believe that bilinguals may have a cognitive advantage from having to consistently juggle two language systems. Because of this mental exercise, they have come to have remarkable attentional control that can be transferred across cognitive domains (linguistic and non-linguistic).

Scholars like Ellen Bialystok have argued that the cognitive advantages associated with bilingualism also have extended benefits that can delay cognitive decline that is associated with healthy aging. In other words, a lifetime of being a bilingual can help to safeguard the individual from cognitive decline that naturally accompanies the aging mind (Bialystok & Craik, 2015).

Work by Bialystok and colleagues (2004) has found that bilinguals were not only able to carry out attentional control more efficiently than monolinguals, but that they unconsciously used such abilities throughout their lives which in turn helped to offset age-related losses in cognitive processes. Although research in this area is still taking hold, we can confirm that there is no reliable evidence suggesting that children acquiring two languages at the same time suffer any cognitive deficits from potential cross-linguistic interferences.

Beyond these cognitive benefits, we must also note that bilingualism has shown benefits in analogical reasoning, mathematical abilities, syntactic complexity, and higher aptitude scores. We have every reason to believe that bilingualism – especially from birth – holds fascinating advantages which will continue to spark intriguing research.

PAUSE AND REFLECT 12.14

Did you or someone you know grow up in a bilingual household? If so, can you remember any language differences from monolingual children? If you don't know anyone, consider finding someone who has and asking them about it.

We will return to discuss cognitive advantages of bilingualism in Chapter 14 Psycholinguistics. For now, while we can't conclude that bilinguals are *smarter* than monolinguals, we can be sure of their superior abilities over monolinguals on a variety of linguistic and non-linguistic tasks.

12.10   Approaches to Studying First Language Acquisition

When researchers became interested in L1 acquisition, their first instinct was to turn to **behaviorism**. Behaviorism is a line of thought in psychology which focuses on an individual's behavior. In terms of L1 acquisition, it was once believed that language was acquired as a set of habits that were based on conditioning. Behaviorists believed that language was acquired due to positive reinforcement to correct productions and imitations.

As you read in Chapter 1 Introducing Linguistics, behaviorism quickly fell out of favor soon after Noam Chomsky sharply criticized B. F. Skinner's view that L1 acquisition was explainable by behaviorist theories. Since this **Chomskyan Revolution** – a period of dramatic shift of theories and methodologies in linguistics following the ground-breaking publication of Chomsky's book *Syntactic structures* (1957) – linguists have become more interested in the mental grammar that underlies language than what speakers do with language. Below, we will discuss some common approaches to studying L1 acquisition.

12.10.1   Generative Approaches

Most of the work that has been informed by Chomsky's theories are **nativist views**. These perspectives argue that L1 acquisition depends on innate knowledge of the properties of language. Similarly, **generative approaches** build on this idea and argue that UG principles – which include the universal properties of all languages – are inborn and that language experience triggers innate knowledge and sets language-specific parameters.

Generativists commonly believe that there is a mechanism that makes language acquisition possible. Chomsky has proposed that this **language acquisition device** starts functioning from birth. Generative approaches to L1 acquisition are interested in studying grammar as an underlying system of rules that allows speakers to generate an infinite combination of structures.

PAUSE AND REFLECT 12.15

The language acquisition device accounts for children's innate predisposition to effective language learning. What do you think is the strongest evidence that supports this claim?

12.10.2   Interactionist/Constructionist Approaches

An alternative to nativist and generative approaches are **interactionist views**. Rather than an innate ability, interactionists argue that language is a social phenomenon. Their views are centered on the importance of communicative and social interaction and place more emphasis on the nature of language-learning experiences.

Researchers who argue in favor of interactionist approaches feel that language emerges because of several things including:

- children's desire to communicate;
- their ability to understand speakers' intentions;
- their ability to learn patterns from language input; and
- their ability to extract information from language input.

Another term for interactionist views has been the position of **constructionism** which interprets language as a result of innate abilities and information provided by the environment.

Connectionist Approaches

One interactionist/constructionist approach to L1 acquisition is **connectionism**, also known as parallel distributed processing or artificial neural networks. This view takes into account both the biological and environmental effects and explains L1 acquisition as the learning of patterns among smaller elements of sound or meaning. According to connectionist views of L1 acquisition it is believed that repeated experience and exposure to language patterns will result in a mental abstraction (i.e., a stored representation of the pattern in question).

Neurologically speaking, connectionism explains that human cognition works through interconnected processing units (neurons) that operate at the same time within a network. Information that is processed, learned, and represented in the mind, is dynamic, connected, and distributed across the network.

Usage-based Approaches

Another prominent and more recent interactionist/constructionist approach to L1 acquisition is **usage-based theory** which is informed by both cognitive and construction-based approaches. The usage-based approach to L1 acquisition argues that L1s are acquired through experience. Instead of drawing on general cognition, usage-based approaches typically emphasize the importance of a small set of cognitive processes, such as categorization, analogy, and chunking to explain how language functions and is structured. Researchers studying L1 development from usage-based approaches argue that children are able to construct utterances based on formulas that ultimately are acquired, based on abilities to learn patterns and understand speakers' intended meanings.

SUMMARY

We began our discussion on L1 acquisition by looking at the development of phonology, vocabulary, morphology, syntax, and communicative skills. A common trend across these linguistic domains seems to be a natural order in which things are acquired. For instance, in phonology, children appear to learn certain sounds before others. As a result, they rely on articulatory processes such as substituting a sound they know (/t/) for another sound they have not yet acquired (/θ/) to say things like *ting* instead of *thing*.

We then identified some factors that affect L1 acquisition. For example, the amount and type of L1 input and the quality of feedback children receive will affect their L1 development *up to a point*. Beyond these external factors, we also looked at internal effects such as innate knowledge and age of acquisition. We noted that exposure to language before the critical period is absolutely essential and in unfortunate cases where language exposure is either minimal or completely lacking, L1 acquisition is extremely difficult. Following this, we turned to a discussion on atypical language development including cases of deafness, blindness, cognitive disabilities, autism spectrum disorders, and developmental language disorders. Although these obstacles cause language impairments, they do not hinder L1 acquisition completely.

Many children are exposed to two L1s from birth. Whereas parents and researchers alike once believed that this would be too cognitively demanding for children, current research revealed a cognitive advantage for bilingual children compared to monolingual children. In fact, the benefit of juggling two languages in one mind may extend to the elderly years to protect against aging effects and degenerative diseases such as Alzheimer's. As more research reveals cognitive benefits of bilingualism, we now realize the importance of encouraging a bilingual environment for children if the opportunity is available.

We concluded the chapter with a conversation on some approaches to studying L1 acquisition. While behavioral approaches dominated L1 acquisition until the Chomskyan revolution, some researchers came to believe that children acquire L1s using innate knowledge of universal properties of language. Others have argued that L1 acquisition is a social phenomenon that relies heavily on language experiences from communicative and social interaction. Most recently, researchers have linked biological and environmental effects through connectionist approaches. Although studies are still ongoing, we have come a long way in the journey of understanding how humans acquire an L1.

EXERCISES

12.1 State whether the following are true or false.

  i.   [p] is acquired before [l]
  ii. [θ] is acquired before [t͡ʃ]
  iii. [ŋ] is acquired before [ɹ]
  iv. [s] is acquired before [z]
  v.   [v] is acquired before [d]

12.2 Look at the data below produced by children ranging in age from two to three years old. What are the articulatory processes you see in the words?

  i.   snake   [nek]
  ii. spoon   [pun]
  iii. go   [do]
  iv. laugh   [læp]

v.   clay   [kej]
vi. broken   [bokən]
vii. twig   [tɪk]
viii.John   [dɑn]
ix. other   [ʌdə]
x.   lion   [jajən]

12.3 The following data show a change in adult pronunciation and a child's pronunciation. What articulatory adjustment(s) has the child made in the examples below?

i.   [læmp] → [jæm]
ii.   [dʌk] → [kʌk]
iii. [sup] → [zup]
iv.   [ɹɑk] → [wɑk]
v.   [lɑk] → [wɑk]
vi.   [d͡ʒ ʌmp] → [dzʌmp]
vii. [θɪŋ] → [tɪŋ]
viii. [bʌmp] → [bʌp]
ix.   [but] → [bu]
x.   [zibɹə] → [dibɹə]

12.4 Children acquire certain words before others. Typically the first categories of words learned are nouns, verbs, adjectives, and social words. Can you think of four or five words in each of these categories that a two-year-old would probably know?

12.5 If a child looks up at the night sky and sees a star but calls it a *light*, what is this an example of?

12.6 A caregiver is reading a story to a two-and-a-half year old whose family has a white horse. They come across a picture of a grey horse and the child points to it and says *donkey!* What is this an example of?

12.7 A three-year-old child has produced the following utterances. Look through the data and then answer the questions that follow.
(1) I going now.
(2) Mommy gave milk to the kitties.
(3) Mommy is a nice kitty-giver.
(4) The gooses want to play with the doggy.
(5) Does Daddy like the fishes?
(6) I leaving now.

i.   In each sentence, identify the grammatical morphemes. Are there any missing grammatical morphemes from the data? Why or why not?
ii.   Which word formation processes are used?
iii. What seems to be a consistent error with the plural –s?
iv.   What do you predict will happen next to the use of the past tense –ed?

12.8 Overgeneralization often occurs when children pluralize nouns. What do you think a child might say instead of the nouns below?

i.   geese
ii.   mice
iii. men
iv.   deer
v.   children
vi.   fish

12.9   A two-year-old child has produced the following utterances. Look through the data and then answer the questions that follow.

(1) Daddy home.
(2) Mommy leave.
(3) Sally funny.
(4) Give treat.
(5) Me hungry.

i.   At what stage of syntactic development do you think this child is?
ii.   What stage do you expect he was in prior to this current stage?
iii.   What should the anticipated next stage be?
iv.   Do you notice any semantic patterns or relations in the data?

12.10 A two-and-a-half-year-old child has produced the following utterances. Look through the data and then answer the questions that follow.

(1) I can't eat it.
(2) Can you give me?
(3) What you can give me?
(4) I like crackers.
(5) Daddy should be home.
(6) Where grandma is?
(7) I'm playing.
(8) Can we eat now?

i.   Do you think the child has acquired auxiliary verbs?
ii.   Does the data show that the child has acquired and/or is using the movement operation correctly?
iii.   Is use of the movement operation limited to certain types of questions? You may want to compare the *yes-no* and *wh*-questions.

12.11 How do conversational and narrative skills differ between a two- to three-year-old and a four- to five-year-old?

12.12 List and describe some of the external and internal factors that can affect L1 acquisition. Which one(s) do you think have the greatest impact on L1 acquisition?

12.13 Steven Pinker (1994) has suggested that hearing children who grow up in homes of deaf parents cannot acquire their L1 simply through TV, radio, or Internet. What does this suggest may be critical to L1 acquisition that we can take from these cases?

12.14 Discuss how the learning of two L1s is different from *learning just one*. What are some effects simultaneous L1 acquisition has on overall language development and cognition? How are monolingual children different from bilingual children?

12.15 Discuss some of the theoretical approaches to studying L1 acquisition. What do you see as strengths and weaknesses of each framework?

REFERENCES

Bates, E. (1976). *Language and context: The acquisition of pragmatics*. New York, NY: Academic Press.

Berko, J. (1958). The child's learning of English morphology. *Word, 14*, 150–177.

Bialystok, E., & Craik, F. (2015). Cognitive consequences of bilingualism: Executive control and cognitive reserve. In J. W. Schwieter (Ed.), *The Cambridge handbook of bilingual processing* (pp. 571–585). Cambridge: Cambridge University Press.

Bialystok, E., & Feng, X. (2011). Language proficiency and its implications for monolingual and bilingual children. In A. Durgunoglu & C. Goldenberg (Eds.), *Language and literacy development in bilingual settings* (pp. 121–138). New York, NY: Guilford.

Bialystok, E., Craik, F., Klein, R., & Viswanathan, M. (2004). Bilingualism, aging, and cognitive control: Evidence from the Simon task. *Psychology and Aging, 19*, 290–303.

Brown, R. (1973). *A first language: The early stages.* Cambridge, MA: Harvard University Press.

Chaika, E. (1989). *Language: The social mirror* (2nd Edition). Cambridge, MA: Newbury House.

Chomsky, N. (1957). *Syntactic structures.* The Hague: Mouton.

Curtiss, S. (1977). *Genie: A psycholinguistic study of the modern-day "wild child."* New York, NY: Academic Press.

Curtiss, S., Fromkin, V., Krashen, S., Rigler, D., & Rigler, M. (1974). The linguistic development of Genie. *Language, 50*(3), 528–554.

Genesee, F., & Nicoladis, E. (2007). Bilingual first language acquisition. In E. Hoff & M. Shatz (Eds.), *Blackwell handbook of language development* (pp. 324–344). Oxford: Blackwell.

Goldfield, B., & Reznick, J. (1990). Early lexical acquisition: Rates, content, and the vocabulary spurt. *Journal of Child Language, 17*, 171–184.

Gopnik, M., & Crago, M. (1991). Familial aggregation of a developmental language disorder. *Cognition, 39*, 1–50.

Harris, M., Barrett, M., Jones, D., & Brookes, S. (1988). Linguistic input and early word naming. *Journal of Child Language, 15*, 77–94.

Hoff, E. (2014). *Language development* (5th Edition). Belmont, CA: Cengage Learning.

Hoff, E., Core, C., Place, S., Rumiche, R., Señor, M., & Parra, M. (2012). Dual language exposure and early bilingual development. *Journal of Child Language, 35*, 1–14.

Lenneberg, E. (1967). *Biological foundations of language.* New York, NY: Wiley.

Locke, J., & Pearson, D. (1992). Vocal learning and the emergence of phonology capacity: A neuro-biological approach. In C. Ferguson, L. Menn, & S. Stoel-Gammon (Eds.), *Phonological development* (pp. 91–129). Timonium, MD: York Press.

Penfield, W., & Roberts, L. (1959). *Speech and brain mechanisms.* Princeton, NJ: Princeton University Press.

Piaget, J. (1926). *The language and thought of the child.* London: Routledge.

Pinker, S. (1994). *The language instinct: The new science of language and mind.* New York, NY: Penguin.

Stark, R. (1986). Pre-speech segmental feature development. In P. Fletcher & M. Garman (Eds.), *Language acquisition* (2nd Edition, pp. 149–173). Cambridge: Cambridge University Press.

Tardif, T., Fletcher, P., Liang, W., Zhang, Z., Kaciroti, N., & Marchman, V. (2008). Baby's first 10 words. *Developmental Psychology, 44*(4), 929–938.

Wolff, S. (2004). The history of autism. *European Child & Adolescent Psychiatry, 13*, 201–208.

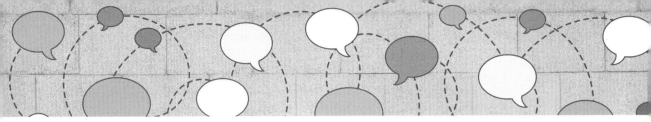

13 Second Language Acquisition

John W. Schwieter

OVERVIEW

In this chapter, you will develop an understanding of the study of second language (L2) acquisition (SLA). Our objectives are to:

- compare and contrast how first languages (L1s) and L2s are acquired;
- explore how sounds, words, and structure develop in an L2;
- learn about internal and external factors that affect SLA;
- gain knowledge about teaching pedagogies that help L2 learning; and
- look at some theoretical approaches to studying SLA.

13.1 What Is Second Language Acquisition?

The study of **second language acquisition (SLA)** investigates the process by which non-native languages are acquired. The most common form of SLA focuses on **sequential language acquisition**, in which an L2 is learned after an L1 has already been acquired. SLA goes well beyond studying how non-native languages are acquired; it also examines questions such as what the language learner comes to know (and not know), why some learners are more successful at learning an L2 than others, and why certain linguistic elements are more easily acquired than others.

As we will see in this chapter, SLA is very interdisciplinary, with strong roots in theoretical linguistics, cognitive psychology, sociology, discourse analysis, and education. Although it is a relatively new field compared to other areas of linguistics, only establishing itself as a field of study in the mid-1900s, research has made huge advances in what we know about how L2s are acquired.

How we study SLA has evolved over time. Just a few decades ago, researchers were mostly concerned with how the L2 was *taught* and less with how it was *acquired*. This position was largely influenced by research in education but as SLA developed into an autonomous research field, it also became more focused on the language learner from a variety of disciplinary perspectives including sociology, psychology, education, linguistics, and anthropology, among others. Today, SLA is concerned with both the process of acquiring an L2 and the many internal and external factors that affect it. Let's first talk about how SLA is different from and similar to L1 acquisition.

13.2 Similarities and Differences from First Language Acquisition

L1 and L2 acquisition both involve learning a linguistic system which contains a set of new sounds, words, and structures. Linguists from both areas are interested in common research questions such as:

- Are learning strategies the same for L1 and L2 learners?
- Is the developmental order of acquisition of sounds, morphemes, and syntax the same for L1 and SLA?
- Does the environment affect learning an L1 and L2 in the same way?

Even with these shared research questions and many others, there are many striking differences between L1 and L2 acquisition. After all, L1 acquisition involves infants and children learning their native language while SLA commonly studies adults learning a non-native language.

This situation alone provides us with two very different sets of language learners (adults and children) who are at different stages of cognitive development. In turn, each requires specific methodologies to study their language acquisition processes. Children are biologically and physiologically different from adults. Beyond these limitations, the research methodologies and approaches that are used to study children vs. adults may be quite distinct. Nonetheless, comparing and contrasting L1 and SLA is an important place to begin our discussion of SLA given that many of its theories have roots in L1 acquisition.

SLA is also unlike L1 acquisition because it is usually acquired after a native language has already been almost or fully established. While this may help with SLA, we will also see that it may cause interference leading to negative effects. Simply put, unlike L1 acquisition, SLA cannot ignore the fully developed linguistic system that already exists. Ironically though, an individual's L1 is not immune to interference; once a learner reaches a certain level of development in an L2, we may likely see L2 effects on the L1.

Personal and cultural factors may also distinguish L1 and SLA from one another. For example, in SLA, personal characteristics such as motivation to learn a non-native language, attitudes towards that language, and even self-esteem, may differentiate it from L1 acquisition. In another example, some adult L2 learners may be worried that the new language may isolate them from their L1 and culture. This may be particularly prevalent among immigrants who are living outside of their home culture.

PAUSE AND REFLECT 13.1

In L1 acquisition, infants learn language in order to carry out daily activities or to satisfy basic biological needs. In L2 acquisition, however, one may learn an L2 to improve the chances of getting a new job. What other reasons do you think motivate people to learn an L2?

Another important difference between L1 and SLA is the **ultimate attainment** of language abilities. For the L1, we ultimately learn it as if it were a human instinct – and it is. However, an L2 may be much more difficult to acquire to the same degree as the L1 despite one's best efforts. In fact, the development of an L2 may even reach a point where it either slows down substantially or stops. When this happens, we usually refer to this as **fossilization**. Although we will talk about some exceptions and individual differences, ultimate attainment in an L2 is almost always inferior to that of an L1.

13.2.1   Interlanguage

One concept which SLA research explores is **interlanguage**. An interlanguage is a developing, dynamic approximation of a language being learned. In other words, an interlanguage is simply the current state of a learner's L2.

An L2 interlanguage can show traces of a speaker's L1. The arrows in Figure 13.1 suggest that both the L1 and L2 influence the development of an L2 interlanguage. For example, an L2 interlanguage may show evidence of L1 phonology (i.e., non-native pronunciation), yet at the same time conform to the syntactic rules of the L2 (i.e., form correct sentence structure).

Figure 13.1 The development of an L2 interlanguage

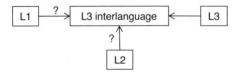

Figure 13.2 The development of an L3 interlanguage

While it is generally accepted that a learner's L1 influences L2 interlanguage, it is still unclear whether the L1, the L2, or a combination of both influences the development of an L3 interlanguage (see Figure 13.2).

PAUSE AND REFLECT 13.2

If an L1 speaker of English who knows L2 Spanish begins learning L3 Italian, do you think he/she will transfer knowledge of Spanish because it is more closely related to Italian? Would your opinion change if – instead of L3 Italian – he/she begins L3 learning German (more closely L3 either the L1 or the L2)?

13.3 Linguistic Development of a Second Language

13.3.1 Phonological Development

Phonology shows us the most obvious influences of an L1 on an L2. In fact, many times when language learners speak their L2, there are sounds that may reveal what their L1 is. For example, an L1 Mandarin speaker probably will not pronounce L2 English the same way as an L1 French speaker. Phonological influences from the L1 affect all areas of L2 sound, from segmental (individual sounds) to prosodic phonology (larger units such as syllables and intonation patterns).

Table 13.1 shows possible pronunciations of the words *goat*, *vote*, and *though* for Spanish and German L1 speakers. Focusing on the first sound of each example ([g], [v], and [ð]), we may predict that because all three languages contain [g] and allow for words to begin with [g], Spanish and German speakers may easily pronounce [got]. The same cannot be said for words beginning with [v] in Spanish or words beginning with [ð] in Spanish and German.

As language learners become more proficient in their L2, they may (or may not) begin to make more native-like sounds. This may require a conscious effort on the part of the learner.

TABLE 13.1 L1 Influences on L2 Pronunciation

English (target)	Spanish L1 speaker	German L1 speaker
[got]	[got]	[got]
[vot]	*[bot]	[vot]
[ðo]	*[do]	*[zo]

Different languages form syllables in different ways. In English, you can have a syllable that begins with /s/ followed by a stop (/p/, /t/, /k/) or a combination of a stop and a liquid (/l/ or /r/). As a result you can pronounce words such as <u>scr</u>eam or <u>Sc</u>otch (Chapter 3 Phonology).

In other languages, syllables are much more restricted. For example Spanish does not allow for syllables to begin with /sp/, /st/, or /sk/. This may explain why we may hear L1 Spanish speakers of L2 English say things such as:

- The baby escreams all the time.
- I am going to the eschool to see an estudent.
- He espeaks Korean very well.

Why do we consider this type of pronunciation error the result of transfer? What is the learner doing (unconsciously) to solve the problem of pronouncing a syllable that is impossible in Spanish?

How words are assigned stress also leads to differences between languages. For example, French words are commonly stressed on the last syllable, and Spanish words on the penultimate syllable. English stress assignment is quite complex because it is related to the weight of the syllable. For example, compare the pronunciation of the underlined vowels in phot<u>o</u>graph and phot<u>o</u>graphy. Differences in stress assignment help to explain why French speakers pronounce the French name Amélie as /amelí/ with stress on the final syllable, Spanish speakers pronounce this name as /amélja/, with stress on the second syllable, and English speakers tend to say /ámeli/, with stress on the first.

The Markedness Differential Hypothesis

An important model explaining L2 phonological development is Eckman's (1977) **Markedness Differential Hypothesis**. This hypothesis is based on the idea of **markedness**. This states that what is *unmarked* in language is more common, more frequent, and/or less complex in world languages. Things *marked* in a language are less common, less frequent, and/or more complex.

The Markedness Differential Hypothesis argues that learners whose L1 contains a marked linguistic feature will have less difficulty learning the unmarked equivalent in the L2 than vice versa. Recall the example from the Eyes on World Languages box on syllable formation in this section where we noticed that English syllable structure is much more complex than Spanish syllable structure. In fact, the most common syllable structure is CV.

Some languages such as Japanese all but prohibit syllables that are not CV while other languages such as English allow for both CV and CCV syllable structure. In terms of markedness, CV is less marked than CCV. So when Japanese L1 speakers learn English they are learning a more marked syllable structure than that which exists in their L1. The Markedness Differential Hypothesis would predict that this may be difficult. On the other hand, an English L1 speaker learning Japanese may not have difficulty with the unmarked CV syllable structure of Japanese.

Support for the Markedness Differential Hypothesis can be seen in **voicing contrast**. Voicing contrast is a change in meaning that occurs from alternating voice and voiceless consonants in the same position in the word. Think about what makes /p̲at/ different from /b̲at/. The dissimilarity is the voicing of the first sound. English voicing contrast can occur in word-initial, -medial, and -final position as can be seen in the examples in Table 13.2.

TABLE 13.2 Voicing Contrasts in English			
Sounds	Word-initial	Word-medial	Word-final
[s] [z]	[s̲u] z̲u] "Sue" "zoo"	[bʌs̲əz] [bʌz̲əz] "busses" "buzzes"	[pis̲] [piz̲] "peace" "peas"
[p] [b]	[p̲ej] [b̲ej] "pay" "bay"	[rowp̲ɪŋ] [rowb̲ɪŋ] "roping" "robing"	[mɑp̲] [mɑb̲] "mop" "mob"
[f] [v]	[f̲ejs] [v̲ejs] "face" "vase"	[sejfəɹ] [sejvəɹ] "safer" "savor"	[sejf̲] [sejv̲] "safe" "save"

PAUSE AND REFLECT 13.3

Take a minute to think about another pair of sounds like those in Table 13.2 that provide voicing contrasts in English. Does your example also have voicing contrasts in all three positions?

As you may have guessed, not all languages have voicing contrast in all of the three positions (word-initial, word-medial, and word-final). In fact, some languages do not have voicing contrast in any of these positions. Languages such as English and French that allow for all three are the most common.

We can create a voicing contrast hierarchy to show that languages which allow for the most marked form (word-final voicing contrast) will also allow for options below it (to the left) but not vice versa:

initial > medial > final

The voicing contrast types lower (to the right) in the hierarchy are less frequent and more marked universally while those higher (to the left) in the hierarchy are more common and less marked.

Table 13.3 presents languages which contain initial, medial, and final voicing contrasts.

In Table 13.3, we see that because English allows for word-final voicing contrasts, it will also allow for medial and initial contrasts. But because German only allows for

TABLE 13.3 The Markedness Differential Hierarchy for Voicing Contrasts (Dinnsen & Eckman, 1975)

Languages with voicing contrast in initial, medial, and final positions.	English, French, Arabic, Swedish, Hungarian	More universally frequent (less marked)
Languages with voicing contrast in initial and medial positions, but not in final position.	German, Polish, Greek, Japanese, Catalan, Russian	
Languages with voicing contrast in initial position, but not in medial and final positions.	Corsican, Sardinian	
Languages with no voice contrast in initial, medial, or final positions.	Korean	Less universally frequent (more marked)

word-medial voicing contrasts, it can only allow for initial but not final contrasts. This may explain why a German L1 speaker of English L2 may pronounce "rat" and "rad" both as [rat]. In fact, studies have shown that an English L1 speaker has no difficulty producing German L2 words which have no voicing contrast in word-final position. On the other hand, a German L1 speaker may have difficulty with voicing contrast in that position in English L2 words. In terms of markedness and voicing contrast, German is more marked than English and French.

13.3.2   Morphological Development

In the 1970s, the main objective for researchers studying morphology in SLA was to establish whether there was a natural order of acquisition for morphemes. Researchers in SLA were largely inspired by L1 acquisition work like Brown's (1973) study of three children which showed that that there was a similar and natural order for acquisition of morphemes in L1 acquisition. When researchers began to investigate morphology in L2, they naturally started by inquiring whether Brown's findings would be true for the acquisition of morphemes in an L2.

The Natural Order Hypothesis

As part of the Monitor Model which we will discuss later in the chapter, Krashen (1982) proposed the **Natural Order Hypothesis**. According to this theory, morphemes are acquired in a predictable sequence of groups as can be seen in Table 13.4. Within these groups, research has shown some variability in ordering.

TABLE 13.4 A Natural Order of Morpheme Acquisition in English

Group 1	present progressive –*ing*	*John runn<u>ing</u>.
	plural –*s*	Two car<u>s</u>.
	copula *be*	John <u>is</u> tall.
Group 2	progressive auxiliary "to be"	John <u>is</u> running.
	articles "the" and "a"	<u>The</u> game is fun.
Group 3	irregular past	John <u>went</u> home.
Group 4	regular past –*ed*	John walk<u>ed</u> to school.
	third-person singular –*s*	John speak<u>s</u> Spanish.
	possessive –'*s*	It is John<u>'s</u> book.

As with other hypotheses in the Monitor Model, the natural order of morpheme acquisition in L2s was not without criticism. Studies later used longitudinal methods which allowed researchers to follow the acquisition order of morphemes across time. They found that there may be more variability in order than Krashen had originally suggested. Typically, the order did not vary much between the groupings in Table 13.4, but for some learners, the acquisition of a particular morpheme could take a lot longer or could be faster due to influence from the L1. For example, if the L1 had morphemes similar to the English possessive –'s, this morpheme would not be as difficult to acquire.

PAUSE AND REFLECT 13.4

Consider the third-person singular /–s/ as in the sentence *He speaks Russian*. L2 speakers of English sometimes leave it out and say things like **He speak Russian*. What can the listener interpret as a result of this error?

Interfaces with Morphology

As interest for investigating a natural order of morpheme acquisition diminished, attention turned towards studying interfaces between aspect, tense, and semantics. Morphology is central in SLA research for the simple fact that many L2 learners find it difficult. For example, it is hard for L1 English speakers to acquire gender agreement in L2 French or Italian. In fact, some studies show that even at high

L2 proficiency levels and after several years, verb agreement errors can still be frequent, as Lardiere (2007) reported from a Chinese L1 speaker of English L2. For this learner, the third person –s and the past tense were often omitted. Lardiere argued that the problem is one of mapping between the abstract functional category *tense* and the correct form. These and other interfaces with morphology continue to catch researchers' attention.

Slabakova (2013) has proposed that morphology forms a bottleneck for learners. They have trouble mapping the abstract functions of the different morphemes to their realization as morphemes. For example, learners know that there is a functional category for tense in English but when producing their L2, they may fail to access the relevant form and produce a sentence that is not marked for past. According to Slabakova, this is in contrast to syntax and semantics that somehow *come for free*. For some researchers, on the other hand, the problem with morphology is evidence of an underlying dissimilarity in the grammar that simply supports a fundamental difference between acquiring an L1 vs. L2.

> **LINGUISTIC TIDBITS: L2 MORPHOLOGY ACQUISITION**
>
> Saying that morphology forms a bottleneck for L2 learners may be clearer if you try to come up with definitions for morphemes like –*ed* and –*s*. Whereas you can easily define an object such as *ball*, functional morphemes have abstract meanings. It makes sense that learners may have trouble acquiring L2 morphology.

13.3.3   Syntactic Development

Like other areas of linguistic development, when it comes to L2 syntax, research has focused on language universals and a natural order in acquisition. Below we discuss a few of these issues.

Markedness and the Accessibility Hierarchy

Work by Keenan & Comrie (1977) shows the predictable nature of world languages. In their study involving L2 learners of English from over 50 L1s, six types of relative clauses were identified. Recall from Chapter 5 Syntax that a relative clause is a subordinate (dependent) clause that provides an independent clause with additional information, but which cannot stand alone as a sentence. The underlined phrase in *I like to learn languages that are challenging*, is an example of a relative clause.

In the study, all languages contained subject relative clauses but beyond this type, access to other relative clauses is restricted and appears to be universal. The researchers put forth an **Accessibility Hierarchy** which showed the degree of markedness for noun phrase relative clauses.

The Accessibility Hierarchy and examples of the six relative clause types can be seen in Table 13.5.

TABLE 13.5 The Accessibility Hierarchy for Relative Clauses

Subject (SU)	The man [who speaks Russian] is smart.	More universally frequent (less marked)
Direct object (DO)	I know the woman [who(m) David loves].	
Indirect object (IO)	I saw the man [who(m) John gave a book to].	
Object of preposition (OPREP)	I know the guy [who(m) John studies with].	
Genitive (GEN)	I have a friend [whose cousin is in Tasmania].	
Object of comparison (OCOMP)	I know the person [who(m) Jim is taller than].	Less universally frequent (more marked)

In the hierarchy, relative clause types lower (to the right) in the hierarchy are less frequent and more marked universally while those higher (to the left) in the hierarchy are more common and less marked. The use of the symbol ">" means "is more accessible than."

SU > DO > IO > OPREP > GEN > OCOMP

As we saw with the hierarchy for voicing contrast, the Accessibility Hierarchy argues that if a language has a certain relative clause type, it will also have all other relative clause types lower in the hierarchy (to the left). Many studies have supported this claim (e.g., Eckman, Bell, & Nelson, 1988; Gass, 1982).

Does learning relative clauses follow a similar path as their hierarchy? If so, can an L2 learner acquire a more marked relative clause type while getting the less-marked ones *for free*? Gass (1982) explored whether or not the knowledge of a more difficult type of relative clause can be applied to easier relative clause positions. In this study, L2 learners who were instructed on subject and direct object relative clauses were compared to L2 learners who were instructed only on object of preposition relative clauses. The results showed that the subject and direct object group improved on these two relative clause types but that the object of preposition group improved on all three relative clause types.

Eckman, Bell, & Nelson (1988) found similar results in their study which included a control group receiving no instruction on relative clauses, and three experimental groups each receiving instruction on one relative clause type: subject; direct object; or object of preposition. Once again, the group which received instruction on the most marked relative clause (object of preposition) also performed better on all three of the relative clause types.

While learners seem to be able to generalize knowledge from more marked to less marked structures, there is no evidence to suggest that the reverse could be possible:

Generalization from less to more difficult relative clauses in the Accessibility Hierarchy does not appear possible.

Generative Linguistics and Universal Principles

Generative linguistics is a theoretical approach that argues for an innate system generally referred to as Universal Grammar or UG (refer back to Chapter 1 Introducing Linguistics). Recall that UG is a mental system made up of a finite set of **principles and parameters** which constrain the number of options open to the learner. With this system of constraints we are able to generate an infinite number of sentences and phrases.

Principles are universal, for example, all active verbs need a subject. However, do not confuse them with the markedness constraints, which depend on the frequency of structures in world languages. **Parameters**, in contrast, are alternatives that UG makes available. It is usually said that learners set parameters, somewhat like setting a light switch to on or off. Setting parameters to the right value will depend on the input. In SLA we talk about resetting parameters, because the learners will already have done this for the native language(s). Although this vision has turned out to be a simplification (e.g., parameters are not necessarily binary), the concept of parameters is still useful in that it allows us to characterize differences between languages. We must note, however, that the features that lead to particular parameters are now considered part of the lexicon.

As we mentioned in Chapter 5 Syntax and Chapter 8 Historical Linguistics, one parameter that has received quite a bit of attention is the **Null-Subject Parameter**. Also known as the Pro-drop Parameter, the Null-Subject Parameter accounts for differences between languages which require subjects to be stated and languages which allow subjects to be unpronounced. In other words, null-subject languages include a pronoun that has no phonological form in their lexicon.

For instance, Spanish and Italian are both null-subject languages, as can be seen in examples (1) and (2), respectively. The subject of both sentences is morphologically marked at the end of verbs instead of through the overt use of a subject pronoun such as *él* (he) or *ella* (she) in Spanish or *egli* (he) or *lei* (she) in Italian (although the addition of these pronouns would still result in grammatical sentences).

> **LINGUISTIC TIDBITS: SUBJECTS AND VERB ENDINGS IN BRAZILIAN PORTUGUESE AND CHINESE**
>
> Portuguese is a pro-drop language. However, Brazilian Portuguese seems to be simplifying its verbs by dropping verb endings. What do you think is happening to subjects? You guessed it: they are becoming much more frequent. This would seem to indicate a relationship between rich verb endings and pro-drop. But wait, Chinese is a pro-drop language, yet Chinese has no verb endings at all! This is because Chinese subjects may be identified by the discourse context and not by the verb.

(1) Comió   rápido.
"[He/she] ate   quickly."

(2) Ha studiato   tutta   la   notte.
[he/she] has studied   all   the   night
"[He/she] has studied all night."

13.4 Factors Affecting Second Language Acquisition

13.4.1 The First Language

L2 learners commonly transfer their knowledge of their L1 to their L2. This tendency may be particularly frequent in the beginning stages of SLA. While we know that not all incorrect L2 output can be traced back to the L1, research suggests that there are indeed subtle influences from the L1 that shape and develop the L2 system in complex ways. In fact, learners may be more likely to transfer L1 knowledge when the L2 is more similar than not.

We have already discussed the Null-Subject Parameter which allows us to predict that an L1 speaker of a [+null subject] language like Spanish who learns another [+null subject] language such as Italian, may find it natural to be able to construct sentences without having an overt subject. In other words, the [+null subject] parameter does not need to be reset and can be transferred for accurate use of the L2.

However, if the same learner whose L1 is [+null subject] is acquiring a [–null subject] language such as French, in which subject pronouns are obligatory, it may be common to observe ungrammatical uses of French because the learner has not adequately reset the null-subject parameter. As expected, if the speaker's L1 had been a [–null subject] language like English, which does not accept sentences without overt subjects, it would be likely, at least at the beginning stages of SLA, that the learner would produce many (if not all) utterances with an overt subject, resulting in a non-native-like and almost redundant form of speech. In fact, as we will see below, these predictions are not necessarily true. English L1 speakers learning Spanish acquire the possibility of omitting subject pronouns quite early, but continue to include pronouns in cases where they are unnecessary.

In these examples, however, regardless of whether the L1 is a [–null subject] or [+null subject] language, each speaker has transferred information about the functionality of the L1 and applied it to the L2.

PAUSE AND REFLECT 13.5

As we saw in Chapter 5 Syntax, object pronouns in English appear after the verb. In French, they attach to the front of the verb.

- I see **him**.
- Je **le** vois.

If transfer occurs, what error in L2 French do you expect an English L1 speaker to produce? What error in L2 English do you expect a French L1 speaker to make, at least initially?

13.4.2 Age

Another factor that may have an impact on SLA is age. You may agree that children have a better chance than adults of acquiring an L2 to a native or near-native level. Not surprisingly, researchers have shown that there is a relationship between age of acquisition and the ultimate attainment of an L2. The support for age effects in SLA predominately stems from the **critical period hypothesis** debate from L1 acquisition which argues that exposure to language must occur before puberty in order to attain native-like proficiency. While this sensitive period is indisputable for the L1, there seem to be mixed results when it comes to the native-like attainment of an L2.

Supporters of a critical period hypothesis in SLA argue that exposure to the L2 may need to occur as early as before the age of six. A number of theories have been presented to explain the cause of a critical period. Some of these have included neurological-based hypotheses discussing lateralization of language in the brain. Others have given cognitive explanations emphasizing processing and/or memory capacity changes, while others have argued for social-based influences such as attachment to the L1 and culture, types of motivation, and the amount and type of language input and interaction.

A number of studies have shown support for age-related effects in SLA. There is general consensus that different linguistic aspects are affected in different ways. Phonology (i.e., native-like pronunciation) seems to be the most susceptible to age effects. Typically, these studies have explored two important variables: *age of onset*, the age at which an individual is exposed to and begins learning an L2; and *length of residence*, the time which an individual spends in the L2 environment. Most of these studies, regardless of the linguistic area studied (i.e., pronunciation, morphology, syntax, ability to judge grammaticality, etc.) have suggested that the age of onset, but not always the length of residence, generally affects L2 performance. These effects may be increasingly more apparent with later exposure to the L2.

A pioneering study by Johnson & Newport (1989) demonstrated that as the age of onset of immigrant L2 learners increased, their ability to judge the grammaticality of sentences in their L2 decreased. These linear effects of age of arrival on the scores of the grammaticality judgement task can be seen in Figure 13.3. The figure shows that L2 learners who arrived in an L2 environment before the age of seven performed at the same level as native speakers. This begins to fall sharply as they arrive later to the L2 environment. Similar age-of-onset effects have also been revealed for pronunciation, morphology, and syntax.

In all, although there has been some disagreement over the extent to which age affects SLA, there are many points on common ground, as Rod Ellis (1994) summarizes below:

- Adult learners have an initial advantage where rate of learning is concerned, particularly in grammar. They will eventually be overtaken by child learners who receive enough exposure to the L2.
- Only child learners are capable of acquiring a native accent in informal learning contexts. Long (1990) puts the critical age at six years, but Scovel (1988) argues for a pre-puberty start. Singleton (1989) points out that children will only acquire a native-like sound system if they receive massive exposure to the L2.

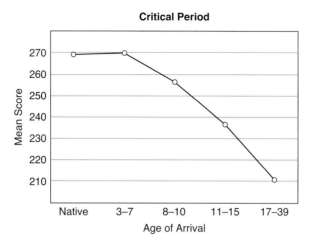

Figure 13.3 The effect of age of arrival on grammaticality judgements in an L2. From: Johnson, J., & Newport, E. (1989). Critical period effects in second language learning: The influence of maturational state on acquisition of ESL. *Cognitive Psychology, 21,* 60–99. Reproduced with permission of Elsevier through PLSclear.

- Children may be more likely to acquire native-like grammatical competence. The critical period for grammar acquisition may be later than for pronunciation (around 15 years). Some adult learners, however, may succeed in acquiring native levels of grammatical accuracy in speech and writing and even full linguistic competence.

- Irrespective of whether native-like proficiency is achieved, children are more likely to reach higher levels of attainment in both pronunciation and grammar than adults.

- The process of acquiring an L2 grammar is not substantially affected by age, but acquiring pronunciation may be.

LINGUISTIC TIDBITS: CRITICAL PERIODS

Critical periods are very common in nature. For example, birds attach to the first moving entity they see after birth (called filial imprinting), identifying it as their mother. In the movie *Fly Away Home* (based on a true story) orphaned Canada geese imprint on a little girl during this critical period and follow her everywhere.

EYES ON WORLD LANGUAGES: GENDER AGREEMENT AND A CRITICAL PERIOD

Many languages have grammatical gender (not to be confused with biological gender which we will discuss later in this chapter). Romance languages along with Greek and German are examples of languages with grammatical gender. In these languages, determiners and adjectives have to agree with their nouns in gender, number, and sometimes case. For example, in the Spanish phrase *the tall boy*, the determiner *the* and the adjective *tall* are marked singular and masculine because they modify the singular masculine noun *boy*.

EYES ON WORLD LANGUAGES: (*cont.*)

Learning languages with gender agreement can be a challenge regardless of whether the L1 has gender agreement (as in French) or not (as in English). In fact, research has shown that both French and English L1 speakers make a similar number of gender errors in L2 Spanish, even though French has gender agreement (Bruhn de Garavito & White, 2002).

Grüter, Lew-Williams, & Fernald (2012) examined knowledge of gender in a group of highly-proficient English L1 speakers of L2 Spanish. Although their comprehension abilities were similar to a balanced-bilingual group, their production abilities were not: the language learners, despite their high proficiency, did not assign correct gender to nouns 20 percent of the time. To further investigate this, the researchers used a *looking-while-listening procedure*. The participants, wearing an eye-tracking device, were shown sets of pictures such as a ball (feminine, *la pelota*) and a shoe (masculine, *el zapato*) while hearing sentences such as *Encuentra la pelota* ("Find the ball"). Eye movements were compared between the two groups and only the L1 speakers of Spanish turned their eyes to the correct picture as soon as they heard the article. In other words, the bilingual group was able to identify pictures using grammatical gender (e.g., *la*) before actually hearing the noun (*pelota*).

Research such as Grüter *et al.* suggests that when it comes to gender agreement, differences between bilinguals and highly proficient language learners arise from fundamental differences in how and when they learned words in the two languages. Infants and adults approach learning words in an L2 differently. Simply put, acquiring grammatical gender (and using it correctly) in an L2 may not proceed the same after the critical period.

PAUSE AND REFLECT 13.6

You may have heard that *children absorb language like a sponge*. Do you think adults can be *sponge-like* too? Why or why not?

13.4.3 Gender

A learner's gender has also been reported to affect SLA. As was discussed in Chapter 9 Sociolinguistics, males and females use language in different ways. For instance, females may use language-learning strategies more often and more efficiently than males. Other differences between males and females have been uncovered in psycholinguistic studies suggesting that the two genders actually process language differently and use distinct types of memory.

In terms of their interaction with other L2 speakers in classroom settings, males – more so than females – admit to having more misunderstandings when matched with females in pair-work. In other words, male students have more difficulty understanding female students than vice versa. Even though both genders work hard to achieve mutual comprehension, males tend to talk more and dominate the conversation. These interactions can influence learners' practice in the L2.

Many studies have also shown that females have more positive attitudes and motivation towards learning an L2. In fact, in the last two decades, some researchers have concentrated on the apparent lack of motivation to study French as an L2 among boys compared to girls. For example, Netten, Riggs, & Hewlett (1999) not only indicated that boys were less likely than girls to study French after Grade 9, among the students who did continue on to study French in Grade 10, the majority of these learners were female by almost a three-to-one ratio.

Kissau's (2006) large-scale study conducted in Ontario examined gender differences in L2 motivation among English-speaking students learning French in Grade 9. The study suggested that the boys were perceived by both teachers and fellow peers as poorer language learners than girls. It is not surprising that Kissau also found that boys perceived themselves as less able to control their success of learning French as an L2 and as less successful than their female counterparts. Males also had more negative perceptions than females towards the L2, a finding also reported in Schwieter's (2008) study of L2 Spanish in the United States.

Kissau's study reminds us that societal influences may be at the root of gender differences in L2 learning: there is simply a lack of encouragement for males to study an L2. Given that similar negative attitudes towards an L2 among adolescent boys have been reported in the United States, England, Ireland, and Hungary (Dörnyei & Clement, 2001; Williams, Burden, & Lanvers, 2002), one wonders whether this may be a universal trend.

13.4.4 Learning Styles

You probably have a preference about how you learn. Studies investigating learning styles among L2 learners have mostly focused on the contrast between field dependent learning vs. field independent learning. Learners who are **field dependent** are said to take a holistic approach to L2 learning in which they may rely on contextual information (i.e., the outer world, situation, etc.) to comprehend and produce language Field dependent learners are also more likely to treat structures as whole units and may learn best in collaborative and social settings.

On the other hand, learners who are **field independent** typically are characterized by preferring an analytic approach in which they rely on inner knowledge and analytical skills, without contextualization from external factors, to help L2 learning. They also may learn more efficiently if they dissect information into smaller components in order to understand the structural (grammatical) function of language.

Take a moment to fill out the self-evaluation of learning styles in the Pause and Reflect 13.7 box to help you better understand your own learning style.

PAUSE AND REFLECT 13.7

Are you a field dependent or field independent learner? Check one box (A–E) for each item (1–6). Boxes A and E indicate that the sentence is very much like you. Boxes B and D indicate that the sentence is more or less like you. Box C indicates that you have no particular inclination one way or the other (adapted from Wyss, 2002).

		A	B	C	D	E	
1	I have no problem concentrating amid noise and confusion.						I need a quiet environment in order to concentrate well.
2	I enjoy analysing grammar structures.						I find grammar analysis tedious and boring.
3	I feel I must understand every word of what I read or hear.						I don't mind reading or listening in the L2 without understanding every single word as long as I *catch* the main idea.
4	I think classroom study is the key to effective language learning.						I think communication is the key to effective language learning.
5	I prefer working alone to working with other people.						I really enjoy working with other people in pairs or groups.
6	Receiving feedback from other people really doesn't affect my learning at all.						I find feedback useful as a means of understanding my problem areas.

Although this checklist is not meant to be a reliable methodology for research, it does provide an idea of what your preferred learning styles may be. Responses towards the left (A) show a preference for field independence while responses more towards the right (E) of the list indicate a preference for field dependence.

Do you agree with your results? Is it possible that learners can be a combination of both or be field independent for learning certain things but field dependent for learning other things?

Both field dependent and independent learning have benefits for SLA. However, some research has found independent learning more conducive to SLA than field dependent learning. Still yet, other studies argue that one style may align better with certain learning environments than another style. For instance, there has been some support for the idea that field independent learning may be useful in formal learning (i.e., classroom settings) and grammar analysis, and that field dependent learning may be most effective in communicative settings (i.e., immersion-based programs).

13.4.5 Aptitude

Do some people have a special ability for language learning? Indeed, if it's possible to be naturally more inclined towards musical, artistic, or any other type of ability, can it be true that linguistic talent could also be a plausible natural ability? The name most associated with research investigating the effects of aptitude on SLA is John Carroll. Carroll defined **aptitude** as the ability to learn a task. Aptitude is separate from achievement, motivation, and general intelligence. Indeed, Carroll argues that **language aptitude** may be an innate quality that provides an individual with the special propensity for learning an L2. However, it is not a requirement for SLA but should be interpreted as a factor that enhances the rate and ease of learning a non-native language.

Two measures of language aptitude are **The Modern Language Aptitude Test (MLAT)** developed by Carroll & Sapon (1959) and the **Pimsleur Language Aptitude Battery (PLAB)** designed by Pimsleur (1966). These two assessments are designed to test one's ability:

- to code sounds so that they can be remembered later;
- to recognize the grammatical function of words in sentences;
- to infer patterns that exist and create a form-to-meaning relationship; and
- to formulate and recall associations between words and concepts (i.e., vocabulary learning).

Language aptitude is a very influential factor in SLA and it has been tested widely. Some researchers such as Gardner & MacIntyre (1992) go as far as saying that "research makes it clear that in the long run, language aptitude is probably the single best predictor of achievement in a second language" (p. 215).

13.4.6   Working Memory

Working memory is the ability to simultaneously store and manipulate information that is relevant to a task at hand (Baddeley, 2003). Studies investigating the interaction between language acquisition and working memory have effectively demonstrated the significant role of working memory in the learning and processing of an L1 and recently these interests have spread to studies in SLA. In fact, some researchers argue that working memory may be more important to SLA than to L1 acquisition.

Many studies have uncovered a correlation between working memory capacity and: L2 reading comprehension; processing of L2 gender and number agreement; the ability to learn from and apply feedback in the L2; and L2 proficiency. Although research on working memory and SLA is still a relatively new area of inquiry, there is a strong indication that it plays a role in the effectiveness and rate of learning an L2.

13.4.7   Context

The learning environment, or **context**, also plays a significant role in SLA. Perhaps some of the most powerful evidence of this comes from studies which compare the effects of classroom-based instruction to study abroad contexts. Although research has demonstrated benefits of both contexts, there also are correlations between context and the specific language abilities associated with that learning environment. In particular, studies comparing L2 learning in traditional classroom settings to study abroad settings have found that individuals in study abroad settings outperform their L2 learner counterparts back in the home country on oral fluency and narrative abilities. Meanwhile, those back home may experience more lexico-grammatical growth.

Other studies have even shown that L2 learners in an abroad context become less sensitive to grammar, at least during the beginning of their program (Schwieter & Klassen, 2016). This suggests that learners may shift their learning strategies to be more communicative rather than focused on grammar due to the demands of the immersive context.

13.4.8 Personalities and Feelings

The intricate personalities and attributes of individuals are perhaps just as complex as the above factors that influence SLA. We will now briefly discuss some of the most studied variables related to this.

Personality

While it has been difficult to find accurate measurements that categorize the personality of individual language learners, there has been general support for the influence of individual character traits. The personality of a human is a complex variable that consists of many interconnected traits that help to characterize the person. Because of the difficult nature of classifying personalities (especially without solid measurements), researchers have had more success in uncovering correlations that exist between individual characteristics and particular linguistic skills.

Some studies have shown that extroverted characteristics such as talkativeness and responsiveness have positive effects on L2 verbal fluency and communication skills. There is also evidence that suggests that introverted characteristics such as being reserved or withdrawn may have positive effects on L2 vocabulary learning. Although at first glance, it would appear as though extroverted personality characteristics may lend themselves better to oral production skills while introverted personalities may assist the development of reading and writing skills, more research is needed to be able to generalize, if at all, the intricate interaction between personality characteristics and SLA.

Affective State

Learners' **affective state** refers to their feelings or emotional condition. If you have ever had a problem that preoccupies your thoughts (i.e., *something is bothering you* or *you can't get something off your mind*), you may have noticed that learning – and any sort of meaningful thinking – is negatively affected. Although a variety of affective factors have been measured (empathy, inhibition, risk-taking, etc.), perhaps among the most studied and pertinent affective states that research in SLA has explored involves the anxiety level of the learners.

Traditionally, **anxiety** has been divided into three types:

- **Trait anxiety** refers to a more permanent predisposition to be anxious. In other words, trait anxiety essentially is the extent to which an individual is an anxious person.
- **State anxiety** is defined as apprehension and nervousness at given moments as a result of a situation (being corrected by the teacher, making errors, etc.).

- **Situation-specific anxiety** refers to particular situations that consistently give rise to anxiety (public speaking, exams, etc.).

Research looking at the effects of anxiety on SLA tend to show that some anxiety may help language learning but that too much may hurt. In other words, there should be some concern on the part of the language learner to be accurate and fluent but too much worry about failure can create obstacles to succeeding.

PAUSE AND REFLECT 13.8

What strategies do you use to learn an L2? Do you:

- Try to find as many occasions as possible to use it?
- Listen to music in the language?
- See movies in the language?

- Memorize phrases?
- Memorize vocabulary and verb forms?
- Other strategies?
  Why do you think your strategies serve as good ways to learn an L2?

Attitudes and Beliefs

Attitude refers to a learner's evaluation of and appreciation for an idea, entity, or situation. It goes without saying that SLA may best occur when an individual has a positive attitude towards the language being learned. In fact, research has demonstrated that positive attitudes towards the native speakers of the L2, their communities and countries, and the attitudes towards language learning in general can all have effects on language learning. Finally, it should be said that learners possess beliefs about how L2s should be learned – or at least, about the best strategies for them personally to learn an L2.

Most commonly, these learning beliefs are a reflection of personal learning experiences. Research investigating L2 learners' attitudes and beliefs is ongoing but in general points to the fact that "it is reasonable to assume that their 'philosophy' dictates their approach to learning and choice of specific learning strategies" (Ellis, 1994, p. 479). With this knowledge, both theoretical and applied implications may help inform L2 teaching practices.

Motivation and Investment

Gardner & Lambert (1959) were among the first researchers to emphasize the importance of motivation as an influential factor in SLA. In the socio-educational model of motivation, there is a distinction between **instrumental motivation**, that is to say, the desire to learn an L2 for practical or utilitarian purposes, and **integrative motivation**, which is the wish to learn an L2 in order to successfully integrate into the L2 community and/or culture. Instrumental motivation refers to situations in which learners are motivated to acquire an L2 based on things such as passing a language certification test or finding a job.

Integrative motivation, in contrast, refers to instances where learners are motivated to acquire an L2 based on things such as wanting to live someday in the country where the language is spoken or having a personal interest in the culture. Both instrumental and integrative motivation have been found to contribute to SLA but there seems to be a slight advantage for having integrative motivation.

Recent studies suggest that the *degree* of motivation may be more important to SLA than the *type* of motivation. Motivation, unlike other factors such as aptitude and personality, is variable and can change from day-to-day and even from one task to the next. Some studies have found that motivation can be modulated by many other factors such as learning context and other social variables such as group dynamics and affective states of peers.

Other researchers go beyond viewing motivation as instrumental or integrative and consider **investment.** Dörnyei (2009) proposed the **L2 Motivation Self System**, a theory rooted in mainstream psychology which includes three main components:

- Ideal L2 Self, which is the L2-specific facet of one's *ideal self*: if the person we would like to become speaks an L2, the *ideal L2 self* is a powerful motivator to learn the L2 because of the desire to reduce the discrepancy between our actual and ideal selves. Traditional integrative and internalized instrumental motives would typically belong to this component.
- Ought-to L2 Self, which concerns the attributes that one believes should be possessed to meet expectations and to avoid possible negative outcomes. This dimension corresponds to Higgins' ought self and to the more extrinsic (i.e., less internalized) types of instrumental motives.
- L2 Learning Experience, which concerns situated, executive motives related to the immediate learning environment and experience such as the impact of the teacher, the curriculum, the peer group, and the experience of success.

Although the construct of motivation continues to be researched and refined (even by some of its original proponents such as Gardner, 2009), it has been criticized for not encompassing the intricate role that power and identity also play in SLA. Bonnie Norton Peirce (1995) has argued that a learner's **investment** refers to the social and historical relationship that language learners build with the L2 and their emerging desire to practice and acquire it.

13.5   Second Language Teaching and Learning

As you can imagine, in L2 classrooms, teaching practices have evolved considerably over the years. In fact, some earlier approaches to the teaching of L2s may seem quite archaic to learners today. Here, we are referring to the teaching of languages that are currently spoken and not to ancient languages such as Latin or Ancient Greek, which are often taught differently than modern languages due to the limitations of their usage in society. Not surprisingly, it is likely that individuals who study languages that are no longer spoken *today* will do so with *yesterday's* teaching pedagogies such as grammar translation. You can read more about early pedagogies such as grammar translation and the audio-lingual method, in 'Delving Deeper' in Chapter 13's resources on the website to accompany this book at www.cambridge.org/introducing-linguistics.

13.5.1   Communicative Language Teaching

Perhaps one of the most common approaches to L2 teaching today is through communicative-based language instruction. Although earlier approaches had many strengths, with one of them being the importance of focus on meaning (i.e., oral communication), they failed to include the importance of focus on form (i.e., grammatical rules). As a result, **communicative language teaching** became – and still is – the preferred teaching method by many language educators. This approach emphasizes the acquisition of communicative competence which includes the knowledge of how to use language in socially and pragmatically appropriate ways.

Communicative competence encompasses several types of knowledge, including grammatical, discourse, sociolinguistic, and strategic competence. Unlike previous approaches, the communicative language teaching approach was one of the first to address all four essential skill areas of language learning (reading, writing, speaking, and listening) although it does not promote explicit grammar instruction.

Five important features that make up communicative language teaching approaches as presented by Nunan (1991) include:

- an emphasis on learning to communicate through interaction in the target language;
- the introduction of authentic texts into the learning situation;
- the provision of opportunities for learners to focus, not only on language but also on the learning process itself;
- an enhancement of the learner's own personal experiences as important contributing elements to classroom learning; and
- an attempt to link classroom language learning with language activities outside the classroom.

More recently, researchers and language educators have begun to elaborate on the effectiveness of including **form-focused instruction** within a framework of communicative language teaching. Form-focused instruction refers to "any pedagogical effort which is used to draw the learners' attention to language form either implicitly or explicitly" (Spada, 1997, p. 73). Under these assumptions, it has generally been accepted that as long as form-focused instruction or grammar instruction (whether directly or indirectly taught) occurs in a meaningful, communicative context, there will be positive effects on SLA.

13.5.2   Task-based Language Teaching

As in communicative language teaching, where focus is on meaningful discourse, task-based approaches view SLA as assisted by activities in which learners participate in communicative steps to carry out a task. For instance, learners may have to communicate the stages necessary to make a hotel reservation or order food at a restaurant. Task-based language teaching draws on sociocultural and interactionist theories and at its core are communicative activities in which language learners participate in authentic, real-world exercises with one another in order to achieve a communication goal.

While task-based language teaching is focused on communication, it commonly draws the learners' attention to linguistic forms and structures implicitly instead of through explicit instruction by the teacher. Some activities which foster the indirect teaching, or at least the noticing, of grammar include those which offer opportunities for language learners to interact with one another in conversational settings in which **breakdowns in communication** may occur. Breakdowns in communication refer to instances where communication is interrupted, potentially due to an L2 learner's incorrect use of the L2 such as incorrect vocabulary, pronunciation, syntax, or other non-native-like forms.

PAUSE AND REFLECT 13.9

While breakdowns in communication may appear problematic, they actually provide the opportunity for L2 learners to give and receive feedback on each other's speech. Doing so may draw their attention to non-native-like forms that may have otherwise gone unnoticed and permit instructors to potentially correct them for a more accurate approximation in the future. Can you think of a time when you either were giving or receiving feedback because of a breakdown in communication?

13.5.3 Processing Instruction

SLA, generally speaking, can be conceptualized as including three main processes: intake, acquisition, and output (Ellis, 2001). In other words, the linguistic data which a language learner internalizes is acquired and subsequently used to produce language. However, this view does not pay attention to the actual processing of input which refers to the initial stage in which learners connect grammar to meaning, for example, by interpreting the role of a noun and its relationship to a verb, among other things.

Bill VanPatten is the scholar most commonly associated with the potential benefits that may arise from exploring the processes involved in converting input into intake. He argues that language input is fundamental in SLA. However, not all input is actually internalized: in other words, not all **input** is truly understood. We use the term **intake** to refer to input that is comprehended and can lead to the reshaping and development of the interlanguage. VanPatten's theory of **input processing** is concerned with two things: how learners perceive and process L2 input, and the psycholinguistic strategies and mechanisms by which learners convert input into intake. Essentially input; processing theory examines a set of internal processing strategies which learners might use to understand language and that ultimately lead to intake.

A pioneering study by VanPatten and Cadierno (1993) demonstrated how the theoretical implications of input processing could be applied to the L2 classroom by arguing for **processing instruction**. Processing instruction is a type of form-focused instruction in which input has been "modified and constructed in a way that pushes learners away from their less than optimal processing strategies, thus creating better intake for development" (VanPatten, 2002, p. 764). Processing instruction, different from other input-based pedagogical interventions, is informed by actual processing and parsing strategies and actively works to move learners away from those that may inhibit acquisition. Benati and Schwieter (2017) argue that processing instruction includes three basic features:

- L2 learners are given explicit information about a linguistic structure or form. Forms and/or structures are presented one at a time.
- Within the linguistic information provided to L2 learners about a target form or structure, learners are also given information on a particular processing principle that may negatively affect their picking up of the form and/or structure during comprehension.
- L2 learners are pushed to process the form and/or structure during structured-input tasks in which the input is manipulated in particular ways to push learners to become dependent on form and/or structure to get meaning (p. 256).

The main differences between traditional instruction and processing instruction in L2 teaching and learning can be seen in Figure 13.4. In (A), traditional approaches to language teaching involve explicit grammatical explanations followed by focused activities to practice output and grammatical rule application. However, in (B), processing instruction exposes language learners to input which is designed to engage learners through **structured input activities**. These latter activities serve as focused practice that has been manipulated in such a way that learners become dependent on forms or structure to derive meaning so that they process grammatical forms in the input and make proper form-meaning connections.

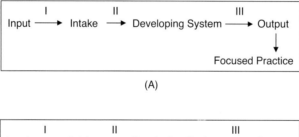

(A)

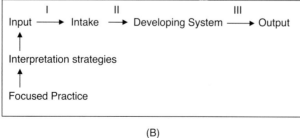

(B)

Figure 13.4 Traditional instruction (A) and processing instruction (B) in second language teaching and learning

In sum, the main differences between traditional instruction (Figure 13.4A) and processing instruction (Figure 13.4B) is that (A) involves presenting learners with explanations regarding the form and then giving them practice in how to make sentences with the relevant grammar point and (B) attempts to alter the processing strategies that language learners use to interpret L2s. While support has been demonstrated for both approaches, research consistently shows that there is a greater advantage for the effectiveness of processing instruction over traditional methods.

13.5.4 Different Types of Language Instruction Programs

A significant number of studies have explored the effectiveness of language programs such as core (i.e., traditional), heritage language maintenance programs, and immersion experiences. We will discuss each of these programs.

PAUSE AND REFLECT 13.10

Stop and think for a moment about your experiences with L2 instruction. What type of program was used in your school?

Core Instruction Programs

We generally refer to educational programs in which the L2 is a single course subject and not the language of instruction for all other course subjects (math, geography, etc.) as **core instruction programs**. While this particular program may not be quite as effective as immersion, for instance, it represents the majority of language education methods in the world today.

In the case of core French or German, for example, learners take the L2 as a course subject and do not necessarily use it as the means of communication in all courses. Many criticisms of core programs have been found, especially concerning whether or not such a small amount of time dedicated to learning the L2 is enough and whether or not the limited input in the target language could ever lead to advanced L2 language abilities. Indeed, many times in core programs, classes may only be a handful of hours per week with the rest of the time – both in and out of school – being in the language of the community.

Heritage Language Maintenance and Submersion Programs

Another language education program option is **heritage language maintenance programs**. In these programs, learners receive instruction in their ancestral or home L1 in order to teach or help maintain that language. Heritage language programs are based on enrichment theory which views bilingualism as being a cognitive and social advantage.

Furthermore, educational theorists have also argued that heritage language maintained in schools can also lead to reduced dropout rates and increased opportunity to develop the basic cognitive skills necessary for functioning in school when compared to **submersion programs** in which learners are placed in classes where the language of instruction (e.g., English) is not the heritage language. Consequently, when a child who has grown up for the first five years of her life speaking Cree or Italian begins school in English, she may suffer a developmental setback that could have a significant impact on the learning trajectory. Heritage language programs attempt to reverse these adverse effects by providing instruction during the first few years in the heritage language and gradually transitioning to instruction which is approximately half in the heritage language and half in the majority language by around grades three to six.

Immersion Programs

Unlike core instruction, **immersion programs** offer all or nearly all instruction subjects in the target language. For example, in the case of French immersion programs in English-speaking regions of Canada, focus is on the teaching *in* French instead of the teaching *of* French. Immersion programs can come in several variations depending on whether the program begins early (e.g., from kindergarten) or later (e.g., from secondary school) or whether the program is partial (i.e., only part of the instruction is in the target language) or full (i.e., all or nearly all of the instruction is in the target language). Generally, the common-sense thought that *more is better than less* and *longer is better than shorter* has been proven accurate in studies comparing early vs. late and partial vs. full immersion programs.

In keeping with some of the theories of SLA discussed above, and in particular, regarding the importance of comprehensible input, it is without a doubt that immersion programs have proven successful because they ensure a significant amount of input which has been modified and contextualized in a way that makes it comprehensible to the language they. However, there are social factors that may also explain their success. Learners in immersion programs find that their L1 and ethnic identity are not under threat and because of this, they have an easier adjustment (Swain & Lapkin, 1985). Furthermore, it must also be considered that because immersion programs are optional, an immersion learner may have been enrolled by their parents who obviously are supporters of bilingualism and bilingual education.

PAUSE AND REFLECT 13.11

How effective are immersion programs? Parents, educators, policy makers, researchers, among others, have commonly wondered just *how native-like* are the L2 abilities of learners who participate in immersion programs. They may also wonder about the effects (negative and positive) on the learners' L1 and general cognition. What are your feelings?

The general consensus about the ultimate state of a learner's L2 in immersion programs depends on whether we are referring to productive or receptive skills. Although it is more than likely that receptive skills such as reading, writing, and discourse competence in the L2 may reach native-like levels in immersion programs, production skills may be a different story. For instance, some researchers have claimed that immersion learners come out of the programs using non-standard forms of the L2 which is a mixture of the L1 and the L2. Although it has been suggested that immersion learners have grammatical errors that are morphosyntactic (e.g., gender of nouns, use of tenses) or pragmatic in nature (e.g., politeness), the fact is their overall receptive skills are native-like and their production skills are very advanced.

In terms of the potential effects of L2 immersion on the L1, the general consensus is that exclusive instruction of the L2 does not imply a diminished capacity for the L1. Although some studies have demonstrated that in early years, learners in L2 immersion programs will have a delay in speaking and writing skills in their L1, these bilinguals catch up to and surpass their monolingual counterparts by roughly the age of 11. See Chapter 12 First Language Acquisition for a discussion on learning two languages from birth.

13.6 Approaches to Studying Second Language Acquisition

Many theoretical approaches have helped to formulate our knowledge base about SLA. Some of the earliest methods of researching SLA took form in the context of behaviorism but soon after favored an approach which sought to predict potential errors that L2 learners would make based on how the L2 was different from the L1. Perhaps it was not until the late 1970s and early 1980s that theoretical approaches to SLA changed from being classified as *early approaches* to *modern approaches*. You can read more about early approaches to SLA such as contrastive analysis and error analysis in 'Delving Deeper' in Chapter 13's resources on the website to accompany this book at www.cambridge.org/introducing-linguistics. We begin our examination of the modern approaches – although some are more outdated than others – that continue to dominate our understanding of the development of an L2.

13.6.1 The Monitor Model

Whereas in the 1950s, research in SLA was dominated by theories of behaviorism and in the 1960s and 1970s by theories that either compared the L1 to the L2 or analyzed the errors produced in the L2, in the early 1980s, research agendas once again shifted. In 1977 and throughout the early 1980s, Stephen Krashen developed the **Monitor Model,** which brought attention to the important role of input in SLA. The Monitor Model argues that language input is the most essential element required to increase linguistic competence when learning an L2.

The Monitor Model originally focused on a single hypothesis known as the **Input Hypothesis**; however, over the years, Krashen's theories were developed and widened to ultimately encompass a series of five hypotheses, which together are still known as the Input Hypothesis, even though only one of the five hypotheses is actually called as such. For the sake of clarity, the preferred term in the literature in the most recent years is the Monitor Model.

The five hypotheses of the Monitor Model emphasize the significance of **comprehensible input** or the understandable language input that is needed for learning. These hypotheses are summarized below:

- **The Acquisition-Learning Hypothesis** holds that while learning is a conscious procedure, acquisition, on the other hand, is a subconscious one that entails the development of underlying linguistic competence. Improvement in language performance depends on acquisition and not on learning.
- **The Natural Order Hypothesis** states that L2s are acquired according to a natural order, regardless of a learner's L1 or instructional interventions. This hypothesis is mostly based on morpheme studies in the 1980s which seemed to show that L2 learners of English acquired morphemes in a similar order. More about this was discussed in Section 13.3.2.
- **The Monitor Hypothesis** argues that an L2 learner has the ability to monitor her speech output when given sufficient time to reflect on it, when the task at hand is about a structural element of the utterance, and when she *knows the rule*. This monitoring stems from what is consciously learned (e.g., in a classroom) and allows the learner to control and correct errors made in the acquired system.
- **The Input Hypothesis**, also known as the Comprehensible Input Hypothesis was at the core of the Monitor Model when it was first developed. It states that SLA requires input (i) that is both comprehensible and sensitive to the language learner's stage of development: it should ideally be slightly above ($i + 1$ level) the current proficiency level of the learners to advance their language abilities.
- **The Affective Filter Hypothesis** posits that affective factors such as motivation and feelings that have a hampering effect on learning such as stress, anxiety, insecurity, embarrassment, cause difficulty in SLA. In instances when the affective filter is *activated*, the ability to acquire language may be constrained.

PAUSE AND REFLECT 13.12

According to the Input Hypothesis what is an important thing you can do when communicating with friends who speak L2 English?

13.6.2   The Output Hypothesis

While one of the main components of the Monitor Model emphasized the important role of input, pioneering work done by Merrill Swain (1995) has focused on output. **The Output Hypothesis** suggests the notion that L2 learners need the opportunity to use language productively and focus on their output instead of using language simply for comprehension (i.e., focus on input).

Swain elaborated output as **comprehensible output**, or language output that is rich enough to "stimulate learners to move from the semantic, open-ended, nondeterministic, strategic processing prevalent in comprehension to the complete grammatical processing needed for accurate production. Output, thus, would seem to have a potentially significant role in the development of syntax and morphology" (Swain, 1995).

13.6.3   The Interaction Hypothesis

Another prominent theoretical approach to SLA focuses on the importance of interaction. **The interaction hypothesis**, mostly informed by the work of Susan Gass and Michael Long in the 1980s, argues that L2 learning occurs when learners participate in conversations in which they encounter difficulties speaking or understanding and must participate in further interaction to reconcile these difficulties.

Interaction forms an important part of L2 development given that it provides the opportunity for learners to seek additional assistance to comprehend the input they receive. This assistance may be requested directly through **clarification requests**. During interaction, learners also have the opportunity to change erroneous language patterns based on direct or indirect correction by their listeners. **Modified output** results when learners change a non-target-like utterance in an attempt to make it become comprehensible input to their listeners.

Finally, interaction involves the important role of feedback. When learners receive **corrective feedback** from their listeners, their attention is drawn to *gaps* that may exist between their linguistic knowledge and the correct target structure. Such feedback can be provided in a variety of ways such as a **recast**, a corrected and/or restated version of a learner's non-target-like utterance.

PAUSE AND REFLECT 13.13

Imagine that your English L2 friend frequently omits the third person –s in English, saying things like *He like chocolate*. What do you think would be more useful: to point out the problem to him/her, to reformulate correctly what he/she has said, or to continue the conversation without addressing or correcting the error?

Researchers have uncovered several benefits to providing an opportunity for meaningful interaction during SLA. In Examples (3)–(5) of exchanges between a native speaker (NS), non-native speaker (NNS), student (S), and teacher (T), you will be able

to identify instances where clarification requests, modified output, and corrective feedback were used to help communication.

(3) NS: there're just a couple more things
    NNS: a sorry? Couple?
    NS: couple more things in the room only just a couple
    NNS: couple? What does it mean couple?
    NS: like two two things two or three things
    NNS: more
    NS: yeah
        (adapted from Mackey & Philp, 1998, p. 339).

In interaction, modified output may arise to correct incorrect utterances as seen in
(4).

(4) NNS: the windows are crozed
    NS: the windows have what?
    NNS: crosed?
    NS: crossed? I'm not sure what you're saying there
    NNS: windows are closed
    NS: oh the windows are closed oh OK sorry
        (adapted from Pica, 1994, p. 514).

Corrective feedback such as a recast may be a subtle way of drawing learners' attention to incorrect utterances in their interlanguage as seen in (5), an exchange between
a student (S) and teacher (T).

(5) S: The boy have many flowers in his basket.
    T: Yes, the boy has many flowers in his basket.
        (adapted from Nicholas, Lightbown, & Spada, 2001, p. 721).

13.6.4 Sociocultural Theory

As originally proposed by Lev Vygotsky in the late 1920s and further refined since the
1990s by researchers such as Lantolf, Swain, and Lapkin, proponents of **sociocultural
approaches** to SLA argue that language development occurs as a result of meaningful
interaction that falls within the language learner's **zone of proximal development**,
that is to say, the theoretical range of language abilities an L2 learner has. Essentially,
the zone of proximal development is the difference between what language learners can
do on their own vs. what they have the ability to do with assistance.

Research investigating SLA from sociocultural perspectives has demonstrated that
when novice language learners are paired with more advanced learners who work
within the novice learners' zone of proximal development, the latter are able to perform
tasks on their own that earlier they were only able to do with assistance. Researchers
claim that novice language learners consequently are able to internalize the guidance

and collaboration of a more capable peer through **scaffolding**, or assisted learning techniques, that elevate learners to a higher proficiency level. Figure 13.5 shows a visualization of second language development as L2 learners progress across developmental zones (i.e., levels).

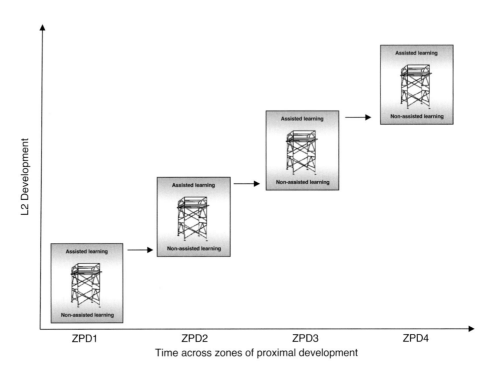

Figure 13.5 Second language learning via assisted learning

13.6.5   Universal Grammar

We have talked about UG throughout this textbook. Research based on UG approaches focuses on how accessible UG is during SLA rather than on the process of L2 development. Two overarching questions that motivate UG research are:

- Does all language acquisition (L1, L2, L3, etc.) in general draw upon the same language learning faculty?
- To what extent does UG remain operational and available to L2 learners?

While the first question has received quite a bit of attention, the second continues to be widely debated. Most researchers agree, however, that the L1 of learners plays an important role. It is generally assumed that when you begin to acquire an L2, the initial state, your starting off point, is the grammar of the L1, and acquisition will consist of slowly changing the properties of the L1 to those close to the L2 in response to input. However, it is important to note that when we speak of changing the properties of the L1 we refer to an unconscious process that is not under our conscious control. Generative approaches, at least until recently, have not been very interested in teaching. However, it is generally assumed that only real communication, and not rule learning, will allow the learner to reset the parameters when necessary.

PAUSE AND REFLECT 13.14

Most recent findings on UG support a *full transfer/full access hypothesis* (Schwartz & Sprouse, 1996) in which the starting point for L2 learning is the L1 but, because there is full access to UG, complete acquisition of the target language is possible.

Imagine that a Chinese speaker is trying to acquire English. English has articles but Chinese does not.

When the learner is exposed to lots of English input that includes articles, he/she will quickly change the parameter to the English version because access to UG is still available. However, this does not happen overnight. What would you expect to hear in the speech of this learner instead of the correct sentence *I have a picture on the table.*

To learn more about SLA and UG, read 'Delving Deeper' in Chapter 13's resources on the website to accompany this book at www.cambridge.org/introducing-linguistics.

Another avenue of research has looked at whether having to process modules of the grammar which are interconnected, for example syntax and pragmatics, leads to variability. This position is referred to as the **Interface Hypothesis** (Sorace, 2011). For example, even beginning learners of L2 Italian or Spanish know that in these languages you can leave out the subject pronoun as we discussed above. The input seems enough for them to learn the syntax associated with null pronouns.

Although leaving out a subject pronoun is learnable in L2 Italian and Spanish, research shows that even the most proficient L2 learners of these languages use subject pronouns differently than native speakers. This difference seems to be due to pragmatic reasons. In other words, L2 learners may be unaware of the circumstances in which it is appropriate to leave out or include subject pronouns. So it seems that it is not the omission of subject pronouns that causes problems, but rather the ability to apply it in the right contexts.

13.6.6   Cognitive Approaches

The Competition Model

The Competition Model, originally developed by Elizabeth Bates and Brian MacWhinney (1989), posits that language learners focus on cues that allow them to compare and contrast properties of different languages. The strength of these cues will vary from language to language. Essentially, the model argues that in SLA, and in particular L2 sentence interpretation, cognitive mechanisms control the activation of representations in the native language that compete with L2 processing. The model also posits that as language learners become more proficient in their L2, they gain an increasingly complete understanding of the meaning of sentences in the target language.

More recently, MacWhinney (2005) made some extensions to the Competition Model in order to account for a greater range of occurrences in language acquisition and bilingualism. Both the original and expanded versions of the model view competition at the core of a set of non-modular interacting forces. However, the expanded version takes this one step further by delineating the exact nature of the various types of competition. In its most contemporary view, language learning is seen as a rich and dynamic procedure which relies on storage, chunking, and support for acquisition of new mental representations.

Processability Theory

Manfred Pienemann's (1998) **Processability Theory** is based on the idea that L2 learners can only produce and comprehend L2 linguistic structures that the current state of the language processor can handle. This is established and constrained by the level of linguistic competence (i.e., L2 proficiency) and perhaps may explain why a beginner L2 learner may feel as though native speakers of the L2 speak so fast. A better explanation according to Processability Theory would argue that the developmental state of the language processor is not ready to intake information at the speed of native-like speech.

The theory argues that SLA requires the acquisition of **procedural skills**, or skills involving a series of discrete responses that have a specific and appropriate sequence in which they should be performed, that are needed to process the L2. In other words, a large part of SLA is that L2 learners must acquire computational routines that operate in accordance to the speaker's linguistic knowledge.

One of the goals of Processability Theory, like many of the theories discussed above, is to understand the ways in which L2 learners restructure their interlanguage to conform to target-like structures. Research has shown that this restructuring is done in stages according to a universal processability hierarchy. These stages proceed according to the cognitive readiness of the learner.

PAUSE AND REFLECT 13.15

In order for English L2 learners to form questions, they must be able to transform declarative sentences. They may first attempt to maintain declarative word order (e.g., *You are hungry?) before applying the appropriate transformation that leads the verb to move to the beginning (e.g., *Are you ~~are~~ hungry?*). Why do you think this is?

SUMMARY

SLA is interested in how humans come to learn a language after their L1. As we have seen, not all linguistic elements in an L2 are easily acquired. According to the idea of markedness, linguistic elements that are *unmarked* in world languages are more common and/or less complex while those *marked* are less common and/or more complex. Studies have shown that learners whose L1 contains a marked feature will have an easier time learning the unmarked L2 equivalent. Universal patterns have allowed us to classify linguistic elements, such as relative clauses, in terms of their frequency and markedness in world languages. There has also been quite a bit of support for a natural order in L2 morpheme acquisition which demonstrates that with some variation, morphemes are learned in predictable sequences of groups.

Learning an L2 does not come without internal and external influences. These effects may be due to the L1, age, gender, learning styles, aptitude, working memory, learning context, personality, affective state, attitudes and beliefs, and motivation and investment. Exploring these factors has been an important part of informing best practices in L2 teaching. Contemporary approaches emphasize a combination of communicative teaching and focus on form. Processing instruction is designed to improve L2 processing strategies by encouraging the conversion of input to intake (i.e., *learning* more from what is *heard*). Innovative approaches most conducive to SLA and the factors that influence it will continue to be a priority in the field.

Several research frameworks have been used to study SLA. Some of these have focused on input while others have centred on output. From these accounts, it is clear that input and output are both essential to SLA. Interactional approaches emphasize the need for learners to interact in the L2 in order to overcome language difficulties. This interaction, according to sociocultural perspectives, ideally should be within the learner's zone of proximal development. Work from UG approaches has shown mixed results when it comes to the extent to which L2 learners have access to their biological language learning faculty, no doubt leaving the door wide open for future research. Cognitive frameworks have viewed SLA as a process of learning new mental representations which is reliant on cognitive competition, storage, and chunking. In all, these research approaches along with refined and new methodologies will continue to drive the future of SLA.

EXERCISES

13.1 Create a table similar to Table 13.1 with at least three examples of errors that L2 learners of English may produce as a result of negative transfer from their L1. If you are unfamiliar with a language other than English, consult with a non-native speaker of English about his/her L2.

13.2 An L2 learner's L1 contains the fricatives /s/ and /f/. If the L2 also contains these sounds plus /θ/ and /x/, which do you think will be acquired first, /θ/ or /x/? Explain your answer.

13.3 An L2 learner's L1 contains the velars /k/ and /x/. If the L2 also contains these sounds plus /g/ and /ɣ/, which do you think will be acquired first: /g/ or /ɣ/? Explain your answer.

13.4 Hungarian words always have stress on the first syllable while Polish words always assign stress to the second-to-last syllable. Which of these words do you think would be more difficult to pronounce for Hungarian and Polish L1 speakers learning English? Explain your answer.

astonish, analysis, replicate, dictate, understanding, conceive, gender, uncover.

13.5 For each row (i)–(iv), rearrange the four columns in the order in which you would expect them to be acquired in L2 English.

i.	three cat<u>s</u>	Gary <u>sang</u>.	Adelle<u>'s</u> chair	<u>the</u> café
ii.	Evan <u>is</u> sitting.	*Evan sitt<u>ing</u>.	He know<u>s</u> Punjabi.	<u>the</u> book
iii.	Jacob play<u>ed</u> a lot.	Jane <u>is</u> dancing.	Becca <u>is</u> smart.	We <u>went</u> home.
iv.	*Molly text<u>ing</u>.	Natalie gain<u>ed</u> weight.	Tara <u>lost</u> the bet.	<u>a</u> game

13.6 The following sentences were produced by English L2 learners. Fill out the table below keeping in mind error analysis. Label error types as *interlingual* (when one language interferes with the other such as negative transfer) or *intralingual* (errors due to influences within the same language such as overgeneralization). This first one (i) has been done for you.

Incorrect sentence	Grammatical subsystem	Description of error	Type of error
i. The man goed out.	morphology	overgeneralization of regular past tense –ed to an irregular verb	intralingual
ii. I drove a car red.			
iii. They no have books.			
iv. Is good to read.			
v. He has thirsty.			
vi. I got my hairs cut.			
vii. Yesterday, I miss the bus.			
viii. Tink about the future.			

13.7 The following sentences were produced both by L1 English-speaking children and adult learners of L2 English. Are these ungrammatical sentences a result of transfer? Why or why not?

i.   *The dog taked the ball.
ii. *The woman haves the book.
iii. *I bringed the homework.

13.8 English and French differ in how they place adverbs in sentences. What explanation could you give to a French speaker learning L2 English as to why (ii) is incorrect but (i) is correct?

i.   Frederick <u>is frequently</u> the cause of the problem.
ii. *Thomas <u>rides frequently</u> his motorcycle.

13.9 In some, but not all, dialects of Arabic, vowels are inserted to the left of problematic clusters of consonants such as [sl]. How do you think a speaker of one of these dialects would pronounce the L2 English words: *plate, sport,* and *translate*?

13.10 For each description, decide which term best identifies it. For (i)-(iii), choose *either field dependent learning* or *field independent learning*. For (iv)-(vi), choose either instrumental motivation or integrative motivation.
i. Learning by using world and situational information
ii. Learning by "the big picture"
iii. Learning by inner knowledge and solving things analytically
iv. Motivation to get a better job.
v. Motivation to be a worldly person.
vi. Motivation to live abroad.

13.11 According to the pro-drop parameter, not all languages require an overt subject. In English, subjects are obligatory, while in Italian and Spanish, they can be omitted. According to the Full Transfer/Full Access to UG Hypothesis (see Chapter 13's 'Delving Deeper' at www.cambridge.org/introducing-linguistics), what errors do you predict a beginning Italian L1 speaker would make learning English? Would an L1 Spanish speaker learning Italian make similar errors? Explain whether you think that Italian and Spanish speakers would eventually converge on the grammar of English.

13.12 In your experience as an L2 learner (or if you are not, talk to someone who is), do you remember occasions where what you had *learned* was more useful than what you had *acquired*? Use the Monitor Model Hypothesis to frame your answer.

13.13 Provide some examples of the types of learning activities that you think would be good scaffolding techniques according to sociocultural approaches to SLA.

13.14 List and describe some factors that affect SLA. Have you or an L2 learner you know had any personal experience with any of these?

13.15 Input, output, and interaction are widely studied issues in SLA. Briefly discuss how they each of them contribute to what we know about how L2s are learned. What teaching techniques or approaches can be used to focus on input, output, and interaction?

REFERENCES

Baddeley, A. (2003). Working memory and language: An overview. *Journal of Communication Disorders*, *36*(3), 189–208.

Bates, E., & MacWhinney, B. (1989). Functionalism and the Competition Model. In B. MacWhinney, & E. Bates (Eds.), *The crosslinguistic study of sentence processing*. New York, NY: Cambridge University Press.

Benati, A., & Schwieter, J. W. (2017). Input Processing and Processing Instruction: Pedagogical and cognitive considerations for L3 acquisition. In T. Angelovska & A. Hahn (Eds.), *L3 syntactic transfer: Models, new developments, and implications* (pp. 253–275). Amsterdam, The Netherlands/Philadelphia, PA: Benjamins.

Brown, R. (1973). *A first language: The early stages*. Cambridge, MA: Harvard University Press.

Bruhn de Garavito, J., & White, L. (2002). L2 acquisition of Spanish DPs: The status of grammatical features. In A. Pérez-Leroux & J. Liceras (Eds.), *The acquisition of Spanish morphosyntax: The L1/L2 connection* (pp. 153–178). Dordrecht: Kluwer.

Carroll, J., & Sapon, S. (1959). *Modern language aptitude test*. New York, NY: Psychological Corporation.

Dinnsen, D., & Eckman, F. (1975). A functional explanation of some phonological typologies. In R. Grossman, L. San, & T. Vance (Eds.), *Functionalism* (pp. 126–134). Chicago, IL: Chicago Linguistic Society.

Dörnyei, Z. (2009). The L2 Motivational Self System. In Z. Dörnyei & E. Ushioda (Eds.), *Motivation, language identity and the L2 self* (pp. 9–42). Bristol: Multilingual Matters.

Dörnyei, Z., & Clément, R. (2001). Motivational characteristics of learning different target languages: Results of a nationwide survey. In Z. Dörnyei & R. Schmidt (Eds.), *Motivation and second language acquisition* (pp. 399–432). Honolulu, HI: University of Hawaii Press.

Eckman, F. (1977). Markedness and the contrastive analysis hypothesis. *Language Learning, 27*, 315–330.

Eckman, F., Bell, L., & Nelson, D. (1988). On the generalization of relative clause instruction in the acquisition of English as a second language. *Applied Linguistics, 9*, 1–20.

Ellis, R. (1994). *The study of second language acquisition*. Oxford: Oxford University Press.

Ellis, R. (2001). *Form-focused instruction and second language learning*. Malden, MA: Blackwell.

Gardner, R. (2009). *Gardner and Lambert (1959): Fifty years and counting*. Paper presented at the Canadian Association of Applied Linguistics Symposium.

Gardner, R., & Lambert, W. (1959). Motivational variables in second language acquisition. *Canadian Journal of Psychology, 13,* 266–272.

Gardner, R., & MacIntyre, P. (1992). A student's contributions to second language learning: Part I: Cognitive variables. *Language Teaching, 25*(1), 211–220.

Gass, S. (1982). From theory to practice. In M. Hines & W. Rutherford (Eds.), *On TESOL '81* (pp. 129–139). Washington, DC: Teachers of English to Speakers of Other Languages.

Grüter, T., Lew-Williams, C., & Fernald, A. (2012). Grammatical gender in L2: A production or a real-time processing problem? *Second Language Research, 28*(2), 191–215.

Johnson, J., & Newport, E. (1989). Critical period effects in second language learning: The influence of maturational state on acquisition of ESL. *Cognitive Psychology, 21,* 60–99.

Keenan, E., & Comrie, B. (1977). Noun phrase accessibility and Universal Grammar. *Linguistic Inquiry, 8,* 63–99.

Kissau, S. (2006). Gender differences in motivation to learn French. *Canadian Modern Language Review, 62*(3), 401–422.

Krashen, S. (1982). *Principles and practice in second language acquisition.* Oxford: Pergamon.

Lardiere, D. (2007). *Ultimate attainment in second language acquisition: a case study.* Mahwah, NJ: Erlbaum.

Long, M. (1990). Maturational constraints on language development. *Studies in Second Language Acquisition, 12,* 251–285.

Mackey, A., & Philp, J. (1998). Conversational interaction and second language development: Recasts, responses, and red herrings? *The Modern Language Journal, 82,* 338–356.

MacWhinney, B. (2005). Extending the competition model. *International Journal of Bilingualism, 9*(7), 69–84.

Netten, J., Riggs, C., & Hewlett, S. (1999). *Choosing French in the senior high school: Grade 9 student attitudes to the study of French in the Western Avalon School District.* St. John's, Canada: Memorial University.

Nicholas, H., Lightbown, P. M., and Spada, N. (2001). Recasts as feedback to language learners. *Language Learning, 51,* 719–758.

Norton Peirce, B. (1995). Social identity, investment, and language learning. *TESOL Quarterly, 29*(1), 9–31.

Nunan, D. (1991). Methods in second language classroom-oriented research: A critical review. *Studies in Second Language Acquisition, 13,* 249–274.

Pica, T. (1994). Research on negotiation: What does it reveal about second-language learning conditions, processes, and outcomes? *Language Learning, 44,* 493–527.

Pienemann, M. (1998). *Language processing and second language development: Processability Theory.* Amsterdam/Philadelphia, PA: Benjamins.

Pimsleur, P. (1966). *Pimsleur Language Aptitude Battery (PLAB).* New York, NY: Harcourt Brace Jovanovich.

Schwartz, B., & Sprouse, R. (1996). L2 cognitive states and the full transfer/full access model. *Second Language Research, 12,* 40–77.

Schwieter, J. W. (2008). Language attitudes and gender: Descriptors and nationalistic ideologies. *The Buckingham Journal of Language and Linguistics, 1*(1), 113–127.

Schwieter, J. W. (2010). Developing second language writing through scaffolding in the ZPD: A magazine project for an authentic audience. *The Journal of College Teaching & Learning, 7*(10), 31–45.

Schwieter, J. W., & Klassen, G. (2016). Linguistic advances and learning strategies in a short-term study abroad experience. *Study Abroad Research in Second Language Acquisition and International Education, 1*(2), 217–247.

Scovel, T. (1988). *A time to speak: A psycholinguistic enquiry into the critical period for human speech.* Rowley, MA: Newbury House.

Singleton (1989). *Language acquisition: The age factor.* Clevedon: Multilingual Matters.

Slabakova, R. (2013). What is easy and what is hard to acquire in a second language: a generative perspective. In M. del Pilar García Mayo, M. Junkal Gutierrez Mangado, & M. Martínez Adrián (Eds.), *Contemporary approaches to second language acquisition*. Amsterdam/Philadelphia, PA: Benjamins.

Sorace, A. (2011). Pinning down the concept of "interface" in bilingualism. *Linguistic Approaches to Bilingualism, 1*(1), 1–33.

Sorensen, A. (1967). Multilingualism in the Northwest Amazon. *American Anthropologist, 69*(6), 670–684.

Spada, N. (1997). Form-focussed instruction and second language acquisition: A review of classroom and laboratory research. *Language Teaching, 30*, 73–87.

Swain, M. (1995). Three functions of output in second language learning. In G. Cook & B. Seidlhofer (Eds.), *Principle and practice in applied linguistics* (pp. 125–144). Oxford: Oxford University Press.

Swain, M., & Lapkin, S. (1985). *Evaluating bilingual education: A Canadian case study*. Clevedon: Multilingual Matters.

VanPatten, B. (2002). Processing instruction: An update. *Language Learning, 52*, 755–803.

VanPatten, B., & Cadierno, T. (1993). Explicit instruction and input processing. *Studies in Second Language Acquisition, 15*, 225–243.

White, L. (1989). *Universal Grammar in second language acquisition*. Amsterdam/Philadelphia, PA: Benjamins.

White, L. (2003). On the nature of interlanguage representation: Universal Grammar in the second language. In C. Doughty & M. Long (Eds.), *The handbook of second language acquisition* (pp. 19–42). Malden, MA: Blackwell.

Williams, M., Burden, R., & Lanvers, U. (2002). 'French is the language of love and stuff': Student perceptions of issues related to motivation in learning a foreign language. *British Educational Research Journal, 28*, 503–528.

Wong, W., & VanPatten, B. (2003). The evidence IN: Drills are OUT. *Foreign Language Annals, 36*, 403–423.

Wyss, R. (2002). Field independent/dependent learning styles and L2 acquisition. *Journal of ELT, 49*, 125–128.

PART 7

LANGUAGE, COGNITION, AND THE BRAIN

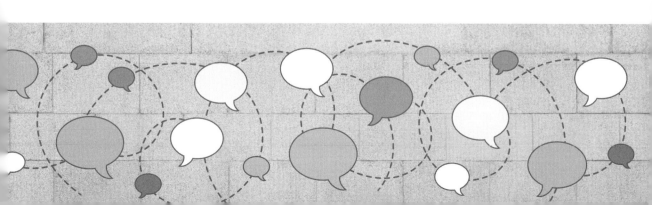

14 Psycholinguistics

Language Processing

John W. Schwieter

OVERVIEW

In this chapter, you will develop an understanding of psycholinguistics. Along the way, you will learn about how humans use their linguistic competence to speak and understand language. In doing so, you will:

- **learn about speech production and comprehension;**
- **explore how sounds, words, and sentences are processed;**
- **consider some of the common methods used to study language processing;**
- **read about how language processing works among bilinguals;** and
- **study current issues and approaches in language processing research.**

14.1 What Is Psycholinguistics?

Psycholinguistics is an interdisciplinary field that intersects with linguistics, psychology, and cognitive science. It can be defined as the study of the cognitive processes and mental representations that are involved in language production, comprehension, and acquisition. Because we have dedicated specific chapters to language acquisition (see Chapter 12 First Language Acquisition and Chapter 13 Second Language Acquisition), in this chapter we will focus on processing during language production and comprehension.

Central to the study of psycholinguistics is understanding how language(s) is/are processed. **Language processing** refers to the real-time use of language, whether to comprehend or to produce.

PAUSE AND REFLECT 14.1

Stop for a moment and think about the incredible ability of the human mind to produce and comprehend speech. Can you think of the many steps required for a person to simply name a picture of a dog?

Let's take an example of two people involved in a conversation. Unconsciously, Person A comes up with a message, plans how to express it, and articulates it to Person B. Person B recognizes the speech sounds, accesses the words and meanings associated with those sounds, and then comprehends what he/she has heard. This procedure has been explained through psycholinguistic modelling. A well-cited example of this is Levelt's (1989) speech production model.

Levelt's speech production model visualizes a *blueprint of a speaker*. The model holds that a speaker uses situational knowledge, or background information, to conceptualize a message to be conveyed. This pre-verbal message allows the speaker to formulate and encode the intended speech and its grammatical and sound properties. The speaker utters the speech which is heard by the listener. Finally, the listener uses sound and grammatical properties to understand what is heard through his/her speech comprehension system.

Although speech production and comprehension are more complex than our very brief discussion of Levelt's model, in the upcoming sections we will expand on how language is processed at the sound, word, and sentence level. At the end of the chapter, we will discuss other relevant theories and models.

Before we begin discussing how sounds, words, and sentences are processed, let us first address the remarkable ability for humans to process language in a bottom-up and top-down manner. Imagine that you are listening to a lecture. Your comprehension of what the speaker is saying will depend on several levels of language processing. At the lowest level, the phonological level, you identify the individual phonemes and the syllables they create. At a higher level, the lexical level, you retrieve the words to which the sounds and syllables belong. At an even higher level, the syntactic level, you organize these words into constituents that adhere to phrase structure rules of the language. Finally, at the highest level, the discourse level, the meaning of sentences is linked to preceding sentences and coherent discourse is formulated.

In this step-by-step example, speech comprehension happens through **bottom-up processing** with lower levels being unaffected by higher ones. In other words, we identify sounds without influence from words, syntax, and discourse; we retrieve words without influence from syntax and discourse; and we construct phrase structure without influence from discourse.

However, consider that in the lecture, you hear the speaker start to say a sentence as in (1). As you proceed to understand the speech through bottom-up processing, you may notice that you can probably fill in the rest of the sentence without even hearing it.

(1)   The dog ran back and forth, from the left to …

Our ability to fill in (1) shows us that we not only use bottom-up processing in language comprehension but we must also be able to employ **top-down processing**. Top-down processing draws on context and higher levels to process information at lower levels. So just as you used syntactic information from *the left* to construct *the right* and not just *right*, you also used semantic and discourse information from the other word pair *back* and *forth* to figure out that what was missing should also be an opposite to the word *left*. Top-down processing, instead of being step-by-step in nature, uses semantic, syntactic, and contextual information to analyze sound in a parallel manner.

So which type of processing is more accurate for language: bottom-up or top-down processing? Both of them are actually correct. We use both bottom-up and top-down processing in language production and comprehension. In Section 14.5, we will return to discuss other ways that the human mind can process linguistic information. For now, keep in mind that language processing seems to be a dynamic and interactive process that requires us to examine it at multiple levels and using several types of methods.

PAUSE AND REFLECT 14.2

If you hear the first two sounds [da] of a word, what are a few of the possibilities that the word could be? Have you used bottom-up or top-down processing to come up with examples?

14.2 Language Processing

Research in psycholinguistics has made huge advances in terms of what we know about how language is processed. In this section, we will talk about key issues related to processing sounds, words, and syntax. To read about how language processing interacts with context and pragmatics, read 'Delving Deeper' in Chapter 14's resources on the website to accompany this book at www.cambridge.org/introducing-linguistics.

14.2.1 Sounds

The sounds we make in human language are fundamental in producing and understanding speech. Although we speak using sounds, these sounds are produced and perceived as a continuous signal of speech. In Chapter 2 Phonetics, we talked a great deal about the articulatory properties of sounds – things like whether they were bilabial, voiced, stops, etc. But it is not articulation that is heard but rather acoustic characteristics of sound. We refer to this auditory information as an acoustic signal or **speech signal**. Oftentimes, psycholinguists researching sound processing are less curious about how sounds are articulated and more intrigued with how sounds are extracted and processed from the speech signal.

Imagine that you travel to a country which speaks a language that you have never heard before. As you listen to this unfamiliar language, it is probably impossible for you to divide up sounds into syllables and syllables into words. In fact, if it weren't for things like pauses, the language would more than likely sound like a continuous (and probably fast) string of unidentifiable noise. It is clear from this example that some phonological knowledge of the language must be known in order to convert continuous sounds into meaningful segments. This is in effect a central research question in sound processing.

We have come to learn that as we hear speech, we are able to identify and process individual sounds only after analyzing their surrounding sound environment.

One of the first studies demonstrating that the surrounding sound environment is important to speech perception was by Schatz (1954). This study found that perception of voiceless stops such as /k/ depends on their sound environment. In the study, the /k/ was removed from tape recordings of the words *keep*, *cop*, and *coop*. It was then added onto the beginning of vowel-consonant sequences such as [-aɹ] and [-ul]. But instead of hearing *car*, the participants in the study overwhelmingly reported hearing *tar*. And instead of *cool*, they said they heard *pool*. The same effect was found when removing /sk/ from words and then adding it onto [-aɹ] and [-ul]. Participants once again heard *star* instead of *scar* and *spool* instead of *school*. Schatz' study showed that an individual sound can be perceived as a number of different phonemes which cannot be determined until the following sounds are processed. In this example, we note that /k/ was perceived as either /p, t, k/ depending on the vowel that follows. Schatz' study is one of the first to show that when we comprehend speech, we do not hear individual sounds, but rather we perceive and analyze a continuum of sounds.

LINGUISTICS TIDBITS: SPEECH PERCEPTION WITH COCHLEAR IMPLANTS

A cochlear implant is a surgically implanted device in the inner ear. It provides sound signals to the brain for individuals who are profoundly deaf or have a severe hearing impairment. The device bypasses the normal processes of spoken speech perception by transmitting signals to implanted electrodes in the cochlea. These signals stimulate the cochlear nerve as would occur among the hearing population. The acoustic input picked up by the device is usually enough for the individual to understand the speech of a familiar voice but when hearing new speakers, there may be difficulties at first. With more exposure to the new speaker, speech perception improves.

Another characteristic we must mention about speech perception is its remarkable ability to adapt to variations of pronunciation. Think about the different ways people may say the word *forty*. Someone from Toronto might say [foɹɾi], someone from Atlanta may pronounce it as [faɹɾi] or [faɾi], and a person from Manchester possibly would say [fɔti]. How are we still able to understand these different pronunciations as the same word? The answer is that our speech perception is flexible to variations in pronunciation. It uses normalization processes that allow for listeners to adjust to various speech rates and individual differences.

PAUSE AND REFLECT 14.3

If we have knowledge of how sounds should be produced, how do you think we adjust to some second language learners' non-native-like pronunciations?

Have you ever noticed that when you read someone's lips while they are speaking, it may be easier to understand what they are saying? This may be especially true when you are in noisy situations, when the speaker is new to you, or when he/she has a non-native accent. The opposite might frustrate you when you hear dubbed-over speech in a foreign film that does not match up to the lip movements of the speakers.

LINGUISTICS TIDBITS: THE MCGURK EFFECT

Play the two-minute YouTube video found at http://www.youtube.com/watch?v=jtsfidRq2tw&t=4s. In the video, you first see and hear someone repeating a single syllable. Next, the audio is removed and you are only able to see the person saying the syllable. Do you notice that you perceive the sounds to be different now? This sound illusion is known as the **McGurk effect** (McGurk & MacDonald, 1976). The effect shows that when a sound is paired with the visual movement of another sound, a third (usually blended) sound will be perceived.

Research shows that we use lip and jaw movements to help facilitate speech perception. This idea is at the core of **motor theory**. As early as the 1950s and stretching into the 1980s, Liberman and colleagues (1957; 1967; 1985) refined motor theory. In their explanation of how speech perception happens, they argue that humans perceive sounds partly, but not exclusively, through analogy with how those sounds are articulated. In other words, our comprehension of sounds has largely to do with our knowledge of how those sounds are produced. We know that when the jaw is wide open, the sound being made is probably an [a] and when the lips are rounded, the sound might be [u] or a few other sounds. This knowledge is what helps us to read lips and assists us in speech perception.

To fully understand the perception of sound, we must go beyond looking at the influence of surrounding sounds (i.e., Schatz, 1954) and our knowledge of articulation movements (i.e., motor theory). One way is to examine the activation levels of other language elements such as words. For example, according to the **TRACE model** (McClelland & Elman, 1986; Elman & McClelland, 1988), several levels of processing – feature level, phoneme level, word level – are all said to be simultaneously active during word recognition. **Activation** spreads from one level to another interactively. Activation refers to the extent to which words, concepts, among other things, are readily available. Levels of activation increase with higher frequency of use. Imagine that you are watching fish swim around in a tank. The concept FISH would have a higher activation level than something you haven't thought about for quite a while. We will return to discuss activation in Section 14.4.2.

An example of how the word *bus* is recognized when it is heard is explained by the TRACE model in Figure 14.1. As soon as the speech signal begins, in this case with the sound /b/, activation will spread to related and overlapping features, phonemes, and words. Arrows show the direction of activation flow and are bidirectional, suggesting that activation spreads and interacts between levels.

As shown in Figure 14.1, among the activated elements when hearing *bus* are words also beginning with /b/ like *bat* or with /ʌ/ as their second sound like *cut*. The activation levels are raised and lowered as necessary until the correct candidates have the highest activation and can be easily selected as a match. In other words, the activation levels of sounds and words that are not needed in the search can be reduced to the point that they no longer interfere with word retrieval. Solid circles, like in the case of the word *sick* suggest that activation has been suppressed because there is no match with the target word *bus*. If these activation levels are not regulated, interference would result in an inappropriate word being activated and retrieved from the mental lexicon. This is

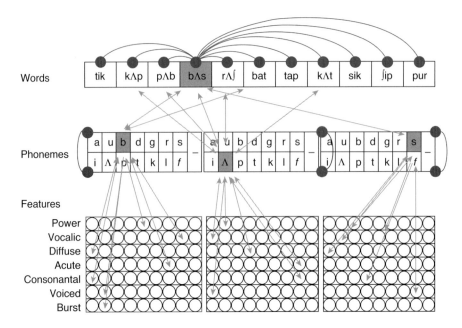

Figure 14.1 The TRACE model of speech perception. From: McClelland, J., Mirman, D., & Holt, L. (2006). Are there interactive processes in speech perception? *Trends in Cognitive Sciences, 10*(8), 363–369. Reproduced with permission of Elsevier through PLSclear.

why activation levels of the traces are modified (either maintained, lowered, or raised) according to the input in the speech signal.

A similar view of the TRACE model which also explains sound processing in the context of dynamic activation is the **cohort model** (Marslen-Wilson, 1990). The model focuses on both speech sounds and the retrieval of the words that make up those sounds. According to the cohort model, we understand a spoken word across three stages. The first stage is a search for and activation of words beginning with the same sound similar to the TRACE model. But unlike the TRACE model which assumes simultaneous processing, the cohort model explains word recognition in a step-by-step fashion.

So, for the word *bus,* the /b/ would first activate a cohort of other words that also start with /b/. These are known as the word-initial cohort. Second, when the next sound is heard, the cohort will adjust and discard the words that no longer match the input. This process of elimination continues until one word is left (i.e., the target word *bus* that matches the acoustic input). This word will also have the highest activation level which can be modulated by things like word frequency and ongoing discourse. In the third stage, the selected word is integrated into the syntactic and semantic context. The cohort model demonstrates that the phoneme is the fundamental element essential for the perception of spoken words.

A final explanation of sound processing that is important to mention takes into account and categorizes articulation and voicing time. This is known as **categorical perception**. According to this line of thought, when sounds are heard, they are categorized by their place of articulation and voice onset time. Recall from Chapter 2 Phonetics that voice onset time refers to the length of time that passes between when a speaker releases a consonant and when the voicing begins on the following vowel or consonant. So, when you hear the sound /b/, you categorize it as a bilabial sound and as one which has faster voice onset times than voiceless stops like /p, t, k/. Categorizing sounds when they are processed by their articulation and voice onset time is yet another way we can explain how sounds are perceived.

Each of the explanations we have given for processing sound has strengths and weaknesses and it is not yet clear which views may be most accurate. Ongoing research will continue to help us understand how sounds are processed.

14.2.2 Words

How does the structure, formation, and meaning of words affect language processing? What cognitive processes allow words to be accessed and recognized? We will discuss these important questions below.

As we said in Chapter 4 Morphology, words consist of one or more morphemes. For example, the words *honeymoon*, *singer*, and *sadness* all consist of two morphemes (*honey + moon*; *sing + –er*; *sad + –ness*). Research has shown that morphemes are independently activated during word recognition. Evidence of this comes from experiments which show that during the visual recognition of multi-morphemic words like *honeymoon*, semantically related words such as *bee* and *sun* are also activated. *Sing* and *music* are likely activated when recognizing *singer*; and *sad* and *happy* might be activated when recognizing *sadness*. Of course, several other words are likely activated as well but these are just a few examples.

Words with only one morpheme such as *dog* also activate related words such as *cat* and *bone*. The interconnectivity of the mental lexicon can also be seen in pseudo-multimorphemic words like *mother* – which even though it does not mean *a person who moths*, activates words related to a moth, like *butterfly*. The related words that are activated in *honeymoon*, *singer*, *sadness*, *dog*, and *mother* are all examples of morphological priming in which a morpheme primes, or activates, a related word. We will talk more about priming in Section 14.3.2.

PAUSE AND REFLECT 14.4

Words that look like they contain more than one morpheme but really don't, such as the example with the word *mother*, can still prime a word like *butterfly*.

If an experiment shows that the word *brother* primes *soup*, do you think *cat* would prime *cattle*? Why or why not?

Lexical access is the process of retrieving a word and information about it (e.g., semantic, syntactic) from the mental lexicon. The **mental lexicon** is a dictionary of information which contains word characteristics including their phonological, syntactic, and semantic properties. One of the earliest explanations of how words are recognized and accessed was Forster's (1976) **search model** as shown in Figure 14.2.

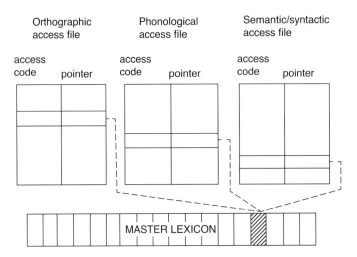

Figure 14.2 The search model. From: Forster, K. (1976). Accessing the mental lexicon. In R. Wales & E. Walker (Eds.), *New approaches to language mechanisms* (pp. 257–287). Amsterdam, The Netherlands: North-Holland. Reproduced with permission of Elsevier through PLSclear.

According to the search model, word recognition is independent from other language processing and is divided into several components called access files. One access file is responsible for phonetic properties of words and another is dedicated to orthographic properties. Both orthographic and phonetic access files are organized in descending order such that more frequent words are searched before lower frequency words. When a word is seen or heard, the input will activate either the orthographic or phonetic access file and a matching word will be identified. Once this occurs, the system follows a pointer to where the word is located in the master lexicon. The system does a post-access check to verify that the correct word has been selected.

Several factors can affect lexical access. For example, research has shown that the speed of word retrieval depends on things like word frequency, phonological neighborhood density, morphological complexity, and lexical ambiguity. Words that are more frequently used will have a higher resting level of activation and according to the search model, will also be higher up on the search list. The **frequency effect** refers to the observation that more frequent words are accessed more quickly and the **recency effect** states that words more recently processed are accessed more rapidly.

A word's phonological neighborhood will also affect lexical processing. A word's **phonological neighborhood** includes all other words that are phonologically similar. So a word like *gate* has a dense neighborhood because there are many similar words:

LINGUISTICS TIDBITS: LEXICAL ACCESS AND THE BRAIN

Significant progress has been made in lexical access research that combines experimental methods with brain imaging technologies. This has provided a more detailed account of how lexical access proceeds. Some studies are using event-related potentials (ERPs) to reveal a fine-grained analysis of lexical access that could not be seen using behavioral techniques alone. We now know that lexical access occurs in stages and that behavioral methods may not fully capture what happens during the earlier stages. Brain measures of lexical access, which are recorded continuously, are able to capture and measure the precise timing and effort needed to process lexical items at early and later stages of lexical processing in real time.

late, gap, get, etc. Research shows that words with more phonological neighbors are retrieved more slowly than words with fewer neighbors. This suggests that more information is required to identify the word being accessed within a denser neighborhood.

Words that are morphologically complex are also slower to be processed than simpler words. Some research has shown that individual morphemes are organized and represented separately in the mind. For instance, *happiness* would be stored as the root word *happy* and the separate representation (i.e., derivational affix) *–ness* would be combined. Evidence for this comes from studies which show that it takes longer to recognize words with pseudomorphemes compared to real morphemes (Taft, 1981). For example, the prefixed word *redo* will be recognized quicker than the pseudo-prefixed word *refer*. Because pseudo-prefixed words take longer to recognize, it is assumed that words are first deconstructed and analyzed in morphological units. So, in the case of *refer, re-* is first removed and the search for *fer* begins. Once this search is unsuccessful, *re-* is reattached and analyzed as the single morpheme *refer*.

Lexical ambiguity can also affect word recognition. Lexical ambiguity can arise when a word has more than one meaning. Experiments have shown that it takes participants longer to recognize ambiguous words compared to unambiguous words. This is likely because more resources are required to process words which activate multiple meanings. Interestingly, though, even when an ambiguous word is found in a sentence which clarifies its meaning, all other possible meanings are still activated for young, typically-developed monolingual speakers only (see Brien & Sabourin, 2012). A classic example of the effects of lexical ambiguity on word recognition is Swinney's (1979) study. In this study, listeners heard sentences containing ambiguous words in contexts with a strong bias toward one of the meanings of the ambiguous word. An example from Swinney's study was:

> Rumor had it that, for years, the government building has been plagued with problems. The man was not surprised when he found several spiders, roaches, and other bugs in the corner of his room (Swinney & Hakes, 1976, p. 686).

Although the word *bugs* is ambiguous, there is a strong bias towards its meaning in this sentence – one which refers to the insect and not the device used to listen or spy. Swinney's (1979) study showed that the word *bugs* not only activated related words such as *ant*, it also activated words like *spy*. This important study shows that even in sentences with biasing contexts, lexically-ambiguous words activate their multiple meanings.

But what happens when a word cannot be accessed? One interesting phenomenon in lexical access which you have probably experienced first-hand is being in a **tip-of-the-tongue (TOT) state**. This happens when we are temporarily unable to retrieve a word from the mental lexicon. If this has happened to you, more than likely, you probably felt frustrated having a word on the tip of your tongue but not being able to retrieve it. This is because it is neither comfortable nor standard for the mind to be in a TOT state. However, the inability to access a word tells psycholinguistics more than just that it feels frustrating. Researchers have found that when participants are in a TOT state, they often will be able to retrieve the word when given a clue about its sound or meaning (Brown, 2012). For example, knowing the first letter or sound of the word will greatly improve the chances of successfully accessing the word. This demonstrates the interconnected nature of the mental lexicon in which things like sound and meaning interact with word processing.

14.2.3   Sentences

When we hear a sentence, we not only perceive the words that make up the sentence but each of these words must be processed and assigned a category (e.g., noun, verb, etc.). **Parsing** is the process of assigning syntactic structure (or phrase structure) to words and/or phrases. Many researchers believe that during parsing, several **processing strategies** are used. These strategies guide language comprehension by assigning grammatical categories to incoming words and determining the syntactic relationship of words within phrases, and phrases within sentences. We unconsciously apply these strategies during sentence processing and they are fairly reliable, although their application may not always be relevant in certain cases.

We can get a better understanding of the parsing strategies involved in sentence processing by looking at what happens when they break down. Let's look more closely at a few of these parsing strategies and also at how ambiguity may take parsing strategies down the wrong path – something commonly called *"the garden path"* in syntactic processing research. Consider the sentences (2)–(5).

(2)   The cat ate the bird and the mouse ran.
(3)   Since Harry always runs five kilometers seem like nothing.
(4)   The responsible people the lectures every day.
(5)   I like fine wines am delightful.

Sentences (2)–(5) are examples of **garden path sentences**. In each of them, you probably had to read them more than once to try to understand them. A garden path sentence is one that is syntactically constructed in a way that often leads to misunderstanding the sentence, causing the reader to backtrack and reparse. You can think of a garden path sentence as a hedge maze – one of those outdoor garden labyrinths made of tall vertical hedges as walls. Just like a hedge maze can lead you to a dead-end and force you to backtrack, a garden path sentence can do the same: it can take parsing strategies down the wrong path. At some point you realize your current interpretation doesn't work and you are forced to reanalyze the sentence..

PAUSE AND REFLECT 14.5

Processing challenges can occur when a sentence does not meet our first expectation as in (i).

(i) The complex houses married and single students and their families.

What trouble, if any, did you have processing this sentence? If you are like most readers, you probably assumed that the main verb was *married* and that the subject was *the complex houses*. Now read the sentence in (ii) and notice how this garden path sentence becomes clearer:

(ii) [$_{NP}$ The complex] [$_{VP}$ houses] [$_{NP}$ married and single students] and [$_{NP}$ their families].

Garden path sentences show us that certain parsing strategies function as general principles in sentence interpretation. It seems as though parsing strategies prefer simplicity whenever possible. The **minimal attachment strategy** states that a minimal amount of syntactic structure should be built. Imagine that as you hear a sentence, your mind is trying to build a syntactic tree diagram of the sentence. Its preference, according to the minimal attachment strategy, would be to build the simplest tree structure with the least amount of syntactic nodes. Syntactic processing uses this strategy to try to group words under the same node and if it is not possible, it builds a new one. For example, read (6) and (7).

(6) The lawyer stated his position clearly.
(7) The lawyer stated his position was accurate.

In sentence (6), the adverb *clearly* is attached to the current constituent [$_{VP}$ stated his position] while (7) is a complement construction which requires building a new constituent [$_{IP}$ his position was accurate]. Reading times for sentences such as (6) are faster than for sentences such as (7). This is because the processing strategy shows preference for trying to place new words under an existing syntactic node. When processing requires that a new node be created, as in (7), more time is needed.

Another processing strategy is that we prefer to parse constituents that we are currently processing. For example, according to the **late closure strategy**, there should be a preference for attaching incoming words to the constituent currently being processed. This is said to help alleviate demands on working memory during parsing. Unfortunately, as can be seen in (8) and (9), this may not always work.

(8) Janine said that Mike will leave yesterday.
(9) Janine says that Mike will leave usually.

When you read (8), more than likely your parsing strategies tried to attach *yesterday* to the constituent currently being processed, [*will leave*]. A garden path effect would likely occur because of the conflict between the future tense and the word *yesterday*. This would probably result in the need to backtrack and attach *yesterday* to the main verb *said*. Similarly, in (9), the future tense and the word *usually* may also conflict and cause you to reparse and correctly assign *usually* with [*Janine says*].

PAUSE AND REFLECT 14.6

As you can see from parsing strategies, the human mind finds ways to complete a task (in this case, to understand sentences). Can you think of another task in which you find that you use strategies to more easily complete the task at hand?

Read 'Delving Deeper' in Chapter 14's resources on the website to accompany this book at www.cambridge.org/introducing-linguistics to learn about another sentence processing strategy called the main clause strategy.

We have not yet talked about to what extent, if at all, certain areas of language processing are independent from others. Here we turn to the idea of **modularity**. Modularity refers to the degree to which language processing is independent from general cognitive processing. In other words, a modular view of syntactic processing would argue that it is unaffected by other levels of processing like sounds and words. Researchers have been interested in whether syntactic parsing operates automatically and independently from other information-processing systems. Frazier (1995) argues in favor of a modular account in which sentence parsing is first processed by a syntactic module that is independent from and unaffected by things like context, meaning, or world knowledge. These factors are said to have an influence only after the parsing is executed by the syntactic module.

An alternative view to modularity is **interactivity**, an account which argues that syntactic processing interacts with and is influenced by other types of processing. Unlike the modular view, researchers who view sentence processing as an interactive procedure argue that parsing involves simultaneous processing of syntactic, lexical, discourse, and non-linguistic information such as background knowledge. For example, Trueswell, Tanenhaus, & Garnsey (1994) suggest that syntactic and contextual information interact during sentence processing. They argue against modular views that hypothesize that initial parsing occurs independent of other processing and information such as context.

Findings on how independent syntactic processing is from other processing types have been controversial and both modular and interactive accounts have received empirical support. Researchers continue to study the degree of interaction between syntactic processing and other types of processing.

EYES ON WORLD LANGUAGES: PROCESSING AMERICAN SIGN LANGUAGE

Do you think that American Sign Language (ASL) shows grammar in the signs that it uses? If you said yes, you are right. In fact, ASL has a rich use of morphology and syntax. For example, in the phrase *tell me*, the movement of the sign *tell* is toward the signer whereas in the phrase *tell you*, the movement is towards the addressee. In other words, the marking of these object pronouns is built into the motion of the sign. When the object pronoun also refers to the subject as in *tell each other*, ASL marks this reciprocity by signing *tell* towards and away from the signer.

Quite a bit of research has compared and contrasted the processing of ASL and English. It is generally accepted that ASL is a separate language from English, however, there are many similarities that exist in terms of their grammatical organization. We even see similarities between processing ASL and English when it comes to the types of errors made by signers and speakers, respectively. You will read more about these naturalistic errors in Section 14.3.1.

14.3   Psycholinguistic Methods

How can we research how language is processed by the mind? There are many techniques that allow us to do this including observing naturally occurring language phenomena or performing experimental and neurological measures. Below you will read about the most common methods of data collection that help us to understand the complex nature of language processing.

14.3.1   Observing Naturalistic Data

Methods that observe natural occurrences of language and the errors that unexpectedly arise in everyday language are very telling of language processing. Below we review some common naturalistic methods used in psycholinguistics.

Slips of the Tongue

Can you think of a time when you accidentally exchanged one sound for a sound from another word (e.g., maybe you said *the mat and couse* instead of *the cat and mouse*)? Have you said the wrong word completely (e.g., *pass me the fork* instead of *pass me the spoon*)? While very much unplanned, and often humorous, these errors are not random. In fact, they are a reflection of language processing. We can learn a great deal from unintentional language slips, which is why it should not be surprising to learn that these naturalistic errors have formed part of psycholinguistic research methods since its earliest days.

Speech errors are a normal part of our language use. It is said that for every 1,000 words we say, we make one or two errors. For the typical person, that is equivalent to making between 7–22 speech errors per day. To psychologists and linguists, these slips of the tongue have been of great interest at least since Rev. William A. Spooner's time at New College, Oxford (1867 until his death). Rev. Spooner became famous for his absent-minded gaffes and accidental (although some may have been intentional) speech errors in which he would switch sounds and morphemes. Even though Rev. Spooner's obituary in 1930 mentions that he was not fond of the reputation he had gained for what became known during his lifetime as **spoonerisms**, we cannot deny that these natural errors tell us something about language processing. The word *spoonerisms* has become synonymous with **slips of the tongue**, an accidental mistake in spoken speech that is a deviation from the intended utterance.

A slip of the tongue can be an accidental exchange of sounds or morphemes or they can also occur to whole words and even phrases. As an example, read sentence (10) and then compare it to the possible slips of the tongue that one might expect in (10a)–(10f).

(10)   I tried to read the book to my grandson.
(10a) I tried to read the book to my <u>b</u>randson.
(10b) I tried to read the <u>g</u>rook to my grandson.
(10c) I <u>read</u>ed to <u>try</u> the book to my grandson.
(10d) I try to read<u>ed</u> the book to my grandson.
(10e) I tried to read the <u>paper</u> to my grandson.
(10f) I tried to read <u>my grandson</u> to <u>the book</u>.

PAUSE AND REFLECT 14.7

Before reading on, can you try to figure out whether the slips of the tongue in (10) involve a sound, morphological, or syntactic error?

Each of the variations of (10) exhibit a different slip of the tongue. For instance, (10a) and (10b) both entail sound errors. To be more specific, (10a) shows the influence of one sound on another: the velar stop [g] in *grandson* changes to [b] due to the enduring influence of the bilabial sound [m] in *my*. We call this type of effect **preserved influence** because the effect comes from a sound already articulated. The slip of the tongue in (10b) shows the influence of one syllable on another: [gr] that we see in *grandson* replaces the onset [b] in *book*. Unlike (10a), the influence in (10b) is in the opposite direction. We call this **anticipatory influence** because the effect comes from a sound not yet articulated.

The slips of the tongue in (10c), (10d), and (10e) are related to morphology. In (10c), there is a stem morpheme exchange in which the stem *read* replaces *try* while the inflectional morpheme *–ed* remains in place. In (10d), however, it is the inflectional morpheme *–ed* which shifts from *try* to *read*. Another morphological speech error can be seen in (10e) where the new word *paper* replaces the target word *book*.

Finally, (10f) shows that even a syntactic error can occur and an entire phrase may switch order with another phrase. This type of slip of the tongue is the least common. Can you think of which types are most common? The answer to this is an equal distribution between sound errors like in (10a) and (10b). The next more common errors are morphological such as the one in (10e).

PAUSE AND REFLECT 14.8

In a slip of the tongue like (10e) in which a new word replaces another word, what do you notice about the relationship between the new word and the word it replaced? What do you think this means?

The slips of the tongue in (10) tell us some key information about language processing. For example, in order for one sound to exchange with another sound that occurs later in the sentence, much or all of the utterance must have been planned out to some degree before speech began. We can also see that morphemes – both bound morphemes like –ed and free morphemes like *book* – are processed and may even function independently.

Slips of the Ear

If slips of the tongue are speech *production* errors, are there also errors of speech *comprehension*? If you have ever misheard something, you probably know that the answer is yes. **Slips of the ear**, also called mishearing, are errors in speech comprehension in which a word or phrase is mistaken for another similar sounding word or phrase. Slips of the ear almost always involve sound perception mistakes that typically involve word boundaries or stress.

Psycholinguists have noticed that sounds misheard in English are often in unstressed syllables and in the middle of a word. This is because in English, about 90 percent of nouns and verbs are stressed on the first syllable. A study by Cutler & Butterfield (1992) showed that when listeners heard words without stress on the first syllable, they were more likely to have a slip of the ear. For example, instead of hearing *conduct ascends uphill*, some participants heard *a duck descends some pill*. For a listener, speech comes in a continuous stream of sounds. Word boundaries must be identified in order to access words from the mental lexicon. Studies like Cutler and Butterfield's show that from slips of the ear,

LINGUISTICS TIDBITS: SLIPS OF THE HAND

Just like slips of the tongue and slips of the ear, in sign language, there can also be slips of the hand(s). In fact, research has shown that when comparing errors between sign language and spoken language, similar types of errors occur such as signing the wrong word. By comparing the naturalistic errors that are produced by users of signed and spoken languages, we see similar principles of language organization that underlie both. The discovery that sign language shows phonological properties similar to those in spoken languages suggests that "human languages universally develop a level of meaningless linguistic structure and a system that organizes this structure" (Emmorey, 2007, p. 704).

we may assume that listeners use clues such as stressed syllables to assist them in separating sounds across word boundaries in speech comprehension.

One drawback of observing naturalistic phenomena is that the researcher has little to no control over when and how often things like slips of the tongue will occur. Many psycholinguists turn to other forms of data collection methods such as those which take place in an experimental lab.

14.3.2   Experimental Methods

Analyzing the behavior of participants in experimental contexts is the most common approach to collecting psycholinguistic data. Unlike the naturalistic data we discussed in 14.3.1, in experimental methods, researchers have control over the context in which human participants process language and the stimuli to which they are exposed. Below we review some common experimental methods used in psycholinguistic research.

Lexical Decision Tasks

In a **lexical decision task**, participants are presented with words and nonwords that are individually displayed on a computer screen in front of them. Participants are asked to simply press a *yes* button if the string of letters they see is a real word or *no* if it is not. Researchers are typically interested in the reaction time (RT) and accuracy of participants' responses. Using these two variables, we are able to gather information about the difficulty of processing – the longer it takes to respond to a stimulus, the more processing is involved.

Lexical decision tasks tell us about the speed and accuracy of access to the mental lexicon. These experiments have consistently shown that more frequent words are responded to more quickly than less frequent words. For example, on average it takes about half a second (500 ms) to process a frequent word such as *shirt* but it may take three-fourths of a second (750 ms) to process a less frequent word such as *sparrow* and even up to a second (1,000 ms) for a very infrequent word such as *alacrity*. This supports what the search model in Figure 14.2 argues: the mental lexicon is organized so that the words that are needed to be accessed more often are readily available and are considered before less frequent words.

Lexical decision tasks can also give us insight into the role of phonology in lexical access. Research has shown that when nonwords are phonologically possible such as *cuperst*, participants respond more slowly than when nonwords are not phonologically possible like *pvrap*. This implies that the knowledge of phonology is used

> **LINGUISTICS TIDBITS: THE SHADOWING TASK**
>
> A **shadowing task** asks participants to listen to sentences and repeat them as quickly as possible and exactly as they were heard. Participants are told that while some sentences are correct, others may have errors like mispronunciations or incorrect inflections. On average, there is a delay of anywhere from 300–800 ms before a participant begins to repeat what they have heard. Interestingly, listeners will often correct errors that were in the original sentences they heard. In fact, listeners are usually unable to say whether the sentences contained errors at all!

to quickly reject words that do not conform to the language's sound rules. While a laborious search happens for phonologically possible nonwords, it is likely that a search is considered unnecessary for nonwords which are not phototactically possible.

Priming

We have said that a more frequent word such as *shirt* is processed faster than a word that is less frequent such as *sparrow*. Would the processing time for *sparrow* be sped up if it were preceded by a semantically related word like *robin*? What if it were preceded by a word with the same onset such as *spot* or by a word with which it rhymes like *pharaoh?* The answer to all of these questions is *yes*. The **priming paradigm** seeks to look at the effect of a priming stimulus, called a **prime**, on the processing of a target stimulus. A prime is usually presented for about 100 ms and is immediately followed by a target stimulus to which a participant must respond.

Using priming techniques in a lexical decision task is an effective way to explore how words are related to one another in the mind. It is now believed that semantically-related words are somehow linked in networks. For example, when a participant sees the word *robin* in the form of a prime, its concept, or the *mental picture*, is activated and this activation is spread to several related concepts. Among these related concepts in the network is the target *sparrow* which is why it is processed more quickly following the prime *robin*. In other words, the target *sparrow* has been pre-activated and is more accessible to be processed, at least temporarily. We call this observed processing facilitation a **priming effect**.

EYES ON WORLD LANGUAGES: PICTURE-WORD INTERFERENCE IN DUTCH-ENGLISH BILINGUALS

If we ask someone to simply name a picture of a truck, it would be pretty easy, right? What if we placed a distracter word next to the picture of the truck? Even with this slight interference, which would probably be seen in the RT, the participant would still be able to say *truck*. If we adapt the task so that the distracter word is presented in the participant's second language, do you think that there would still be interference? The quick answer is *yes*. For bilinguals, there is overwhelming support that both languages are constantly active and competing in the mind during language production and comprehension.

In a well-cited study by Hermans *et al.* (1998), Dutch-English bilinguals participated in a **picture-word interference task** in which they named pictures in one language while these pictures were presented alongside distracter words in the opposite language. For example, a picture of a mountain that was to be named in English was presented with a Dutch distracter word (*berm*), which happened to be phonologically similar to the picture's name (*berg*) in Dutch. The researchers argued that if the irrelevant language (in this case, Dutch) is not active during lexical access in the relevant language (in this case, English), then there should be no differences between processing times to name pictures accompanied by phonologically related vs. non-related distracter words. However, this was not the case. Distracter words that were phonologically similar to the picture's name in the irrelevant language were named more slowly than when distracters were unrelated. Hermans *et al.*'s study shows evidence that during lexical access in one language, the other language cannot be *turned off*.

Timed Reading

Sentence processing can be studied through a common method called a **timed-reading task** in which participants read sentences or parts of sentences that appear on a computer screen in front of them. Among the most frequent timed-reading experiments is the **self-paced reading task**. In this version of the timed-reading task, participants read sentences one word at a time. They advance from one word to the next by pressing the space bar until they reach the end of the sentence. The self-paced reading task allows us to measure the time it takes for participants to process each word within a sentence.

In general, self-paced reading research has found that participants read content words such as nouns and verbs more slowly than function words like conjunctions and prepositions. Studies have also shown slower processing times at the end of clauses and sentences. This is more than likely because more time is needed to incorporate preceding information into a complete clause. A classic study that shows these general trends was done by Stine (1990) who asked adolescent and elderly participants to read sentences such as the one in (11).

(11)   The Chinese, who used to produce kites, used them in order to carry ropes across the rivers.

The RTs for reading the individual words in (11) can be seen in Figure 14.3. Notice that for both young and old readers, the words which took the longest to process were content words such as *Chinese, kites, ropes,* and *rivers.* The opposite is true for function words such as *to, in,* and *the.*

Younger and elderly readers differed, however, in terms of how much time they allocated to sentence boundaries. The study showed that while both younger and elderly readers allocate more time at clausal boundaries, only younger readers do so at sentence boundaries. As you can see in Figure 14.3, the word *kites,* which is at the end of a

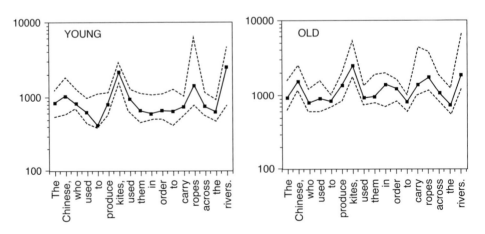

Figure 14.3 Reading time comparisons between young and old readers. From: Stine, E. (1990). On-line processing of written text by younger and older adults. *Psychology and Aging, 5*(1), 68–78. Reproduced with permission of the American Psychological Association through PLSclear.

clausal boundary, is processed at a similar speed for younger and elderly participants, but the word *rivers*, which is at the end of a sentence boundary, is processed more slowly for younger readers. This effect is a reflection of working memory limitations which come with normal aging and prevent allocating more processing time at sentence boundaries.

Eye Tracking

Among the most recent experimental techniques used in psycholinguistics is **eye tracking**. This sophisticated research method uses eye-monitoring cameras to study the details of eye movements during sentence reading and other processes. An eye-tracking device contains a low-intensity infrared light which illuminates participants' eyes and records the reflection of their movement during reading. There are at least three behavioral patterns found in eye tracking experiments in which researchers are interested. These include saccades, fixations, and regressions.

As we read, our eyes do not smoothly progress across words equally in sentences. Instead they engage in **saccades**, or jolting-like eye movements that rapidly propel eye fixations from one point to the next. It is believed that the speed of the saccade to the next fixation point is so fast (usually occurring in 10–20 ms) that visual information is not processed during the jump. The length of the saccade is usually 8–10 letters to the right where it will take a brief pause of 200–250 ms. At this pause, or **fixation** point, two or three words will be processed and then another saccade will occur. The length of the fixation is an index of processing difficulty, with longer fixations implying more difficulty in processing. Sometimes in difficult sentence structures such as in garden path sentences, a saccade may regress in order to reread and reparse the sentence. These regressions are known as **regressive saccades**.

PAUSE AND REFLECT 14.9

If a regressive saccade proceeds to the left in English, in which direction do you think that a regressive saccade moves in Hebrew, a language which is read from right to left?

Let's walk through what some eye-tracking data might look like. Imagine that you are interested in seeing what happens when a reader parses a word that doesn't quite fit in a sentence. To do so, you ask a participant to read (12) while using eye-tracking technology.

(12)   The knight attacked the windmill on his donkey.

As your participant reads (12), his eyes will proceed in saccades like we explained above. But when he comes to the word *windmill*, he realizes that there is a semantic violation because a knight cannot attack a windmill. He will have to go back to see if he read the verb correctly. A regressive saccade to *attacked* shows that he indeed read it correctly the first pass. The reader proceeds a second time, perhaps slightly faster and/or down a different path, until the end of the sentence. At that point, he knows that the words he read were correct; they just simply don't make much sense in this sentence.

From the participant's eye-tracking data shown in Figure 14.4, you see that the steps we just outlined in parsing (12) are as expected.

Figure 14.4 shows that there were ten fixation points, although other readers might have slightly more or less. The time spent at each fixation is relative to the size of the shaded circle. The area we might be most interested in, at least in this example, is what happens at the place of semantic violation (i.e., at the word *windmill*).

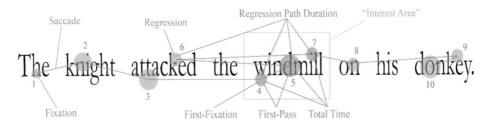

Figure 14.4 Saccades, fixations, and regressions in an eye-tracking example.
From: https://devintxcontent.blob.core.windows.net/showcontent/Speaker%20Presentations%20 Spring%202016/M.%20Miller_The%20Science%20of%20Great%20UI%20-%20 DEVintersection2016.pdf. Reproduced with permission of Mark Miller, Developer Express Inc.

Research using eye tracking has shown that fixations occur more often on content words and less on function words. This is probably why our reader in Figure 14.4 breezed right by the words *the* and *his*. Fixations are also sensitive to word frequency: fixation times are lower for more frequent words and higher for less frequent words, as you can see when comparing *knight* with *on* in Figure 14.4.

Another common trend which eye-tracking experiments have revealed is that, as readers improve their reading skills, "fixation duration decreases, saccade length increases, the number of fixations decreases, and the frequency of regressions decreases" (Rayner, 1998, p. 393). These are characteristics of a *good reader* because it shows that faster and more accurate sentence processing comes with practice.

14.3.3   Neurological Methods

Some of the most promising methods in psycholinguistics study the brain. For instance, innovations in technology have allowed researchers to watch brain activity during language processing. Sophisticated neuroimaging techniques such as Positron Emission Tomography (PET) and Functional Magnetic Resonance Imaging (fMRI) allow us to see dynamic changes in blood flow in the brain. By using these imaging methods, researchers can see which areas of the brain are involved in language processing.

Other methods from neuroscience use electric and magnetic fields to map the time-line of events involved in language processing. For example, electroencephalography (EEG) measures the brain's voltage changes as a response to certain events. These events, known as event-related potentials (ERPs), can reveal a great deal about word retrieval and syntactic processing. We will fully discuss these neurological methods in Chapter 15 Neurolinguistics.

PAUSE AND REFLECT 14.10

What do you think the changes in blood flow in the brain represent in terms of language processing?

14.4 Bilingual Processing

An interconnected world and the fact that the majority of the world's population is bilingual have perked the interest of psycholinguists and linguists to study how the mind processes and represents more than one language. Below we present some issues related to bilingual processing.

14.4.1 The Information Processing Model

Stemming from the 1950s, the **Information Processing Model** explains how humans process information in order to perform tasks such as problem solving and critical thinking. This is said to occur through a systematic model of memory, cognition, and thinking. The model represents perhaps the most researched and widely accepted theories explaining how humans process information based on three main components: sensory memory, working memory, and long-term memory. We will talk more about memory in Section 14.5.1 but let's take a look at what the Information Processing Model says about bilingual processing.

Think back to when you were learning to tie your shoes (although you may not remember it too clearly). This task used to be a controlled process that required you to consciously concentrate on how to perform and successfully complete the task. Now, after you have done it thousands of times, it is probably an automatic process that you can do without even looking at your shoe. **Automatic processing** is an effortless task that requires no conscious attention. **Controlled processing**, however, uses attentional resources under constrained processing to perform a task. The difficulty of the task, amount of attention needed, and processing capacities available, are factors that determine whether controlled processing or automatic processing will be used. According to the Information Processing Model, as language learners become more proficient, they move from controlled processing to automatic processing.

You can think of on-line processing of language as one which occurs in *real-time*. Naturally, comparing the processing involved in one language with that of another language is also an important topic to study. In fact, it seems that processing can differ from language to language. For example, read (13).

(13) Someone shot the maid of the actress that was on the balcony.

Who was on the balcony? From the information given in (13), we cannot be sure. But even though this sentence is ambiguous, English speakers tend to interpret the relative clause *that was on the balcony* as attached to *the actress*, while Spanish speakers (in Spanish) tend to prefer to interpret it as modifying the higher noun, *the maid*. In other words, Spanish and English speakers tend to process these types of sentences differently. This implies that languages may have (at least some) specific ways of being processed.

14.4.2　Word Recognition for Bilinguals

Many of the same theoretical questions in monolingualism have been asked in research on bilinguals. For example, how are words retrieved from the mental lexicon in light of a second language system? Other enduring questions have been more specific to bilingualism such as whether words in both languages are integrated into the same lexicon or whether they have separate lexicons.

A study by van Heuven, Dijkstra, & Grainger (1998) investigated the activation of words and the interference caused from non-target words in both languages. In their study, proficient Dutch-English bilinguals were asked to perform a lexical decision task in each of their languages. The main research question was whether or not lexical decisions in English were slowed down when accompanied by distracter words in either Dutch or English. Indeed, their results showed that the participants judged the English target words as real words *slower* in the presence of interference words in both languages. Van Heuven *et al.* argued that for bilinguals, the L1 and L2 lexicon are integrated and that words in both languages are activated.

The results from van Heuven *et al.* (1998) provided support for the **Bilingual Interactive Activation Model** (BIA Model). The BIA Model is shown in Figure 14.5.

According to the BIA Model, visually presented words simultaneously activate their orthographic and phonological representations. For example, when you see the word *body*, the visual input consisting of four positioned objects (i.e., graphemes) will activate the four letters and sounds that represent them. This in turn activates words and their meanings in both languages. A language node recognizes that the letters and sounds activated match that of English and as such, sends activation and inhibition back down to the word level. At this point, you are able to recognize the word *body* and probably did not notice that sounds and words in both languages were competing during the recognition of the word *body*.

14.4.3　Cognitive Benefits of Bilingual Processing

You may have heard that doing crossword puzzles and other analytic mind-teasers are *good for the brain*. Did you know that these benefits can also come from being a

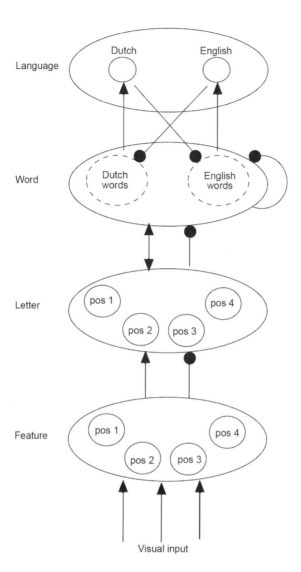

Language

Word

Letter

Feature

Visual input

Figure 14.5 The Bilingual Interactive Activation Model. From: Dijkstra, T., & van Heuven, W. (2002). The architecture of the bilingual word recognition system: From identification to decision. *Bilingualism: Language and Cognition, 5,* 175–197. Reproduced with permission of Cambridge University Press through PLSclear.

bilingual? Recent research, primarily led by Ellen Bialystok, shows that bilingualism incurs cognitive benefits. Her work suggests that bilinguals outperform their monolingual counterparts on a variety of tasks that measure executive functions. **Executive functions** include cognitive processes such as attentional control, working memory, reasoning, problem-solving, and planning. For instance, bilinguals have been shown to outperform monolinguals in working memory tasks, problem-solving tests, adapting to new rules and unpredictable elements in games and tasks, and switching between different tasks, among other things. Bilinguals also show greater metalinguistic awareness or metalinguistic abilities. (see also Brien & Sabourin, 2012).

The cognitive benefits associated with bilingualism, however, may be sensitive to some external factors. For instance, social challenges such as the linguistic situation in school (bilingual vs. monolingual) or in the community (equal value or not given to both languages) may also affect whether bilingualism entails cognitive benefits. Refer back to Chapter 9 Sociolinguistics to read more about bilingualism and language policy.

PAUSE AND REFLECT 14.11

Look back at Figure 14.3 and notice once again the difference in reading times between younger and older readers at the end of the sentence. If the older readers had been bilingual, do you think that they would have allocated more time at the end of the sentence as younger readers did?

LINGUISTICS TIDBITS: SPEECH-LANGUAGE PATHOLOGY

The assessment and treatment of communication disorders is a clinical field called speech-language pathology. A common misconception is that speech therapists only work with pronunciation problems like a child having difficulty saying /ɹ/. However, speech therapists are also trained to treat a range of language disorders that may result from cognitive impairment, reading and writing problems, or social communication difficulties. For example, speech-language pathologists may work with an adult patient with dementia to improve word-finding abilities or with a child with reading and writing difficulties to develop sound-to-spelling relationships. Read 'Delving Deeper' in Chapter 14's resources on the website to accompany this book at www.cambridge.org/introducing-linguistics to read a little on how psycholinguistic models have informed speech-language therapy.

Work by Bialystok and colleagues has also suggested that bilingualism throughout the lifespan can help fight age-related cognitive decline. In other words, the cognitive benefits associated with the constant *juggling* of more than one language in one mind may have lasting effects that can be called upon later in life to help counteract the effects of normal aging (Bialystok & Craik, 2015). In an extensive history of hospital records, Bialystok *et al.* (2007) found a significant difference between the average age at which monolingual and bilingual patients were diagnosed with a type of dementia. The hospital records showed that bilingual patients with dementia experienced the onset of symptoms three to four years later in life than the monolingual patients.

14.5 Current and Ongoing Issues and Debates

Many issues in psycholinguistics have been explained through theoretical models which are used to visualize and explain research findings and to generate new hypotheses. In this last section we will take a look at a few prominent issues and ongoing debates in psycholinguistics. We will first talk about the role of memory in language processing followed by a few explanations and counter explanations of how language processing unfolds in the human mind.

14.5.1 Working Memory and Long-term Memory

Memory refers to the storing and retrieving of information. Even though memory has been widely studied in psychology since the late 1800s, it did not take centre stage in language studies until the mid-1950s. Since then, it has played an important role in research in psycholinguistics. When you stop to think about it, memory is a central component of language. We must remember things just said to us and background knowledge important to the conversation. And just like a printer must temporarily store information before it is printed onto paper, our minds must temporarily store information before it is articulated into speech.

Traditionally, there have been two forms of memory defined: working memory and long-term memory. Let's first look at working memory. Baddeley (1986) defines **working memory** as "the temporary storage of information that is being processed in any range of cognitive tasks" (p. 34). Working memory is used to momentarily store information and perform operations on that information. Perhaps the most accepted model of working memory is by Baddeley & Hitch (1974). In its most current form, as shown in Figure 14.6, working memory is said to contain a central executive and three subsystems: the visuospatial sketchpad, the episodic buffer, and the phonological loop.

The **central executive** acts as a supervisory system that controls the information flow between three fluid subsystems. The central executive is also responsible for multitasking, control, attention, and assigning tasks to the three subsystems. The **visuospatial sketchpad** is accountable for temporarily storing and manipulating visual and visuospatial information. This subsystem is what allows us to do things like form images in our mind and convert words that are read into sounds. The **episodic buffer** subsystem is responsible for forming integrated units that are logically organized and sequenced. So, when someone is telling you a story, the episodic buffer formulates the scene of what happened in your mind. The **phonological loop** is the subsystem

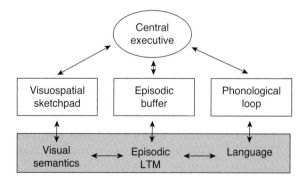

Figure 14.6 A model of working memory. From: Baddeley, A. (2000). The episodic buffer: A new component of working memory? *Trends in Cognitive Sciences, 4,* 417–423. Reproduced with permission of Elsevier through PLSclear.

responsible for sound and storing verbal content. It acts as phonological storage that leaves traces of auditory memories and an articulatory loop which allows for rehearsal and revival of auditory memories.

PAUSE AND REFLECT 14.12

Ask a friend who speaks another language to say a word for you to try and repeat. This is a good way to see how the phonological loop of working memory works. You hear something which the phonological loop must temporarily store and articulate. If you wait several minutes and pronounce the word again, you will probably be less accurate. This is because the auditory memories in the phonological loop are very quick to decay.

Our normal working memory capacity can only hold about seven units of information at a time. One of the most highly cited papers in psychology was "The magical number seven, plus or minus two: Some limits on our capacity for processing information" (Miller, 1956). Named after the author, the *7 ± 2 finding* is frequently referred to as **Miller's Law**.

Now let's turn to **long-term memory** and the types of memory it entails. Long-term memory is the storage that holds permanent information. We can categorize long-term memory as declarative or procedural memory and can further divide declarative memory into episodic memory and semantic memory. For the sake of clarity, we illustrate how long-term memory is conceptualized in Figure 14.7.

Let's comment on the components in Figure 14.7. From your long-term memory, you can recall memories like the facts and events about your last birthday party or memories (probably unconscious) about how to tie your shoes. These two types of memories are essentially the difference between declarative memory and procedural memory, respectively. **Procedural memory** includes memories about the knowledge of tasks that normally do not need to be recalled consciously to perform them. Examples would include remembering how to ride a bike, play a guitar, and make a peace sign with your fingers.

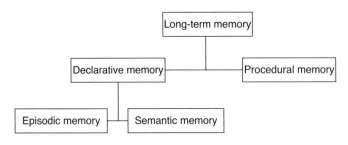

Figure 14.7 Long-term memory

The other main type of long-term memory is **declarative memory**, which refers to explicit memories that can be recalled consciously. As you can see in Figure 14.7, declarative memory can be divided into episodic and semantic memory. You may be able to tell from the names that episodic memory might have something to do with episodes whereas semantic memory may have to do with meaning. This is a fairly accurate observation. **Episodic memory** is a type of long-term memory in which personally experienced information is stored. Episodic memories are personal experiences or events that occurred at a particular time and place. For example, if you remember your exact location, and maybe even at what time, you learned something important, this would form part of your episodic memories. **Semantic memory** is a long-term memory that represents information about words, facts, concepts, symbols, and anything that is not personal-experience based. Your knowledge of the difference between the colors *brown* and *red*, the fact that the American flag has stars and stripes on it, or the meaning of the word *secretary* are all examples of things in your semantic memory.

Working memory (Figure 14.6) and long-term memory (Figure 14.7) are important to our discussion of language processing. Research has shown that the human mind is quite efficient in how it divides language up into units. Instead of temporarily storing a string of seven words, parsing will identify perhaps seven constituents that can be chunked in a way that count as a single unit for working memory. Long-term memory is also essential for our knowledge of the speech sounds we hear and produce along with the meaning of the words these sounds create. These are just some of the reasons why these two types of memory have formed a central part of psycholinguistic research for decades: without memory, there would be no language.

14.5.2   Serial and Parallel Processing

An ongoing debate in psycholinguistics is whether certain processes take place sequentially or whether sets of processes occur simultaneously. For example, does word retrieval occur at the same time as sounds are perceived? Can phrase structure be developed while words are being searched for? These are enduring questions that continue to be asked by researchers and two possibilities are discussed. **Serial processing** explains language processing as a set of processes that occur one at a time. You can think of this like a computer program that works in a step-by-step fashion through a series of non-overlapping processes. This should remind you of our discussion of modularity in Section 14.2.3. **Parallel processing**, on the other hand, argues that several processes occur at the same time during language processing. Unlike serial processing, parallel processes affect and inform one another. As we saw earlier, interactive models make these assumptions. Take a moment to read the horizontal and vertical words in Figure 14.8.

Figure 14.8 Processing an ambiguous letter shape based on context

Did the ambiguous letter in the middle of both words in Figure 14.8 prevent you from reading the words? More than likely, you said *no* but how was your mind able to process the words if they were spelled with a non-letter? How did you recognize the non-letter as an *a* in *bat* but an *h* in *the* when it is physically the same? This question is especially difficult to answer for serial processing. It would seem that we are using context to help identify the ambiguous letter. But in this case, the context is an actual word, either *bat* or *the*. Because the processing of the word is occurring at the same time as you are trying to assign the missing letter, this is evidence of parallel processing in which more than one process occurs simultaneously.

This example also provides support for the top-down processing that we discussed in 14.1: a higher level, in this case the lexical level, is influencing the processing of a lower level, namely letter recognition. Although it is not always the case, often a top-down process is also a parallel process; a bottom-up process is usually serial.

PAUSE AND REFLECT 14.13

On the popular game show *Wheel of Fortune*, contestants solve word puzzles by guessing the missing letters of words. Each round's word puzzle is contextualized by a category (e.g., *Person; Landmark; Headline*). Does this contextualization show an example of serial or parallel processing?

14.5.3   Single- and Dual-route Processing

Another issue in psycholinguistics is whether there is one or more routes of processing. This has especially been tested with respect to reading words. Consider that you are asked to read silently the word *basket*. One way for word recognition to occur is that you recognize the whole word based on the visual input (see Figure 14.9). Another way that you may read the word is that you *sound it out* (see Figure 14.10). Both of these possibilities provide examples of **single-route processing** which argues that one path, but not both, represent potential processing routes.

From what we have read so far, however, do you think that it is possible for processing to occur via both routes at the same time? A **dual-route processing** model such as this would look something like the one in Figure 14.11.

The dual-processing model for reading the word *basket* in Figure 14.11 suggests that the lexicon can be accessed via a phonological (indirect) route or via a direct route. In

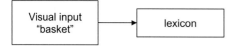

Figure 14.9 Single-route processing through whole-word recognition

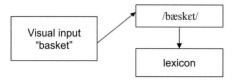

Figure 14.10 Single-route processing through phonological encoding

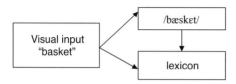

Figure 14.11 Dual-route processing

other words, both routes are active, but one path will be chosen over the other based on things like word length and frequency. Research has shown that longer and less frequent words are more likely to be processed via the phonological route while shorter and more-frequent words usually have direct access to the lexicon. This explains why you have to *sound-out* a new word that you have never seen.

To read about an example of a dual-route processing model, consult 'Delving Deeper' in Chapter 14's resources on the website to accompany this book at www.cambridge .org/introducing-linguistics to.

PAUSE AND REFLECT 14.14

Think back to the eye-tracking methodology we discussed earlier. According to dual-route processing, what do you think eye fixation times would be for words that are processed via the phonological route?

14.5.4 Connectionist Approaches

Up until now, we have discussed models of language processing which make direct reference to linguistic representations and symbols such as phonemes, words, and structural rules. In other words, these models have argued that our linguistic knowledge must access and utilize these elements in order to process language. But not all psycholinguistic models assume this. The last issue we will discuss is **connection-ism**, an alternative approach to the models discussed so far. Connectionism is a way of modelling language as evolving processes of networks that are interconnected and consist of simple units. The most common connectionist approach today is the **parallel distributed processing** (PDP) model. Like parallel processing that we described above, PDP proposes simultaneous processing at multiple levels. However, PDP argues that activation is distributed across neural connections. Connectionists use predictions of PDP to simulate computer models of artificial neural networks that can explain how language processing occurs.

Computer modelling using connectionist approaches allows researchers to replicate the natural behavior of neural networks: that they constantly evolve and adapt over time. This can be clearly seen in the idea of activation. Connectionism argues that everything in the mind has an activation level. Activation, which can be represented numerically by a computer, can increase and spread to other connected units. Repeated activation of a connection not only reinforces and strengthens the connection itself but it also seems to be transferable to similar connections. Think about when you open a program on your computer that you have just turned on. The speed of opening the program will be slower the first time you open it compared to the second or third time. In other words, activating the process needed to open the program made it easier the next time to execute that same process. In language, take the past tense as an example. Rather than subscribing to the idea that we have linguistic knowledge of the past tense, connectionist approaches assume that the neural connections between verbs like *dance-danced* and *sleep-slept* can be built up and even transferred to similar computations in order to generate *study-studied* and *feel-felt*, respectively.

PAUSE AND REFLECT 14.15

Connectionism draws on computational modeling to make predictions about language representation and acquisition. To learn more about computational approaches to language, see Chapter 17 Computational Linguistics..

SUMMARY

Psycholinguistics is the study of the cognitive processes and mental representations that are involved in language production, comprehension, and acquisition. In this chapter, we have discussed several theoretical models of speech production and comprehension. You have learned that both bottom-up and top-down processing are involved in language.

In sound processing, we use auditory information in the speech signal to process linguistic input. Motor theory states that we also use our knowledge of sound articulation and reading lips to comprehend speech. Two important models that explain sound processing and lexical access are the TRACE model and the cohort model. While the TRACE model argues that several levels of processing – feature level, phoneme level, word level – are all said to be active, the cohort model posits that a cohort of words with the same initial sound will be first analyzed followed by a process of elimination until one word is left as the correct target word.

We focused much on the mental lexicon and lexical access in our conversation about word processing. The mental lexicon is the dictionary in your mind which contains word characteristics including their phonological, syntactic, and semantic properties. The search model explains how words from the mental lexicon are recognized. There are factors, however, that could affect this such as word frequency, ambiguity, how recently the word was last accessed, and its phonological neighborhood. When a speaker is temporarily unable to retrieve a word from the mental lexicon, we say that he/she is in a tip-of-the-tongue state.

In sentence processing, parsing is the process of determining the grammaticality of words and phrases and assigning them into their appropriate grammatical category. As we read sentences, we use several parsing strategies to process language and to help overcome the challenges of complex structures such as garden path sentences. These types of sentences often lead to misparsing, causing the reader to backtrack and reparse.

Important data collection techniques in psycholinguistics include naturalistic methods such as analyzing speech errors called slips of the tongue and mishearings known as slips of the ear. Experimental methods include lexical decision tasks, priming experiments, timed-reading tasks such as the self-paced reading task, and eye tracking. As these methods continue to be improved, psycholinguists are better equipped to study ongoing issues and debates such as the role of working memory and long-term memory in language processing; serial and parallel processing; single- and dual-route processing; and connectionist approaches.

EXERCISES

14.1   Decide whether each statement below characterizes serial processing or parallel processing.

   i.   Different levels of processing happen simultaneously.
   ii.   Language comprehension occurs in stages starting with smaller units such as phonological features.
   iii. Processing is better handled bottom-up.
   iv.   Word retrieval occurs at the same time as sound analysis.
   v.   Processing is more step-by-step.

14.2 Fill in the missing words in the sentences below. Did you use a top-down or bottom-up process to do this exercise? Explain your answer.

    i.   Skyler and Davon only see things in _____ and white.
    ii.   The runners for sure _____ run tomorrow at 3:30pm.
    iii. Last year, my sister _____ the best time of her life.
    iv. A _____ is someone who plays the piano.

14.3 Come up with five compound words and talk about how morphemes are represented and processed.

14.4 Do the words below have dense or sparse phonological neighborhoods? How do you know this?

    i.   rate
    ii.   grander
    iii. rat
    iv. sunken

14.5 Think of three words (a noun, verb, and adjective) that are all examples of lexical ambiguity. Next to each of the three words, write their two (or more) meanings.

14.6 What does the tip-of-the-tongue phenomenon imply for the mental lexicon?

14.7 Come up with two short garden path sentences and write each on a piece of paper. Next, find a participant who can read each of the sentences silently. Make sure that he/she holds the paper high enough so that you can watch their eye movements. Write about your mini-experience and what this means for sentence processing.

14.8 Think about and write down a slip-of-the-tongue that you've had. Then, decide which type of slip-of-the-tongue it best represents out of the examples in (10). Finally, using your example, come up with other variations like that you could have also made. For each, identify the linguistic units that change and label whether they are primarily a sound, morphological, or syntactic slip-of-the-tongue.

14.9 In the Cohort model, sounds are perceived one at a time and as sound input continues, words that do not match the input are eliminated. Use the words below as an example to fill in the rest of the table.

Target	Cohort after first two phonemes	Cohort after first three phonemes	Cohort after first four phonemes or point of perception
/vɪdio/			
/ʃit/			
/mɛdɪk/			
/arm/			
/farmɪŋ/			

14.10 Imagine that you are setting up a priming experiment and you must come up with the primes that are to be presented right before the experiment's target words. For each of the target words below, give an example of a semantically related and an unrelated prime. Be careful to control for phonological relatedness (e.g., avoid choosing *plane* as a possible semantically related prime for *train* because it rhymes with the target). In the results of the experiment, which primes do you think would speed up processing times of the target: the semantically related primes or the unrelated primes? Why?

Semantically related prime	Unrelated prime	Target
		train
		tree
		cat
		arm
		doctor
		apple

14.11   For each of the garden path sentences below, state which parsing strategy – late closure or minimal attachment – causes misreading or ambiguity.

  i.   Without her people did not come.
  ii.   While Gary baked the pie cooled on the window ledge.
  iii. Janice saw the letter Sophie was reading in the office.
  iv.   After Janet studied the answers turned out to be wrong.
  v.   The teachers forgot the answer key was online yesterday.

14.12   Describe what motor theory in speech perception is.

14.13   Discuss the role of working memory and long-term memory in language processing.

14.14   Compare and contrast the main predictions put forth by dual-route vs. single-route processing models. How do you think connectionism fits into these two types?

14.15   Bilinguals may outperform monolinguals on a variety of cognitive tasks such as working memory measures, problem-solving tests, and switching between different tasks. Do an Internet search and talk about at least two of the methods or tasks that have shown that bilinguals outperform monolinguals.

REFERENCES

Baddeley, A. (1986). *Working memory*. New York, NY: Oxford University Press.

Baddeley, A. (2000). The episodic buffer: A new component of working memory? *Trends in Cognitive Sciences, 4*, 417–423.

Baddeley, A., & Hitch, G. (1974). Working memory. In G. Bower (Ed.), *Recent advances in learning and motivation* (pp. 47–90). New York, NY: Academic Press.

Bialystok, E., & Craik, F. (2015). Cognitive consequences of bilingualism: Executive control and cognitive reserve. In J. W. Schwieter (Ed.), *The Cambridge handbook of bilingual processing* (pp. 571–585). Cambridge: Cambridge University Press.

Bialystok, E., Craik, F., & Freedman, M. (2007). Bilingualism as a protection against the onset symptoms of dementia. *Neuropsychologia, 45*(2), 459–464.

Brien, C., & Sabourin, L. (2012). Second language effects on ambiguity resolution in the first language. *EUROSLA Yearbook, 12*(1), 191–217.

Brown, A. (2012). *The tip of the tongue state*. New York, NY: Psychology Press.

Cutler, A., & Butterfield, S. (1992). Rhythmic cues to speech segmentation: Evidence from juncture misperception. *Journal of Memory and Language, 31*, 218–236.

Dijkstra, T., & van Heuven, W. (2002). The architecture of the bilingual word recognition system: From identification to decision. *Bilingualism: Language and Cognition, 5*, 175–197.

Elman, J., & McClelland, J. (1988). Cognitive penetration of the mechanisms of perception: Compensation for coarticulation of lexically restored phonemes. *Journal of Memory and Language, 27*, 143–165.

Emmorey, K. (2007). The psycholinguistics of signed and spoken languages: How biology affects processing. In G. Gaskell (Ed.), *The Oxford handbook of psycholinguistics* (pp. 703–721). Oxford: Oxford University Press.

Forster, K. (1976). Accessing the mental lexicon. In R. Wales & E. Walker (Eds.), *New approaches to language mechanisms* (pp. 257–287). Amsterdam: North-Holland.

Forster, K. (1978). Assessing the mental lexicon. In E. Walker (Ed.), *Explorations in the biology of language* (pp. 139–174). Cambridge, MA: MIT Press.

Frazier, L. (1995). Constraint satisfaction as a theory of sentence processing. *Journal of Psycholinguistic Research, 24,* 437–468.

Hermans, D., Bongaerts, T., de Bot, K., & Schreuder, R. (1998). Producing words in a foreign language: can speakers prevent interference from their first language? *Bilingualism: Language and Cognition, 1*(3), 213–230.

Levelt, W. (1989). *Speaking: From intention to articulation.* Cambridge, MA: MIT Press.

Liberman, A., Cooper, F., Shankweiler, D., & Studdert-Kennedy, M. (1967). Perception of the speech code. *Pscyhological Review, 74,* 431–461.

Liberman, A., Harris, K., Hoffman, H., & Griffith, B. (1957). The discrimination of speech sounds within and across phoneme boundaries. *Journal of Experimental Psychology, 54,* 358–368.

Liberman, A., & Mattingly, I. (1985). The motor theory of speech perception revised. *Cognition, 21,* 1–36.

Marslen-Wilson, W. (1990). Activation, competition, and frequency in lexical access. In G. Altmann (Ed.), *Cognitive models of speech processing: Psycholinguistic and computational perspectives* (pp. 148–172). Cambridge, MA: MIT Press.

McClelland, J., & Elman, J. (1986). Interactive processes in speech perception: The TRACE model. In J. McClelland, D. Rumelhart, & the PDP Research Group (Eds.), *Parallel distributed processing: Psychological and biological model* (pp. 58–121). Cambridge, MA: MIT Press.

McClelland, J., Mirman, D., & Holt, L. (2006). Are there interactive processes in speech perception? *Trends in Cognitive Sciences, 10*(8), 363–369.

McGurk, H., & MacDonald, J. (1976). Hearing lips and seeing voices. *Nature, 264,* 746–748.

McLaughlin, B. (1987). *Theories of second-language learning.* London: Edward Arnold.

Miller, G. (1956). The magical number seven, plus or minus two: Some limits on our capacity for processing information. *Psychological Review, 63*(2), 81–97.

Rayner, K. (1998). Eye movements in reading and information processing: 20 years of research. *Psychological Bulletin, 124,* 372–422.

Schatz, C. (1954). The role of context in the perception of stops. *Language, 30,* 47–56.

Stine, E. (1990). On-line processing of written text by younger and older adults. *Psychology and Aging, 5*(1), 68–78.

Swinney, D. (1979). Lexical access during sentence comprehension: (Re)consideration of context effects. *Journal of Verbal Learning and Verbal Behavior, 18,* 645–659.

Swinney, D., & Hakes, D. (1976). Effects of prior context upon lexical access during sentence comprehension. *Journal of Verbal Learning and Verbal Behavior, 15,* 681–689.

Taft, M. (1981). Prefix stripping revisited. *Journal of Verbal Language and Verbal Behavior, 20,* 289–297.

Trueswell, J., Tanenhaus, M., & Garnsey, S. (1994). Semantic influences on parsing: Use of thematic role information in syntactic disambiguation. *Journal of Memory and Language, 33,* 285–318.

van Heuven, W., Dijkstra, T., & Grainger, J. (1998). Orthographic neighborhood effects in bilingual word recognition. *Journal of Memory and Language, 39,* 458–483.

15 Neurolinguistics

Language and the Brain
John W. Schwieter

OVERVIEW

In this chapter, you will develop an understanding of neurolinguistics and will:

- **explore the brain's anatomy and the specific areas that are most involved in language;**
- **discuss methods and technologies used to study language in the brain including lesion studies and autopsies, dichotic listening and split-brain studies, neuroimaging, and measures of the brain's electric and magnetic fields;**
- **study language impairments that have neurological explanations;**
- **learn about rehabilitation of language impairments and in the case of multilinguals, how several languages can recover; and**
- **consider how neurolinguistics has informed our knowledge of theoretical linguistics including our understanding of the mental lexicon, morphology, and syntax.**

15.1   What Is Neurolinguistics?

The area of linguistics which studies the biological and cognitive bases of language is **neurolinguistics**. In other words, neurolinguistics studies language and the brain. This branch of linguistics and neuroscience allows us to learn more about the physiological mechanisms which the brain uses for language. Neurolinguists investigate research questions such as:

- How is language represented in the brain?
- Is there a place in the brain where language is primarily located?
- What are the effects on language of trauma to, or degeneration of, certain areas of the brain? What are the recovery patterns for lost language abilities?
- What makes the human brain specialized and advanced enough for language that other species' brains lack?
- Does language use the same parts of the brain for other non-linguistic tasks such as playing a musical instrument or doing mathematics?
- How is the bilingual brain different from the monolingual brain?

In addition to being highly related to psycholinguistics, neurolinguistics also informs the main branches of linguistics by exploring phenomena such as how the brain:

- separates the speech we hear from background noise (phonetics);
- represents the sound system (phonology);
- stores and accesses morphemes (morphology);
- combines words into phrases (syntax); and
- uses structural and contextual information to comprehend language (semantics).

PAUSE AND REFLECT 15.1

Have you ever heard that one side of the brain is more responsible for language? If so, which side is it? Later in the chapter, we will see whether or not this is true.

15.2   The Human Brain and Language

Is language what makes us human? Although being *human* may have other specialized traits, our ability for language does set us apart from other species. These superior language abilities exist because of our highly developed brain. The brain, along with the spinal cord, are the two main components of the **central nervous system** (see Figure 15.1).

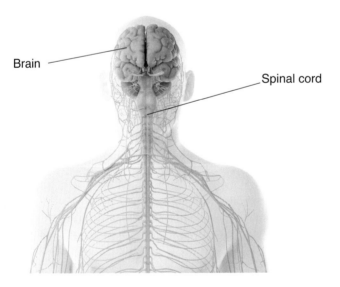

Brain

Spinal cord

Figure 15.1 The central nervous system

Now take a look at Figure 15.2 in which we take a closer look at just the brain. You can see that the brain includes the cerebrum, the cerebellum, and the brain stem. The **cerebellum** helps in coordination, precision, and accuracy of motor functions. The **brain stem** helps to provide motor and sensory actions to the face and neck through cranial nerves. Most studies in neurolinguistics have explored the cerebrum and its many complexities, which we will do below.

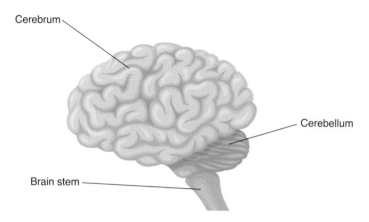

Figure 15.2 The main parts of the brain

EYES ON WORLD LANGUAGES: THE MULTILINGUAL TALENTS OF LANGUAGE SAVANTS

Do some people have a special gift for learning languages? The quick answer to this is *yes*. We have seen some evidence of remarkable linguistic talents among **savants**. These individuals are people who have a mental disability such as autism yet show exceptional brilliance in other areas such as mathematics, memory, music, art, or language. These exceptional talents are far beyond what are considered normal or even excellent abilities. While most savants are born as such, about 10 percent of them have **acquired savant syndrome** in that they show these prodigious skills following neurological problems such as dementia or brain damage.

Christopher is the most documented case of a **language savant**, also called **polyglot savant**. A polyglot is a speaker of multiple languages. Christopher was born in the UK in 1962 and was diagnosed with brain damage at six months. He has a nonverbal IQ of 40–60 – depending on how it is measured – a mental age of a little over nine years, and is unable to care for himself. Christopher also has motor skill problems, so performing tasks such as cutting his fingernails or dressing himself are almost impossible.

EYES ON WORLD LANGUAGES: (*cont.*)

Christopher has been living for many years in an institution for the mentally disabled because he requires round-the-clock care and cannot go places by himself. Even though Christopher faces these difficulties, he has learned over 20 languages without any formal instruction including: Berber, Danish, Dutch, Finnish, French, German, Greek, Hindi, Italian, Norwegian, Polish, Portuguese, Russian, Spanish, Swedish, Turkish, and Welsh, among others.

Neil Smith, a researcher who has been working with Christopher for years, introduced an invented language to him and as predicted, he learned it with extreme ease. However, when Smith presented Christopher with elements of the invented language that were unlike any other natural language and in fact, broke rules of Universal Grammar (UG), he could not learn it – even though they were logical and simple rules which Smith found that people of average or higher IQs were able to learn perfectly. Smith explained that Christopher was unable to learn these irregular language patterns because he lacks the logical and rational skills needed to figure out things outside of his innate language capacity or UG, the latter of which is unaffected by his mental disability. Language savants like Christopher provide us with evidence that linguistic abilities are independent from general intellectual abilities.

15.2.1   The Cerebrum

The uppermost, largest, and primary part of the brain is called the **cerebrum**. The cerebrum controls voluntary actions and is probably what the brain looks like to you when you think about it: a large wrinkled mass inside the skull (see Figure 15.3).

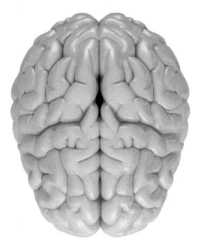

Figure 15.3 The cerebrum as seen from above

In terms of size, you may have heard that your heart is about the size of your fist and that your brain is about the size of both of your fists put together. While this is a good way to conceptualize their approximate size, there is no research that shows an actual correlation between the size of your hands and brain. After all, everyone has different sized hands but these differences are much smaller when it comes to brain size.

While there is research showing a correlation between brain size and gender – with men's brains being slightly larger than women's – there is no conclusive evidence that brain size is related to intelligence. A good example of this is Albert Einstein's brain. When Einstein died in 1955, his brain was secretively removed surgically within eight hours of his death. In 1978, when news revealed that Einstein's brain had been removed and studied, it was reported that the size of his brain was no larger than any ordinary man's. However, neurologists noticed that the regions in his brain responsible for math and spatial perception (i.e., areas in which he excelled) were a staggering 35 percent wider than these regions in the average man's brain.

15.2.2 The Cerebral Cortex

The entire cerebrum is covered in **cerebral cortex**. The word *cortex* is from Latin and means bark, peeling, or rind. You can think of the cortex as a thin layer of tissue that fits over the brain. Although the cortex is only two to four millimetres thick, it is essential for nearly all cognition including things like memory, attention, perception, awareness, thought, and language.

The cerebral cortex consists of **grey matter**, the outer, darker tissue which includes most of the brain's nerve cell bodies. Grey matter that is distributed on the cortex is thought to be involved in cognition and information processing. Just underneath the grey matter is the **white matter** that forms the bulk of the deep parts of the brain. White matter is responsible for learning, distributing stimuli, and coordinating communication between different areas of the brain. Figure 15.4 shows the layered-like characteristic of the brain with grey matter being the outer layer and white matter being the inner layer.

One of the most notable characteristics of the cortex is the folds on its surface that give it its wrinkled-like appearance. There are two important parts of these folds that we should point out: the **sulcus** (plural: sulci) is the place where the cortex is folded inward and the **gyrus** (plural: gyri) is the place where the cortex is folded outward. These folds are also shown in Figure 15.4. You can think of sulci as being valleys and canyons and gyri as being peaks and plateaus.

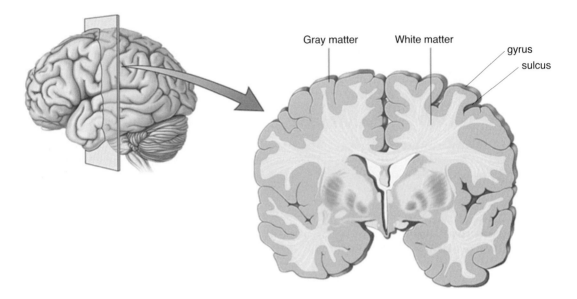

Figure 15.4 Grey matter and white matter. © Creative Commons Attribution-Share Alike 4.0 International.

Some of the sulci are deeper than others, allowing us to distinguish, even with the naked eye, different parts of the brain. For instance, looking back at the cerebrum in Figure 15.3, you can clearly see that the brain is divided into two halves. In fact, the deepest sulcus in the brain is the **longitudinal fissure** which divides the brain into a left hemisphere and a right hemisphere. Let's take a look at the differences between these two halves.

15.2.3   The Two Hemispheres

The two sides of the brain that you saw in Figure 15.3 look as though they are two halves stuck together. In this case, looks do not deceive you. The two sides of the brain are connected mainly by a bundle of about 200 million nerve fibers collectively called the **corpus callosum**. You can think of them as a net connecting the left and right halves of the brain. The corpus callosum is the most complex set of neurons in the human body. Its primary function is to allow the two hemispheres to communicate with one another and to act as one. The connectivity of these neurons and their influence on one another is staggering: each neuron can affect anywhere from 4,000 to 10,000 other neurons. Of the more than ten billion neurons in the brain, about 2 percent of the most sophisticated and complex ones are found in the corpus callosum.

There are quite a few functional differences between the left and right hemispheres, yet they work together in harmony in an undamaged, typically developed brain. In popular psychology and culture, great lengths have been made to assign certain abilities to a respective hemisphere. For example, you may have heard the broad generalization that the left side of the brain is the logical side and the right side is the creative side. While claims like this may have some validity, others are often incorrect given the fact that most brain functions are distributed across both hemispheres.

PAUSE AND REFLECT 15.2

Based on what you have read so far, would you say that you are left- or right-brain dominant? Why?

Other than these functional differences between the right and left hemisphere, we should also mention that each of the hemispheres is responsible for movement and sensation on the opposite side of the body. For example, if you pick up your cell phone with your left hand, the right side of your brain controls this movement. These **contralateral control** duties explain why patients who suffer a paralysis in one hemisphere of the brain show the effects on the opposite side of the body.

15.2.4   The Lobes of the Cortex

In addition to studying the brain in terms of its two hemispheres, we can also learn about it based on its lobes. Stretching across both hemispheres of the brain are four lobes, sections of the cortex that are (fairly) anatomically divided from each other and have distinct functions. Figure 15.5 shows the **frontal**, **parietal**, **occipital**, and

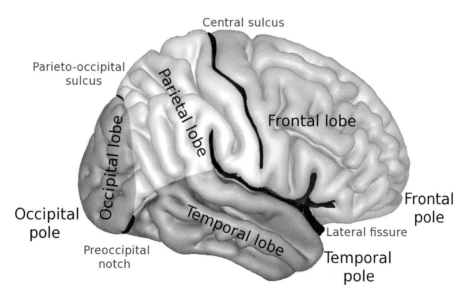

Figure 15.5 Lobes of the cortex. © Creative Commons Attribution-Share Alike 3.0

temporal lobes of the brain along with the sulci, fissures, and notches that identify their boundaries. Although the figure shows the right hemisphere of the brain, recall that the lobes are found in both hemispheres.

Many of the divisions between the lobes can be clearly seen with the naked eye because of the sulci that we discussed above. For instance, if you look again at Figure 15.5, you will see that we have also labeled the parieto-occipital sulcus, central sulcus, lateral fissure, and preoccipital notch. These are all involved in establishing where one lobe ends and another one begins.

TABLE 15.1 Primary Functions of the Lobes of the Cortex

Lobe of the cortex	Primary functions
Frontal	• speaking • voluntary movement and motor performance • planning and predicting future consequences of current actions • making the choice between good and bad actions • controlling socially unacceptable responses • differentiating and finding similarities between things or events
Parietal	• reading • integrating sensory information from various parts of the body • knowing about numbers and their relations • manipulating objects
Occipital	• processing visual input
Temporal	• retaining short- and long-term memories • processing auditory information including words and speech • integrating sensory functions

Each of the lobes has specific responsibilities, although for some tasks like language, more than one lobe is involved. Just as we saw when we tried to describe the main functions of the two hemispheres, keep in mind that the very nature of the brain requires that we interpret the incomplete list of lobe functions in Table 15.1 as variable.

PAUSE AND REFLECT 15.3

Given what you have read about the lobes of the cortex, why do you think that someone may *see stars* when hit in the back of the head?

15.2.5   Is There a Place for Language in the Brain?

Since the early 1800s, researchers such as Franz Joseph Gall began to believe that certain abilities, sensations, and behaviors could be traceable to certain locations in the brain. This theory became known as **localization**. By the mid-1800s, *language* was hypothesized to be one of these abilities. This was believed because patients who typically suffer brain damage in the frontal lobe of the left hemisphere have some sort of language impairment. Because of this, language was argued to be lateralized in the left hemisphere. We use the term **lateralization** to specify whether something (e.g., language) is primarily localized in the left or right hemisphere.

For most right-handed people, language is lateralized in the left hemisphere. While it is impossible to pinpoint the exact location of language in the brain, we do know that there are at least two key areas that are important for language production and comprehension. These include **Broca's area** named after French surgeon Paul Broca in 1861, and **Wernicke's area**, named after German physician Carl Wernicke in 1874. To read more about how being left- or right-handed affects language lateralization , read 'Delving Deeper' in Chapter 15's resources on the website to accompany this book at www.cambridge.org/introducing-linguistics.

We will return to our discussion on Broca's and Wernicke's areas when we explore how damage to these parts leads to language impairment in Section 15.4. For now, we can say that researchers have come a long way in brain research since the 1800s and we now know a wealth of information about what the human brain does with language. For example, we know that:

- Broca's area is involved largely in speech production;
- The primary motor cortex is needed for movement in speech and articulation;
- The primary somatosensory cortex is used in connecting senses with language;
- The inferior parietal lobule is involved in the perception of faces and facial emotions;
- The primary visual cortex along with the angular gyrus are essential for reading;
- Wernicke's area is important for speech comprehension; and
- The primary auditory area is essential for hearing speech sounds.

Figure 15.6 illustrates where these areas are located in the brain.

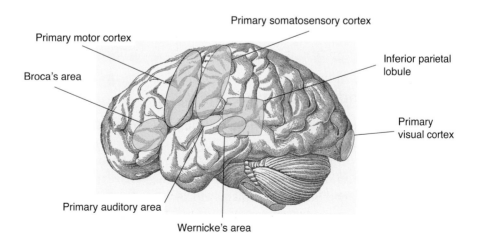

Figure 15.6 Primary Brain Areas Involved in Language

The **angular gyrus** is located between Wernicke's area and the primary visual cortex. It allows us to change visual stimuli into auditory stimuli and vice versa. It is crucial for the ability to read and write. The angular gyrus is what allows the brain to match a spoken word with the object it describes and also with the written form of the word.

LINGUISTICS TIDBITS: IS THIS YOUR BRAIN *ON WORDS*?

The question of what our brain does with just a simple word is actually a complicated one. Research has shown that the entire brain *lights up* when hearing, seeing, speaking, or retrieving words. However, some areas do so more than others: Broca's area when thinking about words, the primary motor cortex when saying words, Wernicke's area when hearing words, and the occipital lobe when reading words. Based on brain imaging, Figure 15.7 shows the most activated areas when your brain is *on words*.

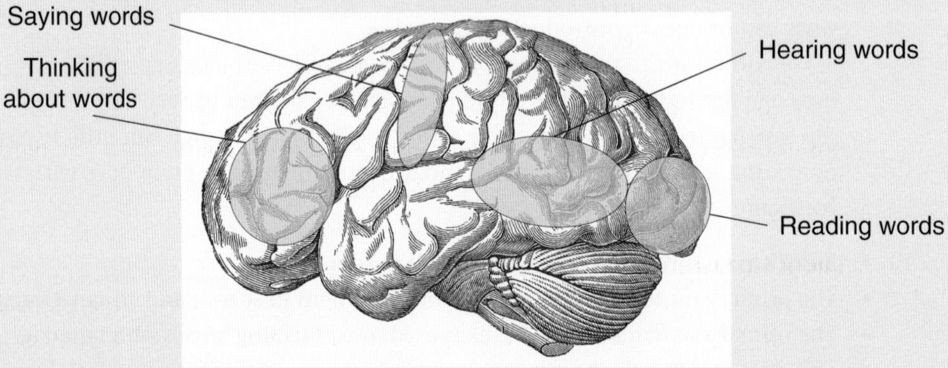

Saying words

Thinking about words

Hearing words

Reading words

Figure 15.7 Word processing in the brain

PAUSE AND REFLECT 15.4

Stop for a moment and see if you can name the four lobes of the brain and their basic functions.

15.3 Methods of Studying the Brain

What are some of the ways we can study language in the brain? Before the birth of technology, we relied mostly on autopsies to learn about language and the brain. These autopsies focused on damaged parts of the brain, or **lesions**, and tried to relate them to any language impairments that the patient might have shown before his/her death. To some extent this method is still used today but with the assistance of innovative methods and advanced technologies.

Today neurolinguists do not have to wait for a patient to die to study how his/her brain works. Instead, they can gather important information about it through behavioral studies and non-invasive neuroimaging. Next, we discuss some of these methods that inform us about language in the brain.

PAUSE AND REFLECT 15.5

Think about what it must have been like in the 1800s to study the brain without the help of things like a computer (or maybe even without electricity!). What participant group do you think would have been the primary informants?

15.3.1 Behavioral Studies on Hemispheric Connections

We can see the contralateral control of the brain by looking at results of behavioral studies. These studies have explored the connection or disconnection of communication between the two hemispheres of the brain. The two most common types of these hemispheric studies are dichotic listening studies and split-brain studies. These methods have been instrumental in understanding the special abilities that differentiate the left and right hemispheres among healthy and damaged brains.

Dichotic Listening Studies

During a dichotic listening task, a participant hears two different auditory stimuli at the same time, one in each ear through headphones. For example, the left ear may hear the word *rain* while the right ear hears *rake*. The same can be done with non-linguistic auditory input: the left ear may hear coughing while the right ear hears barking. Consistent in these studies is a **right ear advantage** such that speech heard through the right ear may seem clearer and louder. In fact, the right ear is able to show this advantage not only for words in the participant's own language but also for nonwords, single syllables, numbers, and even Morse code.

The opposite is true for the left ear: we see a **left ear advantage** when it comes to the perception of non-linguistic sounds such as natural/environmental sounds and melodies. Because we know that sensory information that is received on one side of the body is sent to the opposite side of the brain, we can easily see why each hemisphere perceives and processes input differently.

PAUSE AND REFLECT 15.6

If you are near a telephone or cell phone, pick it up and bring it to one ear as if you were answering it. To which ear did you raise the phone? What does this tell you about an ear advantage?

The accuracy that participants have shown in linguistic and non-linguistic versions of dichotic listening studies suggests that language is lateralized in the left hemisphere.

They also show that the left hemisphere is superior to the right hemisphere when it comes to the perception of linguistic sounds. However, the right hemisphere seems to be better at recognizing nonverbal information. In other words, dichotic listening studies demonstrate that the left hemisphere is specialized for language sounds, not all sounds. But we must be careful, once again, to keep in mind that not all brains are alike. A small number of people may have language lateralized in the right hemisphere. In this case, we would expect a left ear advantage for linguistic input, as shown in earlier work (Kimura, 1961). If you consulted 'Delving Deeper' on the book's accompanying website when we mentioned it in 15.2.5, you probably found out that left-handed and ambidextrous individuals are more likely to show language lateralization in the right hemisphere.

EYES ON WORLD LANGUAGES: THAI AND MANDARIN TONE LATERALIZATION

You have read about the fact that there seems to be a right ear advantage for language sounds like /d/ and a left ear advantage for non-language sounds like the ringing of a bell. But what about languages like Mandarin that we spoke of in Chapter 2 Phonetics that use pitch on individual syllables to differentiate words? Whereas for English speakers, saying the word *cat* with rising or falling pitch will not change the meaning of the word, for Thai and Mandarin words, it might. Take a look at how the four pitch contours of Mandarin tones change the meaning of the word:

[shī]	teacher
[shí]	ten
[shǐ]	history
[shì]	right

For Thai and Mandarin speakers, pitch changes are meaningful, linguistic sounds. Does this suggest that English speakers don't have a left ear advantage for tone but Thai and Mandarin speakers do?

The pioneering study by Van Lancker and Fromkin (1973) indeed found that speakers of tonal languages like Thai and Mandarin perceive tone as part of their language system and thus, show a right ear advantage for it. Speakers of languages without meaningful pitch contours do not hear it as part of their language system and in turn, show a left ear advantage for tone just as they would for something like the sound of a beep or cough.

Split-brain Studies

Recall that the corpus callosum is the bundle of neurons connecting the right and left hemispheres. What do you think would happen if it were to be severed? You probably guessed it: The pathway allowing for communication between the two hemispheres would be blocked. However, sometimes a rare surgical intervention in which the corpus callosum is cut, known as a **callosumectomy**, may be necessary to prevent epileptic seizures from spreading to both hemispheres. The result is known as a **split-brain**.

Although, fortunately, advances in neuropharmacology have introduced much less invasive treatments for patients with epilepsy, we have learned a great deal about how the two sides of the brain communicate with each other from split-brain patients.

Many split-brain patients are able to talk normally but when they are asked to perform tasks that require each side of the brain to communicate with the other, they are unable to do so. This can be seen in early work by Michael Gazzaniga (1970) in which a split-brain patient was unable to name an object he was holding in his left hand but was able to name the object when he was holding it in his right hand.

Given what you already know about the brain's contralateral control, you might realize that something held in the left hand sends a signal to the right side of the brain and something held in the right hand sends a signal to the left side of the brain. But given the fact that for most individuals, language may be lateralized in the left hemisphere, the signals received in the right hemisphere will need to consult with the left hemisphere for linguistic help. This is not possible for a split-brain patient whose corpus callosum has been surgically cut. What is even more intriguing is that while a blind-folded split-brain patient is unable to name what is in his left hand, he is able to describe it and even draw it.

In addition to holding objects in one hand or the other and trying to name them, split-brain patients show similar behavior when reading words or naming pictures. Once again, when using the left visual field – but not vice versa – the patient was unable to read the word or name the picture.

PAUSE AND REFLECT 15.7

If a split-brain patient is holding an orange in his left hand and a grapefruit in his right hand, which one will he be able to name? Why?

Before a surgical intervention such as a callosumectomy, the hemispheric connections and their responsibilities (e.g., for language, memory, etc.) are often assessed in the patient. One task that can be used is the **Wada test**, named after notable Canadian neurologist and epileptologist Juhn Wada. While awake, the patient is injected with a barbiturate anesthetic in the right internal carotid artery to shut down the ability for language and memory in the right hemisphere (or in the left internal carotid artery for the left hemisphere). This test is conducted pre-operatively to evaluate one side of the brain at a time. The language and memory tasks that patients perform during the effects of the injection can predict post-operative side-effects from a callosumectomy. The Wada test is therefore important for surgical planning. Its results help neurosurgeons to spare, as much as possible, language-essential areas for the patient assessed.

15.3.2 Neuroimaging

Some of the first technologies that were used to study language in the brain include tomography (i.e., still pictures). These practices are still relevant today but neurolinguists are now able to study the brain in more dynamic ways using methods which allow them to track blood flow in the brain and measure its electric and magnetic fields. Let's look at some of the most important neuroimaging techniques now being used in research labs and medical centres around the world.

Computerized Axial Tomography

You can think of the still pictures that we just mentioned as what **computerized axial tomography** gives us. Abbreviated as CT scanning, this method typically takes a series of x-rays of the head from several directions. Using a special computer program, CT scanning uses these x-rays to produce a series of black-and-white photographic cross-sections of the brain. The denser a material is, the whiter it will appear in the scan. Tumors can be easily spotted as they would appear as completely white while the rest of the brain would be shades of grey.

The CT scan perhaps has been around the longest of the neuroimaging methods and provides a useful way to identify tumors and lesions. A modern spiral CT scan only takes up to 30 seconds to complete and the results are available in a matter of minutes.

PAUSE AND REFLECT 15.8

Have you or anyone you know ever had an X-ray? What about a CT scan of the head? What were the doctors looking for?

Hemodynamic Neuroimaging

Newer methods using **hemodynamic neuroimaging** to study language in the brain are dominating research in neurolinguistics. This type of technology, unlike CT scanning, produces dynamic images that represent and map changes in blood flow in the brain. In other words, we are given visual displays of the locations in the brain that are active while a participant is performing a variety of tasks, including those related to language. Here, we will discuss two of these methods: Positron Emission Tomography (PET) and Functional Magnetic Resonance Imaging (fMRI). Read 'Delving Deeper' in Chapter 15's resources on the book's accompanying website to read about two other imaging methods known as DTI and fNIRS (www.cambridge .org/introducing-linguistics).

In the somewhat invasive method of **PET**, a participant is injected with radioactive tracers called positron-emitting isotopes. While the participant engages in a variety of cognitive and linguistic activities, these tracers are recorded and mapped in the brain to show the activity that occurs. Unlike CT scanning, PET imaging is capable of detecting areas of the brain at the molecular level. Until fMRI, which we will discuss next, PET scanning provided the best spatial resolution of linguistic tasks in the brain.

While PET has helped neurolinguists to understand the neurotransmitters and other molecules that underlie language in the brain, a much more common neuroimaging method used today is **fMRI**. This method is minimally invasive and can detect and measure some signals in the brain that PET scanning cannot. For fMRI, a participant lies in a scanner with an extremely powerful magnetic field (see Figure 15.8). Because blood is rich in iron, the magnetic fields in the fMRI scanner are able to track changes in blood flow in the brain. An image is reconstructed based on these changes. The image is so spatially accurate that we can distinguish areas of activation that are as little as a millimeter apart. When looking at language, a participant uses visual and/or auditory information to perform spoken tasks into a microphone while in the scanner.

As we just mentioned, fMRI provides researchers with excellent spatial resolution. However, it cannot be used to measure the spatiotemporal dynamics of language. In other words, while it is good at pinpointing where activity occurs, it cannot map its timeline. This is because the changes in the brain that occur in response to a neural activity are too slow (in terms of seconds) to detect changes in real-time processing. This is why many researchers now combine neuroimaging with sensitive temporal measures which we will take a look at next.

15.3.3   Measures of Electric and Magnetic Fields

In addition to the behavioral studies and imaging techniques used to explore the brain, we can also measure the brain's electric and magnetic fields to learn about how it functions and processes language. Below we review three of these important methods: Electroencephalography (EEG), Magnetoencephalography (MEG), and Transcranial Magnetic Stimulation (TMS).

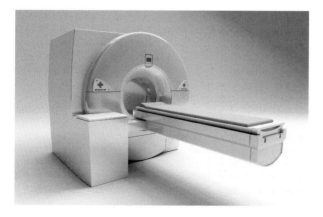

Figure 15.8 A fMRI scanner

Electroencephalography

EEG is a device which allows researchers to measure the brain's voltage changes in milliseconds as a response to certain events. These changes are referred to as event-related potentials (ERPs). An **ERP** is a scalp-recorded electrical response of brain activity that occurs after the presentation of an event stimulus such as a picture, word, or sound. A participant wears a cap – sort of like a hairnet – containing electrodes. The responses to their events are time-locked on to the EEG and are represented by an ERP waveform. So, EEG refers to the device and ERP refers to the data from that device.

EEG gives us waveform activity of the brain, called ERPs, which are plotted with negative voltage upward and positive voltage downward. These ERP waveforms reveal several processing characteristics involved in language functions, such as word retrieval and syntax, and can be seen usually 100–1,000 milliseconds after presentation of the stimulus. One consistent observation is the brain's reaction to an unexpected word where it does not semantically make sense. For example, read the following two sentences:

(1) The scholar criticized the man's <u>proof</u> of the hypothesis.
(2) *The scholar criticized the man's <u>event</u> of the hypothesis.

The underlined word in (1) semantically makes sense while the one in (2) does not. As you read the words *proof* or *event*, your brain reacted differently to each: Probably one was acceptable and one was rejected as ungrammatical. Let's take a look at how your ERPs might have looked using EEG technology. Although we would get slightly different voltages among the four lobes, the general pattern we would expect is seen in Figure 15.9. The figure shows the difference between brain potentials during the 600 ms after reading either the word *proof* (solid line) or *event* (dotted line).

From Figure 15.9, you can see two places where negative voltage rises, around 200 ms and around 400 ms after the critical word. This seems to be consistent for both *proof* and *event*. But what is important to note is the difference at around 400 ms after the critical word: For *event*, there is quite a bit more negativity than for *proof*. This is known as the **N400 effect**, a reliable and normal brain response to words and other stimuli when

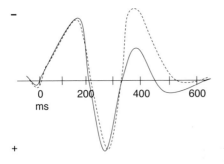

Figure 15.9 The N400 effect shown in the ERPs after reading a word which semantically makes sense in a sentence (solid line) and one which does not (dotted line).

reading sentences. The N400 effect is where we expect to see significant differences in brain activity due to a semantic anomaly. This is why there is more negative voltage around 400 ms after seeing *event* than after seeing *proof*. The N400 effect directly tells us about semantic processing and whether the brain accepts or rejects a word.

PAUSE AND REFLECT 15.9

Come up with another sentence like *The scientist criticized Max's ___ of the theorem.* In your example, provide three possible words that could fill in the blank. These words should show varying degrees of "correctness" (e.g., *proof, event, pizza*). In what order do you think N400 would be least to most negative?

Magnetoencephalography

One of the most promising methods that combines the temporal resolution benefits of EEG and the spatial resolution strengths of fMRI is **MEG**. You can think of MEG technology as being the magnetic imaging equivalent to ERPs. The MEG measures electrophysiological brain activity at milliseconds, or faster, through extremely sensitive detectors called **superconducting quantum interference devices (SQUIDs)**. These SQUIDs are located in a helmet which is lowered onto a participant's head. While the participant is performing linguistic or cognitive tasks, the computer records and images the spatiotemporal resolution in the brain.

Transcranial Magnetic Stimulation

One of the newest methods in studying language and the brain is **TMS**. This technique allows researchers to stimulate small regions of the brain using a magnetic field generator. This single-pulse of magnetic stimulation is passed through a coil that is placed near the head of the participant as seen in Figure 15.10. The coil lets out small electric currents to a very small area of the brain, about 1–1.5 cm². This permits researchers to *turn on and off* certain behaviors in the participant. This can do things like make you twitch your finger or briefly stop pain.

Figure 15.10 Transcranial Magnetic Stimulation

By using TMS, researchers have the opportunity to create temporary lesions in the brain that will show neuronal dysfunction in the same way as brain damage. However, these temporary disturbances are extremely short, with the duration of the stimulation only being about 100 ms. This could be both advantageous and limiting for TMS. The short duration does not give the brain enough time to compensate for the temporary disruption (which is good since it is not a real problem). But, the short duration also may be too brief for researchers to synchronize the disturbed functions with the magnetic field.

By applying TMS pulses repeatedly, the short-term effects of TMS are extended, making it easier to synchronize the measurements. This technique is called **repetitive transcranial magnetic stimulation (rTMS)**. Research has shown that while rTMS is more dangerous than single-pulse TMS, it has the potential to therapeutically treat language and behavioral disorders such as major depression disorder.

15.4 Language Impairments

What happens to language when the brain suffers from a tumor, damage, infection, hemorrhage, or disease? The answer to this is complicated and of course depends on the extent and location of damage. Neurolinguists are conducting ongoing research using some of the methods and technologies described in 15.3 to help answer this question. The main type of language impairment in which neurolinguists are interested includes a spectrum of aphasias which happen to approximately 80,000 people per year.

Broadly defined, **aphasia** is an impairment that affects the production and/or comprehension of language. It is estimated that there are around one million people in North America living with some form of aphasia.

Aphasiology is the study of language impairments that result from disease or damage to the parts of the brain that are vital to language. The most common cause is a stroke but aphasia can also be caused by brain tumors, traumatic brain injury, and progressive neurological disorders such as forms of dementia. A stroke occurs when there is an interruption of blood flow to neurons in the brain that require oxygen and nutrients.

Below, we organize the forms of language disturbances as non-fluent aphasia, fluent aphasia, and primary progressive aphasia. We then discuss language impairments that are primarily related to reading and/or writing abilities. Finally, you will read about how language can recover from these impairments through clinical rehabilitation.

15.4.1 Broca's and Non-fluent Aphasias

As its name suggests, **Broca's aphasia** occurs when damage to the brain is localized in Broca's area, which we identified in Section 15.2.5. This type of aphasia, also known as *non-fluent aphasia*, *motor aphasia*, or *expressive aphasia*, affects speech production but not speech comprehension as much. This is due to the fact that Broca's area is located in the frontal lobe in an area largely responsible for speech articulation.

For Broca's aphasics, speaking is labored and telegraphic, often missing function words such as prepositions (*of, at, to,* etc.), articles (*the, a*), and auxiliaries (*will, could*). Broca's aphasia patients may also have word-finding pauses and ungrammatical word order. The slow speed of their speech makes it impossible for them to have normal intonation and stress patterns when speaking. The example in (3) shows an exchange between a researcher and a patient with Broca's aphasia who tries to explain that he will go to the store with Sandy the next day.

(3) Researcher: Tell me what you will do tomorrow.
     Patient: Store…um…take…Sandy.
                                     "[Sandy will take me to the store]."

Patients with Broca's aphasia suffer from language impairment beyond fluency and phonology. They may also have trouble with morphemes. For instance, their speech may be missing plural (–s), tense (–ed), or comparative (–er) markers. Because Broca's aphasia patients are able to monitor and comprehend their own speech (and that of others), they are normally aware of their speech problems. This perhaps explains why they often attempt to self-correct their speech. Unfortunately, also because of their awareness of their impairment, speaking can be quite frustrating for Broca's aphasia patients and they are more likely than patients with other forms of aphasia to suffer from depression or other negative repercussions. The most severe form of non-fluent aphasia is **global aphasia** in which there is damage to the perisylvian cortex including both Broca's and Wernicke's areas. Because of this, a global aphasic is usually unable to comprehend or produce language. In this case, it is likely that the arcuate fasciculus – the bundle of nerves that connects Broca's and Wernicke's areas – has been damaged. Without this communicative link, the brain is unable to access words (in Wernicke's area) or say them (using Broca's area). Nonetheless, many global aphasic patients may still be able to communicate to a limited extent through facial expressions, gestures, and sounds.

15.4.2 Wernicke's and Fluent Aphasias

When damage to the brain happens in Wernicke's area, another location vital for language, **Wernicke's aphasia** may occur. This type of aphasia, also called *fluent aphasia*, *sensory aphasia*, or *receptive aphasia*, primarily affects the ability to comprehend spoken and written language. This is because Wernicke's area spans the region between the temporal and parietal lobes which are essential for understanding the auditory input we receive. Even though patients with Wernicke's aphasia produce fluent speech, often with correct pronunciation and intonation, what they actually say makes little sense. This is because they not only have problems comprehending language input, but they also are unable to monitor and comprehend the speech that they themselves produce. Furthermore, because meaning plays an important role in connecting thoughts in sentences, the discourse of Wernicke's aphasics is fragmented: One sentence may not have anything to do with the previous. Unlike Broca's aphasics, patients with Wernicke's aphasia are unaware that what they say and write does not make sense.

The example in (4) shows an exchange between a researcher and a patient with Wernicke's aphasia.

(4)   Researcher: Tell me what you will do tomorrow.
       Patient: Generally, it is … my brother is off doing his job
       to do better, when he's looking, the shepherds looking at
       other side. One their big book into her time there. She's
       looking at another time because she's eating too.

Speech is usually fluid for Wernicke's aphasics but there may be times when word retrieval causes them to hesitate. Often, they are unable to come up with the word they are trying to think of and substitute empty words like *those* or *thing*. Word substitutions are quite common for these patients whereas sometimes their substitutions are only slightly related (e.g., *pen* instead of *marker*) or completely unrelated (e.g., *shoe* instead of *marker*). In rare cases, patients with Wernicke's aphasia invent their own words or jargon. In these cases, their speech may include phonemes and intonation patterns from the language in question but contain very few real words. This type of fluent aphasia is called **jargon aphasia**.

PAUSE AND REFLECT 15.10

If you were to listen to a patient who has either Broca's or Wernicke's aphasia, what would you listen for to know which of the two aphasias the patient has?

Another form of a fluent language impairment is **anomic aphasia** which may occur when damage to the brain happens to the angular gyrus. The angular gyrus is an area involved in several processes related to language, memory recall, and attention. Anomic aphasia is characterized by the constant inability to access and produce certain words. This is more common for content words like nouns and verbs than for function words like prepositions.

While there is some degree of anomia in all aphasias, patients who suffer from anomic aphasia constantly find themselves in a tip-of-the-tongue state. You will recall from Chapter 14 Psycholinguistics that we defined the tip-of-the tongue state as a condition in which a word or expression cannot be retrieved from the mental lexicon.

PAUSE AND REFLECT 15.11

A patient has been diagnosed with anomic aphasia and constantly finds himself in a tip-of-the-tongue state. What types of strategies do you think his caregiver may use to help him come up with words in daily life?

LINGUISTICS TIDBITS: APHASIA AMONG DEAF COMMUNITIES

Sign language uses many of the same areas of the brain as spoken communication. Among these are Broca's and Wernicke's areas. Deaf individuals who used sign language before brain damage can be diagnosed with many of the same aphasias as speaking patients. For example, deaf patients with Wernicke's aphasia may have trouble understanding signs while those with Broca's aphasia have difficulties producing signs.

Another language impairment known as **conduction aphasia** may occur when damage is localized in the supramarginal gyrus of the parietal lobe, which is just above Wernicke's area. However, some research suggests that the affected area may be the connection or border between Broca's and Wernicke's areas. Patients with conduction aphasia can understand what they are hearing but are unable to repeat it, especially if what they hear is long and complex. In other words, **receptive** and **expressive abilities** are not so much the problem as is the connection between the two.

When contrasting conduction and global aphasias, remember that conduction aphasia is a type of fluent aphasia in which the predominant impairment is repetition. Global aphasia is a type of nonfluent aphasia which includes expressive and receptive impairments. By *expressive,* we refer to the ability to produce language and by *receptive,* we refer to the ability to understand language. With regard to expressive abilities, we should also mention that pronunciation can be affected (e.g., stuttering, mispronunciations) among patients with global and Broca's aphasias but not so much among patients with conduction aphasia.

15.4.3   Primary Progressive Aphasias

Unlike the impairments we've discussed so far, language impairment may result from a progressive loss of function or death of neurons. Neurodegenerative diseases such as dementia can cause this. **Dementia** is a category of several neurodegenerative diseases in which there is a decline in memory or other thinking skills severe enough to reduce the ability to perform everyday activities. While dementia includes diseases such as Alzheimer's disease and Parkinson's disease, there are some which cause more noticeable language impairments than others, which we will discuss next.

Primary progressive aphasia (PPA) occurs because of a degeneration of the frontal, temporal, and/or parietal regions of the brain which help to control speech and language. This can happen from a variety of degenerative diseases but Alzheimer's, frontotemporal lobar degeneration, and other forms of dementia are the most common cause. Depending on the specific areas of the brain affected, the symptoms will vary allowing us to classify PPA as either: agrammatic, semantic, or logopenic. The majority of patients will have increasing problems expressing themselves even though their memory stays relatively unaffected. Interestingly, though, some patients show evidence that other creative skills such as music and art improve as language abilities decline.

Patients who are **PPA-agrammatic**, also known as *progressive non-fluent aphasia,* have difficulty pronouncing words or producing speech fluently. Even though they cannot maintain the meaning of words, they speak slowly and have a hard time articulating utterances. Articulation may include stuttering, especially if the patient had a childhood stutter. Over time, PPA-agrammatic patients will begin to use shorter and simpler sentences, often leaving out articles and other function words. Eventually, less and less language is used because speech becomes too effortful and many patients become mute. It is believed that the main areas of the brain affected by PPA-agrammatic are the left frontal and temporal lobes.

Another progressive aphasia is **PPA-semantic**, in which patients encounter growing challenges remembering names of people, objects, facts, and words. Semantic memory loss in both speech production and comprehension is the primary symptom of PPA-semantic, although semantic memory seems to be unaffected for day-to-day events. As word meaning becomes more and more impaired, patients will also have trouble understanding conversations. In advanced stages of PPA-semantic, patients may be unable to recognize faces and show personality and behavioral changes that are typical in many types of dementia. It is thought that the main area of the brain affected by PPA-semantic is the left temporal lobe.

The third type of progressive aphasia is **PPA-logopenic** in which patients have growing problems with naming and sentence repetition. Although they are able to produce speech, they do so much more slowly because of word retrieval difficulties and not because of the loss of meaning of words as in PPA-semantic. As the disease progresses, PPA-logopenic patients are eventually unable to retain long or complex sentences and information. It is thought that the main areas of the brain affected by PPA-logopenic are the left temporal and parietal lobes. Alzheimer's disease is the most common cause of PPA-logopenic.

15.4.4   Alexia and Agraphia

Some other forms of language impairment that may or may not accompany the aphasias we just discussed include alexia, also called *acquired dyslexia*, and agraphia, also called *acquired dysgraphia*. These two impairments are related to reading and writing abilities, respectively. Keep in mind that alexia and agraphia are *acquired* impairments that result from brain injury or trauma. They are not the same as dyslexia and dysgraphia which are *developmental* impairments that may be prevalent during childhood development.

Alexia

Alexia is the loss of the ability to read due to brain damage. There are several types of alexia with the most common being **pure alexia**. In pure alexia, patients have severe reading problems while other skills such as speaking, listening comprehension, and writing are typically unaffected. This impairment arises when there is damage to the posterior part of the corpus callosum and the primary visual cortex. Pure alexia affects visual processing but not auditory processing so even though a patient with pure alexia will be able to write, he can't read what he has just written. However, he will be able to understand what he has written if someone else reads or spells it out to him.

A second type of alexia is called **surface dyslexia** in which patients must rely on the pronunciation of written words in order to understand them. They are unable to recognize words as wholes but instead process them according to spelling-to-sound rules. For example, they may be likely to read the word *look* as [luk] or pronounce letters that should remain silent as in saying [ɑtʃej] for the word *ache*. This impairment may result from damage to the temporoparietal region of the left hemisphere.

Perhaps the opposite of surface dyslexia is **phonological dyslexia** which is the selective impairment of the ability to read pronounceable made-up words while the ability to read familiar words is not affected. Unlike patients with surface dyslexia, people who suffer from phonological dyslexia recognize words as wholes and cannot *sound them out*. This language impairment may happen when there is damage to the superior temporal lobe although the specific location varies.

A final type of alexia we must mention is **deep dyslexia**, a severe form of phonological dyslexia. Deep dyslexia is notable by the patient's frequent semantic errors during reading and the inability to read nonwords. These semantic errors while reading words aloud can be of many types: synonyms (saying *doctor* instead of *physician*); antonyms (saying *clean* instead of *dirty*); subordinates (saying *bird* instead of *dove*); superordinates (saying *apple* instead of *fruit*); attributes (saying *orange* instead of *carrot*); or associates (saying *milk* instead of *baby*). The exact place of brain lesions that cause deep dyslexia again vary but often include much of the left frontal lobe.

PAUSE AND REFLECT 15.12

What is the difference between acquired dyslexia and developmental dyslexia?

Agraphia

Whereas alexia affects reading abilities, **agraphia** causes impairments to writing abilities. Often agraphia is split into two categories depending on whether they affect language or motor areas of the brain. **Central agraphia** occurs when there are impairments to both spoken language and to motor and visual skills. Commonly, there are problems with spelling–sound rules and orthographic memory. In other words, patients with central agraphia oftentimes can neither remember how words look when correctly spelled nor spell them out. This form of agraphia is often the result of damage involving the left parietal lobe.

Peripheral agraphia is the impairment of writing abilities due to damage to the motor system. Patients with peripheral agraphia will produce incomplete, effortful writing that includes incorrect or distorted letter formation. Even though their writing may be almost illegible, they are still able to spell fairly well. Poor handwriting is due to damage to the parietal lobe, specifically in the area responsible for the motor planning that is needed for letter formation.

EYES ON WORLD LANGUAGES: GRAPHIC APHASIA AND JAPANESE ORTHOGRAPHY

Japanese aphasia patients show some characteristics that Western aphasics do not and the differences lie within their unique writing system (see Chapter 11 Writing systems). The Japanese writing system consists of two scripts: kanji and kana. Kanji is a set of about 3,000 Chinese characters that do not have a sound-to-script relationship. In other words, kanji characters have been borrowed into Japanese and because of this, the pronunciation of these characters in Japanese is not predictable by their Chinese-rooted script. However, the other Japanese script, kana, is a phonetic script that has a sound-symbol correlation.

Theoretically, Japanese could be written entirely in kana script but because of tradition and other historical reasons, kanji characters are used if there has been one borrowed into Japanese. So, while kanji characters exist for months of the year like March, April, and May, they could be (but are not) written in kana script as shown below.

Kanji		Kana
三月	"March"	さんがつ
四月	"April"	しがつ
五月	"May"	ごがつ

One interesting and rather predictable symptom of Japanese aphasics is that if there is damage to Broca's area, they lose the ability to process kana script yet their kanji reading and writing may be unaffected. If there is damage to Wernicke's area, usually both scripts will remain unaffected but they will be unable to produce meaningful language.

15.4.5 Recovery from Language Impairments

The recovery of impaired language is a long and winding road. Luckily, the more we know about the brain and how it engages with language, the better we become at rehabilitating it after language impairment. Below we take a look at the rehabilitation of language impairments and also some of the recovery patterns for speakers of more than one language.

Rehabilitation of Language Impairment

Aphasia affects every patient slightly differently depending on the exact location of the neurological damage. Because of this, the treatment for aphasics must be customized to every patient. In fact, because each patient's impairment and rehabilitation needs will be different, a team of specialists will normally be involved in the treatment

LINGUISTICS TIDBITS: AN APP FOR EVERYTHING
Aphasia treatment teams have begun using technology in rehabilitation plans. Technology can significantly increase the intensity of treatment because patients can practice a variety of exercises on an app outside of face-to-face sessions. For example, a company called Constant Therapy has developed a free app that helps people who are suffering from speech-language disorders related to diseases such as aphasia and dementia. The app can be used to improve speech comprehension and production along with memory, attention, and reading skills.

plan. For instance, in addition to the speech-language pathologist, others may include a clinical neuropsychologist, physiotherapist, occupational therapist, or social worker.

Most patients are able to recover some or most language skills by working with their speech-language pathologist and treatment team. But as you can imagine, improvement does not happen overnight. Rehabilitation of language may take years but the sooner the treatment plan is put into action, the greater chances of recovery are. It is believed that during the six months or so after trauma, the brain tries to repair damaged neurons and recover from the injury. Helping the brain to do this during this period is essential because if things cannot be repaired, the brain accepts these impairments as the new normal and thus may be much more resistant to treatment.

Naturally, the effectiveness of language rehabilitation for aphasia patients varies depending on many factors including the type and severity of aphasia, treatment intensity, the patient's age, health, motivation, handedness, and educational level. As we become more familiar with what happens when certain areas of the brain are damaged, we get closer to understanding how to rehabilitate the hampering effects.

Recovery Patterns of Language Impairment among Multilinguals

In the case of an aphasia patient who spoke more than one language before suffering damage to the brain, we can ask several interesting questions. Firstly, can one language have aphasia and others not? If more than one language is affected, which language returns first, why, and how well? Do some languages never recover?

Michel Paradis (1977) found that some patients may recover their languages simultaneously, some may recover one language only after other languages have recovered, and other patients recover one language while the other language(s) regress or are never recovered at all. He classifies these patterns as:

- Parallel recovery: languages recover at the same rate;
- Differential recovery: recovery rates differ compared to pre-damage;
- Selective recovery: not all languages are fully recovered;
- Antagonistic recovery: one (or more) language(s) gets worse while another (or others) get better;
- Successive recovery: a language can only recover once another is completely restored; and
- Mixed/blended recovery: languages are mistakenly mixed together, interfering in the recovery process.

When languages are not recovered in parallel, two patterns have been observed. **Ribot's law** (1882) suggests that language recovery replicates the order in which they were acquired. On the other hand, **Pitre's law** (1895) argues that the recovery pattern is determined by how frequently a language was used prior to brain injury or trauma, which may or may not be the first language.

As you can imagine, the number of aphasics who also speak several languages is far fewer than aphasics who speak just one or two languages. Because of this, many studies use case-study approaches that provide us with in-depth information about a small sample. Galloway (1978) conducted a study which examined the language production of a hepta-lingual (named MB) after a major cardiovascular trauma that caused damage to the left posterior temporal and parietal lobes. Table 15.2 shows MB's language acquisition history and Table 15.3 gives information about the language production and comprehension skills that were recovered after trauma.

TABLE 15.2 Hepta-lingual MB's Language Acquisition History (Galloway, 1978)

Age	Place	Language	Environment
0–4	Hungary	Hungarian	Home
3–17	Hungary/Poland/Romania	Hebrew (Biblical)	Hebrew school
4–6	Poland	Polish	Nursery school
6–10	Hungary	Hungarian	Relearn: home, school, friends
10–12	Romania (multilingual neighborhood)	Romanian Yiddish Hungarian	School Hebrew school Home
12–17	Hungary	German/English Hungarian	Formal instruction Home and school
18–19	Austria	German	Concentration camp
19–25	Germany	German	University degree in engineering
25+	United States	English	No formal instruction, learned from news, radio, etc.

TABLE 15.3 Hepta-lingual MB's Language Production and Comprehension after Trauma (Galloway, 1978)

	English	German	Hungarian	Yiddish	Hebrew	Romanian	Polish
Production	Near normal	None	None	None	None	None	None
Comprehension	Normal	Normal	Normal	Normal	Almost none	Almost none	Almost none

> **PAUSE AND REFLECT 15.13**
>
> From Tables 15.2 and 15.3 for patient MB, does Ribot's or Pitre's law more accurately predict language recovery patterns? Explain your answer.

As can be seen in Table 15.3, language production for MB after trauma was near normal in English but not for the other six languages. Comprehension was normal for English and also for German, Hungarian, and Yiddish, but not for Hebrew, Romanian, or Polish. Although Ribot's law has been supported in other studies, these language recovery patterns for MB support Pitre's law with frequency of usage prior to damage predicting language recovery.

How do aphasiologists, then, decide in which language(s) to provide rehabilitation? Paradis and colleagues developed the **Bilingual Assessment Test** (BAT) between 1976–1982, with the objective of comparing "the two languages of a bilingual individual with aphasia so as to reliably and validly determine to what extent and in which aspects one language might be better preserved than another" (Paradis, 2011, p. 428). The BAT includes 32 tasks which collectively assess the implicit linguistic knowledge for comprehension and production. This provides researchers with an idea of the most appropriate rehabilitation strategies and in which language(s). Since its initial conception, it is now available in over 70 languages and versions of it can be downloaded for free at http://www.mcgill.ca/linguistics/research/bat

Without a doubt, the BAT continues to be the most widely used assessment of aphasia in speakers of two or more languages. Its application goes well beyond aphasia and has been used to assess many types of language impairments as a result of several conditions such as Alzheimer's, autism spectrum disorders, multiple sclerosis, and Parkinson's, among many others.

15.5   Theoretical Explanations from Neurolinguistics

What can the knowledge gained from neurolinguistics tell us about how grammar is processed and represented in the brain? In this section we will take a look at the biological evidence and theoretical explanations that intersect with major areas of theoretical linguistics. We organize the section by first describing the biology of words, their sounds, and meaning followed by a discussion on the biocognition of morphology and syntax.

15.5.1   Words, Sound, and Meaning

You may recall that the **lexicon** is the mental dictionary which includes information related to a word's sounds and pronunciation, its meanings, and grammatical properties. From the neuroimaging methods and language impairments that you have read about, researchers have learned that the temporal lobe is important for the lexicon. This is true for the temporal lobes in both the left and right hemispheres – but much more so in the left. PET and fMRI studies have consistently shown activation in the temporal-lobe regions of the brain during lexical tasks of word form and meaning or when reading words or naming pictures. Not surprisingly, when these same areas suffer damage, patients will exhibit severe lexical deficits.

Of course, we cannot generalize that all things related to the lexicon are mostly done in the temporal lobes. Certain lexical functions depend on other areas as well. In fact, studies show that the **supramarginal gyrus** is largely responsible for phonological memory. This is needed to do things like temporarily remember a string of letters or numbers. Whereas the right cerebellum underlies searching for lexical knowledge, the basal ganglia and inferior frontal gyrus which includes Broca's area are needed to retrieve and select lexical knowledge. This means that several areas of the brain work together to process words.

There is evidence from MEG studies showing that the brain responds differently to speech sounds that are phonemically contrastive like [p] vs. [b] than to sounds that are acoustically different but not phonemically distinct such as [p] vs. [pʰ]. ERP studies provide further support for this with permissible sequences of sounds like the [bl] in *black* showing different neurological reflexes than impermissible sequences like [bn] in *bnack*. Interestingly, these same neurological differences show up when the brain responds to correct or incorrect hand or sign formations in sign language. This means that the brain may represent and process spoken and signed language in a similar manner.

PAUSE AND REFLECT 15.14

Given that ERP studies show electric differences to correct or incorrect sequences of sounds, would you expect these to show up in a reaction time study? Explain your answer.

The brain also seems to distinguish between word categories such as nouns vs. verbs. For instance, neuroimaging studies have shown that verbs are strongly linked to the left frontal regions and nouns to the left temporal regions. We are reassured of this again by observing the symptoms of aphasia patients. Patients with left frontal lesions commonly have trouble producing verbs whereas patients with left temporal lesions often have difficulties producing nouns. This could imply that verbs are stored and accessed in the frontal lobe whereas nouns are stored and accessed in the temporal lobe.

The learning of new words depends on the medial temporal lobe including the hippocampus. We again know this from neuroimaging, which shows increased activation of these areas while learning new words, and from patients suffering from language impairment due to brain trauma. The well-cited case of amnesic patient H.M. shows us the effects of having the medial temporal areas surgically removed. After his surgery in 1953, he was unable to learn new words introduced into the language like *cellphone*, *geek*, or *bikini*.

15.5.2 Morphology

You will recall from Chapter 4 Morphology that we made a distinction between inflectional and derivational morphology. Inflectional morphology is a word-formation process (such as affixation) that modifies words in terms of things liked tense, person, number, and gender. For instance, the verb *play* can add the suffix *–ing* to express the present progressive tense, *playing*. Derivational morphology is interested in the processes that build new words based on existing ones. This results in a word with a different category (V → N) and/or different meaning. For example, the prefix *un–* added to *happy* results in *unhappy*. Even though this addition did not change categories (Adjective → Adjective), *happy* and *unhappy* certainly have different meanings. If we add the suffix *–ness* to *happy* to get *happiness*, we see a category change (Adjective → Noun).

Neurolinguistics has provided evidence that not only are inflection and derivation indeed processes that rely on different areas of the brain, but we also know that the brain treats regular forms differently than irregular. In other words, the brain reacts differently to the inflectional affix (e.g., *–ed*) compared to the derivational affix (*–ness*) just as it handles the *–ed* in *jumped* differently than the irregular *ran*. Morphological problems in patients with aphasia show us these differences. Many Broca's aphasics tend to omit inflectional morphemes but may retain most derivational morphemes. When it comes to regular and irregular forms, patients with brain damage to the temporal lobe may have difficulties producing, understanding, or reading irregular inflections like *drank* and *mice* but less so for regulars such as *looked* and *cats*. Contrarily, patients with damage to the frontal lobe may show impairments to regular inflections but not so much for irregulars.

Neuroimaging studies demonstrate additional explanations for these differences. PET work in several languages has found that regular morphological forms elicit activation in Broca's area and the basal ganglia. Irregular forms show activation in other areas such as the left middle temporal gyrus, some parietal regions, and the cerebellum. fMRI studies mirror these findings by showing that regular forms, both inflected and derivational, produce more activation in the Broca's area compared to irregular forms.

The independent nature of the impairments shown for inflectional and derivational morphemes provides evidence for **double dissociation**. Double dissociation refers to cases in which two related mental processes function independently. For example, there is double dissociation between speech production and speech comprehension as shown in the symptoms of patients with Broca's aphasia (trouble with production but not comprehension) and patients with Wernicke's aphasia (trouble with comprehension but not production). In other words, if Patient X has Impairment A but not Impairment B and Patient Y has Impairment B but not Impairment A, we can say that there is double dissociation between Impairments A and B. Research using neuroimaging has shown that when mapping out patients with inflectional morpheme problems and patients with derivational morpheme problems, a clear dissociation can be seen between the two. Neuroimaging on inflectional vs. derivational morpheme impairments has shown that the two related processes function independently in the healthy brain.

Taken together, this body of work shows that speech production and comprehension of irregulars and regulars depends on different brain structures. Irregulars seem to rely on temporal lobe regions while regulars depend on the frontal cortex, particularly Broca's area. This explains why Broca's aphasics have trouble with regular, but not as much with irregular, inflectional and derivational morphology.

PAUSE AND REFLECT 15.15

Given what you know about Wernicke's aphasia, how do you think morphology is affected?

15.5.3 Syntax

Recall from Chapter 5 Syntax that you learned about the difference between the underlying representation, a type of knowledge, and what is actually produced.

Neurolinguistics has helped to prove that the underlying mental representation actually exists. Notice the difference in distance between the movement of *which man* in (5) and *who* in (6). Remember that, when a syntactic element moves, we indicate this by crossing out the copy of the moved element.

(5)   [Which man] did Jerry see ~~which man~~?
(6)   Who ~~who~~ went home?

Many studies show that longer response times are associated with sentences like (5) which have longer movements, in terms of distance, than those like (6). This supports the existence of an underlying representation in which copies are present. Frazier, Clifton, & Randall (1983) showed that when filling in the *gap site* – where we have left a copy – with a word that is semantically related to the moved element, there is increased electrical activity at the gap site (e.g., *Which man did Jerry see [which woman]* vs. *Which man did Jerry see [which table]*). This suggests that there are different brain functions involved in different *wh*-movements.

As you read above, Broca's aphasia patients have difficulties with syntax. Typically, to understand speech, Broca's aphasics must rely on typical subject-verb-object (SVO) word order and they have difficulties when syntactic structure is more complex. This is problematic for sentences like (5) which involve movement. Broca's aphasia patients are likely to comprehend the first DP as the subject of the sentence. Therefore, they would mistakenly think that a man saw Jerry instead of Jerry seeing the man.

Some researchers argue that Broca's aphasia patients rely on word order for meaning because they are unable to perform syntactic transformations like *wh*-movements. It is likely that they also suffer from **agrammatism**, a syndrome in which grammatical abilities are lost and as a result, speech is morphologically and syntactically simplified. Passive voice constructions, like *wh*-questions, involve movement. The sentences in (7) and (8) show the underlying representations before and after movement, respectively.

(7)   was seen Mary by Joan

(8)   Mary was seen ~~Mary~~ by Joan.

According to the view of Grodzinsky (2000), agrammatism involves specific syntactic impairments that prevent the patient from being able to relate elements within a sentence. According to this view, agrammatics would be unable to relate moved objects to their original position (represented in (8) by ~~Mary~~). This explains why they would probably understand that in (8), Mary saw Joan.

Another interesting contribution from neurolinguistics is the extent to which syntax is separate from semantics. Some of this evidence has come from **Jabberwocky** sentences – grammatical sentences that have no meaning due to their use of nonsense words. Read the excerpt of the poem *Jabberwocky* written by Lewis Carroll (1871) in his novel *Through the Looking-Glass, and What Alice Found There* in (9).

(9)   He took his vorpal sword in hand:
Long time the manxome foe he sought—
So rested he by the Tumtum tree,
And stood awhile in thought.

And as in uffish thought he stood,
The Jabberwock, with eyes of flame,
Came whiffling through the tulgey wood,
And burbled as it came!

Even though there are many nonsense words in (9), it does not distract too much from our general understanding of what is happening in the poem. Now read (10) in which we have replaced the nonsense words with real words.

(10)   He took his shining sword in hand:
Long time the skillful foe he sought—
So rested he by the apple tree,
And stood awhile in thought.

And as in profound thought he stood,
The Jabberwock, with eyes of flame,
Came charging through the thorny wood,
And snarled as it came!

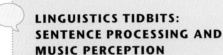

LINGUISTICS TIDBITS: SENTENCE PROCESSING AND MUSIC PERCEPTION

The brain reacts to syntactic violations in language and unexpected chords or instrumental changes in music similarly. While the same areas of the brain are involved, for language this is lateralized in the left hemisphere and for music it is bilateralized, with slightly more activation in the right hemisphere. ERP studies show that word order violations elicit left anterior negativities but that music violations cause right anterior negativities.

From ERP studies, we know that the brain responds differently to speech and non-speech with more activity in the left hemisphere for speech. Oddly enough, the Jabberwocky sentences in (9), which contain several non-speech words, evoke the same ERP patterns as the meaningful sentences in (10). Researchers argue that this demonstrates that the left hemisphere is sensitive to syntactic structure even when there is little or no meaning. One study by Hahne & Jescheniak (2001) showed that participants were even sensitive to syntactic violations in Jabberwocky sentences.

SUMMARY

In this chapter, we first looked at the brain's anatomy in terms of the areas important for language. We identified that for most right-handed people, the left hemisphere is widely responsible for language competence and performance. It is connected to the right hemisphere by the corpus callosum, a network of nerves that permits communication between the two hemispheres. Both of the hemispheres can be divided into four lobes: frontal, parietal, temporal, and occipital, each of which have specific responsibilities. There are still many unanswered questions when it comes to the architecture and functionality of the human brain. In fact, there are still many brain regions that have not yet been charted. Future research will need to explore these regions as technologies continue to improve.

Common methods and technologies used to study the brain include lesion studies and autopsies, dichotic listening and split-brain studies, neuroimaging, and studies measuring the brain's electric and magnetic fields. These methods have given researchers an incredible advantage in better understanding the brain and language. This is especially apparent regarding language impairments that result from acquired brain damage or injury (either instantaneous or progressive). Examples of such impairments that we discussed include forms of aphasia: non-fluent, fluent, and primary progressive. We also looked at language disturbances that are primarily related to reading and writing abilities, called alexia and agraphia, respectively.

Finally, we discussed how neurolinguistics has informed what we know about the mental lexicon – words, their sounds and meanings – along with morphology and syntax. Recent research using state-of-the-art technologies has informed us about which language functions rely on which brain structures. It is without a doubt that future work will further investigate these intriguing functions with more precision and even from molecular and genetic levels.

EXERCISES

15.1 In the diagram below, label the brain's four lobes in the boxes provided. Then, identify the central sulcus, lateral fissure, Broca's area, and Wernicke's area in the remaining spaces.

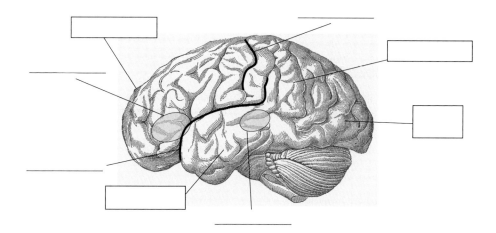

15.2 For each of the following abilities, list whether the frontal, parietal, temporal, or occipital lobe is primarily responsible. There may be more than one lobe for each.

i.   reasoning
ii.   emotions
iii. vision
iv.   reading
v.   hearing
vi.   movement
vii. sensation

15.3 Consider the following scenarios and assume that each of the patients described is right-handed. Then answer the questions about the consequences for language. Hint: remember to keep in mind contralateral control.

i.   A stroke severely damaged Jimmy's right side of the primary visual cortex and corpus callosum. Will he still be able to read?
ii.   Donna suffered a blow to the head that destroyed her left side of the primary visual cortex and corpus callosum. Will she still be able to read?
iii. Gary had a stroke that damaged his left auditory cortex. Will he still be able to comprehend speech?
iv.   Garthaniel has a degenerative disease that progressively affects his primary motor cortex. What language problem will he likely develop?

15.4 Identify which language impairment is most associated with the following symptoms:

i.   inability to produce accurate and fluid speech;
ii.   inability to comprehend written language;
iii. inability to comprehend simple instructions like *Take the book*;
iv.   inability to monitor one's own speech production;
v.   inability to read familiar words but not unfamiliar words.

15.5 Assume that you have language functions which are lateralized in the left hemisphere like most people. For each example below, circle the choice that you would likely hear first and more clearly.

  i.   Left ear: bird singing
        Right ear: car honking
  ii.   Left ear: car honking
        Right ear: bird singing
  iii. Left ear: the word *cat*
        Right ear: the word *dog*
  iv.   Left ear: the word *dog*
        Right ear: the word *cat*

15.6 A split-brain patient is asked to put on a blindfold and then name an object that he is given in his right hand. Can he name the object? Why or why not? What if the object is in his left hand, would that make a difference?

15.7 When it comes to morphology (inflectional vs. derivational; irregular forms vs. regular forms), Broca's aphasics may have predictable difficulties. Decide which of the two words in each pair below a patient with Broca's aphasia will have more trouble producing and briefly say why.

  i.   shortest vs. beautiful
  ii.   walked vs. swam
  iii. slowly vs. taller
  iv.   was vs. studied
  v.   unable vs. John's

15.8 While Broca's aphasia patients usually suffer little problems with language comprehension, there are some syntactic structures that they simply cannot understand. Take a look at the examples below and anticipate what a Broca's aphasic might misunderstand and why.

  i.   What man did Begonia hire?
  ii.   The cat was chased by the dog.
  iii. It was the cat that the dog chased.

15.9 Decide whether a Broca's or Wernicke's aphasia patient would be more likely to produce each of the sentences below.

i.	Examiner:	Tell me where you live.
	Patient:	Well, it's a meender place and it has two … two of them. For dreaming and pinding after supper. And up and down. Four of down and three of up … (Brookshire, 2003, p. 155).
ii.	Examiner:	What's the weather like today?
	Patient:	Fully under the jimjam and on the altigrabber.
		(Brookshire, 2003, p. 155).
iii.	Examiner:	What is the boy doing in this picture?
	Patient:	The boy is catch … the boy is hitch … the boy is hit the ball.
		(Saffran, Schwartz, & Marin, 1980, p. 229).
iv.	Examiner:	Why are you in the hospital?
	Patient:	… All right … From when wine [why] I'm here. What's wrong with me because I … was myself until the taenz took something about the time between me and my regular time in that time and they took the time in that time here and that's when the the time took around here and saw me around in it's started with me no time and I bekan [began] work of nothing else that's the way the doctor find me that way …

(Obler & Gjerlow, 1999, p. 43).

v.   Examiner: What is the girl doing in this picture?
      Patient: Girl ... wants to ... flowers ... flowers and wants to ... The woman ... wants to
                   ... The girl wants to ... the flowers and the woman.
                   (Saffran, Schwartz, & Marin, 1980, p. 234).

15.10   In the table below, put an X in the appropriate coloumns that describe the primary linguistic
        symptoms associated with the acquired language disorders.

	Expressive impairments	Receptive impairments	Pronunciation difficulties
alexia			
Broca's aphasia			
conduction aphasia			
global aphasia			
jargon aphasia			
Wernicke's aphasia			

15.11   In the table below, fill in the location (i.e., the lobe and hemisphere) and function of certain areas of
        the brain.

Area of the brain	Location in the brain	Function in language
angular gyrus		
Broca's area		
corpus callosum		
primary motor cortex		
primary visual cortex		
Wernicke's area		

15.12   Which column of words will an aphasic patient who has agrammatism have more difficulty reading
        and why? What does this tell us about how words are stored and processed in the brain?

(i)	(ii)
cat	not
knot	but
television	may
sing	should
pretty	and

15.13   How are phonological and surface dyslexia different?

15.14   What are the main differences between fluent and non-fluent types of aphasia?

15.15   Why do you think the human brain has been described as two brains in one?

REFERENCES

Brookshire, R. (2003). *Introduction to neurogenic communication disorders* (6ᵗʰ Edition). St. Louis, MO:
    Mosby.
Carroll, L. (1871). *Through the looking-glass, and what Alice found there*. London: Macmillan.

Frazier, L., Clifton, C., & Randall, J. (1983). Filling gaps: Decision principles and structure in sentence comprehension. *Cognition, 13*, 187–222.

Galloway, L. (1978). Language impairment and recovery in polyglot aphasia: A case study of a hepta-lingual. In M. Paradis (Ed.), *Aspects of bilingualism* (pp. 139–148). Columbia, SC: Hornbeam.

Gazzaniga, M. (1970). *The bisected brain.* New York, NY: Appleton-Century-Crofts.

Gopnik, M., & Crago, M. (1991). Familial aggregation of a developmental language disorder. *Cognition, 39*, 1–50.

Grodzinsky, Y. (2000). The neurology of syntax: Language use without Broca's area. *Behavioral and Brain Sciences, 23*(1), 1–71.

Hahne, A., & Jescheniak, J. (2001). What's left if the Jabberwock gets the semantics? An ERP investigation into semantic and syntactic processes during auditory sentence comprehension. *Cognitive Brain Research, 11*(2), 199–212.

Kimura, D. (1961). Cerebral dominance and the perception of verbal stimuli. *Canadian Journal of Psychology, 15*, 166–177.

Neville, H., Nicol, J., Barss, A., Forster, K., Garrett, M. (1991). Syntactically based sentence processing classes: Evidence from event-related brain potentials. *Journal of Cognitive Neuroscience, 3*, 151–165.

Obler, L., & Gjerlow, K. (1999). *Language and the brain.* Cambridge: Cambridge University Press.

Paradis, M. (1977). Bilingualism and aphasia. In H. Whitaker & H. Whitaker (Eds.), *Studies in neurolinguistics* (pp. 65–121). New York, NY: Academic Press.

Paradis, M. (2011). Principles underlying the Bilingual Aphasia Test (BAT) and its uses. *Clinical Linguistics & Phonetics, 25*(6–7), 427–443.

Pitres, A. (1895). Aphasia in polyglots. In M. Paradis (Ed.) (1983), *Readings on aphasia in bilinguals and polyglots* (pp. 26–49). Montreal: Marcel-Dieder.

Ribot, T. (1882). *Diseases of memory: An essay in the positive psychology.* New York, NY: Appleton.

Saffran, E., Schwartz, M., & Marin, O. (1980). Evidence from aphasia: Isolating the components of a production model. In B. Butterworth (Ed.), *Language production* (pp. 221–241). London: Academic Press.

Van Lancker, D., & Fromkin, V. (1973). Hemispheric specialization for pitch and "tone": Evidence from Thai. *Journal of Phonetics, 1*, 101–109.

GLOSSARY

abductive change The creation of a new morphological rule based on a misanalysis of the available data during language acquisition. See also *deductive change*.

abjad A writing system in which each character, or *letter*, represents a consonant.

abugida A writing system in which each character represents a consonant followed by a specific vowel (usually /a/), and other vowels are notated by modifying the basic shape with an addition or deformation.

accessibility hierarchy shows the access to relativization of noun phrases in simple clauses. In the hierarchy, relative clause types lower (to the right) in the hierarchy are less frequent and more marked universally while those higher (to the left) in the hierarchy are more common and less marked.

acquired savant syndrome is a syndrome in which prodigious skills follow neurological problems such as dementia or brain damage.

Acquisition-Learning Hypothesis is part of the Monitor Model which distinguishes between acquisition and learning. While learning is a conscious procedure, acquisition, on the other hand, is a subconscious one that entails the development of underlying linguistic competence.

acronym A word formed from the initials of several words, e.g., *UNICEF*.

activation in psycholinguistics refers to the fact that everything in the mind has an activation level. Activation can increase or decrease as the situation dictates and can also spread to other connecting units.

active sentence is a sentence in which the action of a main verb is preform *by* the subject (i.e., the element with the agent role). Example: *Jeanette sent the message*.

adjective (A) A category of word that typically describes a property of an entity. In English some adjectives exhibit comparative and superlative forms (*big, bigger, biggest*). They generally precede the nouns they modify. Examples: *large, nice, blue*.

adjunct This term refers to a phrase that is not required by the head but is used to include additional, optional information. For example, if I say *I walked in the mud*, the information expressed by the phrase *in the mud* is an adjunct.

adposition An umbrella term for both prepositions and postpositions.

adverb (Adv) Adverbs modify actions or properties. They are often formed by the addition of –*ly*. Examples: *quickly, very, often*.

Affective Filter Hypothesis is part of the Monitor Model which posits that affective factors such as motivation and feelings that have a hampering effect on learning such as stress, anxiety, insecurity, and embarrassment, present a potential difficulty in SLA.

affective state refers to learners' feelings or emotional condition.

affix A bound morpheme that attaches to a base, e.g., *–ed, in–*.

affricates are [–continuous] consonants that are characterized by their slow release of closure. In English, the two affricates are /d͡ʒ/ and /t͡ʃ/

agglutinative language A language in which words have several grammatical morphemes that attach to a root morpheme and each grammatical morpheme has only one distinct meaning.

aggressive signals Signals letting other animals know that a particular animal is feeling aggressive and might be ready to fight.

agrammatism is a syndrome in which grammatical abilities are lost.

agraphia also called *acquired dysgraphia* is the loss of the ability to write due to brain damage.

Akshara In Indic writing, a character that denotes a consonant, or a combination of more than one consonant, with or without a vowel matra.

alarm signals Signals alerting animals to the presence of danger.

alexia also called *acquired dyslexia*, is the loss of the ability to read due to brain damage.

allograph A positional variant of a character, such as ç used instead of σ for /s/ at the end of a word in Greek.

allomorph One of the phonetic forms that a morpheme may take, e.g., the prefix *in–* is realized as [ɪŋ] before the velar stops /k/ and /g/.

allophone Sounds that change their pronunciation based upon a predictable context are allophones. For example, in English, the phoneme /k/ is aspirated [kʰ] at the beginning of a stressed syllable but non-aspirated after /s/.

alphabet A writing system in which each character, or *letter*, represents a consonant or a vowel, usually, but not necessarily, on graphically equal footings.

ambiguous A word, phrase, sentence, or statement that can be interpreted in more than one way, as in the headline *soldier helps dog bite victim*.

amelioration A semantic change by which a word acquires a positive connotation as part of its meaning. Over time, this positive connotation can become part of the word's denotation. Example: The word *knight* goes back to Old English *cniht* "servant, young boy" and acquired the (arguably more positive) meaning "nobleman" via "military servant".

amplitude The amount of movement in a sound wave, similar to intensity.

analogy A type of deductive morphological change that involves the generalization of a formal relationship from one form (or set of forms) to another form (or set of forms). See proportional analogy.

andro-centric generics The use of a male form to refer to a person whose gender is unknown.

angular gyrus is located between Wernicke's area and the visual cortex and is what allows us to change visual stimuli into auditory stimuli and vice versa. It is crucial for the ability to read and write.

aniconic symbol A symbol associated with a meaning arbitrarily.

anomic aphasia is an acquired form of fluent aphasia in which damage to the brain happens to the angular gyrus. Anomic aphasics have constant difficulties accessing and producing certain words.

anterior [+/– anterior] is a feature in phonology that describes sounds that are made in front of the alveopalatal region.

anticipatory (assimilation) A type of sound change in which a segment takes on (a) phonetic feature(s) of a following sound, as if anticipating the following sound.

anticipatory influence in speech errors are when influence comes from a sound that has not yet been articulated.

antonyms Words or phrases expressing opposite senses.

anxiety has been divided into three types: 1) Trait anxiety, a more permanent predisposition to be anxious; 2) State anxiety, apprehension, and nervousness at given moments as a result of a situation; and 3) Situation-specific anxiety refers to particular situations that consistently give rise to anxiety.

aphasia is an impairment which affects the production and/or comprehension of language.

aphasiology is the study of language impairments that result from disease or damage to the parts of the brain that are vital to language.

apocope From Greek *apokopē* "cutting off": a segment (usually an unstressed or weakly stressed vowel) is lost at the end of a word. Example: Old English *mōna* (two syllables) > Modern English *moon* (one syllable).

apology (apologize) is a speech act in which the speaker requests forgiveness for an injury or insult which he/she has caused.

apparent time study The study of language change that compares intergenerational differences.

approximates are sounds that involve a constriction in the vocal tract but do not have complete closure or any frication. In English, the approximate phonemes include the lateral /l/ and the rhotic /ɹ/.

aptitude refers to the ability to learn a task.

arbitrary An arbitrary symbol has no direct connection to what it represents, like the word *green* doesn't tell you anything about what the color green actually looks like.

argument The term argument typically refers to the number of participants in the event described by the sentence. The arguments of a transitive verb are the subject and the complement, for example, <u>Peter</u> ate <u>cake</u>; an intransitive verb only requires a subject, for example, <u>Peter</u> walked.

articulator Any part of the vocal tract that constricts or comes into contact with another articulator to produce a speech sound. Articulators can be passive (do not move) or active (do move).

articulatory processes are systematic alterations to speech so that it fits within one's current sound repertoire and production abilities.

aspect The expression of internal temporal constituency (of events, processes etc.): whether they are complete, ongoing, habitual, etc.

aspectual classes of verbs identify four distinct types of verbs (states, activities, accomplishments, and achievements) that are universal to all languages.

assimilation A type of phonological change or articulatory process in which sounds are influenced by neighboring sounds. In assimilation, a segment takes on some or all of the phonetic features of a preceding or following segment (it becomes "more similar" to a preceding or following segment). Nasalization and palatalization are common assimilatory changes. See also anticipatory, regressive, progressive.

attested In historical linguistics: a language or linguistic form is (directly) attested if there is physical evidence for the language/form, usually written texts, but also recordings or native speakers ("informants").

attitude in SLA refers to a learner's evaluation of and appreciation for an idea, entity, or situation.

auditory channel Signals involving the sending and reception of vibratory information, usually in the form of sound.

autism spectrum disorders are a group of severe developmental disorders which typically include impaired social development, delayed language development, and a strong preference for routine and sameness.

automatic processing is a type of cognitive processing which is effortless and requires no conscious attention.

auxiliary verb (Aux) Auxiliary verbs supply tense and person features to the main verb in the sentence. In English the main auxiliary verbs are *to be* and *to have*, and *to do* in questions and negation.

backformation A word formation process that is the result of historically incorrect morphological analysis on the part of speakers, e.g., *televise* from *television*.

bar-pressing test is a type of timed-reading task in which participants read sentences one word at a time, advancing from one word to the next by pressing the space bar until they reach the end of the sentence.

base The form to which we attach an affix. It may consist of a single root, e.g. *cup* is the base for *cup–s*, *walk* is the base for *walk–ed*; or it may consist of a root with one or more affixes, e.g., *real-ize* is the base for *real-iz-ation*.

basic vocabulary Part of vocabulary, thought to be most stable across time, which includes words for kinship terms (e.g. "mother", "brother"), basic body parts (e.g. "head", "heart"), low numbers (e.g. "three", "five"), pronouns (e.g. "I", "you"), etc.

behaviorism A theory of psychology that argues that all learning is based on responses to stimuli that are followed by some type of reinforcement. In the case of language, reinforcement leads to the formation of appropriate linguistic habits.

Bilingual Assessment Test is a battery of 32 tasks which assess language abilities for comprehension and production. The results help to identify the most appropriate rehabilitation strategies and in which language(s).

Binary Coded Decimal (BCD) (6-bit) One of the earliest character encoding schemes used to encode the 26 (uppercase) letters, ten digits, and a limited number of punctuation characters. BCD (Binary Coded Decimal) was originally used to encode decimal numbers. 6-bit BCD encodes alphanumeric characters.

Bilingual Interactive Activation (BIA) Model is a theoretical account of how bilinguals process and recognize visually-presented words.

blend A compound in which parts of the words are deleted, e.g., *simulcast* from *simultaneous broadcast*.

borrowing consists of the integration of foreign words into a language, e.g., *burrito* from Spanish.

bottom-up processing assumes that input in language is processed first in small units like phonemes and proceeds in a step-by-step manner on to words and phrases until the entire input has been processed. Activation of higher levels such as words and phrases are activated through lower units such as phonemes.

bound morpheme A morpheme that must attach to another element, e.g., the plural marker *–s* which attaches to nouns, the ending *–able* which attaches to verbs.

bound root Roots that only occur in combination with another root, e.g., *cran-* in *cranberry* has no meaning or grammatical function on its own.

brain stem helps to provide motor and sensory actions to the face and neck through cranial nerves.

breakdowns in communication occur in instances where communication is interrupted potentially due to an L2 learner's incorrect use of the L2 such as incorrect vocabulary, pronunciation, syntax, or other non-native-like forms.

Broca's aphasia is an acquired form of non-fluent aphasia which severely affects speech production but not so much comprehension. The speech of a Broca's aphasic is labored and telegraphic and often is missing function words.

Broca's area is an area in the left frontal lobe that is largely responsible for language production.

callosumectomy is a rare surgical intervention in which the corpus callosum is cut or removed in order to prevent or minimize the occurrence of seizures.

calque An expression that is borrowed into another language by translating it word for word, e.g., *new wave* is translated from the French *nouvelle vague*.

Canadian raising A Canadian pronunciation pattern in which diphthongs are shortened and raised before voiceless consonants.

categorical perception is an explanation of sound perception which states that sounds are categorized by their place of articulation and voice onset time.

central agraphia is an acquired form of agraphia that occurs when there are impairments to both spoken language and to motor and visual skills.

central executive is a mental supervisory system that controls the flow of information between the three fluid subsystems: the visuospatial sketchpad, episodic buffer, and phonological loop.

central nervous system includes the spinal cord and the brain.

cerebellum helps in coordination, precision, and accuracy of motor functions.

cerebral cortex is the thin layer of grey tissue that fits over the brain and is responsible for all consciousness including things like memory, attention, perception, awareness, thought, and language.

cerebrum is the uppermost, largest, and primary part of the brain that controls voluntary actions.

chemosensory channel These signals involve the production and reception of odors, as well as taste.

child-directed speech or caregiver speech involves the unconscious adjustments in adult speech that are less complex and many times resemble child's speech.

childhood egocentrism is a theory which argues that although children engage in single conversation, what they actually say has little to do with the previous statement spoken by their conversation partner.

Chomskyan revolution is a period of dramatic shift of theories and methodologies in linguistics following the ground-breaking publication of Noam Chomsky's *Syntactic structures* (1957).

circumfix An affix that has two parts, a prefix and a suffix, which act as a unified morpheme, e.g., the circumfix *ge——t* in German participles such as *ge-mach-t* "made".

clarification requests allow for learners to seek assistance during interaction. As such, they have the opportunity to change erroneous language patterns based on the direct or indirect correction by their listeners.

classifier A grammatical word that makes a noun countable.

clause Like a sentence, a clause has a subject and a verb. A sentence can include several clauses. In the sentence *he said that he was tired*, there are two clauses: [He said] and [he was tired].

clipping consists of shortening longer words or phrases, e.g., *prof* for *professor.*

clicks are sounds that are produced with a closure of the tongue body against the velum or uvula and a second closure at another point in the oral cavity. Less than two percent of world languages use clicks.

clitic Word-like element that must attach to a host, e.g., the object pronouns in French, such as *Je le vois,* "I see it"; the possessive *–s* in English.

cliticization The development of free morphemes into clitics (unstressed elements which are dependent on a preceding or following stressed word). Elements that undergo grammaticalization usually undergo a loss of syntactic freedom and become more restricted in their distribution by turning into clitics or affixes.

closed class A class of words to which you cannot generally add items. Functional categories are closed classes.

coarticulation Active articulation for more than one sound at a time and the effects of this simultaneous activation on the speech sounds.

coda of a syllable The consonant(s) that follow the nucleus.

code-abandonment When a person reverts to their stronger language to ensure successful communication.

code-switching The use of two separate speech varieties in one conversation.

cognate From Latin *co-gnātus* "sharing ancestors, kindred, related". A form F_1 in language L_1 and a form F_2 in language L_2 are cognate if they go back to the same proto-form *F in the reconstructed proto-language *L, where *L is the ancestor of L_1 and L_2.

cognate set A set of cognates from two or more genetically related languages in a lineal or non-lineal descent relationship. See also correspondence, correspondence set.

cognates Words that are similar in sound and meaning across two or more languages due to common descent from the same ancestral form.

coherence refers to the property of texts that makes them make sense in the context in which they occur.

coherent text See *coherence.*

cohesion is a property of how texts hang together and make sense in context. Whereas coherence tends to refer to making sense with respect to the outside world, cohesion refers to texts that make sense because they have cohesive ties or links among entities mentioned in the text.

cohort model is an explanation of auditory word recognition in which a cohort of possible words is first activated based on a word-initial sound. When the next sound of the word is analyzed, non-matching words in the cohort get eliminated. With each successful sound analyzed, the cohort gets smaller until only one word is left as the correct target word.

coinage The invention of new words, e.g., *quark.*

collective monologues are several non-relevant statements made by children who engage in *childhood egocentrism.*

common phonetic features In comparative reconstruction: the phonetic properties shared by corresponding sounds in a cognate set, usually the features that are reconstructed for the corresponding sound in the proto-language.

communication The transfer of information from one entity (the sender) to another (the receiver).

communicative competence encompasses several types of knowledge including grammatical, discourse, sociolinguistic, and strategic competence.

communicative language teaching is a teaching approach that is preferred by many language educators. This approach emphasizes the acquisition of communicative competence which includes the knowledge of how to use language in socially and pragmatically appropriate ways.

comparative method The method used in historical linguistics to reconstruct unattested proto-languages from attested, genetically related languages, and to study and compare the features of the attested languages themselves. See also comparative reconstruction.

comparative reconstruction The reconstruction of unattested proto-languages based on the comparison and study of the features of their attested daughter languages. See also comparative reconstruction method.

comparative reconstruction method A method for comparing words and structures across related languages in order to reconstruct their shared ancestor.

compensatory lengthening A sound change by which a vowel is lengthened when a following consonant is lost (as if to compensate for the loss of the following segment). Example: Sanskrit *paɲʧa* "five" > Hindi *pãːʧ*.

competence The term used to refer to the knowledge speakers have of their language.

Competition Model posits that language is interpreted as the result of a cognitive comparison of a number of linguistic cues that are found within sentences and that L2s are learned through the competition of cognitive mechanisms in the presence of a rich linguistic environment.

complement A complement is an argument that is required by the head, often a verb, in order to complete its meaning.

complementary distribution When allophones are conditioned by the mutually exclusive phonetic contexts in which they are found we say they are in complementary distribution. For example, you will never find [p] in the same phonetic context as [pʰ].

complementizer (Comp) A word that introduces a clause: *and, if, whether*. A complementizer (C) is the head of the phrase that precedes TP.

compositionality The linguistic principle postulating that the meaning of a sentence is a function of the meaning of its grammatical and lexical morphemes, taking their order and syntactic structure into account.

compound A word made up of the combination of two or more words, e.g., *dog house*.

compounding is the process of combining two or more words to create a new word.

comprehensible input is the understandable language input that is needed for learning.

comprehensible output refers to language output that is rich enough to "stimulate learners to move from the semantic, open-ended, nondeterministic, strategic processing prevalent in comprehension to the complete grammatical processing needed for accurate production" (Swain, 1995). See also *Output Hypothesis*.

computational linguistics An interdisciplinary field that processes natural language using computer algorithms.

computerized axial tomography is a series of x-rays of the head from several directions that produces a series of black-and-white cross sectioned images of the brain.

conduction aphasia is an acquired form of fluent aphasia which occurs when damage is localized in the supramarginal gyrus of the parietal lobe. Conduction aphasics are able to understand what they are hearing but are unable to repeat it.

conjunction (Conj) A word used to connect phrases or clauses. In English the common conjunctions are *and, or,* and *but.*

connectionism is a perspective in language acquisition in which repeated experience and exposure to language patterns will result in a mental abstraction (i.e., a stored representation of the pattern in question). Connectionism views language as evolving processes of networks that are interconnected and consist of simple units. See also *connectionist models.*

connectionist models Connectionist models are derived from computer simulations of the brain that are used to test language learning modules. See also *connectionism.*

connotation Emotional and cultural meaning associated with a word in addition to its denotation.

consonant harmony is a type of assimilation, an articulatory process, in which a consonant becomes more like or the same as (duplicates) another consonant in the word.

consonants (pulmonic) are non-vowel sounds that are produced with air pressure from the lungs. They are often described in terms of the place and manner of articulation and voicing.

constituent A constituent consists of a word or group of words that function as a unit in a (hierarchical) syntactic structure. For example, the sentence *the child ate the cake* is made up of two main constituents, the determiner phrase (DP) *the child*, and the verb phrase (VP) *ate the cake*. The VP *ate the cake* is in turn made up of the constituent verb *ate* and the DP *the cake*.

constricted glottis [+/−CG] is a feature in phonology that describes that state of the glottis. For [+CG], the vocal folds are held tightly together such that air cannot pass through momentarily. In English, the only sound that is [+CG] is the glottal stop /ʔ/.

constructionism is an interactionist view which interprets language as a result of innate abilities and information provided by the environment.

context can refer to the learning environment.

contradiction A relationship between propositions where the truth of one necessitates the falsity of the other.

contralateral control explains the functionality of the brain: areas of one side of the brain are responsible for movements on the opposite side of the body.

controlled processing is a type of cognitive processing which uses attentional resources under constrained conditions to perform a task.

conversion The process that changes the category of a word without the addition of derivational affixes, e.g., *bank* (noun), *to bank* (verb).

cooing are pre-speech sounds that infants make which are soft, murmuring sounds characteristic of doves.

Cooperative Principle is the principle, as defined by H. P. Grice, that underlies all communication, stating that speakers aim to be helpful when communicating with each other.

coordination This is a test used to determine whether a string of words forms a constituent in a syntactic structure. Coordination, that is, linking two strings of words by conjunctions such as *and* or *but*, is a good test for constituency because it is not possible to link two elements that do not have the same structure. For example, we cannot link a verb phrase and a noun phrase but we can link two noun phrases such as *a large grey cat and a small kitten* in a sentence such as *I own a large grey cat and a small kitten.*

copy (of a moved element) When an element is moved in syntax it leaves a copy of itself behind. This allows the structural requirements of the different heads to be preserved.

core instruction programs are educational programs in which the L2 is a single course subject and not the language of instruction for all other course subjects (math, geography, etc.).

coronals are sounds that involve the tip or blade of the tongue. Interdentals, alveolars, and post-alveolars are [+coronal], all other segments are [–coronal].

corpus is a large and representative collection of language data, used to study large-scale tendencies.

corpus analysis See *corpus linguistics.*

corpus callosum is a bundle of around 200 million nerve fibers that connects the two sides of the brain and whose primary function is to allow the two hemispheres to communicate with one another and act as one.

corpus linguistics is the study of language using large amounts of data, to find general tendencies and investigate variations across time or language varieties.

corpus planning Efforts made to elaborate the stylistic contexts in which a speech variety is used.

corrective feedback is given from a listener in order to draw the attention of the learner to the to "gaps" that may exist between their linguistic knowledge and the correct target structure.

correspondence A linguistic form X (a phoneme, morpheme, or word) in grammar G_1 diachronically corresponds to a linguistic form Y in grammar G_2 if X can be related to Y through one or more changes which transformed X into Y.

correspondence set A set of diachronically or synchronically corresponding forms, normally used to reconstruct the corresponding proto-forms in the ancestor language (see proto-language) of these forms. See also *cognate set.*

Creole Morphologically and grammatically complex varieties of language that are often developed out of a prior pidgin. A Creole is adopted as vernaculars for entire speech communities and is learned as a first language.

critical period hypothesis In L1 acquisition, the critical period hypothesis argues that the first years of infants' lives are a vital time during which they acquire their L1. If this exposure to input does not occur during this time, they will not be able to achieve complete command of the L1, no matter how much training they receive. In L2 acquisition, it is argued that exposure to language must occur before puberty in order to attain native-like proficiency.

cultural transmission There must be a strong component of learning in a language. We aren't born knowing the language that we speak.

cuneiform A technique for recording a message on a pliable surface by touching the corner of a stylus to it so as to leave a wedge-shaped impression.

daughter languages The languages that are descended from any given proto-language. For example: French, Spanish, Italian, etc., are daughter languages of Proto-Romance.

declarative memory is a type of long-term memory that refers to explicit memories that can be recalled consciously. These can be further divided into episodic or semantic memory.

deductive change Rule extension; the extension of an already existing morphological rule or pattern to an environment where it did not previously apply. Example: English *cactus*, plural *cactuses* instead of *cactus, cacti*. See also *analogy*.

deep dyslexia is a severe form of phonological dyslexia which is notable by the patient's frequent semantic errors during reading and the inability to read nonwords.

deep learning A form of machine learning that attempts to model high-level abstractions in data. It promises to learn the human crafted features that are used to describe the data.

deep structure is the abstract or theoretical representation of phrase and sentence structure.

deictic meaning Meaning pertaining to the time and place of the utterance.

deletion The complete omission of a speech segment or a sequence of sounds in an utterance.

delayed release [+/−DR] is a feature in phonology that describes sounds that have complete constriction followed by a fricative-like release of air. In English, the affricates /d͡ʒ/ and /t͡ʃ/ are [+DR]. All other sounds in English are [−DR].

dementia is a category of several neurodegenerative diseases in which there is a decline in memory or other thinking skills severe enough to reduce the ability to perform everyday activities.

denasalization is an articulatory process in which a nasal consonant is replaced by a non-nasal consonant.

denotation The literal, dictionary meaning of a word.

derivation, derivational morphology The morphological process that builds new words based on existing ones. This is done by attaching affixes which change the meaning and/or category of the base (e.g., the morpheme *–ation* changes a verb such as *realize* into the noun *realiz–ation*).

derivational morphemes are meaningful units that are added to a word to make a new word that has either changed categories (e.g., from a verb to a noun) or means something different. See also *derivation*.

descriptive In linguistics: an approach to the study of language in which the linguistic habits of a speech community and the grammars of its speakers are described as objectively as possible, as opposed to prescriptive approaches.

descriptive grammar A description of how language is actually used. It is often contrasted with *prescriptive grammar*.

determinative See *semantic determinative*.

determiner (D) A functional category that includes articles (*the, a*), demonstratives (*this, that*), and possessives (*my, your*). In English, determiners precede noun phrases.

developmental language disorder is an impairment which is restricted to language and is not accompanied by another cognitive, social, or sensory condition.

diachronic variation In historical linguistics: variation in the syntax, semantics, morphology, or phonology of two grammars G_1 and G_2 which are in a lineal descent relationship, or (informally): variation in the grammar of a language at different stages of its development.

diachrony In historical linguistics: the development of languages *over time*, from Greek *diá* "through, across", *khrónos* "time". Diachronic linguistics studies the changes in speakers' grammars across time, usually grammars that are in a lineal descent relationship.

diacritics IPA symbols that are used to indicate changes in the production of a phone, usually due to neighboring sounds (see Figure 2.6 in the text for a list of the IPA diacritics).

dialogue systems are computational agents that engage in conversation, often performing tasks for humans (adding an event to a calendar, opening an app in a smartphone). Because they are typically activated by saying a specific word or phrase, they are also called voice-activated systems.

diffusion In historical linguistics: the spread of an innovative form that may have arisen through language change through a speaker community. While change in the narrow sense arises during language acquisition, diffusion of innovative forms can take place at any stage of a speaker's lifetime and can have different sources (language change, language contact, etc.).

diffusion tensor imaging (DTI) is a type of MRI which uses senses and tracks water molecules in fiber tracks in the brain.

digital electronic computers A computing device that uses electronic components (like transistors) to represent information discretely.

digraph A sequence of two letters spelling a single sound, such as English *sh* or French *ch* for [ʃ].

diphthongization A sound change that turns a monophthong into a diphthong, e.g., Old English /muːs/ > Modern English /maws/.

directionality approach A way of reconstructing ancestral forms by taking into account which sound changes are common, and which ones are rare or unknown.

discourse analysis is concerned with language use in context, and with how language users produce and understand coherent discourse.

discourse markers are conjunctions, adverbs, and adverbial phrases used to connect ideas and portions of text.

discrete Each symbol has to be a discrete unit, just like the words in the sentence are all discrete units.

displacement A language has to provide information about events that occur in different locations from the speaker or in different time periods, in other words displacement in either space or time.

dissimilation The modification of a speech sound that makes it less similar to nearby speech sounds.

distinctive feature A feature that serves to distinguish between two phonemes or groups of phonemes. For example, the feature [voice] distinguishes between /p/ and /b/.

ditransitive verbs that have three obligatory arguments.

ditransitive verb A verb that requires two arguments besides the subject, i.e., *put a vase on the shelf; give a present to Mary.*

double dissociation refers to cases in which two related mental processes function independently. For example, there is double dissociation between speech production and speech comprehension as shown in the symptoms of patients with Broca's aphasia (trouble with production but not comprehension) and patients with Wernicke's aphasia (trouble with comprehension but not production).

Down syndrome is a chromosomal abnormality that causes moderate to severe mental retardation and a delay of language development.

duality Language has to have smaller units that can be combined into bigger units.

dual-route processing argues that word recognition proceeds both by recognizing the whole word and by "sounding out" its phonemes. One of the two paths will be more efficient and likely be the one utilized.

dummy *do* The term refers to the use of the verb *do* as an auxiliary to move the features of T to the complementizer position (C).

echolalic speech is meaningless repetition of a word or several words previously spoken by another speaker. This may be a characteristic in severe cases of autism.

egressive pulmonic airstream Air pushed out through the vocal tract by the lungs.

ejectives are voiceless consonants that are pronounced by airflow that is initiated in the upper vocal tract by the vocal cords/glottis. In English, there are no ejective sounds.

e-language The linguistic conventions and language use common to a particular speech community. "E" stands for "external" (sc. to the individual) and is usually opposed to I-language.

electroencephalography (EEG) is a device that measures the brain's voltage changes in milliseconds as a response to certain events. These changes are referred to as event-related potentials.

electromagnetic channel Signals involving the sending and detection of electrical pulses.

embedded clause A clause or sentence that does not stand alone but is dependent on another clause, referred to as the main clause. For example, in *I said he was a genius* the clause *he was a genius* is embedded in the main clause *I said*.

emergentism A general theory that proposes that apparent structures spontaneously arise from the interplay of a large combination of factors. The main application in linguistics is found in connectionist models of language learning.

enclisis The process by which a clitic attaches after the host, e.g., the English possessive.

endocentric compound A compound whose meaning is derived from the meaning of the head, e.g., *skateboard* is a type of board.

English as a second language A local English variety that is used as a second variety by communities speaking local languages natively.

entailment A relationship between propositions where the truth of one necessitates the truth of the other.

entities are the people, things, organizations, and ideas mentioned in a text.

epenthesis The addition of a speech sound into a sequence.

episodic buffer is responsible for forming integrated units that are logically organized and sequenced. This subsystem is what allows us to formulate the scene of a story in our mind.

episodic memory is a type of declarative memory of the long-term memory system in which information that is personally experienced is stored. Episodic memories are personal experiences that occurred at a particular time and place.

equipollently framed A type of language where the direction and manner of motion or change are both expressed by equivalent grammatical forms.

etymology The historical development in sound and meaning of a form through time; the study of the history of words (from Greek *étymon* "true").

event-related potentials (ERP) are scalp-recorded electrical potentials of brain activity that occur after the presentation of an "event" stimulus such as a picture, word, or sound.

executive functions include cognitive processes such as attentional control, working memory, reasoning, problem-solving, and planning.

exocentric compound A compound whose meaning cannot be inferred from the meaning of the head, e.g., *highbrow* is not a type of brow.

expressive abilities refer to the ability to produce language. Examples include speaking (or signing) and writing.

eye tracking is a research method which uses eye-monitoring cameras to study the details of eye movements during sentence reading.

feature A property of phones that allows us to generalize across different sounds and to form natural classes. For example, the feature [–voice] characterizes the sounds /p t k f θ s ʃ t͡ʃ/. Features are binary, that is they are present or they are not.

feature (syntax) A syntactic feature is a way of representing an abstract grammatical property. Syntactic features, like phonological features, are often binary. For example, tense can be either [+past] or [–past]; nouns are either [+count] or [–count].

feature matrix A feature matrix is a table that shows, for each feature, the value, either [+] or [–], assigned to each phoneme.

feedback is the modification of language as a basis for improvement and development.

feral children are those who have lived isolated from human contact from a very young age.

field is one of the aspects of register. It refers to the content part of a text, what the participants are talking about.

field dependent learners are said to take a holistic approach to L2 learning in which they may rely on contextual information (i.e., the outer world, situation, etc.) to comprehend and produce language.

field independent learners are said to prefer an analytic approach in which they rely on inner knowledge and analytical skills, without contextualization from external factors, to help L2 learning.

field research is conducted with real people in real situations. This is a common method in studies of Indigenous languages, where the researcher travels to communities where the language is spoken, and interviews speakers. It is also used in sociolinguistic research, where the context and demographic characteristics of the speakers are of importance.

first language (L1) acquisition is the study of infants' and children's development of language from birth.

fixation is a brief pause of eye movement during sentence processing in which two or three words will be processed before jumping to the next fixation point. The length of the fixation is an index of processing difficulty, with longer fixations implying more difficult processing.

food signals Signals letting other animals know about the location of food.

formants A band of frequency in an acoustic signal. Formants F1, F2, F3 measure the acoustic characteristics of a vowel.

form-focused instruction refers to "any pedagogical effort which is used to draw the learners' attention to language form either implicitly or explicitly" (Spada, 1997, p. 73).

fossilization is when the development of an L2 reaches a point where it either slows down substantially or stops.

free morpheme A morpheme that can stand alone, e.g., *cup, moon, run*.

free variation Refers to those cases in which allophones are not conditioned by their phonetic environment. For example, a person may pronounce [pan] with more or less nasalization of the vowel.

frequency The number of cycles per second of a sound wave, measured in hertz.

frequency effect is the observation that more frequent words are accessed more quickly.

fricatives are non-sonorant consonants that are produced with a continuous airflow through the mouth. In English, these are /f v θ ð s z ʃ ʒ h/.

frontal lobe is an area of the brain that is responsible for speaking, voluntary moving and motor performance, planning and predicting future consequences of current actions, making the choice between good and bad actions, and controlling socially unacceptable responses, among other things.

fronting is an articulatory process in which there is moving forward of the place of articulation of a sound.

full access with regard to the access to UG debate, this line of thought states that UG is directly accessible during SLA. We should expect interlanguage grammars to show evidence of being constrained by UG principles and evidence of parameter setting other than those of the L1. In the *full access* account, all aspects of the L2 are acquirable.

functional category A class of words that have no descriptive content: auxiliary verbs, determiners, conjunctions, quantifiers, and complementizers. Functional categories often provide abstract grammatical information, usually with respect to agreement, tense, definiteness, etc. They are often contrasted with *lexical categories*.

functional magnetic resonance imaging (fMRI) is a brain imaging methodology which measures brain activity by detecting changes in blood flow. It is used to study brain anatomy, brain functions, and damaged areas of brains.

functional near-infrared spectroscopy (fNIRS) is a brain imaging methodology which measures the dynamics of blood flow by observing the absorption of near-infrared light.

functional theories (or approaches) Approaches that place emphasis on communicative acts between people in order to explain both acquisition and the use of language in general.

fusional language A language in which morphemes have more than one meaning fused into a single affix.

fuzzy concept is one which does not have precise denotations with clear-cut boundaries. Many adjectives such as *tall* and *beautiful* are fuzzy concepts.

garden path sentences are sentences that are syntactically constructed in a way that leads to misunderstanding them, causing the reader to backtrack and reparse.

gender A feature that is used in some languages to classify words, particularly nouns and pronouns. In English we find gender on third person pronouns only (*he, she, it*), but in some languages all nouns carry gender.

generative approaches are perspectives which build on nativist views and argue that UG principles are inborn and that language experience triggers innate knowledge and sets language-specific parameters.

generative approaches to language Theory of language and language acquisition that presupposes three mechanisms: a genetic component, UG; experience with the language; other rule-governed elements such as processing and learning mechanisms.

generative linguistics is a theoretical approach that argues for an innate system generally referred to as UG.

genetic classification Classification of languages according to their shared descent.

genetic relationship Languages which belong to the same language family because they go back to the same proto-language are considered genetically related (note that "genetic" is used metaphorically here).

genre or text type refers to the different types of text that are possible in a language and in a culture. The genre of a text is defined by its purpose in the context and the stages in which it develops.

gliding is an articulatory process in which a liquid becomes a glide.

glides are sounds that show properties of both consonants and vowels. In English, these include /j/ and /w/.

global aphasia is the most severe form of non-fluent aphasia in which there is damage to the perisylvian cortex including both Broca's and Wernicke's areas. Patients of global aphasia are usually unable to comprehend or produce language.

gloss is an explanatory translation of individual words and phrases.

grammar The underlying unconscious representation of the structure of language in the mind of the speaker. It is a set of rules for how words are assembled into sentences in order to generate language.

grammatical A phrase or sentence that native speakers judge to be possible or well formed in their language.

grammatical meaning The meaning encoded in functional words and morphemes.

grammaticality judgement A native speaker's judgement of whether or not a linguistic utterance is well formed according to the rules of his/her mental grammar.

grammaticalization A process by which free-standing words turn into affixes. Grammaticalization is when lexical items develop into functional items while functional items become clitics or affixes over time.

grapheme An essentially meaningless term often seen in discussions of writing systems.

great vowel shift A set of phonological changes in Middle English which affected the entire vowel system of English. The long high vowels of Middle English underwent diphthongization, while mid-vowels were raised to become high vowels, and low mid-vowels were raised to become mid-vowels.

grey matter is the outer, darker tissue which includes most of the brain's nerve cell bodies and is believed to be involved in cognition and information processing.

gyrus is the place where the cortex is folded outward.

head (morphology) The word that determines the category of the compound, e.g., *black board* is a noun because *board*, the head, is a noun.

head (syntax) The word that determines the properties of a phrase or constituent. For example, the head of a prepositional phrase is a preposition.

head movement Is the operation that displaces a head such as T, V, or N, to a higher position. Heads can only move into head positions.

head-turn procedure is an experimental method that uses a blinking light either on the left or right to attract an infant's attention. Once the infant looks at the blinking light, a speech sample is played until he/she looks away for more than two seconds.

hemispherectomy is a procedure in which one of the two hemispheres of the brain is surgically removed or disabled.

hemodynamic neuroimaging is a neurolinguistics method which provides dynamic images that represent and map changes in blood flow in the brain.

heritage language maintenance programs are language programs in which learners receive instruction in their ancestral L1 in order to teach or help maintain that language. Heritage language programs are based on enrichment theory which views bilingualism as being a cognitive and social advantage.

high amplitude sucking paradigm is an experimental method that relies on infants' sucking reflexes to mark their preference for and discrimination of sounds.

historical records In historical linguistics: **artifacts** that contain linguistic information, usually texts in or about a non-informant language.

holophrase is a single word that is used to refer to multiple words, phrases, or sentences. They are often used by children in the one-word stage.

homographs Words that are spelled the same but pronounced differently.

homonyms Words that are spelled and pronounced the same but have different meanings.

homophones Words that are spelled differently but pronounced the same.

hyponyms Words whose meaning is a subset of, or included in, the meaning of other words.

iconic A symbol that represents some attribute of the thing that it is describing.

iconic symbol A symbol that by its appearance suggests what it represents.

ideogram A symbol that represents a thing or concept (an "idea") rather than a word.

idiolect The mental grammar or knowledge state of one particular individual; your personal I-language.

I-language The internal knowledge state of an individual with respect to language; their mental grammar. Language in this sense is part of the cognitive capacities of an individual's brain. It is usually opposed to E-language.

immersion programs offer all or nearly all instruction subjects in the target language.

imperative mood represents speech indicating the speaker desires something to happen. Imperative sentences are either commands or requests.

imperfect transmission The transmission of a grammar G_1 is "flawed" with respect to some feature(s) during language acquisition, resulting in a new grammar G_2. Imperfect transmission results in language change (see also *misanalysis*).

implicature What is suggested in an utterance, even though not explicitly expressed nor strictly entailed by the utterance. An implicature is the meaning derived from, but not stated in, an utterance.

indicative mood represents speech which the speaker asserts to be true. The indicative mood is used to make factual statements and to ask and is the most common mood in language (compared to the other two moods, subjunctive and imperative).

indexical variability The connection between how a speaker sounds and her speaker identity in a given interaction.

indirect access with regard to the access to UG debate, under this assumption UG is only accessible through the L1.

indirect speech act is one that is expressed in a grammatical form that is not the usual one. For instance, a request is typically expressed as an imperative (in a communal kitchen: "Clean up after yourself"), but can be indirectly conveyed through a statement ("Your dishes will not wash themselves").

infix An affix inserted inside the root, e.g., in Malagasy (Madagascar) the infix *–in–* is inserted in roots such as *folaka* "break", to form the participle *f-in-olaka* "broken".

inflected future A verb form where a future marker is added as a suffix.

inflection, inflectional morphology The process that attaches affixes that do not change the meaning or category of the base. For instance, when adding the past tense *– ed* to the verb walk, the result maintains the same meaning (i.e., walking), the same category (i.e., verb). Inflectional morphology modifies words in terms of things like tense, person, number, and gender.

inflectional morpheme A morpheme that does not change the meaning or category of the base, e.g., the past tense *–ed*.

Information Processing Model explains how humans process information in order to perform tasks such as problem-solving and critical thinking through a systematic model of memory, cognition, and thinking.

initialism When a word formed from the initials of several words is spelled out, e.g., CEO.

innateness hypothesis is the idea that infants are born with the innate and unique ability for language acquisition.

input refers to the linguistic elements to which learners are exposed to but do not always internalize into intake.

Input Hypothesis is part of the Monitor Model which states that SLA requires input (*i*) that is both comprehensible and sensitive to the language learner's proficiency level: **it** should ideally be slightly above (*i* + 1 level) the current proficiency level of the learners to advance their language abilities.

input processing is a theory concerned with two things: how learners perceive and process L2 input and with the psycholinguistic strategies and mechanisms by which learners convert input into intake. Essentially input processing theory examines a set of internal processing strategies which learners might use to understand language and ultimately lead to intake.

instrumental motivation refers to the desire to learn an L2 for practical or utilitarian purposes.

intake refers to input that is comprehended and can lead to the reshaping and development of the interlanguage.

integrative motivation refers to the wish to learn an L2 in order to successfully integrate into the L2 community and/or culture.

intellectual disability is usually diagnosed in a person who has a general IQ of two or more standard deviations below the mean for the population.

intensity A measure of a sound's energy, closely related to amplitude.

Interaction Hypothesis argues that L2 learning occurs when learners participate in conversations in which they encounter difficulties speaking or understanding and must participate in further interaction to reconcile these difficulties.

interactionist views are perspectives of L1 acquisition which argue that language is a social phenomenon. Interactionist views are centered on the importance of communicative and social interaction and place more emphasis on the nature of language-learning experiences.

interactivity in syntactic processing refers to sentence processing interacting with and being influenced by other processing. Parsing simultaneously processes syntactic, lexical discourse, and non-linguistic information such as background knowledge.

Interface Hypothesis is an avenue of research which has looked at whether having to process modules of the grammar which are interconnected, for example syntax and pragmatics, leads to variability.

interlanguage is a developing, dynamic approximation of a language being learned. It is simply the current state of a learner's L2.

internal change A morphological process in which one segment, which does not, on its own, constitute a morpheme, is substituted for another segment, e.g., *begin, began*.

intonation Changes in pitch across the length of an utterance.

intransitive verb A verb that does not require a complement (e.g., *walk, scream, swim*).

introspection refers to a research methodology where the researchers use their own intuitions to arrive at conclusions.

inventory The complete set of sounds (phonetic inventory) or phonemes (phonemic inventory) of a language.

inversion This term is used to refer to those cases in which the auxiliary or modal (or the main verb in some languages) precedes the subject in the linear order of the sentence. It is commonly found in questions in English.

investment refers to the social and historical relationship that language learners build with the L2 and their emerging desire to practice and acquire it.

isolate A language that cannot be classified into a language family.

isolating language A language in which grammatical concepts like tense, number, or grammatical relations are expressed primarily by word order and the use of free-standing words rather than by inflectional morphemes attached to words.

Jabberwocky is made-up language that consists of grammatical sentences that have no meaning due to their use of nonsense words.

jargon aphasia is a rare form of fluent aphasia in which patients' speech may include phonemes and intonation patterns from the language in question but contain very few real words.

kanji The adopted Chinese characters that are used in modern Japanese script.

Koiné A variety that emerged via extensive dialect contact in colonial settings via a process of leveling, mixing, and simplification.

L2 Motivation Self System is a theory rooted in mainstream psychology which includes three main components: Ideal L2 Self; Ought-to L2 Self; and L2 Learning Experience.

label In the ancestry of Egyptian hieroglyphs, labels are tags of ivory with one or two drawings incised or painted on them.

landing site The result of movement, it is the position to which a phrase or head moves.

language refers to both the representation of grammar in the mind of a speaker and the use we make of the grammar in communication.

language acquisition device is a theoretical mechanism that begins functioning from birth and makes language acquisition possible according to nativist and generative approaches.

language aptitude is an innate quality that provides an individual with the special propensity for learning an L2.

language change In historical linguistics: the transmission of a given grammar G_1 during language acquisition is flawed with respect to some feature of that grammar (in its syntax, semantics, morphology, or phonology), resulting in a slightly different grammar G_2. In other words, language change is imperfect transmission.

language death When a language no longer has speakers.

language faculty The sum of mental structures that allow human beings to acquire a language; similar in meaning to UG.

language family Languages that are genetically related by virtue of being descended from a common ancestor language or proto-language belong to the same language family.

language isolate A language with no demonstrable genealogical (or "genetic") relationship with other languages, one that has not been demonstrated to descend from an ancestor common with any other language.

language play is a normal part of L1 conversational skill development in which children use activities such as rhyming and making puns to manipulate and test-out language.

language processing refers to the use of language to express ideas, facts, and feelings and how these expressions are understood.

language savant is a person who has a mental disability such as autism yet shows exceptional brilliance in language acquisition.

language shift When a group abandons its ancestral language.

late closure strategy is a parsing strategy which states that there should be a preference to attach incoming words to the constituent currently being processed.

lateral sounds are formed by the tongue tip touching the roof of the mouth, with air escaping from one or both sides of the tongue. In English, only the /l/ and its allophones are [+lateral].

lateralization is the term used to specify whether something is primarily localized in the left or right hemisphere. It is argued that most right-handed people have language lateralized in the left hemisphere.

lax vowel is slightly shorter in duration and less constricted than a tense vowel. The /i/ in *beat* is a tense vowel while the /ɪ/ in *bit* is lax.

left ear advantage is when non-linguistic sounds such as natural/environmental sounds and melodies heard through the left ear seem clearer and louder.

lenition, lenited In historical linguistics: lenition is a type of sound change that affects consonants, usually stops by making them more sonorous on the sonority scale. A common type of lenition turns stops into (voiced or voiceless) fricatives. Lenition is also called weakening. A sound that has undergone lenition is called a lenited sound.

lesion is a damaged area of the brain which may cause acquired language impairments when found in specific places.

lexeme An abstract unit representing a word or a family of words related by form or meaning. It is generally written in capitals. The words *walk, walks, walked, walking* are represented by the lexeme WALK.

lexical access is the process of retrieving a word and information about it (e.g., semantic, syntactic) from the mental lexicon.

lexical ambiguity arises when a word has two or more meanings that can either be related or not.

lexical categories Categories that have relatively descriptive semantic content and are generally open classes, i.e., nouns, verbs, adjectives, adverbs, and prepositions. Lexical categories are generally contrasted with functional categories.

lexical decision task is an experimental task in which the participant sees or hears strings of letters (words or nonwords) and must decide if it is a real word.

lexical meaning The meaning encoded in words or parts of words.

lexicon is the "mental dictionary" which includes information related to a word's sounds and pronunciation, its meanings, and grammatical properties. It represents the knowledge of words used in a particular language and the grammatical properties that are linked to them.

lineal descent A grammar G2 (e.g., Modern English) corresponds diachronically to an earlier grammar G1 (e.g., Old English) through a series of intermediate changes between G1 and G2.

lingua franca An interim language adopted for communicative purposes by speech communities that have no language in common.

linguistic context The linguistics elements that surround the variants of a variable.

linguistic typology Classification of languages based on various linguistic properties, such as sound inventory, ways of building words out of morphemes, word order, etc.

linguistic variable Two or more ways of saying the same thing (an alternation).

linguistic variant A linguistic form involved in the alternation; subpart of a variable.

linguistics The scientific study of language.

loan word A word which is adapted ("borrowed") from another language, usually by changing the phonology to that of the borrowing language. For example, the English word *mutton* was borrowed from Old French *moton* "mutton; sheep".

localization is the belief that certain abilities, sensations, and behaviors could be traceable to certain locations in the brain. The theory of localization has been extended to language.

logogram In a morphosyllabary, a character used solely for its semantic content and not at all for its phonological content.

longitudinal fissure is the deepest sulcus in the brain which divides it into a left hemisphere and a right hemisphere.

long-term memory is the memory storage that holds permanent information. It is usually divided into episodic memory and semantic memory.

loss of syntactic freedom See *cliticization*.

machine learning Computer programs that learn how to compute by analyzing input-output examples of the problem being solved. This automated method of computer programming differs from the more typical practice of computer programming that is done by humans.

macrofamily A language family consisting of several (large) subfamilies. For example, the Afro-Asiatic language family is the macrofamily of, e.g., the Semitic, Chadic, and Cushitic language families.

magnetoencephalography (MEG) is a device which measures electrophysiological brain activity at milliseconds through extremely sensitive detectors in a helmet.

manner of articulation A description of how the articulators come together to form a particular speech sound.

markedness refers to the frequency, commonality, and universality of elements in language. Things that are "unmarked" in language are more common, more frequent, and/or less complex in world languages. Things "marked" in a language are less common, less frequent, and/or more complex.

Markedness Differential Hypothesis is based on the idea of markedness. Things "unmarked" in language are more common, more frequent, and/or less complex in world languages. Things "marked" in a language are less common, less frequent, and/or more complex. It is argued that learners whose L1 contains a marked linguistic feature will have less difficulty learning the unmarked equivalent in the L2 than vice versa.

mating signals Signals conveying to other animals of the same species the readiness to mate.

matra In Indic writing, an appendage to a consonant akshara denoting a particular following vowel other than /a/.

Maximum Onset Rule A requirement that as many consonants as possible should be syllabified in the onset of a syllable, as long as the resulting sequence is allowed in the language.

McGurk effect is a phenomenon that shows that when a sound is paired with the visual movement of another sound, a third (blended) sound will be perceived.

mechanoreception channel Signals involving a sense of touch, where an animal may be nudging, stroking, or touching another one to send a signal.

mental grammar The internal knowledge state of an individual with respect to their first language(s); the generative component that allows them to generate and parse well-formed linguistic expressions in their first language(s). See also *I-language*.

mental lexicon See *lexicon*.

merge (syntax) In syntax, merge is the operation that consists of combining two elements to form a third. Merge and move are the two main operations used to build phrases and sentences.

merger In historical linguistics, a merger is a sound change by which the phonemic contrast between two (or more) segments is lost and they merge as one and the same segment. Example: In some varieties of North American English, the vowels /ɛ/ and /ɪ/ merge before nasals, so that the words *pen* and *pin* have the same vowel.

mesoclisis The (rare) process by which a clitic attaches after the host before inflectional morphology is added, e.g., some object clitics in Portuguese.

metaphor, metaphorical A metaphor or "figure of speech" is a word (or phrase) that is used in the place of another to draw a comparison between two concepts by pointing out a similarity between them. It is essentially the understanding of one concept in terms of another. Semantic change of lexical items often results from the metaphorical use of nouns, verbs, and adjectives.

metonymy replaces the name of an object or person or event with the name of something else with which it is closely associated.

Miller's law is the observation originally put forth by George Miller (1954) that the number of objects the human working memory can hold is about seven, plus or minus two.

minimal attachment strategy is a parsing strategy which states that the minimal amount of syntactic structure should be built.

minimal pair Consists of a pair of words in a particular language that differ by only one sound segment in the same position. *Fan* and *pan* constitute a minimal pair in English.

modal verb English distinguishes between auxiliary verbs such as *to have* or *to be* and modals. Modals do not exhibit person or tense inflection. However, like auxiliaries they invert in questions. Modals add modality to the interpretation of the main verb. Examples: *can, will, could, may, would, might,* etc.

mode is one of the aspects of register. It refers to how the channel of communication and the interpersonal distance between participants affects language choices.

Modern Language Aptitude Test (MLAT) is a measure of language aptitude developed by Carroll and Sapon (1959).

modified output results when learners change a non-target-like utterance in an attempt to make it become comprehensible input to their listeners.

modularity refers to the degree to which language processing is independent from general cognitive processing. Modular views of sound argue that sound processing is unaffected by other levels of processing.

Monitor Hypothesis is part of the Monitor Model which argues that an L2 learner has the ability to monitor her speech output when given sufficient time to reflect on it, when the task at hand is about a structural element of the utterance, and when she "knows the rule".

Monitor Model argues that language input is the most essential element required to increase linguistic competence when learning an L2. It consists of five hypotheses: The Acquisition-Learning Hypothesis; The Natural Order Hypothesis; The Monitor Hypothesis; The Input Hypothesis; and The Affective Filter Hypothesis.

monophthongization A sound change by which a diphthong becomes a monophthong. Example: Classical Greek *grapʰei* "he/she writes" > Modern Greek *grafi*.

mood grammatical category which conveys the speaker's attitude about the truth value of what the sentence describes.

morpheme The smallest linguistic unit of meaning or function. *Cups* contains two morphemes, *cup* and the plural marker *–s*.

morphological change Change(s) that alter(s) a language's morphological system and inventory of functional items. Morphological change usually affects inflectional and derivational morphemes. See also *abductive* and *deductive change*.

morphology The study of words, how they are formed, and how they relate to other words.

morphophonology The area in which morphology and phonology interact, e.g., the different realizations of the prefix *in–* according to the phoneme that follows it.

morphosyntax The area in which morphology and syntax interact, e.g., the case of clitics.

motor theory is the idea that speech perception happens through analogy to how it is articulated.

move An operation that displaces a constituent (a head or a phrase) from one position in the structure to another, typically higher position. In current theories the constituent leaves behind a copy of itself.

movement test This is a test used to determine whether a string of words forms a constituent in a syntac tic structure. It consists of moving a string of words to a different position in the sentence. For example, *I gave the chocolates to my mother* may be expressed as *To my mother, I gave the chocolates*, showing that *to my mother* is a constituent.

multimodal refers to communication that occurs across different modes. Most communication is, in fact, multimodal. Face-to-face communication relies on facial expression, gestures, and body posture. Online communication makes use of emoticons, emoji, images, video, and layout.

mutual intelligibility A way of defining languages vs. dialects based on whether speakers of two linguistic varieties can understand each other.

N400 effect is a reliable and normal brain response to words and other stimuli when reading sentences. In an ERP, this effect shows an increase in negativity at around 400 ms after the presentation of a stimulus.

named entity recognition The identification of phrases that name entities in text and their classification into categories such as the names of persons, organizations, locations, etc.

narratives are descriptive dialogues in conversation.t

nasals are sounds that are produced when the velum is lowered forcing the air to flow through the nasal cavity. In English, /m/, /n/, and /ŋ/ are the nasal consonants.

nasalization A phonological change by which an oral vowel becomes nasalized before (or, more rarely, after) a nasal stop. The nasal stop may or may not be lost afterwards. Example: Latin *bonus* "good" > French *bon* /bɔ̃/. See also *assimilation*.

nativist views are perspectives which argue that L1 acquisition depends on innate knowledge of the properties of language.

natural class refers to sets of phonemes that share a number of features and participate in certain regularities of the phonological system of a language. For example, /p t k/ form a natural class, they are all aspirated at the beginning of a word or stressed syllable.

natural language A language used by humans in their every-day communication. The use of the modifier "natural" is to distinguish these human languages from artificial languages such as computer programming languages.

Natural Order Hypothesis is part of the Monitor Model which states that L2 morphemes are acquired according to a natural and predictable order, regardless of a learner's L1 or instructional interventions.

negative face is a concept that is part of Politeness Theory. Negative face is the desire to act unimpeded.

Neogrammarian Hypothesis The observation that sound change is regular and exceptionless; "Sound laws suffer no exceptions."

neurolinguistics is the study of the biological and neurocognitive bases of language.

neuroplasticity refers to the brain's ability to change.

New Englishes Second-language varieties of English around the world, spoken and used as stable national forms of the language in many countries around the world (India, Singapore, Nigeria, etc.),

n-gram A sequence of adjacent homogeneous items in text or speech. The items can be phonemes, syllables, letters, or words.

no access with regard to the access to UG debate, argues that UG is no longer available to L2 learners.

non-informant languages Languages that are no longer spoken; there are no native speaker informants that linguists can consult; also informally referred to as "dead languages".

non-lineal descent There is a regular correspondence between features of grammar G_1 and grammar G_2 that are NOT due to a lineal descent relationship $G_1 > G_2$. In these situations, it is legitimate to assume that G_1 and G_2 both descended from a common ancestor language proto-G which may need to be reconstructed. In other words, G_1 and G_2 are genetically related, but neither is descended from the other.

non-standard language An informal speech variety.

non-reduplicated babbling is a characteristic of pre-speech occurring from around nine to14 months of age. Infants combine vowels and consonants into syllable strings without reduplicating them.

noun (N) A category of word that commonly denotes an entity. In English nouns can be singular or plural and are typically preceded by a determiner. Examples: *house, child, water*.

nucleus of a syllable Refers to the [+syllabic] segment, generally a vowel.

null-subject parameter Within the theory of UG, the null subject parameter accounts for differences between languages which require subjects to be stated and languages which allow them to be overtly left out. It is also known as the pro-drop parameter. Examples of null-subject languages are Italian, Spanish, Greek, Japanese, and Navajo. Non-null-subject languages are those like English and French. See also *pro-drop*.

number The distinction between singular and plural. In English nouns are marked for number.

occipital lobe is an area of the brain which is responsible for processing visual input.

one-word stage is a developmental stage in syntax in which children use a single word in cases where adults would say several words.

onomatopoeia Words that attempt to mimic the sounds an object or animal makes, e.g., *quack quack*, for the sound a duck makes.

onset of the syllable The consonant(s) that precede the nucleus.

open class A class of words to which you can add or subtract items. Most lexical categories are open.

oralist method is a training method for deaf children in which they are intensively trained to produce speech and read lips.

orthography The language-specific principles governing how the elements of a script are used to represent the sounds of a language.

Output Hypothesis puts forth the notion that L2 learners need the opportunity to use language productively (i.e., focus on output) instead of using language simply for comprehension (i.e., focus on input). See also *comprehensible output*.

overextension (overgeneralization) errors are the overly broad uses of a word such that it is more general or inclusive than it should be. These mistakes are due to the broad application of a rule in cases where it doesn't apply.

overlapping correspondence A set of cognates from two or more languages in a lineal or non-lineal set descent relationship in which a sound x in language L_1 corresponds to more than one sound in language L_2. For example, after palatalization took place in Old English, an Early Old English /k/ corresponded to /ʧ/ before front vowels, but to /k/ everywhere else.

palatalization In phonetics, palatalization is a process by which velar sounds become fronted (e.g. alveolar, palato-alveolar, interdental), typically though not always before front vowels. In historical linguistics, velars or dental stops may develop a "front" (palatal) co-articulation and/or affrication before front vowels (e.g., Old English cīdan /kiːdan/ > Modern English chide /ʧajd/).

parallel distributed processing is a connectionist model which argues simultaneous processing at multiple levels. Activation spreads and distributes across neural connections.

parallel processing argues that several processes occur at the same time during language processing. These parallel processes affect and inform one another.

parameters are the set of alternatives to UG principles which provide options permitted by a language in question. Parameters are generally linked to differences in the lexicon, interpreted in its broadest sense to include functional categories and features.

parietal lobe is an area of the brain which is responsible for reading, integrating sensory information from various parts of the body, knowing about numbers and their relations, and manipulating objects, among other things.

parsing is the process of assigning syntactic structure (or phrase structure) to words and/or phrases.

parsing strategies guide and assist the language comprehension procedure by assigning grammatical categories to incoming words and determining the syntactic relationship of words within phrases.

partial access with regard to the access to UG debate, this line of thought argues that only some of UG will remain available during SLA. Unlike the indirect access hypothesis, access to UG does not necessarily occur via the L1.

passive sentence is a sentence in which the action of the main verb is done *to* the subject (i.e., the element with the theme role). An example of a passive sentence is *The message was sent by Jeanette.*

past language stages A grammar/variety of a language that is no longer spoken, a "dead language". See non-informant languages.

pejoration A semantic change by which a word acquires a negative connotation as part of its meaning. Over time, this negative connotation can turn into the sole denotation of the word. Example: English *villain* originally meant "villager" (it was borrowed from Old French *vilain* "peasant") and underwent a pejoration.

performance refers to observable language behavior, either in production or comprehension. It is essentially the use of language in different contexts.

performative speech act is one that changes the world once it is uttered (e.g., "I pronounce you husband and wife").

periodic A quality of sound waves that have repeated, regular waves. This contrasts with aperiodic sound waves, which have no repeated pattern.

peripheral agraphia is an acquired form of agraphia in which there is an impairment of writing abilities due to damage to the motor system.

periphery A less typical representative of the concept.

petroglyph A pictogram scratched into a rock face.

philology The study and evaluation of written texts and their origin, history, and linguistic properties and an important tool for the study of historical records in historical linguistics.

phonation Production of sounds with voicing, or the vibration of the vocal folds.

phone A distinct speech sound that may or may not contrast words.

phoneme Is the contrastive sound segment of a specific language. Unlike a phone, a phoneme serves to distinguish between words that have different meaning. For example, the contrast between *pan* and *fan* indicates that both /p/ and /f/ are phonemes in English. Phonemes are written between slashes.

phonemic Related to phonemes, for example, the difference in English between /p/ and /f/ is phonemic.

phonetic complement In morphosyllabic writing, a character whose phonetic reading gives some indication of the pronunciation of the character with which it is associated.

phonetic component In Chinese writing, a portion of a character that gives some indication of its pronunciation.

phonetic environment In historical linguistics/sound change: the phonetic properties of the sounds before and after a particular sound that is undergoing a change. The phonetic environment of a given sound is usually what triggers its change. In nasalization, the sound undergoing the change (an oral vowel) picks up the [+nasal] feature of its phonetic environment (a preceding or following nasal).

phonetically natural In historical linguistics/sound change: "phonetically natural" means that a sound change is conditioned by the properties of its phonetic environment and the way learners analyze this environment during language acquisition.

phonetics The study of human speech sounds.

phonological change Change(s) that affect(s) the phonological system of a given language, also known as sound change.

phonological dyslexia is an acquired form of alexia in which the selective impairment of the ability to read pronounceable nonwords occurs while the ability to read familiar words is not affected.

phonological loop is responsible for sound and storing verbal content. It acts as phonological storage that leaves traces of auditory memories and an articulatory loop which allows for rehearsal and revival of auditory memories.

phonological neighborhood refers to all other words that are phonologically similar to a word.

phonological reduction Also known as "phonological weakening": a fully stressed lexical item can become unstressed or weakly stressed as it changes into a functional item as the result of grammaticalization. Phonological reduction also takes place when free functional items become bound morphemes (clitics, affixes).

phonology The subfield of linguistics that studies how a specific language selects segments (phones) and organizes the sound system.

phrasal or sentence semantics describes the patterns and rules for building sentence meanings.

phrase A word or group of words that functions as a unit in a clause. Often used as a synonym for *constituent*. Examples: *the big, red dog* (noun phrase); *eating cake* (verb phrase); *on the roof* (adjective phrase). All phrases must have a head.

phrase movement is the operation that displaces a phrase such as a DP to another higher position. Phrases typically move into specifiers.

pictogram A simplified, stylized picture that may be used in a visual communication system.

picture-word interference task is an experimental task in which participants name pictures that are accompanied by distracter words that are often manipulated to be related in some way to the target picture.

pidgin A new speech variety that emerges and is used for communication between two linguistically disparate groups. Pidgins are lingua franca forms used by adult speakers for everyday conversation in multilingual settings (e.g. in the Caribbean or East Africa).

Pimsleur Language Aptitude Battery (PLAB) is a measure of language aptitude developed by Pimsleur (1966).

pitch The vibration of the vocal tract due to the vibration from the glottis.

Pitre's law suggests that multilingual patients with language impairments will have language recovery patterns determined by the frequency of language use prior to cerebral insult.

place of articulation The point in the vocal tract where constriction or contact occurs to produce a given speech sound.

politeness theory describes how we manage our social identities and those of others, through language.

polyglot savant See *language savant*.

polysemy A word that has more than one meaning is called polysemous.

positive face is a concept that is part of Politeness Theory. Positive face is the desire to be liked or appreciated by others.

positron emission tomography (PET) is a device which uses radioactive tracers called positron-emitting isotopes that are then recorded while the participant engages in a variety of cognitive and linguistic activities.

postposition preposition-like words that follow rather than precede their noun phrase complement.

poverty of the stimulus refers to the insufficient input that children receive during first language acquisition although they are still able to generate novel utterances.

pragmatic meaning Meaning supplied by the discourse context and knowledge of the world.

pragmatics is the study of meaning in context.

prefix An affix which attaches at the beginning of the base, e.g., *–re* in *re–do* is a prefix.

preposition (P) Prepositions generally express direction, location, etc. In English they are invariable. They typically take a DP or NP as a complement. Examples: *up, under, on*.

prescriptive In linguistics: a normative approach to the study of language by which the linguistic habits and language use of a speech community are compared to a "correct" standard and attempts are made to adjust these habits to that standard. These attempts usually fail. See also *descriptive*.

prescriptive grammar An approach to language that judges elements of language to be incorrect according to some rule decided on by an authority or group of people. It is essentially a set of rules that informs speakers about how they should use language. It is often contrasted with *descriptive grammar*.

prescriptive linguistics A subjective approach of "good" and "bad" language.

preserved influence in speech errors are when influence comes from a sound that has already been articulated.

pre-speech refers to sounds such as crying, burping, and babbling that allow infants to explore their vocal abilities and familiarize themselves with processes they will later use to speak.

presupposition A background belief relating to an utterance, such as existence of the objects mentioned in the utterance. It is essentially a proposition that the speaker assumes to be true.

primary progressive aphasia (PPA) occurs because of a degeneration of the frontal, temporal, and/or parietal regions of the brain which help to control speech and language.

primary progressive aphasia-agrammatic also known as *progressive non-fluent aphasia*, is a language disorder in which patients have difficulty pronouncing words or producing speech fluently. The cause is a degenerative disease.

primary progressive aphasia-logopenic is a language disorder in which patients have growing problems with naming and sentence repetition. The cause is a degenerative disease.

primary progressive aphasia-semantic is a language disorder in which patients encounter growing challenges remembering names of people, objects, facts, and words. The cause is a degenerative disease.

prime is a stimulus which is immediately presented before a target stimulus in order to measure possible processing effects caused by the prime on the target.

priming effect is an implicit memory effect in which a priming stimulus pre-activates a target stimulus, making it temporarily more accessible to be processed.

priming paradigm is an experimental design in which exposure to a priming stimulus influences the processing of a stimulus that immediately follows.

principles are the universal rules of language and form part of UG.

Principles and Parameters A framework in generative linguistic theory that posits that UG provides a set of universal principles shared by all human languages and language-specific parameters. The combination of linguistic constants (principles) and variant parameter settings results in language variation at the syntactic level.

private speech is when children talk to themselves (for different reasons) in order to practice language abilities.

procedural memory is a type of long-term memory that includes memories about the knowledge of tasks that normally do not need to be recalled consciously to perform them. Examples would include remembering how to ride a bike, play a guitar, and make a peace sign with your fingers.

procedural skills are those involving a series of discrete responses that have a specific and appropriate sequence in which they should be performed, that are needed to process the L2.

processability is based on the idea that L2 learners can only produce and comprehend L2 linguistic structures that the current state of the language processor can handle.

Processing Instruction is a type of form-focused instruction in which input has been "modified and constructed in a way that pushes learners away from their less than optimal processing strategies, thus creating better intake for development" (VanPatten, 2002, p. 764).

proclisis The process by which a clitic attaches before the host, e.g., the French object pronouns.

pro-drop (pronoun dropping) A syntactically or pragmatically conditioned property by which some languages allow (subject and/or object) pronouns to be omitted or "dropped" under certain circumstances. See also *null-subject parameter*.

productivity A language has to be able to make up new words. For example, the word "cell phone" did not exist in the English language until recently.

progressive (assimilation) A type of sound change by which a sound takes on some or all of the features of a preceding sound.

progressive non-fluent aphasia See *primary progressive aphasia-agrammatic*.

pronoun A word belonging to the functional category whose function is to stand in for DPs or NPs. Examples: *I, you, he, she; him, her, them; his hers, ours, etc.*

proportional analogy A deductive morphological change that copies a relationship between one set of forms to another set of forms, formally a : b = c : x "a is to b as c is to x, where x is ... " (x = the new, analogical form). Example: English *dive: dived* was replaced by *dive: dove* in analogy with *strive: strove*, etc.

proposition A logical expression, statement, or idea describing a state of affairs in the world.

prosodic stress (sentence stress) refers to stress that can be used to contrast or emphasize words at the sentence level. For example, *Naida danced* **SAL***sa* seems to contrast *salsa* from another type of dance like *merengue* or that Naida doesn't usually dance at all.

Proto-Indo-European The reconstructed proto-language of the Indo-European language **family, spoken ca. 4000 BCE in South Russia and Ukraine.**

Proto-language The language from which all languages of a given language family are descended, usually a reconstructed (not directly attested) language. For example, the Germanic languages (English, German, Dutch, Norwegian, etc.) go back to a reconstructed proto-language called Proto-Germanic.

Proto-(theta) roles is the notion put forth by David Dowty which holds that rather than theta roles (agent, theme, recipient, etc.), there are only two cluster-concepts called proto-agent and proto-patient.

prototype A more typical representative of the concept.

psycholinguistics is the study of the cognitive processes and mental representations that are involved in language production, comprehension, and acquisition.

quantifier A word that denotes quantity: *all, both, each, every, some, etc.*

question and answer test This is a test used to determine whether a string of words forms a constituent in a syntactic structure. It works because the short answer to a question is almost always a constituent of the complete sentence, showing that constituents can often stand alone. For example, in answer to the question *who did you see?* you can say *I saw the dog that belongs to the guy next door*, the complete sentence, or *the dog that belongs to the guy next door*, which is a constituent.

radical In Chinese writing, equivalent to *semantic component*.

r-dropping The loss of the consonant R at the end of a word or before a consonant.

reading Conversion of written text into meaningful content using optical (or tactile, for Braille) input to the brain.

real-time study The study of language change that compares different points in time.

reanalysis Speakers/language acquirers assign a different underlying structure to a string of words or morphemes than the previous generation of speakers, resulting in a slightly different grammar. See *misanalysis, flawed transmission*.

rebracketing A type of reanalysis by which speakers assign a different constituent structure (= different "brackets") to a string of words or morphemes than the previous generation.

recast is a corrected and/or restated version of a learner's non-target-like utterance. In other words, recasts are indirect feedback on language which has adjusted form and/or content of incorrect utterances.

recency effect is the idea that more recent words heard are accessed more rapidly.

receptive abilities refer to the ability to understand language. Examples include speech (or sign) comprehension and reading.

reconstruction, reconstructed In historical linguistics: the recovery of unattested languages and language stage from the study of attested languages, usually by applying the comparative method to attested languages that are genetically related.

recursion Refers to the property of language that consists of embedding (nesting) a structure within another structure of the same type.

redundancy The same message is sent along two or more communication channels.

reduplicated babbling is a characteristic of pre-speech occurring from six to ten months of age. Infants begin to produce true syllables that are usually produced in series of the same consonant and vowel combinations.

reduplication In morphology, reduplication is the process by which part of a word or the whole word is repeated, leading to a change in meaning and/or grammatical category of the base word, e.g., *mumbo-jumbo*. In phonetics, reduplication refers to the articulatory process of assimilation in which syllables are repeated as in [baba] for bottle.

reference The person or object in the outside world that is being pointed to or talked about.

reflexive vocalizations are the earliest vocalizations including crying and vegetative sounds such as breathing, sucking, or sneezing and occur from zero to six weeks of age.

register refers to how language choices are shaped by the specific context of situation. It is the style of the language that may be associated with particular social settings or listeners. Register is defined by three aspects: field, tenor, and mode.

regressive (assimilation) A type of sound change by which a sound takes on some or all of the phonetic features of a following sound; also called anticipatory.

regressive saccades are an extremely rapid eye movement that backtracks in order to reread and reparse the sentence.

relational meaning is the semantic relationship between the referents of the two words.

relative chronology The ordering of phonological rules ("sound laws") which respect each other; the order in which two or more sound changes are applied in a given language.

repetitive transcranial magnetic stimulation (rTMS) is a method which allows researchers to use repetitive pulses to stimulate small regions of the brain using a magnetic field generator coil.

request is a speech act in which a speaker asks someone to do something. The request is not a performative speech act; it simply conveys the speaker's intention.

rhotic sounds form part of approximate consonants. In English, there is only one rhotic sound that is alveolar: /ɹ/.

rhyme (syllable) The unit constituted by the nucleus and the coda.

Ribot's law suggests that multilingual patients with language impairments will have language recovery patterns that replicate the order in which they were acquired.

right ear advantage is when speech heard through the right ear seems clearer and louder. This is found with words, nonwords, single syllables, numbers, and even Morse code.

root (morphology) The morpheme that carries the main meaning of a word and cannot be divided into further parts. Roots belong to lexical categories, i.e., nouns, verbs, adjectives, adverbs, or prepositions. *Plant* is the root of the word *plant–ation–s*.

rounded are sounds that are produced when the lips are protruding and round. Examples in English include /w/ and /u/.

s(atellite)-framed A type of language where the direction of motion or change is encoded (framed) in the satellite.

saccades are unconscious eye movements (jumps) to the left or right which rapidly propel eye fixations from one point to the next.

satellite An element of the verb phrase that is not the verb, for example, an adverb, a prepositional phrase, a participle, or a gerund.

savant is a person who has a mental disability such as autism yet shows exceptional brilliance in other areas such as mathematics, memory, music, art, or language.

scaffolding Refers to assisted learning techniques that help to elevate learners to a higher proficiency level. Scaffolding essentially is the support given during a language learning process which can be in the form of follow-up questions that elicit more information on a topic.

scalar implicature A subset of implicatures involving quantifiers arranged on a scale. Uttering a sentence with the weaker term implies that the stronger terms in the same scale are not true.

schwa the central, lax vowel that only occurs in unstressed syllables. The schwa /ə/ has a very brief duration and is also called a reduced vowel.

science A process of inquiry that follows a systematic approach: forming theories and hypotheses; searching for evidence; evaluating evidence; providing explanations.

script The inventory of characters used in writing a particular language.

Search Model is a model of lexical access in which word recognition is independent from other language processing and is divided into access files, one for words' orthographic properties and another for phonetic properties.

second language acquisition (SLA) investigates the process by which non-native languages are acquired.

semantic bleaching A lexical item loses part or all of its meaning, usually through a grammaticalization process into a functional item (functional categories usually have a more abstract and restricted meaning than lexical categories).

semantic broadening In the course of semantic change, a word comes to refer to a superset ("broader set") than its previous meaning. Example: English *dog*, which originally referred to a specific breed of dog (cp. German *Dogge* "mastiff") and now refers to the superset "dogs".

semantic change Changes in the meaning of lexical and functional categories of a given language, also known as lexical change.

semantic component In Chinese writing, a portion of a character that gives some indication of its meaning; equivalent to *radical*.

semantic determinative In morphosyllabic writing, a character that indicates the superordinate semantic category to which the referent of a logogram belongs.

semantic memory is a type of declarative memory of the long-term memory system that represents information about words, facts, concepts, symbols, and anything that is not personal-experience based.

semantic narrowing In the course of semantic change, a word comes to refer to a subset ("narrower set") than its previous meaning. Example: English *deer* originally meant "animal" (cp. German *Tier* "animal"), but its meaning "narrowed" to refer to only a particular type of animal.

semantics The systematic study of the meaning of linguistic expressions.

semasiography Visual communication not representing language.

sense The linguistic meaning of an expression.

sentence A linguistic expression bigger than a phrase. It is a mental structure dependent on a speaker's knowledge of language.

sequential language acquisition is the most common form of SLA in which an L2 is learned after an L1 has already been acquired.

serial processing explains language processing as a set of processes that occur one at a time, similar to a computer program that works in a step-by-step fashion through a series of non-overlapping processes.

shadowing task requires participants to listen to sentences and repeat them as quickly as possible and exactly as they were heard. The task is used to study behavioral reactions to grammatical and ungrammatical sentences.

simultaneous language acquisition is the process of learning two languages from birth.

single-route processing argues that word recognition proceeds either by recognizing the whole word or by "sounding out" its phonemes, but not both.

sisters in syntax, are two elements merged together on the same level.

slips of the ear or mishearing, are errors in speech comprehension in which a word or phrase is mistaken for another similar-sounding word or phrase.

slips of the tongue are unintentional speech errors in which words and sounds are rearranged (with often humorous results).

social class A ranking that depends on income, education, and occupation.

social network The individuals with whom one interacts on a regular basis.

sociocultural approaches to SLA argue that language development occurs as a result of meaningful interaction that falls within the language learner's zone of proximal development.

sociolinguistics The study of variable properties of human language.

sociophonetics The field of phonetics that examines how variability in speech production can be connected to a speaker's identity.

sonority scale A requirement that, when there are complex onsets or codas, the segments with the highest degree of sonority should be closest to the nucleus.

sonorant is a major class of sounds that includes all vowels, glides, liquids, and nasals. Sonorous sounds are more *easily sung* compared to stops, fricatives, and affricates, for example.

sound change See *phonological change*.

sound correspondences A sound X in grammar G_1 diachronically corresponds to a sound Y in Grammar G_2 if X can be related to Y through one or more changes which transformed X into Y. Sound correspondences are also found in non-lineal descent relationships, e.g., when G_1 and G_2 go back to a common ancestor proto-G.

sound law A particular phonological change that occurs between two grammars which are in a lineal descent relationship. Sound laws are diachronic phonological rules of the type A > B "A turns into B"; A > B/_C "A turns into B before C", etc. and are regular. See also *Neogrammarian Hypothesis*.

specifier Specifier defines a position in a syntactic tree: immediately under XP and to the left of X'. Subjects always merge in the specifier position. Not all phrases project specifiers.

spectogram The visual representation of a sound spectrum and its frequencies.

speech acts are utterances that accomplish something in the world.

speech community A group of speakers who interact and judge language forms in the same way.

speech error See *slips of the tongue*.

speech signal is auditory information also known as the acoustic signal. This is the information actually heard in speech production that will serve as linguistic input to a listener.

speech style The level of formality.

split A type of sound change by which a phoneme "splits" into two different phonemes, usually conditioned by a particular phonetic environment. For example, the Old English palatalization change resulted in a split of Early Old English /k/ into the phonemes /k/ and /ʧ/.

split-brain is when the corpus callosum connecting the two hemispheres of the brain is severed to some degree and the result is the disruption of or interference with the connection between the hemispheres of the brain.

Spoonerisms See *slips of the tongue.*

spread glottis [+/–SG] is a laryngeal feature which describes the glottis as being spread apart [+SG] or not [–SG]. In English, only the aspirated voiceless stops [p t k] and /h/ are [+SG].

standard language A linguistic variety promoted by public institutions, used in formal settings.

status planning Efforts made to improve how a language is viewed/judged by members of a given society.

stopping is an articulatory process in which a fricative becomes a stop.

stops (plosives) are consonants that are produced with a full constriction in the vocal tract followed by a brief burst when they are released into the vowel. In English, the stops are /p b t d k g ʔ/.

stress The pronunciation of a syllable in a word or phrase with greater length, volume, or higher pitch than the surrounding syllables. The syllable bearing the greatest stress in a word is generally marked with the diacritic ˈ preceding it. For example, /ˈwɪn.do/ "window".

stridents are consonants that are produced with high turbulence in the air flow. Strident sounds seem *hissy* or like the sizzling of oil in a pan. In English, the stridents are /s z ʃ ʒ d͡ʒ t͡ʃ/.

structural linguistics The study of invariable properties of human language.

structured input activities serve as focused practice that has been manipulated in such a way that learners become dependent on forms or structure to derive meaning so that they process grammatical forms in the input and make proper form–meaning connections.

subcategorization This term refers to the knowledge found in our mental lexicon regarding the requirements of different types of heads, particularly verbs and prepositions. For example, knowledge that certain verbs require a complement of a certain type.

subgrouping The internal relationships between daughter languages within a language family; the "branching" of the family tree of a given language family.

subject The subject of a sentence in English can be recognized because it agrees with the verb and generally precedes it in statements. Example: The child likes chocolate; the children like chocolate. Subjects are obligatory, although in some languages the subject can remain unpronounced (although it is still present syntactically).

subjunctive mood represents speech which the speaker uses to explore hypothetical, conditional, or imaginary situations. Compared to the indicative and imperative moods, the subjunctive is the least common.

submersion programs are language programs in which learners are placed in classes where the language of instruction (e.g., English) is not the form of communication.

substitution is an articulatory process in which one sound is simply replaced by another sound.

substitution test This is a test used to determine whether a string of words forms a constituent in a syntactic structure. It consists of the grammatical replacement of a string of words by a single word or an expression such as *do so*. For example, we can show that in the sentence *the children next door saw a rabbit*, the string *the children next door* is a constituent because we can replace it by the pronoun *they*, as in *they saw a rabbit*.

suffix An affix which attaches at the end of the base, e.g., *–er* in *teach–er* is a suffix.

sulcus A place where the cortex is folded inward.

superconducting quantum interference devices (SQUIDs) are extremely sensitive detectors that are used to measure electrophysiological brain activity in magnetoencephalography.

suppletion The process by which a grammatical contrast is expressed by the complete replacement of one form by another, e.g., *good, better*.

supramarginal gyrus is largely responsible for phonological memory which is needed to do things like temporarily remember a string of letters or numbers.

suprasegmentals Features such as stress and intonation that apply to an entire utterance rather than to a single segment.

surface dyslexia is an acquired form of alexia in which patients must rely on the pronunciation of written words in order to understand them.

surface structure is the well-formed phrases and sentences that are constructed based on a deep structure.

syllabary A writing system in which each character, or *syllabogram*, represents a syllable, typically a vowel preceded by a consonant, and there is no graphic resemblance between characters representing the same consonant or the same vowel.

syllable A unit of phonological structure that typically consists of a vowel that may be preceded and/or followed by one or more consonants. For example, the word *stops* /stɑps/ is made up of one syllable, the word *tendency* /tɛn.dən.si/ is made up of three. The boundary between syllables is marked with a dot.

syllabic is a major feature class in phonology that describes sounds that form the nucleus of a syllable. All vowels are syllabic, as well as syllabic liquids and syllabic nasals.

syllable deletion is an articulatory process in which a weaker, unstressed syllable is deleted.

syllable simplification is an articulatory process in which consonants that occur in clusters are deleted.

synchronic See *synchrony*.

synchronic variation The linguistic variation between dialects of a particular language (microvariation) or between different languages (macrovariation) at the same synchronic stage.

synchrony (The study of) the properties of speakers' grammars at a given linguistic stage X, without reference to earlier or later stages (from Greek *sýn* "with, together" + *khrónos* "time").

syncope From Greek *synkopē* "cutting short": a segment (usually an unstressed or weakly stressed vowel) is lost in the middle of a word. Example: Latin *populus* "people" > French *peuple*.

synonyms Words that have the same or partially the same sense.

syntactic change Change(s) that affect(s) the syntax of a language, primarily its word order and distribution of functional and lexical items.

syntax The branch of linguistics that studies how sentences and phrases are formed. Syntax can also refer to the knowledge of how words are combined to create phrases, which in turn are used to build sentences.

taboo words Words that speakers avoid or consciously modify because there is a social inhibition or constraint on their use. They are usually words that designate body parts (especially genitalia), swearwords, dangerous animals, and deities (basically everything that people are a little bit afraid of).

tap (flap) a consonant sound that is produced by tapping the tongue tip quickly against the alveolar ridge with no pressure build-up. In English, the only tap is the /ɾ/.

telegraphic stage is a developmental stage in syntax in which the speech of children sounds telegraphic because of its choppiness. Speech lacks bound morphemes and non-lexical categories such as determiners and auxiliaries.

temporal lobe is an area of the brain which is responsible for retaining short- and long-term memories, processing auditory information including words and speech, and integrating sensory functions, among other things.

tenor is one of the aspects of register. It refers to how the relationship between the participants affects language choices.

tense The feature(s) that situate the action of the verb in time in relation to the moment of speaking. In English tense can be expressed by auxiliary verbs, modals, or [+/–past] morphology on the main verb. The tense features are merged under T, which is the head of TP, the sentence.

tense phrase, TP The syntactic phrase that determines tense (finiteness) and agreement on verbs. TP is a functional category.

tense vowels are slightly longer and higher than their lax counterparts. Tense vowels have greater vocal tract construction. The /i/ in _beat_ is a tense vowel while the /ɪ/ in _bit_ is lax.

text In pragmatics and discourse analysis refers to both spoken and written language.

texture is a property of texts that makes them hang together and make sense in context.

thematic (theta) roles Classes of verb arguments dependent on their semantic function in the sentence.

timed-reading task is an experimental task in which participants read sentences or parts of sentences that appear on a computer screen in front of them.

tip-of-the-tongue (TOT) state is a temporary condition in which a word or expression cannot be retrieved from the mental lexicon. One can usually come out of the TOT state when given the first letter, sound, meaning, or some other clue.

tone The use of pitch to distinguish between words.

top-down processing assumes that input in language is processed based on expectations from higher levels such as phrases and words to guide processes of lower levels such as sound.

total communication approach is a training method for deaf children which draws on the oralist method but adds the combination of some signs and gestures.

TRACE model is a connectionist view of language processing in which several levels of processing – feature level, phoneme level, word level – are all said to be simultaneously active. This activation allows them to interact with one another.

transcranial magnetic stimulation (TMS) is a method which allows researchers to use a single pulse to stimulate small regions of the brain using a magnetic field generator coil.

transient sounds Sounds that have a sudden and brief burst of acoustic energy.

transition-relevant place is the end of a unit of conversation; the place where another speaker may take the turn.

transitive (verb) A verb that requires a complement, i.e., *buy a card; sell a house; devour a hamburger.*

trills are consonant sounds that are made by holding the active articulator tense (lips, tongue, etc.) and then exhaling strongly to make the active articulator and the passive articulator vibrate.

turn-constructional units are the minimal units a turn of talk is composed of.

turns are the pieces of a conversation during which a given speaker holds the floor, that is, during which a participant speaks.

turn-taking refers to the process of giving or holding the floor in a conversation.

T-to-C movement In syntax, a movement in which the element in the tense (T) position moves up to the complement (C) position. For example, the word *Does* in the sentence *Does he ~~does~~ sing?* has moved from the T position and landed in C.

two-word stage is a developmental stage in syntax in which children use two words, often two holophrases from the one-word stage.

ultimate attainment is the outcome of language acquisition. Other terms used interchangeably with ultimate attainment are final state, end state, and asymptote.

unaccusative Intransitive verbs whose argument is a Theme.

underextension errors are the overly restricted uses of a word such that it is less inclusive than it should be.

unergative Intransitive verbs whose argument is an Agent.

ungrammatical A phrase or sentences that native speakers reject as possible in their language.

unicode A modern encoding that can represent all of the symbols in most of the world's writing systems. UTF (Unicode Transformation Format) encodes these symbols in variable length formats: UTF-8, as 8, 16, 24, or 32 bits; UTF-16, as 16 or 32 bits; and UTF-32 as 32 bits.

Uniformitarian Principle states that past language stages conform to the same basic principles as contemporary language stages. The Uniformitarian Principle according to Hock, 1986: "The general processes and principles which can be noticed in observable history are applicable in all stages of language history."

Universal Grammar (UG) A set of grammatical principles that are not violated in any human language. In language acquisition, this theory argues that for humans, there is a set of inborn principles that are universal to all languages.

universal listener refers to a healthy newborn infant because of its ability to discriminate non-native phonemic contrasts in any world language. This ability declines within the first year of life.

Universals In linguistics: (abstract) features or properties shared by all human languages. See *Universal Grammar.*

usage-based approach argues that L1s are acquired through experience by emphasizing the importance of a small set of cognitive processes, such as categorization, analogy, and chunking to explain how language functions and is structured.

utterance A concrete use of a linguistic expression in a context.

v(erb)-framed A type of language where the direction of motion or change is encoded (framed) in the verb.

variable domain Specific context where the variants are "interchangeable".

variation Differential language use according to social and linguistic factors.

verb (V) A category of word that typically refers to an action. In English (and many other languages, verbs are distinguished by inflection marking person (third person –*s*) or tense (present and past). They can also follow a modal such as can. Examples: *eat, play, make*.

verb raising In many languages (e.g., French, Portuguese, Italian) the main verb moves out of the VP, going from V to T.

visual channel Signals involving movement of body parts, body posture, and coloration.

visuospatial sketchpad is accountable for temporarily storing and manipulating visual and visuospatial information. This subsystem is what allows us to do things like form images in our mind and convert words to sounds.

vocal play is a characteristic of pre-speech occurring from four to seven-and-a-half months of age. Infants engage in vocal play to test their speech abilities by using different consonant- and vowel-like sounds.

vocal tract The area from the nose and the nasal cavity down to the vocal cords deep in the throat.

voice onset time The length of time that passes between when a speaker releases a consonant and when she begins to voice the following vowel or consonant.

voice-activated systems See *dialogue systems*.

voicing The behavior of the vocal chords during the production of a given sound. Typically *voiced* (vibration of vocal chords) or *unvoiced* (no vibration of vocal chords).

voicing contrast is a change in meaning that occurs from alternating voice and voiceless consonants in a specific position of the word.

vowels are syllabic sounds that are produced with no obstruction of air and are usually voiced.

vowel harmony is a type of assimilation, an articulatory process, in which a vowel becomes more like or the same as (duplicates) another vowel in the word.

wada test is a procedure in which a barbiturate is injected into either the right or left internal carotid artery. This temporarily "turns off" language and memory abilities in either the right or left hemisphere, respectively and allows neurolinguistics to assess language and memory in one hemisphere without communication with the other.

Web the World Wide Web: an information resource that can be accessed via the Internet.

Wernicke's aphasia is an acquired form of fluent aphasia which severely affects speech comprehension but not so much production. The speech of a Wernicke's aphasic is fluent but they have problems comprehending language input and are unable to monitor and understand the speech that they themselves produce.

Wernicke's area is an area found between the left temporal and parietal lobes that is largely responsible for language comprehension.

white matter is the inner, deep part of the brain that is responsible for learning, distributing action potentials, and coordinating communication between different areas of the brain.

***wh*-questions** In contrast to yes/no questions, *wh*-questions include an interrogative such as *who, what, what colour*, etc. These interrogatives always represent phrases.

Williams syndrome is a rare neurodevelopmental disorder which causes mild to moderate intellectual disability.

word is a unit which carries meaning and is the smallest free form in a language.

word embedding A technique that represents words or phrases from a vocabulary as vectors of real numbers. The size of the vector is small compared to the vocabulary size.

word spurt period is a time during which the rate of acquiring new words exponentially increases.

working memory is the ability to simultaneously store and manipulate information that is relevant to a task at hand.

writing (system) is a combination of a script and an orthography of a particular language. It uses more or less permanent marks to represent an utterance in such a way that the utterance can be recovered more or less the same without the intervention of the utterer.

Wug test is a measure which examines acquisition of morphemes. For instance, children are introduced to made-up animals and actions (like *a wug*). The next time they see them, however, they are asked to pluralize the new word (*wugs*) to see if they have acquired the plural –*s* morpheme.

X-bar template is the basic, prototype structure for all phrases in languages. It can be thought of as a blueprint.

zone of proximal development is the theoretical range of language abilities an L2 learner has.

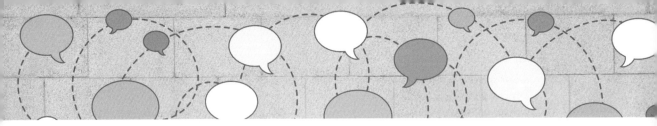

INDEX